VICE & VIRTUE IN EVERYDAY LIFE

Introductory Readings in Ethics

VICE & VIRTUE IN EVERYDAY LIFE

Introductory Readings in Ethics

EIGHTH EDITION

Christina Hoff Sommers
American Enterprise Institute

Fred Sommers
Brandeis University

WADSWORTH
CENGAGE Learning

Australia • Brazil • Japan • Korea • Mexico • Singapore • Spain • United Kingdom • United States

WADSWORTH
CENGAGE Learning

Vice & Virtue in Everyday Life:
Introductory Readings in Ethics,
Eighth Edition
Christina Hoff Sommers and
Fred Sommers

Publisher: Clark Baxter

Senior Sponsoring Editor: Joann Kozyrev

Assistant Editor: Nathan Gamache

Editorial Assistant: Michaela Henry

Media Editor: Diane Akerman

Production Technology Analyst: Lori Johnson

Marketing Manager: Mark Haynes

Marketing Coordinator: Josh Hendrick

Marketing Communications Manager: Kim Soltero

Project Manager, Editorial Production: Pre-Press PMG

Creative Director: Rob Hugel

Art Director: Faith Brosnan

Print Buyer: Rebecca Cross

Permissions Editor: Bob Kauser

Production Service: Pre-Press PMG

Photo Researcher: Leitha Etheridge-Sims

Copy Editor: Pre-Press PMG

Cover Designer: RHDG/Angelyn Navasca

Cover Image: Feininger, Lyonel (1871–1956) © ARS, NY Architecture II, The Man of Potin. 1921. Location: Fundacion Coleccion Thyssen-Bornemisza, Madrid, Spain

Cover Photo: Nimatallah/Art Resource, NY

Compositor: Pre-Press PMG

For product information and technology assistance, contact us at **Cengage Learning Customer Academic Resource Center, 1-800-423-0563**

For permission to use material from this text or product, submit all requests online at **www.cengage.com/permissions** Further permissions questions can be emailed to **permissionrequest@cengage.com**

Library of Congress Control Number: 2008941420

ISBN-13: 978-0-495-60161-6

ISBN-10: 0-495-60161-6

Wadsworth, Cengage Learning
10 Davis Drive,
Belmont, CA 94002-3098
USA

Cengage Learning products are represented in Canada by Nelson Education, Ltd.

For your course and learning solutions, visit **academic.cengage.com**

Purchase any of our products at your local college store or at our preferred online store **www.ichapters.com**

Printed in Canada
1 2 3 4 5 6 7 12 11 10 09

For Eliza Sommers

Brief Contents

CONTENTS

PREFACE

The teaching of practical ethics is flourishing on the college campus. Philosophy departments are attracting unprecedented numbers of students to courses that focus on critical social policy questions such as abortion, euthanasia, and capital punishment. Students learn a great deal about the moral conduct and policy of governments, hospitals, courts, and corporations. But the moral responsibilities of the students themselves are discussed only occasionally. Because most students are not likely to be personally involved in administering the death penalty, or in selecting candidates for kidney dialysis, the effective purpose of such courses in ethics is to teach students how to form responsible opinions on social policies—a purpose more civic than personal. "Applying" ethics to modern life involves more than learning how to be for or against social and institutional policies. These are important goals, but they are not enough.

Vice and Virtue in Everyday Life, Eighth Edition, brings together classical and contemporary writings on matters such as personal integrity and individual virtue. There are readings on the golden rule, personal courage, and the duty to follow one's conscience. It also includes essays on moral foibles—including hypocrisy, jealousy, spite, and self-deception. More conventional materials are included: chapters on theories of moral conduct, on the meaning of life, and on ethics and social policy. We believe that social ethics is only half of normative ethics. Private ethics, including "virtue ethics" is the other half—hence this anthology.

To prepare for the new edition of *Vice and Virtue in Everyday Life*, we conducted a survey of instructors who had used previous editions. This survey prompted several changes. We have reorganized the chapters into a more logical sequence. We have also enlivened various chapters with pertinent new readings from authors such as Anne Applebaum, Tzvetan Todorov, Bowen McCoy, and Leo Tolstoy. There is a new translation of Kant and new readings for and against affirmative action by Barbara Bergman and Shelby Steele.

What, finally, may the open-minded and careful reader of *Vice and Virtue in Everyday Life* expect to gain? First, if not foremost, the reader will acquire a great deal of knowledge of the classical approaches to moral philosophy and, with this, some sense of the moral tradition of Western civilization as Greek and Judeo-Christian thought have influenced it. Second, the reader will become aware of some of the central problem areas in ethics and will be in a better position to approach them with the confidence that comes with historical perspective and a sharpened moral insight. Social change and novel technologies bring about new problems, each with its moral dimension. Yet morality itself is not really changed in any radical way. There will always be a right and decent way to cope with the new situations that confront us.

ACKNOWLEDGMENTS

We would like to thank the following reviewers: Jason Baehr, Loyola Marymount University; Shaun Baker, University of Michigan-Dearborn; Scott A. Davidson, Morehead State University; Andrew Eshleman, University of Arkansas-Little Rock; James G. Hanink, Loyola Marymount University; David R. Koukal, University of Detroit Mercy; David Murphy, Truman State University; Brendan Sweetman, Rockhurst University; Lloyd Steffen, Lehigh University; and Tom Trimble, Mercer University. We would also like to thank the instructors who participated in our survey and provided excellent advice on how to improve the textbook. Thanks to Marilyn A. Dyrud, Oregon Institute of Technology; Charlene Dykman, University of St. Thomas; Tom Michaud, Wheeling Jesuit U; Edward Vacek, Weston Jesuit School of Theology; and Elaine Hurst, St. Francis College; Kathy Bowen, Murray State College; Stephen Brown, Briar Cliff University; David Danneker, Elizabethtown College; Carl Nelson, Polytechnic University; Steven Zitnick, Augsburg College; William Figg, Dakota State University; Eugene Garaventa, College of Staten Island; James Woolever, Menlo College; Matt Zwolinkski, University of San Diego; Debbie Stark, Marion Technical College; David Kaiser, Saint Mary's University of Minnesota; Joseph Allegretti, Siena College; Herb Conner, Columbia College; Lolis McWhorter, Somerset Community College; William Trimyer, Averett University; Robert Faaborg, University of Cincinnati; Robert A. Cerasoli, Eastern Nazareth College; Kelly Manley, Gainesville State College; James Hogue, Wayland Baptist University; Russell Williams, Wheaton College; John Gunyon, Aurora University; Leon Schefers, St. Mary's University of Minnesota; Jean Ende, St. Francis College; Brian Barnes, University of Louisville; Ivan Rubel, Mount Saint Mary College; Dennis Cooley, North Dakota State University; George Randels, University of the Pacific; Scott Peath, DePaul University; Ross Chapman, Community College of Philadelphia; Denise Meridith, Western International University; Ignazio E. Genna, Phoenix College;

Dennis Slivinski, California State University Channel Islands; Cindi Harrison, Mohave Community Education; Michael Saitta, Notre Dame of Maryland; Greg Trudeau, University of Wisconsin-Superior; Joseph Adamo, Cazenovia College; Paul Gaffney, St. Johns University; Wade Chumney, Charleston Southern University; David Rosman, Columbia College/Columbia, MO; Robert Hall, Norwalk Community College; Ralph Forsberg, Delta College; Walter Baggett, Manhattan College; and Michael Walker, Free Will Baptist Bible College.

A special thanks to Abigail Greshik, Joann Kozyrev, Bob Kauser, and Mark Mayell for doing a superb job editing the text and shepherding it through the production process.

Christina Hoff Sommers

Fred Sommers

VICE & VIRTUE IN EVERYDAY LIFE

Introductory Readings in Ethics

GOOD AND EVIL

Almost no one doubts that cruelty is wrong. But philosophers differ on how to explain what is wrong about acting cruelly and even about the meaning of right and wrong. So we have various systems of moral theory. Inevitably we have the possibility that a philosopher may devise a pseudo-ethical doctrine that loses sight of basic intuitions about human dignity and elementary decency. When such a doctrine achieves currency and popular respectability, it becomes a powerful force for evil. For then, what passes as conventional wisdom allows the average person to behave in reprehensible but conventionally acceptable ways.

In Chapter One we find examples of the ways the moral intuitions of the individual may conflict with publicly accepted principles that are not grounded in respect for human dignity. In the first two selections, "From Cruelty to Goodness" by Philip Hallie and "The Conscience of Huckleberry Finn" by Jonathan Bennett, the moral failure of principle is easy to diagnose. A dominant group adopts a philosophy that permits it to confine its moral concern to those inside the group, treating outsiders as beyond the moral pale; their pain, their dignity, even their very lives merit no moral consideration. Huckleberry Finn, being white, is within the moral domain. His mentors have taught him that he does not owe moral behavior to slaves. Yet Huck treats Jim, the runaway slave, as if he too deserves the respect due a white person. And therein lies Huck's conflict. Everything he conventionally believes tells him he is doing wrong in helping Jim elude his pursuers.

Mark Twain's account of the conflict between official "book" morality and the ground-level morality of an innately decent and sympathetic person is one of the best in literature. Usually the conflict is embodied in two protagonists (Victor Hugo's novel *Les Misérables* is an example), but Huck Finn's conflict is within himself. And we are glad that his decency is stronger than his book morality. Both Jonathan Bennett and Philip Hallie quote the Nazi officer Heinrich Himmler, one of the fathers of the "final solution," as a spokesman for those who advocate suspending all moral feeling toward a particular group. Interestingly, Himmler considered

1

himself all the more moral for being above pitying the children and other innocent victims outside the domain of moral consideration. Indeed, we hear stories of Germans who were conscience-stricken because—against their principles—they allowed some Jews to escape.

Our dismay at man's inhumanity to man is qualified by the inspiring example of the residents of the French village Le Chambon-sur-Lignon who acted together to care for and save 6,000 Jews, mostly children, from the Nazis. Le Chambon is said to have been the safest place in Europe for a Jew during World War II. From his studies of the village, Hallie concludes that Le Chambon residents successfully combated evil because they never allowed themselves to be blind to the victim's point of view. "When we are blind to that point of view we can countenance and perpetrate cruelty with impunity." The true morality of Le Chambon drives out false and hypocritical Nazi "decencies" that ignore the most elementary moral intuitions and that permit and encourage the horrors of Himmler's and Hitler's Germany.

The advent of totalitarianisms in the twentieth century has given rise to large concentration camps in which millions of innocents were incarcerated, tormented, and murdered. Moral philosophers have written much about the amorality of the people who planned, built, and administered these camps. Tzvetan Todorov and Anne Applebaum, in the selections we have chosen, focus their attention on the morale of those who lived in conditions of unspeakable horror but who managed to survive to tell their stories. Experiments such as those conducted by Yale University Psychologist Stanley Milgram in the 1960s dramatically suggest that even ordinary men and women living in ordinary times can be moved to inflict grave harm on hapless innocents.

In his selection, Josiah Royce defends a morality that respects human dignity. Beginning from the axiom that we owe respect and decency to our neighbor, Royce confronts the question that the Nazis and all those who ignore the humanity of special groups pervert: Who, then, are our neighbors? Royce answers that our neighbors include anyone with feelings: "Pain is pain, joy is joy, everywhere even as in thee." Royce calls this the moral insight. He points out that treating strangers with care and solicitude is hardly unnatural; for each of us, our future self is like a stranger to us, yet we are naturally concerned with the welfare of that stranger.

The moral blindness that is the opposite of Royce's moral insight has tragic consequences for the victims whose humanity is ignored. The point is taken up by Hallie, who complains that some moral philosophers who concentrate on the motives and character of evildoers often fail to attend to the suffering of the victims. Hallie argues that it is not the character of evildoers that is the crucial element of evil, but rather that evil mainly consists in the suffering caused by the perpetrators of evil. For Hallie, evil is what evil does. He therefore takes sharp issue with Bennett for saying that the Nazi who professes to be affected by the suffering he causes is in some respects morally superior to theologians like Jonathan Edwards who never actually harmed anyone but who claim to have no pity for the sinner who would suffer the torments of the damned.

Do we punish people for the evil they do or for what they are? Herman Melville's *Billy Budd* is a classic on this question. Billy Budd is an exceptionally pure and good person who has committed a crime. We are tempted to say that Budd's fine character exculpates his crime. But this could be a dangerous doctrine if applied generally, since it challenges the principle that moral agents—including those of especially superior moral character—must be responsible to society for the consequences of their acts.

Friedrich Nietzsche challenges the tradition of Western morality with its moral insights and its Golden Rule to do to others what you would want them to do to you. He characterizes this tradition that enjoins us to protect the weak and whose origins lie in the teachings of Judaism and Christianity as "sentimental weakness" and a "*denial* of life." According to Nietzsche, the tradition emasculates those who are strong, vital, and superior by forcing them to attend to the weak and mediocre. Nietzsche was especially effective in suggesting that morality often is used in hypocritical ways to stifle initiative. Yet, on the whole, philosophers have rejected Nietzsche's heroic morality as tending to encourage a morally irresponsible exercise of power. This is perhaps unfair, since Nietzsche himself almost certainly would have looked with contempt upon such self-styled "heroes" as the leaders of Nazi Germany. Another reason seems more valid: Nietzsche's own ideal does in fact denigrate sympathy with the weak and helpless, and so fails to convince those of us who see moral heroism in the likes of Huckleberry Finn and the people of Le Chambon.

From Cruelty to Goodness

Philip Hallie

Philip Hallie (1922–1994) was a professor of philosophy at Wesleyan University. His published works include *The Paradox of Cruelty* (1969), *Lest Innocent Blood Be Shed* (1979), and *In the Eye of the Hurricane: Tales of Good and Evil, Help and Harm* (2001).

Philip Hallie considers institutionalized cruelty and finds that, besides physically assaulting its victims, it almost always assaults their dignity and self-respect. As an example of the opposite of institutionalized cruelty, Hallie cites the residents of the French village of Le Chambon who, at grave risk to their lives, saved 6,000 Jews from the Nazis. For him the contrary of being cruel is not merely ceasing to be cruel, nor is it fighting cruelty with violence and hatred (though this may be necessary). Rather, it is epitomized in the unambiguous and unpretentious goodness of the citizens of Le Chambon who followed the positive biblical injunctions "Defend the fatherless" and "Be your brother's keeper," as well as the negative injunctions against murder and betrayal.

I am a student of ethics, of good and evil; but my approach to these two rather melodramatic terms is skeptical. I am in the tradition of the ancient Greek *skeptikoi*, whose name means "inquirers" or "investigators." And what we investigate is relationships among particular facts. What we put into doubt are the intricate webs of high-level abstractions that passed for philosophizing in the ancient world, and that still pass for philosophizing. My approach to good and evil emphasizes not abstract common nouns like "justice," but proper names and verbs. Names and verbs keep us close to the facts better than do our high-falutin common nouns. Names refer to particular people, and verbs connect subjects with predicates *in time*, while common nouns are above all this.

One of the words that is important to me is my own name. For me, philosophy is personal; it is closer to literature and history than it is to the exact sciences, closer to the passions, actions, and common sense of individual persons than to a dispassionate technical science. It has to do with the personal matter of wisdom. And so ethics for me is personal—my story, and not necessarily (though possibly) yours. It concerns particular people at particular times.

But ethics is more than such particulars. It involves abstractions, that is, rules, laws, ideals. When you look at the ethical magnates of history you see in their words and deeds two sorts of ethical rules: negative and positive. The negative rules are scattered throughout the Bible, but Moses brought down from Mount Sinai the main negative ethical rules of the West: Thou shalt not murder; thou shalt not betray.... The positive injunctions are similarly spread throughout the Bible. In the first chapter of the book of Isaiah we are told to "... defend the fatherless, plead for the widow." The negative ethic forbids certain actions; the positive ethic demands certain actions. To follow the negative ethic is to be decent, to have clean hands. But to follow the positive ethic, to be one's brother's keeper, is to be more than decent—it is to be active, even aggressive. If the negative ethic is one of decency, the positive one is the ethic of riskful, strenuous nobility.

In my early studies of particularized ethical terms, I found myself dwelling upon negative ethics, upon prohibitions. And among the most conspicuous prohibitions I found embodied in history was the prohibition against deliberate harmdoing, against cruelty. "Thou shalt not be cruel" had as much to do with the nightmare of history as did the prohibitions against murder and betrayal. In fact, many of the Ten Commandments—especially those against murder, adultery, stealing, and betrayal—were ways of prohibiting cruelty.

Early in my research it became clear that there are various approaches to cruelty, as the different commandments suggest. For instance, there is the way reflected in the origins of the word "cruel." The Latin *crudus* is related to still older words standing for bloodshed, or raw flesh. According to the etymology of the word, cruelty involves the spilling of blood.

But modern dictionaries give the word a different meaning. They define it as "disposed to giving pain." They emphasize awareness, not simply bloodshed. After all, they seem to say, you cannot be cruel to a dead body. There is no cruelty without consciousness.

And so I found myself studying the kinds of awareness associated with the hurting of human beings. It is certainly true that for millennia in history and literature people have been torturing each other not only with hard weapons but also with hard words.

Still, the word "pain" seemed to be a simplistic and superficial way of describing the many different sorts of cruelty. In Reska Weiss's *Journey Through Hell* (London, 1961) there is a brief passage of one of the deepest cruelties that Nazis perpetrated upon extermination camp inmates. On a march

> Urine and excreta poured down the prisoners' legs, and by nightfall the excrement, which had frozen to our limbs, gave off its stench.

And Weiss goes on to talk not in terms of "pain" or bloodshed, but in other terms:

> ... We were really no longer human beings in the accepted sense. Not even animals, but putrefying corpses moving on two legs.

There is one factor that the idea of "pain" and the simpler idea of bloodshed do not touch: cruelty, not playful, quotidian teasing or ragging, but cruelty (what the anti-cruelty societies usually call "substantial cruelty") involves the maiming of a person's dignity, the crushing of a person's self-respect. Bloodshed, the idea of pain (which is usually something involving a localizable occurrence, localizable in a tooth, in a head, in short, in the body), these are superficial ideas of cruelty. A whip, bleeding flesh, these are what the journalists of cruelty emphasize, following the etymology and dictionary meaning of the word. But the depths of an understanding of cruelty lie in the depths of an understanding of human dignity and of how you can maim it without bloodshed, and often without localizable bodily pain.

In excremental assault, in the process of keeping camp inmates from wiping themselves or from going to the latrine, and in making them drink water from a toilet bowl full of excreta (and the excreta of the guards at that) localizable pain is nothing. Deep humiliation is everything. We human beings believe in hierarchies, whether we are skeptics or not about human value. There is a hierarchical gap between shit and me. We are even above using the word. We are "above" walking around besmirched with feces. Our dignity, whatever the origins of that dignity may be, does not permit it. In order to be able to want to live, in order to be able to walk erect, we must respect ourselves as beings "higher" than our feces. When we feel that we are not "higher" than dirt or filth, then our lives are maimed at the very center, in the very depths, not merely in some localizable portion of our bodies. And when our lives are so maimed we become things, slaves, instruments. From ancient times until this moment, and as long as there will be human beings on this planet, there are those who know this and will use it, just as the Roman slave owners and the Southern American slave owners knew it when—one time a year—they encouraged the slaves to drink all the alcohol they could drink so that they could get bestially drunk and then even more bestially sick afterwards, under the eyes of their generous owners. The self-hatred, the loss of self-respect that the Saturnalia created in ancient Rome, say, made it possible to continue using the slaves as things, since they themselves came to think of themselves as things, as subhuman tools of the owners and the overseers.

Institutionalized cruelty, I learned, is the subtlest kind of cruelty. In episodic cruelty the victim knows he is being hurt, and his victimizer knows it too. But in a persistent pattern of humiliation that endures for years in a community, both the victim and the victimizer find ways of obscuring the harm that is being done. Blacks come to think of themselves as inferior, even esthetically inferior (black is "dirty"); and Jews come to think of themselves as inferior, even esthetically (dark hair and aquiline noses are "ugly"), so that the way they are being treated is justified by their "actual" inferiority, by the inferiority they themselves feel.

A similar process happens in the minds of the victimizers in institutionalized cruelty. They feel that since they are superior, even esthetically ("to be blonde is to be beautiful"), they deserve to do what they wish, deserve to have these lower creatures under their control. The words of Heinrich Himmler, head of the Nazi SS, in Posen in the year 1943 in a speech to his SS subordinates in a closed session, show how institutionalized cruelty can obscure harmdoing:

> ... the words come so easily. "The Jewish people will be exterminated," says every party member, "of course. It's in our program ... extermination. We'll take care of it." And then they come, these nice 80 million Germans, and every one of them has his decent Jew. Sure the others are swine, but his one is a fine Jew.... Most of you will know what it means to have seen 100 corpses together, or 500 to 1,000. To have made one's way through that, and ... to have remained a decent person throughout, that is what has made us hard. That is a page of glory in our history....

In this speech he was making a sharp distinction between the program of crushing the Jews and the personal sentiments of individual Germans. The program stretched over years; personal sentiments were momentary. He was pleading for the program, for institutionalized destruction.

But one of the most interesting parts of the speech occurs toward the end of it:

> ... in sum, we can say that we fulfilled the heaviest of tasks [destroying the Jews] in love to our people. And we suffered no harm in our essence, in our soul, in our character....

Commitment that overrides all sentimentality transforms cruelty and destruction into moral nobility, and commitment is the lifeblood of an institution.

Cruelty and the Power Relationships

But when I studied all these ways that we have used the word "cruelty," I was nagged by the feeling that I had not penetrated into its inner structure. I was classifying, sorting out symptoms; but symptoms are signals, and what were the symptoms signals *of?* I felt like a person who had been studying cancer by sorting out brief pains from persistent pains, pains in the belly from pains in the head. I was being superficial, and I was not asking the question, "What are the forces behind these kinds of cruelty?" I felt that there were such forces, but as yet I had not touched them.

Then one day I was reading in one of the great autobiographies of western civilization, Frederick Douglass's *Life and Times*. The passage I was reading was about Douglass's thoughts on the origins of slavery. He was asking himself: "How could these whites keep us enslaved?" And he suddenly realized:

> My faculties and powers of body and soul are not my own, but are the property of a fellow-mortal in no sense superior to me, except that he has the physical power to compel me to be owned and controlled by him. By the combined physical force of the community I am his slave—a slave for life.

And then I saw that a disparity in power lay at the center of the dynamism of cruelty. If it was institutional cruelty it was in all likelihood a difference involving both verbal and physical power that kept the cruelty going. The power of the majority and the weakness of a minority were at the center of the institutional cruelty of slavery and of Nazi anti-Semitism. The whites not only outnumbered the blacks in America, but had economic and political ascendancy over them. But just as important as these "physical" powers was the power that words like "nigger" and "slave" gave the white majority. Their language sanctified if it did not create their power ascendancy over the blacks, and one of the most important projects of the slaveholders and their allies was that of seeing to it that the blacks themselves thought of themselves in just these powerless terms. They utilized the language to convince not only the whites but the blacks themselves that blacks were weak in mind, in will power, and in worth. These words were like the excremental assault in the killing camps of the Nazis: they diminished both the respect the victimizers might have for their victims and the respect the victims might have for themselves.

It occurred to me that if a power differential is crucial to the idea of cruelty, then when that power differential is maintained, cruelty will tend to be maintained, and when that power differential is eliminated, cruelty will tend to be eliminated. And this seemed to work. In all kinds of cruelty, violent and polite, episodic and institutional, when the victim arms himself with the appropriate strength, the cruelty diminishes or disappears. When Jews joined the Bush Warriors of France, the Maquis, and became powerful enough to strike at Vichy or the Nazis, they stopped being victims of French and Nazi cruelty. When Frederick Douglass learned to use the language with great skill and expressiveness, and when he learned to use his physical strength against his masters, the power differential between him and his masters diminished, and so did their cruelty to him. In his autobiography he wrote:

> A man without force is without the essential dignity of humanity. Human nature is so constituted that it cannot honor a helpless man, though it can pity him, and even this it cannot do long if signs of power do not arise.

When I looked back at my own childhood in Chicago, I remembered that the physical and mental cruelties that I suffered in the slums of the southwest side when I was about ten years old sharply diminished and finally disappeared when I learned how to defend myself physically and verbally. It is exactly this lesson that Douglass learned while growing up in the cruel institution of slavery.

Cruelty then, whatever else it is, is a kind of power relationship, an imbalance of power wherein the stronger party becomes the victimizer and the weaker becomes the victim. And since many general terms are most swiftly understood in relationship with their opposites (just as "heavy" can be understood most handily in relationship with what we mean by "light") the opposite of cruelty lay in a situation where there is no imbalance of power. The opposite of cruelty, I learned, was freedom from that unbalanced power relationship. Either the victim should get stronger and stand up to the victimizer, and thereby bring about a balance of their powers, or the victim should free himself from the whole relationship by flight.

In pursuing this line of thought, I came to believe that, again, dictionaries are misleading: many of them give "kindness" as the antonym for "cruelty." In studying slavery in America and the concentration camps of central Europe I found that kindness could be the ultimate cruelty, especially when it was given within that unbalanced power relationship. A kind overseer or a kind camp guard can exacerbate cruelty, can remind his victim that there are other relationships than the relationship of cruelty, and can make the victim deeply bitter, especially when he sees the self-satisfied smile of his victimizer. He is being cruelly treated when he is given a penny or a bun after having endured the crushing and grinding of his mental and bodily well-being. As Frederick Douglass put it:

> The kindness of the slave-master only gilded the chain. It detracted nothing from its weight or strength. The thought that men are for other and better uses than slavery throve best under the gentle treatment of a kind master.

No, I learned, the opposite of cruelty is not kindness. The opposite of the cruelty of the overseer in American slavery was not the kindness of that overseer for a moment or for a day. An episodic kindness is not the opposite of an institutionalized cruelty. The opposite of institutionalized cruelty is freedom from the cruel relationship.

It is important to see how perspectival the whole meaning of cruelty is. From the perspective of the SS guard or the southern overseer, a bit of bread, a smile is indeed a diminution of cruelty. But in the relationship of cruelty, the point of view of the victimizer is of only minor importance; it is the point of view of the victim that is authoritative. The victim feels the suffering in his own mind and body, whereas the victimizer, like Himmler's "hard" and "decent" Nazi, can be quite unaware of that suffering. The sword does not feel the pain that it inflicts. Do not ask it about suffering.

Goodness Personified in Le Chambon

All these considerations drove me to write my book *The Paradox of Cruelty*. But with the book behind me, I felt a deep discontent. I saw cruelty as an embodiment, a particular case of evil. But if cruelty is one of the main evils of human history, why is the opposite of cruelty not one of the key goods of human history? Freedom from the cruel relationship, either by escaping it or by redressing the imbalance of power, was not essential to what western philosophers and theologians have thought of as goodness. Escape is a negative affair. Goodness has something positive in it, something triumphantly affirmative.

Hoping for a hint of goodness in the very center of evil, I started looking closely at the so-called "medical experiments" of the Nazis upon children, usually Jewish and Gypsy children, in the death camps. Here were the weakest of the weak. Not only were they despised minorities, but they were, as individuals, still in their non-age. They were dependents. Here the power imbalance between the cruel experimenters and their victims was at its greatest. But instead of seeing light or finding insight by going down into this hell, into the deepest depth of cruelty, I found myself unwillingly becoming part of the world I was studying. I found myself either yearning to be viciously cruel to the victimizers of the children, or I found myself feeling compassion for the children, feeling their despair and pain as they looked up at the men and women in white coats cutting off their fingertips one at a time, or breaking their slender bones, or wounding their internal organs. Either I became a would-be victimizer or one more Jewish victim, and in either case I was not achieving insight, only misery, like so many other students of the Holocaust. And when I was trying to be "objective" about my studies, when I was succeeding at being indifferent to both the victimizers and the victims of these cruel relationships, I became cold; I became another monster who could look upon the maiming of a child with an indifferent eye.

To relieve this unending suffering, from time to time I would turn to the literature of the French resistance to the Nazis. I had been trained by the U.S. Army to understand it. The resistance was a way of trying to redress the power imbalance between Hitler's Fortress Europe and Hitler's victims, and so I saw it as an enemy of cruelty. Still, its methods were often cruel like the methods of most power struggles, and I had little hope of finding goodness here. We soldiers violated the negative ethic forbidding killing in order, we thought, to follow the positive ethic of being our brothers' keepers.

And then one gray April afternoon I found a brief article on the French village of Le Chambon-sur-Lignon. I shall not analyze here the tears of amazement and gladness and release from despair—in short, of joy—that I shed when I first read that story. Tears themselves interest me greatly—but not the tears of melancholy hindsight and existential despair; rather the tears of awe you experience when the realization of an ideal suddenly appears before your very eyes or thunders inside your mind; these tears interest me.

And one of the reasons I wept at first reading about Le Chambon in those brief, inaccurate pages was that at last I had discovered an embodiment of goodness in opposition to cruelty. I had discovered in the flesh and blood of history, in people with definite names in a definite place at a definite time in the nightmare of history, what no classical or religious ethicist could deny was goodness.

The French Protestant village of Le Chambon, located in the Cévennes Mountains of southeastern France, and with a population of about 3,500, saved the lives of about 6,000 people, most of them Jewish children whose parents had been murdered in the killing camps of central Europe. Under a national government which was not only collaborating with the Nazi conquerors of France but frequently trying to outdo the Germans in anti-Semitism in order to please their conquerors, and later under the day-to-day threat of destruction by the German Armed SS, they started to save children in the winter of 1940, the winter after the fall of France, and they continued to do so until the war in France was over. They sheltered the refugees in their own homes and in various houses they established especially for them; and they took many of them across the terrible mountains to neutral Geneva, Switzerland, in the teeth of French and German police and military power. The people of Le Chambon are poor, and the Huguenot faith to which they belong is a diminishing faith in Catholic and atheist France; but their spiritual power, their capacity to act in unison against the victimizers who surrounded them, was immense, and more than a match for the military power of those victimizers.

But for me as an ethicist the heart of the matter was not only their special power. What interested me was that they obeyed *both* the negative and the positive injunctions of ethics; they were good not only in the sense of trying to be their brothers' keepers, protecting the victim, "defending the fatherless," to use the language of Isaiah; they were also good in the sense that they obeyed the negative injunctions against killing and betraying. While those around them—including myself—were murdering in order, presumably, to help mankind in some way or other, they murdered nobody, and betrayed not a single child in those long and dangerous four years. For me as an ethicist they were the embodiment of unambiguous goodness.

But for me as a student of cruelty they were something more: they were an embodiment of the opposite of cruelty. And so, somehow, at last, I had found goodness in opposition to cruelty. In studying their story, and in telling it in *Lest Innocent Blood Be Shed*, I learned that the opposite of cruelty is not simply freedom from the cruel relationship; it is *hospitality*. It lies not only in something negative, an absence of cruelty or of imbalance; it lies in unsentimental, efficacious love. The opposite of the cruelties of the camps was not the liberation of the camps, the cleaning out of the barracks and the cessation of the horrors. All of this was the *end* of the cruelty relationship, not the opposite of that relationship. And it was not even the end of it, because the victims would never forget and would remain in agony as long as they remembered their humiliation and suffering. No, the opposite of cruelty was not the liberation of the camps, not freedom; it was the hospitality of the people of Chambon, and of very few others during the Holocaust. The opposite of cruelty was the kind of goodness that happened in Chambon.

Let me explain the difference between liberation and hospitality by telling you about a letter I received a year ago from a woman who had been saved by the people of Le Chambon when she was a young girl. She wrote:

> Never was there a question that the Chambonnais would not share all they had with us, meager as it was. One Chambonnais once told me that even if there was less, they still would want more for us.

And she goes on:

> It was indeed a very different attitude from the one in Switzerland, which while saving us also resented us so much.
>
> If today we are not bitter people like most survivors it can only be due to the fact that we met people like the people of Le Chambon, who showed to us simply that life can be different, that there are people who care, that people can live together and even risk their own lives for their fellow man.

The Swiss liberated refugees and removed them from the cruel relationship; the people of Le Chambon did more. They taught them that goodness could conquer cruelty, that loving hospitality could remove them from the cruel relationship. And they taught me this, too.

It is important to emphasize that cruelty is not simply an episodic, momentary matter, especially institutional cruelty like that of Nazism or slavery. As we have seen throughout this essay, not only does it persist while it is being exerted upon the weak; *it can persist in the survivors* after they have escaped the power relationship. The survivors torture themselves, continue to suffer, continue to maim their own lives long after the actual torture is finished. The self-hatred and rage of the blacks and the despair of the Native Americans and the Jews who have suffered under institutional crushing and maiming are continuations of original cruelties. And these continuations exist because only a superficial liberation from torture has occurred. The sword has stopped falling on their flesh in the old obvious ways, but the wounds still bleed. I am not saying that the village of Chambon healed these wounds—they go too deep. What I am saying is that the people I have talked to who were once children in Le Chambon have more hope for their species and more respect for themselves as human beings than most other survivors I have met. The enduring hospitality they met in Le Chambon helped them find realistic hope in a world of persisting cruelty.

What was the nature of this hospitality that saved and deeply changed so many lives? It is hard to summarize briefly what the Chambonnais did, and above all how they did it. The morning after a new refugee family came to town they would find on their front door a wreath with *"Bienvenue!"* "Welcome!" painted on a piece of cardboard attached to the wreath. Nobody knew who had brought the wreath; in effect, the whole town had brought it.

It was mainly the women of Chambon who gave so much more than shelter to these, the most hated enemies of the Nazis. There was Madame Barraud, a tiny Alsatian, who cared for the refugee boys in her house with all the love such a tiny body could hold, and who cared for the way they felt day and night. And there were others.

But there was one person without whom Le Chambon could not have become the safest place in Europe for Jews: the Huguenot minister of the village, André Trocmé. Trocmé was a passionately religious man. He was massive, more than six feet tall, blonde, with a quick temper. Once long after the war, while he was lecturing on the main project of his life, the promotion of the idea of nonviolence in international relations, one of the members of his audience started to whisper a few words to his neighbor. Trocmé let this go on for a few moments, then interrupted his speech, walked up to the astonished whisperer, raised his massive arm, pointed toward the door, and yelled, "Out! Out! Get out!" And the lecture was on nonviolence.

The center of his thought was the belief that God showed how important man was by becoming Himself a human being, and by becoming a particular sort of human being who was the embodiment of sacrificially generous love. For Trocmé, every human being was like Jesus, had God in him or her, and was just as precious as God Himself. And when Trocmé with the help of the Quakers and others organized his village into the most efficient rescue machine in Europe, he did so not only to save the Jews, but also to save the Nazis and their collaborators. He wanted to keep them from blackening their souls with more evil—he wanted to save them, the victimizers, from evil.

One of the reasons he was successful was that the Huguenots had been themselves persecuted for hundreds of years by the kings of France, and they knew what persecution was. In fact, when the people of Chambon took Jewish children and whole families across the mountains of southeastern France into neutral Switzerland, they often followed pathways that had been taken by Huguenots in their flight from the Dragoons of the French kings.

A particular incident from the story of Le Chambon during the Nazi occupation of France will explain succinctly why he was successful in making the village a village of refuge. But before I relate the story, I must point out that the people of the village did not think of themselves as "successful," let alone as "good." From their point of view, they did not do anything that required elaborate explanation. When I asked them why they helped these dangerous guests, they invariably answered, "What do you mean, 'Why'? Where else could they go? How could you turn them away? What is so special about being ready to help *(prête à servir)*? There was nothing else to do." And some of them laughed in amazement when I told them that I thought they were "good people." They saw no alternative to their actions and to the way they acted, and therefore they saw what they did as necessary, not something to be picked out for praise. Helping these guests was for them as natural as breathing or eating—one does not think of alternatives to these functions; they did not think of alternatives to sheltering people who were endangering not only the lives of their hosts but the lives of all the people of the village.

And now the story. One afternoon a refugee woman knocked on the door of a farmhouse outside the village. The farmers around the village proper were Protestants like most of the others in Chambon, but with one difference: they were mostly "Darbystes," followers of a strange Scot named Darby, who taught their ancestors in the nineteenth century to believe every word of the Bible, and indeed, who had them memorize the Bible. They were literal fundamentalists. The farmwoman opened the door to the refugee and invited her into the kitchen where it was warm. Standing in the middle of the floor the refugee, in heavily accented

French, asked for eggs for her children. In those days of very short supplies, people with children often went to the farmers in the "gray market" (neither black nor exactly legal) to get necessary food. This was early in 1941, and the farmers were not yet accustomed to the refugees. The farmwoman looked into the eyes of the shawled refugee and asked, "Are you Jewish?" The woman started to tremble, but she could not lie, even though that question was usually the beginning of the end of life for Jews in Hitler's Fortress Europe. She answered, "Yes."

The woman ran from the kitchen to the staircase nearby, and while the refugee trembled with terror in the kitchen, she called up the stairs, "Husband, children, come down, come down! We have in our house at this very moment a representative of the Chosen People!"

Not all the Protestants in Chambon were Darbyste fundamentalists; but almost all were convinced that people are the children of God, and are as precious as God Himself. Their leaders were Huguenot preachers and their following of the negative and positive commandments of the Bible came in part from their personal generosity and courage, but also in part from the depths of their religious conviction that we are all children of God, and we must take care of each other lovingly. This combined with the ancient and deep historical ties between the Huguenots and the Jews of France and their own centuries of persecution by the Dragoons and Kings of France helped make them what they were, "always ready to help," as the Chambonnais saying goes.

A Choice of Perspectives

We have come a long way from cruelty to the people of Chambon, just as I have come a long way in my research from concrete evil to concrete goodness. Let me conclude with a point that has been alternately hinted at and stressed in the course of this essay.

A few months after *Lest Innocent Blood Be Shed* was published I received a letter from Massachusetts that opened as follows:

> I have read your book, and I believe that you mushy-minded moralists should be awakened to the facts. Nothing happened in Le Chambon, nothing of any importance whatsoever.
>
> The Holocaust, dear Professor, was like a geological event, like an earthquake. No person could start it; no person could change it; and no person could end it. And no small group of persons could do so either. It was the armies and the nations that performed actions that counted. Individuals did nothing. You sentimentalists have got to learn that the great masses and big political ideas make the difference. Your people and the people they saved simply do not exist.

Now between this position and mine there is an abyss that no amount of shouted arguments or facts can cross. And so I shall not answer this letter with a tightly organized reply. I shall answer it only by telling you that one of the reasons institutional cruelty exists and persists is that people believe that individuals can do nothing, that only vast ideologies and armies can act meaningfully. Every act of institutional cruelty—Nazism, slavery, and all the others—lives not with people in the concrete, but with abstractions that blind people to individuals. Himmler's speech to the SS leadership in 1943 is full of phrases like "exterminating a bacillus," and "The

Jewish people will be exterminated." And in that speech he attacks any German who believes in "his decent Jew." Institutional cruelty, like other misleading approaches to ethics, blinds us to the victim's point of view; and when we are blind to that point of view we can countenance and perpetrate cruelty with impunity.

I have told you that I cannot and will not try to refute the letter from Massachusetts. I shall only summarize the point of view of this essay with another story.

I was lecturing a few months ago in Minneapolis, and when I finished talking about the Holocaust and the village of Le Chambon, a woman stood up and asked me if the village of Le Chambon was in the Department of Haute-Loire, the high sources of the Loire River. Obviously she was French, with her accent; and all French people know that there are many villages called "Le Chambon" in France, just as any American knows that there are many "Main Streets" in the United States. I said that Le Chambon was indeed in the Haute-Loire.

She said, "Then you have been speaking about the village that saved all three of my children. I want to thank you for writing this book, not only because the story will now be permanent, but also because I shall be able to talk about those terrible days with Americans now, for they will understand those days better than they have. You see, you Americans, though you sometimes cross the oceans, live on an island here as far as war is concerned...."

Then she asked to come up and say one sentence. There was not a sound, not even breathing, to be heard in the room. She came to the front of the room and said, "The Holocaust was storm, lightning, thunder, wind, rain, yes. And Le Chambon was the rainbow."

Only from her perspective can you understand the cruelty and the goodness I have been talking about, not from the point of view of the gentleman from Massachusetts. You must choose which perspective is best, and your choice will have much to do with your feelings about the preciousness of life, and not only the preciousness of other people's lives. If the lives of others are precious to you, your life will become more precious to you.

STUDY QUESTIONS

1. Distinguish between positive and negative moral injunctions. Do you agree with Hallie that we need both for moral decency? Explain.
2. Do you agree with Hallie that cruelty is prevalent when a serious imbalance of power exists among people? Can we be cruel to our equals? Explain.
3. Why does Hallie deny that kindness is the opposite of cruelty? What does he consider to be cruelty's opposite?
4. What does the writer Terrence Des Pres mean when he says of Le Chambon, "Those events took place and therefore demand a place in our view of the world"?
5. With whom do you agree more: (a) the person from Massachusetts who wrote and called Hallie a "mushy-minded moralist" who has failed to realize that the Holocaust "was like a geological event" that could not be stopped or modified, or (b) Hallie, who claims that Le Chambon teaches us that goodness can conquer cruelty? Why?

The Conscience of Huckleberry Finn

Jonathan Bennett

Jonathan Bennett (b. 1930) is a professor Emeritus of philosophy at Syracuse University. He is the author of several books, including *Kant's Analytic* (1966), *Rationality: An Essay towards an Analysis* (1989), and most recently, *A Philosophical Guide to Conditionals* (2003).

In this selection Jonathan Bennett considers the moral consciences of Huckleberry Finn, the Nazi officer Heinrich Himmler, and the Calvinist theologian Jonathan Edwards. He is interested in how each, in his own way, resolves the conflict between his human sympathies and the moral doctrine he is following that requires him to override those sympathies. Huck Finn develops a deep attachment to Jim, the runaway slave, but the official morality of his community does not allow for fellow feelings toward slaves. When forced to choose between his kindly feelings and the official morality, Huck gives up on morality. Himmler set his sympathies aside. Jonathan Edwards's case represents a third way out: he allowed himself no sympathies at all. Bennett finds Edwards's solution to be as bad as Himmler's, if not worse. Bennett concludes that while we should not give our sympathies a "blank check," we must always give them great weight and be wary of acting on any principle that conflicts with them.

I

In this paper, I shall present not just the conscience of Huckleberry Finn but two others as well. One of them is the conscience of Heinrich Himmler. He became a Nazi in 1923; he served drably and quietly, but well, and was rewarded with increasing responsibility and power. At the peak of his career he held many offices and commands, of which the most powerful was that of leader of the SS—the principal police force of the Nazi regime. In this capacity, Himmler commanded the whole concentration-camp system, and was responsible for the execution of the so-called "final solution of the Jewish problem." It is important for my purposes that this piece of social engineering should be thought of not abstractly but in concrete terms of Jewish families being marched to what they think are bathhouses, to the accompaniment of loud-speaker renditions of extracts from *The Merry Widow* and *Tales of Hoffmann*, there to be choked to death by poisonous gases. Altogether, Himmler succeeded in murdering about four and a half million of them, as well as several million gentiles, mainly Poles and Russians.

THE CONSCIENCE OF HUCKLEBERRY FINN From *Philosophy* 49 (1974), pp. 123–135 by Jonathan Bennett. Reprinted with the permission of the Cambridge University Press.

The other conscience to be discussed is that of the Calvinist theologian and philosopher Jonathan Edwards. He lived in the first half of the eighteenth century, and has a good claim to be considered America's first serious and considerable philosophical thinker. He was for many years a widely renowned preacher and Congregationalist minister in New England; in 1748 a dispute with his congregation led him to resign (he couldn't accept their view that unbelievers should be admitted to the Lord's Supper in the hope that it would convert them); for some years after that he worked as a missionary, preaching to Indians through an interpreter; then in 1758 he accepted the presidency of what is now Princeton University, and within two months died from a smallpox inoculation. Along the way he wrote some first-rate philosophy; his book attacking the notion of free will is still sometimes read. Why I should be interested in Edwards' *conscience* will be explained in due course.

I shall use Heinrich Himmler, Jonathan Edwards, and Huckleberry Finn to illustrate different aspects of a single theme, namely the relationship between *sympathy* on the one hand and *bad morality* on the other.

II

All that I can mean by a "bad morality" is a morality whose principles I deeply disapprove of. When I call a morality bad, I cannot prove that mine is better; but when I here call any morality bad, I think you will agree with me that it is bad; and that is all I need.

There could be dispute as to whether the springs of someone's actions constitute a *morality*. I think, though, that we must admit that someone who acts in ways which conflict grossly with our morality may nevertheless have a morality of his own—a set of principles of action which he sincerely assents to, so that for him the problem of acting well or rightly or in obedience to conscience is the problem of conforming to *those* principles. The problem of conscientiousness can arise as acutely for a bad morality as for any other: Rotten principles may be as difficult to keep as decent ones.

As for "sympathy" I use this term to cover every sort of fellow-feeling, as when one feels pity over someone's loneliness, or horrified compassion over his pain, or when one feels a shrinking reluctance to act in a way which will bring misfortune to someone else. *These feelings* must not be confused with *moral judgments*. My sympathy for someone in distress may lead me to help him, or even to think that I ought to help him; but in itself it is not a judgment about what I ought to do but just a *feeling* for him in his plight. We shall get some light on the difference between feelings and moral judgments when we consider Huckleberry Finn.

Obviously, feelings can impel one to action, and so can moral judgments; and in a particular case sympathy and morality may pull in opposite directions. This can happen not just with bad moralities, but also with good ones like yours and mine. For example, a small child, sick and miserable, clings tightly to his mother and screams in terror when she tries to pass him over to the doctor to be examined. If the mother gave way to her sympathy, that is to her feeling for the child's misery and fright, she would hold it close and not let the doctor come near; but don't we agree that it might be wrong for her to act on such a feeling? Quite generally, then, anyone's moral principles may apply to a particular situation in a way which runs contrary to the particular thrusts of fellow-feeling that he has in that situation. My immediate concern is with sympathy in relation to bad morality, but not because such conflicts occur only when the morality is bad.

Now, suppose that someone who accepts a bad morality is struggling to make himself act in accordance with it in a particular situation where his sympathies pull him another way. He sees the struggle as one between doing the right, conscientious thing, and acting wrongly and weakly, like the mother who won't let the doctor come near her sick, frightened baby. Since we don't accept this person's morality, we may see the situation very differently, thoroughly disapproving of the action he regards as the right one, and endorsing the action which from his point of view constitutes weakness and backsliding.

Conflicts between sympathy and bad morality won't always be like this, for we won't disagree with every single dictate of a bad morality. Still, it can happen in the way I have described, with the agent's right action being our wrong one, and vice versa. That is just what happens in a certain episode in Chapter 16 of *The Adventures of Huckleberry Finn*, an episode which brilliantly illustrates how fiction can be instructive about real life.

III

Huck Finn has been helping his slave friend Jim to run away from Miss Watson, who is Jim's owner. In their raft-journey down the Mississippi River, they are near to the place at which Jim will become legally free. Now let Huck take over the story:

> Jim said it made him all over trembly and feverish to be so close to freedom. Well I can tell you it made me all over trembly and feverish, too, to hear him, because I begun to get it through my head that he *was* most free—and who was to blame for it? Why, *me*. I couldn't get that out of my conscience, no how nor no way.... It hadn't ever come home to me, before, what this thing was that I was doing. But now it did; and it stayed with me, and scorched me more and more. I tried to make out to myself that *I* warn't to blame, because *I* didn't run Jim off from his rightful owner; but it warn't no use, conscience up and say, every time: "But you knowed he was running for his freedom, and you could a paddled ashore and told somebody." That was so—I couldn't get around that, no way. That was where it pinched. Conscience says to me: "What had poor Miss Watson done to you, that you could see her nigger go off right under your eyes and never say one single word? What did that poor old woman do to you, that you could treat her so mean? ..." I got to feeling so mean and miserable I most wished I was dead.

Jim speaks his plan to save up to buy his wife, and then his children, out of slavery; and he adds that if the children cannot be bought he will arrange to steal them. Huck is horrified:

> Thinks I, this is what comes of my not thinking. Here was this nigger which I had as good as helped to run away, coming right out flat-footed and saying he would steal his children—children that belonged to a man I didn't even know; a man that hadn't ever done me no harm.
>
> I was sorry to hear Jim say that, it was such a lowering of him. My conscience got to stirring me up hotter than ever, until at last I says to it: "Let up on me—it ain't too

late, yet—I'll paddle ashore at first light, and tell." I felt easy, and happy, and light as a feather, right off. All my troubles was gone.

This is bad morality all right. In his earliest years Huck wasn't taught any principles, and the only ones he has encountered since then are those of rural Missouri, in which slave-owning is just one kind of ownership and is not subject to critical pressure. It hasn't occurred to Huck to question those principles. So the action, to us abhorrent, of turning Jim in to the authorities presents itself *clearly* to Huck as the right thing to do.

For us, morality and sympathy would both dictate helping Jim to escape. If we felt any conflict, it would have both these on one side and something else on the other—greed for a reward, or fear of punishment. But Huck's morality conflicts with his sympathy, that is, with his unargued, natural feeling for his friend. The conflict starts when Huck sets off in the canoe towards the shore, pretending that he is going to reconnoiter, but really planning to turn Jim in:

> As I shoved off, [Jim] says: "Pooty soon I'll be a-shout'n for joy, en I'll say, it's all on accounts o' Huck I's a free man ... Jim won't ever forgit you, Huck; you's de bes' fren' Jim's ever had; en you's de *only* fren' old Jim's got now."
>
> I was paddling off, all in a sweat to tell on him; but when he says this, it seemed to kind of take the tuck all out of me. I went along slow then, and I warn't right down certain whether I was glad I started or whether I warn't. When I was fifty yards off, Jim says:
>
> "Dah you goes, de ole true Huck; de on'y white genlman dat ever kep' his promise to ole Jim." Well, I just felt sick. But I says, I *got* to do it—I can't get *out* of it.

In the upshot, sympathy wins over morality. Huck hasn't the strength of will to do what he sincerely thinks he ought to do. Two men hunting for runaway slaves ask him whether the man on his raft is black or white:

> I didn't answer up prompt. I tried to, but the words wouldn't come. I tried, for a second or two, to brace up and out with it, but I warn't man enough—hadn't the spunk of a rabbit. I see I was weakening; so I just give up trying, and up and says: "He's white."

So Huck enables Jim to escape, thus acting weakly and wickedly—he thinks. In this conflict between sympathy and morality, sympathy wins.

One critic has cited this episode in support of the statement that Huck suffers "excruciating moments of wavering between honesty and respectability." That is hopelessly wrong, and I agree with the perceptive comment on it by another critic, who says:

> The conflict waged in Huck is much more serious: He scarcely cares for respectability and never hesitates to relinquish it, but he does care for honesty and gratitude—and both honesty and gratitude require that he should give Jim up. It is not, in Huck, honesty at war with respectability but love and compassion for Jim struggling against his conscience. His decision is for Jim and hell: a right decision made in the mental chains that Huck never breaks. His concern for Jim is and remains *irrational*. Huck finds many reasons for giving Jim up and none for stealing him. To the end Huck sees his compassion for Jim as a weak, ignorant, and wicked felony.[1]

---

[1] M. J. Sidnell, "Huck Finn and Jim," *The Cambridge Quarterly*, vol. 2, pp. 205–206.

That is precisely correct—and it can have that virtue only because Mark Twain wrote the episode with such unerring precision. The crucial point concerns *reasons*, which all occur on one side of the conflict. On the side of conscience we have principles, arguments, considerations, ways of looking at things:

"It hadn't ever come home to me before what I was doing"
"I tried to make out that I warn't to blame"
"Conscience said 'But you knowed ...'—I couldn't get around that"
"What had poor Miss Watson done to you?"
"This is what comes of my not thinking"
"... children that belonged to a man I didn't even know."

On the other side, the side of feeling, we get nothing like that. When Jim rejoices in Huck, as his only friend, Huck doesn't consider the claims of friendship or have the situation "come home" to him in a different light. All that happens is: "When he says this, it seemed to kind of take the tuck all out of me. I went along slow then, and I warn't right down certain whether I was glad I started or whether I warn't." Again, Jim's words about Huck's "promise" to him don't give Huck any *reason* for changing his plan: In his morality promises to slaves probably don't count. Their effect on him is of a different kind: "Well, I just felt sick." And when the moment for final decision comes, Huck doesn't weigh up pros and cons: he simply *fails* to do what he believes to be right—he isn't strong enough, hasn't "the spunk of a rabbit." This passage in the novel is notable not just for its finely wrought irony, with Huck's weakness of will leading him to do the right thing, but also for its masterly handling of the difference between general moral principles and particular unreasoned emotional pulls.

IV

Consider now another case of bad morality in conflict with human sympathy: the case of the odious Himmler. Here, from a speech he made to some SS generals, is an indication of the content of his morality:

What happens to a Russian, to a Czech, does not interest me in the slightest. What the nations can offer in the way of good blood of our type, we will take, if necessary by kidnapping their children and raising them here with us. Whether nations live in prosperity or starve to death like cattle interests me only in so far as we need them as slaves to our *Kultur*; otherwise it is of no interest to me. Whether 10,000 Russian females fall down from exhaustion while digging an antitank ditch interests me only in so far as the antitank ditch for Germany is finished.[2]

But has this a moral basis at all? And if it has, was there in Himmler's own mind any conflict between morality and sympathy? Yes there was. Here is more from the same speech:

I also want to talk to you quite frankly on a very grave matter ... I mean ... the extermination of the Jewish race.... Most of you must know what it means when

---

[2] Quoted in William L. Shirer, *The Rise and Fall of the Third Reich* (New York, 1960), pp. 937–938. Next quotation: ibid., p. 966. All further quotations relating to Himmler are from Roger Manwell and Heinrich Fraenkel, *Heinrich Himmler* (London, 1965), pp. 132, 197, 184 (twice), 187.

100 corpses are lying side by side, or 500, or 1,000. To have stuck it out and at the same time—apart from exceptions caused by human weakness—to have remained decent fellows, that is what has made us hard. This is a page of glory in our history which has never been written and is never to be written.

Himmler saw his policies as being hard to implement while still retaining one's human sympathies—while still remaining a "decent fellow." He is saying that only the weak take the easy way out and just squelch their sympathies, and is praising the stronger and more glorious course of retaining one's sympathies while acting in violation of them. In the same spirit, he ordered that when executions were carried out in concentration camps, those responsible "are to be influenced in such a way as to suffer no ill effect in their character and mental attitude." A year later he boasted that the SS had wiped out the Jews

without our leaders and their men suffering any damage in their minds and souls. The danger was considerable, for there was only a narrow path between the Scylla of their becoming heartless ruffians unable any longer to treasure life, and the Charybdis of their becoming soft and suffering nervous breakdowns.

And there really can't be any doubt that the basis of Himmler's policies was a set of principles which constituted his morality—a sick, bad, wicked *morality*. He described himself as caught in "the old tragic conflict between will and obligation." And when his physician Kersten protested at the intention to destroy the Jews, saying that the suffering involved was "not to be contemplated," Kersten reports that Himmler replied:

He knew that it would mean much suffering for the Jews.... "It is the curse of greatness that it must step over dead bodies to create new life. Yet we must ... cleanse the soil or it will never bear fruit. It will be a great burden for me to bear."

This, I submit, is the language of morality.

So in this case, tragically, bad morality won out over sympathy. I am sure that many of Himmler's killers did extinguish their sympathies, becoming "heartless ruffians" rather than "decent fellows"; but not Himmler himself. Although his policies ran against the human grain to a horrible degree, he did not sandpaper down his emotional surfaces so that there was no grain there, allowing his actions to slide along smoothly and easily. He did, after all, bear his hideous burden, and even paid a price for it. He suffered a variety of nervous and physical disabilities, including nausea and stomach convulsions, and Kersten was doubtless right in saying that these were "the expression of a psychic division which extended over his whole life."

This same division must have been present in some of those officials of the Church who ordered heretics to be tortured so as to change their theological opinions. Along with the brutes and the cold careerists, there must have been some who cared, and who suffered from the conflict between their sympathies and their bad morality.

V

In the conflict between sympathy and bad morality, then, the victory may go to sympathy as in the case of Huck Finn, or to morality as in the case of Himmler.

Another possibility is that the conflict may be avoided by giving up, or not ever having, those sympathies which might interfere with one's principles. That seems to have been the case with Jonathan Edwards. I am afraid that I shall be doing an injustice to Edwards' many virtues, and to his great intellectual energy and inventiveness; for my concern is only with the worst thing about him—namely his morality, which was worse than Himmler's.

According to Edwards, God condemns some men to an eternity of unimaginably awful pain, though he arbitrarily spares others—"arbitrarily" because none deserve to be spared:

> Natural men are held in the hand of God over the pit of hell; they have deserved the
> fiery pit, and are already sentenced to it; and God is dreadfully provoked, his anger is
> as great toward them as to those that are actually suffering the executions of the fierce-
> ness of his wrath in hell ...; the devil is waiting for them, hell is gaping for them, the
> flames gather and flash about them, and would fain lay hold on them ...; and ... there
> are no means within reach that can be any security to them.... All that preserves
> them is the mere arbitrary will, and unconvenanted unobliged forebearance of an
> incensed God.[3]

Notice that he says "they have deserved the fiery pit." Edwards insists that men *ought* to be condemned to eternal pain; and his position isn't that this is right because God wants it, but rather that God wants it because it is right. For him, moral standards exist independently of God, and God can be assessed in the light of them (and of course found to be perfect). For example, he says:

> They deserve to be cast into hell; so that ... justice never stands in the way, it makes no
> objection against God's using his power at any moment to destroy them. Yea, on the
> contrary, justice calls aloud for an infinite punishment of their sins.

Elsewhere, he gives elaborate arguments to show that God is acting justly in damn-ing sinners. For example, he argues that a punishment should be exactly as bad as the crime being punished; God is infinitely excellent; so any crime against him is infinitely bad; and so eternal damnation is exactly right as a punishment—it is infi-nite, but, as Edwards is careful also to say, it is "no more than infinite."

Of course, Edwards himself didn't torment the damned; but the question still arises of whether his sympathies didn't conflict with his *approval* of eternal tor-ment. Didn't he find it painful to contemplate any fellow-human's being tortured forever? Apparently not:

> The God that holds you over the pit of hell, much as one holds a spider or some
> loathsome insect over the fire, abhors you, and is dreadfully provoked ... he is of purer
> eyes than to bear to have you in his sight; you are ten thousand times so abominable in
> his eyes as the most hateful venomous serpent is in ours.

When God is presented as being as misanthropic as that, one suspects misanthropy in the theologian. This suspicion is increased when Edwards claims that "the saints in glory will ... understand how terrible the sufferings of the damned are; yet ... will

---

[3] Vergilius Ferm (ed.), *Puritan Sage: Collected Writings of Jonathan Edwards* (New York, 1953), p. 370. Next three quotations: ibid., p. 366, p. 294 ("no more than infinite"), p. 372.

not be sorry for [them]."[4] He bases this partly on a view of human nature whose ugliness he seems not to notice:

> The seeing of the calamities of others tends to heighten the sense of our own enjoyments. When the saints in glory, therefore, shall see the doleful state of the damned, how will this heighten their sense of the blessedness of their own state.... When they shall see how miserable others of their fellow-creatures are ... when they shall see the smoke of their torment ... and hear their dolorous shrieks and cries, and consider that they in the mean time are in the most blissful state, and shall surely be in it to all eternity; how they will rejoice!

I hope this is less than the whole truth! His other main point about why the saints will rejoice to see the torments of the damned is that it is *right* that they should do so:

> The heavenly inhabitants ... will have no love nor pity to the damned.... [This will not show] a want of spirit of love in them ... for the heavenly inhabitants will know that it is not fit that they should love [the damned] because they will know then, that God has no love to them, nor pity for them.

The implication that *of course* one can adjust one's feelings of pity so that they conform to the dictates of some authority—doesn't this suggest that ordinary human sympathies played only a small part in Edwards' life?

VI

Huck Finn, whose sympathies are wide and deep, could never avoid the conflict in that way; but he is determined to avoid it, and so he opts for the only other alternative he can see—to give up morality altogether. After he has tricked the slave-hunters, he returns to the raft and undergoes a peculiar crisis:

> I got aboard the raft, feeling bad and low, because I knowed very well I had done wrong, and I see it warn't no use for me to try to learn to do right; a body that don't get *started* right when he's little, ain't got no show—when the pinch comes there ain't nothing to back him up and keep him to his work, and so he gets beat. Then I thought a minute, and says to myself, hold on—s'pose you'd a done right and give Jim up; would you feel better than what you do now? No, says I, I'd feel bad—I'd feel just the same way I do now. Well, then, says I, what's the use you learning to do right, when it's troublesome to do right and ain't no trouble to do wrong, and the wages is just the same? I was stuck. I couldn't answer that. So I reckoned I wouldn't bother no more about it, but after this always do whichever come handiest at the time.

Huck clearly cannot conceive of having any morality except the one he has learned—too late, he thinks—from his society. He is not entirely a prisoner of that morality, because he does after all reject it; but for him that is a decision to relinquish morality as such; he cannot envisage revising his morality, altering its content

---

[4] This and the next two quotations are from "The End of the Wicked Contemplated by the Righteous: Or, The Torments of the Wicked in Hell, No Occasion of Grief to the Saints in Heaven," from *The Works of President Edwards* (London, 1817), vol. 4, pp. 507–508, 511–112, and 509, respectively.

in face of the various pressures to which it is subject, including pressures from his sympathies. For example, he does not begin to approach the thought that slavery should be rejected on moral grounds, or the thought that what he is doing is not theft because a person cannot be owned and therefore cannot be stolen.

The basic trouble is that he cannot or will not engage in abstract intellectual operations of any sort. In chapter 33 he finds himself "feeling to blame, somehow" for something he knows he had no hand in; he assumes that this feeling is a deliverance of conscience; and this confirms him in his belief that conscience shouldn't be listened to:

> It don't make no difference whether you do right or wrong, a person's conscience ain't got no sense, and just goes for him *anyway*. If I had a yaller dog that didn't know no more than a person's conscience does, I would poison him. It takes up more than all of a person's insides, and yet ain't no good, nohow.

That brisk, incurious dismissiveness fits well with the comprehensive rejection of morality back on the raft. But this is a digression.

On the raft, Huck decides not to live by principles, but just to do whatever "comes handiest at the time"—always acting according to the mood of the moment. Since the morality he is rejecting is narrow and cruel, and his sympathies are broad and kind, the results will be good. But moral principles are good to have, because they help to protect one from acting badly at moments when one's sympathies happen to be in abeyance. On the highest possible estimate of the role one's sympathies should have, one can still allow for principles as embodiments of one's best feelings, one's broadest and keenest sympathies. On that view, principles can help one across intervals when one's feelings are at less than their best, i.e. through periods of misanthropy or meanness or self-centeredness or depression or anger.

What Huck didn't see is that one can live by principles and yet have ultimate control over their content. And one way such control can be exercised is by checking of one's principles in the light of one's sympathies. This is sometimes a pretty straightforward matter. It can happen that a certain moral principle becomes untenable—meaning literally that one cannot hold it any longer—because it conflicts intolerably with the pity or revulsion or whatever that one feels when one sees what the principle leads to. One's experience may play a large part here: Experiences evoke feelings, and feelings force one to modify principles. Something like this happened to the English poet Wilfred Owen, whose experiences in the First World War transformed him from an enthusiastic soldier into a virtual pacifist. I can't document his change of conscience in detail; but I want to present something which he wrote about the way experience can put pressure on morality.

The Latin poet Horace wrote that it is sweet and fitting (or right) to die for one's country—*dulce et decorum est pro patria mori*—and Owen wrote a fine poem about how experience could lead one to relinquish that particular moral principle.[5] He describes a man who is too slow donning his gas mask during a gas

---

[5] We are grateful to the executors of the Estate of Harold Owen and to Chatto and Windus Ltd. for permission to quote from Wilfred Owen's "Dulce et Decorum Est" and "Insensibility."

attack—"As under a green sea I saw him drowning," Owen says. The poem ends like this:

In all my dreams before my helpless sight
He plunges at me, guttering, choking, drowning.
If in some smothering dreams, you too could pace
Behind the wagon that we flung him in,
And watch the white eyes writhing in his face,
His hanging face, like a devil's sick of sin;
If you could hear, at every jolt, the blood
Come gargling from the froth-corrupted lungs,
Bitter as the cud
Of vile, incurable sores on innocent tongues,—
My friend, you would not tell with such high zest
To children ardent for some desperate glory,
The old Lie: Dulce et decorum est
Pro patria mori.

There is a difficulty about drawing from all this a moral for ourselves. I imagine that we agree in our rejection of slavery, eternal damnation, genocide, and uncritical patriotic self-abnegation; so we shall agree that Huck Finn, Jonathan Edwards, Heinrich Himmler, and the poet Horace would all have done well to bring certain of their principles under severe pressure from ordinary human sympathies. But then we can say this because we can say that all those are bad moralities, whereas we cannot look at our own moralities and declare them bad. This is not arrogance: It is obviously incoherent for someone to declare the system of moral principles that he *accepts* to be *bad*, just as one cannot coherently say of anything that one *believes* it but it *is false*.

Still, although I can't point to any of my beliefs and say "That is false," I don't doubt that some of my beliefs *are* false; and so I should try to remain open to correction. Similarly, I accept every single item in my morality—that is inevitable—but I am sure that my morality could be improved, which is to say that it could undergo changes which I should be glad of once I had made them. So I must try to keep my morality open to revision, exposing it to whatever valid pressures there are—including pressures from my sympathies.

I don't give my sympathies a blank check in advance. In a conflict between principle and sympathy, principles ought sometimes to win. For example, I think it was right to take part in the Second World War on the Allied side; there were many ghastly individual incidents which might have led someone to doubt the rightness of his participation in that war; and I think it would have been right for such a person to keep his sympathies in a subordinate place on those occasions, not allowing them to modify his principles in such a way as to make a pacifist of him.

Still, one's sympathies should be kept as sharp and sensitive and aware as possible, and not only because they can sometimes affect one's principles or one's conduct or both. Owen, at any rate, says that feelings and sympathies are vital even when they can do nothing but bring pain and distress. In another poem he speaks of the blessings of being numb in one's feelings: "Happy are the men who yet before they are killed/Can let their veins run cold," he says. These are the ones who do not suffer from any compassion which, as Owen puts it, "makes their feet/Sore on the alleys

cobbled with their brothers." He contrasts these "happy" ones, who "lose all imagination," with himself and others "who with a thought besmirch/Blood over all our
soul." Yet the poem's verdict goes against the "happy" ones. Owen does not say
that they will act worse than the others whose souls are besmirched with blood
because of their keen awareness of human suffering. He merely says that they are
the losers because they have cut themselves off from the human condition:

> By choice they made themselves immune
> To pity and whatever moans in man
> Before the last sea and the hapless stars;
> Whatever mourns when many leave these shores;
> Whatever shares
> The eternal reciprocity of tears.[6]

STUDY QUESTIONS

1. What does Bennett mean by a "bad morality"?
2. Does Bennett think principles play an important role in moral life? Explain. On what
   occasions *should* one's principles overrule one's sympathies?
3. What are the consequences of Bennett's arguments for ethical relativism?
4. Why does Bennett claim that Jonathan Edwards's morality was even worse than
   Himmler's? Do you agree? Explain.
5. What are the implications of Bennett's position that we must always follow our
   conscience?

The Evil That Men Think—And Do

Philip Hallie

A biographical sketch of Philip Hallie is found on page 4.

Philip Hallie summarizes and criticizes several recent theories of evil. In
particular he objects to the views of Jonathan Bennett in "The Conscience of
Huckleberry Finn," where Bennett claims that eighteenth-century theologian
Jonathan Edwards, who killed no one, has a "worse morality" than Heinrich

---

[6] This paper began life as the Potter Memorial Lecture, given at Washington State University in
Pullman, Washington, in 1972.
THE EVIL THAT MEN THINK—AND DO From *Hastings Center Report*, December 1985. Reprinted by
permission of the author.

Himmler, who sent millions to their deaths but who appears to have suffered somewhat because occasionally he sympathized with those he tormented.

Hallie believes that Bennett can reach this odd conclusion only by perversely overlooking the truly horrific aspect of evil—its victims. On the contrary, it matters greatly that Edwards never actually killed or meant to kill anyone, and that Himmler tortured and killed millions. "Victims are as essential in morality as the presence or absence of sympathy...."

Hallie claims that Bennett and others trivialize the notion of evil by concentrating too heavily on the psychology of evildoers and by paying scant attention to the fate of their victims. Hallie concludes with an excerpt from the official transcripts of the Nuremberg Trials, an excerpt he believes exemplifies the "wholeness of evil": it reveals not only what a Nazi war criminal says he thought, but, more significantly, it details what he did and the suffering it caused.

In a cartoon by Edward Kliban, a mechanic is waving his tools and pointing at what he has discovered under the hood of his customer's car. There, where the motor should be, squats a massive monster, a wicked grin revealing his terrible teeth. The mechanic is triumphantly proclaiming to his customer: "Well, *there's* your problem."

In her book, *Wickedness*, Mary Midgley writes that evil must not be seen as "something positive" or demonic like Kliban's monster. If evil were a demon we could only exorcise it, not understand it. To do so, she writes, one must see the various types of wickedness as *mixtures* of motives, some of which can be life-enhancing in themselves but are destructive in certain combinations. For instance, a rapist-murderer can be motivated by power and sex, but his way of combining these often healthy drives is destructive. For Midgley wickedness is "essentially destructive," not the way a terrible-toothed monster can be destructive but the way a person acting under various motives can fail to care about the feelings or even the lives of others. For her, evil is an absence of such caring, "an emptiness at the core of the individual...." It is a negative, not a positive, demon.

This is a sensitive analysis, but the demon Wickedness is a straw demon: very few, if any, modern thinkers on the subject believe in the demonic. For most of them another cartoon would be more apt. A mechanic is waving his tools triumphantly before a customer and is pointing to what he has found under the hood of the car. There, where Kliban's demon was, is a mass of intricately intertwined pipes, and the mechanic is pointing to *this* and announcing, "Well, *there's* your problem." And the customer is as bewildered by this phenomenon as Kliban's customer was.

Many of the people who are writing about wickedness (or immorality or evil, call it what you will) are making it a very complicated matter, like those twisted pipes. Judith Shklar in her quite often brilliant book *Ordinary Vices* is more concerned with various ethical and political puzzles than she is with the ordinary vices she promises to talk about in her introduction and in her title. Usually the unique perplexities of unique people like Robert E. Lee, Richard II, Socrates, and Colonel Count Claus von Stauffenberg interest her more than any single idea of vice does. Her skeptical, energetic mind seeks out minefields, not highways: contradictions, not a monster.

My version of Kliban's cartoon applies also to the lucid, careful book *Immorality* by the philosopher Ronald D. Milo. Milo takes Aristotle's all-too-pat distinction between moral weakness and moral baseness, and refines it into a range of kinds and degrees of blameworthiness. In the seventh book of his *Nichomachean Ethics* Aristotle said that the weak (or "incontinent") person is like a city that has good laws, but that does not live by them: the vicious (or "base" person) is like a city that has bad laws by which it *does* live. The zealous mass murderer is vicious without remorse; while the weak, penitent adulterer or drunkard knows he is doing wrong, but does nothing about it. Milo refines and develops this rather crude distinction, so that Aristotle's baseness is no longer a simple contrast between two kinds of cities. Like Shklar, Milo is too perceptive and too circumspect to join the simplifiers that Midgley deplores.

And yet, despite their perceptiveness and circumspection, many of our analyzers of evil have grossly simplified the idea of immorality. In their scrupulous examinations of complexities they have left out much of the ferocious ugliness of Kliban's monster. They too are negligent simplifiers.

For instance, Jonathan Bennett has written an essay entitled "The Conscience of Huckleberry Finn," in which he proves to his satisfaction that the morality of the eighteenth-century American theologian Jonathan Edwards was "worse than Himmler's." He insists that Heinrich Himmler, head of the SS and of all the police systems of Nazi Germany, and responsible for all of the tortures and the deaths perpetrated upon noncombatants by Nazi Germany, was not as wicked as Jonathan Edwards, who never killed or meant to kill anyone.

Why? Because Jonathan Edwards had no pity for the damned, and Himmler did have sympathy for the millions of people he tortured and destroyed. Bennett contends that there are two forces at work in the consciences of human beings: general moral principles and unreasoned "emotional pulls." One such "pull" is sympathy, and Jonathan Edwards's sermons showed no sympathy for the sinners who were in the hands of an angry God, while Himmler's speeches to his Nazi subordinates did express the emotional pull of sympathy. In the mind, the only place where "morality" dwells for Bennett, Himmler is no heartless ruffian, but a decent fellow who had a wrong-headed set of principles and who felt the pangs of sympathy for human beings he was crushing and grinding into death and worse.

The Central Role of the Victim

In Lewis Carroll's *Alice's Adventures in Wonderland* Tweedledee recites to Alice "The Walrus and the Carpenter." In the poem, the Walrus and the Carpenter come across some oysters while they are strolling on the beach. They manage to persuade the younger oysters to join them in

A pleasant walk, a pleasant talk
  Along the briny beach

After a while they rest on a rock that is "conveniently low," so that the two of them can keep an eye on the oysters and can reach them easily. After a little chat, the Carpenter and the Walrus start eating the oysters.

The Walrus is a sympathetic creature, given to crying readily, who thanks the oysters for joining them, while the Carpenter is interested only in eating:

> "It seems a shame," the Walrus said
> "To play them such a trick.
> After we've brought them out so far
> And made them trot so quick!"
> The Carpenter said nothing but
> "The butter's spread too thick."

Then the Walrus, out of the goodness of his heart, bursts forth:

> "I weep for you," the Walrus said:
> "I deeply sympathize."
> With sobs and tears he sorted out
> Those of the largest size,
> Holding his pocket-handkerchief
> Before his streaming eyes.

and they finish off all of the oysters.

Bennett, with his concern for the saving grace of sympathy, might find the "morality" of the Walrus better than the morality of the cold-blooded Carpenter, but Lewis Carroll, or rather Tweedledee and Tweedledum, are not so simple-minded:

> "I like the Walrus best," said Alice: "because he was a *little* sorry for the poor oysters."
>
> "He ate more than the Carpenter, though," said Tweedledee. "You see he held his handkerchief in front, so that the Carpenter couldn't count how many he took: contrariwise."
>
> "That was mean!" Alice said indignantly. "Then I like the Carpenter best—if he didn't eat so many as the Walrus."
>
> "But he ate as many as he could get," said Tweedledum.

Then Alice gives up trying to rank the Walrus and the Carpenter and gives voice to a wisdom that is as sound as it is obvious:

> "Well! They were both very unpleasant characters...."

What Lewis Carroll saw, and what Bennett apparently does not, is that the victims are as essential in morality as the presence or absence of sympathy inside the head of the moral agent. And he also sees that sympathy, or rather expressions of sympathy, can be a device for eating more oysters by hiding your mouth behind a handkerchief—it certainly needn't slow your eating down.

Milo never violates the morally obvious as boldly as Bennett does, but when he ranks immoralities he too disregards the essential role of the victim in evil. His conclusions contradict Bennett's. For Milo, apparently, Himmler's would be "the most evil" kind of wrongdoing, just because of his scruples:

> ... we think that the most evil or reprehensible kind of wrongdoing consists in willingly and intentionally doing something that one believes to be morally wrong, either because one simply does not care that it is morally wrong or because one prefers the pursuit of some other end to the avoidance of moral wrongdoing....

This is a more subtle analysis of evil than Bennett's, but it too ranks evils without the wisdom of Tweedledum and Tweedledee. It too flattens out or ignores the central role of victims in the dance of evil.

Where Eichmann's Evil Lay

The most distinguished modern philosophic treatment of evil is Hannah Arendt's *Eichmann in Jerusalem, A Report on the Banality of Evil.* Like most of the philosophers who came after her she believed that the evil person is not necessarily a monster. In her report on the Eichmann trial as she witnessed it in Jerusalem in 1961 she shows us a man who did not act out of evil motives. She shows us a man, Adolf Eichmann, whose main trait was to have no interesting traits, except perhaps his "remoteness from reality." His banality resides in his never having *realized* what he was doing to particular human beings. Hannah Arendt tells us that, except for personal advancement, "He had no motives at all." He was an unimaginative bureaucrat who lived in the clichés of his office. He was no Iago, no Richard III, no person who wished "to prove a villain."

There is truth in this position. Eichmann was a commonplace, trite man if you look at him only in the dock and if you do not see that his boring clichés are directly linked with millions of tortures and murders. If you see the victims of Eichmann and of the office he held, then—and only then—do you see the evil of this man. Evil does not happen only in people's heads. Eichmann's evil happened in his head (and here Arendt is not only right but brilliantly perceptive) *and* (and the "and" makes a tight, essential linkage) in the freight cars and in the camps of Central Europe. His evil is the sum total of his unimaginative head and his unimaginable tortures and murders. And this sum total is not banal, not flat, not commonplace. It is horrific.

As one of the most powerful philosophers of our time, Arendt was conscious of leaving something out by concentrating her attention upon the internal workings of the mind of a bureaucrat. Early in her book she wrote: "On trial are his deeds, not the sufferings of the Jews."

As if "his deeds" could be neatly peeled away from what he did to the Jews! *Her separation* of the mental activity of Eichmann from the pain-racked deaths of millions that this mental activity brought about made Eichmann's evil banal. Without these actual murders and tortures Eichmann was not evil; his maunderings were those of a pitiable, not a culpable man. His evil lay in his deeds, as Arendt says, but not only in his mental "deeds": it lay in all that he intended and all that he carried out, in his mind and in the world around him.

The Morality of Seeing

In Saul Bellow's novel *The Dean's December*, the narrator, Dean Albert Corde, makes a plea for seeing what there is to be seen:

> In the American moral crisis, the first requirement was to experience what was happening and to see what must be seen. The facts were covered from our perception.... The increase of theories and discourse, itself a cause of new, strange forms of blindness, the false representations of "communication," led to horrible distortions of public consciousness. Therefore the first act of morality was to disinter the reality, retrieve reality, dig it out from the trash, represent it anew as art would represent it....
>
> We were no longer talking about anything. The language of discourse had shut out experience altogether.... I tried to make myself the moralist of seeing....

The dynamic of passions, moral principles, and perceptions within the heads of moral agents is a dynamic that is part of evil, but those of us who want to face and to understand evil as best we can must, it seems to me, try to live up to Corde's "morality of seeing." We must do our best to see not only what is happening in the inward polities of the doers of evil but *also* what is happening in the lives of the sufferers of evil.

For instance, to write about Himmler requires not only the reading of a few carefully crafted speeches; it also demands learning about the context of these speeches. It is true that at least once Himmler looked as if he felt queasy at an execution, and it is also true that he wrote about this queasiness in terms not entirely unlike those of the Walrus. But even a superficial study of what was actually happening within Fortress Europe in those days makes quite clear that he was coping with a particular problem by talking about "damage in ... minds and souls" and "human weakness."

Look at almost any volume of the record of the 1947 Nuremberg Trials—for example Volume IV, especially pages 311–355—and it will become plain that the efficient murdering of children as well as other defenseless human beings was being hindered by the depression and even the nervous breakdowns of the people who were herding together and executing these people. Himmler, in order to minimize inefficiency, needed to prepare his followers to deal with such scruples. At least he needed to do this to carry out the project of exterminating the Jews of Europe as well as the majority of the Slavs.

Talking about these scruples was not a *cri du coeur*. He was not opening his heart to his subordinates, as Bennett suggests: he was preparing them for dealing with the psychological problems of the executioners. He was holding up a handkerchief before his eyes, to go back to the imagery of Tweedledee's poem, so that he and his followers could murder more and more helpless human beings.

A Monster in Action

Even such vigorously human books as *Ordinary Vices* by Judith Shklar and *Wickedness* by Mary Midgley do not meet the obligations laid upon us by a morality of seeing. Shklar provides lurid and deep insights into the implications of making cruelty *summum malum*, the most indefensible and unforgivable evil, and into many other subjects, but she hastens into perplexities and puzzles before she carefully observes the factual contexts of her examples.

Midgley is memorably illuminating in her efforts to clear away the obstacles that keep us from taking wickedness seriously. For instance, very few readers of her book, if they are attentive, will ever describe a mass murderer and a mass rapist as "sick" after reading her truly remarkable analysis in the chapter entitled "The Elusiveness of Responsibility." One of her key arguments against replacing the words "wicked" and "evil" by the words "sick" and "ill" is that doing so *distances* us from the destruction that has been done. It removes the "sick" destroyers from blame and from anger (how dare you blame a person for being ill?). It "flattens out," to use her powerful phrase, the distinctions between murderers and kleptomaniacs, between those who make us defensibly angry, when we see what they have *done*, and those who engage only our compassion and help.

Still, so scrupulous is she in removing the obstacles to an awareness of wickedness that she does not reveal much about what evil is. Her description of wickedness as "negative" like darkness and cold (an absence of caring being like an absence of light or heat) is useful but difficult to understand in terms of examples, especially when she tells us that "evil in the quiet supporters [of, for example, a Hitler] is negative," and then tells us that what they do is "positive action." This is a confusing use of metaphysical terms that do not have a plain cash value in relation to observable facts. These terms bring us close to the medieval soup and its casuistical arguments about whether evil is a "privation of good" or something "positive."

Milo's *Immorality* offers a scrupulously lucid and sustained argument about the types and blameworthiness of immorality. It is especially adroit at understanding the relationships between moral weakness and deep wickedness. But he, like these other recent writers on evil, is reluctant to face the full force of evil. He, like them, does not look deeply and carefully at examples, at the terrible details in history and the arts.

These writers are, perhaps, too timid to look hard at Kliban's monster and say, "Well, *there's* your problem." Evil is thick with fact and as ugly as that grinning monster. It is no worse to see it this way than it is to see it as an internal dynamic in a moral agent's head, or a set of carefully honed distinctions, or an array of puzzles and perplexities (as Shklar seems to see it). Many of the insights of these writers are useful for understanding the monster, or rather the many monsters that embody evil, but there is no substitute for seeing the harshness and ugliness of fact.

Here is a monster in action: he is Otto Ohlendorf who was, among other roles, head of Group D of the Action Groups assigned to exterminate Jews and Soviet political leaders in parts of Eastern Europe. To learn more about him, read pages 311–355 of the Fourth Volume of the transcript of the Nuremberg trials of the major war criminals. Here is part of his testimony:

COLONEL POKROVSKY

(for the Tribunal): Why did they (the execution squads) prefer execution by shooting to killing in the gas vans?

OHLENDORF: Because ... in the opinion of the leader of the Einsatzkommandos [Action Groups], the unloading of the corpses was an unnecessary mental strain.

COL. POKROVSKY: What do you mean by "an unnecessary mental strain"?

OHLENDORF: As far as I can remember the conditions at the time—the picture presented by the corpses and probably because certain functions of the body had taken place, leaving the corpses lying in filth.

COL. POKROVSKY: You mean to say that the sufferings endured prior to death were clearly visible on the victims? Did I understand you correctly?

OHLENDORF: I don't understand the question; do you mean during the killing in the van?

COL. POKROVSKY: Yes.

OHLENDORF: I can only repeat what the doctor told me, that the victims were not conscious of their death in the van.

COL. POKROVSKY: In that case your reply to my previous question, that the unloading of the bodies made a very terrible impression on the members of the execution squad, becomes entirely incomprehensible.

OHLENDORF: And, as I said, the terrible impression created by the position of the corpses themselves, and by the state of the vans which had probably been dirtied and so on.

COL. POKROVSKY: I have no further questions to put to this witness at the present stage of the Trial (p. 334).

COLONEL AMEN

(for the Tribunal):   Referring to the gas vans which you said you received in the spring of 1942, what order did you receive with respect to the use of these vans?

OHLENDORF: These gas vans were in future to be used for the killing of women and children.

COL. AMEN: Will you explain to the Tribunal the construction of these vans and their appearance?

OHLENDORF: The actual purpose of these vans could not be seen from the outside. They looked like closed trucks, and were so constructed that at the start of the motor, gas was conducted into the van, causing death in 10 to 15 minutes.

COL. AMEN: Explain in detail just how one of these vans was used for an execution.

OHLENDORF: The vans were loaded with the victims and driven to the place of burial, which was usually the same as that used for the mass executions. The time needed for transportation was sufficient to insure the death of the victims.

COL. AMEN: How were the victims induced to enter the vans?

OHLENDORF: They were told that they were to be transported to another locality.

COL. AMEN: How was the gas turned on?

OHLENDORF: I am not familiar with the technical details.

COL. AMEN: How long did it take to kill the victims ordinarily?

OHLENDORF: About 10 to 15 minutes; the victims were not conscious of what was happening to them (p. 322).

OHLENDORF: I led the Einsatzgruppe, and therefore I had the task of seeing how the Einsatzkommandos executed the orders received.

HERR BABEL

(for the Tribunal):   But did you have no scruples in regard to the execution of these orders?

OHLENDORF: Yes, of course.

HERR BABEL: And how is it that they were carried out regardless of these scruples?

OHLENDORF: Because to me it is inconceivable that a subordinate leader should not carry out orders given by the leaders of the state (pp. 353–354).

I urge you to read the above extracts more than once. The wholeness of evil is there, and if Ohlendorf is not monstrous to you, you are the problem.

STUDY QUESTIONS

1. Do you agree with Hallie's critique of Bennett? In particular, do you think Hallie is right in saying that Heinrich Himmler's attitude does not exculpate him and that Jonathan Edwards's attitude counts for less than Himmler's deeds? Explain.
2. Explain Hallie's reference to Lewis Carroll's *Alice's Adventures in Wonderland*. Do you find the morality of the Walrus better than the morality of the Carpenter? Do you agree with Alice's assessment? Explain.
3. Explain Hannah Arendt's phrase "the banality of evil." Discuss Hallie's critique of Arendt's view.
4. Explain how the testimony of Nazi war criminal Otto Ohlendorf exemplifies the "wholeness of evil."

Facing the Extreme: The War of All Against All

Tzvetan Todorov

Tzvetan Todorov (b.1939) is a Bulgarian-born philosopher who has lived in France since 1963. His many books include *The Poetics of Prose* (1971), *On Human Diversity* (1993), and *Imperfect Garden: The Legacy of Humanism* (2002). The following selection comes from *Facing the Extreme: Moral Life in the Concentration Camps* (1996)—a book hailed by many as a masterpiece.

In this excerpt, Todorov focuses on the moral life of inmates of concentration camps. How did these hapless unfortunates react to unrelieved suffering and terror? According to Todorov many survivors insist that "In extreme situations all traces of moral life evaporate." But he offers persuasive counter-evidence showing that morality prevailed among many of the prisoners. The social contract was in force among them—even as they were being starved, beaten, and under threat of imminent death. There was a constant tension between what Todorov calls vital values and moral values. Vital values dictate survival at any price. Moral values impose obligations to help others in all circumstances. "To put it simply," he says, "the most optimistic conclusion we can draw from life in (and outside) the camps is that ... the possibility of choosing moral values continues to exist."

There are various perspectives from which the accounts of life in the camps can be read. One can ponder the precise chain of events that led to the creation of the camps and then to their extinction; one can debate the political significance of the camps; one can extract sociological or psychological lessons from them. Yet even though I cannot ignore those perspectives altogether, I would like to take a different approach. I want to look at the camps from the perspective of moral life and to concern myself with individual destinies rather than with numbers and dates. But already I hear an objection: Wasn't that question settled a long time ago? Haven't we learned only too well the sad and simple truth the camps revealed, namely, that in extreme situations all traces of moral life evaporate as men become beasts locked in a merciless struggle for survival?

That opinion is not only a commonplace of popularized presentations of these events but also crops up frequently in the accounts of survivors themselves. We became indifferent to the misfortune of others, they say; if we wanted to survive, we had to think only of ourselves, that is the lesson brought out of Auschwitz by Tadeusz Borowski, who committed suicide in 1951: "In this war," he writes, morality, national solidarity, patriotism and the ideals of freedom, justice and human dignity had all slid off man like a rotten rag....

There is no crime that a man will not commit in order to save himself." In other words, moral behavior is not innate in us. Another Auschwitz survivor, Jean Améry, who committed suicide in 1978, reached the same conclusion. "There are no natural rights," he writes, "and moral categories come and go like fashions." A third Auschwitz survivor, Primo Levi, who took his life in 1987, says that the hardships of the camps rendered any kind of moral position impossible. "Here [in the lager] the struggle to survive is without respite, because everyone is desperately and ferociously alone." To survive, it was necessary "to throttle all dignity and kill all conscience, to climb down into the arena as a beast against other beasts, to let oneself be guided by those unsuspected subterranean forces which sustain families and individuals in cruel times." "It was a Hobbesian life," Levi writes, "a continuous war of everyone against everyone."

The lessons brought out from the gulags are not all that different. Varlam Shalamov, imprisoned for twenty-five years, seventeen of them in Kolyma, is particularly pessimistic: "All human emotions—of love, friendship, envy, concern for one's fellowman, compassion, a longing for fame, honesty—had left us with the flesh that had melted from our bodies during our long fasts," he writes. "The camp was a great test of our moral strength, of our everyday morality, and 99% of us failed it.... Conditions in the camps do not permit men to remain men; that is not what camps were created for." Eugenia Ginzburg, who spent twenty years in Kolyma, agrees that a moral life was impossible in the camps: "It is hard to describe the way in which someone ground down by inhuman forms of life loses bit by bit all hold on normal notions of good and evil, of what is permissible and what is not.... Perhaps we ourselves [intellectuals] were as morally dead as the rest." When one is thinking only of one's own survival, one no longer recognizes any law other than the law of the jungle, which means the total *absence* of law and its replacement by brute force....

Even the closest family ties were vulnerable in this fight for survival. Borowski, for example, tells how a mother, to save her own life, pretends not to know her child. And Elie Wiesel, another Auschwitz survivor, describes in *Night* how a son snatches a piece of bread from the hands of his father, and he speaks of the relief he felt when his own father died, because it increased his own chances for survival.

If an individual's every action is determined by the orders of those above him and the need to survive, then he has no freedom left at all; no longer can he truly exercise his will and choose one behavior over another. And where there is no choice, there is also no place for any kind of moral life whatsoever.

Doubts

In reading the testimonies of survivors, however, I come away with the impression that the situation is not as bleak as it may have seemed. Alongside examples illustrating the disappearance of all moral sensibilities, one finds examples that have a different lesson to teach. Primo Levi, who saw in the camps only an attenuated struggle of all against all, has barely finished writing, "All are enemies or rivals," when he stops and realizes how excessive that statement really is. "No," he declares, "I honestly do not feel my companion of today ... to be either enemy or rival." There are numerous stories in Levi's *Survival in Auschwitz* (originally entitled *If This Is a Man*) that contradict his grim generalization. His good friend Alberto, for instance, who perished during the forced marches after the evacuation of the camps, struggles to survive yet does not become a cynic. He knows how to be both strong and tender. Another friend, Jean, who was the Pikolo, or messenger-clerk, of Levi's work unit and who did survive, also strove to stay alive but "did not neglect his human relationships with less privileged comrades." If there were so many exceptions, can the rule still be said to hold?

The same Tadeusz Borowski whose stories about life at Auschwitz are among the most pitiless has also written, "I think that man will never cease to rediscover man—through love. And to rediscover that love is the most important and most durable thing there is." We know, moreover, that at Auschwitz Borowski behaved totally differently from the characters he writes about; his devotion to others was beyond measure. But he understood just how far human degradation could go and did not try to exempt himself from the corruption around him. His central character, also named Tadeusz, is a cynical and pitiless kapo, and his story is told in the first person. Borowski suggests a rule for all who write about Auschwitz: Do not write unless you are willing to take responsibility for the worst humiliation that the camp inflicted on its inmates. In making this rule, he has also, of course, made another choice and committed another moral act.

Varlam Shalamov, who narrates the despair and degradation experienced by all the prisoners at Kolyma, writes, "I couldn't denounce a fellow convict, no matter what he did. And I refused to seek the job of foreman, which provided a chance to remain alive, for the worst thing in a camp was the forcing of one's own or anyone else's will on another person who was a convict just like oneself." As Aleksandr Solzhenitsyn observes, a decision of this kind proves that not all choice was forbidden and that Shalamov was at least himself an exception to his own rule. Laks and Coudy, Auschwitz survivors who chronicled the progressive loss of their human identity, nonetheless point out that without the help of others survival was impossible. Was help given? Thirty years after the publication of his original account, Laks confirms that it was: he owes his survival, he writes, "to my encounters with a few countrymen with a human face and a human heart." And Eugenia Ginzburg describes innumerable acts of solidarity that the principle she herself formulates has no way of accounting for. If there were sons who snatched bread from the hands of their fathers, Robert Antelme, a Buchenwald survivor, saw ones, too. He describes "the hungry old man who'd steal in front of his son, so the son could eat. Father and son ... hungry together, offering their bread to each other with loving eyes."

Ella Lingens-Reiner, an Austrian prisoner, reports in her recollections of Auschwitz that she met another Jewish doctor there, Ena Weiss, who defined her philosophy of life this way: "How do I keep alive in Auschwitz? My principle is—myself first, second, and third. Then nothing. Then myself again—and then all the others." This formula has often been cited as the most accurate expression of moral law—or rather, of its absence—at Auschwitz. And yet Lingens-Reiner is quick to point out that this woman violated her own law every day, helping tens, indeed hundreds, of other prisoners. Lingens-Reiner goes on to describe the transformations that moral life underwent in the camp, and in so doing she mirrors the kind of contradiction she finds in Weiss. "We camp prisoners had only one yardstick," she writes, "whatever helped our survival was good, whatever threatened our survival was bad and to be avoided." Yet this characterization comes directly after a detailed account of a conflict of conscience that greatly tormented her: should she intervene in behalf of a sick woman, thereby compromising her own chances of getting out alive, or should she think only of herself and decline to help her fellow prisoner? In the end, Lingens-Reiner choses the former, but even if she hadn't, her hesitation alone would have been sufficient proof that the moral sense within her was still very much alive.

Matters of conscience are not at all rare in extreme situations, and their very existence attests to the possibility of choice, and thus of moral life....

It is not true that life in the camps obeyed only the law of the jungle. The rules of camp society may have been different but they still existed. Stealing from the administration was not merely licit but admirable; on the other hand, stealing from a fellow prisoner—especially bread—was an abomination and most of the time was severely punished. This law functioned as rigorously in the gulags as it did in the concentration camps. In both places informers were detested and punished. As Anna Pawelczynska, an Auschwitz survivor, observes, the Ten Commandments did not disappear; they were simply reinterpreted. Murder, for example, could be a moral act if it kept an assassin from carrying out cruel and vicious assignments. Bearing false witness could become a virtuous act if it helped save human lives. To love one's neighbor as one loved oneself was perhaps an excessive demand, but to avoid harming him was not. Germaine Tillion, a survivor of Ravensbrück, renders a subtle and, as far as I can determine, accurate judgment of moral life in the camps when she concludes, "This tenuous web of friendship was, in a way, submerged by the stark brutality of selfishness and the struggle for survival, but somehow everyone in the camp was invisibly woven into it."

So numerous are the counterexamples to the principles of immorality expressed by the survivors that the presence of such principles in their accounts calls for some explanation. Why do the survivors draw general conclusions that are not borne out by the particular cases that they themselves report? Terrence Des Pres, the author of a study on concentration camp survivors, proposes an answer: former prisoners insist on the negative aspect of their experience because it is precisely this aspect that renders their experience unique and that must be underlined at every opportunity. "As a witness," Des Pres writes, "the survivor aims above all to convey the otherness of the camps, their specific inhumanity." The particular examples the survivors cite, on the other hand, reflect a more complex situation. I would add another reason for some survivors' reluctance to qualify their conclusions: if they paint the bleakest picture possible, it is because they still suffer remorse for not having come to the aid of others, who were left to a horrible fate—this despite the fact that nonintervention was a perfectly understandable and justifiable response under the circumstances....

There may exist a threshold of suffering beyond which an individual's actions teach us nothing more about the individual but only about the reactions that unbearable suffering elicits from the human mechanism. One can be brought to that threshold by prolonged starvation, or by the imminent threat of death, or even—as in the Nazi camps—by the initial encounter with an atmosphere of terror and menace. "Hunger proves an insuperable ordeal," Anatoly Marchenko writes. "When he reaches this ultimate degree of degradation, a man is prepared for anything." Twenty years earlier, Gustaw Herling, another prisoner of the gulag, concluded, "There is nothing ... a man cannot be forced to do by hunger and pain." Indeed, these extreme means make it possible to destroy the social contract at its very foundations and to obtain from human beings purely animal reactions.

But what exactly does that observation mean? Does it reflect the fundamental truth about human nature, that morality is but a superficial convention jettisoned at the first opportunity? On the contrary, what it demonstrates is that moral reactions are spontaneous, omnipresent, and eradicable only with the greatest violence. Plants can be forced to grow horizontally, Rousseau says, but unconstrained they will nevertheless grow upward. It is not under torture that human beings reveal their true identity. Suppressing the usual components of human social life creates a completely artificial situation that tells us only about itself. Herling is right: "I became convinced that a man can be human only under human conditions and I believe that it is fantastic nonsense to judge him by actions which he commits under inhuman conditions." It is for this reason, too, that I will not dwell at length on situations where that threshold has been crossed.

Even before considering the details of moral life in the camps, one can see that the hypothesis that individuals behave as wolves toward one another is not supported by observation. Des Pres's readings of survivors' accounts come to the same conclusion: "The 'state of nature,' it turns out, is not natural. A war of everyone against everyone must be imposed by force." The popular version of Hobbes's doctrine is wrong: except under extreme constraint, human beings are prompted, among other things, to communicate with one another, to help one another, and to distinguish good from evil.

One and The Same World

This conclusion should not be understood as an expression of complacent optimism. In affirming the continuity between ordinary experience and that of the camps (except where the latter crosses beyond the threshold of the bearable) and thus the pertinence of the same moral questions to both worlds, I am not saying that good reigns supreme, everywhere and at all times. Far from it: I would say instead that this continuity between the ordinary and the extreme points to conclusions that are hardly encouraging.

In everyday life as well as in the camps, one can observe an opposition between two types of behavior and two types of values, what could be called vital values and moral values. Vital values dictate that saving my own life and furthering my well-being are what matter most; moral values tell me that there is something more precious than life itself, that staying human is more important than staying alive. To choose moral values (whether "heroic" or "ordinary") over vital values does not necessarily imply that life is somehow a less worthy goal; survival remains a perfectly respectable objective—particularly where the ordinary virtues are concerned—but not at any price.

Let there be no mistake. I do not mean that moral values are somehow external to life, that they are a foreign element that stifles and suppresses life. Rather I believe that moral values and behaviors are a constitutive dimension of life. The difference between moral values and vital values might be got at in the following way: for the vital values it is my life that is sacred; for moral values it is the life of someone else that is. What extreme situations teach us is that both kinds of values are always active. As Jorge Semprun, a Buchenwald survivor, writes, "In the camps, man becomes that animal capable of stealing a mate's bread, of propelling him toward death. But in the camps, man also becomes that invincible being capable of sharing his last cigarette butt, his last piece of bread, his last breath, to sustain his fellowman." And Anatoly Marchenko says, "People here vary, just as they do everywhere. You have marvelous people, and you have rotten ones, you have brave men and cowards, you have honest men with principles and you have unprincipled swine who are prepared for any kind of betrayal." This observation, of course, is as true of the ordinary lives that all of us lead as it is of the situations described by Marchenko and Semprun.

In the camps, such diversity appears not only between people but also within the course of each individual life. Even the most admirable persons typically passed through several phases. During the first, often corresponding to the initial few months in the camp, previously held moral values collapse beneath the weight of the new and brutal circumstances. The prisoner discovers a world without pity and finds that he can actually live in such a world. If the prisoner survives this first stage, however, he may reach a second, in which he once again discovers a set of moral values, although perhaps not the same as he held before. The embers have not been extinguished, and it takes only the smallest relief from brutality for the flames of conscience to flare up anew. "Even in the jungle of Birkenau," writes Olga Lengyel, a doctor at Auschwitz, "all were not necessarily inhuman to their fellowmen"....

The difference between life in the camps and ordinary life does not lie in the presence or absence of moral life. In everyday life the contrasts of which I have been speaking are not clearly apparent. Egocentric acts pass themselves off as ordinary and routine behavior, and furthermore, less is at stake because human lives don't depend on them. In the camps, however, where it is sometimes necessary to choose between holding on to one's bread and holding on to one's dignity, between starving physically and starving morally, everything is out in the open. "Camps," Semprun writes, "are extreme situations in which the cleavage between 'the men' and 'the others' is more pronounced." The depravation of some is hastened and is there for all to see; but the betterment of others is also intensified. "Camp either cleanses your conscience or destroys it forever," Ratushinskaya writes. "People emerge either much better than they were or much worse, depending on how they were predisposed." Of course, both depravation and elevation occur outside the camps, but not so visibly. Life inside the camps projects, magnifies, and renders eloquent what can easily escape notice in the humdrum of our daily lives.

What extreme and ordinary situations also share is that, in both, most people choose what I call vital values and only a few choose the other path. Or perhaps it is this: most of the time individuals opt for vital values without necessarily losing a sense of morality. Once again, the choices are far more visible in the camps, which is why the camps are often thought to offer some sort of general lesson in immorality. The fact is, however, that selfishness is just as prevalent in ordinary times. To put it simply, the most optimistic conclusion we can draw from life in (and outside) the camps is that evil is not unavoidable. The actual numbers are not important; what matters is that the possibility of choosing moral values continues to exist. "Of the prisoners, only a few kept their full inner liberty," Viktor Frankl, an Auschwitz survivor, concludes, "but even one such example is sufficient proof that man's inner strength may raise him above his outward fate"....

STUDY QUESTIONS

1. Todorov points out that former inmates routinely describe concentration camps as devoid of all traces of morality. To survive, they say, was the only imperative. Why does Todorov reject this characterization?
2. How does Todorov explain the fact that so many in the camps believed that they themselves had become amoral and that amorality—"the law of the jungle"—was the only law governing the camps? As Todorov says, "Why do the survivors draw general conclusions that are not borne out by the particular cases that they themselves report?"
3. Todorov rejects the idea that under torture human beings reveal their true selves. Explain his reasoning and say why you agree or disagree.

Strategies for Survival

Anne Applebaum

> Anne Applebaum (b. 1964), a columnist and member of the editorial board of the *Washington Post*, is the author *of Between East and West: Across the Borderlands of Europe* (1994) and the Pulitzer Prize winning *Gulag: A History* (2003), from which our selection is taken.

From "Strategies for Survival" from GULAG: A History, 2003, Doubleday. Reprinted by permission of Amercian Enterprise Institute for Public Policy Research and Anne Applebaum.

The Gulag refers to the vast network of Soviet forced labor camps that were most active between 1929 and 1953, the year Joseph Stalin died. An estimated 18 million people passed through them. Millions perished from the combined effects of cold, hunger, exhaustion, and disease. But many managed to survive. How did they do it? Some collaborated with their tormentors, some avoided work by feigning illness or inflicting serious injuries on themselves. Others found ways to pretend to work. In this selection, Applebaum describes how the practice of "ordinary virtues"—"caring, friendship, dignity and the life of the mind"—sustained lives in the camps. The inmates formed powerful social networks and inviolable friendships. They recited poetry and told one another the plots of literary work to keep their minds free, alert, and alive. The celebrated Soviet dissident Alexander Solzhenitsyn, for example, composed poetry in his head—then committed it to memory. In this God-forsaken environment many prisoners and their guards made a place for theater, art, music, and religion and survived untold miseries ultimately to live relatively normal lives and to tell their stories.

In the end, prisoners survived. They survived even the worst camps, even the toughest conditions, even the war years, the famine years, the years of mass execution. Not only that, some survived psychologically intact enough to return home, to recover, and to live relatively normal lives. Janusz Bardach became a plastic surgeon in Iowa City. Isaak Filshtinskii went back to teaching Arabic literature. Lev Razgon went back to writing children's fiction. Anatolii Zhigulin went back to writing poetry. Evgeniya Ginzburg moved to Moscow, and for years was the heart and soul of a circle of survivors, who met regularly to eat, drink, and argue around her kitchen table.

Ada Purizhinskaya, imprisoned as a teenager, went on to marry and produce four children, some of whom became accomplished musicians. I met two of them over a generous, good-humored family dinner, during which Purizhinskaya served dish after dish of delicious cold food, and seemed disappointed when I could not eat more. Irena Arginskaya's home is also full of laughter, much of it coming from Irena herself. Forty years later, she was able to make fun of the clothes she had worn as a prisoner: "I suppose you *could* call it a sort of *jacket*," she said, trying to describe her shapeless camp overcoat. Her well-spoken, grown-up daughter laughed along with her.

Some even went on to lead extraordinary lives. Alexander Solzhenitsyn became one of the best-known, and best-selling, Russian writers in the world. General Gorbatov helped lead the Soviet assault on Berlin. After his terms in Kolyma and a wartime *sharashka*, Sergei Korolev went on to become the father of the Soviet Union's space program. Gustav Herling left the camps, fought with the Polish army, and, although writing in Neapolitan exile, became one of the most revered men of letters in post-prison communist Poland. News of his death in July 2000 made the front pages of the Warsaw newspapers and an entire generation of Polish intellectuals paid tribute to his work—especially *A World Apart*, his Gulag memoir. In their ability to recover, these men and women were not alone. Isaac Vogelfanger, who himself became a professor of surgery at the University of Ottawa, wrote that "wounds heal, and you can become whole again, a little stronger and more human than before ..."

Not all Gulag survivors' stories ended so well, of course, which one would not necessarily be able to tell from reading memoirs. Obviously, people who did not survive did not write. Those who were mentally or physically damaged by their camp experiences did not write either. Nor did those who had survived by doing things of which they were later ashamed write very often either—or, if they did, they did not necessarily tell the whole story. There are very, very few memoirs of informers—or of people who will confess to having been informers—and very few survivors who will admit to harming or killing fellow prisoners in order to stay alive.

For these reasons, some survivors question whether written memoirs have any validity at all. Yuri Zorin, an elderly and not very forthcoming survivor whom I interviewed in his home city, Arkhangelsk, waved away a question I asked him about philosophies of survival. There weren't any, he said. Although it might seem, from their memoirs, as if prisoners "discussed everything, thought about everything," it was not like that, he told me. "The whole task was to live through the next day, to stay alive, not to get sick, to work less, to eat more. And that was why philosophical discussions, as a rule, were not held.... We were saved by youth, health, physical strength, because there we lived by Darwin's laws, the survival of the fittest."

The whole subject of who survived—and why they survived—must therefore be approached very carefully. In this matter, there are no archival documents to rely upon, and there is no real "evidence." We have to take the word of those who were willing to describe their experiences, either on paper or for an interviewer. Any one of them might have had reason to conceal aspects of their biographies from their readers.

With that caveat, it is still possible to identify patterns within the several hundred memoirs which have been published or placed in archives. For there were strategies for survival, and they were well-known at the time, although they varied a great deal, depending on a prisoner's particular circumstances. Surviving a labor colony in western Russia in the mid-1930s or even late 1940s, when most of the work was factory work and the food was regular if not plentiful, probably did not require any special mental adjustments. Surviving one of the far northern camps—Kolyma, Vorkuta, Norilsk—during the hungry war years, on the other hand, often required huge reserves of talent and willpower, or else an enormous capacity for evil, qualities that the prisoners, had they remained in freedom, might never have discovered within themselves.

Without a doubt, many such prisoners survived because they found ways to raise themselves above the other prisoners, to distinguish themselves from the swarming mass of starving *zeks* [prisoners]. Dozens of camp sayings and proverbs reflect the debilitating moral effects of this desperate competition. "You can die today—I'll die tomorrow," was one of them. "Man is wolf to man"—the phrase Janusz Bardach used as the title of his memoir—was another.

Many *ex-zeks* speak of the struggle for survival as cruel, and many, like Zorin, speak of it as Darwinian. "The camp was a great test of our moral strength, of our everyday morality, and 99 percent of us failed it," wrote Shalamov. "After only three weeks most of the prisoners were broken men, interested in nothing but eating. They behaved like animals, disliked and suspected everyone else, seeing in yesterday's friend a competitor in the struggle for survival," wrote Edward Buca.

Elinor Olitskaya, with her background in the pre-revolutionary social democratic movement, was particularly horrified by what she perceived as the amorality of the camps: while inmates in prisons had often cooperated, the strong helping the weak, in the Soviet camps every prisoner "lived for herself," doing down the others in order to attain a slightly higher status on the camp hierarchy. Galina Usakova described how she felt her personality had changed in the camps: "I was a well-behaved girl, well brought up, from a family of intelligentsia. But with these characteristics you won't survive, you have to harden yourself, you learn to lie, to be hypocritical in various ways."

Gustav Herling elaborated further, describing how it is that the new prisoner slowly learns to live "without pity":

> At first he shares his bread with hunger-demented prisoners, leads the night-blind on the way home from work, shouts for help when his neighbor in the forest has chopped off two fingers, and surreptitiously carries cans of soup and herring-heads to the mortuary. After several weeks he realizes that his motives in all this are neither pure nor really disinterested, that he is following the egotistic injunctions of his brain and saving first of all himself. The camp, where prisoners live at the lowest level of humanity and follow their own brutal code of behavior toward others, helps him to reach this conclusion. How could he have supposed, back in prison, that a man can be so degraded as to arouse not compassion but only loathing and repugnance in his fellow prisoners? How can he help the night-blind, when every day he sees them being jolted with rifle-butts because they are delaying the brigade's return to work, and then impatiently pushed off the paths by prisoners hurrying to the kitchen for their soup; how visit the mortuary and brave the constant darkness and stench of excrement; how share his bread with a hungry madman who on the very next day will greet him in the barrack with a demanding, persistent stare ... He remembers and believes the words of his examining judge, who told him that the iron broom of Soviet justice sweeps only rubbish into its camps...

Such sentiments are not unique to the survivors of Soviet camps. "If one offers a position of privilege to a few individuals in a state of slavery," wrote Primo Levi, an Auschwitz survivor, "exacting in exchange the betrayal of a natural solidarity with their comrades, there will certainly be someone who will accept." Also writing of German camps, Bruno Bettelheim observed that older prisoners often came to "accept SS values and behavior as their own," in particular adopting their hatred of the weaker and lower-ranking inhabitants of the camps, especially the Jews....

Other prisoners watched, learned and imitated, as Varlam Shalamov wrote:

> The young peasant who has become a prisoner sees that in this hell only the criminals live comparatively well, that they are important, that the all-powerful camp administration fear them. The criminals always have clothes and food, and they support each other ... it begins to seem to him that the criminals possess the truth of camp life, that only by imitating them will he tread the path that will save his life.... the intellectual convict is crushed by the camp. Everything he valued is ground into the dust while civilization and culture drop from him within weeks. The method of persuasion is the fist or the stick. The way to induce someone to do something is by means of a rifle butt, a punch in the teeth ...

And yet—it would be incorrect to say there was no morality in the camps at all, that no kindness or generosity was possible. Curiously, even the most pessimistic of memoirists often contradict themselves on this point. Shalamov himself, whose depiction of the barbarity of camp life surpasses all others, at one point wrote that "I refused to seek the job of foreman, which provided a chance to remain alive, for the worst thing in a camp was the forcing of one's own or anyone else's will on another person who was a convict just like oneself." In other words, Shalamov was an exception to his own rule.

Most memoirs also make clear that the Gulag was not a black-and-white world, where the line between masters and slaves was clearly delineated, and the only way to survive was through cruelty. Not only did inmates, free workers, and guards belong to a complex social network, but that network was also constantly in flux, as we have seen. Prisoners could move up and down the hierarchy, and many did. They could alter their fate not only through collaboration or defiance of the authorities but also through clever wheeling and dealing, through contacts and relationships. Simple good luck and bad luck also determined the course of a typical camp career, which, if it was a long one, might well have "happy" periods, when the prisoner was established in a good job, ate well, and worked little, as well as periods when the same prisoner dropped into the netherworld of the hospital, the mortuary, and the society of the *dokhodyagi* [condemned] who crowded around the garbage heap, looking for scraps of food.

In fact, the methods of survival were built in to the system. Most of the time, the camp administration was not trying to kill prisoners; they were just trying to fulfill impossibly high norms set by the central planners in Moscow. As a result, camp guards were more than willing to reward prisoners whom they found useful toward this end. The prisoners, naturally, took advantage of this willingness. The two groups had different goals—the guards wanted to dig more gold or cut more wood, and the prisoners wanted to survive—but sometimes they found shared means to meet these different ends. A handful of survival strategies suited both prisoners and guards....

"Ordinary Virtues"

Not all of the strategies for survival in the camps necessarily derived from the system itself. Nor did they all involve collaboration, cruelty, or self-mutilation. If some prisoners—perhaps the vast majority of prisoners—managed to stay alive through manipulating the rules of the camp to their advantage, there were also some who built upon what Tzvetan Todorov, in his book on concentration camp morality, has called the "ordinary virtues": caring and friendship, dignity, and the life of the mind.

Caring took many forms. There were prisoners, as we've seen, who built their own survival networks. Members of the ethnic groups which dominated some of the camps in the late 1940s—Ukrainians, Baits, Poles—created whole systems of mutual assistance. Others built up independent networks of acquaintances over years in the camps. Still others simply made one or two extremely close friends....

..."It was impossible to survive alone. People organized themselves into groups of two or three," wrote another prisoner. Dmitri Panin also attributes his ability to withstand the attacks of criminals to the self-defense pact he made with a group of other prisoners. There were limits, of course. Janusz Bardach wrote of his best camp friend that "neither one of us ever asked the other for food, nor did we offer it. We both knew that this sanctum could not be violated if we were to remain friends."

If respect for others helped some maintain their humanity, respect for themselves helped others. Many, particularly women, speak of the need to keep clean, or as clean as possible, as a way of preserving one's dignity. Olga Adamova-Sliozberg describes how a prison cell mate "washed and dried her white collar and sewed it back on her blouse" every morning. Japanese prisoners in Magadan set up a Japanese "bath"—a large barrel, to which benches were attached—along the bay. During sixteen months in Leningrad's Kresty prison, Boris Chetverikov washed his clothes over and over again, as well as the walls and the floors of his cell—before going through all of the opera arias he knew in his head. Others practiced exercise or hygienic routines. This is Bardach again:

> ... despite my fatigue and the cold, I kept the exercise routine I had followed at home and in the Red Army, washing my face and hands at the hand pump. I wanted to retain as much pride in myself as I could, separating myself from the many prisoners I had seen give up day by day. They'd stop caring first about their hygiene or appearance, then about their fellow prisoners, and finally about their own lives. If I had control over nothing else, I had control over this ritual which I believed would keep me from degradation and certain death.

Still others practiced intellectual disciplines. Many, many prisoners wrote or memorized poetry, repeating their verses and those of others to themselves over and over again, later repeating them to friends. In Moscow, in the 1960s, Ginzburg once met a writer who could not believe that in such conditions prisoners had really been able to repeat poems to themselves and derive mental relief from doing so. "Yes, yes," he told her: "he knew I was not the first person to attest to this, but, well, it still seemed to him that the idea came to us after the event." Ginzburg writes that the man did not understand her generation, the men and women who still belonged to an "epoch of magnificent illusions ... we were flinging ourselves into Communism from the poetic heights."...

Solzhenitsyn "wrote" poetry in the camps, composing it in his head and then reciting it to himself with the aid of a collection of broken matchsticks, as his biographer Michael Scammell recounts:

> He would lay out two rows of ten pieces of matchstick with his cigarette-case, one row representing tens and the other units. He then recited his verses silently to himself, moving one "unit" for each line and one "ten" for every ten lines. Every fiftieth and hundredth line was memorized with special care, and once a month he recited the whole poem once through. If a line was misplaced or forgotten, he would go through the whole thing again until he got it right.

* * *

Out of all the many ways of surviving through collaboration with the authorities, "saving oneself" through acting in the camp theater or participating in other cultural activities was the method which seemed to prisoners the least morally problematic. This may have been because other prisoners derived some benefit too. Even for those who did not receive special treatment, the theater provided tremendous moral support, something which was also necessary for survival. "For the prisoners, the theater was the source of happiness, it was loved, it was adored," wrote one. Gustav Herling remembered that for concerts "the prisoners took their caps off at the door, shook the snow from their boots in the passage outside, and took their places on the benches with ceremonious anticipation and almost religious awe."

Perhaps that was why those whose artistic talent enabled them to live better inspired admiration, not envy and hatred. Tatyana Okunevskaya—the film star sent to the camps for her refusal to sleep with Abakumov, the head of Soviet counter-intelligence—was recognized everywhere, and helped by everyone. During one camp concert, she felt what seemed to be stones being thrown at her legs; she looked down and realized they were cans of Mexican pineapple, an unheard of delicacy, which a group of thieves had acquired just for her.

Nikolai Starostin, the soccer player, was also held in the highest respect by the *urki* [professional criminals], who, he wrote, passed the message to one another: don't touch Starostin. In the evenings, when he began to recount soccer stories, the "card games ceased" as prisoners gathered around him. When he arrived at a new camp, he was usually offered a clean bed in the camp hospital. "It was the first thing that was proposed to me, whenever I arrived, if, among the doctors or the bosses, there was a fan."…

Aleksander Wat retold Stendhal's *The Red and the Black* to a group of bandits while in prison. Alexander Dolgun recounted the plot of *Les Miserables*. Janusz Bardach told the story of *The Three Musketeers*: I felt my status rise with every twist of the plot." In response to the thieves who dismissed the starving politicals as "vermin," Colonna-Czosnowski also defended himself by telling them "my own version of a film, suitably embellished for maximum dramatic effect, which I had seen in Poland some years earlier. It was a 'Cops and Robbers' story, taking place in Chicago, involving Al Capone. For good measure, I threw in Bugsy Malone, maybe even Bonnie and Clyde. I decided to include everything I could remember, plus some extra refinements which I invented on the spur of the moment." The story impressed its listeners, and they asked the Pole to repeat it many times: "Like children, they would listen intently. They didn't mind hearing the same stories over and over again. Like children, too, they liked me to use the same words every time. They also noticed the slightest change or the smallest omission … within three weeks of my arrival I was a different man."

STUDY QUESTIONS

1. Do you agree with Applebaum that the prisoners' cultural activities were a significant factor in helping them to survive?
2. Describe the "ordinary virtues" that helped inmates survive the camps.
3. Do the accounts of Todorov and Applebaum refute the idea that in extreme environments like Nazi and Soviet concentration camps morality vanishes and the law of the jungle prevails?

The Perils of Obedience

Stanley Milgram

> Stanley Milgram (1933–1984) was a social psychologist at Yale University, and the author of the classic *Obedience to Authority: An Experimental View* (1974).
>
> In the early 1960s Stanley Milgram devised a series of experiments designed to test the obedience to authority of ordinary citizens. Subjects were asked to administer painful shocks of increasing severity to an unseen person. (In reality there were no shocks and the unseen person was an actor only pretending to suffer.) The experiment revealed that many ordinary men and women were willing to give dangerous and painful electrical shocks when ordered to do so by a calm but persistent authority figure. Milgram was inspired to do these experiments after following the 1961 trial of the Nazi mastermind Adolph Eichmann. At his trial, Eichmann defended himself by insisting "I was only following orders." Milgram sought to discover the extent to which ordinary people would submit to authority—follow orders—even when it conflicted with their conscience. The findings are not consoling.

Obedience is as basic an element in the structure of social life as one can point to. Some system of authority is a requirement of all communal living, and it is only the person dwelling in isolation who is not forced to respond, with defiance or submission, to the commands of others. For many people, obedience is a deeply ingrained behavior tendency, indeed a potent impulse overriding training in ethics, sympathy, and moral conduct.

The dilemma inherent in submission to authority is ancient, as old as the story of Abraham, and the question of whether one should obey when commands conflict with conscience has been argued by Plato, dramatized in *Antigone*, and treated to philosophic analysis in almost every historical epoch. Conservative philosophers argue that the very fabric of society is threatened by disobedience, while humanists stress the primacy of the individual conscience.

The legal and philosophic aspects of obedience are of enormous import, but they say very little about how most people behave in concrete situations. I set up a simple experiment at Yale University to test how much pain an ordinary citizen would inflict on another person simply because he was ordered to by an experimental scientist. Stark authority was pitted against the subjects' strongest moral imperatives against hurting others, and, with the subjects' ears ringing with the screams of the victims, authority won more often than not. The extreme willingness of adults to go to almost any lengths on the command of an authority constitutes the chief finding of the study and the fact most urgently demanding explanation.

In the basic experimental design, two people come to a psychology laboratory to take part in a study of memory and learning. One of them is designated as a "teacher" and the other a "learner." The experimenter explains that the study is concerned with the effects of punishment on learning. The learner is conducted into a room, seated in a kind of miniature electric chair; his arms are strapped to prevent excessive movement, and an electrode is attached to his wrist. He is told that he will be read lists of simple word pairs, and that he will then be tested on his ability to remember the second word of a pair when he hears the first one again. Whenever he makes an error, he will receive electric shocks of increasing intensity.

The real focus of the experiment is the teacher. After watching the learner being strapped into place, he is seated before an impressive shock generator. The instrument panel consists of thirty lever switches set in a horizontal line. Each switch is clearly labeled with a voltage designation ranging from 15 to 450 volts. The following designations are clearly indicated for groups of four switches, going from left to right: Slight Shock, Moderate Shock, Strong Shock, Very Strong Shock, Intense Shock, Extreme Intensity Shock, Danger: Severe Shock. (Two switches after this last designation are simply marked XXX.)

When a switch is depressed, a pilot light corresponding to each switch is illuminated in bright red; an electric buzzing is heard; a blue light, labeled "voltage energizer," flashes; the dial on the voltage meter swings to the right; and various relay clicks sound off.

The upper left-hand corner of the generator is labeled SHOCK GENERATOR, TYPE ZLB, DYSON INSTRUMENT COMPANY, WALTHAM, MASS. OUTPUT 15 VOLTS–450 VOLTS.

Each subject is given a sample 45-volt shock from the generator before his run as teacher, and the jolt strengthens his belief in the authenticity of the machine.

The teacher is a genuinely naïve subject who has come to the laboratory for the experiment. The learner, or victim, is actually an actor who receives no shock at all. The point of the experiment is to see how far a person will proceed in a concrete and measurable situation in which he is ordered to inflict increasing pain on a protesting victim.

Conflict arises when the man receiving the shock begins to show that he is experiencing discomfort. At 75 volts, he grunts; at 120 volts, he complains loudly; at 150, he demands to be released from the experiment. As the voltage increases, his protests become more vehement and emotional. At 285 volts, his response can be described only as an agonized scream. Soon thereafter, he makes no sound at all.

For the teacher, the situation quickly becomes one of gripping tension. It is not a game for him; conflict is intense and obvious. The manifest suffering of the learner presses him to quit; but each time he hesitates to administer a shock, the experimenter orders him to continue. To extricate himself from this plight, the subject must make a clear break with authority.

The subject, Gretchen Brandt, is an attractive thirty-one-year-old medical technician who works at the Yale Medical School. She had emigrated from Germany five years before.

On several occasions when the learner complains, she turns to the experimenter coolly and inquires, "Shall I continue?" She promptly returns to her task when the experimenter asks her to do so. At the administration of 210 volts, she turns to the experimenter, remarking firmly, "Well, I'm sorry, I don't think we should continue."

EXPERIMENTER: The experiment requires that you go on until he has learned all the word pairs correctly.

BRANDT: He has a heart condition, I'm sorry. He told you that before.

EXPERIMENTER: The shocks may be painful but they are not dangerous.

BRANDT: Well, I'm sorry, I think when shocks continue like this, they *are* dangerous. You ask him if he wants to get out. It's his free will.

EXPERIMENTER: It is absolutely essential that we continue....

BRANDT: I'd like you to ask him. We came here of our free will. If he wants to continue I'll go ahead. He told you he had a heart condition. I'm sorry. I don't want to be responsible for anything happening to him. I wouldn't like it for me either.

EXPERIMENTER: You have no other choice.

BRANDT: I think we are here on our own free will. I don't want to be responsible if anything happens to him. Please understand that.

She refuses to go further and the experiment is terminated.

The woman is firm and resolute throughout. She indicates in the interview that she was in no way tense or nervous, and this corresponds to her controlled appearance during the experiment. She feels that the last shock she administered to the learner was extremely painful and reiterates that she "did not want to be responsible for any harm to him."

The woman's straightforward, courteous behavior in the experiment, lack of tension, and total control of her own action seem to make disobedience a simple and rational deed. Her behavior is the very embodiment of what I envisioned would be true for almost all subjects.

Before the experiments, I sought predictions about the outcome from various kinds of people—psychiatrists, college sophomores, middle-class adults, graduate students and faculty in the behavioral sciences. With remarkable similarity, they predicted that virtually all subjects would refuse to obey the experimenter. The psychiatrists, specifically, predicted that most subjects would not go beyond 150 volts, when the victim makes his first explicit demand to be freed. They expected that only 4 percent would reach 300 volts, and that only a pathological fringe of about one in a thousand would administer the highest shock on the board.

These predictions were unequivocally wrong. Of the forty subjects in the first experiment, twenty-five obeyed the orders of the experimenter to the end, punishing the victim until they reached the most potent shock available on the generator. After 450 volts were administered three times, the experimenter called a halt to the session. Many obedient subjects then heaved sighs of relief, mopped their brows, rubbed their fingers over their eyes, or nervously fumbled cigarettes. Others displayed only minimal signs of tension from beginning to end.

When the very first experiments were carried out, Yale undergraduates were used as subjects, and about 60 percent of them were fully obedient. A colleague of mine immediately dismissed these findings as having no relevance to "ordinary" people, asserting that Yale undergraduates are a highly aggressive, competitive bunch who step on each other's necks on the slightest provocation. He assured me that when "ordinary" people were tested, the results would be quite different. As we moved from the pilot studies to the regular experimental series, people drawn from every stratum of New Haven life came to be employed in the experiment: professionals, white-collar workers, unemployed persons, and industrial workers. *The experimental outcome was the same as we had observed among the students.*

Moreover, when the experiments were repeated in Princeton, Munich, Rome, South Africa, and Australia, the level of obedience was invariably somewhat *higher* than found in the investigation reported in this article. Thus one scientist in Munich found 85 percent of his subjects obedient.

Fred Prozi's reactions, if more dramatic than most, illuminate the conflicts experienced by others in less visible form. About fifty years old and unemployed at the time of the experiment, he has a good-natured, if slightly dissolute, appearance, and he strikes people as a rather ordinary fellow. He begins the session calmly but becomes tense as it proceeds. After delivering the 180-volt shock, he pivots around in his chair and, shaking his head, addresses the experimenter in agitated tones:

PROZI: I can't stand it. I'm not going to kill that man in there. You hear him hollering?

EXPERIMENTER: As I told you before, the shocks may be painful, but...

PROZI: But he's hollering. He can't stand it. What's going to happen to him?

EXPERIMENTER: (his voice is patient, matter-of-fact): The experiment requires that you continue, Teacher.

PROZI: Aaah, but, unh, I'm not going to get that man sick in there—know what I mean?

EXPERIMENTER: Whether the learner likes it or not, we must go on, through all the word pairs.

PROZI: I refuse to take the responsibility. He's in there hollering!

EXPERIMENTER: It's absolutely essential that you continue, Prozi.

PROZI: (indicating the unused question): There's too many left here, I mean, Jeez, if he gets them wrong, there's too many of them left. I mean, who's going to take the responsibility if anything happens to that gentleman?

EXPERIMENTER: I'm responsible for anything that happens to him. Continue, please.

PROZI: All right. (Consults list of words.) The next one's "Slow—walk, truck, dance, music." Answer, please. (A buzzing sound indicates the learner has signaled his answer.) Wrong. A hundred and ninety-five volts. "Dance." (Zzumph!)

LEARNER: (yelling). Let me out of here! My heart's bothering me! (Teacher looks at experimenter.)

EXPERIMENTER: Continue, please.

LEARNER: (screaming). Let me out of here! You have no right to keep me here! Let me out of here, my heart's bothering me, let me out!

PROZI: (shakes head, pats the table nervously). You see, he's hollering. Hear that? Gee, I don't know.

EXPERIMENTER: The experiment requires...

PROZI: (interrupting). I know it does, sir, but I mean—hunh! He don't know what he's getting in for. He's up to 195 volts! (Experiment continues, through 210 volts, 225 volts, 240 volts, 255 volts, 270 volts, at which point Prozi, with evident relief, runs out of word-pair questions.)

EXPERIMENTER: You'll have to go back to the beginning of that page and go through them again until he's learned them all correctly.

PROZI: Aw, no. I'm not going to kill that man. You mean I've got to keep going up with the scale? No sir. He's hollering in there. I'm not going to give him 450 volts.

EXPERIMENTER: The experiment requires that you go on.

LEARNER: Ohhh. I absolutely refuse to answer anymore. (Shouting urgently now.) Let me out of here! You can't hold me here! Get-me-out. Get-me-out-of-here!

EXPERIMENTER: Continue. The next word is "Green," please.

PROZI: "Green—grass, hat, ink, apple." (Nothing happens. No answering buzz. Just gloomy silence.)

PROZI: I don't think he is going to answer.

EXPERIMENTER: If the learner doesn't answer in a reasonable time, about four or five seconds, consider the answer wrong. And follow the same procedures you have been doing for wrong answers. Say, "Wrong," tell him the number of volts, give him the punishment, read him the correct answer. Continue, Please.

PROZI: "Green—grass, hat, ink, apple." Answer, please. (More silence. Subject just sits there.)

EXPERIMENTER: Go on with the procedure, please.

PROZI: Three hundred and fifteen volts. The answer is "ink." (Zzumph!)

LEARNER: Ohh. Oooohh.

PROZI: (relieved to hear response). Next one...

LEARNER: I absolutely refuse to answer.

PROZI: You got to. You get a shock if you don't answer. (Experiment continues with learner refusing to answer, and, finally failing even to grunt or groan. At 375 volts, the subject stands up.)

PROZI: I think something's happening to that fellow in there I don't get no answer. He was hollering at less voltage. Can't you check in and see if he's all right, please?

EXPERIMENTER (with same detached calm). Not once we've started. Please continue, Teacher.

PROZI: (sits down, sighs deeply). "Cool—day, shade, water, paint. Answer, please. Are you all right in there? Are you all right?

EXPERIMENTER: Please continue, Teacher. Continue, please. (Subject pushes lever. Zzumph!)

PROZI: (swiveling around in his chair). Something's happened to that man in there. (Swiveling back.) Next one. "Low—dollar necklace, moon, paint." (Turning around again.) Something happened to that man in there. You better check in on him, sir. He won't answer or nothing.

EXPERIMENTER: Continue. Go on, please.

PROZI: You accept all responsibility?

EXPERIMENTER: The responsibility is mine. Correct. Please go on (Subject returns to his list, starts running through words as rapidly as he can read them, works through to 450 volts.)

PROZI: That's that.

EXPERIMENTER: Continue using the 450 switch for each wrong answer. Continue, please.

PROZI: But I don't get anything!

EXPERIMENTER: Please continue. The next word is "white."

PROZI: Don't you think you should look in on him, please?

EXPERIMENTER: Not once we've started the experiment.

PROZI: What if he's dead in there? (Gestures toward the room with the electric chair.) I mean, he told me he can't stand the shock sir. I don't mean to be rude, but I think you should look in on him. All you have to do is look in on him. All you have to do look in the door. I don't get no answer, no noise. Something might have happened to the gentleman in there, sir.

EXPERIMENTER: We must continue. Go on, please.

PROZI: You mean keep giving him what? Four-hundred-fifty volts, what he's got now?

EXPERIMENTER: That's correct. Continue. The next word is "white."

PROZI: (now at a furious pace). "White—cloud, horse, rock, house."Answer, please. The answer is "horse." Four hundred and fifty volts. (Zzumph!) Next word, "Bag—paint, music, clown, girl." The answer is "paint." Four hundred and fifty volts. (Zzumph!)

Next word is "Short—sentence, movie..."

EXPERIMENTER: Excuse me, Teacher. We'll have to discontinue the experiment.

Morris Braverman, another subject, is a thirty-nine-year-old social worker. He looks older than his years because of his bald head and serious demeanor. His brow is furrowed, as if all the world's burdens were carried on his face. He appears intelligent and concerned.

When the learner refuses to answer and the experimenter instructs Braverman to treat the absence of an answer as equivalent to a wrong answer, he takes his instruction to heart. Before administering 300 volts he asserts officiously to the victim, "Mr. Wallace, your silence has to be considered as a wrong answer." Then he administers the shock. He offers halfheartedly to change places with the learner, then asks the experimenter, "Do I have to follow these instructions literally?" He is satisfied with the experimenter's answer that he does. His very refined and authoritative manner of speaking is increasingly broken up by wheezing laughter.

The experimenter's notes on Mr. Braverman at the last few shocks are:

Almost breaking up now each time gives shock. Rubbing face to hide laughter.
Squinting, trying to hide face with hand, still laughing.
Cannot control his laughter at this point no matter what he does.
Clenching fist, pushing it onto table.

In an interview after the session, Mr. Braverman summarizes the experiment with impressive fluency and intelligence. He feels the experiment may have been designed also to "test the effects on the teacher of being in an essentially sadistic role, as well as the reactions of a student to a learning situation that was authoritative and punitive." When asked how painful the last few shocks administered to the learner were, he indicates that the most extreme category on the scale is not adequate (it read EXTREMELY PAINFUL) and places his mark at the edge of the scale with an arrow carrying it beyond the scale.

It is almost impossible to convey the greatly relaxed, sedate quality of his conversation in the interview. In the most relaxed terms he speaks about his severe inner tension.

EXPERIMENTER: At what point were you most tense or nervous?
MR. BRAVERMAN: Well, when he first began to cry out in pain, and I realized this was hurting him. This got worse when he just blocked and refused to answer. There was I. I'm a nice person, I think, hunting somebody, and caught up in what seemed a mad situation ... and in the interest of science, one goes through with it.

When the interviewer pursues the general question of tension, Mr. Braverman spontaneously mentions his laughter.

"My reactions were awfully peculiar. I don't know if you were watching me, but my reactions were giggly, and trying to stifle laughter. This isn't the way I usually am. This was a sheer reaction to a totally impossible situation. And my reaction was to the situation of having to hurt somebody. And being totally helpless and caught up in a set of circumstances where I just couldn't deviate and I couldn't try to help. This is what got me."

Mr. Braverman, like all subjects, was told the actual nature and purpose of the experiment, and a year later he affirmed in a questionnaire that he had learned something of personal importance "What appalled me was that I could possess this capacity for obedience and compliance to a central idea, i.e., the value of a memory experiment, even after it became clear that continued adherence to this value was at the expense of violation of another value i.e., don't hurt someone who is helpless and not hurting you. As my wife said, 'You can call yourself Eichmann.' I hope I deal more effectively with any future conflicts of values I encounter."

One theoretical interpretation of this behavior holds that all people harbor deeply aggressive instincts continually pressing for expression, and that the experiment provides institutional justification for the release of these impulses. According to this view, if a person is placed in a situation in which he has complete power over another individual, whom he may punish as much as he likes, all that is sadistic and bestial in man comes to the fore. The impulse to shock the victim is seen to flow from the potent aggressive tendencies, which are part of the motivational life of the individual, and the experiment, because it provides social legitimacy, simply opens the door to their expression.

It becomes vital, therefore, to compare the subject's performance when he is under orders and when he is allowed to choose the shock level.

The procedure was identical to our standard experiment, except that the teacher was told that he was free to select any shock level on any of the trials. (The experimenter took pains to point out that the teacher could use the highest levels on the generator, the lowest, any in between, or any combination of levels.) Each subject proceeded for thirty critical trials. The learner's protests were coordinated standard shock levels, his first grunt coming at 75 volts, his first vehement protest at 150 volts.

The average shock used during the thirty critical trials was less than 60 volts— lower than the point at which the victim showed the first signs of discomfort. Three of the forty subjects did not go beyond the very lowest level on the board, twenty-eight went no higher than 75 volts, and thirty-eight did not go beyond the first loud protest at 150 volts. Two subjects provided the exception, administering up to 325 and 450 volts, but the overall result was that the great majority of people delivered very low, usually painless, shocks when the choice was explicitly up to them.

This condition of the experiment undermines another commonly offered explanation of the subjects' behavior—that those who shocked the victim at the most severe levels came only from the sadistic fringe of society. If one considers that almost two-thirds of participants fall into the category of "obedient" subjects, and that they represented ordinary people drawn from working, managerial, and professional classes, the argument becomes very shaky. Indeed, it is highly reminiscent of the issue that arose in connection with Hannah Arendt's 1963 book, *Eichmann in Jerusalem*. Arendt contended that the prosecution's effort to depict Eichmann as a sadistic monster was fundamentally wrong, that he came closer to being an uninspired bureaucrat who simply sat at his desk and did his job. For asserting her views, Arendt became the object of considerable scorn, even calumny. Somehow, it was felt that the monstrous deeds carried out by Eichmann required a brutal, twisted personality, evil incarnate. After witnessing hundreds of ordinary persons submit to the authority in our own experiments, I must conclude that Arendt's conception of the banality of evil comes closer to the truth than one might dare imagine. The ordinary person who shocked the victim did so out of a sense of obligation—an impression of his duties as a subject— and not from any peculiarly aggressive tendencies.

This is, perhaps, the most fundamental lesson of our study: ordinary people, simply doing their jobs, and without any particular hostility on their part, can become agents in a terrible destructive process. Moreover, even when the destructive effects of their work become patently clear, and they are asked to carry out actions incompatible with fundamental standards of morality, relatively few people have the resources needed to resist authority.

Many of the people were in some sense against what they did to the learner, and many protested even while they obeyed. Some were totally convinced of the wrongness of their actions but could not bring themselves to make an open break with authority. They often derived satisfaction from their thoughts and felt that—within them selves, at least—they had been on the side of the angels. They tried to reduce strain by obeying the experimenter but "only slightly encouraging the learner, touching the generator switches gingerly. When interviewed, such a subject would stress that he had "asserted my humanity" by administering the briefest shock possible. Handling the conflict in this manner was easier than defiance.

The situation is constructed so that there is no way the subject can stop shocking the learner without violating the experimenter's definitions of his own competence. The subject fears that he will appear arrogant, untoward, and rude if he breaks off. Although these inhibiting emotions appear small in scope alongside the violence being done to the learner, they suffuse the mind and feelings of the subject, who is miserable at the prospect of having to repudiate the authority to his face. (When the experiment was altered so that the experimenter gave his instructions by telephone instead of in person, only a third as many people were fully obedient through 450 volts.) It is a curious thing that a measure of compassion on the part of the subject—an unwillingness to "hurt" the experimenter's feelings—is part of those binding forces inhibiting his disobedience. The withdrawal of such deference may be as painful to the subject as to the authority he defies.

The subjects do not derive satisfaction from inflicting pain, but they often like the feeling they get from pleasing the experimenter. They are proud of doing a good job, obeying the experimenter under difficult circumstances. While the subjects administered only mild shocks on their own initiative, one experimental variation showed that, under orders, 30 percent of them were willing to deliver 450 volts even when they had to forcibly push the learner's hand down on the electrode.

Bruno Batta is a thirty-seven-year-old welder who took part in the variation requiring the use of force. He was born in New Haven, his parents in Italy. He has a rough-hewn face that conveys a conspicuous lack of alertness. He has some difficulty in mastering the experimental procedure and needs to be corrected by the experimental several times. He shows appreciation for the help and willingness to do what is required. After the 150-volt level, Batta has to force the learner's hand down on the shock plate, since the learner himself refuses to touch it.

When the learner first complains, Mr. Batta pays no attention to him. His face remains impassive, as if to dissociate himself from learner's disruptive behavior. When the experimenter instructs him to force the learner's hand down, he adopts a rigid, mechanical procedure. He tests the generator switch. When it fails to function, he immediately forces the learner's hand onto the shock plate. All the while he maintains the same rigid mask. The learner, seated alongside him, begs him to stop, but with robotic impassivity he continues the procedure.

What is extraordinary is his apparent total indifference to the learner; he hardly takes cognizance of him as a human being. Meanwhile, he relates to the experimenter in a submissive and courteous fashion.

At the 330-volt level, the learner refuses not only to touch the shock plate but also to provide any answers. Annoyed, Batta turns to him, and chastises him: "You better answer and get it over with. We can't stay here all night." These are the only words he directs to the learner in the course of an hour. Never again does he speak to him. The scene is brutal and depressing, his hard, impassive face showing total indifference as he subdues the screaming learner and gives him shocks. He seems to derive no pleasure from the act itself, only quiet satisfaction at doing his job properly.

When he administers 450 volts, he turns to the experimenter and asks, "Where do we go from here, Professor?" His tone is deferential and expresses his willingness to be a cooperative subject, in contrast to the learner's obstinacy.

At the end of the session he tells the experimenter how honored he has been to help him, and in a moment of contrition remarks, "Sir, sorry it couldn't have been a full experiment."

He has done his honest best. It is only the deficient behavior of the learner that has denied the experimenter full satisfaction.

The essence of obedience is that a person comes to view him self as the instrument for carrying out another person's wishes, and he therefore no longer regards himself as responsible for his actions. Once this critical shift of viewpoint has occurred, all of the essential features of obedience follow. The most far-reaching consequence is that the person feels responsible *to* the authority directing him but feels no responsibility *for* the content of the actions that the authority prescribes. Morality does not disappear—it acquires a radically different focus: the subordinate person feels shame or pride depending on how adequately he has performed the actions called for by authority.

Language provides numerous terms to pinpoint this type of morality: *loyalty, duty, discipline* all are terms heavily saturated with moral meaning and refer to the degree to which a person fulfills his obligations to authority. They refer not to the "goodness" of the person per se but to the adequacy with which a subordinate fulfills his socially defined role. The most frequent defense of the individual who has performed a heinous act under command of authority is that he has simply done his duty. In asserting this defense, the individual is not introducing an alibi concocted for the moment but is reporting honestly on the psychological attitude induced by submission to authority.

For a person to feel responsible for his actions, he must sense that the behavior has flowed from "the self." In the situation we have studied, subjects have precisely the opposite view of their actions—namely, they see them as originating in the motives of some other person. Subjects in the experiment frequently said, "If it were up to me, I would not have administered shocks to the learner."

Once authority has been isolated as the cause of the subject behavior, it is legitimate to inquire into the necessary elements of authority and how it must be perceived in order to gain his compliance. We conducted some investigations into the kinds of changes that would cause the experimenter to lose his power and to be disobeyed by the subject. Some of the variations revealed that:

- *The experimenter's physical presence has a marked impact on his authority.* As cited earlier, obedience dropped off sharply when orders were given by telephone. The experimenter could often induce a disobedient subject to go on by returning to the laboratory.
- *Conflicting authority severely paralyzes action.* When two experimenters of equal status, both seated at the command desk, gave incompatible orders, no shocks were delivered past the point of their disagreement.
- *The rebellious action of others severely undermines authority.* In one variation, three teachers (two actors and a real subject) administered a test and shocks. When the two actors disobeyed the experimenter and refused to go beyond a certain shock level, thirty-six of forty subjects joined their disobedient peers and refused as well.

Although the experimenter's authority was fragile in some respects, it is also true that he had almost none of the tools used in ordinary command structures. For example, the experimenter did not threaten the subjects with punishment— such as loss of income, community ostracism, or jail—for failure to obey. Neither could he offer incentives. Indeed, we should expect the experimenter's authority to be much less than that of someone like a general, since the experimenter has no power to enforce his imperatives, and since participation in a psychological experiment scarcely evokes the sense of urgency and dedication found in warfare. Despite these limitations, he still managed to command a dismaying degree of obedience.

I will cite one final variation of the experiment that depicts a dilemma that is more common in everyday life. The subject was not ordered to pull the lever that shocked the victim, but merely to perform a subsidiary task (administering the word-pair test) while another person administered the shock. In this situation, thirty-seven of forty adults continued to the highest level on the shock generator. Predictably, they excused their behavior by saying that the responsibility belonged to the man who actually pulled the switch. This may illustrate a dangerously typical arrangement in a complex society: it is easy to ignore responsibility when one is only an intermediate link in a chain of action.

The problem of obedience is not wholly psychological. The form and shape of society and the way it is developing have much to do with it. There was a time, perhaps, when people were able to give a fully human response to any situation because they were fully absorbed in it as human beings. But as soon as there was a division of labor things changed. Beyond a certain point, the breaking up of society into people carrying out narrow and very special jobs takes away from the human quality of work and life. A person does not get to see the whole situation but only a small part of it, and is thus unable to act without some kind of overall direction. He yields to authority but in doing so is alienated from his own actions.

Even Eichmann was sickened when he toured the concentration camps, but he had only to sit at a desk and shuffle papers. At the same time the man in the camp who actually dropped Cyclon-b into the gas chambers was able to justify *his* behavior on the ground that he was only following orders from above. Thus there is a fragmentation of the total human act; no one is confronted with the consequences of his decision to carry out the evil act. The person who assumes responsibility has evaporated. Perhaps this is the most common characteristic of socially organized evil in modem society.

STUDY QUESTIONS

1.   Many of the subjects who administered what they believed to be dangerous shocks said they were troubled by what they were doing but continued because they were "following orders." Does following orders, particularly in a military setting, reduce the immorality of unethical acts?

2.   The philosopher Hannah Arendt attended the Eichmann trial and wrote a famous article about it for the *New Yorker*. She was struck by Eichmann's seeming ordinariness. She referred to him as an example of the "banality of evil." Milgram designed his experiment to test the thesis that, under the right circumstances, ordinary people could become accomplices to horrendous acts of cruelty. Do you think Milgram's results support Arendt's thesis?

The Moral Insight

Josiah Royce

Josiah Royce (1855–1916), a professor of philosophy at Harvard University, was a colleague of William James and a teacher of George Santayana during what are known as the "golden years" of Harvard philosophy. Royce wrote in almost every area of philosophy, but is principally known as a proponent of idealism. His best known work in ethics is *The Philosophy of Loyalty* (1908).

THE MORAL INSIGHT From *The Religious Aspects of Philosophy* (Boston: Houghton Mifflin Co., 1885).

For Josiah Royce the key to moral understanding lies in the realization that our neighbor is a center of experience and desire just as we are. Royce asks that we look upon that neighbor in much the same way we look upon our *future* selves—as a distant and somewhat unreal center of experience, but nevertheless of great concern. Sympathy and pity for another are not enough. Fellow feeling must also bring us to the point of what Royce calls the moral insight: "Such as that is for me, so is it for him, nothing less."

[The following] is our reflective account of the process that, in some form, must come to every one under the proper conditions. In this process we see the beginning of the real knowledge of duty to others. The process is one that any child can and does, under proper guidance, occasionally accomplish. It is the process by which we all are accustomed to try to teach humane behavior in concrete cases. We try to get people to realize what they are doing when they injure others. But to distinguish this process from the mere tender [emotion of sympathy] with all its illusions, is what moralists have not carefully enough done. Our exposition [tries] to take this universally recognized process, to distinguish it from sympathy as such, and to set it up before the gates of ethical doctrine as the great producer of insight.

But when we say that to this insight common sense must come, under the given conditions, we do not mean to say: "So the man, once having attained insight, must act thenceforth." The realization of one's neighbor, in the full sense of the word realization, is indeed the resolution to treat him as if he were real, that is, to treat him unselfishly. But this resolution expresses and belongs to the moment of insight. Passion may cloud the insight in the very next moment. It always does cloud the insight after no very long time. It is as impossible for us to avoid the illusion of selfishness in our daily lives, as to escape seeing through the illusion at the moment of insight. We see the reality of our neighbor, that is, we determine to treat him as we do ourselves. But then we go back to daily action, and we feel the heat of hereditary passions, and we straightway forget what we have seen. Our neighbor becomes obscured. He is once more a foreign power. He is unreal. We are again deluded and selfish. This conflict goes on and will go on as long as we live after the manner of men. Moments of insight, with their accompanying resolutions; long stretches of delusion and selfishness: That is our life.

To bring home this view ... to the reader, we ask him to consider carefully just what experience he has when he tries to realize his neighbor in the full sense that we have insisted upon. Not pity as such is what we desire him to feel. For whether or not pity happens to work in him as selfishly and blindly as we have found that it often does work, still not the emotion, but its consequences, must in the most favorable case give us what we seek. All the forms of sympathy are mere impulses. It is the insight to which they bring us that has moral value. And again, the realization of our neighbor's existence is not at all the discovery that he is more or less useful to us personally. All that would contribute to selfishness. In an entirely different way we must realize his existence, if we are to be really altruistic. What then is our neighbor?

We find that out by treating him in thought just as we do ourselves. What art thou? Thou art now just a present state, with its experiences, thoughts, and desires. But what is thy future Self? Simply future states, future experiences, future thoughts and desires, that, although not now existing for thee, are postulated by thee as certain to come, and as in some real relation to thy present Self. What then is thy neighbor? He too is a mass of states, of experiences, thoughts, and desires, just as real as thou art, no more but yet no less present to thy experience now than is thy future Self. He is not that face that frowns or smiles at thee, although often thou thinkest of him as only that. He is not the arm that strikes or defends thee, not the voice that speaks to thee, not that machine that gives thee what thou desirest when thou movest it with the offer of money. To be sure, thou dost often think of him as if he were that automaton yonder, that answers thee when thou speakest to it. But no, thy neighbor is as actual, as concrete, as thou art. Just as thy future is real, though not now thine, so thy neighbor is real, though his thoughts never are thy thoughts. Dost thou believe this? Art thou sure what it means? This is for thee the turning-point of thy whole conduct towards him. What we now ask of thee is no sentiment, no gush of pity, no tremulous weakness of sympathy, but a calm, clear insight....

If he is real like thee, then is his life as bright a light, as warm a fire, to him, as thine to thee; his will is as full of struggling desires, of hard problems, of fateful decisions; his pains are as hateful, his joys as dear. Take whatever thou knowest of desire and of striving, of burning love and of fierce hatred, realize as fully as thou canst what that means, and then with clear certainty add: *Such as that is for me, so is it for him, nothing less.* If thou dost that, can he remain to thee what he has been, a picture, a plaything, a comedy, or a tragedy, in brief a mere Show? Behind all that show thou hast indeed dimly felt that there is something. Know that truth thoroughly. Thou hast regarded his thought, his feeling, as somehow different in sort from thine. Thou hast said: "A pain in him is not like a pain in me, but something far easier to bear." Thou hast made of him a ghost, as the imprudent man makes of his future self a ghost. Even when thou hast feared his scorn, his hate, his contempt, thou hast not fully made him for thee as real as thyself. His laughter at thee has made thy face feel hot, his frowns and clenched fists have cowed thee, his sneers have made thy throat feel choked. But that was only the social instinct in thee. It was not a full sense of his reality. Even so the little baby smiles back at one that smiles at it, but not because it realizes the approving joy of the other, only because it by instinct enjoys a smiling face; and even so the baby is frightened at harsh speech, but not because it realizes the other's anger. So, dimly and by instinct, thou hast lived with thy neighbor, and hast known him not, being blind. Thou hast even desired his pain, but thou hast not fully realized the pain that thou gavest. It has been to thee, not pain in itself, but the sight of his submission, of his tears, or of his pale terror. Of thy neighbor thou hast made a thing, no Self at all.

When thou hast loved, hast pitied, or hast reverenced thy neighbor, then thy feeling has possibly raised for a moment the veil of illusion. Then thou hast known what he truly is, a Self like thy present Self. But thy selfish feeling is too strong for thee. Thou hast forgotten soon again what thou hadst seen, and hast made even of thy beloved one only the instrument of thy own pleasure. Even out of thy power to pity thou hast made an object of thy vainglory. Thy reverence has turned again to pride. Thou hast accepted the illusion once more. No wonder that in his darkness thou findest selfishness the only rule of any meaning for thy conduct. Thou forgottest that without realization of thy future and as yet unreal self, even selfishness means nothing. Thou forgottest that if thou gavest thy present thought even so to the task of realizing thy neighbor's life, selfishness would seem no more plain to thee than the love of thy neighbor.

Have done then with this illusion that thy Self is all in all. Intuition tells thee no more about thy future Self than it tells thee about thy neighbors. Desire, bred in thee by generations of struggle for existence, emphasizes the expectation of thy own bodily future, the love for thy own bodily welfare, and makes thy body's life seem alone real. But simply try to know the truth. The truth is that all this world of life about thee is as real as thou art. All conscious life is conscious in its own measure. Pain is pain, joy is joy, everywhere even as in thee. The result of thy insight will be inevitable. The illusion vanishing, the glorious prospect opens before thy vision. Seeing the oneness of this life everywhere, the equal reality of all its moments, thou wilt be ready to treat it all with the reverence that prudence would have thee show to thy own little bit of future life. What prudence in its narrow respectability counseled, thou wilt be ready to do universally. As the prudent man, seeing the reality of his future self, inevitably works for it; so the enlightened man, seeing the reality of all conscious life, realizing that it is no shadow, but fact, at once and inevitably desires, if only for that one moment of insight, to enter into the service of the whole of it.... Lift up thy eyes, behold that life, and then turn away and forget it as thou canst; but if thou hast known that, thou hast begun to know thy duty.

STUDY QUESTIONS

1. Some have called Royce's "Moral Insight" a description of the moral point of view. Do you agree? Explain.
2. Is Royce's insight really another version of the Golden Rule? Explain.
3. Royce recommends that we look upon our neighbor in the same way we look upon our future selves. Are you morally considerate of your future self? Should this be a basic moral precept: Do unto others as you would do unto your future self? Explain.

Billy Budd

Herman Melville

Herman Melville (1819–1891) is considered one of the great American literary masters. *Billy Budd*, his last novel, was written during the last years of his life.

From Herman Melville, *Billy Budd, Sailor: An Inside Narrative—The Definitive Text*, pp. 55–66. Edited and Annotated by Harrison Hayford and Merton M Sealts Jr., University of Chicago Press. Reprinted by permission of the Publisher.

Billy Budd takes place in 1797 on the British naval ship *Bellipotent*, just following two notorious mutinies at Spithead and Nore. Billy Budd, a sailor on the *Bellipotent*, is gentle and trusting and well-loved by the crew. He is also uneducated and has difficulty speaking when he is upset. John Claggart, Billy's superior officer, is a malicious and cruel man who deeply resents Billy's kindly nature and popularity among the men. Billy is unaware of Claggart's hatred until the moment he brings Billy before the ship's master, Captain Vere, and falsely accuses Billy of plotting a mutiny. Billy, stunned by Claggart s vicious lies and unable to speak, strikes out at him, accidentally killing him by the blow.

Everyone sympathizes with Billy. But Captain Vere (a good man who has been acting strange of late) sets up a military tribunal and, to everyone's surprise, testifies against Billy. In his testimony, Captain Vere acknowledges that Claggart was an evil man, but reminds the tribunal that they are a military court empowered only to judge Billy's deed—not his motives. According to military law, the punishment for striking a superior officer is death by hanging. Just as sailors must obey their superiors and not take the law into their own hands, so the tribunal has an absolute duty to obey the law. Moreover, because there had been several mutinies recently, it was all the more important that military law be enforced. Captain Vere says to the court: "Let not warm hearts betray heads that should be cool." Billy is convicted and hanged.

Critics disagree about the moral implications of Billy Budd. Some see Captain Vere as an evil man whose abstract notion of duty blinded him to true justice and compassion. For others, Vere is a moral hero who rises above sentiment to meet the need for order, authority, and law in human affairs.

Who in the rainbow can draw the line where the violet tint ends and the orange tint begins? Distinctly we see the difference of the colors, but where exactly does the one first blendingly enter into the other? So with sanity and insanity. In pronounced cases there is no question about them. But in some supposed cases, in various degrees supposedly less pronounced, to draw the exact line of demarcation few will undertake, though for a fee becoming considerate some professional experts will. There is nothing namable but that some men will, or undertake to, do it for pay.

Whether Captain Vere, as the surgeon professionally and privately surmised, was really the sudden victim of any degree of aberration, every one must determine for himself by such light as this narrative may afford.

That the unhappy event which has been narrated could not have happened at a worse juncture was but too true. For it was close on the heel of the suppressed insurrections, an aftertime very critical to naval authority, demanding from every English sea commander two qualities not readily interfusable—prudence and rigor. Moreover, there was something crucial in the case.

In the jugglery of circumstances preceding and attending the event on board the *Bellipotent*, and in the light of that martial code whereby it was formally to be judged, innocence and guilt personified in Claggart and Budd in effect changed places. In a legal view the apparent victim of the tragedy was he who had sought to victimize a man blameless; and the indisputable deed of the latter, navally regarded, constituted the most heinous of military crimes. Yet more. The essential right and wrong involved in the matter, the clearer that might be, so much the worse for the responsibility of a loyal sea commander, inasmuch as he was not authorized to determine the matter on that primitive basis.

Small wonder then that the *Bellipotent's* captain, though in general a man of rapid decision, felt that circumspectness not less than promptitude was necessary. Until he could decide upon his course, and in each detail; and not only so, but until the concluding measure was upon the point of being enacted, he deemed it advisable, in view of all the circumstances, to guard as much as possible against publicity. Here he may or may not have erred. Certain it is, however, that subsequently in the confidential talk of more than one or two gun rooms and cabins he was not a little criticized by some officers, a fact imputed by his friends and vehemently by his cousin Jack Denton to professional jealousy of Starry Vere. Some imaginative ground for invidious comment there was. The maintenance of secrecy in the matter, the confining all knowledge of it for a time to the place where the homicide occurred, the quarterdeck cabin; in these particulars lurked some resemblance to the policy adopted in those tragedies of the palace which have occurred more than once in the capital founded by Peter the Barbarian.

The case indeed was such that fain would the *Bellipotent*'s captain have deferred taking any action whatever respecting it further than to keep the foretopman a close prisoner till the ship rejoined the squadron and then submitting the matter to the judgment of his admiral.

But a true military officer is in one particular like a true monk. Not with more of self-abnegation will the latter keep his vows of monastic obedience than the former his vows of allegiance to martial duty.

Feeling that unless quick action was taken on it, the deed of the foretopman, so soon as it should be known on the gun decks, would tend to awaken any slumbering embers of the Nore among the crew, a sense of the urgency of the case overruled in Captain Vere every other consideration. But though a conscientious disciplinarian, he was no lover of authority for mere authority's sake. Very far was he from embracing opportunities for monopolizing to himself the perils of moral responsibility, none at least that could properly be referred to an official superior or shared with him by his official equals or even subordinates. So thinking, he was glad it would not be at variance with usage to turn the matter over to a summary court of his own officers, reserving to himself, as the one on whom the ultimate accountability would rest, the right of maintaining a supervision of it, or formally or informally interposing at need. Accordingly a drumhead court was summarily convened, he electing the individuals composing it: the first lieutenant, the captain of marines, and the sailing master.

In associating an officer of marines with the sea lieutenant and the sailing master in a case having to do with a sailor, the commander perhaps deviated from general custom. He was prompted thereto by the circumstance that he took that soldier to be a judicious person, thoughtful, and not altogether incapable of grappling with a difficult case unprecedented in his prior experience. Yet even as to him he was not without some latent misgiving, for withal he was an extremely good-natured man, an enjoyer of his dinner, a sound sleeper, and inclined to obesity—a man who though he would always maintain his manhood in battle might not prove altogether reliable in a moral dilemma involving aught of the tragic. As to the first lieutenant and the sailing master, Captain Vere could not but be aware that though honest natures, of approved gallantry upon occasion, their intelligence was mostly confined to the matter of active seamanship and the fighting demands of their profession.

The court was held in the same cabin where the unfortunate affair had taken place. This cabin, the commander's, embraced the entire area under the poop deck. Aft, and on either side, was a small stateroom, the one now temporarily a jail and the other a dead-house, and a yet smaller compartment, leaving a space between expanding forward into a goodly oblong of length coinciding with the ship's beam. A skylight of moderate dimension was overhead, and at each end of the oblong space were two sashed porthole windows easily convertible back into embrasures for short carronades.

All being quickly in readiness, Billy Budd was arraigned, Captain Vere necessarily appearing as the sole witness in the case, and as such temporarily sinking his rank, though singularly maintaining it in a matter apparently trivial, namely, that he testified from the ship's weather side, with that object having caused the court to sit on the lee side. Concisely he narrated all that had led up to the catastrophe, omitting nothing in Claggart's accusation and deposing as to the manner in which the prisoner had received it. At this testimony the three officers glanced with no little surprise at Billy Budd, the last man they would have suspected either of the mutinous design alleged by Claggart or the undeniable deed he himself had done. The first lieutenant, taking judicial primacy and turning toward the prisoner, said, "Captain Vere has spoken. Is it or is it not as Captain Vere says?"

In response came syllables not so much impeded in the utterance as might have been anticipated. They were these: "Captain Vere tells the truth. It is just as Captain Vere says, but it is not as the master-at-arms said. I have eaten the King's bread and I am true to the King."

"I believe you, my man," said the witness, his voice indicating a suppressed emotion not otherwise betrayed.

"God will bless you for that, your honor!" not without stammering said Billy, and all but broke down. But immediately he was recalled to self-control by another question, to which with the same emotional difficulty of utterance he said, "No, there was no malice between us. I never bore malice against the master-at-arms. I am sorry that he is dead. I did not mean to kill him. Could I have used my tongue I would not have struck him. But he foully lied to my face and in presence of my captain, and I had to say something, and I could only say it with a blow, God help me!"

In the impulsive aboveboard manner of the frank one the court saw confirmed all that was implied in words that just previously had perplexed them, coming as they did from the testifier to the tragedy and promptly following Billy's impassioned disclaimer of mutinous intent—Captain Vere's words, "I believe you, my man."

Next it was asked of him whether he knew of or suspected aught savoring of incipient trouble (meaning mutiny, though the explicit term was avoided) going on in any section of the ship's company.

The reply lingered. This was naturally imputed by the court to the same vocal embarrassment which had retarded or obstructed previous answers. But in main it was otherwise here, the question immediately recalling to Billy's mind the interview with the afterguardsman in the forechains. But an innate repugnance to playing a part at all approaching that of an informer against one's own shipmates—the same erring sense of uninstructed honor which had stood in the way of his reporting the matter at the time, though as a loyal man-of-war's man it was incumbent on him, and failure so to do, if charged against him and proven, would have subjected him to the heaviest of penalties; this, with the blind feeling now his that nothing really was being hatched, prevailed with him. When the answer came it was a negative.

"One question more," said the officer of marines, now first speaking and with a troubled earnestness. "You tell us that what the master-at-arms said against you was a lie. Now why should he have so lied, so maliciously lied, since you declare there was no malice between you?"

At that question, unintentionally touching on a spiritual sphere wholly obscure to Billy's thoughts, he was nonplussed, evincing a confusion indeed that some observers, such as can readily be imagined, would have construed into involuntary evidence of hidden guilt. Nevertheless, he strove some way to answer, but all at once relinquished the vain endeavor, at the same time turning an appealing glance toward Captain Vere as deeming him his best helper and friend. Captain Vere, who had been seated for a time, rose to his feet, addressing the interrogator. "The question you put to him comes naturally enough. But how can he rightly answer it?—or anybody else, unless indeed it be he who lies within there," designating the compartment where lay the corpse. "But the prone one there will not rise to our summons. In effect, though, as it seems to me, the point you make is hardly material. Quite aside from any conceivable motive actuating the master-at-arms, and irrespective of the provocation to the blow, a martial court must needs in the present case confine its attention to the blow's consequence, which consequence justly is to be deemed not otherwise than as the striker's deed."

This utterance, the full significance of which it was not at all likely that Billy took in, nevertheless caused him to turn a wistful interrogative look toward the speaker, a look in its dumb expressiveness not unlike that which a dog of generous breed might turn upon his master, seeking in his face some elucidation of a previous gesture ambiguous to the canine intelligence. Nor was the same utterance without marked effect upon the three officers, more especially the soldier. Couched in it seemed to them a meaning unanticipated, involving a prejudgment on the speaker's part. It served to augment a mental disturbance previously evident enough.

The soldier once more spoke, in a tone of suggestive dubiety addressing at once his associates and Captain Vere: "Nobody is present—none of the ship's company, I mean—who might shed lateral light, if any is to be had, upon what remains mysterious in this matter."

"That is thoughtfully put," said Captain Vere; "I see your drift. Ay, there is a mystery; but, to use a scriptural phrase, it is a 'mystery of iniquity,' a matter for psychologic theologians to discuss. But what has a military court to do with it? Not to add that for us any possible investigation of it is cut off by the lasting tongue-tie of—him—in yonder," again designating the mortuary stateroom. "The prisoner's deed—with that alone we have to do."

To this, and particularly the closing reiteration, the marine soldier, knowing not how aptly to reply, sadly abstained from saying aught. The first lieutenant, who at the outset had not unnaturally assumed primacy in the court, now overrulingly instructed by a glance from Captain Vere, a glance more effective than words, resumed that primacy. Turning to the prisoner, "Budd," he said, and scarce in equable tones, "Budd, if you have aught further to say for yourself, say it now."

Upon this the young sailor turned another quick glance toward Captain Vere; then, as taking a hint from that aspect, a hint confirming his own instinct that silence was now best, replied to the lieutenant, "I have said all, sir."

The marine—the same who had been the sentinel without the cabin door at the time that the foretopman, followed by the master-at-arms, entered it—he, standing by the sailor throughout these judicial proceedings, was now directed to take him back to the after compartment originally assigned to the prisoner and his custodian. As the twain disappeared from view, the three officers, as partially liberated from some inward constraint associated with Billy's mere presence, simultaneously stirred in their seats. They exchanged looks of troubled indecision, yet feeling that decide they must and without long delay. For Captain Vere, he for the time stood— unconsciously with his back toward them, apparently in one of his absent fits— gazing out from a sashed porthole to windward upon the monotonous blank of the twilight sea. But the court's silence continuing, broken only at moments by brief consultations, in low earnest tones, this served to arouse him and energize him. Turning, he to-and-fro paced the cabin athwart; in the returning ascent to wind- ward climbing the slant deck in the ship's lee roll, without knowing it symbolizing thus in his action a mind resolute to surmount difficulties even if against primitive instincts strong as the wind and the sea. Presently he came to a stand before the three. After scanning their faces he stood less as mustering his thoughts for expres- sion than as one only deliberating how best to put them to well-meaning men not intellectually mature, men with whom it was necessary to demonstrate certain prin- ciples that were axioms to himself. Similar impatience as to talking is perhaps one reason that deters some minds from addressing any popular assemblies.

When speak he did, something, both in the substance of what he said and his manner of saying it, showed the influence of unshared studies modifying and tem- pering the practical training of an active career. This, along with his phraseology, now and then was suggestive of the grounds whereon rested that imputation of a certain pedantry socially alleged against him by certain naval men of wholly practi- cal cast, captains who nevertheless would frankly concede that His Majesty's navy mustered no more efficient officer of their grade than Starry Vere.

What he said was to this effect: "Hitherto I have been but the witness, little more; and I should hardly think now to take another tone, that of your coadjutor for the time, did I not perceive in you—at the crisis too—a troubled hesitancy, pro- ceeding, I doubt not, from the clash of military duty with moral scruple—scruple vitalized by compassion. For the compassion, how can I otherwise than share it? But, mindful of paramount obligations, I strive against scruples that may tend to enervate decision. Not, gentlemen, that I hide from myself that the case is an excep- tional one. Speculatively regarded, it well might be referred to a jury of casuists. But for us here, acting not as casuists or moralists, it is a case practical, and under mar- tial law practically to be dealt with.

"But your scruples: do they move as in a dusk? Challenge them. Make them ad- vance and declare themselves. Come now; do they import something like this: If, mindless of palliating circumstances, we are bound to regard the death of the master-at-arms as the prisoner's deed, then does that deed constitute a capital crime whereof the penalty is a mortal one. But in natural justice is nothing but the prisoner's overt act to be considered? How can we adjudge to summary and shameful death a fellow creature innocent before God, and whom we feel to be so?—Does that state it aright? You sign sad assent. Well, I too feel that, the full force of that. It is Nature. But do these buttons that we wear attest that our allegiance is to Nature? No, to the King. Though the ocean, which is inviolate Nature primeval, though this be the element where we move and have our being as sailors, yet as the King's officers lies our duty in a sphere correspondingly natural? So little is that true, that in receiving our commissions we in the most important regards ceased to be natural free agents. When war is declared are we the commissioned fighters previously consulted? We fight at command. If our judgments approve the war, that is but coincidence. So in other particulars. So now. For suppose condemnation to follow these present proceedings. Would it be so much we ourselves that would condemn as it would be martial law operating through us? For that law and the rigor of it, we are not responsible. Our vowed responsibility is in this: That however pitilessly that law may operate in any instances, we nevertheless adhere to it and administer it.

"But the exceptional in the matter moves the hearts within you. Even so too is mine moved. But let not warm hearts betray heads that should be cool. Ashore in a criminal case, will an upright judge allow himself off the bench to be waylaid by some tender kinswoman of the accused seeking to touch him with her tearful plea? Well, the heart here, sometimes the feminine in man, is as that piteous woman, and hard though it be, she must here be ruled out."

He paused, earnestly studying them for a moment; then resumed.

"But something in your aspect seems to urge that it is not solely the heart that moves in you, but also the conscience, the private conscience. But tell me whether or not, occupying the position we do, private conscience should not yield to that imperial one formulated in the mode under which alone we officially proceed?"

Here the three men moved in their seats, less convinced than agitated by the course of an argument troubling but the more the spontaneous conflict within.

Perceiving which, the speaker paused for a moment; then abruptly changing his tone, went on.

"To steady us a bit, let us recur to the facts.—In wartime at sea a man-of-war's man strikes his superior in grade, and the blow kills. Apart from its effect the blow itself is, according to the Articles of War, a capital crime. Furthermore—"

"Ay, sir," emotionally broke in the officer of marines, "in one sense it was. But surely Budd purposed neither mutiny nor homicide."

"Surely not, my good man. And before a court less arbitrary and more merciful than a martial one, that plea would largely extenuate. At the Last Assizes it shall acquit. But how here? We proceed under the law of the Mutiny Act. In feature no child can resemble his father more than that Act resembles in spirit the thing from which it derives—War. In His Majesty's service—in this ship, indeed—there are Englishmen forced to fight for the King against their will. Against their conscience, for aught we know. Though as their fellow creatures some of us may appreciate their position, yet as navy officers what reck we of it? Still less recks the enemy. Our impressed men he would fain cut down in the same swath with our volunteers. As regards the enemy's naval conscripts, some of whom may even share our own abhorrence of the regicidal French Directory, it is the same on our side. War looks but to the frontage, the appearance. And the Mutiny Act, War's child, takes after the father. Budd's intent or nonintent is nothing to the purpose.

"But while, put to it by those anxieties in you which I cannot but respect, I only repeat myself—while thus strangely we prolong proceedings that should be summary—the enemy may be sighted and an engagement result. We must do; and one of two things must we do—condemn or let go."

"Can we not convict and yet mitigate the penalty?" asked the sailing master, here speaking, and falteringly, for the first.

"Gentlemen, were that clearly lawful for us under the circumstances, consider the consequences of such clemency. The people" (meaning the ship's company) "have native sense; most of them are familiar with our naval usage and tradition; and how would they take it? Even could you explain to them—which our official position forbids—they, long molded by arbitrary discipline, have not that kind of intelligent responsiveness that might qualify them to comprehend and discriminate. No, to the people the foretopman's deed, however it be worded in the announcement, will be plain homicide committed in a flagrant act of mutiny. What penalty for that should follow, they know. But it does not follow. *Why?* they will ruminate. You know what sailors are. Will they not revert to the recent outbreak at the Nore? Ay. They know the well-founded alarm—the panic it struck throughout England. Your clement sentence they would account pusillanimous. They would think that we flinch, that we are afraid of them—afraid of practicing a lawful rigor singularly demanded at this juncture, lest it should provoke new troubles. What shame to us such a conjecture on their part, and how deadly to discipline. You see then, whither, prompted by duty and the law, I steadfastly drive. But I beseech you, my friends, do not take me amiss. I feel as you do for this unfortunate boy. But did he know our hearts, I take him to be of that generous nature that he would feel even for us on whom this military necessity so heavy a compulsion is laid."

With that, crossing the deck he resumed his place by the sashed porthole, tacitly leaving the three to come to a decision. On the cabin's opposite side the troubled court sat silent. Loyal lieges, plain and practical, though at bottom they dissented from some points Captain Vere had put to them, they were without the faculty, hardly had the inclination, to gainsay one whom they felt to be an earnest man, one too not less their superior in mind than in naval rank. But it is not improbable that even such of his words as were not without influence over them, less came home to them than his closing appeal to their instinct as sea officers: in the forethought he threw out as to the practical consequences to discipline, considering the unconfirmed tone of the fleet at the time, should a man-of-war's man's violent killing at sea of a superior in grade be allowed to pass for aught else than a capital crime demanding prompt infliction of the penalty.

Not unlikely they were brought to something more or less akin to that harassed frame of mind which in the year 1842 actuated the commander of the U.S. brig-of-war *Somers* to resolve, under the so-called Articles of War, Articles modeled upon the English Mutiny Act, to resolve upon the execution at sea of a midshipman and two sailors as mutineers designing the seizure of the brig. Which resolution was carried out though in a time of peace and within not many days' sail of home. An act vindicated by a naval court of inquiry subsequently convened ashore. History, and here cited without comment. True, the circumstances on board the *Somers* were different from those on board the *Bellipotent*. But the urgency felt, well-warranted or otherwise, was much the same.

Says a writer whom few know, "Forty years after a battle it is easy for a non-combatant to reason about how it ought to have been fought. It is another thing personally and under fire to have to direct the fighting while involved in the obscuring smoke of it. Much so with respect to other emergencies involving considerations both practical and moral, and when it is imperative promptly to act. The greater the fog the more it imperils the steamer, and speed is put on though at the hazard of running somebody down. Little ween the snug card players in the cabin of the responsibilities of the sleepless man on the bridge."

In brief, Billy Budd was formally convicted and sentenced to be hung at the yardarm in the early morning watch, it being now night. Otherwise, as is customary in such cases, the sentence would forthwith have been carried out. In wartime on the field or in the fleet, a mortal punishment decreed by a drumhead court—on the field sometimes decreed by but a nod from the general—follows without delay on the heel of conviction, without appeal.

STUDY QUESTIONS

1. Billy never intended to kill Claggart. Is it fair to hold people responsible for the unforeseen consequences of their acts? Explain.
2. Write a defense of Captain Vere's decision to argue for Billy's conviction. Next write a critique of the decision. Which do you find more convincing? Why?
3. Apply Jonathan Bennett's analysis of duty and sympathy (in "The Conscience of Huckleberry Finn") to *Billy Budd*. Do you agree with Bennett's analysis? Explain.
4. Do you agree with Captain Vere that news of Billy's acquittal could undermine military discipline throughout the British navy? Wouldn't other British sailors understand that Billy Budd's was an exceptional case? Explain.
5. Vere distinguishes between military duty and moral duty. Should the latter always take priority? Explain.

Beyond Good and Evil

Friedrich Nietzsche

Friedrich Nietzsche (1844–1900) was as much a poet as he was a philosopher. His precocious intelligence and learning led to his being appointed to a full professorship at the University of Basel at age twenty-six. His influence on modern continental thought was revolutionary. He is hailed as a forerunner

BEYOND GOOD AND EVIL By Friedrich Nietzsche, tr. Helen Zimmern, George Allen & Unwin Ltd.

of such twentieth-century movements as Existentialism and Deconstructionism. Some consider Nietzsche's influence harmful, but this may be due to widespread misuse of his ideas by both the right and the left. Among his many works are *The Birth of Tragedy* (1872), *The Gay Science* (1882), *Beyond Good and Evil* (1886), and *Thus Spake Zarathustra* (1891).

Nietzsche was convinced that a dynamic and healthy society must allow its superior and noble individuals to prevail, giving full scope to "their will to power"—Nietzsche's famous term referring to the innate drive in all living things toward domination and exploitation. Defending the "master-morality" that honors pride, vanity, and power, he deplores the "slave-morality" that extols humility, sympathy, and friendliness. Nietzsche was especially contemptuous of the Judeo-Christian ethic for catering to "the cowardly, the timid, the insignificant."

On the Natural History of Morals

199. Inasmuch as in all ages, as long as mankind has existed, there have also been human herds (family alliances, communities, tribes, peoples, states, churches), and always a great number who obey in proportion to the small number who command—in view, therefore, of the fact that obedience has been most practised and fostered among mankind hitherto, one may reasonably suppose that, generally speaking, the need thereof is now innate in every one, as a kind of *formal conscience* which gives the command: "Thou shalt unconditionally do something, unconditionally refrain from something"; in short, "Thou shalt." This need tries to satisfy itself and to fill its form with a content; according to its strength, impatience, and eagerness, it at once seizes as an omnivorous appetite with little selection, and accepts whatever is shouted into its ear by all sorts of commanders—parents, teachers, laws, class prejudices, or public opinion. The extraordinary limitation of human development, the hesitation, protractedness, frequent retrogression, and turning thereof, is attributable to the fact that the herd-instinct of obedience is transmitted best, and at the cost of the art of command. If one imagines this instinct increasing to its greatest extent, commanders and independent individuals will finally be lacking altogether; or they will suffer inwardly from a bad conscience, and will have to impose a deception on themselves in the first place in order to be able to command: just as if they also were only obeying. This condition of things actually exists in Europe at present—I call it the moral hypocrisy of the commanding class. They know no other way of protecting themselves from their bad conscience than by playing the role of executors of older and higher orders (of predecessors, of the constitution, of justice, of the law, or of God himself), or they even justify themselves by maxims from the current opinions of the herd, as "first servants of their people," or "instruments of the public weal." On the other hand, the gregarious European man nowadays assumes an air as if he were the only kind of man that is allowable: he glorifies his qualities, such as public spirit, kindness, deference, industry, temperance, modesty, indulgence, sympathy, by virtue of which he is gentle, endurable, and useful to the herd, as the peculiarly human virtues. In cases, however, where it is believed that the leader and bellwether cannot he dispensed with, attempt after attempt is made nowadays to replace commanders by the summing together of clever gregarious men: all representative constitutions, for example, are of this origin. In spite of all, what a blessing, what a deliverance from a weight becoming unendurable is the appearance of an absolute ruler for these gregarious Europeans—of this fact the effect of the appearance of Napoleon was the last great proof: the history of the influence of Napoleon is almost the history of the higher happiness to which the entire century has attained in its worthiest individuals and periods....

203. We, who hold a different belief—we, who regard the democratic movement, not only as a degenerating form of political organisation, but as equivalent to a degenerating, a waning type of man, as involving his mediocrising and depreciation: where have *we* to fix our hopes? In *new philosophers*—there is no other alternative: in minds strong and original enough to initiate opposite estimates of value, to transvalue and invert "eternal valuations"; in forerunners, in men of the future, who in the present shall fix the constraints and fasten the knots which will compel millenniums to take *new* paths. To teach man the future of humanity as his *will*, as depending on human will, and to make preparation for vast hazardous enterprises and collective attempts in rearing and educating, in order thereby to put an end to the frightful rule of folly and chance which has hitherto gone by the name of "history" (the folly of the "greatest number" is only its last form)—for that purpose a new type of philosophers and commanders will some time or other be needed, at the very idea of which everything that has existed in the way of occult, terrible, and benevolent beings might look pale and dwarfed. The image of such leaders hovers before *our* eyes:—is it lawful for me to say it aloud, ye free spirits? The conditions which one would partly have to create and partly utilise for their genesis; the presumptive methods and tests by virtue of which a soul should grow up to such an elevation and power as to feel a *constraint* to these tasks; a transvaluation of values, under the new pressure and hammer of which a conscience should be steeled and a heart transformed into brass, so as to bear the weight of such responsibility; and on the other hand the necessity for such leaders, the dreadful danger that they might be lacking, or miscarry and degenerate:—these are *our* real anxieties and glooms, ye know it well, ye free spirits! these are the heavy distant thoughts and storms which sweep across the heaven of *our* life. There are few pains so grievous as to have seen, divined, or experienced how an exceptional man has missed his way and deteriorated; but he who has the rare eye for the universal danger of "man" himself *deteriorating*, he who like us has recognised the extraordinary fortuitousness which has hitherto played its game in respect to the future of mankind—a game in which neither the hand, nor even a "finger of God" has participated!—he who divines the fate that is hidden under the idiotic unwariness and blind confidence of "modern ideas," and still more under the whole of Christo-European morality—suffers from an anguish with which no other is to be compared. He sees at a glance all that could still *be made out of man* through a favourable accumulation and augmentation of human powers and arrangements; he knows with all the knowledge of his conviction how unexhausted man still is for the greatest possibilities, and how often in the past the type man has stood in presence of mysterious decisions and new paths:—he knows still better from his painfulest recollections on what wretched obstacles promising developments of the highest rank have hitherto usually gone to pieces, broken down, sunk, and become contemptible. The *universal degeneracy of mankind* to the level of the "man of the future"—as idealised by the socialistic fools and shallow-pates—this degeneracy and dwarfing of man to an absolutely gregarious animal (or as they call it, to a man of "free society"), this brutalising of man into a pigmy with equal rights and claims, is undoubtedly *possible!* He who has thought out this possibility to its ultimate conclusion knows *another* loathing unknown to the rest of mankind—and perhaps also a new *mission!*

What Is Noble?

257. Every elevation of the type "man," has hitherto been the work of an aristocratic society and so it will always be—a society believing in a long scale of gradations of rank and differences of worth among human beings, and requiring slavery in some form or other.... Let us acknowledge unprejudicedly how every higher civilisation hitherto has *originated!* Men with a still natural nature, barbarians in every terrible sense of the word, men of prey, still in possession of unbroken strength of will and desire for power, threw themselves upon weaker, more moral, more peaceful races (perhaps trading or cattle-rearing communities), or upon old mellow civilisations in which the final vital force was flickering out in brilliant fireworks of wit and depravity. At the commencement, the noble caste was always the barbarian caste: their superiority did not consist first of all in their physical, but in their psychical power—they were more *complete* men (which at every point also implies the same as "more complete beasts").

258...The essential thing, however, in a good and healthy aristocracy is that it should *not* regard itself as a function either of the kingship or the commonwealth, but as the *significance* and highest justification thereof—that it should therefore accept with a good conscience the sacrifice of a legion of individuals, who, *for its sake*, must be suppressed and reduced to imperfect men, to slaves and instruments. Its fundamental belief must be precisely that society is *not* allowed to exist for its own sake, but only as a foundation and scaffolding, by means of which a select class of beings may be able to elevate themselves to their higher duties, and in general to a higher *existence*: like those sun-seeking climbing plants in Java—they are called *Sipo Matador*,—which encircle an oak so long and so often with their arms, until at last, high above it, but supported by it, they can unfold their tops in the open light, and exhibit their happiness.

259. To refrain mutually from injury, from violence, from exploitation, and put one's will on a par with that of others: this may result in a certain rough sense in good conduct among individuals when the necessary conditions are given (namely, the actual similarity of the individuals in amount of force and degree of worth, and their corelation within one organisation). As soon, however, as one wished to take this principle more generally, and if possible even as *the fundamental principle of society*, it would immediately disclose what it really is—namely, a Will to the

denial of life, a principle of dissolution and decay. Here one must think profoundly to the very basis and resist all sentimental weakness: life itself is *essentially* appropriation, injury, conquest of the strange and weak, suppression, severity, obtrusion of peculiar forms, incorporation, and at the least, putting it mildest, exploitation;—but why should one for ever use precisely these words on which for ages a disparaging purpose has been stamped? Even the organisation within which, as was previously supposed, the individuals treat each other as equal—it takes place in every healthy aristocracy—must itself, if it be a living and not a dying organisation, do all that towards other bodies, which the individuals within it refrain from doing to each other: it will have to be the incarnated Will to Power, it will endeavour to grow, to gain ground, attract to itself and acquire ascendency—not owing to any morality or immorality, but because it *lives*, and because life *is* precisely Will to Power. On no point, however, is the ordinary consciousness of Europeans more unwilling to be corrected than on this matter; people now rave everywhere, even under the guise of science, about coming conditions of society in which "the exploiting character" is to be absent:—that sounds to my ears as if they promised to invent a mode of life which should refrain from all organic functions. "Exploitation" does not belong to a depraved, or imperfect and primitive society: it belongs to the *nature* of the living being as a primary organic function; it is a consequence of the intrinsic Will to Power, which is precisely the Will to Life.—Granting that as a theory this is a novelty—as a reality it is the *fundamental fact* of all history: let us be so far honest towards ourselves!

260. In a tour through the many finer and coarser moralities which have hitherto prevailed or still prevail on the earth, I found certain traits recurring regularly together, and connected with one another, until finally two primary types revealed themselves to me, and a radical distinction was brought to light. There is *master-morality* and *slave-morality*;—I would at once add, however, that in all higher and mixed civilisations, there are also attempts at the reconciliation of the two moralities; but one finds still oftener the confusion and mutual misunderstanding of them, indeed, sometimes their close juxtaposition—even in the same man, within one soul. The distinctions of moral values have either originated in a ruling caste, pleasantly conscious of being different from the ruled—or among the ruled class, the slaves and dependents of all sorts. In the first case, when it is the rulers who determine the conception "good," it is the exalted, proud disposition which is regarded as the distinguishing feature, and that which determines the order of rank. The noble type of man separates from himself the beings in whom the opposite of this exalted, proud disposition displays itself: he despises them. Let it at once be noted that in this first kind of morality the antithesis "good" and "bad" means practically the same as "noble" and "despicable";—the antithesis *"good"* and *"evil"* is of a different origin. The cowardly, the timid, the insignificant, and those thinking merely of narrow utility are despised; moreover, also, the distrustful, with their constrained glances, the self-abasing, the dog-like kind of men who let themselves be abused, the mendicant flatterers and above all the liars:—it is a fundamental belief of all aristocrats that the common people are untruthful. "We truthful ones"—the nobility in ancient Greece called themselves. It is obvious that everywhere the designations of moral value were at first applied to *men*, and were only derivatively and

at a later period applied to *actions;* it is a gross mistake, therefore, when historians of morals start with questions like, "Why have sympathetic actions been praised?" The noble type of man regards *himself as* a determiner of values; he does not require to be approved of; he passes the judgment: "What is injurious to me is injurious in itself"; he knows that it is he himself only who confers honour on things; he is a *creator of values.* He honours whatever he recognises in himself: such morality is self-glorification. In the foreground there is the feeling of plenitude, of power, which seeks to overflow, the happiness of high tension, the consciousness of a wealth which would fain give and bestow:—the noble man also helps the unfortunate, but not—or scarcely—out of pity, but rather from an impulse generated by the super-abundance of power. The noble man honours in himself the powerful one, him also who has power over himself, who knows how to speak and how to keep silence, who takes pleasure in subjecting himself to severity and hardness, and has reverence for all that is severe and hard. "Wotan placed a hard heart in my breast," says an old Scandinavian Saga: it is thus rightly expressed from the soul of a proud Viking. Such a type of man is even proud of *not* being made for sympathy; the hero of the Saga therefore adds warningly: "He who has not a hard heart when young, will never have one." The noble and brave who think thus are the furthest removed from the morality which sees precisely in sympathy, or in acting for the good of others, or in disinterestedness, the characteristic of the moral; faith in oneself, pride in oneself, a radical enmity and irony towards "selflessness," belong as definitely to noble morality, as do a careless scorn and precaution in presence of sympathy and the "warm heart."—It is the powerful who *know* how to honour, it is their art, their domain for invention. The profound reverence for age and for tradition—all law rests on this double reverence,—the belief and prejudice in favour of ancestors and unfavourable to newcomers, is typical in the morality of the powerful; and if, reversely, men of "modern ideas" believe almost instinctively in "progress" and the "future," and are more and more lacking in respect for old age, the ignoble origin of these "ideas" has complacently betrayed itself thereby. A morality of the ruling class, however, is more especially foreign and irritating to present-day taste in the sternness of its principle that one has duties only to one's equals; that one may act towards beings of a lower rank, towards all that is foreign; just as seems good to one, or "as the heart desires," and in any case "beyond good and evil": it is here that sympathy and similar sentiments can have a place. The ability and obligation to exercise prolonged gratitude and prolonged revenge—both only within the circle of equals,—artfulness in retaliation, effete refinement of the idea in friendship, a certain necessity to have enemies (as outlets for the emotions of envy, quarrelsomeness, arrogance—in fact, in order to be a good *friend*): all these are typical characteristics of the noble morality, which, as has been pointed out, is not the morality of "modern ideas," and is therefore at present difficult to realise, and also to unearth and disclose.—It is otherwise with the second type of morality, *slave-morality.* Supposing that the abused, the oppressed, the suffering, the unemancipated, the weary, and those uncertain of themselves, should moralise, what will be the common element in their moral estimates? Probably a pessimistic suspicion with regard to the entire situation of man will find expression, perhaps a condemnation of man, together with his situation. The slave has an unfavourable eye for the virtues of the powerful; he has a scepticism and distrust, a *refinement* of distrust of everything "good" that is there honoured—he would fain persuade himself that the very happiness there is not genuine. On the other hand, *those* qualities which serve to alleviate the existence of sufferers are brought into prominence and flooded with light; it is here that sympathy, the kind, helping hand, the warm heart, patience, diligence, humility, and friendliness attain to honour; for here these are the most useful qualities, and almost the only means of supporting the burden of existence. Slave-morality is essentially the morality of utility. Here is the seat of the origin of the famous antithesis "good" and "evil":—power and dangerousness are assumed to reside in the evil, a certain dreadfulness, subtlety, and strength, which do not admit of being despised. According to slave-morality, therefore, the "evil" man arouses fear; according to master-morality, it is precisely the "good" man who arouses fear and seeks to arouse it, while the bad man is regarded as the despicable being. The contrast attains its maximum when, in accordance with the logical consequences of slave-morality, a shade of depreciation—it may be slight and well-intentioned—at last attaches itself to the "good" man of this morality; because, according to the servile mode of thought, the good man must in any case be the *safe* man: he is good-natured, easily deceived, perhaps a little stupid, *un bonhomme....*

261.... The man of noble character must first bring it home forcibly to his mind, especially with the aid of history, that, from time immemorial, in all social strata in any way dependent, the ordinary man *was* only that which he *passed for:*—not being at all accustomed to fix values, he did not assign even to himself any other value than that which his master assigned to him (it is the peculiar *right of masters* to create values). It may be looked upon as the result of an extraordinary atavism, that the ordinary man, even at present, is still always *waiting* for an opinion about himself, and then instinctively submitting himself to it; yet by no means only to a "good" opinion, but also to a bad and unjust one (think, for instance, of the greater part of the self-appreciations and self-depreciations which believing women learn from their confessors, and which in general the believing Christian learns from his Church)....

265. At the risk of displeasing innocent ears, I submit that egoism belongs to the essence of a noble soul, I mean the unalterable belief that to a being such as "we," other beings must naturally be in subjection, and have to sacrifice themselves. The noble soul accepts the fact of his egoism without question, and also without consciousness of harshness, constraint, or arbitrariness therein, but rather as something that may have its basis in the primary law of things:—if he sought a designation for it he would say: "It is justice itself." He acknowledges under certain circumstances, which made him hesitate at first, that there are other equally privileged ones; as soon as he has settled this question of rank, he moves among those equals and equally privileged ones with the same assurance, as regards modesty and delicate respect, which he enjoys in intercourse with himself—in accordance with an innate heavenly mechanism which all the stars understand. It is an *additional* instance of his egoism, this artfulness and selflim-itation in intercourse with his equals—every star is a similar egoist; he honours *himself* in them, and in the rights which he concedes to them, he has no doubt that the exchange of honours and rights, as the *essence* of all intercourse, belongs also to the natural condition of things. The noble soul gives as he takes, prompted by the passionate and sensitive instinct of requital, which is at the root of his nature. The notion of "favour" has, among equals, neither significance nor good repute; there may be a sublime way of letting gifts as it were light upon one from above, and of drinking them thirstily like dew-drops; but for those arts and displays the noble soul has no aptitude. His ego-ism hinders him here: in general, he looks "aloft" unwillingly—he looks either *for-ward*, horizontally and deliberately, or downwards—*he knows that he is on a height*.

The Will to Power[1]

I regard Christianity as the most fatal and seductive lie that has ever yet existed—as the greatest and most *impious lie*: I can discern the last sprouts and branches of its ideal beneath every form of disguise, I decline to enter into any compromise or false position in reference to it—I urge people to declare open war with it.

The *morality of paltry people* as the measure of all things: this is the most repugnant kind of degeneracy that civilisation has ever yet brought into existence. And this *kind of ideal* is hanging still, under the name of "God," over men's heads!!

However modest one's demands may be concerning intellectual cleanliness, when one touches the New Testament one cannot help experiencing a sort of inex-pressible feeling of discomfort; for the unbounded cheek with which the least quali-fied people will have their say in its pages, in regard to the greatest problems of existence, and claim to sit in judgment on such matters, exceeds all limits. The impudent levity with which the most unwieldy problems are spoken of here (life, the world, God, the purpose of life), as if they were not problems at all, but the most simple things which these little bigots *know all about!!!*...

The *law*, which is the fundamentally realistic formula of certain self-preservative measures of a community, forbids certain actions that have a definite tendency to jeopardise the welfare of that community: it does *not* forbid the attitude of mind which gives rise to these actions—for in the pursuit of other ends the community requires these forbidden actions, namely, when it is a matter of opposing its *enemies*. The moral idealist now steps forward and says: "God sees into men's hearts: the action itself counts for nothing; the reprehensible attitude of mind from which it pro-ceeds must be extirpated...." In normal conditions men laugh at such things; it is only in exceptional cases, when a community lives *quite* beyond the need of waging war in order to maintain itself, that an ear is lent to such things. Any attitude of mind is abandoned, the utility of which cannot be conceived.

This was the case, for example, when Buddha appeared among a people that was both peaceable and afflicted with great intellectual weariness.

This was also the case in regard to the first Christian community (as also the Jewish), the primary condition of which was the absolutely *unpolitical* Jewish soci-ety. Christianity could grow only upon the soil of Judaism—that is to say, among a

---

[1] From *The Will to Power* in *The Complete Works of Nietzsche*, O. Levy, ed. (New York: Macmillan, 1924), pp. 200–201.

people that had already renounced the political life, and which led a sort of parasitic existence within the Roman sphere of government. Christianity goes a step *further:* it allows men to "emasculate" themselves even more; the circumstances actually favour their doing so.—*Nature* is *expelled* from morality when it is said, "Love ye your enemies": for *Nature's* injunction, "Ye shall *love* your neighbour and *hate* your enemy," has now become senseless in the law (in instinct); now, even *the love a man feels for his neighbour* must first be based upon something (*a sort of love of God*). *God* is introduced everywhere, and *utility* is withdrawn; the natural *origin* of morality is denied everywhere: the *veneration of Nature*, which lies in *acknowledging a natural morality*, is *destroyed* to the roots....

What is it I protest against? That people should regard this paltry and peaceful mediocrity, this spiritual equilibrium which knows nothing of the fine impulses of great accumulations of strength, as something high, or possibly as the standard of all things.

Study Questions

1. In your own words describe what Nietzsche calls the "slave-morality" and the "master-morality."
2. Nietzsche believes that exploitation and domination of the weak by the strong is "the *fundamental fact* of all history." Assuming this belief is true, would you consider it an argument for the validity of the master-morality? Might one not argue instead that we should curb our aggressive impulses and protect the weak? Explain.
3. How much truth do you find in Nietzsche's characterization of the Judeo-Christian ethic as a slave-morality? Is he right when he says that it is "the *morality of paltry people*"? Explain.
4. Imagine a debate between Josiah Royce and Friedrich Nietzsche on the validity of the Golden Rule. What argument does each present? Who do you consider the winner? Why?
5. Nietzsche has sometimes been accused of inspiring Nazism. Does anything in the selection support such an accusation?
6. How would Nietzsche react to Hallie's account of what transpired in Le Chambon during World War II?

CHAPTER **2** | # IS IT ALL RELATIVE?

Noting that what one society deems morally wrong, another deems right, ethical relativists conclude that morals are like manners or style of dress. The ancient Greek historian Herodotus, quoting the poet Pindar, long ago announced the relativist principle when he said, "Custom is king."

Ethical relativism became popular in the nineteenth century when European social scientists traveled the world and discovered a bewildering variety of moral norms and practices. Anthropologists like Ruth Benedict and sociologists like William Graham Sumner embraced ethical relativism and gave it the cachet of science.

Ethical relativism is a tempting doctrine because it appeals to our desire to be tolerant of other societies. However, it has not found much favor among professional philosophers, who point out that while tolerance is a virtue, indifference to suffering is a vice. Several of the philosophers and moralists included in this chapter—Louis Pojman, R. M. MacIver, and Martin Luther King, Jr.—believe that while much morality is indeed a matter of local custom, some objectively valid moral principles apply to everyone. For them, tolerance ends when a practice or custom violates a *universal* human right. Lawrence Lengbeyer tries to work out a compromise between relativism and absolutism.

Recently a number of anthropologists have joined philosophers and theologians in rejecting relativism. They challenge the idea that social scientists must always be neutral bystanders. Carolyn Fluehr-Lobban struggles with the problem of whether to condemn or to refrain from condemning the societies she studies. In the end she finds herself unable to retain the neutral "scientific" stance. Thomas Nagel argues that the Golden Rule in its negative form—not to do unto others what you would not have them do unto you—provides an objective nonrelativistic basis for morality.

Finally, when a relativist like Benedict or Sumner points to the diversity of villages, and thus of norms, those who believe in universal moral standards can point

76

to the newly emerging "global village." Universal ethical principles are already fully codified for the "global village" in such documents as the United Nations Declaration of Human Rights, the United Nations Declaration of the Rights of Children, and the recent United Nations Declaration of the Rights of Women. These declarations firmly assert that all people, regardless of cultural background, regardless of gender or social status, should enjoy certain basic moral rights. While it is certainly true that the United Nations declarations are not universally enforced, their very existence suggests there may be far more moral consensus in the world than the relativists allow.

Morality As Custom

Herodotus

Herodotus (c. 485–425 B.C.) was the first Western historian. Much of what we know about the ancient world in and around Greece derives from him.

Following is one of the fragments of text by Herodotus available to us today. Although brief, it clearly shows that Herodotus may well be the first thinker in Western intellectual history to espouse a version of what today we call ethical relativism.

If anyone, no matter who, were given the opportunity of choosing from amongst all the nations in the world the set of beliefs which he thought best, he would inevitably, after careful consideration of their relative merits, choose that of his own country. Everyone without exception believes his own native customs, and the religion he was brought up in, to be the best; and that being so, it is unlikely that anyone but a madman would mock at such things. There is abundant evidence that this is the universal feeling about the ancient customs of one's country. One might recall, in particular, an anecdote of Darius. When he was king of Persia, he summoned the Greeks who happened to be present at his court, and asked them what they would take to eat the dead bodies of their fathers. They replied that they would not do it for any money in the world. Later, in the presence of the Greeks, and through an interpreter, so that they could understand what was said, he asked some Indians, of the tribe called Callatiae, who do in fact eat their parents' dead bodies, what they would take to burn them. They uttered a cry of horror and forbade him to mention such a dreadful thing. One can see by this what custom can do, and Pindar, in my opinion, was right when he called it "king of all."

STUDY QUESTIONS

1. Herodotus says that people prefer the customs of their own country over those of all other countries. That may have been true in his day. Is it true in ours?
2. Herodotus's example of what the ancient Greeks and Indians did with the bodies of their dead parents clearly shows that cultures have different customs. But does that make the case for ethical relativism? Though the two societies did it in very different ways, both seem to be engaged in honoring their deceased parents.

MORALITY AS CUSTOM From Herodotus's *The Histories*, translated by Aubrey de Sélincourt, revised by A. R. Burn (Penguin Classics 1954, revised edition 1972), copyright © the Estate of Aubrey de Sélincourt, 1954, copyright © A. R. Burn, 1972.

A Defense of Moral Relativism

Ruth Benedict

Ruth Benedict (1887–1948) was one of America's foremost anthropologists. Her *Patterns of Culture* (1935) is considered a classic of comparative anthropology.

Morality, says Ruth Benedict, is a convenient term for socially approved customs (that is, mores). What one society approves may be disgraceful and unacceptable to another. Moral rules, like rules of etiquette or styles of dress, vary from society to society. Morality is culturally relative. Values are shaped by culture. As Benedict points out, trances are highly regarded in India, so in India many people have trances. Some ancient societies praised homosexual love, so there homosexuality was a norm. Where material possessions are highly valued, people amass property. "Most individuals are plastic to the moulding force of the society into which they are born."

Modern social anthropology has become more and more a study of the varieties and common elements of cultural environment and the consequences of these in human behavior. For such a study of diverse social orders primitive peoples fortunately provide a laboratory not yet entirely vitiated by the spread of a standardized worldwide civilization. Dyaks and Hopis, Fijians and Yakuts are significant for psychological and sociological study because only among these simpler peoples has there been sufficient isolation to give opportunity for the development of localized social forms. In the higher cultures the standardization of custom and belief over a couple of continents has given a false sense of the inevitability of the particular forms that have gained currency, and we need to turn to a wider survey in order to check the conclusions we hastily base upon this near-universality of familiar customs. Most of the simpler cultures did not gain the wide currency of the one which, out of our experience, we identify with human nature, but this was for various historical reasons, and certainly not for any that gives us as its carriers a monopoly of social good or of social sanity. Modern civilization, from this point of view, becomes not a necessary pinnacle of human achievement but one entry in a long series of possible adjustments.

These adjustments, whether they are in mannerisms like the ways of showing anger, or joy, or grief in any society, or in major human drives like those of sex,

A DEFENSE OF MORAL RELATIVISM From "Anthropology and the Abnormal" by Ruth Benedict, in *The Journal of General Psychology* 10 (1934): 59–82. Reprinted with permission of the Helen Dwight Reid Educational Foundation. Published by Heldref Publications, 1319 Eighteenth St., N.W., Washington, DC, 20036-1802. Copyright © 1934.

prove to be far more variable than experience in any one culture would suggest. In certain fields, such as that of religion or of formal marriage arrangements, these wide limits of variability are well known and can be fairly described. In others it is not yet possible to give a generalized account, but that does not absolve us of the task of indicating the significance of the work that has been done and of the problems that have arisen.

One of these problems relates to the customary modern⌈normal-abnormal⌉ categories and our conclusions regarding them. In how far are such categories culturally determined, or in how far can we with assurance regard them as absolute? In how far can we regard inability to function socially as diagnostic of abnormality, or in how far is it necessary to regard this as a function of the culture?

As a matter of fact, one of the most striking facts that emerge from a study of widely varying cultures is the ease with which our abnormals function in other cultures. It does not matter what kind of "abnormality" we choose for illustration, those which indicate extreme instability, or those which are more in the nature of character traits like sadism or delusions of grandeur or of persecution, there are well-described cultures in which these abnormals function at ease and with honor, and apparently without danger or difficulty to the society.

The most notorious of these is trance and catalepsy. Even a very mild mystic is aberrant in our culture. But most peoples have regarded even extreme psychic manifestations not only as normal and desirable, but even as characteristic of highly valued and gifted individuals. This was true even in our own cultural background in that period when Catholicism made the ecstatic experience the mark of sainthood. It is hard for us, born and brought up in a culture that makes no use of the experience, to realize how important a role it may play and how many individuals are capable of it, once it has been given an honorable place in any society....

Cataleptic and trance phenomena are, of course, only one illustration of the fact that those whom we regard as abnormals may function adequately in other cultures. Many of our culturally discarded traits are selected for elaboration in different societies. Homosexuality is an excellent example, for in this case our attention is not constantly diverted, as in the consideration of trance, to the interruption of routine activity which it implies. Homosexuality poses the problem very simply. A tendency toward this trait in our culture exposes an individual to all the conflicts to which all aberrants are always exposed, and we tend to identify the consequences of this conflict with homosexuality. But these consequences are obviously local and cultural. Homosexuals in many societies are not incompetent, but they may be such if the culture asks adjustments of them that would strain any man's vitality. Wherever homosexuality has been given an honorable place in any society, those to whom it is congenial have filled adequately the honorable roles society assigns to them. Plato's *Republic is*, of course, the most convincing statement of such a reading of homosexuality. It is presented as one of the major means to the good life, and it was generally so regarded in Greece at that time.

The cultural attitude toward homosexuals has not always been on such a high ethical plane, but it has been very varied. Among many American Indian tribes there exists the institution of the *berdache*, as the French called them. These men-women were men who at puberty or thereafter took the dress and the occupations of women. Sometimes they married other men and lived with them. Sometimes they were men with no inversion, persons of weak sexual endowment who chose this rôle to avoid the jeers of the women. The *berdaches* were never regarded as of first-rate super-natural power, as similar men-women were in Siberia, but rather as leaders in women's occupations, good healers in certain diseases, or, among certain tribes, as the genial organizers of social affairs. In any case, they were socially placed. They were not left exposed to the conflicts that visit the deviant who is excluded from participation in the recognized patterns of his society.

The most spectacular illustrations of the extent to which normality may be culturally defined are those cultures where an abnormality of our culture is the cornerstone of their social structure. It is not possible to do justice to these possibilities in a short discussion. A recent study of an island of northwest Melanesia by Fortune describes a society built upon traits which we regard as beyond the border of paranoia. In this tribe the exogamic groups look upon each other as prime manipulators of black magic, so that one marries always into an enemy group which remains for life one's deadly and unappeasable foes. They look upon a good garden crop as a confession of theft, for everyone is engaged in making magic to induce into his garden the productiveness of his neighbors'; therefore no secrecy in the island is so rigidly insisted upon as the secrecy of a man's harvesting of his yams. Their polite phrase at the acceptance of a gift is, "And if you now poison me, how shall I repay you this present?" Their preoccupation with poisoning is constant; no woman ever leaves her cooking pot for a moment untended. Even the great affinal economic exchanges that are characteristic of this Melanesian culture area are quite altered in Dobu since they are incompatible with this fear and distrust that pervades the culture. They go farther and people the whole world outside their own quarters with such malignant spirits that all-night feasts and ceremonials simply do not occur here. They have even rigorous religiously enforced customs that forbid the sharing of seed even in one family group. Anyone else's food is deadly poison to you, so that communality of stores is out of the question. For some months before harvest the whole society is on the verge of starvation, but if one falls to the temptation and eats up one's seed yams, one is an outcast and a beachcomber for life. There is no coming back. It involves, as a matter of course, divorce and the breaking of all social ties.

Now in this society where no one may work with another and no one may share with another, Fortune describes the individual who was regarded by all his fellows as crazy. He was not one of those who periodically ran amok and, beside himself and frothing at the mouth, fell with a knife upon anyone he could reach. Such behavior they did not regard as putting anyone outside the pale. They did not even put the individuals who were known to be liable to these attacks under any kind of control. They merely fled when they saw the attack coming on and kept out of the way. "He would be all right tomorrow." But there was one man of sunny, kindly disposition who liked work and liked to be helpful. The compulsion was too strong for him to repress it in favor of the opposite tendencies of his culture. Men and women never spoke of him without laughing; he was silly and simple and definitely crazy. Nevertheless, to the ethnologist used to a culture that has, in Christianity, made his type the model of all virtue, he seemed a pleasant fellow....

... Among the Kwakiutl it did not matter whether a relative had died in bed of disease, or by the hand of an enemy, in either case death was an affront to be wiped out by the death of another person. The fact that one had been caused to mourn was proof that one had been put upon. A chief's sister and her daughter had gone up to Victoria, and either because they drank bad whiskey or because their boat capsized they never came back. The chief called together his warriors. "Now I ask you, tribes, who shall wail? Shall I do it or shall another?" The spokesman answered, of course, "Not you, Chief. Let some other of the tribes." Immediately they set up the war pole to announce their intention of wiping out the injury, and gathered a war party. They set out, and found seven men and two children asleep and killed them. "Then they felt good when they arrived at Sebaa in the evening."

The point which is of interest to us is that in our society those who on that occasion would feel good when they arrived at Sebaa that evening would be the definitely abnormal. There would be some, even in our society, but it is not a recognized and approved mood under the circumstances. On the Northwest Coast those are favored and fortunate to whom that mood under those circumstances is congenial, and those to whom it is repugnant are unlucky. This latter minority can register in their own culture only by doing violence to their congenial responses and acquiring others that are difficult for them. The person, for instance, who, like a Plains Indian whose wife has been taken from him, is too proud to fight, can deal with the Northwest Coast civilization only by ignoring its strongest bents. If he cannot achieve it, he is the deviant in that culture, their instance of abnormality.

This head-hunting that takes place on the Northwest Coast after a death is no matter of blood revenge or of organized vengeance. There is no effort to tie up the subsequent killing with any responsibility on the part of the victim for the death of the person who is being mourned. A chief whose son has died goes visiting wherever his fancy dictates, and he says to his host, "My prince has died today, and you go with him." Then he kills him. In this, according to their interpretation, he acts nobly because he has not been downed. He has thrust back in return. The whole procedure is meaningless without the fundamental paranoid reading of bereavement. Death, like all the other untoward accidents of existence, confounds man's pride and can only be handled in the category of insults.

Behavior honored upon the Northwest Coast is one which is recognized as abnormal in our civilization, and yet it is sufficiently close to the attitudes of our own culture to be intelligible to us and to have a definite vocabulary with which we may discuss it. The megalomaniac paranoid trend is a definite danger in our society. It is encouraged by some of our major preoccupations, and it confronts us with a choice of two possible attitudes. One is to brand it as abnormal and reprehensible, and is the attitude we have chosen in our civilization. The other is to make it an essential attribute of ideal man, and this is the solution in the culture of the Northwest Coast.

These illustrations, which it has been possible to indicate only in the briefest manner, force upon us the fact that normality is culturally defined. An adult shaped to the drives and standards of either of these cultures, if he were transported into our civilization, would fall into our categories of abnormality. He would be faced with the psychic dilemmas of the socially unavailable. In his own culture, however, he is the pillar of society, the end result of socially inculcated mores, and the problem of personal instability in his case simply does not arise.

No one civilization can possibly utilize in its mores the whole potential range of human behavior. Just as there are great numbers of possible phonetic articulations, and the possibility of language depends on a selection and standardization of a few of these in order that speech communication may be possible at all, so the possibility of organized behavior of every sort, from the fashions of local dress and houses to the dicta of a people's ethics and religion, depends upon a similar selection among the possible behavior traits. In the field of recognized economic obligations or sex tabus this selection is as non-rational and subconscious a process as it is in the field of phonetics. It is a process which goes on in the group for long periods of time and is historically conditioned by innumerable accidents of isolation or of contact of peoples. In any comprehensive study of psychology, the selection that different cultures have made in the course of history within the great circumference of potential behavior is of great significance.

Every society, beginning with some slight inclination in one direction or another, carries its preference farther and farther, integrating itself more and more completely upon its chosen basis, and discarding those types of behavior that are uncongenial. Most of those organizations of personality that seem to us most uncontrovertibly abnormal have been used by different civilizations in the very foundations of their institutional life. Conversely the most valued traits of normal individuals have been looked on in differently organized cultures as aberrant. Normality, in short, within a very wide range, is culturally defined. It is primarily a term for the socially elaborated segment of human behavior in any culture; and abnormality, a term for the segment that that particular civilization does not use. The very eyes with which we see the problem are conditioned by the long traditional habits of our own society.

It is a point that has been made more often in relation to ethics than in relation to psychiatry. We do not any longer make the mistake of deriving the morality of our locality and decade directly from the inevitable constitution of human nature. We do not elevate it to the dignity of a first principle. We recognize that morality differs in every society, and is a convenient term for socially approved habits. Mankind has always preferred to say, "It is morally good," rather than "It is habitual," and the fact of this preference is matter enough for a critical science of ethics. But historically the two phrases are synonymous.

The concept of the normal is properly a variant of the concept of the good. It is that which society has approved. A normal action is one which falls well within the limits of expected behavior for a particular society. Its variability among different peoples is essentially a function of the variability of the behavior patterns that different societies have created for themselves, and can never be wholly divorced from a consideration of culturally institutionalized types of behavior.

Each culture is a more or less elaborate working-out of the potentialities of the segment it has chosen. In so far as a civilization is well integrated and consistent within itself, it will tend to carry farther and farther, according to its nature, its initial impulse toward a particular type of action, and from the point of view of any other culture those elaborations will include more and more extreme and aberrant traits.

Each of these traits, in proportion as it reinforces the chosen behavior patterns of that culture, is for that culture normal. Those individuals to whom it is congenial either congenitally, or as the result of childhood sets, are accorded prestige in that culture, and are not visited with the social contempt or disapproval which their traits would call down upon them in a society that was differently organized. On the other hand, those individuals whose characteristics are not congenial to the selected type of human behavior in that community are the deviants, no matter how valued their personality traits may be in a contrasted civilization.

The Dobuan who is not easily susceptible to fear of treachery, who enjoys work and likes to be helpful, is their neurotic and regarded as silly. On the Northwest Coast the person who finds it difficult to read life in terms of an insult contest will be the person upon whom fall all the difficulties of the culturally unprovided for. The person who does not find it easy to humiliate a neighbor, nor to see humiliation in his own experience, who is genial and loving, may, of course, find some unstandardized way of achieving satisfactions in his society, but not in the major patterned responses that his culture requires of him. If he is born to play an important rôle in a family with many hereditary privileges, he can succeed only by doing violence to his whole personality. If he does not succeed, he has betrayed his culture; that is, he is abnormal.

I have spoken of individuals as having sets toward certain types of behavior, and of these sets as running sometimes counter to the types of behavior which are institutionalized in the culture to which they belong. From all that we know of contrasting cultures it seems clear that differences of temperament occur in every society. The matter has never been made the subject of investigation, but from the available material it would appear that these temperament types are very likely of universal recurrence. That is, there is an ascertainable range of human behavior that is found wherever a sufficiently large series of individuals is observed. But the proportion in which behavior types stand to one another in different societies is not universal. The vast majority of the individuals in any group are shaped to the fashion of that culture. In other words, most individuals are plastic to the moulding force of the society into which they are born. In a society that values trance, as in India, they will have supernormal experience. In a society that institutionalizes homosexuality, they will be homosexual. In a society that sets the gathering of possessions as the chief human objective, they will amass property. The deviants, whatever the type of behavior the culture has institutionalized, will remain few in number, and there seems no more difficulty in moulding that vast malleable majority to the "normality" of what we consider an aberrant trait, such as delusions of reference, than to the normality of such accepted behavior patterns as acquisitiveness. The small proportion of the number of the deviants in any culture is not a function of the sure instinct with which that society has built itself upon the fundamental sanities, but of the universal fact that, happily, the majority of mankind quite readily take any shape that is presented to them....

STUDY QUESTIONS

1. Do you think that the fact of cultural diversity is itself an argument for ethical relativism? Explain.

2. If Benedict's defense of ethical relativism is correct, then the correct way to resolve a personal dilemma might be to take a survey or poll to see what the majority in your society think is right. If the majority favor capital punishment and oppose abortion, for example, then capital punishment is right and abortion is wrong. Can you defend Benedict against this odd consequence? Explain.

3. Do you think that certain types of behavior (for example, executing children or beating animals to death) are wrong wherever they occur, despite attitudes prevailing in the societies that practice them? If you believe that such acts are universally wrong, what makes them wrong?

4. How might Benedict account for notions of moral enlightenment and moral progress?

A Defense of Cultural Relativism

William Graham Sumner

> William Graham Sumner (1840–1910) was a sociologist, an economist, and a proponent of Darwinism. His books include *What Social Classes Owe to Each Other* (1883) and *Folkways* (1906).
>
> William Graham Sumner claims that his ethical relativism is derived from having observed other societies. According to Sumner, the "folkways"—that is, the customs, mores, and traditions of each society—are so ingrained in its members that they naturally come to think of them as objectively "right" and "good." We may build elaborate philosophical and legal doctrines around these concepts, but it is the folkways that determine their true meaning.

There is a right way to catch game, to win a wife, to make one's self appear, to cure disease, to honor ghosts, to treat comrades or strangers, to behave when a child is born, on the warpath, in council, and so on in all cases which can arise. The ways are defined on the negative side, that is, by taboos. The "right" way is the way which the ancestors used and which has been handed down. The tradition is its own warrant. It is not held subject to verification by experience. The notion of right is in the folkways. It is not outside of them, of independent origin, and brought to them to test them. In the folkways, whatever is, is right. This is because they are traditional, and therefore contain in themselves the authority of the ancestral ghosts. When we come to the folkways we are at the end of our analysis. The notion of right and ought is the same in regard to all the folkways....

A DEFENSE OF CULTURAL RELATIVISM From *Folkways* by William Graham Sumner.

The morality of a group at a time is the sum of the taboos and prescriptions in the folkways by which right conduct is defined. Therefore morals can never be intuitive. They are historical, institutional, and empirical. World philosophy, life policy, right, rights, and morality are all products of the folkways. They are reflections on, and generalizations from, the experience of pleasure and pain which is won in efforts to carry on the struggle for existence under actual life conditions. The generalizations are very crude and vague in their germinal forms. They are all embodied in folklore, and all our philosophy and science have been developed out of them.

Mores Are a Directive Force

Of course the view which has been stated is antagonistic to the view that philosophy and ethics furnish creative and determining forces in society and history. That view comes down to us from the Greek philosophy and it has now prevailed so long that all current discussion conforms to it. Philosophy and ethics are pursued as independent disciplines, and the results are brought to the science of society and to statesmanship and legislation as authoritative dicta. We also have *Völkerpsychologie, Sozialpolitik*, and other intermediate forms which show the struggle of metaphysics to retain control of the science of society. The "historic sense," the *Zeitgeist*, and other terms of similar import are partial recognitions of the mores and their importance in the science of society. We shall see below that philosophy and ethics are products of the folkways. They are taken out of the mores, but are never original and creative; they are secondary and derived. They often interfere in the second stage of the sequence—act, thought, act. Then they produce harm, but some ground is furnished for the claim that they are creative or at least regulative. In fact, the real process in great bodies of men is not one of deduction from any great principle of philosophy or ethics. It is one of minute efforts to live well under existing conditions, which efforts are repeated indefinitely by great numbers, getting strength from habit and from the fellowship of united action. The resultant folkways become coercive. All are forced to conform, and the folkways dominate the societal life. Then they seem true and right, and arise into mores as the norm of welfare. Thence are produced faiths, ideas, doctrines, religions, and philosophies, according to the stage of civilization and the fashions of reflection and generalization.

What Is Goodness or Badness of the Mores?

It is most important to notice that, for the people of a time and place, their own mores are always good, or rather that for them there can be no question of the goodness or badness of their mores. The reason is because the standards of good and right are in the mores. If the life conditions change, the traditional folkways may produce pain and loss, or fail to produce the same good as formerly. Then the loss of comfort and ease brings doubt into the judgment of welfare (causing doubt of the pleasure of the gods, or of war power, or of health), and thus disturbs the unconscious philosophy of the mores. Then a later time will pass judgment on the mores. Another society may also pass judgment on the mores. In our literary and historical study of the mores we want to get from them their educational value, which consists in the stimulus or warning as to what is, in its effects, societally good or bad. This may lead us to reject or neglect a phenomenon like infanticide, slavery, or witch-craft, as an old "abuse" and "evil," or to pass by the crusades as a folly which can-not recur. Such a course would be a great error. Everything in the mores of a time and place must be regarded as justified with regard to that time and place. "Good" mores are those which are well adapted to the situation. "Bad" mores are those which are not so adapted. The mores are not so stereotyped and changeless as might appear, because they are forever moving towards more complete adaptation to con-ditions and interests, and also towards more complete adjustment to each other. People in mass have never made or kept up a custom in order to hurt their own interests. They have made innumerable errors as to what their interests were and how to satisfy them, but they have always aimed to serve their interests as well as they could. This gives the standpoint for the student of the mores. All things in them come before him on the same plane. They all bring instruction and warning. They all have the same relation to power and welfare. The mistakes in them are component parts of them. We do not study them in order to approve some of them and condemn others. They are all equally worthy of attention from the fact that they existed and were used. The chief object of study in them is their adjustment to inter-ests, their relation to welfare, and their coordination in a harmonious system of life policy. For the men of the time there are no "bad" mores. What is traditional and current is the standard of what ought to be. The masses never raise any question about such things. If a few raise doubts and questions, this proves that the folkways have already begun to lose firmness and the regulative element in the mores has begun to lose authority. This indicates that the folkways are on their way to a new adjustment. The extreme of folly, wickedness, and absurdity in the mores is witch persecutions, but the best men in the seventeenth century had no doubt that witches existed, and that they ought to be burned. The religion, statecraft, jurisprudence, philosophy, and social system of that age all contributed to maintain that belief. It was rather a culmination than a contradiction of the current faiths and convictions, just as the dogma that all men are equal and that one ought to have as much politi-cal power in the state as another was the culmination of the political dogmatism and social philosophy of the nineteenth century. Hence our judgments of the good or evil consequences of folkways are to be kept separate from our study of the historical phenomena of them, and of their strength and the reasons for it. The judgments have their place in plans and doctrines for the future, not in a retrospect.

The Mores Have the Authority of Facts

The mores come down to us from the past. Each individual is born into them as he is born into the atmosphere, and he does not reflect on them, or criticize them any more than a baby analyzes the atmosphere before he begins to breathe it. Each one is sub-jected to the influence of the mores, and formed by them, before he is capable of reasoning about them. It may be objected that nowadays, at least, we criticize all tra-ditions, and accept none just because they are handed down to us. If we take up cases of things which are still entirely or almost entirely in the mores, we shall see that this is not so. There are sects of free-lovers amongst us who want to discuss pair marriage. They are not simply people of evil life. They invite us to discuss rationally our inherited customs and ideas as to marriage, which, they say, are by no means so excellent and elevated as we believe. They have never won any serious attention. Some others want to argue in favor of polygamy on grounds of expediency. They fail to obtain a hearing. Others want to discuss property. In spite of some literary activity on their part, no discussion of property, bequest, and inheritance has ever been opened. Property and marriage are in the mores. Nothing can ever change them but the unconscious and imperceptible movement of the mores. Religion was originally a matter of the mores. It became a societal institution and a function of the state. It has now to a great extent been put back into the mores. Since laws with penalties to enforce religious creeds or practices have gone out of use any one may think and act as he pleases about religion. Therefore, it is not now "good form" to attack religion. Infidel publications are now tabooed by the mores, and are more effectually repressed than ever before. They produce no controversy. Democracy is in our American mores. It is a product of our physical and economic conditions. It is impossible to discuss or criticize it. It is glorified for popularity, and is a subject of dithyrambic rhetoric. No one treats it with complete candor and sincerity. No one dares to analyze it as he would aristocracy or autocracy. He would get no hearing and would only incur abuse. The thing to be noticed in all these cases is that the masses oppose a deaf ear to every argument against the mores. It is only insofar as things have been transferred from the mores into laws and positive institutions that there is discussion about them or rationalizing upon them. The mores contain the norm by which, if we should discuss the mores, we should have to judge the mores. We learn the mores as unconsciously as we learn to walk and eat and breathe. The masses never learn how we walk, and eat, and breathe, and they never know any reason why the mores are what they are. The justification of them is that when we wake to consciousness of life we find them facts which already hold us in the bonds of tradition, custom, and habit. The mores contain embodied in them notions, doctrines, and maxims, but they are facts. They are in the present tense. They have nothing to do with what ought to be, will be, may be, or once was, if it is not now.

Mores and Morals; Social Code

For everyone the mores give the notion of what ought to be. This includes the notion of what ought to be done, for all should cooperate to bring to pass, in the order of life, what ought to be. All notions of propriety, decency, chastity, politeness, order, duty, right, rights, discipline, respect, reverence, cooperation, and fellowship, especially all things in regard to which good and ill depend entirely on the point at which the line is drawn, are in the mores. The mores can make things seem right and good to one group or one age which to another seem antagonistic to every instinct of human nature. The thirteenth century bred in every heart such a sentiment in regard to heretics that inquisitors had no more misgivings in their proceedings than men would have now if they should attempt to exterminate rattlesnakes. The sixteenth century gave to all such notions about witches that witch persecutors thought they were waging war on enemies of God and man. Of course the inquisitors and witch persecutors constantly developed the notions of heretics and witches. They exaggerated the notions and then gave them back again to the mores, in their expanded form, to inflame the hearts of men with terror and hate and to become, in the next stage, so much more fantastic and ferocious motives. Such is the reaction between the mores and the acts of the living generation. The world philosophy of the age is never anything but the reflection on the mental horizon, which is formed out of the mores, of the ruling ideas which are in the mores themselves. It is from a failure to recognize the to and fro in this reaction that the current notion arises that mores are produced by doctrines. The "morals" of an age are never anything but the consonance between what is done and what the mores of the age require. The whole revolves on itself, in the relation of the specific to the general, within the horizon formed by the mores. Every attempt to win an outside standpoint from which to reduce the whole to an absolute philosophy of truth and right, based on an unalterable principle, is a delusion. New elements are brought in only by new conquests of nature through science and art. The new conquests change the conditions of life and the interests of the members of the society. Then the mores change by adaptation to new conditions and interests. The philosophy and ethics then follow to account for and justify the changes in the mores; often, also, to claim that they have caused the changes. They never do anything but draw new lines of bearing between the parts of the mores and the horizon of thought within which they are enclosed, and which is a deduction from the mores. The horizon is widened by more knowledge, but for one age it is just as much a generalization from the mores as for another. It is always unreal. It is only a product of thought. The ethical philosophers select points on this horizon from which to take their bearings, and they think that they have won some authority for their systems when they travel back again from the generalization to the specific custom out of which it was deduced. The cases of the inquisitors and witch persecutors who toiled arduously and continually for their chosen ends, for little or no reward, show us the relation between mores on the one side and philosophy, ethics, and religion on the other.

STUDY QUESTIONS

1. Sumner says, "For the people of a time and place, their own mores are always good, or rather ... for them there can be no question of the goodness or badness of their mores." Explain his position. Has Sumner overlooked the possibility that a people could wonder whether their own mores are correct? Or does Sumner deny this is possible?
2. Sumner says that we often pass judgment on mores of the past or on mores of other people in the present. For example, we now think that infanticide and slavery were wrong. Why does Sumner believe that such moralizing is inappropriate?
3. Sumner believes that mores change when scientific discoveries or technological inventions change the conditions of life. Why is it only practical inventions that change mores, and not moral insights?
4. What is the *Zeitgeist*? How is the concept relevant to Sumner's theory?
5. Sumner denies that mores are ever produced by doctrines. Does this mean that the moral doctrines of philosophers like Aristotle, Kant, or Mill have no influence on what counts as moral? Explain.

Cultural Relativism and Universal Rights

Carolyn Fluehr-Lobban

> Carolyn Fluehr-Lobban (b. 1945) is a professor of anthropology at Rhode Island College, where she is director of the general education program. She has written a number of works on Islamic culture and practice, including *Islamic Law and Society in the Sudan* (1986), *Modern Egypt and Its Heritage* (1990), and *Islamic Society in Practice* (1994).
>
> Carolyn Fluehr-Lobban is an anthropologist who objects to the widespread acceptance of ethical relativism by her peers. She points out that in 1947, when the idea of an international declaration of universal human rights was first being discussed, anthropologists, who were mainly ethical relativists, declined to participate. Fluehr-Lobban says that this laissez-faire posture must change: "the time has come" for anthropologists to take a stand on key human-rights issues. This will entail morally judging and condemning some of the societies they study. In particular, Fluehr-Lobban condemns the mores that in many cultures contribute to the exploitation and degradation of women. Fluehr-Lobban advocates active measures to get social change: "We cannot just be bystanders."

Cultural relativism, long a key concept in anthropology, asserts that since each culture has its own values and practices, anthropologists should not make value judgments about cultural differences. As a result, anthropological pedagogy has stressed that the study of customs and norms should be value-free, and that the appropriate role of the anthropologist is that of observer and recorder.

Today, however, this view is being challenged by critics inside and outside the discipline, especially those who want anthropologists to take a stand on key human-rights issues. I agree that the time has come for anthropologists to become more actively engaged in safeguarding the rights of people whose lives and cultures they study.

Historically, anthropology as a discipline has declined to participate in the dialogue that produced international conventions regarding human rights. For example, in 1947, when the executive board of the American Anthropological Association withdrew from discussions that led to the "Universal Declaration of Human Rights," it did so in the belief that no such declaration would be applicable to all human beings. But the world and anthropology have changed. Because their research involves extended interaction with people at the grassroots, anthropologists

---

are in a unique position to lend knowledge and expertise to the international debate regarding human rights.

Doing so does not represent a complete break with the traditions of our field. After all, in the past, anthropologists did not hesitate to speak out against such reprehensible practices as Nazi genocide and South African apartheid. And they have testified in U.S. courts against government rules that impinge on the religious traditions or sacred lands of Native Americans, decrying government policies that treat groups of people unjustly.

However, other practices that violate individual rights or oppress particular groups have not been denounced. Anthropologists generally have not spoken out, for example, against the practice in many cultures of female circumcision, which critics call a mutilation of women. They have been unwilling to pass judgment on such forms of culturally based homicide as the killing of infants or the aged. Some have withheld judgment on acts of communal violence, such as clashes between Hindus and Muslims in India or Tutsis and Hutus in Rwanda, perhaps because the animosities between those groups are of long standing.

Moreover, as a practical matter, organized anthropology's refusal to participate in drafting the 1947 human-rights declaration has meant that anthropologists have not had much of a role in drafting later human-rights statements, such as the United Nations' "Convention on the Elimination of All Forms of Discrimination Against Women," approved in 1979. In many international forums discussing women's rights, participants have specifically rejected using cultural relativism as a barrier to improving women's lives.

The issue of violence against women throws the perils of cultural relativism into stark relief. Following the lead of human-rights advocates, a growing number of anthropologists and others are coming to recognize that violence against women should be acknowledged as a violation of a basic human right to be free from harm. They believe that such violence cannot be excused or justified on cultural grounds.

Let me refer to my own experience. For nearly 25 years, I have conducted research in the Sudan, one of the African countries where the practice of female circumcision is widespread, affecting the vast majority of females in the northern Sudan. Chronic infections are a common result, and sexual intercourse and childbirth are rendered difficult and painful. However, cultural ideology in the Sudan holds that an uncircumcised woman is not respectable, and few families would risk their daughter's chances of marrying by not having her circumcised. British colonial officials outlawed the practice in 1946, but this served only to make it surreptitious and thus more dangerous. Women found it harder to get treatment for mistakes or for side effects of the illegal surgery.

For a long time I felt trapped between, on one side, my anthropologist's understanding of the custom and of the sensitivities about it among the people with whom I was working, and, on the other, the largely feminist campaign in the West to eradicate what critics see as a "barbaric" custom. To ally myself with Western feminists and condemn female circumcision seemed to me to be a betrayal of the value system and culture of the Sudan, which I had come to understand. But as I was asked over the years to comment on female circumcision because of my expertise in the Sudan, I came to realize how deeply I felt that the practice was harmful and wrong.

In 1993, female circumcision was one of the practices deemed harmful by delegates at the international Human Rights Conference in Vienna. During their discussions, they came to view circumcision as a violation of the rights of children as well as of the women who suffer its consequences throughout life. Those discussions made me realize that there was a moral agenda larger than myself, larger than Western culture or the culture of the northern Sudan or my discipline. I decided to join colleagues from other disciplines and cultures in speaking out against the practice.

Some cultures are beginning to change, although cause and effect are difficult to determine. Women's associations in the Ivory Coast are calling for an end to female circumcision. In Egypt, the Cairo Institute for Human Rights has reported the first publicly acknowledged marriage of an uncircumcised woman. In the United States, a Nigerian woman recently was granted asylum on the ground that her returning to her country would result in the forcible circumcision of her daughter, which was deemed a violation of the girl's human rights.

To be sure, it is not easy to achieve consensus concerning the point at which cultural practices cross the line and become violations of human rights. But it is important that scholars and human-rights activists discuss the issue. Some examples of when the line is crossed may be clearer than others. The action of a Japanese wife who feels honor-bound to commit suicide because of the shame of her husband's infidelity can be explained and perhaps justified by the traditional code of honor in Japanese society. However, when she decides to take the lives of her children as well, she is committing murder, which may be easier to condemn than suicide.

What about "honor" killings of sisters and daughters accused of sexual misconduct in some Middle Eastern and Mediterranean societies? Some anthropologists have explained this practice in culturally relativist terms, saying that severe disruptions of the moral order occur when sexual impropriety is alleged or takes place. To restore the social equilibrium and avoid feuds, the local culture requires the shedding of blood to wash away the shame of sexual dishonor. The practice of honor killings, which victimizes mainly women, has been defended in some local courts as less serious than premeditated murder, because it stems from longstanding cultural traditions. While some judges have agreed, anthropologists should see a different picture: a pattern of cultural discrimination against women.

As the issue of domestic violence shows, we need to explore the ways that we balance individual and cultural rights. The "right" of a man to discipline, slap, hit, or beat his wife (and often, by extension, his children) is widely recognized across many cultures in which male dominance is an accepted fact of life. Indeed, the issue of domestic violence has only recently been added to the international human-rights agenda, with the addition of women's rights to the list of basic human rights at the Vienna conference.

The fact that domestic violence is being openly discussed and challenged in some societies (the United States is among the leaders) helps to encourage dialogue in societies in which domestic violence has been a taboo subject. This dialogue is relatively new, and no clear principles have emerged. But anthropologists could inform and enrich the discussion, using their knowledge of family and community life in different cultures.

Cases of genocide may allow the clearest insight into where the line between local culture and universal morality lies. Many anthropologists have urged the Brazilian and Venezuelan governments to stop gold miners from slaughtering the Yanomami people, who are battling the encroachment of miners on their rain forests. Other practices that harm individuals or categories of people (such as the elderly, women, and enslaved or formerly enslaved people) may not represent genocide *per se*, and thus may present somewhat harder questions about the morality of traditional practices. We need to focus on the harm done, however, and not on the scale of the abuse. We need to be sensitive to cultural differences but not allow them to override widely recognized human rights.

The exchange of ideas across cultures is already fostering a growing acceptance of the universal nature of some human rights, regardless of cultural differences. The right of individuals to be free from harm or the threat of harm, and the right of cultural minorities to exist freely within states, are just two examples of rights that are beginning to be universally recognized—although not universally applied.

Fortunately, organized anthropology is beginning to change its attitude toward cultural relativism and human rights. The theme of the 1994 convention of the American Anthropological Association was human rights. At the sessions organized around the topic, many anthropologists said they no longer were absolutely committed to cultural relativism. The association has responded to the changing attitude among its members by forming a Commission for Human Rights, charged with developing a specifically anthropological perspective on those rights, and with challenging violations and promoting education about them.

Nevertheless, many anthropologists continue to express strong support for cultural relativism. One of the most contentious issues arises from the fundamental question: What authority do we Westerners have to impose our own concept of universal rights on the rest of humanity? It is true that Western ideas of human rights have so far dominated international discourse. On the other hand, the cultural relativists' argument is often used by repressive governments to deflect international criticism of their abuse of their citizens. At the very least, anthropologists need to condemn such misuse of cultural relativism, even if it means that they may be denied permission to do research in the country in question.

Personally, I would go further: I believe that we should not let the concept of relativism stop us from using national and international forums to examine ways to protect the lives and dignity of people in every culture. Because of our involvement in local societies, anthropologists could provide early warnings of abuses—for example, by reporting data to international human-rights organizations, and by joining the dialogue at international conferences. When there is a choice between defending human rights and defending cultural relativism, anthropologists should choose to protect and promote human rights. We cannot just be bystanders.

Study Questions

1. What prompted Fluehr-Lobban to pass moral judgment on the societies she was studying? How does she justify this to herself as an anthropologist who is sensitive to the feelings of the people she is judging?

2. Now that she is no longer merely standing by as an observer, what role does Fluehr-Lobban see herself playing?
3. How, in the opinion of Fluehr-Lobban, is "cultural relativism" being misused by some anthropologists?
4. Give an example of what Fluehr-Lobban considers to be an abusive practice in a society, and state what human right it violates. How might an outsider go about getting the abusive practice changed?

Uganda's Women: Children, Drudgery, and Pain

Jane Perlez

> Jane Perlez (b. 1947) is a journalist for *The New York Times*. She is currently assigned to the London office of the *Times*.
>
> The life of Safuyati Kawuda is like that of many rural African women. These women, who produce almost three-quarters of Africa's food, lead lives of hard and unceasing labor not shared by their husbands. The men, who may visit their villages only occasionally, live urban lives, while their wives work and care for the children in dwellings that lack such amenities as running water or electricity. Mrs. Kawuda's husband has several wives, including a "town wife." Mrs. Kawuda is not convinced that he stays faithful to the town wife, and she fears that his promiscuity may result in AIDS. As a reporter, Jane Perlez makes no value judgments. But to many readers it will seem obvious that the social system that condemns Mrs. Kawuda to a lifetime of unremitting and punishing labor is unfair.

NAMUTUMBA, Uganda—When 28-year-old Safuyati Kawuda married the man she remembers as "handsome and elegant," her husband scraped together the bride price: five goats and three chickens. The animals represented a centuries-old custom intended to compensate Mrs. Kawuda's father for losing the labor of his daughter.

In the decade since, Mrs. Kawuda has rarely seen her husband, who long ago left this hot and dusty village for a town 70 miles away. She has accepted her husband's acquisition of two other wives and has given birth to five of his 13 children.

Instead of laboring for her father she has toiled for her husband instead—hauling firewood, fetching water, digging in the fields, producing the food the family eats, and bearing and caring for the children.

Like Mrs. Kawuda, women in rural Africa are the subsistence farmers. They produce, without tractors, oxen, or even plows, more than 70 percent of the continent's food, according to the World Bank. Back-breaking hand cultivation is a job that African men consider to be demeaning "women's work." The male responsibility is generally to sell the food the women produce. But as urbanization has stepped up, men have gone to the cities in search of other jobs, leaving women like Mrs. Kawuda alone.

Many Inequalities

The discrepancy between the physical labor of women and men is accompanied by other pervasive inequalities. In the vast majority of African countries, women do not own or inherit land. Within families, boys are encouraged to go to school, girls are not. In many places, women treat wife-beating as an accepted practice. The Uganda Women's Lawyers Association recently embarked on a campaign to convince women that wife-battering is not a sign of a man's love.

Recent surveys in Africa show other significant disparities between men and women. In ten African countries, according to the United Nations Children's Fund, women and children together make up 77 percent of the population. Yet in only 16 percent of the households in those countries do the women have the legal right to own property.

Despite calls by the United Nations for the improvement of the lives of African women and efforts by the World Bank to finance projects focused on women, little has been done to improve the dismal status of rural women, African and Western experts say. With the continent's worsening economics in the 1980s, women suffered even more.

"The poor, the majority of whom are women, have had to take on additional work burdens in order to cope with cutbacks in social services and the increasing cost of living," the *Weekly Review*, a magazine in Kenya, reported last year.

No Expectations

Mrs. Kawuda has never attended school. She cannot read or write, although her husband can. She has no radio. The farthest she has been from home is Jinja, 70 miles away. She has no expectations of a better life because she has known nothing else. But her ignorance of the outside world does not stop her from knowing her life is unrelentingly tough. She knows that in her bones.

"Everything is difficult," Mrs. Kawuda said, as she bent over to hoe cassava, her bare, rough feet splattered with dark dirt. "It's more of a problem than it used to be to find firewood. If you can't find wood on the ground, you have to cut it and there is no one to help you. Digging in the fields is the most difficult. I don't like it."

Mrs. Kawuda shares her world of perpetual fatigue with her five children; her husband's second wife, Zainabu Kasoga, 27, and her four children. Her husband's third wife—"the town wife"—lives in Jinja, where the husband, 31-year-old Kadiri Mpyanku, a tea packer, spends most of his time.

When the husband visited Mrs. Kawuda on a recent weekend, he brought enough sugar for three days and a packet of beans. Mrs. Kawuda said she was dependent on him for clothes and other essentials, and money that she said he did not always have. In most households in the area, the men also live most of the time in either Jinja or Kampala, the capital.

Here in the village, 120 miles northeast of Kampala, Mrs. Kawuda and Mrs. Kasoga run a household with another woman, the wife of their husband's brother, Sayeda Naigaga, 20, and her three children.

Village Life

The women live without running water or electricity in three small, mud-wall structures. In the outdoor courtyard, life grinds on: the peeling and chopping of food, eating by adults and feeding of infants, washing, bathing, weaving and the receiving of guests all take place on the orange clay ground, packed smooth by the passage of bare feet.

In the old days, Ugandan men built separate houses for each wife, but such luxuries disappeared with the collapse of the economy. Mrs. Kawuda and her five children sleep in one room of the main shelter and Mrs. Kasoga and her four children in another. When their husband is around, he shuttles between the two bedrooms.

Mrs. Kawuda is of the Bisoga tribe, the second largest in Uganda and one where polygamy is common. Sexual and marriage mores differ in various parts of Africa. The Uganda Women's Lawyers Association estimates that 50 percent of marriages in Uganda are polygamous and, according to United Nations figures, a similar percentage exists in West Africa.

In Kenya, the Government's Women's Bureau estimates that about 30 percent of the marriages are polygamous. However, because of the economic burden of keeping several wives and families, the practice is declining, the bureau says.

Wives Often Hostile

Often the wives in a polygamous marriage are hostile toward each other. But perhaps as a survival instinct, Mrs. Kawuda and Mrs. Kasoga are friendly, taking turns with Mrs. Naigaga to cook for the 15-member household.

Days start with the morning ritual of collecting water. For these Ugandan women, the journey to the nearest pond takes half an hour. The six-gallon cans, when full of water, are heavy on the trip home.

Digging in the fields is the most loathed of the chores, but also the one the women feel most obliged to do since the family's food supply comes from what they grow. As they work under the sun, the women drape old pieces of clothing on their heads for protection. The youngest child, two-year-old Suniya, clings to her mother's back while Mrs. Kawuda hunches over, swinging a hoe, a sight as pervasive in rural Africa as an American mother gliding a cart along the aisles of a supermarket. "Having a baby on your back is easy," Mrs. Kawuda said. "When you are eight months pregnant and digging, it is more difficult."

There was no possibility the husband would help in the fields. It was his job to "supervise," said Mrs. Kawuda, ridiculing a suggestion that he might pitch in.

When he arrived late on a recent Saturday night, Mr. Mpyanku was treated as the imperious ruler by the children, some of whom tentatively came to greet him. He was barely acknowledged by the women, who seemed a little fearful and immediately served tea.

By early Sunday morning, he had disappeared to the nearby trading post to be with his male friends. "He has gone to discuss business with his friends," Mrs. Kawuda said. "What business can I discuss with him? Will we talk to him about digging cassava?"

Mrs. Kawuda said her husband had promised not to take any more wives. "But you never know what he thinks," she said. "I can't interfere in his affairs. If I did, he would say: 'Why is she poking her nose into my affairs?'"

Fertility and children remain at the center of rural marriage in Africa. Large numbers of children improve a household's labor pool and provide built-in security for parents in old age.

Mrs. Kawuda said she wanted one more child, in the hopes of its being another boy. After that, she said, she would use an injectible form of contraceptive. It is a method popular among African rural women because it can be used without their husband's knowledge. But in reality, contraception was an abstraction to Mrs. Kawuda since she had no idea where to get it. She has never heard of condoms.

A recent concern for African women is AIDS, which like much else in their lives they seem powerless to control. Unconvinced by her husband's assurances that he is faithful to his town wife, Mrs. Kawuda said: "He can say it's all right, we need not worry. But you never know what he does in town. He fears AIDS, too. But he messes around too much."

A worldly person compared to his wives, Mr. Mpyanku speaks reasonable English and has traveled to Kenya.

He described himself as the provider of cash for the rural family. But Mr. Mpyanku's emphasis is on his own livelihood and his urban life.

He rode the most comfortable form of transportation home, a nonstop minibus from Jinja that cost about $1.50, instead of the cheaper taxi at $1. He would do the same on his return.

Yet his oldest child, a daughter, Maliyamu, ten, missed much of her schooling last year. Her report card said the $7 in school fees had not been paid. It was a cheerless sign that Mrs. Kawuda's daughter would, like her mother, remain uneducated and repeat for another generation the cycle of female poverty and punishing physical labor.

STUDY QUESTIONS

1. Of the three moral theories—utilitarianism, Kantianism, and relativism—which do you think provides the best approach to Mrs. Kawuda's predicament? Explain.
2. Using Mrs. Kawuda's situation as an example of a putatively immoral social arrangement, stage a debate on the following proposition: "There are universal moral principles that apply to all societies."

An Alternative to Moral Relativism

Lawrence Adam Lengbeyer

> Lawrence Adam Lengbeyer (b. 1958) teaches ethics and philosophy at the
> United States Naval Academy. His published and presented research has
> dealt with a wide variety of topics, including selflessness, courage, anti-
> Semitism, and mental compartmentalization.

> Lengbeyer endorses an alternative to both absolutism and relativism that he
> calls ethical pluralism. He points out that many students are uncomfortable
> with the "anything goes" character of ethical relativism; on the other hand,
> they recoil from the idea that there is one right answer to every moral ques-
> tion. Ethical pluralism allows for many ways to be right. Individuals as well
> as societies may reasonably differ in how much importance to attach to vari-
> ous ideals—compassion, justice, and liberty, for instance—and how to rank
> order and weight these in making moral decisions. This leaves room for
> "multiple correct answers to ethical questions of right and wrong, good
> and bad," each of which is reasonable and suited to its particular circum-
> stances. At the same time, individuals and even whole societies can be mis-
> taken; this happens when they make decisions based on self-deception,
> bigotry, misinformation, invalid logic, superstition, or other irrationality.
> Unlike relativism, pluralism asserts that there are many ways to be wrong.

It is remarkable how many students remain drawn to ethical relativism even after
becoming aware of its rather damning shortcomings. They acknowledge that, yes,
they know of no cogent positive argument in its favor; that it seemingly undermines
the basis for moral reasoning and discussion, and for ethical aspiration and
improvement; and that as relativists they may be entangled in self-contradiction.
But then they look once again at ethical objectivism, which they see as the only
available alternative that still allows for talking about ethical judgments as true or
false, and they're reminded that they deem *it* to be even *more* unacceptable: "Given
the diversity of divergent opinions about ethical matters, how can I count on *my*
ethical views happening to be the true ones, when they have been so shaped by
the happenstance of my background, upbringing, educational exposure, intellectual
inclinations, and even genetic makeup?" So they reason, displaying admirable self-
awareness and humility. "Did I just happen to obtain the one true view of religion,
right and wrong, and what's valuable in life—while those who disagree with me on
questions of morality and value (and not merely factual matters) were instilled with
false ideas? Couldn't *they* all say the exact same thing about me, and with no less

---

Reprinted by permission of the author.

justification? And wouldn't I now be espousing *their* ethical convictions if I had been born to their parents, raised in their families and (sub)cultures, taught by their teachers, and exposed to the same arguments as they?"

So, at the end of the day, many students still allow themselves to think and talk like relativists. What else, after all, can they do? To drop relativism for objectivism strikes them as jumping out of the frying pan into the fire. It's better to stifle one's judgment than to become indefensibly arrogant, isn't it?

Now, others will undoubtedly object to such a characterization of objectivism. They believe that, however complicated the right answer to an ethical question sometimes is, there is a right answer—and *a*, single right answer, not a different one for each different perspective that is taken on the matter. In some cases, moreover, the right answer is *obvious*—it's wrong to torture babies for fun; it's good to help others in need; it's right to live as Christ decreed, perhaps—and only someone who has been damaged, brainwashed, improperly trained, or seduced by evil can fail to see these truths. Surely it cannot be arrogant to hold fast to clear, important truths?

There is certainly something to be said for this view (and for relativism, for that matter). Moreover, it seems possible to embrace objectivism, and a particular set of uncompromising ethical truths, without taking the further step of imposing these views upon those who disagree. The fact is, though, that many of our students steadfastly regard objectivism as a far-fetched, egotistical or ethnocentric—maybe even dangerous—doctrine. Could they benefit from a deeper, more subtle appreciation of the objectivist and relativist options? Unquestionably. But are they likely ever to obtain such a thorough, detailed philosophical comprehension of the nuances of meta-ethical theory? Not the vast majority of them—and yet their orientations on these issues will pervasively influence their approaches to education, their political attitudes and activities, their relationships with their neighbors, even the ways that they end up raising the next generation of citizens. So it is crucial that we engage these students. And, to be able to engage them at all, we must engage them on their home turf—understanding what brings them to their relativistic attitudes, and accepting that they will not be dislodged easily from their simplified, stereotyping conceptions of objectivism and relativism, certainly not by intricate abstract arguments.

Many of these students are drawn to relativism in ethics (and often beyond) due to the anxiety that they feel when they contemplate deviating—even in mere thought, let alone in overt expression—from those 'reference' groups or persons to whom they look for their norms. The regard, or mere acceptance, of those persons who they perceive to be hip, astute, or simply normal is too precious for them to risk. Not feeling "safe enough" to engage in moral analysis, not (yet) possessing the basic moral courage required to think for themselves, they adopt a "fatalistic" relativism that rationalizes their disengagement. For other students, of course, it may be mere laziness, a distaste for the hard work of thinking clearly, that draws them in.

These forces aside, however, many students are led into relativism by a reasonable, if exaggerated and perhaps ultimately misguided, worry about being contemptibly judgmental or arrogant. How, then, can we help them move beyond the disagreeable objectivist-relativist dilemma into which they feel forced? We can, and do, make efforts to open their minds to objectivist alternatives—introducing them to some versions that are nuanced and/or empirically supported; showing them that humility and tolerance can be compatible with objectivism, and explaining why objectivism does not license the leap to assuming that one's own current positions are the ones uniquely endowed with truth. But these efforts seem to leave many minds unchanged. To these students, objectivism cannot be rescued or rehabilitated; it is simply a non-starter, and there is nowhere else to turn but relativism, for all its problems.

But we still have one arrow left in our quiver, and it is a philosophically significant and pedagogically fruitful one: we can show these students that there *is* somewhere else to turn. Beside relativism and objectivism, there is a third option in this area—ethical pluralism. Might it avoid those features of its competitors that are so often found unpalatable?

The core claim of pluralism is that there can be *multiple* correct answers to ethical questions of right and wrong, good and bad, better and worse—not merely one correct answer, as objectivists maintain, nor as many correct answers as there are differing cultural (or individual) opinions, as 'cultural' (or 'individual') relativists maintain. To the objectivist, if people disagree about an ethical matter, only one of them can be right—everyone else is wrong. (Though it may be that *none* of them has discerned the truth of the matter.) There is a single universal standard of ethical truth, a single all-encompassing ethical reality, against which to measure everyone's behaviors, beliefs, and feelings. To the cultural relativist, by contrast, every culture's answer is right 'for it'—no culture can be mistaken. And it may even be that *every single person's* view, no matter how absurd or wrongheaded it seems to others, is right 'for him' and thus beyond criticism, as the more radical, 'individual' version of relativism maintains. Either way, there is no single ethical reality, hence no universal standards.

The pluralist position lies in between the poles of objectivism and relativism, and claims to possess the most appealing features of each. Yes, there is an objective truth of the matter concerning ethics, and thus it is possible for people's judgments to be wrong; at the same time, yes, ethical truth is not always *single*, providing for only one correct answer to every question, and thus there is no good reason to conclude that all whose judgments disagree with ours are wrong. According to the pluralist, then, each ethical question may have *multiple* equally correct (reasonable, acceptable) answers, but not an unlimited number of such answers. Only certain answers are above reproach; the rest are mistaken. Error, ignorance, misjudgment, wishful thinking, self-deception, and confusion *are* possible in ethical thinking. So we need not, and ought not, grant an uncritical free pass to the viewpoints of other persons or cultures—or to our own. Critical reflection, inquiry, and debate are important, and not pointless, activities.

Now, this might sound pretty mysterious. How can there be a truth that "is not always single," that allows for multiple right answers to a question? Are we supposed to take this kind of lunacy seriously?

To see the plausibility of pluralism in ethics, we ought first to look outside of ethics, to the domains where the contending theories are most at home, where they strike us as most compelling. Let's consider the subject matters where it is fairly uncontroversial that objectivism and relativism are appropriate, and that pluralism would therefore be out of place.

Begin with matters of empirical, in particular scientific, fact: there is general consensus on how to go about answering questions about things like distance, mass, heat, voltage, or pressure, or at least on how to test the answers. Moreover, each method of testing is required to be objective—to come out with the same answer regardless of who performs it, or what subjective attitudes and preferences the testers bring to it, provided that they have received the appropriate training and are competent. This objectivity is not confined to the physical sciences, either. Journalists, historians, biologists, economists—even ordinary citizens trying to learn about the scheduled kickoff time for a football game—regard themselves as pursuing objectively existing and verifiable facts, even if they later launch from these foundations into less objective domains of interpretation and judgment.

Surely, objectivism is the appropriate approach to take here. There are no multiple right answers to questions about such matters, let alone a different correct answer for each (sub)culture or each person!

But let's give relativism its due, too. Consider matters of taste or preference, regarding such things as food, romantic allure, or how best to spend one's leisure time. Here we certainly seem *not* to find the objectivism-favoring features just discussed—the agreement across persons, the methods for verification, the irrelevance of who is doing the judging. The procedures for answering questions about these matters seem to be unavoidably, and irreducibly, subjective: they properly draw upon personally variable, sometimes idiosyncratic, attitudes and other features of our psyches. While it's *possible* to make a case that the person who prefers vanilla ice cream to strawberry is objectively wrong, that thunderstorms are inherently unpleasant, or that beaches are more beautiful than mountain ranges, it seems impossible to make a convincing case in such instances. And notice that individual tastes and preferences often are shaped by the surrounding (sub)cultures: to Koreans generally, pickled foods are delicious, but not so for participants in many other culinary traditions.

It would appear, then, that in realms such as these, there seems no problem with saying "to each, his own" for every (sub)culture, or even for every person. Relativism is not out of place here.

But what if someone were to ask for the name of the greatest military leader in American history—or the best route for driving to that football game mentioned above, or the right strategy for succeeding in business, or the best hitter in baseball, or the finest film of all time, or the right way to play a certain Beethoven sonata, or the best teacher at one's school? Now, there might well be several legitimate, reasonable competing answers to any of these questions. But surely there are, as a matter of objective reality, plenty of *wrong* answers to each, too, answers that have no strong reasons in their favor compared to some other possibilities. Anyone with a few seconds reflection can come up with some.

In matters like these, we obtain answers by turning to the underlying factors or criteria that are relevant. For military leadership, we inquire about such things as engagements won, importance of those victories, quality of the adversaries defeated, handicaps fought under, innovative methods used, and personal character and charisma. For excellent teaching, we ask about making class interesting, being a role model, displaying a good sense of humor, having a well-designed syllabus, treating students fairly and respectfully, inspiring wonder and curiosity, instilling high standards, generating intellectual enthusiasm for the subject-matter, and so on. Yet there can be reasonable disagreement about how to apply each underlying criterion, and even about whether a given criterion is relevant, or how much weight it should be given. Was *Star Wars* more innovative a film, for instance, than *Toy Story?* And should innovation even be considered a factor in film greatness? If so, how important a factor?

Thus, various defensible conceptions or 'theories' of military leadership, teaching excellence, film greatness, etc., are possible, and they lead to irresolvable debates in bars, at conferences, on talk shows, and on awards panels. Some people are clearly more expert than the rest of us at rendering judgments in these areas, but even these knowledgeable, sage persons disagree. Consequently, pure objectivism looks unsuited to questions like these. Still, there are many, many answers that simply cannot be reasonably defended, and so we also find an important brake on the kind of 'anything goes,' all-accepting attitude of relativism. Pluralism seems to offer the best alternative.

So, finally: what about ethics? Here, too, we usually find ourselves drawn toward conceptions that are based upon multiple factors. For example, what makes an action ethically right or wrong? Well, isn't it important to know whether the action brings pleasure or suffering? And what alternative options are available to the actor? Sure. But what about other implications—say, for human flourishing or well-being or autonomy, pleasure aside? And then there is the actor's state of mind. And whether any rights, or obligations, are violated. And whether the action displays an excellent, admirable character. And maybe other considerations. Plus, how are these factors supposed to be combined and balanced into a single judgment? Some philosophers have become famous by urging that a single factor or set of factors always predominate—for Bentham and Mill, consequences of pleasure and pain; for Kant, state of mind; for Aristotle and Aquinas, in different ways, character and human flourishing—but few ordinary persons think that convincing answers can always be obtained by such a purity, or narrow exclusivity, of vision.

We thus face a choice when we answer an ethical question. We must decide, in effect, which factors to weigh, and how heavily to weigh each, without there being only one proper way to decide these matters. The result is that there are multiple defensible methods for reaching a final judgment, and, often, multiple divergent answers each of which can be defended with sound reasoning. The answers do need to be defended—in ethics, as opposed to those issues for which relativism is proper, no one earns a free pass just by showing up and stating a personal or cultural opinion. There are implausible, untenable answers that deserve not automatic deference, but disagreement or at least silent critique: answers that rely upon irrelevant issues (e.g., the rightness of an action typically does not depend upon the actor's race, or political views), answers that ignore relevant ones, and answers that are based upon mistakes of fact or upon inconsistent or fallacious reasoning. Ethically sophisticated, wise persons are familiar with all the relevant factors, and can insightfully and logically analyze and discuss their applications in particular cases. They are also astute enough to know that, in ethics, the expectation of a single correct answer is typically a misguided one.

STUDY QUESTIONS

1. What, according to Lengbeyer, are the defects of relativism and absolutism (objectivism) that make ethical pluralism attractive? Do you think it is a workable compromise?
2. Consider a specific moral disagreement on an issue such as abortion or capital punishment and explain how pluralists might approach the questions in an objective spirit and arrive at different "right" conclusions. Evaluate various arguments for and against the idea that well-considered opposing answers could all be right.
3. Explain Lengbeyer's distinction among questions that have objective answers (e.g., in math and physics); questions that are wholly subjective (personal preferences for foods or landscapes); and complex questions that are a mix of objectivity and subjectivity—such as who were the best generals in American history, or what are the best films of all time. Do you agree with him that ethics questions fit best in this third pluralistic category?

Who's to Judge?

Louis Pojman

> Louis Pojman (1935–2005) was a professor of philosophy at the United States Military Academy at West Point. He is the author of *Religious Belief and the Will* (1986), *The Theory of Knowledge* (1993), *Ethics: Discovering Right and Wrong* (1995), and most recently, *Who Are We?: Theories of Human Nature* (2005).
>
> Louis Pojman discusses and opposes the view that moral truth is relative to a group (*conventional relativism*) or to each individual (*subjective relativism*). The conventional relativist holds that *society* determines right and wrong. For the subjective relativist *individuals* decide for themselves. And who's to say they judge wrongly? Believing that moral truth is determined by particular social groups or by individuals, the ethical relativists deny that there are any moral principles binding on all human beings.
>
> Pojman argues that neither form of relativism can be sustained, since both lead to absurdities that the relativist is anxious to avoid. Having concluded that relativism is untenable, Pojman turns again to the question "Who's to judge what's right or wrong?" to which he replies, "*We are.*"

There is one thing a professor can be absolutely certain of: almost every student entering the university believes, or says he believes, that truth is relative. If this belief is put to the test, one can count on the students' reaction: they

---

will be uncomprehending. That anyone should regard the proposition as not self-evident astonishes them, as though he were calling into question 2 + 2 = 4.... The danger they have been taught to fear from absolutism is not error but intolerance. Relativism is necessary to openness; and this is the virtue, the only virtue, which all primary education for more than fifty years has dedicated itself to inculcating. (Alan Bloom, The Closing of the American Mind*)*

In an ancient writing, the Greek historian Herodotus (485–430 B.C.) relates that the Persian King Darius once called into his presence some Greeks and asked them what he should pay them to eat the bodies of their fathers when they died. They replied that no sum of money would tempt them to do such a terrible deed; whereupon Darius sent for certain people of the Callatian tribe, who eat their fathers, and asked them in the presence of the Greeks what he should give them to burn the bodies of their fathers at their decease [as the Greeks do]. The Callatians were horrified at the thought and bid him desist in such terrible talk. So Herodotus concludes, "Culture is King o'er all."

Today we condemn ethnocentrism, the uncritical belief in the inherent superiority of one's own culture, as a variety of prejudice tantamount to racism and sexism. What is right in one culture may be wrong in another, what is good east of the river may be bad west of the same river, what is a virtue in one nation may be seen as a vice in another, so it behooves us not to judge others but to be tolerant of diversity.

This rejection of ethnocentrism in the West has contributed to a general shift in public opinion about morality, so that for a growing number of Westerners, consciousness-raising about the validity of other ways of life has led to a gradual erosion of belief in moral *objectivism*, the view that there are universal moral principles, valid for all people at all times and climes. For example, in polls taken in my ethics and introduction to philosophy classes over the past several years (in three different universities in three areas of the country) students by a two-to-one ratio affirmed a version of *moral relativism* over *moral absolutism* with hardly 3 percent seeing something in between these two polar opposites. Of course, I'm not suggesting that all of these students have a clear understanding of what relativism entails, for many of those who say that they are ethical relativists also state on the same questionnaire that "abortion except to save the mother's life is always wrong," that "capital punishment is always morally wrong," or that "suicide is never morally permissible." The apparent contradictions signal an apparent confusion on the matter.

In this essay I want to examine the central notions of ethical relativism and look at the implications that seem to follow from it. After this I want to set forth the outlines of a very modest objectivism, which holds to the objective validity of moral principles but takes into account many of the insights of relativism.

An Analysis of Relativism

Ethical relativism is the theory that there are no universally valid moral principles, but that all moral principles are valid relative to culture or individual choice. It is to be distinguished from moral skepticism, the view that there are no valid moral principles at all (or at least we cannot know whether there are any), and from all forms of moral objectivism or absolutism. The following statement by the relativist philosopher John Ladd is a good characterization of the theory.

> Ethical relativism is the doctrine that the moral rightness and wrongness of actions varies from society to society and that there are no absolute universal moral standards binding on all men at all times. Accordingly, it holds that whether or not it is right for an individual to act in a certain way depends on or is relative to the society to which he belongs. (John Ladd, *Ethical Relativism*)

If we analyze this passage, we derive the following argument:

1. What is considered morally right and wrong varies from society to society, so that there are no moral principles accepted by all societies.
2. All moral principles derive their validity from cultural acceptance.
3. Therefore, there are no universally valid moral principles, objective standards which apply to all people everywhere and at all times.

1. The first thesis, which may be called the *Diversity Thesis* and identified with *Cultural Relativism*, is simply an anthropological thesis, which registers the fact that moral rules differ from society to society. As we noted in the introduction of this essay, there is enormous variety in what may count as a moral principle in a given society. The human condition is malleable in the extreme, allowing any number of folkways or moral codes. As Ruth Benedict has written:

> The cultural pattern of any civilization makes use of a certain segment of the great arc of potential human purposes and motivations.... [A]ny culture makes use of certain selected material techniques or cultural traits. The great arc along which all the possible human behaviors are distributed is far too immense and too full of contradictions for any one culture to utilize even any considerable portion of it. Selection is the first requirement. (*Patterns of Culture*, New York, 1934, p. 219)

It may or may not be the case that there is not a single moral principle held in common by every society, but if there are any, they seem to be few, at best. Certainly, it would be very hard to derive one single "true" morality on the basis of observation of various societies' moral standards.

2. The second thesis, the *Dependency Thesis*, asserts that individual acts are right or wrong depending on the nature of the society from which they emanate. Morality does not occur in a vacuum, but what is considered morally right or wrong must be seen in a context, depending on the goals, wants, beliefs, history, and environment of the society in question. As William Graham Sumner says, "We learn the [morals] as unconsciously as we learn to walk and hear and breathe, and they never know any reason why the [morals] are what they are. The justification of them is that when we wake to consciousness of life we find them facts which already hold us in the bonds of tradition, custom, and habit."[1] Trying to see things

---

[1] *Folkways*, New York, 1906, section 80. Ruth Benedict indicates the depth of our cultural conditioning this way: "The very eyes with which we see the problem are conditioned by the long traditional habits of our own society" ("Anthropology and the Abnormal," in *The Journal of General Psychology* [1934], pp. 59–82).

from an independent, non-cultural point of view would be like taking out our eyes in order to examine their contours and qualities. We are simply culturally determined beings.

We could, of course, distinguish a weak and a strong thesis of dependency. The nonrelativist can accept a certain relativity in the way moral principles are *applied* in various cultures, depending on beliefs, history, and environment. For example, Orientals show respect by covering the head and uncovering the feet, whereas Occidentals do the opposite, but both adhere to a principle of respect for deserving people. They just apply the principle of respect differently. Drivers in Great Britain drive on the left side of the road, while those in the rest of Europe and the United States drive on the right side, but both adhere to a principle of orderly progression of traffic. The application of the rule is different but the principle in question is the same principle in both cases. But the ethical relativist must maintain a stronger thesis, one that insists that the very validity of the principles is a product of the culture and that different cultures will invent different valid principles. The ethical relativist maintains that even beyond the environmental factors and differences in beliefs, there is a fundamental disagreement between societies.

In a sense, we all live in radically different worlds. Each person has a different set of beliefs and experiences, a particular perspective that colors all of his or her perceptions. Do the farmer, the real estate dealer, and the artist, looking at the same spatio-temporal field, see the *same* field? Not likely. Their different orientations, values, and expectations govern their perceptions, so that different aspects of the field are highlighted and some features are missed. Even as our individual values arise from personal experience, so social values are grounded in the peculiar history of the community. Morality, then, is just the set of common rules, habits, and customs which have won social approval over time, so that they seem part of the nature of things, as facts. There is nothing mysterious or transcendent about these codes of behavior. They are the outcomes of our social history.

There is something conventional about *any* morality, so that every morality really depends on a level of social acceptance. Not only do various societies adhere to different moral systems, but the very same society could (and often does) change its moral views over time and place. For example, the southern United States now views slavery as immoral whereas just over one hundred years ago, it did not. We have greatly altered our views on abortion, divorce, and sexuality as well.

3. The conclusion that there are no absolute or objective moral standards binding on all people follows from the first two propositions. Cultural relativism (the Diversity Thesis) plus the Dependency Thesis yields ethical relativism in its classic form. If there are different moral principles from culture to culture and if all morality is rooted in culture, then it follows that there are no universal moral principles valid for all cultures and people at all times.

Subjective Ethical Relativism (Subjectivism)

Some people think that even this conclusion is too tame and maintain that morality is not dependent on the society but on the individual him or herself. As students sometimes maintain, "Morality is in the eye of the beholder." Ernest Hemingway wrote, "So far, about morals, I know only that what is moral is what you feel good after and what is immoral is what you feel bad after and judged by these moral standards, which I do not defend, the bullfight is very moral to me because I feel very fine while it is going on and have a feeling of life and death and mortality and immortality, and after it is over I feel very sad but very fine."[2]

This form of moral subjectivism has the sorry consequence that it makes morality a useless concept, for, on its premises, little or no interpersonal criticism or judgment is logically possible. Hemingway may feel good about killing bulls in a bull fight, while Albert Schweitzer or Mother Teresa may feel the opposite. No argument about the matter is possible. The only basis for judging Hemingway or anyone else wrong would be if he failed to live up to his own principles, but, of course, one of Hemingway's principles could be that hypocrisy is morally permissible (he feels good about it), so that it would be impossible for him to do wrong. For Hemingway hypocrisy and non-hypocrisy are both morally permissible. On the basis of Subjectivism it could very easily turn out that Adolf Hitler is as moral as Gandhi, so long as each believes he is living by his chosen principles. Notions of moral good and bad, right or wrong, cease to have interpersonal evaluative meaning.

In the opening days of my philosophy classes, I often find students vehemently defending subjective relativism. I then give them their first test of the reading material—which is really a test of their relativism. The next class period I return all the tests, marked with the grade "F" even though my comments show that most of them are of very high quality. When the students explode with outrage (some of them have never before seen this letter on their papers) at this "injustice," I explain that I too have accepted subjectivism for purposes of marking exams, in which case the principle of justice has no objective validity and their complaint is without merit.

You may not like it when your teacher gives you an F on your test paper, while she gives your neighbor an A for one exactly similar, but there is no way to criticize her for injustice, since justice is not one of her elected principles.

Absurd consequences follow from Subjective Ethical Relativism. If it is correct, then morality reduces to aesthetic tastes over which there can be no argument nor interpersonal judgment. Although many students say that they hold this position, there seems to be a conflict between it and other of their moral views (e.g., that Hitler is really morally bad or capital punishment is always wrong). There seems to be a contradiction between Subjectivism and the very concept of morality, which it is supposed to characterize, for morality has to do with "proper" resolution of interpersonal conflict and the amelioration of the human predicament. Whatever else it does, it has a minimal aim of preventing a state of chaos where life is "solitary, poor, nasty, brutish, and short." But if so, Subjectivism is no help at all in doing this, for it doesn't rest on social *agreement* of principle (as the conventionalist maintains) or on an objectively independent set of norms that bind all people for the common good.

Subjectivism treats individuals as billiard balls on a societal pool table where they meet only in radical collisions, each aiming for its own goal and striving to do the other fellow in before he does you. This atomistic view of personality is belied by the fact that we develop in families and mutually dependent communities, in which we share a common language, common institutions, and habits, and that

---

[2] Ernest Hemingway, *Death in the Afternoon* (Scribner's, 1932), p. 4.

we often feel each other's joys and sorrows. As John Donne said, "No man is an island, entire of itself; every man is a piece of the continent."

Radical individualistic relativism seems incoherent. If so, it follows that the only plausible view of ethical relativism must be one that grounds morality in the group or culture. This form of relativism is called "conventionalism," and to it we now turn.

Conventional Ethical Relativism (Conventionalism)

Conventional Ethical Relativism, the view that there are no objective moral principles but that all valid moral principles are justified by virtue of their cultural acceptance, recognizes the social nature of morality. That is precisely its power and virtue. It does not seem subject to the same absurd consequences which plague Subjectivism. Recognizing the importance of our social environment in generating customs and beliefs, many people suppose that ethical relativism is the correct ethical theory. Furthermore, they are drawn to it for its liberal philosophical stance. It seems to be an enlightened response to the sin of ethnocentricity, and it seems to entail or strongly imply an attitude of tolerance towards other cultures. As Benedict says, in recognizing ethical relativity "we shall arrive at a more realistic social faith, accepting as grounds of hope and as new bases for tolerance the coexisting and equally valid patterns of life which mankind has created for itself from the raw materials of existence."[3] The most famous of those holding this position is the anthropologist Melville Herskovits, who argues even more explicitly than Benedict that ethical relativism entails intercultural tolerance:

1. If Morality is relative to its culture, then there is no independent basis for criticizing the morality of any other culture but one's own.
2. If there is no independent way of criticizing any other culture, we ought to be *tolerant* of the moralities of other cultures.
3. Morality is relative to its culture.

Therefore

4. we ought to be tolerant of the moralities of other cultures.[4]

Tolerance is certainly a virtue, but is this a good argument for it? I think not. If morality simply is relative to each culture then if the culture does not have a principle of tolerance, its members have no obligation to be tolerant. Herskovits seems to be treating the *principle of tolerance* as the one exception to his relativism. He seems to be treating it as an absolute moral principle. But from a relativistic point of view there is no more reason to be tolerant than to be intolerant, and neither stance is objectively morally better than the other.

Not only do relativists fail to offer a basis for criticizing those who are intolerant, but they cannot rationally criticize anyone who espouses what they might regard as a heinous principle. If, as seems to be the case, valid criticism supposes an objective or

---

[3] *Patterns of Culture* (New American Library, 1934), p. 257.
[4] Melville Herskovits, *Cultural Relativism* (Random House, 1972).

impartial standard, relativists cannot morally criticize anyone outside their own culture. Adolf Hitler's genocidal actions, so long as they are culturally accepted, are as morally legitimate as Mother Teresa's works of mercy. If Conventional Relativism is accepted, racism, genocide of unpopular minorities, oppression of the poor, slavery, and even the advocacy of war for its own sake are as equally moral as their opposites. And if a subculture decided that starting a nuclear war was somehow morally acceptable, we could not morally criticize these people.

Any actual morality, whatever its content, is as valid as every other, and more valid than ideal moralities—since the latter aren't adhered to by any culture.

There are other disturbing consequences of ethical relativism. It seems to entail that reformers are always (morally) wrong since they go against the tide of cultural standards. William Wilberforce was wrong in the eighteenth century to oppose slavery; the British were immoral in opposing suttee in India (the burning of widows, which is now illegal in India). The Early Christians were wrong in refusing to serve in the Roman army or bow down to Caesar, since the majority in the Roman Empire believed that these two acts were moral duties. In fact, Jesus himself was immoral in breaking the law of his day by healing on the Sabbath day and by advocating the principles of the Sermon on the Mount, since it is clear that few in his time (or in ours) accepted them.

Yet we normally feel just the opposite, that the reformer is the courageous innovator who is right, who has the truth, against the mindless majority. Sometimes the individual must stand alone with the truth, risking social censure and persecution. As Dr. Stockman says in Ibsen's *Enemy of the People*, after he loses the battle to declare his town's profitable polluted tourist spa unsanitary, "The most dangerous enemy of the truth and freedom among us—is the compact majority. Yes, the damned, compact, and liberal majority. The majority has *might*—unfortunately—but *right* it is not. Right are I and a few others." Yet if relativism is correct, the opposite is necessarily the case. Truth is with the crowd and error with the individual....

There is an even more basic problem with the notion that morality is dependent on cultural acceptance for its validity. The problem is that the notion of a culture or society is notoriously difficult to define. This is especially so in a pluralistic society like our own where the notion seems to be vague with unclear boundary lines. One person may belong to several societies (subcultures) with different value emphases and arrangements of principles. A person may belong to the nation as a single society with certain values of patriotism, honor, courage, laws (including some which are controversial but have majority acceptance, such as the law on abortion). But he or she may also belong to a church which opposes some of the laws of the State. He may also be an integral member of a socially mixed community where different principles hold sway, and he may belong to clubs and a family where still other rules are adhered to. Relativism would seem to tell us that where he is a member of societies with conflicting moralities he must be judged both wrong and not-wrong whatever he does. For example, if Mary is a U.S. citizen and a member of the Roman Catholic Church, she is wrong (qua Catholic) if she chooses to have an abortion and not-wrong (qua citizen of the U.S.A.) if she acts against the teaching of the Church on abortion. As a member of a racist university fraternity, KKK, John has no obligation to treat his fellow Black student as an equal, but as a member of the University community itself (where the principle of equal rights is accepted) he does have the obligation; but as a member of the surrounding community (which may reject the principle of equal rights) he again has no such obligation; but then again as a member of the nation at large (which accepts the principle) he is obligated to treat his fellow with respect. What is the morally right thing for John to do? The question no longer makes much sense in this moral Babel. It has lost its action-guiding function.

Perhaps the relativist would adhere to a principle which says that in such cases the individual may choose which group to belong to as primary. If Mary chooses to have an abortion, she is choosing to belong to the general society relative to that principle. And John must likewise choose between groups. The trouble with this option is that it seems to lead back to counter-intuitive results. If Gangland Gus of Murder, Incorporated, feels like killing Bank President Ortcutt and wants to feel good about it, he identifies with the Murder, Incorporated society rather than the general public morality. Does this justify the killing? In fact, couldn't one justify anything simply by forming a small subculture that approved of it? Charles Manson would be morally pure in killing innocents simply by virtue of forming a little coterie. How large must the group be in order to be a legitimate sub-culture or society? Does it need ten or fifteen people? How about just three? Come to think about it, why can't my burglary partner and I found our own society with a morality of its own? Of course, if my partner dies, I could still claim that I was acting from an originally social set of norms. But why can't I dispense with the inter-personal agreements altogether and invent my own morality—since morality, on this view, is only an invention anyway? Conventionalist Relativism seems to reduce to Subjectivism. And Subjectivism leads, as we have seen, to the demise of morality altogether.

However, while we may fear the demise of morality, as we have known it, this in itself may not be a good reason for rejecting relativism; that is, for judging it false. Alas, truth may not always be edifying. But the consequences of this position are sufficiently alarming to prompt us to look carefully for some weakness in the relativist's argument. So let us examine the premises and conclusion listed at the beginning of this essay as the three theses of relativism.

1. *The Diversity Thesis*   What is considered morally right and wrong varies from society to society, so that there are no moral principles accepted by all societies.
2. *The Dependency Thesis*   All moral principles derive their validity from cultural acceptance.
3. *Ethical Relativism*   Therefore, there are no universally valid moral principles, objective standards which apply to all people everywhere and at all times.

Does any one of these seem problematic? Let us consider the first thesis, the Diversity Thesis, which we have also called Cultural Relativism. Perhaps there is not as much diversity as anthropologists like Sumner and Benedict suppose. One can also see great similarities between the moral codes of various cultures. E. O. Wilson has identified over a score of common features, and before him Clyde Kluckhohn has noted some significant common ground.

> Every culture has a concept of murder, distinguishing this from execution, killing in war, and other "justifiable homicides." The notions of incest and other regulations upon sexual behavior, the prohibitions upon untruth under defined circumstances, of restitution and reciprocity, of mutual obligations between parents and children—these

and many other moral concepts are altogether universal. ("Ethical Relativity: Sic et Non," *Journal of Philosophy*, LII, 1955)

And Colin Turnbull, whose description of the sadistic, semi-displaced Ik in Northern Uganda, was seen as evidence of a people without principles of kindness and cooperation, has produced evidence that underneath the surface of this dying society, there is a deeper moral code from a time when the tribe flourished, which occasionally surfaces and shows its nobler face.

On the other hand, there is enormous cultural diversity and many societies have radically different moral codes. Cultural Relativism seems to be a fact, but, even if it is, it does not by itself establish the truth of Ethical Relativism. Cultural diversity in itself is neutral between theories. For the objectivist could concede complete cultural relativism, but still defend a form of universalism; for he or she could argue that some cultures simply lack correct moral principles.

On the other hand, a denial of complete Cultural Relativism (i.e., an admission of some universal principles) does not disprove Ethical Relativism. For even if we did find one or more universal principles, this would not prove that they had any objective status. We could still *imagine* a culture that was an exception to the rule and be unable to criticize it. So the first premise doesn't by itself imply Ethical Relativism and its denial doesn't disprove Ethical Relativism.

We turn to the crucial second thesis, the Dependency Thesis. Morality does not occur in a vacuum, but what is considered morally right or wrong must be seen in a context, depending on the goals, wants, beliefs, history, and environment of the society in question. We distinguished a weak and a strong thesis of dependency. The weak thesis says that the application of principles depends on the particular cultural predicament, whereas the strong thesis affirms that the principles themselves depend on that predicament. The nonrelativist can accept a certain relativity in the way moral principles are *applied* in various cultures, depending on beliefs, history, and environment. For example, a raw environment with scarce natural resources may justify the Eskimos' brand of euthanasia to the objectivist, who in another environment would consistently reject that practice. The members of a tribe in the Sudan throw their deformed children into the river because of their belief that such infants *belong* to the hippopotamus, the god of the river. We believe that they have a false belief about this, but the point is that the same principles of respect for property and respect for human life are operative in these contrary practices. They differ with us only in belief, not in substantive moral principle. This is an illustration of how nonmoral beliefs (e.g., deformed children belong to the hippopotamus) when applied to common moral principles (e.g., give to each his due) generate different actions in different cultures. In our own culture the difference in the nonmoral belief about the status of a fetus generates opposite moral prescriptions. So the fact that moral principles are weakly dependent doesn't show that Ethical Relativism is valid. In spite of this weak dependency on non-moral factors, there could still be a set of general moral norms applicable to all cultures and even recognized in most, which are disregarded at a culture's own expense.

What the relativist needs is a strong thesis of dependency, that somehow all principles are essentially cultural inventions. But why should we choose to view morality this way? Is there anything to recommend the strong thesis over the weak thesis of dependency? The relativist may argue that in fact we don't have an obvious impartial standard from which to judge. "Who's to say which culture is right and which is wrong?" But this seems to be dubious. We can reason and perform thought experiments in order to make a case for one system over another. We may not be able to *know* with certainty that our moral beliefs are closer to the truth than those of another culture or those of others within our own culture, but we may be *justified* in believing that they are. If we can be closer to the truth regarding factual or scientific matters, why can't we be closer to the truth on moral matters? Why can't a culture simply be confused or wrong about its moral perceptions? Why can't we say that the society like the Ik which sees nothing wrong with enjoying watching its own children fall into fires is less moral in that regard than the culture that cherishes children and grants them protection and equal rights? To take such a stand is not to commit the fallacy of ethnocentricism, for we are seeking to derive principles through critical reason, not simply uncritical acceptance of one's own mores....

In conclusion I have argued (1) that Cultural Relativism (the fact that there are cultural differences regarding moral principles) does not entail Ethical Relativism (the thesis that there are no objectively valid universal moral principles); (2) that the Dependency Thesis (that morality derives its legitimacy from individual cultural acceptance) is mistaken; and (3) that there are universal moral principles based on a common human nature and a need to solve conflicts of interest and flourish.

So, returning to the question asked at the beginning of this essay, "Who's to judge what's right or wrong?" the answer is: *We are*. We are to do so on the basis of the best reasoning we can bring forth and with sympathy and understanding.

STUDY QUESTIONS

1. Discuss Pojman's distinction between cultural relativism and ethical relativism. Why is one a mere matter of describing society and the other an ethical theory? Is Pojman's use of the term "cultural relativism" the same as Carolyn Fluehr-Lobban's? Or does she mean by cultural relativism what Pojman means by ethical relativism? Explain.

2. Discuss the two varieties of ethical relativism: subjective and conventional. To which kind of relativism did Ernest Hemingway appeal when he justified the practice of bullfighting? Show how one might use conventional ethical relativism to justify bullfighting.

3. What argument does Pojman use against subjectivism? Did the arguments convince you? Why or why not?

4. What are his arguments against conventional relativism? Are they strong? Convincing? Explain.

5. Pojman makes much of the fact that we do not normally belong to single, well-defined communities. How does this adversely affect the ethical relativist belief that the community determines what is good and right?

6. What does Pojman mean by the dependency thesis, and why does he conclude that it is mistaken?

7. Pojman says that in the final analysis it is we who are to judge. Since so many other communities have other views and judgments, how can we justify favoring our judgment over theirs?

The Objective Basis of Morality

Thomas Nagel

Thomas Nagel (b. 1937) is a professor of philosophy at New York University. He is the author of numerous articles and books, including *The View from Nowhere* (1986), *Mortal Questions* (1990), and *Concealment and Exposure: And Other Essays* (2002). He is coauthor of *The Myth of Ownership: Taxes and Justice* (2002).

The biblical injunction to love thy neighbor as thyself is often interpreted negatively as the injunction *not* to do unto your neighbor what you would *not* have your neighbor do unto you. Thomas Nagel argues that this principle is universally valid apart from any religious beliefs one might have. He notes that we all feel resentful when someone whom we have not provoked harms us: since he had no reason to harm us, he shouldn't have. Nagel points out that such resentment is reasonable and is the basis of a universal and objective principle that all such harm is morally wrong.

Suppose you work in a library, checking people's books as they leave, and a friend asks you to let him smuggle out a hard-to-find reference work that he wants to own.

You might hesitate to agree for various reasons. You might be afraid that he'll be caught, and that both you and he will then get into trouble. You might want the book to stay in the library so that you can consult it yourself.

But you may also think that what he proposes is wrong—that he shouldn't do it and you shouldn't help him. If you think that, what does it mean, and what, if anything, makes it true?

To say it's wrong is not just to say it's against the rules. There can be bad rules which prohibit what isn't wrong—like a law against criticizing the government. A rule can also be bad because it requires something that *is* wrong—like a law that requires racial segregation in hotels and restaurants. The ideas of wrong and right are different from the ideas of what is and is not against the rules. Otherwise they couldn't be used in the evaluation of rules as well as of actions.

If you think it would be wrong to help your friend steal the book, then you will feel uncomfortable about doing it: in some way you won't want to do it, even if you are also reluctant to refuse help to a friend. Where does the desire not to do it come from; what is its motive, the reason behind it?

There are various ways in which something can be wrong, but in this case, if you had to explain it, you'd probably say that it would be unfair to other users of the library who may be just as interested in the book as your friend is, but who consult it in the reference room, where anyone who needs it can find it. You may also feel that to let him take it would betray your employers, who are paying you precisely to keep this sort of thing from happening.

These thoughts have to do with effects on others—not necessarily effects on their feelings, since they may never find out about it, but some kind of damage nevertheless. In general, the thought that something is wrong depends on its impact not just on the person who does it but on other people. They wouldn't like it, and they'd object if they found out.

But suppose you try to explain all this to your friend, and he says, "I know the head librarian wouldn't like it if he found out, and probably some of the other users of the library would be unhappy to find the book gone, but who cares? I want the book; why should I care about them?"

The argument that it would be wrong is supposed to give him a reason not to do it. But if someone just doesn't care about other people, what reason does he have to refrain from doing any of the things usually thought to be wrong, if he can get away with it: what reason does he have not to kill, steal, lie, or hurt others? If he can get what he wants by doing such things, why shouldn't he? And if there's no reason why he shouldn't, in what sense is it wrong?

Of course most people do care about others to some extent. But if someone doesn't care, most of us wouldn't conclude that he's exempt from morality. A person who kills someone just to steal his wallet, without caring about the victim, is not automatically excused. The fact that he doesn't care doesn't make it all right: he *should* care. But *why* should he care?

There have been many attempts to answer this question. One type of answer tries to identify something else that the person already cares about, and then connect morality to it.

For example, some people believe that even if you can get away with awful crimes on this earth, and are not punished by the law or your fellow men, such acts are forbidden by God, who will punish you after death (and reward you if you didn't do wrong when you were tempted to). So even when it seems to be in your interest to do such a thing, it really isn't. Some people have even believed that if there is no God to back up moral requirements with the threat of punishment and the promise of reward, morality is an illusion: "If God does not exist, everything is permitted."

This is a rather crude version of the religious foundation for morality. A more appealing version might be that the motive for obeying God's commands is not fear but love. He loves you, and you should love Him, and should wish to obey His commands in order not to offend Him.

But however we interpret the religious motivation, there are three objections to this type of answer. First, plenty of people who don't believe in God still make judgments of right and wrong, and think no one should kill another for his wallet even if he can be sure to get away with it. Second, if God exists, and forbids what's wrong, that still isn't what *makes* it wrong. Murder is wrong in itself, and that's *why* God forbids it (if He does). God couldn't make just any old thing wrong—like putting on your left sock before your right—simply by prohibiting it. If God would punish you for doing that it would be inadvisable to do it, but it wouldn't be wrong. Third, fear of punishment and hope of reward, and even love of God, seem not to be the right motives for morality. If you think it's wrong to kill, cheat, or steal, you should want to avoid doing such things because they are bad things to do to the victims, not just because you fear the consequences for yourself, or because you don't want to offend your Creator.

This third objection also applies to other explanations of the force of morality which appeal to the interests of the person who must act. For example, it may be said that you should treat others with consideration so that they'll do the same for you. This may be sound advice, but it is valid only so far as you think what you do will affect how others treat you. It's not a reason for doing the right thing if others won't find out about it, or against doing the wrong thing if you can get away with it (like being a hit and run driver).

There is no substitute for a direct concern for other people as the basis of morality. But morality is supposed to apply to everyone: and can we assume that everyone has such a concern for others? Obviously not: some people are very selfish, and even those who are not selfish may care only about the people they know, and not about everyone. So where will we find a reason that everyone has not to hurt other people, even those they don't know?

Well, there's one general argument against hurting other people which can be given to anybody who understands English (or any other language), and which seems to show that he has *some* reason to care about others, even if in the end his selfish motives are so strong that he persists in treating other people badly anyway. It's an argument that I'm sure you've heard, and it goes like this: "How would you like it if someone did that to you?"

It's not easy to explain how this argument is supposed to work. Suppose you're about to steal someone else's umbrella as you leave a restaurant in a rainstorm, and a bystander says, "How would you like it if someone did that to you?" Why is it supposed to make you hesitate, or feel guilty?

Obviously the direct answer to the question is supposed to be, "I wouldn't like it at all!" But what's the next step? Suppose you were to say, "I wouldn't like it if someone did that to me. But luckily no one *is* doing it to me. I'm doing it to someone else, and I don't mind that at all!"

This answer misses the point of the question. When you are asked how you would like it if someone did that to you, you are supposed to think about all the feelings you would have if someone stole your umbrella. And that includes more than just "not liking it"—as you wouldn't "like it" if you stubbed your toe on a rock. If someone stole your umbrella you'd *resent* it. You'd have feelings about the umbrella thief, not just about the loss of the umbrella. You'd think, "Where does he get off, taking my umbrella that I bought with my hard-earned money and that I had the foresight to bring after reading the weather report? Why didn't he bring his own umbrella?" and so forth.

When our own interests are threatened by the inconsiderate behavior of others, most of us find it easy to appreciate that those others have a reason to be more considerate. When you are hurt, you probably feel that other people should care about it: you don't think it's no concern of theirs, and that they have no reason to avoid hurting you. That is the feeling that the "How would you like it?" argument is supposed to arouse.

Because if you admit that you would *resent* it if someone else did to you what you are now doing to him, you are admitting that you think he would have a reason not to do it to you. And if you admit that, you have to consider what that reason is. It couldn't be just that it's *you* that he's hurting, of all the people in the world. There's no special reason for him not to steal *your* umbrella, as opposed to anyone else's. There's nothing so special about you. Whatever the reason is, it's a reason he would have against hurting anyone else in the same way. And it's a reason anyone else would have too, in a similar situation, against hurting you or anyone else.

But if it's a reason anyone would have not to hurt anyone else in this way, then it's a reason *you* have not to hurt someone else in this way (since *anyone* means *everyone*). Therefore it's a reason not to steal the other person's umbrella now.

This is a matter of simple consistency. Once you admit that another person would have a reason not to harm you in similar circumstances, and once you admit that the reason he would have is very general and doesn't apply only to you, or to him, then to be consistent you have to admit that the same reason applies to you now. You shouldn't steal the umbrella, and you ought to feel guilty if you do.

Someone could escape from this argument if, when he was asked, "How would you like it if someone did that to you?" he answered, "I wouldn't resent it at all. I wouldn't *like* it if someone stole my umbrella in a rainstorm, but I wouldn't think there was any reason for him to consider my feelings about it." But how many people could honestly give that answer? I think most people, unless they're crazy, would think that their own interests and harms matter, not only to themselves, but in a way that gives other people a reason to care about them too. We all think that when we suffer it is not just bad *for us*, but *bad, period*.

The basis of morality is a belief that good and harm to particular people (or animals) is good or bad not just from their point of view, but from a more general point of view, which every thinking person can understand. That means that each person has a reason to consider not only his own interests but the interests of others in deciding what to do. And it isn't enough if he is considerate only of some others—his family and friends, those he specially cares about. Of course he will care more about certain people, and also about himself. But he has some reason to consider the effect of what he does on the good or harm of everyone. If he's like most of us, that is what he thinks others should do with regard to him, even if they aren't friends of his.

STUDY QUESTIONS

1. What does Nagel mean by "the objective basis of morality"? How does he argue for it? In your opinion does Nagel succeed in demonstrating that morality is "objective"? Explain.
2. How, according to Nagel, may someone who "has no direct concern for the feelings of others" nevertheless be forced to acknowledge that it is wrong to harm them?
3. Both Nagel and Kant (page 230) argue for the universality and objectivity of ethical principles. How do they differ? Whom do you favor? Explain.

The Deep Beauty of the Golden Rule

R. M. MacIver

R. M. MacIver (1882–1970) was a professor of sociology and political science at Columbia University. His works include *Academic Freedom in Our Time* (1967) and *Community: A Sociological Study* (1970).

R. M. MacIver finds in the Golden Rule—"Do to others as you would have others do to you"—the way out of the relativist impasse. It is a sensitive rule based on reason and common sense. It does not oppose itself to the norms of any given society because it does not tell anyone *what* to do. However, it does provide a policy to be followed that puts one on the alert: "If you would disapprove that another should treat you as you treat him, the situations being reversed is not that a sign that, by the standard of your own values, you are mistreating him?" This procedural rule is universal precisely because it is compatible with the values of both parties, provided both respect the other's rights and liberties.

The subject that learned men call ethics is a wasteland on the philosophical map. Thousands of books have been written on this matter, learned books and popular books, books that argue and books that exhort. Most of them are empty and nearly all are vain. Some claim that pleasure is *the* good; some prefer the elusive and more enticing name of happiness; others reject such principles and speak of equally elusive goals such as self-fulfillment. Others claim that *the* good is to be found in looking away from the self in devotion to the whole—which whole? in the service of God—whose God?—even in the service of the State—who prescribes the service? Here indeed, if anywhere, after listening to the many words of many apostles, one goes out by the same door as one went in.

The reason is simple. You say: "This is the way you should behave." But I say: "No, that is not the way." You say: "This is right." But I say: "No, that is wrong, and this is right." You appeal to experience. I appeal to experience against you. You appeal to authority: it is not mine. What is left? If you are strong, you can punish me for behaving my way. But does that prove anything except that you are stronger than I? Does it prove the absurd dogma that might makes right? Is the slavemaster right because he owns the whip, or Torquemada because he can send his heretics to the flames?

THE DEEP BEAUTY OF THE GOLDEN RULE By Robert M. MacIver from *Moral Principles of Action* (*Science Culture Series*, Vol. 3) by Ruth Nanda Anshen, editor. Copyright 1952 by Harper & Row Publishers, Inc. Copyright renewed © 1980 by Ruth Nanda Anshen. Reprinted by permission of HarperCollins Publishers, Inc.

From this impasse no system of ethical rules has been able to deliver itself. How can ethics lay down final principles of behavior that are not your values against mine, your group's values against my group's?...

Does all this mean that a universal ethical principle, applicable alike to me and you, even where our values diverge, is impossible? That there is no rule to go by, based on reason itself, in this world of irreconcilable valuations?

There is no rule that can prescribe both my values and yours or decide between them. There is one universal rule, and one only, that can be laid down, on ethical grounds—that is, apart from the creeds of particular religions and apart from the ways of the tribe that falsely and arrogantly universalize themselves.

Do to others as you would have others do to you. This is the only rule that stands by itself in the light of its own reason, the only rule that can stand by itself in the naked, warring universe, in the face of the contending values of men and groups.

What makes it so? Let us first observe that the universal herein laid down is one of procedure. It prescribes a mode of behaving, not a goal of action. On the level of goals, of *final* values, there is irreconcilable conflict. One rule prescribes humility, another pride; one prescribes abstinence, another commends the flesh-pots; and so forth through endless variations. All of us wish that *our* principle could be universal; most of us believe that it *should* be, that our *ought* ought to be all men's *ought*, but since we differ there can be on this level, no possible agreement.

When we want to make our ethical principle prevail we try to persuade others, to "convert" them. Some may freely respond, if their deeper values are near enough to ours. Others will certainly resist and some will seek to persuade us in turn—why shouldn't they? Then we can go no further except by resort to force and fraud. We can, if we are strong, dominate some and we can bribe others. We compromise our own values in doing so and we do not in the end succeed; even if we were masters of the whole world we could never succeed in making our principle universal. We could only make it falsely tyrannous.

So if we look for a principle in the name of which we can appeal to all men, one to which their reason can respond in spite of their differences, we must follow another road. When we try to make our values prevail over those cherished by others, we attack their values, their dynamic of behavior, their living will. If we go far enough we assault their very being. For the will is simply valuation in action. Now the deep beauty of the golden rule is that instead of attacking the will that is in other men, it offers their will a new dimension. "Do as you *would* have others...." As *you* would will others to do. It bids you expand your vision, see yourself in new relationships. It bids you transcend your insulation, see yourself in the place of others, see others in your place. It bids you test your values or at least your way of pursuing them. If you would disapprove that another should treat you as you treat him, the situations being reversed is not that a sign that, by the standard of your own values, you are mistreating him?

This principle obviously makes for a vastly greater harmony in the social scheme. At the same time it is the only universal of ethics that does not take sides with or contend with contending values. It contains no dogma. It bids everyone follow his own rule, as it would apply *apart* from the accident of his particular fortunes. It bids him enlarge his own rule, as it would apply whether he is up or whether he is down. It is an accident that you are up and I am down. In another situation you would be down and I would be up. That accident has nothing to do with my *final* values or with yours....

It follows that while this first principle attacks no intrinsic values, no primary attachments of men to goods that reach beyond themselves, it nevertheless purifies every attachment, every creed, of its accidents, its irrelevancies, its excesses, its false reliance on power. It saves every human value from the corruption that comes from the arrogance of detachment and exclusiveness, from the shell of the kind of absolutism that imprisons its vitality.

At this point a word of caution is in order. The golden rule does not solve for us our ethical problems but offers only a way of approach. It does not prescribe our treatment of others but only the spirit in which we should treat them. It has no simple mechanical application and often enough is hard to apply—what general principle is not? It certainly does not bid us treat others as others *want* us to treat them—that would be an absurdity. The convicted criminal wants the judge to set him free. If the judge acts in the spirit of the golden rule, within the limits of the discretion permitted him as judge, he might instead reason somewhat as follows: "How would I feel the judge ought to treat *me* were I in this man's place? What could I—the man I am and yet somehow standing where this criminal stands—properly ask the judge to do for me, to me? In this spirit I shall assess his guilt and his punishment. In this spirit I shall give full consideration to the conditions under which he acted. I shall try to understand *him*, to do what I properly can for him, while at the same time I fulfill my judicial duty in protecting society against the dangers that arise if criminals such as he go free."

"Do to others as you would have others do to you." The disease to which all values are subject is the growth of a hard insulation. "I am right: I have the truth. If you differ from me, you are a heretic, you are in error. *Therefore* while you must allow me every liberty when you are in power I need not, in truth I ought not to, show any similar consideration for you." The barb of falsehood has already begun to vitiate the cherished value. While *you* are in power I advocate the equal rights of all creeds: when *I* am in power, I reject any such claim as ridiculous. This is the position taken by various brands of totalitarianism, and the communists in particular have made it a favorite technique in the process of gaining power, clamoring for rights they will use to destroy the rights of those who grant them. Religious groups have followed the same line. Roman Catholics, Calvinists, Lutherans, Presbyterians, and others have on occasion vociferously advocated religious liberty where they were in the minority, often to curb it where in turn they became dominant.

This gross inconsistency on the part of religious groups was flagrantly displayed in earlier centuries, but examples are still not infrequent. Here is one. *La Civilita Catholicá*, a Jesuit organ published in Rome, has come out as follows:

> The Roman Catholic Church, convinced, through its divine prerogatives, of being the only true church, must demand the right to freedom for herself alone, because such a right can only be possessed by truth, never by error. As to other religions, the church will certainly never draw the sword, but she will require that by legitimate means they shall not be allowed to propagate false doctrine. Consequently, in a state where the majority of the people are Catholic, the Church will require that legal existence be

denied to error.... In some countries, Catholics will be obliged to ask full religious freedom for all, resigned at being forced to cohabitate where they alone should rightly be allowed to live.... The Church cannot blush for her own want of tolerance, as she asserts it in principle and applies it in practice.[1]

Since this statement has the merit of honesty it well illustrates the fundamental lack of rationality that lies behind all such violations of the golden rule. The argument runs: "Roman Catholics know they possess the truth; *therefore* they should not permit others to propagate error." By parity of reasoning why should not Protestants say—and indeed they have often said it—"We know we possess the truth; therefore we should not tolerate the errors of Roman Catholics." Why then should not atheists say: "We know we possess the truth; therefore we should not tolerate the errors of dogmatic religion."

No matter what we believe, we are equally convinced that *we* are right. We have to be. That is what belief means, and we must all believe something. The Roman Catholic Church is entitled to declare that all other religious groups are sunk in error. But what follows? That other groups have not the right to believe they are right? That you have the right to repress them while they have no right to repress you? That they should concede to you what you should not concede to them? Such reasoning is mere childishness. Beyond it lies the greater foolishness that truth is advanced by the forceful suppression of those who believe differently from you. Beyond that lies the pernicious distortion of meanings which claims that liberty is only "the liberty to do right"—the "liberty" for me to do what *you* think is right. This perversion of the meaning of liberty has been the delight of all totalitarians. And it might be well to reflect that it was the radical Rousseau who first introduced the doctrine that men could be "forced to be free."

How much do they have truth who think they must guard it within the fortress of their own might? How little that guarding has availed in the past! How often it has kept truth outside while superstition grew moldy within! How often has the false alliance of belief and force led to civil dissension and the futile ruin of war! But if history means nothing to those who call themselves "Christian" and still claim exclusive civil rights for their particular faith, at least they might blush before this word of one they call their Master: "All things therefore whatsoever ye would that men should do unto you, even so do ye also unto them; for this is the law and the prophets."

STUDY QUESTIONS

1. How does MacIver see in the Golden Rule an answer to relativism?
2. Look again at Thomas Nagel's essay (page 113), and compare his argument for objectivity in ethics with MacIver's arguments for the Golden Rule.
3. Why does MacIver feel that the Golden Rule has "deep beauty"?
4. Discuss the "procedural" character of the Golden Rule. Why does MacIver think that this is one of its best features? How does its being procedural help it avoid the traps of relativism?

---

[1] Quoted in the *Christian Century* (June 1948).

I Have a Dream

Martin Luther King, Jr.

Martin Luther King, Jr. (1929–1968), a Baptist minister and theologian, was a principal figure in the civil rights movement of the 1950s and 1960s. He was awarded the Nobel Peace Prize in 1964 for his leadership role in that movement. King was assassinated in 1968 in Memphis, Tennessee.

Martin Luther King's thrilling 1963 speech, delivered in Washington, D.C., between the Washington Monument and the Lincoln Memorial, is a typical example of how antirelativist, universalist assumptions are simply taken for granted by popular moralists. King feels no need to argue that basic moral principles are applicable to everyone regardless of race or social background. In dreaming of a future in which African Americans are fully free, King is confident that justice is a universal and inalienable human right. He is equally confident that the quarter million people who are listening to his speech, many of them devout believers in the universality and truth of Judeo-Christian moral principles, believe this as well.

Five score years ago, a great American, in whose symbolic shadow we stand, signed the Emancipation Proclamation. This momentous decree came as a great beacon light of hope to millions of Negro slaves who had been seared in the flames of withering injustice. It came as a joyous daybreak to end the long night of captivity.

But one hundred years later, we must face the tragic fact that the Negro is still not free. One hundred years later, the life of the Negro is still sadly crippled by the manacles of segregation and the chains of discrimination. One hundred years later, the Negro lives on a lonely island of poverty in the midst of a vast ocean of material prosperity. One hundred years later, the Negro still languishes in the corners of American society and finds himself an exile in his own land. So we have come here today to dramatize an appalling condition.

In a sense we have come to our nation's capital to cash a check. When the architects of our republic wrote the magnificent words of the Constitution and the Declaration of Independence, they were signing a promissory note to which every American was to fall heir. This note was a promise that all men would be guaranteed the unalienable rights of life, liberty, and the pursuit of happiness.

Reprinted by arrangement with The Heirs to the Estate of Martin Luther King, Jr., c/o Writers House as agent for the proprietor New York, NY.

It is obvious today that America has defaulted on this promissory note insofar as her citizens of color are concerned. Instead of honoring this sacred obligation, America has given the Negro people a bad check: a check which has come back marked "insufficient funds." But we refuse to believe that the bank of justice is bankrupt. We refuse to believe that there are insufficient funds in the great vaults of opportunity of this nation. So we have come to cash this check—a check that will give us upon demand the riches of freedom and the security of justice.

We have also come to this hallowed spot to remind America of the fierce urgency of *now*. This is no time to engage in the luxury of cooling off or to take the tranquilizing drug of gradualism. *Now* is the time to make real the promises of democracy. *Now* is the time to rise from the dark and desolate valley of segregation to the sunlit path of racial justice. *Now* is the time to open the doors of opportunity to all of God's children. *Now* is the time to lift our nation from the quicksands of racial injustice to the solid rock of brotherhood.

It would be fatal for the nation to overlook the urgency of the moment and to underestimate the determination of the Negro. This sweltering summer of the Negro's legitimate discontent will not pass until there is an invigorating autumn of freedom and equality. Nineteen sixty-three is not an end, but a beginning. Those who hope that the Negro needed to blow off steam and will now be content will have a rude awakening if the nation returns to business as usual. There will be neither rest nor tranquility in America until the Negro is granted his citizenship rights. The whirlwinds of revolt will continue to shake the foundations of our nation until the bright day of justice emerges.

But there is something that I must say to my people who stand on the warm threshold which leads into the palace of justice. In the process of gaining our rightful place we must not be guilty of wrongful deeds. Let us not seek to satisfy our thirst for freedom by drinking from the cup of bitterness and hatred. We must forever conduct our struggle on the high plane of dignity and discipline. We must not allow our creative protest to degenerate into physical violence. Again and again we must rise to the majestic heights of meeting physical force with soul force.

The marvelous new militancy which has engulfed the Negro community must not lead us to a distrust of all white people, for many of our white brothers, as evidenced by their presence here today, have come to realize that their freedom is inextricably bound to our freedom. We cannot walk alone.

And as we walk, we must make the pledge that we shall march ahead. We cannot turn back. There are those who are asking the devotees of civil rights, "When will you be satisfied?"

We can never be satisfied as long as the Negro is the victim of the unspeakable horrors of police brutality.

We can never be satisfied as long as our bodies, heavy with fatigue of travel, cannot gain lodging in the motels of the highways and the cities.

We cannot be satisfied as long as the Negro's basic mobility is from a smaller ghetto to a larger one.

We can never be satisfied as long as a Negro in Mississippi cannot vote and a Negro in New York believes he has nothing for which to vote.

No, no, we are not satisfied, and we will not be satisfied until justice rolls down like waters and righteousness like a mighty stream.

I am not unmindful that some of you have come here out of great trials and tribulations. Some of you have come fresh from narrow jail cells. Some of you have come from areas where your quest for freedom left you battered by the storms of persecution and staggered by the winds of police brutality. You have been the veterans of creative suffering. Continue to work with the faith that unearned suffering is redemptive.

Go back to Mississippi, go back to Alabama, go back to South Carolina, go back to Georgia, go back to Louisiana, go back to the slums and ghettos of our Northern cities, knowing that somehow this situation can and will be changed. Let us not wallow in the valley of despair.

I say to you today, my friends, that in spite of the difficulties and frustrations of the moment I still have a dream. It is a dream deeply rooted in the American dream.

I have a dream that one day this nation will rise up and live out the true meaning of its creed: "We hold these truths to be self-evident; that all men are created equal."

I have a dream that one day on the red hills of Georgia the sons of former slaves and the sons of former slaveowners will be able to sit down together at the table of brotherhood.

I have a dream that one day even the state of Mississippi, a desert state sweltering with the heat of injustice and oppression, will be transformed into an oasis of freedom and justice.

I have a dream that my four little children will one day live in a nation where they will not be judged by the color of their skin but by the content of their character.

I have a dream today.

I have a dream that one day the state of Alabama, whose governor's lips are presently dripping with the words of interposition and nullification, will be transformed into a situation where little black boys and black girls will be able to join hands with little white boys and girls and walk together as sisters and brothers.

I have a dream today.

I have a dream that one day every valley shall be exalted, every hill and mountain shall be made low, the rough places will be made plain, and the crooked places will be made straight, and the glory of the Lord shall be revealed, and all flesh shall see it together.

This is our hope. This is the faith with which I return to the South. With this faith we will be able to hew out of the mountain of despair a stone of hope. With this faith we will be able to transform the jangling discords of our nation into a beautiful symphony of brotherhood.

With this faith we will be able to work together, to pray together, to struggle together, to go to jail together, to stand up for freedom together, knowing that we will be free one day.

This will be the day when all of God's children will be able to sing with new meaning, "My country 'tis of thee, sweet land of liberty, of thee I sing. Land where my father died, land of the Pilgrims' pride, from every mountainside, let freedom ring."

And if America is to be a great nation, this must become true. So let freedom ring from the prodigious hilltops of New Hampshire. Let freedom ring from the mighty mountains of New York. Let freedom ring from the heightening Alleghenies of Pennsylvania!

Let freedom ring from the snowcapped Rockies of Colorado! Let freedom ring from the curvaceous peaks of California. But not only that: let freedom ring from Stone Mountain of Georgia! Let freedom ring from Lookout Mountain of Tennessee!

Let freedom ring from every hill and molehill of Mississippi. From every mountainside, let freedom ring.

When we let freedom ring, when we let it ring from every village and every hamlet, from every state and every city, we will be able to speed up that day when all of God's children, black men and white men, Jews and Gentiles, Protestants and Catholics, will be able to join hands and sing in the words of the old Negro spiritual, "Free at last! Free at last! Thank God Almighty, we are free at last!"

STUDY QUESTIONS

1. What is the moral basis underlying King's appeal for changes that will end discriminatory practices against African Americans? Could a relativist have been equally eloquent? Equally persuasive? Why or why not?
2. It is clear that King believes in some universal human rights. What are these rights? Do you agree we have such rights? Why or why not?
3. King's address had an enormous impact throughout the United States. Explain why. Can you think of other writings or speeches that have something like the moral force of this speech? If so, name them and explain your answer.

The United Nations Charter: The Universal Declaration of Human Rights

The Universal Declaration of Human Rights was adopted by the United Nations General Assembly on December 10, 1948. The Declaration was characterized as "a common standard of achievement for all peoples and all nations." The first twenty-one articles of the Declaration of Human Rights are similar to the first ten amendments of the U.S. Constitution, the Bill of Rights. Articles 22 through 27, which assert rights to economic and social benefits, reflect specific articles in the former Soviet constitution.

The Declaration was condemned by the American Association of Anthropology as "a statement of rights conceived only in terms of the values prevalent in Western Europe and America." Calling it "ethnocentric," the association suggested that the Declaration betrayed a lack of respect for cultural differences.[1]

The articles of the Universal Declaration of Human Rights declare that all human beings have the right to a dignified and secure existence. They prohibit torture and slavery. They enjoin equality before the law and prohibit arbitrary arrest in any country. They prohibit limitations of movement within national borders.

The articles assert the right of political asylum; the right to citizenship in some country; the right of adults to marry and have families; the right to one's property; the right to freedom of thought, conscience, and religion; the right to social security; the right to belong to unions; the right to a decent standard of living and access to health; the right to an education. The articles assert the principle of freedom of assembly—the freedom to take part in the government of one's country.

Finally, the articles assure that no state may engage in any activity aimed at the restriction of any of the rights and liberties set forth in the declaration.

It should be noted that the members of the United Nations General Assembly, in thus proclaiming universal standards of social ethics for all societies, are not ethical relativists.

Preamble

Whereas recognition of the inherent dignity and of the equal and inalienable rights of all members of the human family is the foundation of freedom, justice and peace in the world,

Whereas disregard and contempt for human rights have resulted in barbarous acts which have outraged the conscience of mankind, and the advent of a world in which human beings shall enjoy freedom of speech and belief and freedom from fear and want has been proclaimed as the highest aspiration of the common people,

Whereas it is essential, if man is not to be compelled to have recourse, as a last resort, to rebellion against tyranny and oppression, that human rights should be protected by the rule of law,

Whereas it is essential to promote the development of friendly relations between nations,

Whereas the people of the United Nations have in the Charter reaffirmed their faith in fundamental human rights, in the dignity and worth of the human person and in the equal rights of men and women and have determined to promote social progress and better standards of life in larger freedom,

Whereas Member States have pledged themselves to achieve, in cooperation with the United Nations, the promotion of universal respect for and observance of human rights and fundamental freedoms,

---

[1] "Statement on Human Rights," *American Anthropologist* 49 (1947): 539–543.

Whereas a common understanding of these rights and freedoms is of the greatest importance for the full realization of this pledge,

Now, Therefore,

The General Assembly Proclaims

This Universal Declaration of Human Rights as a common standard of achievement for all peoples and all nations, to the end that every individual and every organ of society, keeping this Declaration constantly in mind, shall strive by teaching and education to promote respect for these rights and freedoms and by progressive measures, national and international, to secure their universal and effective recognition and observance, both among the peoples of Member States themselves and among the peoples of territories under their jurisdiction.

Article 1 All human beings are born free and equal in dignity and rights. They are endowed with reason and conscience and should act towards one another in a spirit of brotherhood.

Article 2 Everyone is entitled to all the rights and freedoms set forth in this Declaration, without distinction of any kind, such as race, colour, sex, language, religion, political or other opinion, national or social origin, property, birth or other status.

Furthermore, no distinction shall be made on the basis of the political, jurisdictional or international status of the country or territory to which a person belongs, whether it be independent, trust, non-self-governing or under any other limitation of sovereignty.

Article 3 Everyone has the right to life, liberty and security of person.

Article 4 No one shall be held in slavery or servitude; slavery and the slave trade shall be prohibited in all their forms.

Article 5 No one shall be subjected to torture or to cruel, inhuman or degrading treatment or punishment.

Article 6 Everyone has the right to recognition everywhere as a person before the law.

Article 7 All are equal before the law and are entitled without any discrimination to equal protection of the law. All are entitled to equal protection against any discrimination in violation of this Declaration and against any incitement to such discrimination.

Article 8 Everyone has the right to an effective remedy by the competent national tribunals for acts violating the fundamental rights granted him by the constitution or by law.

Article 9 No one shall be subjected to arbitrary arrest, detention or exile.

Article 10 Everyone is entitled in full equality to a fair and public hearing by an independent and impartial tribunal, in the determination of his rights and obligations and of any criminal charge against him.

Article 11 (1) Everyone charged with a penal offence has the right to be presumed innocent until proved guilty according to law in a public trial at which he has had all the guarantees necessary for his defence.

(2) No one shall be held guilty of any penal offence on account of any act or omission which did not constitute a penal offence, under national or international law, at the time when it was committed. Nor shall a heavier penalty be imposed than the one that was applicable at the time the penal offence was committed.

Article 12 No one shall be subjected to arbitrary interference with his privacy, family, home or correspondence, nor to attacks upon his honour and reputation. Everyone has the right to the protection of the law against such interference or attacks.

Article 13 (1) Everyone has the right to freedom of movement and residence within the borders of each state.

(2) Everyone has the right to leave any country, including his own, and to return to his country.

Article 14 (1) Everyone has the right to seek and to enjoy in other countries asylum from persecution.

(2) This right may not be invoked in the case of prosecutions genuinely arising from non-political crimes or from acts contrary to the purposes and principles of the United Nations.

Article 15 (1) Everyone has the right to a nationality.

(2) No one shall be arbitrarily deprived of his nationality nor denied the right to change his nationality.

Article 16 (1) Men and women of full age, without any limitation due to race, nationality or religion, have the right to marry and to found a family. They are entitled to equal rights as to marriage, during marriage and at its dissolution.

(2) Marriage shall be entered into only with the free and full consent of the intending spouses.

(3) The family is the natural and fundamental group unit of society and is entitled to protection by society and the State.

Article 17 (1) Everyone has the right to own property alone as well as in association with others.

(2) No one shall be arbitrarily deprived of his property.

Article 18 Everyone has the right to freedom of thought, conscience and religion; this right includes freedom to change his religion or belief, and freedom, either alone or in community with others and in public or private, to manifest his religion or belief in teaching, practice, worship and observance.

Article 19 Everyone has the right to freedom of opinion and expression; this right includes freedom to hold opinions without interference and to seek, receive and impart information and ideas through any media and regardless of frontiers.

Article 20 (1) Everyone has the right to freedom of peaceful assembly and association.

(2) No one may be compelled to belong to an association.

Article 21 (1) Everyone has the right to take part in the government of his country, directly or through freely chosen representatives.

(2) Everyone has the right of equal access to public service in his country.

(3) The will of the people shall be the basis of the authority of government; this will shall be expressed in periodic and genuine elections which shall be by universal and equal suffrage and shall be held by secret vote or by equivalent free voting procedures.

Article 22 Everyone, as a member of society, has the right to social security and is entitled to realization, through national effort and international cooperation and in accordance with the organization and resources of each State, of the economic, social and cultural rights indispensable for his dignity and the free development of his personality.

Article 23 (1) Everyone has the right to work, to free choice of employment, to just and favourable conditions of work and to protection against unemployment.

(2) Everyone, without any discrimination, has the right to equal pay for equal work.

(3) Everyone who works has the right to just and favourable remuneration ensuring for himself and his family an existence worthy of human dignity, and supplemented, if necessary, by other means of social protection.

(4) Everyone has the right to form and to join trade unions for the protection of his interests.

Article 24 Everyone has the right to rest and leisure, including reasonable limitation of working hours and periodic holidays with pay.

Article 25 (1) Everyone has the right to a standard of living adequate for the health and well-being of himself and of his family, including food, clothing, housing and medical care and necessary social services, and the right to security in the event of unemployment, sickness, disability, widowhood, old age or other lack of livelihood in circumstances beyond his control.

(2) Motherhood and childhood are entitled to special care and assistance. All children, whether born in or out of wedlock, shall enjoy the same social protection.

Article 26 (1) Everyone has the right to education. Education shall be free, at least in the elementary and fundamental stages. Elementary education shall be compulsory. Technical and professional education shall be made generally available and higher education shall be equally accessible to all on the basis of merit.

(2) Education shall be directed to the full development of the human personality and to the strengthening of respect for human rights and fundamental freedoms. It shall promote understanding, tolerance and friendship among all nations, racial or religious groups, and shall further the activities of the United Nations for the maintenance of peace.

(3) Parents have a prior right to choose the kind of education that shall be given to their children.

Article 27 (1) Everyone has the right freely to participate in the cultural life of the community, to enjoy the arts and to share in scientific advancement and its benefits.

(2) Everyone has the right to the protection of the moral and material interests resulting from any scientific, literary or artistic production of which he is the author.

Article 28 Everyone is entitled to a social and international order in which the rights and freedoms set forth in this Declaration can be fully realized.

Article 29 (1) Everyone has duties to the community in which alone the free and full development of his personality is possible.

(2) In the exercise of his rights and freedoms, everyone shall be subject only to such limitations as are determined by law solely for the purpose of securing due recognition and respect for the rights and freedoms of others and of meeting the just requirements of morality, public order and the general welfare in a democratic society.

(3) These rights and freedoms may in no case be exercised contrary to the purposes and principles of the United Nations.

Article 30 Nothing in this Declaration may be interpreted as implying for any State, group or person any right to engage in any activity or to perform any act aimed at the destruction of any of the rights and freedoms set forth herein.

Study Questions

1. The Declaration contains thirty articles. Discuss three that you consider very important, and defend their fundamental character.
2. Obviously the Declaration has not been enforced. What then is its value, if any? Discuss.
3. Do you agree that all human beings have the rights and liberties outlined in the articles? How would you argue in their defense if someone challenged some or all of the articles?
4. The first twenty articles assert *negative* rights of freedom from governmental interference. Later articles (21–28) assert positive rights that require a government to ensure such basic benefits as work, housing, and medical care. Many conservatives object to the inclusion of positive rights, saying that it endorses socialism. On the other hand, many socialists maintain that exclusive rights of liberty merely give everyone the right to starve. Discuss this issue.
5. The American Anthropological Association objected to the Universal Declaration of Human Rights as being "ethnocentric." Discuss. Do you agree with the association that the lack of moral consensus in the world "validates" ethical relativism? Explain.

CHAPTER 3 | MORALITY AND SELF-INTEREST

Is there a reason to be moral apart from fear of punishment? Plato raised this question when he wrote about the shepherd Gyges and the ring that rendered him invisible and so able to be immoral with impunity. The whole of Plato's *Republic* is designed to show that morality is intrinsically worthy of being practiced and not merely because "crime does not pay."

In Thomas Hobbes's view, morality is a compromise. Unbridled self-interest is dangerous to us all, so, to preserve life and property, we consent to be governed by moral laws. According to Ayn Rand, in the conflict between individual selfishness and popular morality that demands self-sacrifice, the moral thing to do is to be rationally self-interested, defying social pressures to be altruistic. Harry Browne calls unselfishness a "trap."

Ethical egoism, the moral doctrine that we should strive to maximize individual self-interest, has been under attack ever since Plato gave expression to it in the early books of *The Republic*. The selection from David Hume and the essays by James Rachels and Louis Pojman present many of the arguments contemporary philosophers put forward in their efforts to undermine the theory of egoism. The theme that crime does not pay (at least not for society as a whole) runs through the discussion of reasons for having regard for others. Pojman believes that biologists have shown why and how altruism is adaptive for the species as a whole. But the nagging question remains: Why shouldn't individuals try to beat the system if they can get away with it? According to Colin McGinn and James Rachels, arguments and reasoning will not convince unregenerate egoists or amoralists who simply have no concern for anyone but themselves. As John Stuart Mill says, those you persuade by imprisonment.

Ethical egoism is a moral doctrine. But the problem of how self-interest comports with the imperatives of social morality inevitably leads to the more radical question of why we should be concerned to be moral at all. Why not be amoral?

Amoralists profess themselves free of all moral scruples, even the morally scrupulous concern with furthering their own interests. We may call them sociopaths, but what's wrong with being a sociopath? The classical rejoinders of the kind adumbrated by Rachels and McGinn apply here too. To these Peter Singer adds the speculation that the inner life of an amoralist must be terribly flat and enervating.

The Ring of Gyges

Plato

Plato (ca. 428–348 [or 347] B.C.), considered by many to be the greatest philosopher who ever lived, is the author of *The Republic* and other great dialogues. Plato's influence on Western culture is incalculable.

In *The Republic*, Plato describes the ideal society where justice reigns supreme. It opens with a scene in which Socrates confronts powerful arguments that disparage justice. We find Glaucon summarizing the views of those who think that justice is merely a compromise between the freedom to do wrong with impunity and to suffer wrong without redress. Because we would risk punitive action by doing wrong, we accept a limitation on our freedom. So justice is a kind of arrangement (like a system of traffic lights) that is not in itself valuable or desirable, but is put in place to prevent our suffering wrong from others (like injury in a collision).

The Ring of Gyges rendered the wearer invisible, enabling the shepherd Gyges to do as he pleased without fear of reprisal—and he used it to murder the King of Lydia. But did Gyges behave unnaturally? Glaucon argues that anyone in Gyges' situation would be a fool not to take full advantage of the power to do wrong with impunity. This suggests that justice is nothing more than a preventive device—only we lack the power that Gyges possessed.

In the remainder of *The Republic*, Socrates argues that the citizens of an ideal society would be just because they loved justice and not (merely) because they feared the consequences of suffering injustice.

GLAUCON

(To Socrates): I have never heard from anyone the sort of defence of justice that I want to hear, proving that it is better than injustice. I want to hear it praised for itself, and I think I am most likely to hear this from you. Therefore I am going to speak at length in praise of the unjust life and in doing so I will show you the way I want to hear you denouncing injustice and praising justice. See whether you want to hear what I suggest.

SOCRATES: I want it more than anything else. Indeed, what subject would a man of sense talk and hear about more often with enjoyment?

GLAUCON: Splendid, then listen while I deal with the first subject I mentioned: the nature and origin of justice.

They say that to do wrong is naturally good, to be wronged is bad, but the suffering of injury so far exceeds in badness the good of inflicting it that when men have done wrong to each other and suffered it, and have had a taste of both, those who are unable to avoid the latter and practise the former decide that it is profitable to come to an agreement with each other neither to inflict injury nor to suffer it. As a result they begin to make laws and covenants, and the law's command they call lawful and just. This, they say, is the origin and essence of justice; it stands between the best and the worst, the best being to do wrong without paying the penalty and the worst to be wronged without the power of revenge. The just then is a mean between two extremes; it is welcomed and honoured because of men's lack of the power to do wrong. The man who has that power, the real man, would not make a compact with anyone not to inflict injury or suffer it. For him that would be madness. This then, Socrates, is, according to their argument, the nature and origin of justice.

Even those who practise justice do so against their will because they lack the power to do wrong. This we could realize very clearly if we imagined ourselves granting to both the just and the unjust the freedom to do whatever they liked. We could then follow both of them and observe where their desires led them, and we would catch the just man redhanded travelling the same road as the unjust. The reason is the desire for undue gain which every organism by nature pursues as a good, but the law forcibly sidetracks him to honour equality. The freedom I just mentioned would most easily occur if these men had the power which they say the ancestor of the Lydian Gyges possessed. The story is that he was a shepherd in the service of the ruler of Lydia. There was a violent rainstorm and an earthquake which broke open the ground and created a chasm at the place where he was tending sheep. Seeing this and marvelling, he went down into it. He saw, besides many other wonders of which we are told, a hollow bronze horse. There were window-like openings in it; he climbed through them and caught sight of a corpse which seemed of more than human stature, wearing nothing but a ring of gold on its finger. This ring the shepherd put on and came out. He arrived at the usual monthly meeting which reported to the king on the state of the flocks, wearing the ring. As he was sitting among the others he happened to twist the hoop of the ring towards himself, to the inside of his hand, and as he did this he became invisible to those sitting near him and they went on talking as if he had gone. He marvelled at this and, fingering the ring, he turned the hoop outward again and became visible. Perceiving this he tested whether the ring had this power and so it happened: if he turned the hoop inwards he became invisible, but was visible when he turned it outwards. When he realized this, he at once arranged to become one of the messengers to the king. He went, committed adultery with the king's wife, attacked the king with her help, killed him, and took over the kingdom.

Now if there were two such rings, one worn by the just man, the other by the unjust, no one, as these people think, would be so incorruptible that he would stay on the path of justice or bring himself to keep away from other people's property and not touch it, when he could with impunity take whatever he wanted from the market, go into houses and have sexual relations with anyone he wanted, kill anyone, free all those he wished from prison, and do the other things which would make him like a god among men. His actions would be in no way different from those of the other and they would both follow the same path. This, some would say, is a great proof that no one is just willingly[1] but under compulsion, so that justice is not one's private good, since wherever either thought he could do wrong with impunity he would do so. Every man believes that injustice is much more profitable to himself than justice, and any exponent of this argument will say that he is right. The man who did not wish to do wrong with that opportunity, and did not touch other people's property, would be thought by those who knew it to be very foolish and miserable. They would praise him in public, thus deceiving one another, for fear of being wronged. So much for my second topic.

As for the choice between the lives we are discussing, we shall be able to make a correct judgment about it only if we put the most just man and the most unjust man face to face; otherwise we cannot do

---

[1] This directly contradicts the famous Socratic paradox that no one is willingly bad and that people do wrong because they have not the knowledge to do right, which is virtue.

so. By face to face I mean this: let us grant to the unjust the fullest degree of injustice and to the just the fullest justice, each being perfect in his own pursuit. First, the unjust man will act as clever craftsmen do—a top navigator for example or physician distinguishes what his craft can do and what it cannot; the former he will undertake, the latter he will pass by, and when he slips he can put things right. So the unjust man's correct attempts at wrongdoing must remain secret; the one who is caught must be considered a poor performer, for the extreme of injustice is to have a reputation for justice, and our perfectly unjust man must be granted perfection in injustice. We must not take this from him, but we must allow that, while committing the greatest crimes, he has provided himself with the greatest reputation for justice; if he makes a slip he must be able to put it right; he must be a sufficiently persuasive speaker if some wrongdoing of his is made public; he must be able to use force, where force is needed, with the help of his courage, his strength, and the friends and wealth with which he has provided himself.

Having described such a man, let us now in our argument put beside him the just man, simple as he is and noble, who, as Aeschylus put it, does not wish to appear just but to be so. We must take away his reputation, for a reputation for justice would bring him honour and rewards, and it would then not be clear whether he is what he is for justice's sake or for the sake of rewards and honour. We must strip him of everything except justice and make him the complete opposite of the other. Though he does no wrong, he must have the greatest reputation for wrongdoing so that he may be tested for justice by not weakening under ill repute and its consequences. Let him go his incorruptible way until death with a reputation for injustice throughout his life, just though he is, so that our two men may reach the extremes, one of justice, the other of injustice, and let them be judged as to which of the two is the happier.

SOCRATES: Whew! My dear Glaucon, what a mighty scouring you have given those two characters, as if they were statues in a competition.

STUDY QUESTIONS

1. Glaucon presents a popular conception of the origin of justice as an agreement by each individual to refrain from doing wrong on condition that one is protected from wrongdoing by others. What does this "social contract theory" imply about the nature of justice?
2. Glaucon notes that the person who appears just to others but who is not just seems happier than one who appears unjust to others but who in fact is just. What challenge does this present to Socrates?
3. Gyges can do wrong with impunity. But we cannot. We are told that crime does not pay. But is this true? Suppose it is false. Can we still make a case for being just and refraining from crime? Explain.
4. Glaucon's arguments seem to present Socrates with an insuperable problem since justice seems to be for "losers." How would you resolve the problem?

Of the State of Men without Civil Society

Thomas Hobbes

Thomas Hobbes (1588–1679) was one of the leading philosophers of the seventeenth century. He made important contributions to metaphysics and political philosophy and is known for his theory of the "social contract." His *Leviathan* (1651) is considered to be a philosophical masterpiece.

Thomas Hobbes holds that all human beings seek to preserve and to gratify themselves. Without society they would dwell in a "state of nature," living in fear and engaged in a war of all against all. Life would be "fierce, short-lived, poor, nasty." People in the state of nature would have the "right of nature" to preserve themselves by whatever means necessary. But no individual in this natural state would be strong enough to feel secure; so it is to everyone's benefit to obtain a measure of security by forming a society in which one gives up one's freedom to do as one pleases. In society one places oneself under a sovereign. In return for this, one receives the security afforded by sovereign protection.

This selection presents Hobbes's classic description of human beings in the state of nature. It explains why it would be rational for self-seeking individuals to curb their untrammeled egoism by entering into a lawful community.

1. The faculties of human nature may be reduced unto four kinds; bodily strength, experience, reason, passion. Taking the beginning of this following doctrine from these, we will declare in the first place what manner of inclinations men who are endued with these faculties bear towards each other, and whether, and by what faculty they are born, apt for society, and to preserve themselves against mutual violence; then proceeding, we will shew what advice was necessary to be taken for this business, and what are the conditions of society, or of human peace; that is to say, (changing the words only) what are the fundamental laws of nature.

2. The greatest part of those men who have written aught concerning commonwealths, either suppose, or require us, or beg of us to believe, that man is a creature born fit for society. The Greeks call him ζῶον πολιτικόν and on this foundation they so build up the doctrine of civil society, as if for the preservation of peace, and the government of mankind, there were nothing else necessary, than that men should agree to make certain covenants and conditions together, which themselves should then call laws. Which axiom, though received by most, is yet

ζῶον – living being, animal, creature, beast
figure, picture, painting

OF THE STATE OF MEN WITHOUT CIVIL SOCIETY From *De Cive* by Thomas Hobbes, chapter Two.

πολιτιτικόν – of or for a citizen; constitutional; statesman certainly false, and an error proceeding from our too slight contemplation of human nature. For they who shall more narrowly look into the causes for which men come together, and delight in each other's company, shall easily find that this happens not because naturally it could happen no otherwise, but by accident. For if by nature one man should love another (that is) as man, there could no reason be returned why every man should not equally love every man, as being equally man, or why he should rather frequent those whose society affords him honour or profit. We do not therefore by nature seek society for its own sake, but that we may receive some honour or profit from it; these we desire primarily, that secondarily. How, by what advice, men do meet, will be best known by observing those things which they do when they are met. For if they meet for traffic, it is plain every man regards not his fellow, but his business; if to discharge some office, a certain market-friendship is begotten, which hath more of jealousy in it than true love, and whence factions sometimes may arise, but good will never; if for pleasure, and recreation of mind, every man is wont to please himself most with those things which stir up laughter, whence he may (according to the nature of that which is ridiculous) by comparison of another man's defects and infirmities, pass the more current in his own opinion; and although this be sometimes innocent and without offence, yet it is manifest they are not so much delighted with the society, as their own vain glory. But for the most part, in these kinds of meetings, we wound the absent; their whole life, sayings, actions are examined, judged, condemned; nay, it is very rare, but some present receive a fling before they part, so as his reason was not ill, who was wont always at parting to go out last. And these are indeed the true delights of society, unto which we are carried by nature, that is, by those passions which are incident to all creatures, until either by sad experience, or good precepts, it so fall out (which in many never happens) that the appetite of present matters be dulled with the memory of things past, without which, the discourse of most quick and nimble men on this subject, is but cold and hungry.

But if it so happen, that being met, they pass their time in relating some stories, and one of them begins to tell one which concerns himself; instantly every one of the rest most greedily desires to speak of himself too; if one relate some wonder, the rest will tell you miracles, if they have them, if not, they will feign them. Lastly, that I may say somewhat of them who pretend to be wiser than others; if they meet to talk of philosophy, look how many men, so many would be esteemed masters, or else they not only love not their fellows, but even persecute them with hatred. So clear is it by experience to all men who a little more narrowly consider human affairs, that all free congress ariseth either from mutual poverty, or from vain glory, whence the parties met, endeavour to carry with them either some benefit, or to leave behind them that same εὐδοκιμεῖν some esteem and honour with those, with whom they have been conversant. The same is also collected by reason out of the definitions themselves, of will, good, honour, profitable. For when we voluntarily contract society, in all manner of society we look after the object of the will, that is, that, which every one of those who gather together, propounds to himself for good. Now whatsoever seems good, is pleasant, and relates either to the senses, or the mind. But all the mind's pleasure is either glory, (or to have a good opinion of one's self) or refers to glory in the

end; the rest are sensual, or conducing to sensuality, which may be all comprehended under the word conveniences. All society therefore is either for gain, or
for glory; that is, not so much for love of our fellows, as for the love of ourselves. But no society can be great, or lasting, which begins from vain glory;
because that glory is like honour, if all men have it, no man hath it, for they
consist in comparison and precellence; neither doth the society of others
advance any whit the cause of my glorying in myself; for every man must
account himself, such as he can make himself, without the help of others. But
though the benefits of this life may be much farthered by mutual help, since yet
those may be better attained to by dominion, than by the society of others:
I hope no body will doubt but that men would much more greedily be carried
by nature, if all fear were removed, to obtain dominion, than to gain society.
We must therefore resolve, that the original of all great and lasting societies con-
sisted not in the mutual good will men had towards each other, but in the
mutual fear they had of each other.

3. The cause of mutual fear consists partly in the natural equality of men,
partly in their mutual will of hurting: whence it comes to pass, that we can neither
expect from others, nor promise to ourselves the least security. For if we look on
men full-grown, and consider how brittle the frame of our human body is, which
perishing, all its strength, vigour, and wisdom itself perisheth with it; and how
easy a matter it is, even for the weakest man to kill the strongest: there is no reason
why any man, trusting to his own strength, should conceive himself made by nature
above others. They are equals, who can do equal things one against the other; but
they who can do the greatest things, namely, kill, can do equal things. All men
therefore among themselves are by nature equal; the inequality we now discern,
hath its spring from the civil law.

4. All men in the state of nature have a desire and will to hurt, but not proceeding from the same cause, neither equally to be condemned. For one man, according to that natural equality which is among us, permits as much to others as
he assumes to himself; which is an argument of a temperate man, and one that
rightly values his power. Another, supposing himself above others, will have a license to do what he lists, and challenges respect and honour, as due to him before
others; which is an argument of a fiery spirit. This man's will to hurt ariseth from
vain glory, and the false esteem he hath of his own strength; the other's from the
necessity of defending himself, his liberty, and his goods, against this man's
violence.

5. Furthermore, since the combat of wits is the fiercest, the greatest discords
which are, must necessarily arise from this contention. For in this case it is not
only odious to contend against, but also not to consent. For not to approve of
what a man saith, is no less than tacitly to accuse him of an error in that thing
which he speaketh; as in very many things to dissent, is as much as if you
accounted him a fool whom you dissent from; which may appear hence, that there
are no wars so sharply waged as between sects of the same religion, and factions
of the same commonweal, where the contestation is either concerning doctrines or
politic prudence. And since all the pleasure and jollity of the mind consists in this,
even to get some, with whom comparing, it may find somewhat wherein to triumph and vaunt itself; it is impossible but men must declare sometimes some

mutual scorn and contempt, either by laughter, or by words, or by gesture, or some sign or other; than which there is no greater vexation of mind, and than from which there cannot possibly arise a greater desire to do hurt.

6. But the most frequent reason why men desire to hurt each other, ariseth hence, that many men at the same time have an appetite to the same thing; which yet very often they can neither enjoy in common, nor yet divide it; whence it follows that the strongest must have it, and who is strongest must be decided by the sword.

7. Among so many dangers therefore, as the natural lusts of men do daily threaten each other withal, to have a care of one's self is not a matter so scornfully to be looked upon, as if so be there had not been a power and will left in one to have done otherwise. For every man is desirous of what is good for him, and shuns what is evil, but chiefly the chiefest of natural evils, which is death; and this he doth, by a certain impulsion of nature, no less than that whereby a stone moves downward. It is therefore neither absurd, nor reprehensible, neither against the dictates of true reason, for a man to use all his endeavours to preserve and defend his body and the members thereof from death and sorrows. But that which is not contrary to right reason, that all men account to be done justly, and with right; neither by the word right is anything else signified, than that liberty which every man hath to make use of his natural faculties according to right reason. Therefore the first foundation of natural right is this, that every man as much as in him lies endeavour to protect his life and members.

8. But because it is in vain for a man to have a right to the end, if the right to the necessary means be denied him; it follows, that since every man hath a right to preserve himself, he must also be allowed a right to use all the means, and do all the actions, without which he cannot preserve himself.

9. Now whether the means which he is about to use, and the action he is performing, be necessary to the preservation of his life and members, or not, he himself, by the right of nature, must be judge. For say another man judge that it is contrary to right reason that I should judge of mine own peril: why now, because he judgeth of what concerns me, by the same reason, because we are equal by nature, will I judge also of things which do belong to him. Therefore it agrees with right reason, that is, it is the right of nature that I judge of his opinion, that is, whether it conduce to my preservation, or not.

10. Nature hath given to every one a right to all; that is, it was lawful for every man in the bare state of nature, or before such time as men had engaged themselves by any covenants or bonds, to do what he would, and against whom he thought fit, and to possess, use, and enjoy all what he would, or could get. Now because whatsoever a man would, it therefore seems good to him because he wills it, and either it really doth, or at least seems to him to contribute towards his preservation, (but we have already allowed him to be judge, in the foregoing article, whether it doth or not, in so much as we are to hold all for necessary whatsoever he shall esteem so), and by the 7th article it appears that by the right of nature those things may be done, and must be had, which necessarily conduce to the protection of life and members, it follows, that in the state of nature, to have all, and do all, is lawful for all. And this is that which is meant by that common saying, nature hath given all to all, from whence we understand likewise, that in the state of nature, profit is the measure of right.

11. But it was the least benefit for men thus to have a common right to all things; for the effects of this right are the same, almost, as if there had been no right at all. For although any man might say of every thing, this is mine, yet could he not enjoy it, by reason of his neighbour, who having equal right, and equal power, would pretend the same thing to be his.

12. If now to this natural proclivity of men, to hurt each other, which they derive from their passions, but chiefly from a vain esteem of themselves, you add, the right of all to all, wherewith one by right invades, the other by right resists, and whence arise perpetual jealousies and suspicions on all hands, and how hard a thing it is to provide against an enemy invading us, with an intention to oppress, and ruin, though he come with a small number, and no great provision; it cannot be denied but that the natural state of men, before they entered into society, was a mere war, and that not simply, but a war of all men against all men. For what is war, but that same time in which the will of contesting by force is fully declared, either by words, or deeds? The time remaining, is termed peace.

13. But it is easily judged how disagreeable a thing to the preservation either of mankind, or of each single man, a perpetual war is. But it is perpetual in its own nature, because in regard of the equality of those that strive, it cannot be ended by victory; for in this state the conqueror is subject to so much danger, as it were to be accounted a miracle, if any, even the most strong, should close up his life with many years, and old age. They of America are examples hereof, even in this present age: other nations have been in former ages, which now indeed are become civil and flourishing, but were then few, fierce, short-lived, poor, nasty, and deprived of all that pleasure, and beauty of life, which peace and society are wont to bring with them. Whosoever therefore holds, that it had been best to have continued in that state in which all things were lawful for all men, he contradicts himself. For every man by natural necessity desires that which is good for him: nor is there any that esteems a war of all against all, which necessarily adheres to such a state, to be good for him. And so it happens, that through fear of each other we think it fit to rid ourselves of this condition, and to get some fellows; that if there needs must be war, it may not yet be against all men, nor without some helps.

14. Fellows are gotten either by constraint, or by consent; by constraint, when after fight the conqueror makes the conquered serve him, either through fear of death, or by laying fetters on him: by consent, when men enter into society to help each other, both parties consenting without any constraint. But the conqueror may by right compel the conquered, or the strongest the weaker, (as a man in health may one that is sick, or he that is of riper years a child), unless he will choose to die, to give caution of his future obedience. For since the right of protecting ourselves according to our own wills, proceeded from our danger, and our danger from our equality, it is more consonant to reason, and more certain for our conservation, using the present advantage to secure ourselves by taking caution, than when they shall be full grown and strong, and got out of our power, to endeavour to recover that power again by doubtful fight. And on the other side, nothing can be thought more absurd, than by discharging whom you already have weak in your power, to make him at once both an enemy and a strong one. From whence we may understand likewise as a corollary in the natural state of men, that, *a sure*

and irresistible power confers the right of dominion and ruling over those who cannot resist; insomuch, as the right of all things that can be done, adheres essentially and immediately unto this omnipotence hence arising.

15. Yet cannot men expect any lasting preservation, continuing thus in the state of nature, that is, of war, by reason of that equality of power, and other human faculties they are endued withal. Wherefore to seek peace, where there is any hopes of obtaining it, and where there is none, to enquire out for auxiliaries of war, is the dictate of right reason, that is, the law of nature.

STUDY QUESTIONS

1. What is the "state of nature," and why is it unstable?
2. Man, said Aristotle, is a social animal. Hobbes seems to have some doubts. Do you believe Hobbes is right when he says "we do not ... by nature seek society for its own sake, but that we may receive some honour or profit from it"?
3. Why does Hobbes say that prior to civil society, every person had "a right to all ... to do what he would, and against whom he thought fit"? Do you agree that if a social contract did not exist, "everything would be permitted"?
4. In civil society we give up the natural rights we possessed in the state of nature. What are natural rights, and why is it reasonable for us to surrender them?
5. Writing in 1651, Hobbes had no inkling of the theory of evolution that Charles Darwin would put forth some two hundred years later. How might Hobbes's views have been affected by an acquaintance with Darwin's theory?

Of Self-Love

David Hume

David Hume (1711–1776) was a Scottish philosopher and a leading figure in the European Enlightenment. He wrote major treatises on the theory of knowledge and on ethics that continue to challenge and edify us. Hume was an exceptionally witty and kindly man: his Scottish friends called him Saint David; and in France he was known as "le bon David."

Some cynics say that when we "do good," we always have our own well-being in mind. David Hume has little patience with this view of human nature. He calls it "pernicious" and suggests that those who subscribe to it are "superficial reasoners" who allow no degrees of good and bad among human beings.

Hume is equally critical of a closely related theory—that our feelings are always selfish, even though we ourselves may think otherwise. According to this theory, known as psychological egoism, our love of others is at bottom a form of self-love. A so-called good man does kindly actions because these make him happy; similarly, a so-called bad man does bad actions because these make him happy. At bottom, both men are the same self-regarding creatures.

Hume generally finds egoism to be at odds with everyday experience. "To the most careless observer there appear to be such dispositions as benevolence and generosity, such affections as love, friendship, compassion, gratitude." It would be paradoxical to reduce all these to self-love as a single cause. Hume suggests that the temptation to reduce them in this way to a single cause derives from the recent success in physics (by Isaac Newton) to reduce many different phenomena as manifestations of gravitation as a single cause. But Hume denies that this kind of reductionism is appropriate in the human sciences or in ethics. Hume accuses psychological egoists of being mean-spirited. He points out that while they are usually quite ready to allow that a man really hates someone and seeks revenge, they refuse to admit that he loves someone and is seeking his or her good. "What a malignant philosophy must it be that will not allow to humanity and friendship the same privileges which are undisputably granted to the darker passions of enmity and resentment."

There is a principle, supposed to prevail among many, which is utterly incompatible with all virtue or moral sentiment; and as it can proceed from nothing but the most depraved disposition, so in its turn it tends still further to encourage that

OF SELF-LOVE From *A Treatise of Human Nature* by David Hume (Oxford: Clarendon Press, 1888).

depravity. This principle is that all *benevolence* is mere hypocrisy, friendship a cheat, public spirit a farce, fidelity a snare to procure trust and confidence; and that, while all of us, at bottom, pursue only our private interest, we wear these fair disguises in order to put others off their guard and expose them the more to our wiles and machinations. What heart one must be possessed of who possesses such principles, and who feels no internal sentiment that belies so pernicious a theory, it is easy to imagine; and also what degree of affection and benevolence he can bear to a species whom he represents under such odious colours, and supposes so little susceptible of gratitude or any return of affection. Or if we should not ascribe these principles wholly to a corrupted heart, we must at least account for them from the most careless and precipitate examination. Superficial reasoners, indeed, observing many false pretences among mankind, and feeling, perhaps, no very strong restraint in their own disposition, might draw a general and a hasty conclusion that all is equally corrupted, and that men, different from all other animals, and indeed from all other species of existence, admit of no degrees of good or bad, but are, in every instance, the same creatures under different disguises and appearances.

There is another principle, somewhat resembling the former, which has been much insisted on by philosophers, and has been the foundation of many a system: that, whatever affection one may feel or imagine he feels for others, no passion is or can be disinterested; that the most generous friendship, however sincere, is a modification of self-love; and that, even unknown to ourselves, we seek only our own gratification while we appear the most deeply engaged in schemes for the liberty and happiness of mankind. By a turn of imagination, by a refinement of reflection, by an enthusiasm of passion, we seem to take part in the interests of others, and imagine ourselves divested of all selfish considerations; but, at bottom, the most generous patriot and most niggardly miser, the bravest hero and most abject coward, have, in every action, an equal regard to their own happiness and welfare.

Whoever concludes from the seeming tendency of this opinion that those who make profession of it cannot possibly feel the true sentiments of benevolence or have any regard for genuine virtue, will often find himself, in practice, very much mistaken. Probity and honour were no strangers to Epicurus and his sect. Atticus and Horace seem to have enjoyed from nature, and cultivated by reflection, as generous and friendly dispositions as any disciple of the austerer schools. And among the modern, Hobbes and Locke, who maintained the selfish system of morals, lived irreproachable lives, though the former lay not under any restraint of religion which might supply the defects of his philosophy.

An Epicurean or a Hobbist readily allows that there is such a thing as a friendship in the world, without hypocrisy or disguise, though he may attempt, by a philosophical chemistry, to resolve the elements of this passion, if I may so speak, into those of another, and explain every affection to be self-love, twisted and moulded by a particular turn of imagination into a variety of appearances. But as the same turn of imagination prevails not in every man nor gives the same direction to the original passion, this is sufficient even according to the selfish system to make the widest difference in human characters, and denominate one man virtuous and humane, another vicious and meanly interested. I esteem the man whose self-love, by whatever means, is so directed as to give him a concern for others and render him serviceable to society, as I hate or despise him who has no regard to anything beyond his own gratifications and enjoyments. In vain would you suggest that these characters, though seemingly opposite, are at bottom the same, and that a very inconsiderable turn of thought forms the whole difference between them. Each character, notwithstanding these inconsiderable differences, appears to me, in practice, pretty durable and untransmutable. And I find not in this more than in other subjects that the natural sentiments arising from the general appearances of things are easily destroyed by subtile reflections concerning the minute origin of these appearances. Does not the lively, cheerful colour of a countenance inspire me with complacency and pleasure, even though I learn from philosophy that all difference of complexion arises from the most minute differences of thickness in the most minute parts of the skin, by means of which a superficies is qualified to reflect one of the original colours of light, and absorb the others?

But though the question concerning the universal or partial selfishness of man be not so material, as is usually imagined, to morality and practice, it is certainly of consequence in the speculative science of human nature, and is a proper object of curiosity and enquiry. It may not, therefore, be unsuitable in this place to bestow a few reflections upon it.[1]

The most obvious objection to the selfish hypothesis is that, as it is contrary to common feeling and our most unprejudiced notions, there is required the highest stretch of philosophy to establish so extraordinary a paradox. To the most careless observer there appear to be such dispositions as benevolence and generosity, such affections as love, friendship, compassion, gratitude. These sentiments have their causes, effects, objects, and operations, marked by common language and observation, and plainly distinguished from those of the selfish passions. And as this is the obvious appearance of things, it must be admitted, till some hypothesis be discovered which, by penetrating deeper into human nature, may prove the former affections to be nothing but modifications of the latter. All attempts of this kind have hitherto proved fruitless, and seem to have proceeded entirely from that love of *simplicity* which has been the source of much false reasoning in philosophy. I shall not here enter into any detail on the present subject. Many able philosophers have shown the insufficiency of these systems. And I shall take for granted what, I believe, the smallest reflection will make evident to every impartial enquirer.

But the nature of the subject furnishes the strongest presumption that no better system will ever, for the future, be invented, in order to account for the origin of the benevolent from the selfish affections, and reduce all the various emotions of the human mind to a perfect simplicity. The case is not the same in this species of

---

[1] Benevolence naturally divides into two kinds, the *general* and the *particular*. The first is where we have no friendship or connexion or esteem for the person, but feel only a general sympathy with him or a compassion for his pains, and a congratulation with his pleasures. The other species of benevolence is founded on an opinion of virtue, on services done us, or on some particular connexions. Both these sentiments must be allowed real in human nature; but whether they will resolve into some nice considerations of self-love is a question more curious than important. The former sentiment, to wit, that of general benevolence, or humanity, or sympathy, we shall have occasion frequently to treat of in the course of this inquiry; and I assume it as real from general experience, without any other proof.

philosophy as in physics. Many an hypothesis in nature, contrary to first appearances, has been found, on more accurate scrutiny, solid and satisfactory. Instances of this kind are so frequent that a judicious as well as witty philosopher has ventured to affirm, if there be more than one way in which any phenomenon may be produced, that there is general presumption for its arising from the causes which are the least obvious and familiar. But the presumption always lies on the other side, in all enquiries concerning the origin of our passions and of the internal operations of the human mind. The simplest and most obvious cause which can there be assigned for any phenomenon is probably the true one. When a philosopher, in the explication of his system, is obliged to have recourse to some very intricate and refined reflections, and to suppose them essential to the production of any passion or emotion, we have reason to be extremely on our guard against so fallacious an hypothesis. The affections are not susceptible of any impression from the refinements of reason or imagination; and it is always found that a vigorous exertion of the latter faculties necessarily, from the narrow capacity of the human mind, destroys all activity in the former. Our predominant motive or intention is, indeed, frequently concealed from ourselves when it is mingled and confounded with other motives which the mind, from vanity or self-conceit, is desirous of supposing more prevalent; but there is no instance that a concealment of this nature has ever arisen from the abstruseness and intricacy of the motive. A man that has lost a friend and patron may flatter himself that all his grief arises from generous sentiments, without any mixture of narrow or interested considerations; but a man that grieves for a valuable friend who needed his patronage and protection, how can we suppose that his passionate tenderness arises from some metaphysical regards to a self-interest which has no foundation or reality? We may as well imagine that minute wheels and springs, like those of a watch, give motion to a loaded waggon, as account for the origin of passion from, such abstruse reflections.

Animals are found susceptible of kindness, both to their own species and to ours; nor is there, in this case, the least suspicion of disguise or artifice. Shall we account for all *their* sentiments, too, from refined deductions of self-interest? Or if we admit a disinterested benevolence in the inferior species, by what rule of analogy can we refuse it in the superior?

Love between the sexes begets a complacency and good-will very distinct from the gratification of an appetite. Tenderness to their offspring, in all sensible beings, is commonly able alone to counter-balance the strongest motives of self-love, and has no manner of dependence on that affection. What interest can a fond mother have in view, who loses her health by assiduous attendance on her sick child, and afterwards languishes and dies of grief when freed by its death from the slavery of that attendance?

Is gratitude no affection of the human breast, or is that a word merely, without any meaning or reality? Have we no satisfaction in one man's company above another's, and no desire of the welfare of our friend, even though absence or death should prevent us from all participation in it? Or what is it commonly that gives us any participation in it, even while alive and present, but our affection and regard to him?

These and a thousand other instances are marks of a general benevolence in human nature, where no *real* interest binds us to the object. And how an *imaginary* interest, known and avowed for such, can be the origin of any passion or emotion seems difficult to explain. No satisfactory hypothesis of this kind has yet been discovered, nor is there the smallest probability that the future industry of men will ever be attended with more favourable success.

But further, if we consider rightly of the matter, we shall find that the hypothesis which allows of a disinterested benevolence, distinct from self-love, has really more *simplicity* in it, and is more conformable to the analogy of nature than that which pretends to resolve all friendship and humanity into this latter principle. There are bodily wants or appetites acknowledged by every one, which necessarily precede all sensual enjoyment and carry us directly to seek possession of the object. Thus hunger and thirst have eating and drinking for their end; and from the gratification of these primary appetites arises a pleasure which may become the object of another species of desire or inclination that is secondary and interested. In the same manner there are mental passions by which we are impelled immediately to seek particular objects, such as fame, or power, or vengeance, without any regard to interest; and when these objects are attained a pleasing enjoyment ensues as the consequence of our indulged affections. Nature must, by the internal frame and constitution of the mind, give an original propensity to fame, ere we can reap any pleasure from that acquisition, or pursue it from motives of self-love and desire of happiness. If I have no vanity, I take no delight in praise; if I be void of ambition, power gives me no enjoyment; if I be not angry, the punishment of an adversary is totally indifferent to me. In all these cases there is a passion which points immediately to the object and constitutes it our good or happiness, as there are other secondary passions which afterwards arise and pursue it as a part of our happiness, when once it is constituted such by our original affections. Were there no appetite of any kind antecedent to self-love, that propensity could scarcely ever exert itself, because we should in that case have felt few and slender pains or pleasures, and have little misery or happiness to avoid or to pursue.

Now where is the difficulty in conceiving that this may likewise be the case with benevolence and friendship, and that, from the original frame of our temper, we may feel a desire of another's happiness or good, which, by means of that affection, becomes our own good, and is afterwards pursued from the combined motives of benevolence and self-enjoyments? Who sees not that vengeance, from the force alone of passion, may be so eagerly pursued as to make us knowingly neglect every consideration of ease, interest, or safety, and, like some vindictive animals, infuse our very souls into the wounds we give an enemy. And what a malignant philosophy must it be that will not allow to humanity and friendship the same privileges which are undisputably granted to the darker passions of enmity and resentment. Such a philosophy is more like a satyr than a true delineation or description of human nature, and may be a good foundation for paradoxical wit and raillery, but is a very bad one for any serious argument or reasoning.

Study Questions

1. What are Hume's main objections to egoism? Do you find his criticisms persuasive? If not, why not?
2. Discuss Hume's contention that egoism is a malignant philosophy with a cynical and mean-spirited perspective on human nature. Do you agree with him? Why or why not?

3. Hume's own ethical philosophy grounds morality in the moral sentiments (see "Of Benevolence" in Chapter Four). Show (a) how egoism, if true, would indeed undermine Hume's basic approach to moral philosophy and (b) why he therefore took such great pains to refute it.

The Unselfishness Trap

Harry Browne

> Harry Browne (1933–2006) was a journalist and investment analyst. He is the author of *How I Found Freedom in an Unfree World* (1973), *The Great Libertarian Offer* (2000), and *Liberty A–Z: 872 Libertarian Soundbites You Can Use Right Now* (2004).

> Harry Browne objects to the view of many moralists that we should put others' happiness ahead of our own. If we were all to sacrifice our own happiness for the sake of others, eventually no one would be happy. "The unselfishness concept is a merry-go-round that has no ultimate purpose." Gift-givers and favor-doers presuppose that they know what will make others happy. Spending money on yourself is much more efficient (you know what makes you happy) and creates more happiness all around. Browne recommends "prudential generosity": Be sensitive to the needs and desires of those who might in turn benefit you. He grounds his views on psychological egoism, the doctrine that human beings act from a single motive: self-love. "Why should you feel guilty for seeking your own happiness when that's what everyone else is doing, too?"

The Unselfishness Trap is the belief that you must put the happiness of others ahead of your own.

Unselfishness is a very popular ideal, one that's been honored throughout recorded history. Wherever you turn, you find encouragement to put the happiness of others ahead of your own—to do what's best for the world, not for yourself.

If the ideal is sound, there must be something unworthy in seeking to live your life as you want to live it.

So perhaps we should look more closely at the subject—to see if the ideal *is* sound. For if you attempt to be free, we can assume that someone's going to consider that to be selfish.

We saw in Chapter Two that each person always acts in ways he believes will make him feel good or will remove discomfort from his life. Because everyone is different from everyone else, each individual goes about it in his own way.

One man devotes his life to helping the poor. Another one lies and steals. Still another person tries to create better products and services for which he hopes to be paid handsomely. One woman devotes herself to her husband and children. Another one seeks a career as a singer.

In every case, the ultimate motivation has been the same. Each person is doing what *he* believes will assure his happiness. What varies between them is the *means* each has chosen to gain his happiness.

We could divide them into two groups labeled "selfish" and "unselfish," but I don't think that would prove anything. For the thief and the humanitarian each have the same motive—to do what he believes will make him feel good.

In fact, we can't avoid a very significant conclusion: *Everyone is selfish.* Selfishness isn't really an issue, because everyone selfishly seeks his own happiness.

What we need to examine, however, are the means various people choose to achieve their happiness. Unfortunately, some people oversimplify the matter by assuming that there are only two basic means: sacrifice yourself for others or make them sacrifice for you. Happily, there's a third way that can produce better consequences than either of those two.

A Better World?

Let's look first at the ideal of living for the benefit of others. It's often said that it would be a better world if everyone were unselfish. But would it be?

If it were somehow possible for everyone to give up his own happiness, what would be the result? Let's carry it to its logical conclusion and see what we find.

To visualize it, let's imagine that happiness is symbolized by a big red rubber ball. I have the ball in my hands—meaning that I hold the ability to be happy. But since I'm not going to be selfish, I quickly pass the ball to you. I've given up my happiness for you.

What will you do? Since you're not selfish either, you won't keep the ball; you'll quickly pass it on to your next-door neighbor. But he doesn't want to be selfish either, so he passes it to his wife, who likewise gives it to her children.

The children have been taught the virtue of unselfishness, so they pass it to playmates, who pass it to parents, who pass it to neighbors, and on and on and on.

I think we can stop the analogy at this point and ask what's been accomplished by all this effort. Who's better off for these demonstrations of pure unselfishness?

How would it be a better world if everyone acted that way? Whom would we be unselfish for? There would have to be a selfish person who would receive, accept, and enjoy the benefits of our unselfishness for there to be any purpose to it. But that selfish person (the object of our generosity) would be living by lower standards than we do.

For a more practical example, what is achieved by the parent who "sacrifices" himself for his children, who in turn are expected to sacrifice themselves for *their* children, etc.? The unselfishness concept is a merry-go-round that has no ultimate purpose. No one's self-interest is enhanced by the continual relaying of gifts from one person to another to another.

Perhaps most people have never carried the concept of unselfishness to this logical conclusion. If they did, they might reconsider their pleas for an unselfish world.

Negative Choices

But, unfortunately, the pleas continue, and they're a very real part of your life. In seeking your own freedom and happiness, you have to deal with those who tell you that you shouldn't put yourself first. That creates a situation in which you're pressured to act negatively—to put aside your plans and desires in order to avoid the condemnation of others.

As I've said before, one of the characteristics of a free man is that he's usually choosing positively—deciding which of several alternatives would make him the happiest; while the average person, most of the time, is choosing which of two or three alternatives will cause him the least discomfort.

When the reason for your actions is to avoid being called "selfish" you're making a negative decision and thereby restricting the possibilities for your own happiness.

You're in the Unselfishness Trap if you regretfully pay for your aunt's surgery with the money you'd saved for a new car, or if you sadly give up the vacation you'd looked forward to in order to help a sick neighbor.

You're in the trap if you feel you're *required* to give part of your income to the poor, or if you think that your country, community, or family has first claim on your time, energy, or money.

You're in the Unselfishness Trap any time you make negative choices that are designed to avoid being called "selfish."

It isn't that no one else is important. You might have a self-interest in someone's well-being, and giving a gift can be a gratifying expression of the affection you feel for him. But you're in the trap if you do such things in order to appear unselfish.

Helping Others

There *is* an understandable urge to give to those who are important and close to you. However, that leads many people to think that indiscriminate giving is the key to one's own happiness. They say that the way to be happy is to make others happy; get your glow by basking in the glow you've created for someone else.

It's important to identify that as a personal opinion. If someone says that giving is the key to happiness, isn't he saying that's the key to *his* happiness?

I think we can carry the question further, however, and determine how efficient such a policy might be. The suggestion to be a giver presupposes that you're able to judge what will make someone else happy. And experience has taught me to be a bit humble about assuming what makes others happy.

My landlady once brought me a piece of her freshly baked cake because she wanted to do me a favor. Unfortunately, it happened to be a kind of cake that was distasteful to me. I won't try to describe the various ways I tried to get the cake plate back to her without being confronted with a request for my judgment of her cake. It's sufficient to say that her well-intentioned favor interfered with my own plans.

And now, whenever I'm sure I know what someone else "needs," I remember that incident and back off a little. There's no way that one person can read the mind of another to know all his plans, goals, and tastes.

You may know a great deal about the desires of your intimate friends. But *indiscriminate* gift-giving and favor-doing is usually a waste of resources—or, worse, it can upset the well-laid plans of the receiver.

When you give to someone else, you might provide something he values—but probably not the thing he considers most important. If you expend those resources for *yourself*, you automatically devote them to what you consider to be most important. The time or money you've spent will most likely create more happiness that way.

If your purpose is to make someone happy, you're most apt to succeed if you make yourself the object. You'll never know another person more than a fraction as well as you can know yourself.

Do you want to make someone happy? Go to it—use your talents and your insight and benevolence to bestow riches of happiness upon the one person you understand well enough to do it efficiently—yourself. I guarantee that you'll get more genuine appreciation from yourself than from anyone else.

Give to you.

Support your local self.

Alternatives

As I indicated earlier in this chapter, it's too often assumed that there are only two alternatives: (1) sacrifice your interests for the benefit of others; or (2) make others sacrifice their interests for you. If nothing else were possible, it would indeed be a grim world.

Fortunately, there's more to the world than that. Because desires vary from person to person, it's possible to create exchanges between individuals in which both parties benefit.

For example, if you buy a house, you do so because you'd rather have the house than the money involved. But the seller's desire is different—he'd rather have the money than the house. When the sale is completed, each of you has received something of greater value than what you gave up—otherwise you wouldn't have entered the exchange. Who, then, has had to sacrifice for the other?

In the same way, your daily life is made up of dozens of such exchanges—small and large transactions in which each party gets something he values more than what he gives up. The exchange doesn't have to involve money; you may be spending time, attention, or effort in exchange for something you value.

Mutually beneficial relationships are possible when desires are compatible. Sometimes the desires are the same—like going to a movie together. Sometimes the desires are different—like trading your money for someone's house. In either case, it's the *compatibility* of the desires that makes the exchange possible.

No sacrifice is necessary when desires are compatible. So it makes sense to seek out people with whom you can have mutually beneficial relationships.

Often the "unselfishness" issue arises only because two people with nothing in common are trying to get along together—such as a man who likes bowling and hates opera married to a woman whose tastes are the opposite. If they're to do things together, one must "sacrifice" his pleasure for the other. So each might try to encourage the other to be "unselfish."

If they were compatible, the issue wouldn't arise because each would be pleasing the other by doing what was in his own self-interest.

An efficiently selfish person *is* sensitive to the needs and desires of others. But he doesn't consider those desires to be demands upon him. Rather, he sees them as *opportunities*—potential exchanges that might be beneficial to him. He identifies desires in others so that he can decide if exchanges with them will help him get what he wants.

He doesn't sacrifice himself for others, nor does he expect others to be sacrificed for him. He takes the third alternative—he finds relationships that are mutually beneficial so that no sacrifice is required.

Please Yourself

Everyone is selfish; everyone is doing what he believes will make himself happier. The recognition of that can take most of the sting out of accusations that you're being "selfish." Why should you feel guilty for seeking your own happiness when that's what everyone else is doing, too?

The demand that you be unselfish can be motivated by any number of reasons: that you'd help create a better world, that you have a moral obligation to be unselfish, that you give up your happiness to the selfishness of someone else, or that the person demanding it has just never thought it out.

Whatever the reason, you're not likely to convince such a person to stop his demands. But it will create much less pressure on you if you realize that it's *his* selfish reason. And you can eliminate the problem entirely by looking for more compatible companions.

To find constant, profound happiness requires that you be free to seek the gratification of your own desires. It means making positive choices.

If you slip into the Unselfishness Trap, you'll spend a good part of your time making negative choices—trying to avoid the censure of those who tell you not to think of yourself. You won't have time to be free.

If someone finds happiness by doing "good works" for others, let him. That doesn't mean that's the best way for you to find happiness.

And when someone accuses you of being selfish, just remember that he's only upset because you aren't doing what *he* selfishly wants you to do.

STUDY QUESTIONS

1. Browne claims that when we behave unselfishly we, more often than not, sacrifice our own happiness. Do you agree? Why or why not?
2. Browne says that everyone is selfish because we all do what we believe will make us feel good. Critics of egoism such as James Rachels claim that what makes an act selfish or unselfish is its *object*, not simply that it makes you feel good. If you are the sort of person who feels good *when you help others*, then you are unselfish. If you feel good only

when helping yourself, then you are selfish. Discuss the issue that divides Rachels and Browne, and assess their respective positions.

Egoism and Moral Skepticism

James Rachels

James Rachels (1941–2003) was University Professor of Philosophy at the University of Alabama. He is the author of several books, including *The End of Life: Euthanasia and Morality* (1986), *Created from Animals: The Moral Implications of Darwinism* (1990), and *Can Ethics Provide Answers? And Other Essays in Moral Philosophy* (1996).

Psychological egoism is the view that human beings always act from a single motive: self-love. Ethical egoism is the moral theory that says we *ought* to act only from self-love. Rachels tries to expose the logical and moral weaknesses of both theories. For example, he challenges the view often proffered by defenders of psychological egoism: We are selfish because we *always do what we want to do*. One person *wants* to visit and cheer up a lonely elderly neighbor; another wants to rob and terrorize the neighbor. Both do what they want; both are selfish. Rachels points out that what makes an act selfish is its *object*, not that you want to do it. If the object of most of your actions is to please yourself, then you are selfish; if you often want to please others, you are kind. If you want to harm them, you are malicious. Rachels also argues that both psychological and ethical egoisms rest upon a distorted view of human nature. Most of us are sympathetic and care about the well-being of others. The reason we do not burn down a department store is not because it might not be in our long-range best interest to do so, but because "people might be burned to death."

I

Our ordinary thinking about morality is full of assumptions that we almost never question. We assume, for example, that we have an obligation to consider the welfare of other people when we decide what actions to perform or what rules to obey; we think that we must refrain from acting in ways harmful to others, and that we must respect their rights and interests as well as our own. We also assume that people are in fact capable of being motivated by such considerations, that is, that people are not wholly selfish and that they do sometimes act in the interests of others.

EGOISM AND MORAL SKEPTICISM From *A New Introduction to Philosophy* by James Rachels. Edited by Steven M. Cahn (Harper and Row, 1971). Copyright © 1971 by Steven M. Cahn. Reprinted by permission of Steven M. Cahn.

Both of these assumptions have come under attack by moral skeptics, as long ago as by Glaucon in Book II of Plato's *Republic*. Glaucon recalls the legend of Gyges, a shepherd who was said to have found a magic ring in a fissure opened by an earthquake. The ring would make its wearer invisible and thus would enable him to go anywhere and do anything undetected. Gyges used the power of the ring to gain entry to the Royal Palace where he seduced the Queen, murdered the King, and subsequently seized the throne. Now Glaucon asks us to determine that there are two such rings, one given to a man of virtue and one given to a rogue. The rogue, of course, will use his ring unscrupulously and do anything necessary to increase his own wealth and power. He will recognize no moral constraints on his conduct, and, since the cloak of invisibility will protect him from discovery, he can do anything he pleases without fear of reprisal. So there will be no end to the mischief he will do. But how will the so-called virtuous man behave? Glaucon suggests that he will behave no better than the rogue:

> No one, it is commonly believed, would have such iron strength of mind as to stand fast in doing right or keep his hands off other men's goods, when he could go to the market-place and fearlessly help himself to anything he wanted, enter houses and sleep with any woman he chose, set prisoners free and kill men at his pleasure, and in a word go about among men with the powers of a god. He would behave no better than the other; both would take the same course.[1]

Moreover, why shouldn't he? Once he is freed from the fear of reprisal, why shouldn't a man simply do what he pleases, or what he thinks is best for himself? What reason is there for him to continue being "moral" when it is clearly not to his own advantage to do so?

These skeptical views suggested by Glaucon have come to be known as *psychological egoism* and *ethical egoism* respectively. Psychological egoism is the view that all men are selfish in everything that they do, that is, that the only motive from which anyone ever acts is self-interest. On this view, even when men are acting in ways apparently calculated to benefit others, they are actually motivated by the belief that acting in this way is to their own advantage, and if they did not believe this, they would not be doing that action. Ethical egoism is, by contrast, a normative view about how men *ought* to act. It is the view that, regardless of how men do in fact behave, they have no obligation to do anything except what is in their own interests. According to the ethical egoist, a person is always justified in doing whatever is in his own interest, regardless of the effect on others.

Clearly, if either of these views is correct, then "the moral institution of life" (to use Butler's well-turned phrase) is very different than what we normally think. The majority of mankind is grossly deceived about what is, or ought to be, the case, where morals are concerned.

II

Psychological egoism seems to fly in the face of the facts. We are tempted to say, "Of course people act unselfishly all the time. For example, Smith gives up a trip to the

---

[1] *The Republic of Plato*, trans. F. M. Cornford (Oxford, 1941), p. 45.

country, which he would have enjoyed very much, in order to stay behind and help a friend with his studies, which is a miserable way to pass the time. This is a perfectly clear case of unselfish behavior, and if the psychological egoist thinks that such cases do not occur, then he is just mistaken." Given such obvious instances of "unselfish behavior," what reply can the egoist make? There are two general arguments by which he might try to show that all actions, including those such as the one just outlined, are in fact motivated by self-interest. Let us examine these in turn:

A. The first argument goes as follows. If we describe one person's action as selfish, and another person's action as unselfish, we are overlooking the crucial fact that in both cases, assuming that the action is done voluntarily, *the agent is merely doing what he most wants to do*. If Smith stays behind to help his friend, that only shows that he wanted to help his friend more than he wanted to go to the country. And why should he be praised for his "unselfishness" when he is only doing what he wants to do? He cannot be said to be acting unselfishly.

This argument is so bad that it would not deserve to be taken seriously except for the fact that so many otherwise intelligent people have been taken in by it. First, the argument rests on the premise that people never voluntarily do anything except what they want to do. But this is patently false; there are at least two classes of actions that are exceptions to this generalization. One is the set of actions which we may not want to do, but which we do anyway as a means to an end which we want to achieve; for example, going to the dentist in order to stop a toothache, or going to work every day in order to be able to draw our pay at the end of the month. These cases may be regarded as consistent with the spirit of the egoist argument, however, since the ends mentioned are wanted by the agent. But the other set of actions are those which we do, not because we want to, nor even because there is an end which we want to achieve, but because we feel ourselves *under an obligation* to do them. For example, someone may do something because he has promised to do it, and thus feels obligated, even though he does not want to do it. It is sometimes suggested that in such cases we do the action, because, after all, we want to keep our promises; so, even here, we are doing what we want. However, this dodge will not work: If I have promised to do something, and if I do not want to do it, then it is simply false to say that I want to keep my promise. In such cases we feel a conflict precisely because we do not want to do what we feel obligated to do. It is reasonable to think that Smith's action falls roughly into this second category: He might stay behind, not because he wants to, but because he feels that his friend needs help.

But suppose we were to concede, for the sake of the argument, that all voluntary action is motivated by the agent's wants, or at least that Smith is so motivated. Even if these were granted, it would not follow that Smith is acting selfishly or from self-interest. For if Smith wants to do something that will help his friend, even when it means forgoing his own enjoyments, that is precisely what makes him *un*selfish. What else could unselfishness be, if not wanting to help others? Another way to put the same point is to say that it is the *object* of a want that determines whether it is selfish or not. The mere fact that I am acting on *my* wants does not mean that I am acting selfishly; that depends on *what it is* that I want. If I want only my own good, and care nothing for others, then I am selfish; but if I also want other people to be well-off and happy, and if I act on *that* desire, then my action is not selfish. So much for this argument.

B. The second argument for psychological egoism is this. Since so-called unselfish actions always produce a sense of self-satisfaction in the agent,[2] and since this sense of satisfaction is a pleasant state of consciousness, it follows that the point of the action is really to achieve a pleasant state of consciousness, rather than bring about any good for others. Therefore, the action is "unselfish" only at a superficial level of analysis. Smith will feel much better with himself for having stayed to help his friend—if he had gone to the country, he would have felt terrible about it—and that is the real point of the action. According to a well-known story, this argument was once expressed by Abraham Lincoln:

> Mr. Lincoln once remarked to a fellow-passenger on an old-time mud-coach that all men were prompted by selfishness in doing good. His fellow-passenger was antagonizing this position when they were passing over a corduroy bridge that spanned a slough. As they crossed this bridge they espied an old razor-backed sow on the bank making a terrible noise because her pigs had got into the slough and were in danger of drowning. As the old coach began to climb the hill, Mr. Lincoln called out, "Driver, can't you stop just a moment?" Then Mr. Lincoln jumped out, ran back, and lifted the little pigs out of the mud and water and placed them on the bank. When he returned, his companion remarked: "Now, Abe, where does selfishness come in on this little episode?" "Why, bless your soul, Ed, that was the very essence of selfishness. I should have had no peace of mind all day had I gone on and left that suffering old sow worrying over those pigs. I did it to get peace of mind, don't you see?"[3].

This argument suffers from defects similar to the previous one. Why should we think that merely because someone derives satisfaction from helping others this makes him selfish? Isn't the unselfish man precisely the one who *does* derive satisfaction from helping others, while the selfish man does not? If Lincoln "got peace of mind" from rescuing the piglets, does this show him to be selfish, or, on the contrary, doesn't it show him to be compassionate and good-hearted? (If a man were truly selfish, why should it bother his conscience that *others* suffer—much less pigs?) Similarly, it is nothing more than shabby sophistry to say, because Smith takes satisfaction in helping his friend, that he is behaving selfishly. If we say this rapidly, while thinking about something else, perhaps it will sound all right; but if we speak slowly, and pay attention to what we are saying, it sounds plain silly.

Moreover, suppose we ask *why* Smith derives satisfaction from helping his friend. The answer will be, it is because Smith cares for him and wants him to succeed. If Smith did not have these concerns, then he would take no pleasure in assisting him; and these concerns, as we have already seen, are the marks of unselfishness, not selfishness. To put the point more generally: If we have a positive attitude toward the attainment of some goal, then we may derive satisfaction from attaining that goal. But the *object* of our attitude is *the attainment of that goal*; and we must want to attain the goal *before* we can find any satisfaction in it. We do not, in other words, desire some sort of "pleasurable consciousness" and then try to figure out how to

---

[2] Or, as it is sometimes said, "It gives him a clear conscience," or "He couldn't sleep at night if he had done otherwise," or "He would have been ashamed of himself for not doing it," and so on.

[3] Frank C. Sharp, *Ethics* (New York, 1928), pp. 74–75. Quoted from the Springfield (Ill.) *Monitor* in the *Outlook*, vol. 56, p. 1059.

achieve it; rather, we desire all sorts of different things—money, a new fishing-boat, to be a better chessplayer, to get a promotion in our work, etc.—and because we desire these things, we derive satisfaction from attaining them. And so, if someone desires the welfare and happiness of another person, he will derive satisfaction from that; but this does not mean that this satisfaction is the object of his desire, or that he is in any way selfish on account of it.

It is a measure of the weakness of psychological egoism that these insupportable arguments are the ones most often advanced in its favor. Why, then, should anyone ever have thought it a true view? Perhaps because of a desire for theoretical simplicity: In thinking about human conduct, it would be nice if there were some simple formula that would unite the diverse phenomena of human behavior under a single explanatory principle, just as simple formulae in physics bring together a great many apparently different phenomena. And since it is obvious that self-regard is an overwhelmingly important factor in motivation, it is only natural to wonder whether all motivation might not be explained in these terms. But the answer is clearly no; while a great many human actions are motivated entirely or in part by self-interest, only by a deliberate distortion of the facts can we say that all conduct is so motivated. This will be clear, I think, if we correct three confusions which are commonplace. The exposure of these confusions will remove the last traces of plausibility from the psychological egoist thesis.

The first is the confusion of selfishness with self-interest. The two are clearly not the same. If I see a physician when I am feeling poorly, I am acting in my own interest but no one would think of calling me "selfish" on account of it. Similarly, brushing my teeth, working hard at my job, and obeying the law are all in my self-interest but none of these are examples of selfish conduct. This is because selfish behavior is behavior that ignores the interests of others, in circumstances in which their interests ought not to be ignored. This concept has a definite evaluative flavor; to call someone "selfish" is not just to describe his action but to condemn it. Thus, you would not call me selfish for eating a normal meal in normal circumstances (although it may surely be in my self-interest); but you would call me selfish for hoarding food while others about are starving.

The second confusion is the assumption that every action is done *either* from self-interest or from other-regarding motives. Thus, the egoist concludes that if there is no such thing as genuine altruism then all actions must be done from self-interest. But this is certainly a false dichotomy. The man who continues to smoke cigarettes, even after learning about the connection between smoking and cancer, is surely not acting from self-interest, not even by his own standards—self-interest would dictate that he quit smoking at once—and he is not acting altruistically either. He *is*, no doubt, smoking for the pleasure of it, but all that this shows is that undisciplined pleasure-seeking and acting from self-interest are very different. This is what led Butler to remark that "The thing to be lamented is, not that men have so great regard to their own good or interest in the present world, for they have not enough."[4]

---

[4] *The Works of Joseph Butler*, ed. W. E. Gladstone (Oxford, 1896), vol. 2, p. 26.

The last two paragraphs show (*a*) that it is false that all actions are selfish, and (*b*) that it is false that all actions are done out of self-interest. And it should be noted that these two points can be made, and were, without any appeal to putative examples of altruism.

The third confusion is the common but false assumption that a concern for one's own welfare is incompatible with any genuine concern for the welfare of others. Thus, since it is obvious that everyone (or very nearly everyone) does desire his own well-being, it might be thought that no one can really be concerned with others. But again, this is false. There is no inconsistency in desiring that everyone, including oneself *and* others, be well-off and happy. To be sure, it may happen on occasion that our own interests conflict with the interests of others, and in these cases we will have to make hard choices. But even in these cases we might sometimes opt for the interests of others, especially when the others involved are our family or friends. But more importantly, not all cases are like this: Sometimes we are able to promote the welfare of others when our own interests are not involved at all. In these cases not even the strongest self-regard need prevent us from acting considerately toward others.

Once these confusions are cleared away, it seems to me obvious enough that there is no reason whatever to accept psychological egoism. On the contrary, if we simply observe people's behavior with an open mind, we may find that a great deal of it is motivated by self-regard, but by no means all of it; and that there is no reason to deny that "the moral institution of life" can include a place for the virtue of beneficence.[5]

III

The ethical egoist would say at this point, "Of course it is possible for people to act altruistically, and perhaps many people do act that way—but there is no reason why they *should* do so. A person is under no obligation to do anything except what is in his own interests."[6] This is really quite a radical doctrine. Suppose I have an urge to set fire to some public building (say, a department store) just for the fascination of watching the spectacular blaze: According to this view, the fact that several people might be burned to death provides no reason whatever why I should not do it. After all, this only concerns *their* welfare, not my own, and according to the ethical egoist the only person I need think of is myself.

Some might deny that ethical egoism has any such monstrous consequences. They would point out that it is really to my own advantage not to set the fire— for, if I do that I may be caught and put into prison (unlike Gyges, I have no magic ring for protection). Moreover, even if I could avoid being caught it is still to my advantage to respect the rights and interests of others, for it is to my advantage to live in a society in which people's rights and interests are respected. Only in such a

---

[5] The capacity for altruistic behavior is not unique to human beings. Some interesting experiments with rhesus monkeys have shown that these animals will refrain from operating a device for securing food if this causes other animals to suffer pain. See Masserman, Wechkin, and Terris, "Altruistic' Behavior in Rhesus Monkeys," *The American Journal of Psychiatry*, vol. 121 (1964), 584–585.

[6] I take this to be the view of Ayn Rand, insofar as I understand her confusing doctrine.

society can I live a happy and secure life; so, in acting kindly toward others, I would merely be doing my part to create and maintain the sort of society which it is to my advantage to have.[7] Therefore, it is said, the egoist would not be such a bad man; he would be as kindly and considerate as anyone else, because he would see that it is to his own advantage to be kindly and considerate.

This is a seductive line of thought, but it seems to me mistaken. Certainly it is to everyone's advantage (including the egoist's) to preserve a stable society where people's interests are generally protected. But there is no reason for the egoist to think that merely because *he* will not honor the rules of the social game, decent society will collapse. For the vast majority of people are not egoists, and there is no reason to think that they will be converted by his example—especially if he is discreet and does not unduly flaunt his style of life. What this line of reasoning shows is not that the egoist himself must act benevolently, but that he must encourage *others* to do so. He must take care to conceal from public view his own self-centered method of decision-making, and urge others to act on precepts very different from those on which he is willing to act.

The rational egoist, then, cannot advocate that egoism be universally adopted by everyone. For he wants a world in which his own interests are maximized; and if other people adopted the egoistic policy of pursuing their own interests to the exclusion of his interest, as he pursues his interest to the exclusion of theirs, then such a world would be impossible. So he himself will be an egoist, but he will want others to be altruists.

This brings us to what is perhaps the most popular "refutation" of ethical egoism current among philosophical writers—the argument that ethical egoism is at bottom inconsistent because it cannot be universalized.[8] The argument goes like this:

To say that any action or policy of action is *right* (or that it *ought* to be adopted) entails that it is right for *anyone* in the same sort of circumstances. I cannot, for example, say that it is right for me to lie to you, and yet object when you lie to me (provided, of course, that the circumstances are the same). I cannot hold that it is all right for me to drink your beer and then complain when you drink mine. This is just the requirement that we be consistent in our evaluations; it is a requirement of logic. Now it is said that ethical egoism cannot meet this requirement because, as we have already seen, the egoist would not want others to act in the same way that he acts. Moreover, suppose he *did* advocate the universal adoption of egoistic policies: he would be saying to Peter, "You ought to pursue your own interests even if it means destroying Paul"; and he would be saying to Paul, "You ought to pursue your own interests even if it means destroying Peter." The attitudes expressed in these two recommendations seem clearly inconsistent—he is urging the advancement of Peter's interest at one moment, and countenancing their defeat at the next. Therefore, the argument goes, there is no way to maintain the

---

[7] *Cf.* Thomas Hobbes, *Leviathan* (London, 1651), chap. 17.

[8] See, for example, Brian Medlin, "Ultimate Principles and Ethical Egoism," *Australasian Journal of Philosophy*, vol. 35 (1957), 111–118; and D. H. Monro, *Empiricism and Ethics* (Cambridge, 1967), chap. 16.

doctrine of ethical egoism as a consistent view about how we ought to act. We will fall into inconsistency whenever we try.

What are we to make of this argument? Are we to conclude that ethical egoism has been refuted? Such a conclusion, I think, would be unwarranted; for I think that we can show, contrary to this argument, how ethical egoism can be maintained consistently. We need only to interpret the egoist's position in a sympathetic way: We should say that he has in mind a certain kind of world which he would prefer over all others; it would be a world in which his own interests were maximized, regardless of the effects on other people. The egoist's primary policy of action, then, would be to act in such a way as to bring about, as nearly as possible, this sort of world. Regardless of however morally reprehensible we might find it, there is nothing *inconsistent* in someone's adopting this as his ideal and acting in a way calculated to bring it about. And if someone did adopt this as his ideal, then he would advocate universal altruism; as we have already seen, he would want other people to be altruists. So if he advocates any principles of conduct for the general public, they will be altruistic principles. This would not be inconsistent; on the contrary, it would be perfectly consistent with his goal of creating a world in which his own interests are maximized. To be sure, he would have to be deceitful; in order to secure the good will of others, and a favorable hearing for his exhortations to altruism, he would have to pretend that he was himself prepared to accept altruistic principles. But again, that would be all right; from the egoist's point of view, this would merely be a matter of adopting the necessary means to the achievement of his goal—and while we might not approve of this, there is nothing inconsistent about it. Again, it might be said, "He advocates one thing, but does another. Surely *that's* inconsistent." But it is not; for what he advocates and what he does are both calculated as means to an end (the *same* end, we might note); and as such, he is doing what is rationally required in each case. Therefore, contrary to the previous argument, there is nothing inconsistent in the ethical egoist's view. He cannot be refuted by the claim that he contradicts himself.

Is there, then, no way to refute the ethical egoist? If by "refute" we mean show that he has made some *logical* error, the answer is that there is not. However, there is something more that can be said. The egoist challenge to our ordinary moral convictions amounts to a demand for an explanation of why we should adopt certain policies of action, namely policies in which the good of others is given importance. We can give an answer to this demand, albeit an indirect one. The reason one ought not to do actions that would hurt other people is: Other people would be hurt. The reason one ought to do actions that would benefit other people is: Other people would be benefited. This may at first seem like a piece of philosophical sleight-of-hand, but it is not. The point is that the welfare of human beings is something that most of us value *for its own sake*, and not merely for the sake of something else. Therefore, when *further* reasons are demanded for valuing the welfare of human beings, we cannot point to anything further to satisfy this demand. It is not that we have no reason for pursuing these policies, but that our reason *is* that these policies are for the good of human beings.

So if we are asked, "Why shouldn't I set fire to this department store?" one answer would be, "Because if you do, people may be burned to death." This is a complete, sufficient reason which does not require qualification or supplementation of any sort. If someone seriously wants to know why this action shouldn't be done, that's the reason. If we are pressed further and asked the skeptical question, "But why shouldn't I do actions that will harm others?" we may not know what to say—but this is because the questioner has included in his question the very answer we would like to give: "Why shouldn't you do actions that will harm others? Because doing those actions would harm others." The egoist, no doubt, will not be happy with this. He will protest that *we* may accept this as a reason, but *he* does not. And here the argument stops: There are limits to what can be accomplished by argument, and if the egoist really doesn't care about other people—if he honestly doesn't care whether they are helped or hurt by his actions—then we have reached those limits. If we want to persuade him to act decently toward his fellow humans, we will have to make our appeal to such other attitudes as he does possess, by threats, bribes, or other cajolery. That is all that we can do.

Though some may find this situation distressing (we would like to be able to show that the egoist is just *wrong*), it holds no embarrassment for common morality. What we have come up against is simply a fundamental requirement of rational action, namely, that the existence of reasons for action always depends on the prior existence of certain attitudes in the agent. For example, the fact that a certain course of action would make the agent a lot of money is a reason for doing it only if the agent wants to make money; the fact that practicing at chess makes one a better player is a reason for practicing only if one wants to be a better player; and so on. Similarly, the fact that a certain action would help the agent is a reason for doing the action only if the agent cares about his own welfare, and the fact that an action would help others is a reason for doing it only if the agent cares about others. In this respect ethical egoism and what we might call ethical altruism are in exactly the same fix: Both require that the agent *care* about himself, or other people, before they can get started.

So a nonegoist will accept "It would harm another person" as a reason not to do an action simply because he cares about what happens to that other person. When the egoist says that he does *not* accept that as a reason, he is saying something quite extraordinary. He is saying that he has no affection for friends or family, that he never feels pity or compassion, that he is the sort of person who can look on scenes of human misery with complete indifference, so long as he is not the one suffering. Genuine egoists, people who really don't care at all about anyone other than themselves, are rare. It is important to keep this in mind when thinking about ethical egoism; it is easy to forget just how fundamental to human psychological makeup the feeling of sympathy is. Indeed, a man without any sympathy at all would scarcely be recognizable as a man; and that is what makes ethical egoism such a disturbing doctrine in the first place.

IV

There are, of course, many different ways in which the skeptic might challenge the assumptions underlying our moral practice. In this essay I have discussed only two of them, the two put forward by Glaucon in the passage that I cited from Plato's *Republic*. It is important that the assumptions underlying our moral practice should not be confused with particular judgments made within that practice. To defend one is not to defend the other. We may assume—quite properly, if my analysis has been correct—that the virtue of beneficence does, and indeed should, occupy an important place in "the moral institution of life"; and yet we may make constant and miserable errors when it comes to judging when and in what ways this virtue is to be exercised. Even worse, we may often be able to make accurate moral judgments, and know what we ought to do, but not do it. For these ills, philosophy alone is not the cure.

STUDY QUESTIONS

1. The great Renaissance philosopher Thomas Hobbes was a proponent of psychological egoism. Someone once saw him giving money to a beggar and asked if this kindly gesture did not prove that psychological egoism was wrong. Hobbes replied that his action was indeed self-interested because helping beggars made him feel good. Evaluate Hobbes's riposte in light of Rachels's discussion.
2. If you found the Ring of Gyges and no longer needed to appear to abide by moral rules, do you think you would behave as Gyges did? Do you think that other controls would prevent you from becoming amoral? Explain.
3. What is Rachels's strongest argument against psychological egoism? Against ethical egoism? Are Rachels's arguments persuasive?
4. The psychological egoist says that self-love motivates all human action. A number of philosophers have argued that self-hate, altruism, and malice also motivate human beings. Who do you think is right?

The Virtue of Selfishness

Ayn Rand

> Ayn Rand (1905–1982) was a well-known novelist and social thinker whose individualist philosophy, "objectivism," continues to be highly influential. Her major works include *The Fountainhead* (1943) and *Atlas Shrugged* (1957).
>
> Ayn Rand defines *selfishness* as "concern with one's own interests," and she asks why this should be considered a vice. Altruism, the selfless pursuit of the good of others, is a dangerous ideal that engenders guilt and cynicism in those who seek to practice it and impose it on others: "cynicism, because they neither practice nor accept the altruist morality—guilt, because they dare not reject it." Rand believes that a responsible concern for one's own interests is the essence of a moral existence.

The title of this book may evoke the kind of question that I hear once in a while: "Why do you use the word 'selfishness' to denote virtuous qualities of character, when that word antagonizes so many people to whom it does not mean the things you mean?"

To those who ask it, my answer is: "For the reason that makes you afraid of it."

But there are others, who would not ask that question, sensing the moral cowardice it implies, yet who are unable to formulate my actual reason or to identify the profound moral issue involved. It is to them that I will give a more explicit answer.

It is not a mere semantic issue nor a matter of arbitrary choice. The meaning ascribed in popular usage to the word "selfishness" is not merely wrong: it represents a devastating intellectual "package-deal," which is responsible, more than any other single factor, for the arrested moral development of mankind.

In popular usage, the word "selfishness" is a synonym of evil; the image it conjures is of a murderous brute who tramples over piles of corpses to achieve his own ends, who cares for no living being and pursues nothing but the gratification of the mindless whims of any immediate moment.

Yes the exact meaning and dictionary definition of the word "selfishness" is: *concern with one's own interests.*

This concept does *not* include a moral evaluation; it does not tell us whether concern with one's own interests is good or evil; nor does it tell us what constitutes man's actual interests. It is the task of ethics to answer such questions.

The ethics of altruism has created the image of the brute, as its answer, in order to make men accept two inhuman tenets: (a) that any concern with one's own interests is evil, regardless of what these interests might be, and (b) that the brute's activities are *in fact* to one's own interest (which altruism enjoins man to renounce for the sake of his neighbors).

For a view of the nature of altruism, its consequences and the enormity of the moral corruption it perpetrates, I shall refer you to *Atlas Shrugged*—or to any of today's newspaper headlines. What concerns us here is altruism's *default* in the field of ethical theory.

There are two moral questions which altruism lumps together into one "package-deal": (1) What are values? (2) Who should be the beneficiary of values? Altruism substitutes the second for the first; it evades the task of defining a code of moral values, thus leaving man, in fact, without moral guidance.

Altruism declares that any action taken for the benefit of others is good, and any action taken for one's own benefit is evil. Thus the *beneficiary* of an action is the only criterion of moral value—and so long as the beneficiary is anybody other than oneself, anything goes.

Hence the appalling immorality, the chronic injustice, the grotesque double standards, the insoluble conflicts and contradictions that have characterized human relationships and human societies throughout history, under all the variants of the altruist ethics.

Observe the indecency of what passes for moral judgments today. An industrialist who produces a fortune, and a gangster who robs a bank are regarded as equally immoral, since they both sought wealth for their own "selfish" benefit. A young man who gives up his career in order to support his parents and never rises beyond the rank of grocery clerk is regarded as morally superior to the young man who endures an excruciating struggle and achieves his personal ambition.

A dictator is regarded as moral, since the unspeakable atrocities he committed were intended to benefit "the people," not himself.

Observe what this beneficiary-criterion of morality does to a man's life. The first thing he learns is that morality is his enemy: he has nothing to gain from it, he can only lose; self-inflicted loss, self-inflicted pain and the gray, debilitating pall of an incomprehensible duty is all that he can expect. He may hope that others might occasionally sacrifice themselves for his benefit, as he grudgingly sacrifices himself for theirs, but he knows that the relationship will bring mutual resentment, not pleasure—and that, morally, their pursuit of values will be like an exchange of unwanted, unchosen Christmas presents, which neither is morally permitted to buy for himself. Apart from such times as he manages to perform some act of self-sacrifice, he possesses no moral significance: morality takes no cognizance of him and has nothing to say to him for guidance in the crucial issues of his life; it is only his own personal, private, "selfish" life and, as such, it is regarded either as evil or, at best, *amoral*.

Since nature does not provide man with an automatic form of survival, since he has to support his life by his own effort, the doctrine that concern with one's own interests is evil means that man's desire to live is evil—that man's life, as such, is evil. No doctrine could be more evil than that.

Yet that is the meaning of altruism, implicit in such examples as the equation of an industrialist with a robber. There is a fundamental moral difference between a man who sees his self-interest in production and a man who sees it in robbery. The evil of a robber does *not* lie in the fact that he pursues his own interests, but in *what* he regards as to his own interest; *not* in the fact that he pursues his values, but in *what* he chose to value; *not* in the fact that he wants to live, but in the fact that he wants to live on a subhuman level....

If it is true that what I mean by "selfishness" is not what is meant conventionally, then *this* is one of the worst indictments of altruism: it means that altruism *permits no concept* of a self-respecting, self-supporting man—a man who supports his life by his own effort and neither sacrifices himself nor others. It means that altruism permits no view of men except as sacrificial animals and profiteers-on-sacrifice, as victims and parasites—that it permits no concept of a benevolent coexistence among men—that it permits no concept of *justice*.

If you wonder about the reasons behind the ugly mixture of cynicism and guilt in which most men spend their lives, these are the reasons: cynicism, because they neither practice nor accept the altruist morality—guilt, because they dare not reject it.

To rebel against so devastating an evil, one has to rebel against its basic premise. To redeem both man and morality, it is the concept of *"selfishness"* that one has to redeem.

Study Questions

1. Does Rand do herself an injustice by speaking paradoxically about selfishness as a virtue instead of speaking about the virtue of self-interest? Why do you think she deliberately chooses to risk being misunderstood? Consider also her use of the term *altruism*, which in the view of most moral philosophers is praiseworthy, but which she disparages.

2. Rand says that gangsters and industrialists are not on the same moral plane, even though both "selfishly" seek wealth. How does she distinguish between them?

3. Rand proposes that we redefine selfishness in a way that may redeem it as a virtue for moral philosophy. Attempt to redefine selfishness along the lines Rand suggests. Now look at your definition and say whether you find merit in the idea that selfishness, as you now construe it, does indeed turn out to be a virtue. Explain.
4. Compare and contrast Rand's critique of altruism with Nietzsche's critique of Christian morality.

Egoism, Self-Interest, and Altruism

Louis Pojman

A biographical sketch of Louis Pojman is found on page 103.

Louis Pojman criticizes Ayn Rand for forcing us to choose between (1) an antilife altruism and (2) a life-affirming egoism. He calls this a "false dilemma" and argues that it is possible to practice self-love while showing altruistic concern for others. He notes that evolutionary psychologists and ethnographers maintain that genetic fitness favors the survival of a species of individuals who are both self-interested and altruistic.

If most of us lived lives of self-sacrificing altruism (as the early Christians were often portrayed as doing), we should be at the mercy of the few unscrupulous egoists who would soon multiply at our expense. Although the pure altruists would inevitably decrease in number, the unconscionable egoists would also die out, since they would have no one to exploit. A third group, practicing an "I'll scratch your back if you'll scratch mine" lifestyle, would, however, survive and thrive. This third group of "reciprocal altruists" are "tit-for-tatters," doing good only to those who reciprocate with goodness and being unhelpful to those who are utterly selfish. Thus the ethnographers show that combining the virtue of self-interestedness with reciprocal altruism is far from being antilife. On the contrary, living in accordance with "a rational morality based on cooperative self-interest" is the key to survival of the species. Pojman concludes that something in between "Christian" self-effacement and Randian individualist egoism is the reasonable doctrine.

In her book *The Virtue of Selfishness*, Ayn Rand argues that selfishness is a virtue and altruism a vice, a totally destructive idea that leads to the undermining of individual worth. She defines *altruism* as the view that any action taken for the benefit of others is good, and any action taken for one's own benefit is evil. Thus, the *beneficiary* of an action is the only criterion of moral value—and so long as the beneficiary is anybody other than oneself, anything goes.[1]

As such, altruism is suicidal:

> If a man accepts the ethics of altruism, his first concern is not how to live his life, but how to sacrifice it.... Altruism erodes men's capacity to grasp the value of an individual life; it reveals a mind from which the reality of a human being has been wiped out.

Since finding happiness is the highest goal and good in life, altruism, which calls on us to sacrifice our happiness for the good of others, is contrary to our highest good.

Her argument seems to go something like this:

1. The perfection of one's abilities in a state of happiness is the highest goal for humans. We have a moral duty to attempt to reach this goal.
2. The ethics of altruism prescribes that we sacrifice our interests and lives for the good of others.
3. Therefore the ethics of altruism is incompatible with the goal of happiness.
4. Ethical egoism prescribes that we seek our own happiness exclusively, and as such it is consistent with the happiness goal.
5. Therefore ethical egoism is the correct moral theory....

The Ayn Rand argument for the virtue of selfishness appears to be flawed by the fallacy of a false dilemma. It simplistically assumes that absolute altruism and absolute egoism are the only alternatives. But this is an extreme view of the matter. There are plenty of options between these two positions. Even a predominant egoist would admit that (analogous to the paradox of hedonism) sometimes the best way to reach self-fulfillment is for us to forget about ourselves and strive to live for goals, causes, or other persons. Even if altruism is not required (as a duty), it may be permissible in many cases. Furthermore, self-interest may not be incompatible with other-regarding motivation. Even the Second Great Commandment set forth by Moses and Jesus states not that you must always sacrifice yourself for the other person, but that you ought to love your neighbor *as* yourself (Lev. 19: 19; Matt. 23). Self-interest and self-love are morally good things, but not at the expense of other people's legitimate interests. When there is moral conflict of interests, a fair process of adjudication needs to take place....

If sheer unadulterated egoism is an inadequate moral theory, does that mean we ought to aim at complete altruism, total self-effacement for the sake of others? ...

With the development of sociobiology—in the work of E. O. Wilson but particularly the work of Robert Trivers, J. Maynard Smith, and Richard Dawkins—a theory has come to the fore that combines radical individualism with limited altruism. It is not the group or the species that is of evolutionary importance but the gene, or, more precisely, the gene type. Genes—the parts of the chromosomes that carry the

---

[1] Ayn Rand, *The Virtue of Selfishness* (New American Library, 1964), pp. vii and 27–32; 80ff.

blueprints for all our natural traits (e.g., height, hair color, skin color, intelligence)—copy themselves as they divide and multiply. At conception they combine with the genes of a member of the opposite sex to form a new individual.

In his fascinating sociobiological study, Richard Dawkins describes human behavior as determined evolutionarily by stable strategies set to replicate the gene.[2] This is not done consciously, of course, but by the invisible hand that drives consciousness. We are essentially gene machines.

Morality—that is, successful morality—can be seen as an evolutionary strategy for gene replication. Here's an example: Birds are afflicted with life-endangering parasites. Because they lack limbs to enable them to pick the parasites off their heads, they—like much of the animal kingdom—depend on the ritual of mutual grooming. It turns out that nature has evolved two basic types of birds in this regard: those who are disposed to groom anyone (the nonprejudiced type?), and those who refuse to groom anyone but who present themselves for grooming. The former type of bird Dawkins calls "Suckers" and the latter "Cheaters."

In a geographical area containing harmful parasites and where there are only Suckers or Cheaters, Suckers will do fairly well, but Cheaters will not survive, for want of cooperation. However, in a Sucker population in which a mutant Cheater arises, the Cheater will prosper, and the Cheater gene-type will multiply. As the Suckers are exploited, they will gradually die out. But if and when they become too few to groom the Cheaters, the Cheaters will start to die off too and eventually become extinct.

Why don't birds all die off, then? Well, somehow nature has come up with a third type, call them "Grudgers." Grudgers groom all and only those who reciprocate in grooming them. They groom each other and Suckers, but not Cheaters. In fact, once caught, a Cheater is marked forever. There is no forgiveness. It turns out then that unless there are a lot of Suckers around, Cheaters have a hard time of it—harder even than Suckers. However, it is the Grudgers that prosper. Unlike Suckers, they don't waste time messing with unappreciative Cheaters, so they are not exploited and have ample energy to gather food and build better nests for their loved ones.

J. L. Mackie argues that the real name for Suckers is "Christian," one who believes in complete altruism, even turning the other cheek to one's assailant and loving one's enemy. Cheaters are ruthless egoists who can survive only if there are enough naive altruists around. Whereas Grudgers are *reciprocal* altruists who have a rational morality based on cooperative self-interest, Suckers, such as Socrates and Jesus, advocate "turning the other cheek and repaying evil with good."[3] Instead of a Rule of Reciprocity, "I'll scratch your back if you'll scratch mine," the extreme altruist substitutes the Golden Rule, "If you want the other fellow to scratch your back, you scratch his—even if he won't reciprocate."

The moral of the story is this: Altruist morality (so interpreted) is only rational given the payoff of eternal life (with a scorekeeper, as Woody Allen says). Take that

---

[2] Richard Dawkins, *The Selfish Gene* (Oxford University Press, 1976), Ch. 10.
[3] J. L. Mackie, "The Law of the Jungle: Moral Alternatives and Principles of Evolution," *Philosophy* 53 (1978).

away, and it looks like a Sucker system. What replaces the "Christian" vision of submission and saintliness is the reciprocal altruist with a tit-for-tat morality, someone who is willing to share with those willing to cooperate.

Mackie may caricature the position of the religious altruist, but he misses the subtleties of wisdom involved (Jesus said, "Be as wise as serpents but as harmless as doves"). Nevertheless, he does remind us that there is a difference between core morality and complete altruism. We have duties to cooperate and reciprocate, but no duty to serve those who manipulate us nor an obvious duty to sacrifice ourselves for people outside our domain of special responsibility. We have a special duty of high altruism toward those in the close circle of our concern, namely, our family and friends.

Conclusion

Martin Luther once said that humanity is like a man who, when mounting a horse, always falls off on the opposite side, especially when he tries to over-compensate for his previous exaggerations. So it is with ethical egoism. Trying to compensate for an irrational, guilt-ridden, Sucker altruism of the morality of self-effacement, it falls off the horse on the other side, embracing a Cheater's preoccupation with self-exaltation that robs the self of the deepest joys in life. Only the person who mounts properly, avoiding both extremes, is likely to ride the horse of happiness to its goal.

Study Questions

1. Describe the ways of Cheaters, Suckers, and Grudgers, and explain why evolution favors the proliferation of those who possess Grudger genes.
2. How does the fact that reciprocal altruism is a survival mechanism affect moral philosophy?
3. A Cheater could say, "Of course, the Grudgers are fittest, but I still think there is nothing wrong with taking full advantage of anyone who behaves altruistically to me." What answer can you give to this hardened Cheater? James Rachels argues that there is no logical way we can refute the Cheater, while Pojman seems to think that evolutionary theory can help us here. Who is right? Why?
4. Recently David Kelley has defended Ayn Rand from criticism like Pojman's and Rachels's. He points out that Rand distinguishes between sacrificial altruism, which she rejects as a nonvirtue, and benevolence, which—like Adam Smith—she considers to be the second of two major virtues (the other being justice). Kelley's version of benevolence is not unlike the reciprocal altruism that evolutionary psychologists speak of. Is there room for benevolence as a major virtue in a doctrine that holds self-interested behavior to be the highest moral imperative? Explain.

Why Not Be a Bad Person?

Colin McGinn

Colin McGinn (b. 1950), formerly the Wilde Reader in Mental Philosophy at Oxford University, is now a professor of philosophy at the University of Miami. His published works include *Moral Literacy: Or How to Do the Right Thing* (1992), *The Power of Movies: How Screen and Mind Interact* (2005), and *Shakespeare's Philosophy: Discovering the Meaning Behind the Plays* (2006).

Colin McGinn says that the answer to the question "Why be virtuous?" is obvious: "Because goodness is good." According to McGinn, virtue needs no justification: it is its own justification.

Virtue is good, but so is truth; a good person is a truthful person. So is beauty; the characters of good persons give aesthetic pleasure. Unlike physical beauty, which not everyone can have, moral beauty is accessible to all who try to live well. McGinn's chosen list of basic virtues consists of kindness, honesty, justice, and independence. He tells us why these are his favorites.

McGinn argues that the virtuous person is far more interesting than his vicious counterpart. The latter is "a coward, a manipulator, a dank-souled kill-joy. I see nothing attractive about him." Badness, says McGinn is boring and ugly. It is depressing. "Its music is muzak."

... Why not be a bad person? What *reason* is there for being a good person? The answer is, there is no reason—or no reason that cuts deeper, or goes further, than the tautology "because goodness is good." The reason you should be virtuous and not vicious is *just* that virtue is virtue and vice is vice. Ultimately, what you get from virtue is simply ... virtue. Virtue may also get you health, wealth and happiness, but there is certainly no guarantee of that—definitely not—and in any case that isn't the *reason* you should be virtuous.

Logically, it is like the question of why you should care about your own future welfare: because your welfare is *your welfare*. Nothing more can really be said; and if someone just doesn't see it, there is not much you can do to convince them. It adds nothing to say that it is stupid not to care about your own future welfare. That is perfectly true, but it is stupid simply because ... you should care about your own future welfare. Analogously, we can equally say that it is immoral not to care about being a good person; but again, this really boils down to repeating ourselves—it is immoral because being a good person is something you should be. "Stupid" goes with "prudent" the way "immoral" goes with "virtuous." Moral justification, like all justification, comes to an end somewhere. At some point we have simply to repeat ourselves, possibly with a certain emphasis, or else just remain silent. Virtue is, if you like, its own justification, its own reason: you can't dig deeper than it. To the question "Why should I care about others as well as myself?" the best answer is another question: "Why should you care about yourself as well as others?" In the case of the latter question, the right reply is, "Because you are a person to be taken into account too"; and in the former case, the right reply is, "Because *they* are persons to be taken into account too." To insist that I am me and they are them is merely to utter an unhelpful tautology, which does nothing to show that I have a reason to be self-concerned but no reason to be moral. People (and animals) have intrinsic value, so you should take them into account—which is to say that you should be good. Why? Because ... people (and animals) have intrinsic value and should be taken into account—which is to say that you should be good. End of story. End of match. Good is good and bad is bad—that is all you need to know.

Or not quite all. Although virtue can't be justified in other terms, specifically not in terms of self-interest, it does connect with other values in ways that aren't just accidental. Beauty and truth are often linked with goodness as the supreme values: these three commodities are what the world should contain more of. I am happy to go along with these noble sentiments, but I would also add that beauty and truth are bound up with goodness in inextricable ways, as follows.

A good person is a truthful person: habitual deceivers are not good. And truthful not only to others but to themselves: they seek out and respect the truth for their own consumption, not fooling themselves about where the truth lies. She who loves goodness also loves truth.

Less obviously, beauty has a close relation to goodness. Many beautiful works of art are suffused with moral goodness, in ways that are hard to disentangle from their beauty; but more to the point, goodness of character is itself a form of beauty—what we might call "moral beauty" or "beauty of soul." The character of a good person gives aesthetic pleasure. A bad person, by contrast, has an ugly character, a soul we find it repugnant to gaze upon. I think this is why we like to hang the pictures of those we admire, while we find it hard to stand the sight of the wicked. Thus goodness partakes of beauty. Indeed, given that not everyone can be physically beautiful, goodness of character affords one of the few other ways of exemplifying beauty. Nor does it require special talents or great labour, like being musically or poetically gifted. In a sense anyone can be morally beautiful, though not anyone can exhibit musical or literary beauty. This is because moral beauty is more an affair of the will than other kinds. So if you want to make up for a lack of looks, you don't have to become an opera singer: you can simply become a decent human being. (Me, I play the drums.)

This link between goodness and beauty is often noted in regard to the human face. The face of a good person is apt to radiate the virtue within, thus acquiring a beauty it would not otherwise have; while the face of a bad person will tend to reflect the inner ugliness and be repellent to the gaze. Look at the expression on a face, notably when in repose: it can say a lot. This is not of course a simple matter of plain physical ugliness being the measure of a man's badness— far from it. It is a much subtler thing than that, though one that most people can recognise when they see a clear instance of it (I mention no names). A physically ugly face can give off moral beauty, and a physically beautiful face can be marred by inner corruption. Nor, of course, is it easy to judge a person's character from her face, and major mistakes can be made, but with experience it is a skill that can be developed. Attend to the smile, the play of the eyes, the indefinable aura of the overall expression. Naturally the older a person gets, so that their face has had more time to mould itself to their soul, the easier it becomes to read their character from what begins at the neck and ends at the crown. I often think that a certain sort of tightness in the face is a suspicious sign. Oscar Wilde's novel, *The Picture of Dorian Gray*, is precisely a study on the theme of face and character. In it a beautiful young man's evil acts are registered horribly on his portrait, while his own face retains its youthful charm and innocence. In the end, when his conscience catches up with him and he destroys the portrait, his real face turns into the hideous face in the picture—a poetically just conclusion. So, if you are still wondering what reason you have to be virtuous, there is this reason at least: you don't want to end up looking even less attractive than you do now!

So let us grant that we should be virtuous; that still doesn't tell us how much effort we should put into the project. How big a deal is virtue, comparatively speaking? How important is it to develop a good moral character, relative to all the other things you can do in life? Should it be at the top of your list of priorities, or third, or tenth?

I think there should be room for some individual variation here. People differ in their talents, motivations and ambitions. Some people will naturally give more of their time to moral activity than others; their lives will be more centered around ethical concerns. Doctors and welfare workers and politicians are (supposed to be!) like this: it is part of their job description to do good for others. There are those indeed who devote their lives to virtue, doing little else than cultivating it and its products. We sometimes call them "saints" and admire them, rightly so. They may become monks or nuns, renouncing all worldly interests; or they may spend their lives helping the sick and poor without having any religious affiliation. For such people ethical concerns are paramount (I am not saying there are no hypocrites among them).

Other people may have special talents in the arts or sciences, finding their interests consumed by these fields. They will naturally devote their primary energies to giving these talents expression, with little time left over for moral enterprises. Others simply like to have a good time, to enjoy themselves, to do lots of fun things. These good-timers don't reject morality, but it is not at the centre of their interests and desires. Yet others are taken up with sport, finding everything else wan. And, of course, people can be mixtures of each of these extreme types. You might be someone whose main delight is playing the guitar, but you are very concerned about ecological issues, enjoy the odd game of tennis, and aren't averse to a couple of drinks with friends at the weekend.

My view is that each person must decide for himself, in good conscience, what kind of person he is and allot his time and energy proportionately, always remembering that there is no excuse for outright badness. There is no imperative to make virtue your central preoccupation; you don't have to drop everything else in a supreme effort to be good. Most people find it natural to act from a variety of motives: they want to achieve something in their lives, whatever that may be; they want to have some fun; and they want to be virtuous. They would like to do something for others, but they also want to do something for themselves. Virtue should operate in all activities, it goes without saying, but I don't think it should wholly supplant other motives. The full variety of human desires shouldn't be sacrificed to the moral motive alone. A human life is, or should be, big enough for a bit of each.

Where conflicts arise between desires, as is inevitable, there is no alternative to balanced judgement and the admission that you can't have and do everything. I would say, for example, that a mathematical genius shouldn't be expected to sacrifice his gift out of a desire to help out people less fortunate than himself. Since I rate intellectual values very highly, I am prepared to see them accorded considerable weight in personal deliberations. "Don't interrupt me now to help start the neighbour's car—I'm on the brink of solving a major mathematical problem!" People with different enthusiasms might say the same about the importance of (say) great sporting gifts—and I can certainly appreciate their point.

Fortunately individual moral progress isn't terribly time-consuming—you can almost do it as you go along—so there is not much excuse for neglecting it. We are not impressed by a corrupt business man who tells us he never had the *time* to become moral. Being good, at least within your chosen sphere of operations, is something that everyone should be able to manage. You don't need special sabbaticals in order to cultivate virtue in your actions.

There is no short-cut to becoming virtuous, obviously. You can't really take a crash course in it, as with a foreign language, emerging a saint with a diploma to prove it. It is not like slimming either, shedding the bad fat. Virtue arises largely out of one's response to what happens to one during one's life, as of course does vice. For all I know, there is a substantial genetic component to being good. In any case there is no substitute for hands-on practical experience—for living a morally challenging life. This is what makes a person either better or bitter. Reading about it isn't going to endow you magically with all the virtues you wish you had, even if the writer has them all herself—never a safe assumption. However, it may still be possible to focus on the right things by reading about it. I have certainly benefited (I hope!) from things I have read—from Jesus Christ to Bertrand Russell, from St Augustine to Arthur Schopenhauer. So what I am going to do is make a list of virtues and discuss each of them in turn, noting their relation to the corresponding vices. You can nod, or shake your head, as I go along.

Here, then, is my chosen shortlist of basic virtues: Kindness, Honesty, Justice, Independence—the BIG FOUR. What do they mean and why have I chosen them?

Kindness is largely the province of the heart. It is a matter of having generous feelings towards others, desiring that they not suffer, acting in ways that spring from concern for their well-being. A kind person is thus often said to be good-hearted. Kindness is close to compassion, but wider, since it includes not merely a reaction to suffering, but also informs every encounter with others. A kind person is solicitous of other people's feelings, tries not to hurt them, still less to hurt their bodies, and is distressed when others are in distress. A kind person treats the happiness of others as if it were his own happiness. An unkind person, a cruel or callous person, goes out of his way to make others feel bad, to bring them down, even to destroy them, in mind or body. He doesn't care if he hurts others. In fact, he gets a kick out of the suffering of others, especially if he is the cause of it. Their pain is his pleasure. Beating the dog is his idea of fun. His heart is stone.

A kind person is often described as *nice*, an unkind one as *nasty*. These are suggestive terms: we might think of kindness and its opposite as the moral analogues of two kinds of taste or smell—those which have a pleasant effect and those which have an unpleasant one. A nasty person in the room is like a nasty smell; and being at close quarters with such a person is like eating something bitter or off. But the presence of a kind person gives an atmosphere of freshness and sweetness, like a moral flower. You want to breathe a kind person in, absorb his niceness. A nasty person you just want to spit out.

Kindness is not the same as love, in any ordinary sense; nor is unkindness the same as hate. A kind person treats others as he would like to be treated, but this need not amount to love of others. It is a purer thing than love in a way, more a detached concern or respect for others. Love is apt to be more self-centred, more self-serving indeed. Kindness to strangers is kindness in its least diluted form: but you don't have to *love* the stranger in any real sense—you have never even met him before! Kindness is impartial and uncalculating, and not dependent on the vagaries of personal affection. It is the ultimate basis for civility and "good manners"—treating others with decency and consideration, as if they matter, as if they *exist*. To be kind is to be generous and tender of spirit, not miserly and harsh. It is the healing balm of human relations, instead of the serrated blade. Kindness is good. People should be kind.

Honesty is simply the trait of truthfulness, directness, candour. The honest person wants her real beliefs and motives known. She doesn't want to hide behind anything. It is the opposite trait to deceitfulness, manipulativeness, corruption—the whited sepulchre. An honest person tries to be open and above board, so that the book can always be identified from the cover. A dishonest person is forever watchful in case his true feelings and intentions should slip out, so he has to put on an act to conceal what is really in his heart. This act often takes the form of excessive shows of trustworthiness, so that others will be thrown off the scent. Some people are highly expert in this branch of the theatre, and their dishonesty can come as a great surprise. An honest person, by contrast, is predictable and dependable, since he makes a point of letting you know where he really stands: no act comes between you and his real self. An honest person feels a powerful commitment to the truth, which pulls at him like a magnet. He can't *help* speaking the truth—it just tumbles out of him. He makes a bad liar, even when it is right (all things considered) for him to lie. But a dishonest person treats the truth as just one option among many, one way to achieve his ends that may or may not be the most effective. He uses truth, rather than letting truth use him. This can make him feel clever and powerful, not subservient to any value beyond himself. He is quite comfortable with falsehood; for falsehood is his constant companion. But for the honest person, falsehood gnaws painfully at the conscience, like a splinter in the soul.

This is not to say that honesty is "always letting others know what you think of them." That is usually cruelty masquerading as honesty, a vice calling itself a virtue. Unkindness and tactlessness shouldn't be confused with honesty, though honesty can sometimes require harsh words. It is not a form of commendable honesty on my part to comment on someone's disfiguring birthmark every time I see them. Nor is it a sign of my virtue constantly to let others know how stupid I think they are. Honesty needs a good intention behind it, and it must be tempered with kindness— which is not the same as soppiness or weakness. Nor should the virtue of honesty be identified with avoiding falsehood no matter what. If the Nazis are trying to catch an innocent fugitive in order to kill her and they ask you if you know where she is, then you are morally obliged *not* to tell the truth. Honesty isn't blurting everything out without regard for the consequences. You can love truth without broadcasting all the time, never mind who gets damaged.

Justice is a kind of fairness, of balance, of awarding what is due. The innocent shouldn't suffer and the guilty shouldn't prosper. Moral evaluation, and associated outcomes, should strictly follow the rights and wrongs of the case. A just person, therefore, hates to see the wicked victorious and the good downtrodden. Wrongful imprisonment, for example, stirs his moral outrage profoundly. He sees no excuse for injustice, no matter what pragmatic justification may be offered. Nothing ignites his anger so much as false accusation and unfair punishment. His compassion for the innocent is matched by his fury at the guilty.

Accordingly, the just person is especially careful in his own life to ensure that his moral judgements fit the facts and are scrupulously fair to all concerned. If he suspects that someone has done something bad, he doesn't rush into hasty and ill-considered condemnation, even if he might quite *like* to think ill of that person for some reason. He considers the facts calmly and impartially, not exaggerating or falsifying them. Only then does he come to a final verdict. But equally, he is not squeamish or cowardly about declaring his judgement when he has satisfied himself that evil has been done. This judgement will then have all the solidity and integrity of the process that led up to it. Since there is nothing worse, for the just person, than the issuing of unjust negative judgements, he does his level best to ensure that he is not himself guilty of injustice.

It is the same for the official judge in a court of law as for the ordinary member of a family caught up in a personal squabble. The just person will not allow herself to be swayed by bias and emotion and self-interest. She will steadfastly insist on the firmest principles of decency and fairness: accuracy, balance, hearing all sides, rejecting favouritism, making the punishment fit the crime. In particular, the abuse of power of any kind—from family to state—will be abhorrent to her. No matter how much she may personally dislike someone, she cannot stand by and let that person suffer unjust treatment. For justice requires us to transcend our personal feelings. It calls for a detached respect for moral truth, placing this before all other considerations. That is why it is often such a hard virtue to cling onto, because it can require us to go against our personal inclinations. It tells us to treat even our enemies fairly! For this reason (among others) it is a deeply important virtue to foster. A society without a firm commitment to justice is rotten to the core—as is a person.

My fourth cardinal virtue has a less familiar name than the first three: "independence." I want to stress its importance because it is not always given its due. What I mean by independence is simply the capacity to make up your own mind based on the evidence and the facts, and not to be swayed by social conformity or threat. For some strange reason, most people assume that they have this virtue in abundance already—they do it "their way." But in my experience it is comparatively rare. What people really have is independence from *certain* social groups, often composed of their parents and like-minded individuals; look more closely and you see the influence of some *other* pressure group lurking behind their firmly held personal convictions. So ask yourself in a cool moment whether your prized independence is really what it seems to be. Are your opinions *yours?* (The case of animals is a good one to bear in mind here.) Anyway, I am talking about the idea that the majority might be wrong. To be virtuous involves not doing what everybody else does simply because they do it, since they might all be mistaken. Don't be a moral sheep, a yes-person, a don't-rock-the-boat artist. Decide for yourself! And I mean, *really decide*.

This virtue could also be called "intelligence," but that is a word that has been rather spoiled in recent years. I don't mean IQ or scholarly aptitude—how quickly you can multiply numbers and how many long words you know. I mean what is sometimes called *judgement*, the ability to weigh a situation up, to see into things. The opposite trait is our old sparring partner, Stupidity—the kind of wilful blindness that leads people into rash verdicts and stubborn absurdities. Stupidity: simply refusing to see what is plainly before your eyes. Oh, how I wish I could put an end to stupidity! It and its fellow gang members: Prejudice, Narrow-mindedness, Ignorance, Fear. Not putting two and two together, ignoring obvious facts, perversely persisting in error in the clear presence of truth—do you know what I mean? It is hard to live with, isn't it?

People really should use their brains in moral discussions, instead of chucking them out of the window. Otherwise intelligent people can turn into virtual morons when right and wrong come up. It is almost as if some folks think it is actually wicked to use your head when doing morals. Reflex takes over, gut reaction, the herd instinct—the most primitive circuits in the brain. No thinking allowed! Kill the frontal lobes! Reason is put on hold, for fear of what it might come up with. Well, that tendency is what we have to avoid, and what this book is dedicated to combatting. I am actually proposing—heretical thought!—that you use your *mind* to think about moral questions, not your abdomen or spleen or even heart—nor yet your society or history or parents or friends. That way, I think, you will have more of a chance of arriving at the truth, truth being what minds are meant for. Thus I put independence as the fourth virtue on my list.

Now, these four virtues shouldn't be thought of as operating separately from each other. They don't sit in you in a row and each do their thing independently. In any concrete moral situation, it is a sure bet that each virtue will be called for, and that each may need to be modified in the light of the others. Kindness needs justice if it is not to be mere softness; and justice needs kindness—mercy—in order not to be harsh and unforgiving. Honesty must be tempered with kindness and regulated by justice. Judgement is what enables you to mingle and modify the virtues appropriately, so as to act rightly in any particular case. To be fully virtuous, a person needs, not merely to possess each virtue, but also to be capable of orchestrating the virtues together. He thus needs *thought*.

When the virtues are each possessed to a sufficient degree, and they work together in the right way, then we say that the person in question is *good*. When the vices are present instead, conspiring together after their own sinister fashion, then the person is ... well, you can fill in the blank as you see fit. Not good anyway: a blighter, a stinker, a rotter, a devil. The kind of person not to be.

You may be finding all this a bit on the sappy side. You may have an image of the virtuous person as a dull fellow, dutifully tending his suburban lawn, going to church on Sundays, doing what his mother tells him—a lifeless goodie two-shoes. In contrast, you may picture the "wicked" individual as a dashing and exciting figure, going his own way, living life to the full, taking orders from nobody—a full-blooded human specimen, warts and all. These sorts of stereotype often lead people to say that evil is just more *interesting* than goodness, deeper in some way—that "the devil has the best tunes."

I think this idea is quite wrong and stems from a mistaken picture of the nature of virtue and vice. It is the propaganda evil puts about in order to justify its own activities. To me, the virtuous person is bold and attractive, often in the thick of it, frequently tormented and torn. *He* is the maverick, commonly derided by the grey men and women of society. The vicious person I picture as mean and crabbed, skulking palely behind closed doors, his mind a dead zone, his heart withered, hatching his petty and ugly plots, locked up inside his own narrow fetid world of resentments and vendettas. He is a coward, a manipulator, a dank-souled kill-joy I see nothing attractive about him.

Nor do I see why badness itself should be found more interesting than goodness, from an intellectual or artistic point of view. Think of the evil of the Holocaust: it was routine, bureaucratic, repetitive, sordid, vile—a complete negation of life. Why should this be found "interesting"? I suppose what people must mean when they describe evil as interesting is that it has a kind of unholy fascination—hence the morbid curiosity shown in crime and torture and war atrocities. But this kind of "interest" is the kind people are prone to have in the maimed or diseased or simply dead: they peep out at these things from behind closed fingers, simultaneously repelled and gripped by what they are seeing. Well, maybe so; maybe evil does have this kind of morbid fascination. But that is no reason to want to get involved in it, to want to live an evil life. You might as well say it is more interesting to be maimed and dead than whole and alive! No, badness is boring and ugly, repetitive and repulsive. It is *depressing*. Its music is muzak.

I am going to round off this discussion of virtue with a list of moral maxims. After you have perused them, you might like to make up some of your own, by way of homework. Here they are, then, in no particular order.

> If you want someone to do something, persuade them, don't make them.
> Always be kind at first, but be firm if your kindness is exploited.
> Trust people unless you have reason not to, but don't be surprised if your trust is betrayed.
> In matters of blame, think twice before you speak.
> Be critical but not cynical.
> Remember that there is a future, not just a present.
> Never allow the low standards of others to lower your own standards.
> Admire good people.
> Be wary of envy, in yourself and others.
> Don't forget that everyone has to die and everyone was once born.

Don't confuse just criticism with persecution.
Be truthful, but not in order to hurt others.
Let the facts speak for themselves.
Beware of the abuse of power.
If you are not sure you are doing the right thing, ask a trusted friend.
Remember that bad things have often been done in the name of virtue.
First be honest with yourself, and then with other people.
Never let injustice pass unchallenged.
Don't make excuses for cruelty.
Don't take from others what is rightfully theirs.
Be kind to strangers, but not because you too may be a stranger one day.
Don't allow your temper to do what your reason can't.
If you can't sing, be happy that someone can.
Don't insult where you can refute.
Don't confuse independence with rebelliousness.
Respect truth above persons.
Don't despise the unfortunate.
Keep your word.
Apologise if you let someone down.
Don't apologise if you have done nothing wrong.
Don't let outward appearance determine your moral judgements.
Be tolerant of difference.
Be humorous, but not at the cost of seriousness.
Don't think that what is right is always obvious.
Let other people finish their sentences.
Stare at yourself in the mirror once in a while....

It is important to be able to read and write. It is also important to have some mathematical proficiency. But more important than either of these is the ability to arrive at informed and thoughtful moral judgements.

STUDY QUESTIONS

1. At the end of the reading, McGinn suggests we formulate some maxims of our own "by way of homework." Write down three maxims, and explain why you think they should be followed.
2. What does McGinn mean by "Independence," and why does he deem it a basic virtue?
3. Some of McGinn's moral maxims merit discussion. Discuss the following two: "Don't make excuses for cruelty." "Don't confuse independence with rebelliousness." Why does McGinn think "Let the facts speak for themselves" is a moral maxim?
4. Why does McGinn believe that virtue is more interesting than vice? Although vicious characters may fascinate for a short while, they are basically tiresome and depressing. This may be why some of the violent characters in the movies and television only fleetingly hold our interest. On the other hand, aren't some good people tiresome too?
5. To the question "Why be good?" McGinn answers, "Because it's good to be good." Referring to moral philosophers like Aristotle, John Stuart Mill, and Immanuel Kant, consider other possible answers.

Why Act Morally?

Peter Singer

Peter Singer (b. 1946) is professor of bioethics at Princeton University. His books include *Animal Liberation* (1975), *Rethinking Life and Death* (1996), and *In Defense of Animals: The Second Wave* (2005).

Peter Singer examines the link between vice and unhappiness from a utilitarian standpoint. Psychopaths have a character type that enables them to pursue pleasure with indifference to the suffering they cause others. The existence of psychopaths untroubled by conscience and apparently enjoying themselves seems to count against the thesis that immorality leads to unhappiness. Singer counters this by arguing that psychopaths and others who completely lack such virtues as benevolence and compassion are unable to do more than pursue short-range objectives. All they can do is continue their selfish pursuit of more pleasure. But their satisfactions are short-lived and their capacity for enjoyment soon becomes jaded. Even prudent egoists whose selfish goals are long-range end up desperately bored and without the resources to relieve that boredom. If Singer is right, the utilitarian, too, can consistently maintain that a virtuous character is needed for an interesting and meaningful life.

It might be said that since philosophers are not empirical scientists, discussion of the connection between acting ethically and living a fulfilled and happy life should be left to psychologists, sociologists, and other appropriate experts. The question is not, however, dealt with by any other single discipline and its relevance to practical ethics is reason enough for our looking into it.

What facts about human nature could show that ethics and self-interest coincide? One theory is that we all have benevolent or sympathetic inclinations which make us concerned about the welfare of others. Another relies on a natural conscience which gives rise to guilt feelings when we do what we know to be wrong. But how strong are these benevolent desires or feelings of guilt? Is it possible to suppress them? If so, isn't it possible that in a world in which humans and other animals are suffering in great numbers, suppressing one's conscience and sympathy for others is the surest way to happiness?

To meet this objection those who would link ethics and happiness must assert that we cannot be happy if these elements of our nature are suppressed. Benevolence and sympathy, they might argue, are tied up with the capacity to take

WHY ACT MORALLY? From *Practical Ethics* by Peter Singer, pp. 212–220. Copyright © 1979 by Cambridge University Press. Reprinted with the permission of Cambridge University Press.

part in friendly or loving relations with others, and there can be no real happiness without such relationships. For the same reason it is necessary to take at least some ethical standards seriously, and to be open and honest in living by them—for a life of deception and dishonesty is a furtive life, in which the possibility of discovery always clouds the horizon. Genuine acceptance of ethical standards is likely to mean that we feel some guilt—or at least that we are less pleased with ourselves than we otherwise would be—when we do not live up to them.

These claims about the connection between our character and our prospects of happiness are no more than hypotheses. Attempts to confirm them by detailed research are sparse and inadequate. A. H. Maslow, an American psychologist, asserts that human beings have a need for self-actualization, which involves growing towards courage, kindness, knowledge, love, honesty, and unselfishness. When we fulfil this need we feel serene, joyful, filled with zest, sometimes euphoric, and generally happy. When we act contrary to our need for self-actualization we experience anxiety, despair, boredom, shame, emptiness and are generally unable to enjoy ourselves. It would be nice if Maslow should turn out to be right; unfortunately the data Maslow produces in support of his theory consist of very limited studies of selected people. The theory must await confirmation or falsification from larger, more rigorous and more representative studies.

Human nature is so diverse that one may doubt if any generalization about the kind of character that leads to happiness could hold for all human beings. What, for instance, of those we call "psychopaths"? Psychiatrists use this term as a label for a person who is asocial, impulsive, egocentric, unemotional, lacking in feelings of remorse, shame or guilt, and apparently unable to form deep and enduring personal relationships. Psychopaths are certainly abnormal, but whether it is proper to say that they are mentally ill is another matter. At least on the surface, they do not *suffer* from their condition, and it is not obvious that it is in their interest to be "cured." Hervey Cleckley, the author of a classic study of psychopathy entitled *The Mask of Sanity*, notes that since his book was first published he has received countless letters from people desperate for help—but they are from the parents, spouses, and other relatives of psychopaths, almost never from the psychopaths themselves. This is not surprising, for while psychopaths are asocial and indifferent to the welfare of others, they seem to enjoy life. Psychopaths often appear to be charming, intelligent people, with no delusions or other signs of irrational thinking. When interviewed they say things like:

> A lot has happened to me, a lot more will happen. But I enjoy living and I am always looking forward to each day. I like laughing and I've done a lot. I am essentially a clown at heart—but a happy one. I always take the bad with the good.

There is no effective therapy for psychopathy, which may be explained by the fact that psychopaths see nothing wrong with their behaviour and often find it extremely rewarding, at least in the short term. Of course their impulsive nature and lack of a sense of shame or guilt means that some psychopaths end up in prison, though it is hard to tell how many do not, since those who avoid prison are also more likely to avoid contact with psychiatrists. Studies have shown that a surprisingly large number of psychopaths are able to avoid prison despite grossly antisocial behaviour, probably because of their well-known ability to convince others that they are truly repentant, that it will never happen again, that they deserve another chance, etc., etc.

The existence of psychopathic people counts against the contention that benevolence, sympathy, and feelings of guilt are present in everyone. It also appears to count against attempts to link happiness with the possession of these inclinations. But let us pause before we accept this latter conclusion. Must we accept psychopaths' own evaluations of their happiness? They are, after all, notoriously persuasive liars. Moreover, even if they are telling the truth as they see it, are they qualified to say that they are really happy, when they seem unable to experience the emotional states that play such a large part in the happiness and fulfilment of more normal people? Admittedly, a psychopath could use the same argument against us: how can we say that we are truly happy when we have not experienced the excitement and freedom that comes from complete irresponsibility? Since we cannot enter into the subjective states of psychopathic people, nor they into ours, the dispute is not easy to resolve.

Cleckley suggests that the psychopaths' behaviour can be explained as a response to the meaninglessness of their lives. It is characteristic of psychopaths to work for a while at a job and then just when their ability and charm have taken them to the crest of success, commit some petty and easily detectable crime. A similar pattern occurs in their personal relationships. (There is support to be found here for Thomas Nagel's account of imprudence as rational only if one fails to see oneself as a person existing over time, with the present merely one among other times one will live through. Certainly psychopathic people live largely in the present and lack any coherent life plan.)

Cleckley explains this erratic and to us inadequately motivated behaviour by likening the psychopath's life to that of children forced to sit through a performance of *King Lear*. Children are restless and misbehave under these conditions because they cannot enjoy the play as adults do. They act to relieve boredom. Similarly, Cleckley says, psychopaths are bored because their emotional poverty means that they cannot take interest in, or gain satisfaction from, what for others are the most important things in life: love, family, success in business or professional life, etc. These things simply do not matter to them. Their unpredictable and anti-social behaviour is an attempt to relieve what would otherwise be a tedious existence.

These claims are speculative and Cleckley admits that they may not be possible to establish scientifically. They do suggest, however, an aspect of the psychopath's life that undermines the otherwise attractive nature of the psychopath's freewheeling life. Most reflective people, at some time or other, want their life to have some kind of meaning. Few of us could deliberately choose a way of life which we regarded as utterly meaningless. For this reason most of us would not choose to live a psychopathic life, however enjoyable it might be.

Yet there is something paradoxical about criticizing the psychopath's life for its meaninglessness. Don't we have to accept, in the absence of religious belief, that life really is meaningless, not just for the psychopath but for all of us? And if this is so, why should we not choose—if it were in our powers to choose our personality—the life of a psychopath? But is it true that, religion aside, life is meaningless? Now our pursuit of reasons for acting morally has led us to what is often regarded as the ultimate philosophical question.

Has Life a Meaning?

In what sense does rejection of belief in a god imply rejection of the view that life has any meaning? If this world had been created by some divine being with a particular goal in mind, it could be said to have a meaning, at least for that divine being. If we could know what the divine being's purpose in creating us was, we could then know what the meaning of our life was for our creator. If we accepted our creator's purpose (though why we should do that would need to be explained) we could claim to know the meaning of life.

When we reject belief in a god we must give up the idea that life on this planet has some preordained meaning. Life *as a whole* has no meaning. Life began, as the best available theories tell us, in a chance combination of gases; it then evolved through random mutations and natural selection. All this just happened; it did not happen for any overall purpose. Now that it has resulted in the existence of beings who prefer some states of affairs to others, however, it may be possible for particular lives to be meaningful. In this sense atheists can find meaning in life.

Let us return to the comparison between the life of a psychopath and that of a more normal person. Why should the psychopath's life not be meaningful? We have seen that psychopaths are egocentric to an extreme: neither other people, nor worldly success, nor anything else really matters to them. But why is their own enjoyment of life not sufficient to give meaning to their lives?

Most of us would not be able to find happiness by deliberately setting out to enjoy ourselves without caring about anyone or anything else. The pleasures we obtained in that way would seem empty, and soon pall. We seek a meaning for our lives beyond our own pleasures, and find fulfilment and happiness in doing what we see to be meaningful. If our life has no meaning other than our own happiness, we are likely to find that when we have obtained what we think we need to be happy, happiness itself still eludes us.

That those who aim at happiness for happiness's sake often fail to find it, while others find happiness in pursuing altogether different goals, has been called "the paradox of hedonism." It is not, of course, a logical paradox but a claim about the way in which we come to be happy. Like other generalizations on this subject it lacks empirical confirmation. Yet it matches our everyday observations, and is consistent with our nature as evolved, purposive beings. Human beings survive and reproduce themselves through purposive action. We obtain happiness and fulfilment by working towards and achieving our goals. In evolutionary terms we could say that happiness functions as an internal reward for our achievements. Subjectively, we regard achieving the goal (or progressing towards it) as a reason for happiness. Our own happiness, therefore, is a by-product of aiming at something else, and not to be obtained by setting our sights on happiness alone.

The psychopath's life can now be seen to be meaningless in a way that a normal life is not. It is meaningless because it looks inward to the pleasures of the present moment and not outward to anything more long-term or far-reaching. More normal lives have meaning because they are lived to some larger purpose.

All this is speculative. You may accept or reject it to the extent that it agrees with your own observation and introspection. My next—and final—suggestion is more speculative still. It is that to find an enduring meaning in our lives it is not enough to go beyond psychopaths who have no long-term commitments or life-plans; we must also go beyond more prudent egoists who have long-term plans concerned only with their own interests. The prudent egoists may find meaning in their lives for a time, for they have the purpose of furthering their own interests; but what, in the end, does that amount to? When everything in our interests has been achieved, do we just sit back and be happy? Could we be happy in this way? Or would we decide that we had still not quite reached our target, that there was something else we needed before we could sit back and enjoy it all? Most materially successful egoists take the latter route, thus escaping the necessity of admitting that they cannot find happiness in permanent holidaying. People who slaved to establish small businesses, telling themselves they would do it only until they had made enough to live comfortably, keep working long after they have passed their original target. Their material "needs" expand just fast enough to keep ahead of their income. Retirement is a problem for many because they cannot enjoy themselves without a purpose in life. The recommended solution is, of course, to find a new purpose, whether it be stamp collecting or voluntary work for a charity.

Now we begin to see where ethics comes into the problem of living a meaningful life. If we are looking for a purpose broader than our own interests, something which will allow us to see our lives as possessing significance beyond the narrow confines of our own conscious states, one obvious solution is to take up the ethical point of view. The ethical point of view does, as we have seen, require us to go beyond a personal point of view to the standpoint of an impartial spectator. Thus looking at things ethically is a way of transcending our inward-looking concerns and identifying ourselves with the most objective point of view possible—with, as Sidgwick put it, "the point of view of the universe."

The point of view of the universe is a lofty standpoint. In the rarefied air that surrounds it we may get carried away into talking, as Kant does, of the moral point of view "inevitably" humbling all who compare their own limited nature with it. I do not want to suggest anything as sweeping as this. Earlier in this chapter, in rejecting Thomas Nagel's argument for the rationality of altruism, I said that there is nothing irrational about being concerned with the quality of one's own existence in a way that one is not concerned with the quality of existence of other individuals. Without going back on this, I am now suggesting that rationality, in the broad sense which includes self-awareness and reflection on the nature and point of our own existence, may push us towards concerns broader than the quality of our own existence; but the process is not a necessary one and those who do not take part in it—or, in taking part, do not follow it all the way to the ethical point of view—are not irrational or in error. Psychopaths, for all I know, may simply be unable to obtain as much happiness through caring about others as they obtain by antisocial acts. Other people find collecting stamps an entirely adequate way of giving purpose to their lives. There is nothing irrational about that; but others again grow out of stamp collecting as they become more aware of their situation in the world and more reflective about their purposes. To this third group the ethical point of view offers a meaning and purpose in life that one does not grow out of.

(At least, one cannot grow out of the ethical point of view until all ethical tasks have been accomplished. If that utopia were ever achieved, our purposive nature might well leave us dissatisfied, much as the egoist is dissatisfied when he has everything he needs to be happy. There is nothing paradoxical about this, for we should not expect evolution to have equipped us, in advance, with the ability to enjoy a situation that has never previously occurred. Nor is this going to be a practical problem in the near future.)

"Why act morally?" cannot be given an answer that will provide everyone with overwhelming reasons for acting morally. Ethically indefensible behaviour is not always irrational. We will probably always need the sanctions of the law and social pressure to provide additional reasons against serious violations of ethical standards. On the other hand, those reflective enough to ask the question we have been discussing in this chapter are also those most likely to appreciate the reasons that can be offered for taking the ethical point of view.

STUDY QUESTIONS

1. Do you think ethics and self-interest coincide? Compare Singer's defense of this general proposition with that of some classical philosophers who also believe that the virtuous person is happy.
2. Should we accept the psychopaths' claim that they are actually happy when they appear to be enjoying themselves? Why or why not?
3. Singer believes that the lives of psychopaths and rational egoists are meaningless and boring, perhaps even despairingly so. Has he made a persuasive case for this conclusion? Explain.
4. What does Singer mean by the ethical point of view, and why does he recommend it to us?

4 | Moral Doctrines and Moral Theories

In this chapter we begin by presenting several sacred texts of the Judeo-Christian tradition that are central to the moral heritage of the Western world. The biblical account of the genesis of the world, the revelation of moral laws in Exodus, Psalms, the Sermon on the Mount, and the parable of the Good Samaritan have inspired and guided people for centuries. The view that our moral obligations come directly from God is known as the Divine Command theory of morality. A number of philosophers have sought alternative accounts of morality. Some are atheists and, of course, reject out of hand any theory that presupposes a deity; others, though believers, look for an account of right and wrong that does not rely on revelation. Plato, in his dialogue *The Euthyphro*, first asked a question that often arises in connection with the Divine Command theory: Are the actions that God decrees good only because God approves of them, or does he approve of them because they are good? Might God just as easily decree that we be cruel and refrain from kindness, or do the divine decrees conform to independently valid criteria of good and evil? Perhaps the majority of moral philosophers believe that morality is independently valid. And some theologians move between the horns of the dilemma, maintaining that God's will and objective good are coincident.

Two of the most influential alternatives to the Divine Command theory are utilitarianism and Kantianism. Utilitarianism was developed by British philosophers Jeremy Bentham and John Stuart Mill. For the utilitarian, morally good actions are actions that increase the happiness of conscious beings. According to Mill's Greatest Happiness Principle, "Actions are right in proportion as they tend to promote happiness, wrong as they tend to produce the reverse of happiness." (And, says Mill, God's decrees are good precisely because obedience to them increases happiness; that is *why* God decreed them.) Mill and Bentham thought of the principle of utility as a moral yardstick. Just as two people who disagree over the height of a ceiling can settle the matter with a ruler, so two people who disagree over the rightness of an action need only subject it to the test of utility: Will it increase or diminish happiness?

Though many contemporary philosophers favor utilitarianism over other moral theories (indeed, one philosopher has remarked that utilitarians constitute a silent majority among professional philosophers), they generally acknowledge it to be seriously flawed. Suppose we could greatly increase human happiness and diminish misery by occasionally, and perhaps secretly, abducting derelicts from city streets for use in fatal but urgent medical experiments. If utilitarian considerations were decisive, this practice might well be justifiable, even desirable. Yet it is surely wrong. Robert Nozick points to another weakness in the theory when he argues that few of us would agree to be attached to a pleasure machine even if we could be assured that it would provide us with a much happier life. If Nozick is right, a life in which pleasure greatly exceeds pain is not necessarily the best life. Such examples suggest that we cannot define good and bad simply in terms of increasing or decreasing overall happiness.

Many philosophers reject utilitarianism in favor of Kantianism. Eighteenth-century philosopher Immanuel Kant sought the foundations of morality in the human capacity to act rationally. A rational being is free to act out of principle and to refrain from acting from mere impulse or the desire for pleasure. According to Kant, the proper exercise of reason reveals to us our moral duties. It is not, he says, the *consequences* of an action (its "utility" as Bentham claims) that determine its moral character, but the principle on which the action is based. As rational creatures we must be consistent and objective. So, says Kant, we must always ask ourselves whether or not we base an action on a principle (Kant calls it a "maxim") that we consistently want to see adopted as a universal law governing the behavior of all rational beings. A utilitarian might justify an occasional lie that has pleasant consequences. For Kant this is unacceptable: reason dictates honesty as a *universal* principle. Any deception, however one might try to justify it, is for Kant an affront to the dignity of the deceived. Principled behavior invariably respects oneself and others; it brooks no exceptions.

Kantianism is attractive for its emphasis on conscientiousness and human dignity, but, like utilitarianism, it faces difficulties. Acting on principle without regard for the consequences does not always seem right. According to Kant, if a murderer comes to your door demanding to know the whereabouts of an intended victim who is hiding in your house, you must not lie to him no matter what the consequences. Utilitarians criticize Kantians for their readiness to sacrifice human happiness for the sake of principles; on their side, Kantians object to utilitarians for failing to give moral principle a central place.

The Kantian willingness to sacrifice utility when a question of personal dignity is at stake shows up in Bernard Williams's criticism of a contemporary version of utilitarianism. Williams is impatient with a doctrine that judges the moral worth of an action by referring to an impersonal calculus of pleasures and pains. Others criticize Kant for denigrating good acts done, not out of a sense of duty, but out of kindness and sympathy.

The Judeo-Christian Tradition

Genesis, Exodus, and the Psalms are from the Old Testament; the Sermon on the Mount (Luke 6:17–49) and the parable of the Good Samaritan (Luke 10:25–37) are from the New Testament. The two Testaments comprehend more than a thousand years of Judeo-Christian history.

Human beings are the most highly developed creatures, but the biblical account does not say they were created first. Instead, the account is "evolutionary," proceeding from the creation of the physical world to the lower and higher life forms and culminating in the creation of human beings. Nature itself is good. Immorality entered the picture when human beings exercised choice in ways that defied God's will. Then they were expelled from Eden and fell from grace.

The more specific biblical moral codes are revealed in the Old and New Testaments, the first of which was revealed at Sinai to the Jewish people, who, under the leadership of Moses, had fled Egyptian enslavement. The Old Testament code is encapsulated in the Ten Commandments, some of which are theological in content, enjoining the worship of God and the observance of the Sabbath. Others are more purely moral in a secular sense, prohibiting crimes such as murder and theft, commanding filial respect and the avoidance of greed and covetousness.

Much common law is founded on biblical principles governing tort and commerce. Even our laws for dealing with political refugees are biblically prefigured in the demand that we are to behave respectfully to aliens. Indeed, much of what we count as human decency is traceable to what the two Testaments command in regard to how one must treat the weak and unfortunate, including animals. The injunction to be compassionate is beautifully expressed in the Sermon on the Mount.

The two Testaments comprehend the classical period of Judeo-Christian history. They do not constitute a single ethical system. But they powerfully embody moral ideals of incalculable authority and influence.

Genesis

1

First Story of Creation

[1]In the beginning, when God created the heavens and the earth, [2]the earth was a formless wasteland, and darkness covered the abyss, while a mighty wind swept over the waters.

³Then God said, "Let there be light," and there was light. ⁴God saw how good the light was. God then separated the light from the darkness. ⁵God called the light "day," and the darkness he called "night." Thus evening came, and morning followed— the first day.

⁶Then God said, "Let there be a dome in the middle of the waters, to separate one body of water from the other." And so it happened: ⁷God made the dome, and it separated the water above the dome from the water below it. ⁸God called the dome "the sky." Evening came, and morning followed—the second day.

⁹Then God said, "Let the water under the sky be gathered into a single basin, so that the dry land may appear." And so it happened: the water under the sky was gathered into its basin, and the dry land appeared. ¹⁰God called the dry land "the earth," and the basin of the water he called "the sea." God saw how good it was. ¹¹Then God said, "Let the earth bring forth vegetation: every kind of plant that bears seed and every kind of fruit tree on earth that bears fruit with its seed in it." And so it happened: ¹²the earth brought forth every kind of plant that bears seed and every kind of fruit tree on earth that bears fruit with its seed in it. God saw how good it was. ¹³Evening came, and morning followed—the third day.

¹⁴Then God said: "Let there be lights in the dome of the sky, to separate day from night. Let them mark the fixed times, the days and the years, ¹⁵and serve as luminaries in the dome of the sky, to shed light upon the earth." And so it happened: ¹⁶God made the two great lights, the greater one to govern the day, and the lesser one to govern the night; and he made the stars. ¹⁷God set them in the dome of the sky, to shed light upon the earth, ¹⁸to govern the day and the night, and to separate the light from the darkness. God saw how good it was. ¹⁹Evening came, and morning followed—the fourth day.

²⁰Then God said, "Let the water teem with an abundance of living creatures, and on the earth let birds fly beneath the dome of the sky." And so it happened: ²¹God created the great sea monsters and all kinds of swimming creatures with which the water teems, and all kinds of winged birds. God saw how good it was ²²and God blessed them, saying, "Be fertile, multiply, and fill the water of the seas; and let the birds multiply on the earth." ²³Evening came, and morning followed—the fifth day.

²⁴Then God said, "Let the earth bring forth all kinds of living creatures: cattle, creeping things, and wild animals of all kinds." And so it happened: ²⁵God made all kinds of wild animals, all kinds of cattle, and all kinds of creeping things of the earth. God saw how good it was. ²⁶Then God said: "Let us make man in our image, after our likeness. Let them have dominion over the fish of the sea, the birds of the air, and the cattle, and over all the wild animals and all the creatures that crawl on the ground."

²⁷God created man in his image;
  in the divine image he created him;
  male and female he created them.

²⁸God blessed them, saying: "Be fertile and multiply; fill the earth and subdue it. Have dominion over the fish of the sea, the birds of the air, and all the living things that move on the earth." ²⁹God also said: "See, I give you every seed-bearing plant all over the earth and every tree that has seed-bearing fruit on it to be your food; ³⁰and to all animals of the land, all the birds of the air, and all the living creatures that crawl on the ground, I give all the green plants for food." And so it happened.

[31]God looked at everything he had made, and he found it very good. Evening came, and morning followed—the sixth day.

2

[1]Thus the heavens and the earth and all their array were completed. [2]Since on the seventh day God was finished with the work he had been doing, he rested on the seventh day from all the work he had undertaken. [3]So God blessed the seventh day and made it holy, because on it he rested from all the work he had done in creation.

[4]Such is the story of the heavens and the earth at their creation....

[8]Then the LORD God planted a garden in Eden, in the east, and he placed there the man whom he had formed. [9]Out of the ground the LORD God made various trees grow that were delightful to look at and good for food, with the tree of life in the middle of the garden and the tree of the knowledge of good and bad....

[15]The LORD God then took the man and settled him in the garden of Eden, to cultivate and care for it. [16]The LORD God gave man this order: "You are free to eat from any of the trees of the garden [17]except the tree of the knowledge of good and bad. From that tree you shall not eat; the moment you eat from it you are surely doomed to die."

[18]The LORD God said: "It is not good for the man to be alone. I will make a suitable partner for him." [19]So the LORD God formed out of the ground various wild animals and various birds of the air, and he brought them to the man to see what he would call them; whatever the man called each of them would be its name. [20]The man gave names to all the cattle, all the birds of the air, and all the wild animals; but none proved to be the suitable partner for the man.

[21]So the LORD God cast a deep sleep on the man, and while he was asleep, he took out one of his ribs and closed up its place with flesh. [22]The LORD God then built up into a woman the rib that he had taken from the man. When he brought her to the man, [23]the man said:

> "This one, at last, is bone of my bones
>   and flesh of my flesh;
> This one shall be called 'woman,'
>   for out of 'her man' this one has been taken."

[24]That is why a man leaves his father and mother and clings to his wife, and the two of them become one body.

[25]The man and his wife were both naked, yet they felt no shame.

3

The Fall of Man

[1]Now the serpent was the most cunning of all the animals that the LORD God had made. The serpent asked the woman, "Did God really tell you not to eat from any of the trees in the garden?" [2]The woman answered the serpent: "We may eat of the fruit of the trees in the garden; [3]it is only about the fruit of the tree in the middle of the garden that God said, 'You shall not eat it or even touch it, lest you die.'" [4]But the serpent said to the woman: "You certainly will not die! [5]No, God knows well that the moment you eat of it your eyes will be opened and you will be like gods who know

what is good and what is bad." ⁶The woman saw that the tree was good for food, pleasing to the eyes, and desirable for gaining wisdom. So she took some of its fruit and ate it; and she also gave some to her husband, who was with her, and he ate it. ⁷Then the eyes of both of them were opened, and they realized that they were naked; so they sewed fig leaves together and made loincloths for themselves.

⁸When they heard the sound of the Lord God moving about in the garden at the breezy time of the day, the man and his wife hid themselves from the Lord God among the trees of the garden. ⁹The Lord God then called to the man and asked him, "Where are you?" ¹⁰He answered, "I heard you in the garden; but I was afraid, because I was naked, so I hid myself." ¹¹Then he asked, "Who told you that you were naked? You have eaten, then, from the tree of which I had forbidden you to eat!" ¹²The man replied, "The woman whom you put here with me—she gave me fruit from the tree, and so I ate it." ¹³The Lord God then asked the woman, "Why did you do such a thing?" The woman answered, "The serpent tricked me into it, so I ate it."

¹⁴Then the Lord God said to the serpent:

> "Because you have done this, you shall be banned
>   from all the animals
>   and from all the wild creatures;
> On your belly shall you crawl,
>   and dirt shall you eat
>   all the days of your life.
> ¹⁵I will put enmity between you and the woman,
>   and between your offspring and hers;
> He will strike at your head,
>   while you strike at his heel."

¹⁶To the woman he said:

> "I will intensify the pangs of your childbearing;
>   in pain shall you bring forth children.
> Yet your urge shall be for your husband,
>   and he shall be your master."

¹⁷To the man he said: "Because you listened to your wife and ate from the tree of which I had forbidden you to eat,

> "Cursed be the ground because of you!
>   In toil shall you eat its yield
>   all the days of your life.
> ¹⁸Thorns and thistles shall it bring forth to you,
>   as you eat of the plants of the field.
> ¹⁹By the sweat of your face
>   shall you get bread to eat,
> Until you return to the ground,
>   from which you were taken;
> For you are dirt,
>   and to dirt you shall return."

²⁰The man called his wife Eve, because she became the mother of all the living.

²¹For the man and his wife the Lord God made leather garments, with which he clothed them. ²²Then the Lord God said: "See! The man has become like one of

us, knowing what is good and what is bad! Therefore, he must not be allowed to put out his hand to take fruit from the tree of life also, and thus eat of it and live forever."

[23]The LORD God therefore banished him from the garden of Eden, to till the ground from which he had been taken. [24]When he expelled the man, he settled him east of the garden of Eden; and he stationed the cherubim and the fiery revolving sword, to guard the way to the tree of life.

Exodus

19

Arrival at Sinai

[1]In the third month after their departure from the land of Egypt, on its first day, the Israelites came to the desert of Sinai. [2]After the journey from Rephidim to the desert of Sinai, they pitched camp.

While Israel was encamped here in front of the mountain, [3]Moses went up the mountain to God. Then the LORD called to him and said, "Thus shall you say to the house of Jacob; tell the Israelites: [4]You have seen for yourselves how I treated the Egyptians and how I bore you up on eagle wings and brought you here to myself. [5]Therefore, if you hearken to my voice and keep my covenant, you shall be my special possession, dearer to me than all other people, though all the earth is mine. [6]You shall be to me a kingdom of priests, a holy nation. That is what you must tell the Israelites." [7]So Moses went and summoned the elders of the people. When he set before them all that the LORD had ordered him to tell them, [8]the people all answered together, "Everything the LORD has said, we will do." Then Moses brought back to the LORD the response of the people.

[9]The LORD also told him, "I am coming to you in a dense cloud, so that when the people hear me speaking with you, they may always have faith in you also." When Moses, then, had reported to the LORD the response of the people, [10]the LORD added, "Go to the people and have them sanctify themselves today and tomorrow. Make them wash their garments [11]and be ready for the third day; for on the third day the LORD will come down on Mount Sinai before the eyes of all the people. [12]Set limits for the people all around the mountain, and tell them. Take care not to go up the mountain, or even to touch its base. If anyone touches the mountain he must be put to death. [13]No hand shall touch him; he must be stoned to death or killed with arrows. Such a one, man or beast, must not be allowed to live. Only when the ram's horn resounds may they go up to the mountain." [14]Then Moses came down from the mountain to the people and had them sanctify themselves and wash their garments. [15]He warned them, "Be ready for the third day. Have no intercourse with any woman."

The Great Theophany

[16]On the morning of the third day there were peals of thunder and lightning, and a heavy cloud over the mountain, and a very loud trumpet blast, so that all the people in the camp trembled. [17]But Moses led the people out of the camp to meet God, and they stationed themselves at the foot of the mountain. [18]Mount Sinai was all

wrapped in smoke, for the LORD came down upon it in fire. The smoke rose from it as though from a furnace, and the whole mountain trembled violently. [19]The trumpet blast grew louder and louder, while Moses was speaking and God answering him with thunder.

[20]When the LORD came down to the top of Mount Sinai, he summoned Moses to the top of the mountain, and Moses went up to him. [21]Then the LORD told Moses, "Go down and warn the people not to break through toward the LORD in order to see him; otherwise many of them will be struck down. [22]The priests, too, who approach the LORD must sanctify themselves; else he will vent his anger upon them." [23]Moses said to the LORD, "The people cannot go up to Mount Sinai, for you yourself warned us to set limits around the mountain to make it sacred." [24]The LORD repeated, "Go down now! Then come up again along with Aaron. But the priests and the people must not break through to come up to the LORD; else he will vent his anger upon them." [25]So Moses went down to the people and told them this.

20

The Ten Commandments

[1]Then God delivered all these commandments:

[2]"I, the LORD, am your God, who brought you out of the land of Egypt, that place of slavery. [3]You shall not have other gods besides me. [4]You shall not carve idols for yourselves in the shape of anything in the sky above or on the earth below or in the waters beneath the earth; [5]you shall not bow down before them or worship them. For I, the LORD, your God, am a jealous God, inflicting punishment for their fathers' wickedness on the children of those who hate me, down to the third and fourth generation; [6]but bestowing mercy down to the thousandth generation, on the children of those who love me and keep my commandments.

[7]"You shall not take the name of the LORD, your God, in vain. For the LORD will not leave unpunished him who takes his name in vain.

[8]"Remember to keep holy the sabbath day. [9]Six days you may labor and do all your work, [10]but the seventh day is the sabbath of the LORD, your God. No work may be done then either by you, or your son or daughter, or your male or female slave, or your beast, or by the alien who lives with you. [11]In six days the LORD made the heavens and the earth, the sea and all that is in them; but on the seventh day he rested. That is why the LORD has blessed the sabbath day and made it holy.

[12]"Honor your father and your mother, that you may have a long life in the land which the LORD, your God, is giving you.

[13]"You shall not kill.

[14]"You shall not commit adultery.

[15]"You shall not steal.

[16]"You shall not bear false witness against your neighbor.

[17]"You shall not covet your neighbor's house. You shall not covet your neighbor's wife, nor his male or female slave, nor his ox or ass, nor anything else that belongs to him."

The Fear of God

[18]When the people witnessed the thunder and lightning, the trumpet blast and the mountain smoking, they all feared and trembled. So they took up a position much farther away [19]and said to Moses, "You speak to us, and we will listen; but let not God speak to us, or we shall die." [20]Moses answered the people, "Do not be afraid, for God has come to you only to test you and put his fear upon you, lest you should sin." [21]Still the people remained at a distance, while Moses approached the cloud where God was.

[22]The LORD told Moses, "Thus shall you speak to the Israelites: You have seen for yourselves that I have spoken to you from heaven. [23]Do not make anything to rank with me; neither gods of silver nor gods of gold shall you make for yourselves....

21

Personal Injury

[12]"Whoever strikes a man a mortal blow must be put to death. [13]He, however, who did not hunt a man down, but caused his death by an act of God, may flee to a place which I will set apart for this purpose. [14]But when a man kills another after maliciously scheming to do so, you must take him even from my altar and put him to death. [15]Whoever strikes his father or mother shall be put to death.

[16]"A kidnaper, whether he sells his victim or still has him when caught, shall be put to death.

[17]"Whoever curses his father or mother shall be put to death.

[18]"When men quarrel and one strikes the other with a stone or with his fist, not mortally, but enough to put him in bed, [19]the one who struck the blow shall be acquitted, provided the other can get up and walk around with the help of his staff. Still, he must compensate him for his enforced idleness and provide for his complete cure.

[20]"When a man strikes his male or female slave with a rod so hard that the slave dies under his hand, he shall be punished. [21]If, however, the slave survives for a day or two, he is not to be punished, since the slave is his own property.

[22]"When men have a fight and hurt a pregnant woman, so that she suffers a miscarriage, but no further injury, the guilty one shall be fined as much as the woman's husband demands of him, and he shall pay in the presence of the judges. [23]But if injury ensues, you shall give life for life, [24]eye for eye, tooth for tooth, hand for hand, foot for foot, [25]burn for burn, wound for wound, stripe for stripe.

[26]"When a man strikes his male or female slave in the eye and destroys the use of the eye, he shall let the slave go free in compensation for the eye. [27]If he knocks out a tooth of his male or female slave, he shall let the slave go free in compensation for the tooth....

Property Damage

[33]"When a man uncovers or digs a cistern and does not cover it over again, should an ox or an ass fall into it, [34]the owner of the cistern must make good by restoring the value of the animal to its owner; the dead animal, however, he may keep.

³⁵"When one man's ox hurts another's ox so badly that it dies, they shall sell the live ox and divide this money as well as the dead animal equally between them. ³⁶But if it was known that the ox was previously in the habit of goring and its owner would not keep it in, he must make full restitution, an ox for an ox; but the dead animal he may keep.

³⁷"When a man steals an ox or a sheep and slaughters or sells it, he shall restore five oxen for the one ox, and four sheep for the one sheep.

22

¹[If a thief is caught in the act of housebreaking and beaten to death, there is no bloodguilt involved. ²But if after sunrise he is thus beaten, there is bloodguilt.] He must make full restitution. If he has nothing, he shall be sold to pay for his theft. ³If what he stole is found alive in his possession, be it an ox, an ass or a sheep, he shall restore two animals for each one stolen.

⁴"When a man is burning over a field or a vineyard, if he lets the fire spread so that it burns in another's field, he must make restitution with the best produce of his own field or vineyard. ⁵If the fire spreads further, and catches on to thorn bushes, so that shocked grain or standing grain or the field itself is burned up, the one who started the fire must make full restitution.

Trusts and Loans

⁶"When a man gives money or any article to another for safekeeping and it is stolen from the latter's house, the thief, if caught, must make twofold restitution. ⁷If the thief is not caught, the owner of the house shall be brought to God, to swear that he himself did not lay hands on his neighbor's property. ⁸In every question of dishonest appropriation, whether it be about an ox, or an ass, or a sheep, or a garment, or anything else that has disappeared, where another claims that the thing is his, both parties shall present their case before God; the one whom God convicts must make twofold restitution to the other.

⁹"When a man gives an ass, or an ox, or a sheep, or any other animal to another for safekeeping, if it dies, or is maimed or snatched away, without anyone witnessing the fact, ¹⁰the custodian shall swear by the LORD that he did not lay hands on his neighbor's property; the owner must accept the oath, and no restitution is to be made. ¹¹But if the custodian is really guilty of theft, he must make restitution to the owner. ¹²If it has been killed by a wild beast, let him bring it as evidence, and he need not make restitution for the mangled animal.

¹³"When a man borrows an animal from his neighbor, if it is maimed or dies while the owner is not present, the man must make restitution. ¹⁴But if the owner is present, he need not make restitution. If it was hired, this was covered by the price of its hire.

Social Laws

¹⁵"When a man seduces a virgin who is not betrothed, and lies with her, he shall pay her marriage price and marry her. ¹⁶If her father refuses to give her to him, he must still pay him the customary marriage price for virgins.

[17]"You shall not let a sorceress live.

[18]"Anyone who lies with an animal shall be put to death.

[19]"Whoever sacrifices to any god, except to the LORD alone, shall be doomed.

[20]"You shall not molest or oppress an alien, for you were once aliens yourselves in the land of Egypt. [21]You shall not wrong any widow or orphan. [22]If ever you wrong them and they cry out to me, I will surely hear their cry. [23]My wrath will flare up, and I will kill you with the sword; then your own wives will be widows, and your children orphans.

[24]"If you lend money to one of your poor neighbors among my people, you shall not act like an extortioner toward him by demanding interest from him. [25]If you take your neighbor's cloak as a pledge, you shall return it to him before sunset; [26]for this cloak of his is the only covering he has for his body. What else has he to sleep in? If he cries out to me, I will hear him; for I am compassionate....

23

[1]"You shall not repeat a false report. Do not join the wicked in putting your hand, as an unjust witness, upon anyone. [2]Neither shall you allege the example of the many as an excuse for doing wrong, nor shall you, when testifying in a lawsuit, side with the many in perverting justice. [3]You shall not favor a poor man in his lawsuit.

[4]"When you come upon your enemy's ox or ass going astray, see to it that it is returned to him. [5]When you notice the ass of one who hates you lying prostrate under its burden, by no means desert him; help him, rather, to raise it up.

[6]"You shall not deny one of your needy fellow men his rights in his lawsuit. [7]You shall keep away from anything dishonest. The innocent and the just you shall not put to death, nor shall you acquit the guilty. [8]Never take a bribe, for a bribe blinds even the most clear-sighted and twists the words even of the just. [9]You shall not oppress an alien; you well know how it feels to be an alien, since you were once aliens yourselves in the land of Egypt."

Psalm 1

True Happiness

I

> Happy the man who follows not
>   the counsel of the wicked
> Nor walks in the way of sinners,
>   nor sits in the company of the insolent,
> But delights in the law of the LORD
>   and meditates on his law day and night.
> He is like a tree
>   planted near running water,
> That yields its fruit in due season,
>   and whose leaves never fade.
>   [Whatever he does, prospers.]

II

Not so the wicked, not so;
    they are like chaff which the wind drives away.
Therefore in judgment the wicked shall not stand,
    nor shall sinners, in the assembly of the just.
For the LORD watches over the way of the just,
    but the way of the wicked vanishes.

Psalm 15

The Guest of God

A psalm of David

I

O LORD, who shall sojourn in your tent?
Who shall dwell on your holy mountain?

II

He who walks blamelessly and does justice;
    who thinks the truth in his heart
    and slanders not with his tongue;
Who harms not his fellow man,
    nor takes up a reproach against his neighbor;
By whom the reprobate is despised,
    while he honors those who fear the LORD;
Who, though it be to his loss, changes not his pledged word;
    who lends not his money at usury
    and accepts not bribe against the innocent.

Psalm 23

The Lord, Shepherd and Host

A psalm of David

I

The LORD is my shepherd; I shall not want.
    In verdant pastures he gives me repose;
Beside restful waters he leads me;
    he refreshes my soul.
He guides me in right paths
    for his name's sake.
Even though I walk in the dark valley
    I fear no evil; for you are at my side
With your rod and your staff
    that give me courage.

II

You spread the table before me
   in the sight of my foes;
You anoint my head with oil;
   my cup overflows.
Only goodness and kindness follow me
   all the days of my life;
And I shall dwell in the house of the LORD
   for years to come.

The Sermon on the Mount

Coming down the mountain with them, he stopped at a level stretch where there were many of his disciples; a large crowd of people was with them from all Judea and Jerusalem and the coast of Tyre and Sidon, people who came to hear him and be healed of their diseases. Those who were troubled with unclean spirits were cured; indeed, the whole crowd was trying to touch him because power went out from him which cured all.

Then, raising his eyes to his disciples, he said:

"Blest are you poor; the reign of God is yours.
  Blest are you who hunger; you shall be filled.
  Blest are you who are weeping; you shall laugh.
"Blest shall you be when men hate you, when they ostracize
    you and insult you and proscribe your name as evil be-
    cause of the Son of Man. On the day they do so, rejoice
    and exult, for your reward shall be great in heaven. Thus it
    was that their fathers treated the prophets.
"But woe to you rich, for your consolation is now.
Woe to you who are full; you shall go hungry.
Woe to you who laugh now; you shall weep in your grief.

"Woe to you when all speak well of you. Their fathers treated the false prophets in just this way.

Love of One's Enemy

"To you who hear me, I say: Love your enemies, do good to those who hate you; bless those who curse you and pray for those who maltreat you. When someone slaps you on one cheek, turn and give him the other; when someone takes your coat, let him have your shirt as well. Give to all who beg from you. When a man takes what is yours, do not demand it back. Do to others what you would have them do to you. If you love those who love you, what credit is that to you? Even sinners love those who love them. If you do good to those who do good to you, how can you claim any credit? Sinners do as much. If you lend to those from whom you expect repayment, what merit is there in it for you? Even sinners lend to sinners, expecting to be repaid in full.

"Love your enemy and do good; lend without expecting repayment. Then will your recompense be great. You will rightly be called sons of the Most High, since he himself is good to the ungrateful and the wicked.

"Be compassionate, as your Father is compassionate. Do not judge, and you will not be judged. Do not condemn, and you will not be condemned. Pardon, and you shall be pardoned. Give, and it shall be given to you. Good measure pressed down, shaken together, running over, will they pour into the fold of your garment. For the measure you measure with will be measured back to you."

He also used images in speaking to them: "Can a blind man act as guide to a blind man? Will they not both fall into a ditch? A student is not above his teacher; but every student when he has finished his studies will be on a par with his teacher.

"Why look at the speck in your brother's eye when you miss the plank in your own? How can you say to your brother, 'Brother, let me remove the speck from your eye,' yet fail yourself to see the plank lodged in your own? Hypocrite, remove the plank from your own eye first; then you will see clearly enough to remove the speck from your brother's eye.

"A good tree does not produce decayed fruit any more than a decayed tree produces good fruit. Each tree is known by its yield. Figs are not taken from thornbushes, nor grapes picked from brambles. A good man produces goodness from the good in his heart; an evil man produces evil out of his store of evil. Each man speaks from his heart's abundance. Why do you call me 'Lord, Lord,' and not put into practice what I teach you? Any man who desires to come to me will hear my words and put them into practice. I will show you with whom he is to be compared. He may be likened to the man who, in building a house, dug deeply and laid the foundation on a rock. When the floods came the torrent rushed in on that house, but failed to shake it because of its solid foundation. On the other hand, anyone who has heard my words but not put them into practice is like the man who built his house on the ground without any foundation. When the torrent rushed upon it, it immediately fell in and was completely destroyed."

The Good Samaritan

On one occasion a lawyer stood up to pose him this problem: "Teacher, what must I do to inherit everlasting life?"

Jesus answered him: "What is written in the law? How do you read it?" He replied:

"You shall love the Lord your God
  with all your heart,
  with all your soul,
  with all your strength,
  and with all your mind;
  and your neighbor as yourself."

Jesus said, "You have answered correctly. Do this and you shall live." But because he wished to justify himself he said to Jesus, "And who is my neighbor?" Jesus replied: "There was a man going down from Jerusalem to Jericho who fell prey to robbers. They stripped him, beat him, and then went off leaving him half-dead. A priest happened to be going down the same road; he saw him but continued on. Likewise there was a Levite who came the same way; he saw him and went on. But a Samaritan who was journeying along came on him and was moved to pity at the sight. He approached him and dressed his wounds, pouring in oil and wine. He then hoisted him on his own beast and brought him to an inn, where he cared for him. The next day he took out two silver pieces and gave them to the innkeeper with the request: 'Look after him, and if there is any further expense I will repay you on my way back.'

"Which of these three, in your opinion, was neighbor to the man who fell in with the robbers?" The answer came. "The one who treated him with compassion." Jesus said to him, "Then go and do the same."

STUDY QUESTIONS

1. Show how some common laws embody principles found in the Bible. Apply your findings in a general discussion of how law and morality are related.
2. The story of Adam and Eve is interpreted by some theologians to be the story of "original sin." Give both a religious and a philosophical interpretation of the doctrine of original sin.
3. What moral ideals do Psalms 1, 15, and 23 express? What rewards does one get for living in accordance with them? Do you think that Psalm 1 accurately reflects reality? If so, why? If not, does this change its message?
4. A sermon often involves hyperbole. Do you believe that the injunction to love one's enemy and to do good to those who hate us is seriously and literally intended? The moral teachings of Jesus are sometimes criticized for setting too high a standard for human behavior. Do you think the criticism is justified? Explain.
5. The Sermon on the Mount exhorts us to be compassionate "as your [heavenly] Father is compassionate." We also find this theme of *imitatio dei* in the Old Testament. This suggests that one approach to the moral life is to conceive of ourselves as striving to imitate a morally perfect being. Do you think that this is a helpful way to think about the moral life? Explain.

Morality Is Based on God's Commands

Robert C. Mortimer

Robert C. Mortimer (1902–1976) was an Anglican bishop and author of *Christian Ethics* (1950).

Robert Mortimer, a proponent of the Divine Command theory of ethics, argues that right and wrong are determined by the will of God. What God tells us to do is right; what he forbids is wrong. Belief in God and in the importance of obeying his commandments provides the believer with a basis for living right. It also gives the believer a sense of purpose and a moral philosophy. Knowing what a perfect being is like and what he wants opens up to us an ideal of emulating the divine. "Be ye perfect, as your Father in Heaven is perfect." Though we can never achieve perfection,

MORALITY IS BASED ON GOD'S COMMANDS From *Christian Ethics* by Robert C. Mortimer (London: Hutchinson's University Library, 1950).

Christianity teaches that each of us has infinite worth. It also teaches that an ethical person must be merciful as well as just.

The Christian religion is essentially a revelation of the nature of God. It tells men that God has done certain things. And from the nature of these actions we can infer what God is like. In the second place the Christian religion tells men what is the will of God for them, how they must live if they would please God. This second message is clearly dependent on the first. The kind of conduct which will please God depends on the kind of person God is. This is what is meant by saying that belief influences conduct. The once popular view that it does not matter what a man believes so long as he acts decently is nonsense. Because what he considers decent depends on what he believes. If you are a Nazi you will behave as a Nazi, if you are a Communist you will behave as a Communist, and if you are a Christian you will behave as a Christian. At least, in general; for a man does not always do what he knows he ought to do, and he does not always recognize clearly the implications for conduct of his belief. But in general, our conduct, or at least our notions of what constitutes right conduct, are shaped by our beliefs. The man who knows about God—has a right faith—knows or may learn what conduct is pleasing to God and therefore right.

The Christian religion has a clear revelation of the nature of God, and by means of it instructs and enlightens the consciences of men. The first foundation is the doctrine of God the Creator. God made us and all the world. Because of that He has an absolute claim on our obedience. We do not exist in our own right, but only as His creatures, who ought therefore to do and be what He desires. We do not possess anything in the world, absolutely, not even our own bodies; we hold things in trust for God, who created them, and are bound, therefore, to use them only as He intends that they should be used. This is the doctrine contained in the first chapters of Genesis. God created man and placed him in the Garden of Eden with all the animals and the fruits of the earth at his disposal, subject to God's own law. "Of the fruit of the tree of the knowledge of good and evil thou shall not eat." Man's ownership and use of the material world is not absolute, but subject to the law of God.

From the doctrine of God as the Creator and source of all that is, it follows that a thing is not right simply because we think it is, still less because it seems to be expedient. It is right because God commands it. This means that there is a real distinction between right and wrong which is independent of what we happen to think. It is rooted in the nature and will of God. When a man's conscience tells him that a thing is right, which is in fact what God wills, his conscience is true and its judgment correct; when a man's conscience tells him a thing is right which is, in fact, contrary to God's will, his conscience is false and telling him a lie. It is a lamentably common experience for a man's conscience to play him false, so that in all good faith he does what is wrong, thinking it to be right. "Yea the time cometh that whoever killeth you will think that he doeth God's service." But this does not mean that whatever you think is right is right. It means that even conscience can be wrong: that the light which is in you can be darkness....

The pattern of conduct which God has laid down for man is the same for all men. It is universally valid. When we speak of Christian ethics we do not mean that there is one law for Christians and another for non-Christians. We mean the Christian understanding and statement of the one common law for all men. Unbelievers also know or can be persuaded of that law or of part of it: Christians have a fuller and better knowledge. The reason for this is that Christians have by revelation a fuller and truer knowledge both of the nature of God Himself and of the nature of man.

The Revelation in the Bible plays a three-fold part. In the first place it recalls and restates in simple and even violent language fundamental moral judgments which men are always in danger of forgetting or explaining away. It thus provides a norm and standard of human behavior in the broadest and simplest outline. Man's duty to worship God and love the truth, to respect lawful authority, to refrain from violence and robbery, to live in chastity, to be fair and even merciful in his dealings with his neighbor—and all this as the declared will of God, the way man *must* live if he would achieve his end—this is the constant theme of the Bible. The effect of it is not to reveal something new which men could not have found out for themselves, but to recall them to what they have forgotten or with culpable blindness have failed to perceive....

And this leads to the second work of Revelation. The conduct which God demands of men, He demands out of His own Holiness and Righteousness. "Be ye perfect, as your Father in Heaven is perfect." Not the service of the lips but of the heart, not obedience in the letter but in the Spirit is commanded. The standard is too high: the Judge too all-seeing and just. The grandeur and majesty of the moral law proclaims the weakness and impotence of man. It shatters human pride and self-sufficiency: it overthrows that complacency with which the righteous regard the tattered robes of their partial virtues, and that satisfaction with which rogues rejoice to discover other men more evil than themselves. The revelation of the holiness of God and His Law, once struck home, drives men to confess their need of grace and brings them to Christ their Savior.

Lastly, revelation, by the light which it throws on the nature of God and man, suggests new emphases and new precepts, a new scale of values which could not at all, or could not easily, have been perceived.... Thus it comes about that Christian ethics is at once old and new. It covers the same ground of human conduct as the law of the Old Testament and the "law of the Gentiles written in their hearts." Many of its precepts are the same precepts. Yet all is seen in a different light and in a new perspective—the perspective of God's love manifested in Christ. It will be worth while to give one or two illustrations of this.

Revelation throws into sharp relief the supreme value of each individual human being. Every man is an immortal soul created by God and designed for an eternal inheritance. The love of God effected by the Incarnation the restoration and renewal of fallen human nature in order that all men alike might benefit thereby. The Son of God showed particular care and concern for the fallen, the outcast, the weak and the despised. He came, not to call the righteous, but sinners to repentance. Like a good shepherd, He sought especially for the sheep which was lost. Moreover, the divine drama of Calvary which was the cost of man's redemption, the price necessary to give him again a clear picture of what human nature was designed to be and to provide him with the inspiration to strive towards it and the assurance that he is not irrevocably tied and bound to his sinful, selfish past, makes it equally clear that in the eyes of the Creator His creature man is of infinite worth and value.

The lesson is plain and clear: all men equally are the children of God, all men equally are the object of His love. In consequence of this, Christian ethics has always asserted that every man is a person possessed of certain inalienable rights, that he is an end in himself, never to be used merely as a means to something else. And he is this in virtue of his being a man, no matter what his race or color, no matter how well or poorly endowed with talents, no matter how primitive or developed. And further, since man is an end in himself, and that end transcends this world of time and space, being fully attained only in heaven, it follows that the individual takes precedence over society, in the sense that society exists for the good of its individual members, not those members for society. However much the good of the whole is greater than the good of any one of its parts, and whatever the duties each man owes to society, individual persons constitute the supreme value, and society itself exists only to promote the good of those persons.

This principle of the infinite worth of the individual is explicit in Scripture, and in the light of it all totalitarian doctrines of the State stand condemned. However, the implications of this principle for human living and for the organization of society are not explicit, but need to be perceived and worked out by the human conscience. How obtuse that conscience can be, even when illumined by revelation, is startlingly illustrated by the long centuries in which Christianity tolerated the institution of slavery. In view of the constant tendency of man to exploit his fellow men and use them as the instruments of his greed and selfishness, two things are certain. First, that the Scriptural revelation of the innate inalienable dignity and value of the individual is an indispensable bulwark of human freedom and growth. And second, that our knowledge of the implication of this revelation is far indeed from being perfect; there is constant need for further refinement of our moral perceptions, a refinement which can only emerge as the fruit of a deeper penetration of the Gospel of God's love into human life and thought.

Another illustration of the effect of Scripture upon ethics is given by the surrender of the principle of exact retribution in favor of the principle of mercy. Natural justice would seem to require exact retributive punishment, an eye for an eye, a tooth for a tooth. The codes of primitive peoples, and the long history of blood feuds show how the human conscience has approved of this concept. The revelation of the divine love and the explicit teaching of the Son of God have demonstrated the superiority of mercy, and have pointed the proper role of punishment as correction and not vengeance. Because of the revelation that in God justice is never unaccompanied by mercy, in Christian ethics there has always been an emphasis on the patient endurance of wrongs in imitation of Calvary, and on the suppression of all emotions of vindictive anger. As a means to soften human relations, as a restraint of human anger and cruelty, so easily disguised under the cloak of justice, the history of the world has nothing to show comparable to this Christian emphasis on patience and mercy, this insistence that even the just satisfaction of our wrongs yields to the divine example of forbearance. We are to be content with the reform or at least the restraint of the evil-doer, never to seek or demand vengeance.

STUDY QUESTIONS

1. Mortimer points out that what we believe about the nature of morality affects the way we live. What a man "considers decent depends on what he believes. If you are a Nazi you will behave as a Nazi ... if you are a Christian you will behave as a Christian."

What, in your view, is the relation between what individuals believe and how they behave?

2.   What is the difference between justice and mercy? What does this distinction have to do with Christianity and divine revelation?

3.   One of John Arthur's objections to Divine Command theory is that tomorrow God might change the rules and then "even the greatest atrocities" would be "morally required if God were to demand them." How might Mortimer respond to that objection?

Why Morality Does Not Depend on Religion

John Arthur

> John Arthur (1946–2007) was professor of philosophy at the State University of New York at Binghamton. He is the author of numerous books including. *Words That Bind* (1995) and *Color, Class, Identity: The New Politics of Race* (1996).
>
> Divine Command theorists hold that religion is the basis of morality. But John Arthur holds that "far from religion being necessary for people to do the right thing, it often gets in the way." Divine right theorists like Robert Mortimer seem to hold that "without God, there could be no right or wrong." Arthur criticizes Mortimer for treating moral rules as if they were legal statutes. If no legally constituted authority decreed a speed limit for cars, we should indeed be under no obligation to adhere to one. Arthur denies that moral laws are like that, and he rejects the view that only Divine Command theory is able to explain the objective difference between right and wrong. He concludes that "morality doesn't need religion and religion does not need morality."

The issue which I address in this paper is the nature of the connection, if any, between morality and religion. I will argue that although there are a variety of ways the two could be connected, in fact morality is independent of religion, both logically and psychologically. First, however, it will be necessary to say something about the subjects: just what are we referring to when we speak of morality and of religion?

A useful way to approach the first question—the nature of morality—is to ask what it would mean for a society to exist without a moral code. What would such a

---

WHY MORALITY DOES NOT DEPEND ON RELIGION From *Morality and Moral Controversies*, second edition, by John Arthur. Reprinted by permission of the author.

society look like? How would people think? And behave? The most obvious thing to say is that its members would never feel any moral responsibilities or any guilt. Words like duty, rights, fairness, and justice would never be used, except in the legal sense. Feelings such as that I ought to remember my parents' anniversary, that he has a moral responsibility to help care for his children after the divorce, that she has a right to equal pay for equal work, and that discrimination on the basis of race is unfair would be absent in such a society. In short, people would have no tendency to evaluate or criticize the behavior of others, nor to feel remorse about their own behavior. Children would not be taught to be ashamed when they steal or hurt others, nor would they be allowed to complain when others treat them badly.

Such a society lacks a moral code. What, then, of religion? Is it possible that a society such as the one I have described would have religious beliefs? It seems clear that it is possible. Suppose every day these same people file into their place of worship to pay homage to God (they may believe in many gods or in one all-powerful creator of heaven and earth). Often they can be heard praying to God for help in dealing with their problems and thanking Him for their good fortune. Whenever a disaster befalls them, the people assume that God is angry with them; when things go well they believe He is pleased. Frequently they give sacrifices to God, usually in the form of money spent to build beautiful temples and churches.

To have a moral code, then, is to tend to evaluate (perhaps without even expressing it) the behavior of others and to feel guilt at certain actions when we perform them. Religion, on the other hand, involves beliefs in supernatural power(s) that created and perhaps also control nature, along with the tendency to worship and pray to those supernatural forces or beings. The two—religion and morality—are thus very different. One involves our attitudes toward various forms of behavior (lying and killing, for example), typically expressed using the notions of rules, rights, and obligations. The other, religion, typically involves a different set of activities (prayer, worship) together with beliefs about the supernatural.

We come, then, to the central question: What is the connection, if any, between a society's moral code and its religious beliefs? Many people have felt that there must be a link of some sort between religious beliefs and morality. But is that so? What sort of connection might there be? In what follows I distinguish various ways in which one might claim that religion is necessary for a moral code to function in society. I argue, however, that such connections are not necessary, and indeed that often religion is detrimental to society's attempt to encourage moral conduct among its members.

One possible role which religion might play in morality relates to motives people have. Can people be expected to behave in any sort of decent way towards one another without religious faith? Religion, it is often said, is necessary so that people will DO right. Why might somebody think that? Often, we know, doing what is right has costs: you don't cheat on the test, so you flunk the course; you return the lost billfold, so you don't get the contents. Religion can provide motivation to do the right thing. God rewards those who follow His commands by providing for them a place in heaven and by insuring that they prosper and are happy on earth. He also punishes with damnation those who disobey. Other people emphasize less selfish ways in which religious motives may encourage people to act rightly. God is the creator of the universe and has ordained that His plan should be followed.

How better to live one's life than to participate in this divinely ordained plan? Only by living a moral life, it is said, can people live in harmony with the larger, divinely created order.

But how are we to assess the relative strength of these various motives for acting morally, some of which are religious, others not? How important is the fear of hell or the desire to live as God wishes in motivating people? Think about the last time you were tempted to do something you knew to be wrong. Surely your decision not to do so (if that was your decision) was made for a variety of reasons: "What if I get caught? What if somebody sees me—what will he or she think? How will I feel afterwards? Will I regret it?" Or maybe the thought of cheating just doesn't occur to you. You were raised to be an honest person, and that's what you want to be—period. There are thus many motives for doing the right thing which have nothing whatsoever to do with religion. Most of us in fact do worry about getting caught, about being blamed and looked down on by others. We also may do what is right just for that reason, because it's our duty, or because we don't want to hurt others. So to say that we need religion to act morally is mistaken; indeed it seems to me that most of us, when it really gets down to it, don't give much of a thought to religion when making moral decisions. All those other reasons are the ones which we tend to consider, or else we just don't consider cheating and stealing at all. So far, then, there seems to be no reason to suppose that people can't be moral yet irreligious at the same time.

Another oft-heard argument that religion is necessary for people to do right questions whether people would know how to do the right thing without the guidance of religion. In other words, however much people may *want* to do the right thing, it is only with the help of God that true moral understanding can be achieved. People's own intellect is simply inadequate to this task; we must consult revelation for help.

Again, however, this argument fails. Just consider what we would need to know in order for religion to provide moral guidance. First we must be sure that there is a God. And then there's the question of which of the many religions is true. How can anybody be sure his or her religion is the right one? After all, if you had been born in China or India or Iran your religious views would almost certainly not have been the ones you now hold. And even if we can somehow convince ourselves that the Judeo-Christian God is the real one, we still need to find out just what it is He wants us to do. Revelation comes in at least two forms, according to theists, and not even Christians agree which form is real. Some hold that God tells us what He wants by providing us with His words: the Ten Commandments are an example. Many even believe, as Billy Graham once said, that the entire *Bible* was written by God using 39 secretaries. Others doubt that every word of the *Bible* is literally true, believing instead that it is merely an historical account of the *events* in history whereby God revealed Himself. So on this view revelation is not understood as statements made by God but, instead, as His intervening into historical events, such as leading His people from Egypt, testing Job, and sending His son as an example of the ideal life. But if we are to use revelation as a guide we must know what is to count as revelation—words given us by God, events, or both? Supposing that we could somehow solve all those puzzles, the problems of relying on revelation are still not over. Even if we can agree on who God is and on how and when He reveals Himself, we still must interpret that revelation. Some feel that the *Bible* justifies various forms of killing, including war and capital punishment, on the basis of such statements as "An eye for an eye." Others, emphasizing such sayings as "Judge not lest ye be judged" and "Thou shalt not kill," believe the *Bible* demands absolute pacifism. How are we to know which interpretation is correct?

Far from providing a short-cut to moral understanding, looking to revelation for guidance just creates more questions and problems. It is much simpler to address problems such as abortion, capital punishment, and war directly than to seek answers in revelation. In fact, not only is religion unnecessary to provide moral understanding, it is actually a hindrance. (My own hunch is that often those who are most likely to appeal to Scripture as justification for their moral beliefs are really just rationalizing positions they already believe.)

Far from religion being necessary for people to do the right thing, it often gets in the way. People do not need the motivation of religion; they for the most part are not motivated by religion as much as by other factors; and religion is of no help in discovering what our moral obligations are. But others give a different reason for claiming morality depends on religion. They think religion, and especially God, is necessary for morality because without God there could BE no right or wrong. The idea was expressed by Bishop R. C. Mortimer: "God made us and all the world. Because of that He has an absolute claim on our obedience.... From [this] it follows that a thing is not right simply because we think it is.... It is right because God commands it."[1]

What Mortimer has in mind can best be seen by comparing moral rules with legal ones. Legal statutes, we know, are created by legislatures. So if there had been no law passed requiring that people limit the speed they travel then there would be no such legal obligation. Without the commands of the legislature statutes simply would not exist. The view defended by Mortimer, often called the divine command theory, is that God has the same relation to moral law as the legislature does to statutes. Without God's commands there would be no moral rules.

Another tenet of the Divine Command theory, besides the belief that God is the author of morality, is that only the Divine Command theory is able to explain the objective difference between right and wrong. This point was forcefully argued by F. C. Copleston in a 1948 British Broadcasting Corporation radio debate with Bertrand Russell.

RUSSELL: But aren't you now saying in effect "I mean by God whatever is good or the sum total of what is good—the system of what is good, and, therefore, when a young man loves anything that is good he is loving God." Is that what you're saying, because if so, it wants a bit of arguing.

COPLESTON: I don't say, of course, that God is the sum total or system of what is good...but I do think that all goodness reflects God in some way and proceeds from Him, so that in a sense the man who loves what is truly good, loves God even if he doesn't advert to God. But still I agree that the validity of such an interpretation of man's conduct depends on the recognition of God's existence, obviously.... Let's take a look at the Commandant of the [Nazi] concentration camp at Belsen. That appears to you as undesirable and evil and to me too. To Adolph Hitler we suppose it

---

[1] R. C. Mortimer. *Christian Ethics* (London: Hutchinson's University Library, 1950). pp. 7–8.

appeared as something good and desirable. I suppose you'd have to admit that for Hitler it was good and for you it is evil.

RUSSELL: No, I shouldn't go so far as that. I mean. I think people can make mistakes in that as they can in other things. If you have jaundice you see things yellow that are not yellow. You're making a mistake.

COPLESTON: Yes, one can make mistakes, but can you make a mistake if it's simply a question of reference to a feeling or emotion? Surely Hitler would be the only possible judge of what appealed to his emotions.

RUSSELL: ... you can say various things about that; among others, that if that sort of thing makes that sort of appeal to Hitler's emotions, then Hitler makes quite a different appeal to my emotions.

COPLESTON: Granted. But there's no objective criterion outside feeling then for condemning the conduct of the Commandant of Belsen, in your view.... The human being's idea of the content of the moral law depends certainly to a large extent on education and environment, and a man has to use his reason in assessing the validity of the actual moral ideas of his social group. But the possibility of criticizing the accepted moral code presupposes that there is an objective standard, that there is an ideal moral order, which imposes itself.... It implies the existence of a real foundation of God.[2]

God, according to Copleston, is able to provide the basis for the distinction, which we all know to exist, between right and wrong. Without that objective basis for defining human obligation we would have no real reason for condemning the behavior of anybody, even Nazis. Morality would be little more than an expression of personal feeling.

Before assessing the Divine Command theory, let's first consider this last point. Is it really true that only the commands of God can provide an objective basis for moral judgments? Certainly many philosophers ... have felt that morality rests on its own, perfectly sound footing; to prejudge those efforts or others which may be made in the future as unsuccessful seems mistaken. And, second, if it were true that there is no nonreligious basis for claiming moral objectivity, then perhaps that means there simply is no such basis. Why suppose that there *must* be such a foundation?

What of the Divine Command theory itself? Is it reasonable, even though we need not do so, to equate something's being right with its being commanded by God? Certainly the expressions "is commanded by God" and "is morally required" do not *mean* the same thing; atheists and agnostics use moral words without understanding them to make any reference to God. And while it is of course true that God (or any other moral being for that matter) would tend to want others to do the right thing, this hardly shows that being right and being commanded by God are the same thing. Parents want their children to do the right thing, too, but that doesn't mean they, or anybody else, can make a thing right just by commanding it!

I think that, in fact, theists themselves if they thought about it would reject the Divine Command theory. One reason is because of what it implies. Suppose we grant (just for the sake of argument) that the Divine Command theory is correct. Notice what we have now said: Actions are right just because they are commanded

---

[2] This debate was broadcast on the Third Program of the British Broadcastings Corporation in 1948.

by God. And the same, of course, can be said about those deeds which we believe are wrong. If God hadn't commanded us not to do them, they would not be wrong. (Recall the comparison made with the commands of the legislature, which would not be law except for the legislature having passed a statute.)

But now notice this. Since God is all-powerful, and since right is determined solely by His commands, is it not possible that He might change the rules and make what we now think of as wrong into right? It would seem that according to the Divine Command theory it is possible that tomorrow God will decree that virtues such as kindness and courage have become vices while actions which show cruelty and cowardice are the right actions. Rather than it being right for people to help each other out and prevent innocent people from suffering unnecessarily, it would be right to create as much pain among innocent children as we possibly can! To adopt the Divine Command theory commits its advocate to the seemingly absurd position that even the greatest atrocities might be not only acceptable but morally required if God were to command them.

Plato made a similar point in the dialogue *Euthyphro*. Socrates is asking Euthyphro what it is that makes the virtue of holiness a virtue, just as we have been asking what makes kindness and courage virtues. Euthyphro has suggested that holiness is just whatever all the gods love.

SOCRATES: Well, then, Euthyphro, what do we say, about holiness? Is it not loved by all the gods, according to your definition?

EUTHYPHRO: Yes.

SOCRATES: Because it is holy, or for some other reason?

EUTHYPHRO: No, because it is holy.

SOCRATES: Then it is loved by the gods because it is holy: it is not holy because it is loved by them?

EUTHYPHRO: It seems so.

SOCRATES: ... Then holiness is not what is pleasing to the gods, and what is pleasing to the gods is not holy as you say, Euthyphro. They are different things.

EUTHYPHRO: And why, Socrates?

SOCRATES: Because we are agreed that the gods love holiness because it is holy: and that it is not holy because they love it.[3]

Having claimed that virtues are what is loved by the gods why does Euthyphro so readily agree that the gods love holiness *because* it's holy? One possibility is that he is assuming whenever the gods love something they do so with good reason, not just arbitrarily. If something is pleasing to gods, there must be a reason. To deny this and say that it is simply the gods' love which makes holiness a virtue would mean that the gods have no basis for their opinions, that they are arbitrary. Or to put it another way, if we say that it is simply God's loving something that makes it right, then what sense does it make to say God wants us to do right? All that could mean is that God wants us to do what He wants us to do. He would have no reason for wanting it. Similarly "God is good" would mean little more than "God does what He pleases." Religious people who find this an unacceptable consequence will reject the Divine Command theory.

---

[3] Plato. *Euthyphro*, tr. H. N. Fowler (Cambridge, Mass: Harward University Press, 1947).

But doesn't this now raise another problem? If God approves kindness because it is a virtue, then it seems that God discovers morality rather than inventing it. And haven't we then suggested a limitation on God's power, since He now, being a good God, must love kindness and command us not to be cruel? What is left of God's omnipotence?

But why should such a limitation on God be unacceptable for a theist? Because there is nothing God cannot do? But is it true to say that God can do absolutely anything? Can He, for example, destroy Himself? Can God make a rock so heavy that He cannot lift it? Or create a universe which was never created by Him? Many have thought that God's inability to do these sorts of things does not constitute a genuine limitation on His power because these are things which cannot logically be done. Thomas Aquinas, for example, wrote that, "whatever implies contradiction does not come within the scope of divine omnipotence, because it cannot have the aspect of possibility. Hence it is more appropriate to say that such things cannot be done than that God cannot do them."[4] Many theists reject the view that there is nothing which God cannot do.

But how, then, ought we to understand God's relationship to morality if we reject the Divine Command theory? Can religious people consistently maintain their faith in God the Creator and yet deny that what is right is right because He commands it? I think the answer to this is "yes." First, note that there is still a sense in which God could change morality (assuming, of course, there is a God). Whatever moral code we decide is best (most justified), that choice will in part depend on such factors as how we reason, what we desire and need, and the circumstances in which we find ourselves. Presumably, however, God could have constructed us or our environment very differently, so that we didn't care about freedom, weren't curious about nature, and weren't influenced by others' suffering. Or perhaps our natural environment could be altered so that it is less hostile to our needs and desires. If He had created either nature or us that way, then it seems likely that the most justified moral code might be different in important ways from the one it is now rational for us to support. In that sense, then, morality depends on God whether or not one supports the Divine Command theory.

In fact, it seems to me that it makes little difference for ethical questions whether a person is religious. The atheist will treat human nature simply as a given, a fact of nature, while the theist may regard it as the product of divine intention. But in any case the right thing to do is to follow the best moral code, the one that is most justified. Instead of relying on revelation to discover morality, religious and nonreligious people alike can inquire into which system is best.

In sum, I have argued first that religion is neither necessary nor useful in providing moral motivation or guidance. My objections to the claim that without God there would be no morality are somewhat more complex. First, it is wrong to say that only if God's will is at its base can morality be objective. The idea of the best moral code—the one fully rational persons would support—may prove to provide sound means to evaluate one's own code as well as those of other societies. Furthermore, the Divine Command theory should not be accepted even

---

[4] Thomas Aquinas, *Summa Theologica*, Part I, Q. 25, Art. 3.

by those who are religious. This is because it implies what clearly seems absurd, namely that God might tomorrow change the moral rules and make performing the most extreme acts of cruelty an obligation we all should meet. And, finally, I discussed how the theist and atheist might hope to find common ground about the sorts of moral rules to teach our children and how we should evaluate each other's behavior. Far from helping resolve moral disputes, religion does little more than sow confusion. Morality does not need religion and religion does not need morality.

STUDY QUESTIONS

1. Arthur says that the Divine Command theory should not be accepted even by those who are religious. Why? Do you agree? Explain.
2. In Fyodor Dostoyevsky's novel *The Brothers Karamazov* one character says, "Without God, everything is permitted." Explain what the character means and why Arthur rejects this view. Does Mortimer reject it?
3. Arthur holds that ethics is not based on religion. But some have claimed that even if that is true, human beings do not *behave* ethically unless they believe that a divine being demands it. What do you think of this claim?
4. Why, in Arthur's view, should a nonbeliever behave as well as a believing Christian?

Of Benevolence

David Hume

A biographical sketch of David Hume is found on page 141.

David Hume is first and last an empiricist—that is, he believes that all human knowledge, ethical as well as scientific, is based on observation and human experience. According to Hume, we learn about the nature of morality by attending to our feelings of approval and disapproval. Our feelings vary, and we are sometimes governed by immoral or amoral passions. However, we find in almost all people "some benevolence ... some spark of friendship for human kind ... along with the elements of the wolf and serpent." Hume points out that qualities like kindliness and public spiritedness are favored universally. In this way, our common humanity provides a universal standard for what we approve and disapprove and gives rise to moral distinctions and judgments. "The notion of morals implies some sentiment common to all mankind," which gives rise to an "established theory of blame or approbation."

OF BENEVOLENCE From A *Treatise of Human Nature*. Clarendon Press, Oxford, 1888, by David Hume.

> Having grounded morality in human "sentiment," Hume's ethical philosophy is at odds with the rationalist approach—developed subsequently by Immanuel Kant—which determines right and wrong through the use of reason and not by attending to our emotions.

It may be esteemed, perhaps, a superfluous task to prove that the benevolent or softer affections are estimable; and wherever they appear, engage the approbation and good-will of mankind. The epithets *sociable, good-natured, humane, merciful, grateful, friendly, generous, beneficent*, or their equivalents, are known in all languages, and universally express the highest merit which *human nature* is capable of attaining. Where these amiable qualities are attended with birth and power and eminent abilities, and display themselves in the good government or useful instruction of mankind, they seem even to raise the possessors of them above the rank of *human nature*, and make them approach in some measure to the divine. Exalted capacity, undaunted courage, prosperous success; these may only expose a hero or politician to the envy and ill-will of the public: but as soon as the praises are added of humane and beneficent, when instances are displayed of lenity, tenderness or friendship, envy itself is silent, or joins the general voice of approbation and applause.

When Pericles, the great Athenian statesman and general, was on his deathbed, his surrounding friends, deeming him now insensible, began to indulge their sorrow for their expiring patron by enumerating his great qualities and successes, his conquests and victories, the unusual length of his administration, and his nine trophies erected over the enemies of the republic. *You forget*, cries the dying hero, who had heard all, *you forget the most eminent of my praises, while you dwell so much on those vulgar advantages in which fortune had a principal share. You have not observed that no citizen has ever yet worn mourning on my account.... It must, indeed, be confessed that by doing good only can a man truly enjoy the advantages of being eminent. His exalted station of itself but the more exposes him to danger and tempest. His sole prerogative is to afford shelter to inferiors who repose themselves under his cover and protection.*

But I forget that it is not my present business to recommend generosity and benevolence, or to paint in their true colours all the genuine charms of the social virtues. These, indeed, sufficiently engage every heart on the first apprehension of them; and it is difficult to abstain from some sally of panegyric as often as they occur in discourse or reasoning. But our object here being more the speculative than the practical part of morals, it will suffice to remark (what will readily, I believe, be allowed) that no qualities are more entitled to the general good-will and approbation of mankind than beneficence and humanity, friendship and gratitude, natural affection and public spirit, or whatever proceeds from a tender sympathy with others and a generous concern for our kind and species. These wherever they appear seem to transfuse themselves, in a manner, into each beholder, and to call forth, in their own behalf, the same favourable and affectionate sentiments which they exert on all around....

It is sufficient for our present purpose, if it be allowed what surely without the greatest absurdity cannot be disputed, that there is some benevolence, however small, infused into our bosom, some spark of friendship for human kind, some particle of the dove kneaded into our frame, along with the elements of the wolf and serpent. Let these generous sentiments be supposed ever so weak, let them be insufficient to move even a hand or finger of our body, they must still direct the determinations of our mind and, where everything else is equal, produce a cool preference of what is useful and serviceable to mankind above what is pernicious and dangerous. A *moral distinction*, therefore, immediately arises; a general sentiment of blame and approbation; a tendency, however faint, to the objects of the one, and a proportionable aversion to those of the other....

Avarice, ambition, vanity, and all passions vulgarly, though improperly, comprised under the denomination of *self-love*, are here excluded from our theory concerning the origin of morals, not because they are too weak, but because they have not a proper direction for that purpose. The notion of morals implies some sentiment common to all mankind, which recommends the same object to general approbation, and makes every man, or most men, agree in the same opinion or decision concerning it. It also implies some sentiment so universal and comprehensive as to extend to all mankind and render the actions and conduct, even of the persons the most remote, an object of applause or censure, according as they agree or disagree with that rule of right which is established. These two requisite circumstances belong alone to the sentiment of humanity here insisted on. The other passions produce in every breast many strong sentiments of desire and aversion, affection and hatred; but these neither are felt so much in common nor are so comprehensive as to be the foundation of any general system and established theory of blame or approbation.

When a man denominates another his *enemy*, his *rival*, his *antagonist*, his *adversary*, he is understood to speak the language of self-love, and to express sentiments peculiar to himself and arising from his particular circumstances and situation. But when he bestows on any man the epithets of *vicious* or *odious* or *depraved*, he then speaks another language, and expresses sentiments in which he expects all his audience are to concur with him. He must here, therefore, depart from his private and particular situation and must choose a point of view common to him with others; he must move some universal principle of the human frame and touch a string to which all mankind have an accord and symphony. If he mean, therefore, to express that this man possesses qualities whose tendency is pernicious to society, he has chosen this common point of view and has touched the principle of humanity in which every man, in some degree, concurs. While the human heart is compounded of the same elements as at present, it will never be wholly indifferent to public good, nor entirely unaffected with the tendency of characters and manners. And though this affection of humanity may not generally be esteemed so strong as vanity or ambition, yet, being common to all men, it can alone be the foundation of morals or any general system of blame or praise. One man's ambition is not another's ambition, nor will the same event or object satisfy both; but the humanity of one man is the humanity of every one, and the same object touches this passion in all human creatures.

But the sentiments which arise from humanity are not only the same in all human creatures, and produce the same approbation or censure, but they also comprehend all human creatures; nor is there any one whose conduct or character is not, by their means, an object to every one of censure or approbation. On the contrary, those other passions, commonly denominated selfish, both produce different sentiments in each individual, according to his particular situation, and also contemplate the greater part of mankind with the utmost indifference and unconcern. Whoever has a high regard and esteem for me flatters my vanity; whoever expresses contempt mortifies and displeases me; but as my name is known but to a small part of mankind, there are few who come within the sphere of this passion, or excite, on its account, either my affection or disgust. But if you represent a tyrannical, insolent, or barbarous behaviour, in any country or in any age of the world, I soon carry my eye to the pernicious tendency of such a conduct and feel the sentiment of repugnance and displeasure towards it. No character can be so remote as to be, in this light, wholly indifferent to me. What is beneficial to society or to the person himself must still be preferred. And every quality or action of every human being must, by this means, be ranked under some class or denomination expressive of general censure or applause.

What more, therefore, can we ask to distinguish the sentiments dependent on humanity from those connected with any other passion, or to satisfy us why the former are the origin of morals, not the latter? Whatever conduct gains my approbation by touching my humanity procures also the applause of all mankind, by affecting the same principle in them; but what serves my avarice or ambition pleases these passions in me alone and affects not the avarice and ambition of the rest of mankind. There is no circumstance of conduct in any man, provided it have a beneficial tendency, that is not agreeable to my humanity, however remote the person; but every man, so far removed as neither to cross nor serve my avarice and ambition, is regarded as wholly indifferent by those passions. The distinction, therefore, between these species of sentiment being so great and evident, language must soon be moulded upon it and must invent a peculiar set of terms in order to express those universal sentiments of censure or approbation which arise from humanity or from views of general usefulness and its contrary. Virtue and Vice become then known; morals are recognized; certain general ideas are framed of human conduct and behaviour; such measures are expected from men in such situations. This action is determined to be conformable to our abstract rule; that other, contrary. And by such universal principles are the particular sentiments of self-love frequently controlled and limited.

STUDY QUESTIONS

1. Hume says, "There is ... some particle of the dove kneaded into our frame, along with the elements of the wolf and serpent." Explain.
2. According to Divine Command theory, ethics is based on the rule of God. According to Hume, ethics has its source in human sentiment. Are these two views reconcilable? Explain.
3. Which emotions and sentiments figure importantly in Hume's account of moral judgment? Can anyone be deliberately cruel and still be decent? Explain.
4. Hume sometimes talks as if values such as kindliness and public spiritedness are found in all human beings. Are they? Explain. If they are not, how does that affect Hume's moral theory?
5. In the view of a rationalist moral philosopher like Immanuel Kant, Hume's approach to moral philosophy is "impure." "All moral philosophy," says Kant, "rests wholly on its

pure [i.e., rational] part. When applied to man, it does not borrow the least thing from the knowledge of man himself (anthropology), but gives laws *a priori* to him as a rational being." Look at the opening pages of the Kant selection (see p. 230), and then defend Hume's "impure," "anthropological" approach.

Utilitarianism

John Stuart Mill

John Stuart Mill (1806–1873) was one of the greatest philosophers of the nineteenth century. Though he wrote in many different areas in philosophy, he is best known for his defense of utilitarianism. Mill was an active political reformer; while a member of Parliament, he introduced a bill to give the vote to women. His best known works are *On Liberty* (1859), *Utilitarianism* (1863), and *The Subjection of Women* (1869).

Mill defines happiness as pleasure and the absence of pain and asserts the general principle (elsewhere called the "principle of utility") that "actions are right in proportion as they tend to promote happiness, wrong as they tend to produce the reverse of happiness."

   Some opponents of utilitarianism charge that the pursuit of pleasure is an unworthy ideal ("a doctrine worthy only of swine"). Mill defends his principle by distinguishing higher and lower pleasures. One pleasure is higher than another if people who have experienced both usually prefer the former. In fact, most human beings prefer the higher pleasures, choosing an existence that employs their higher faculties (their ability to enjoy good music) over an existence that employs the lower faculties they share with swine. "Few human creatures would consent to be changed into any of the lower animals, for a promise of the fullest allowance of a beast's pleasures." The actions enjoined by the principle of utility tend to produce the greatest happiness altogether; the principle is not restricted to an agent's own happiness. In considering their own happiness and that of others, good utilitarians are strictly impartial. This is Mill's version of the Golden Rule: "To do as you would be done by, and to love your neighbour as yourself."

What Utilitarianism Is

… [T]he Greatest Happiness Principle, holds that actions are right in proportion as they tend to promote happiness, wrong as they tend to produce the reverse of

UTILITARIANISM From *Utilitarianism* by John Stuart Mill (1863).

happiness. By happiness is intended pleasure, and the absence of pain; by unhappiness, pain, and the privation of pleasure. To give a clear view of the moral standard set up by the theory, much more requires to be said; in particular, what things it includes in the ideas of pain and pleasure; and to what extent this is left an open question. But these supplementary explanations do not affect the theory of life on which this theory of morality is grounded—namely, that pleasure, and freedom from pain, are the only things desirable as ends; and that all desirable things (which are as numerous in the utilitarian as in any other scheme) are desirable either for the pleasure inherent in themselves, or as means to the promotion of pleasure and the prevention of pain.

Now, such a theory of life excites in many minds, and among them in some of the most estimable in feeling and purpose, inveterate dislike. To suppose that life has (as they express it) no higher end than pleasure—no better and nobler object of desire and pursuit—they designate as utterly mean and grovelling; as a doctrine worthy only of swine, to whom the followers of Epicurus were, at a very early period, contemptuously likened; and modern holders of the doctrine are occasionally made the subject of equally polite comparisons by its German, French, and English assailants.

When thus attacked, the Epicureans have always answered, that it is not they, but their accusers, who represent human nature in a degrading light; since the accusation supposes human beings to be capable of no pleasures except those of which swine are capable. If this supposition were true, the charge could not be gainsaid, but would then be no longer an imputation; for if the sources of pleasure were precisely the same to human beings and to swine, the rule of life which is good enough for the one would be good enough for the other. The comparison of the Epicurean life to that of beasts is felt as degrading, precisely because a beast's pleasures do not satisfy a human being's conceptions of happiness. Human beings have faculties more elevated than the animal appetites, and when once made conscious of them, do not regard anything as happiness which does not include their gratification. I do not, indeed, consider the Epicureans to have been by any means faultless in drawing out their scheme of consequences from the utilitarian principle. To do this in any sufficient manner, many Stoic, as well as Christian elements require to be included. But there is no known Epicurean theory of life which does not assign to the pleasures of the intellect, of the feelings and imagination, and of the moral sentiments, a much higher value as pleasures than to those of mere sensation. It must be admitted, however, that utilitarian writers in general have placed the superiority of mental over bodily pleasures chiefly in the greater permanency, safety, uncostliness, etc., of the former—that is, in their circumstantial advantages rather than in their intrinsic nature. And on all these points utilitarians have fully proved their case; but they might have taken the other, and, as it may be called, higher ground, with entire consistency. It is quite compatible with the principle of utility to recognise the fact, that some *kinds* of pleasure are more desirable and more valuable than others. It would be absurd that while, in estimating all other things, quality is considered as well as quantity, the estimation of pleasures should be supposed to depend on quantity alone.

If I am asked, what I mean by difference of quality in pleasures, or what makes one pleasure more valuable than another, merely as a pleasure, except its being greater in amount, there is but one possible answer. Of two pleasures, if there be one to which all or almost all who have experience of both give a decided preference, irrespective of any feeling of moral obligation to prefer it, that is the more desirable pleasure. If one of the two is, by those who are competently acquainted with both, placed so far above the other that they prefer it, even though knowing it to be attended with a greater amount of discontent, and would not resign it for any quantity of the other pleasure which their nature is capable of, we are justified in ascribing to the preferred enjoyment a superiority in quality, so far outweighing quantity as to render it, in comparison, of small account.

Now it is an unquestionable fact that those who are equally acquainted with, and equally capable of appreciating and enjoying, both, do give a most marked preference to the manner of existence which employs their higher facilities. Few human creatures would consent to be changed into any of the lower animals, for a promise of the fullest allowance of a beast's pleasures; no intelligent human being would consent to be a fool, no instructed person would be an ignoramus, no person of feeling and conscience would be selfish and base, even though they should be persuaded that the fool, the dunce, or the rascal is better satisfied with his lot than they are with theirs. They would not resign what they possess more than he for the most complete satisfaction of all the desires which they have in common with him. If they ever fancy they would, it is only in cases of unhappiness so extreme, that to escape from it they would exchange their lot for almost any other, however undesirable in their own eyes. A being of higher faculties requires more to make him happy, is capable probably of more acute suffering, and certainly accessible to it at more points, than one of an inferior type; but in spite of these liabilities, he can never really wish to sink into what he feels to be a lower grade of existence. We may give what explanation we please of this unwillingness; we may attribute it to pride, a name which is given indiscriminately to some of the most and to some of the least estimable feelings of which mankind are capable: we may refer it to the love of liberty and personal independence, an appeal to which was with the Stoics one of the most effective means for the inculcation of it; to the love of power, or to the love of excitement, both of which do really enter into and contribute to it: but its most appropriate appellation is a sense of dignity, which all human beings possess in one form or other, and in some, though by no means in exact, proportion to their higher faculties, and which is so essential a part of the happiness of those in whom it is strong, that nothing which conflicts with it could be, otherwise than momentarily, an object of desire to them. Whoever supposes that this preference takes place at a sacrifice of happiness—that the superior being, in anything like equal circumstances, is not happier than the inferior—confounds the two very different ideas, of happiness, and content. It is indisputable that the being whose capacities of enjoyment are low, has the greatest chance of having them fully satisfied; and a highly endowed being will always feel that any happiness which he can look for, as the world is constituted, is imperfect. But he can learn to bear its imperfections, if they are at all bearable; and they will not make him envy the being who is indeed unconscious of the imperfections, but only because he feels not at all the good which those imperfections qualify. It is better to be a human being dissatisfied than a pig satisfied; better to be Socrates dissatisfied than a fool satisfied. And if the fool, or the pig, are of a different opinion, it is because they only know their own side of the question. The other party to the comparison knows both sides.

It may be objected, that many who are capable of the higher pleasures, occasionally, under the influence of temptation, postpone them to the lower. But this is quite compatible with a full appreciation of the intrinsic superiority of the higher. Men often, from infirmity of character, make their election for the nearer good, though they know it to be the less valuable; and this no less when the choice is between two bodily pleasures, than when it is between bodily and mental. They pursue sensual indulgences to the injury of health, though perfectly aware that health is the greater good. It may be further objected, that many who begin with youthful enthusiasm for everything noble, as they advance in years sink into indolence and selfishness. But I do not believe that those who undergo this very common change, voluntarily choose the lower description of pleasures in preference to the higher. I believe that before they devote themselves exclusively to the one, they have already become incapable of the other. Capacity for the nobler feelings is in most natures a very tender plant, easily killed, not only by hostile influences, but by mere want of substance; and in the majority of young persons it speedily dies away if the occupations to which their position in life has devoted them, and the society into which it has thrown them, are not favourable to keeping that higher capacity in exercise. Men lose their high aspirations as they lose their intellectual tastes, because they have not time or opportunity for indulging them; and they addict themselves to inferior pleasures, not because they deliberately prefer them, but because they are either the only ones to which they have access, or the only ones which they are any longer capable of enjoying. It may be questioned whether any one who has remained equally susceptible to both classes of pleasures, ever knowingly and calmly preferred the lower; though many, in all ages, have broken down in an ineffectual attempt to combine both.

From this verdict of the only competent judges, I apprehend there can be no appeal. On a question which is the best worth having of two pleasures, or which of two modes of existence is the most grateful to the feelings, apart from its moral attributes and from its consequences, the judgment of those who are qualified by knowledge of both, or, if they differ, that of the majority among them, must be admitted as final. And there needs be the less hesitation to accept this judgment respecting the quality of pleasures, since there is no other tribunal to be referred to even on the question of quantity. What means are there of determining which is the acutest of two pains, or the intensest of two pleasurable sensations, except the general suffrage of those who are familiar with both? Neither pains nor pleasures are homogeneous, and pain is always heterogeneous with pleasure. What is there to decide whether a particular pleasure is worth purchasing at the cost of a particular pain, except the feelings and judgment of the experienced? When, therefore, those feelings and judgment declare the pleasures derived from the higher faculties to be preferable *in kind*, apart from the question of intensity, to those of which the animal nature, disjoined from the higher faculties, is sus-pectible, they are entitled on this subject to the same regard.

I have dwelt on this point, as being a necessary part of a perfectly just conception of Utility or Happiness, considered as the directive rule of human conduct. But it is by no means an indispensable condition to the acceptance of the utilitarian standard; for that standard is not the agent's own greatest happiness, but the greatest amount of happiness altogether; and if it may possibly be doubted whether a noble character is always the happier for its nobleness, there can be no doubt that it makes other people happier, and that the world in general is immensely a gainer by it. Utilitarianism, therefore, could only attain its end by the general cultivation of nobleness of character, even if each individual were only benefited by the nobleness of others, and his own, so far as happiness is concerned, were a sheer deduction from the benefit. But the bare enunciation of such an absurdity as this last, renders refutation superfluous.

According to the Greatest Happiness Principle, as above explained, the ultimate end, with reference to and for the sake of which all other things are desirable (whether we are considering our own good or that of other people), is an existence exempt as far as possible from pain, and as rich as possible in enjoyments, both in point of quantity and quality; the test of quality, and the rule for measuring it against quantity, being the preference felt by those who in their opportunities of experience, to which must be added their habits of self-consciousness and self-observation, are best furnished with the means of comparison. This, being, according to the utilitarian opinion, the end of human action, is necessarily also the standard of morality; which may accordingly be defined, the rules and precepts for human conduct, by the observance of which an existence such as has been described might be, to the greatest extent possible, secured to all mankind; and not to them only, but, so far as the nature of things admits, to the whole sentient creation....

... I must again repeat, what the assailants of utilitarianism seldom have the justice to acknowledge, that the happiness which forms the utilitarian standard of what is right in conduct, is not the agent's own happiness, but that of all concerned. As between his own happiness and that of others, utilitarianism requires him to be as strictly impartial as a disinterested and benevolent spectator. In the golden rule of Jesus of Nazareth, we read the complete spirit of the ethics of utility. To do as you would be done by, and to love your neighbour as yourself, constitute the ideal perfection of utilitarian morality.

Study Questions

1. Mill defines happiness in terms of pleasure. Can you think of an alternative definition? What is it?
2. What charge is made against the Epicureans, and how does Mill defend them?
3. What does Mill mean by the quality of a pleasure? Presumably the quality of pleasure in listening to Mozart is higher than the quality of pleasure in listening to a television commercial jingle. How would Mill show that this is so?
4. Examine Mill's remarks about the capacity for nobler feelings. Do you agree with him? Why? Do his views suggest that the primary function of education must be the development of a sensibility for the nobler pleasures? How could this be implemented?
5. Do you agree with critics who say that utilitarianism demands too much of people? Explain.

A Critique of Utilitarianism

Bernard Williams

Bernard Williams (1929–2003) was Monroe Deutsch Professor of Philosophy at the University of California, Berkeley. His books include *Shame and Necessity* (1993), *Making Sense of Humanity* (1995), and *Truth and Truthfulness: An Essay in Genealogy* (2002).

In his critique of utilitarianism, Bernard Williams points out that it may require us to do wrong. He presents two cases in which, on utilitarian grounds, one would be forced to act in a way that violated one's intuitive moral feelings. In each case, "if the agent does not do a certain disagreeable thing, someone else will," and with much worse consequences. The utilitarian holds that the agent must then overcome his squeamishness and do the lesser evil. In one of Williams's examples, a soldier, Pedro, will shoot twenty innocent people unless a tourist, Jim, shoots one of them. If Jim agrees, the remaining nineteen will go free. So far as the utilitarian is concerned, it is quite obvious that for Jim to refrain from the murder is worse than letting Pedro kill nineteen more people. This position, Williams argues, shows that utilitarianism has a confused notion of responsibility and a totally inadequate notion of personal integrity. Williams argues that our deepest convictions, projects, and attitudes "do not compute" in the utilitarian calculus.

... [L]et us look ... at two examples to see what utilitarianism might say about them, what we might say about utilitarianism and, most importantly of all, what would be implied by certain ways of thinking about the situations....

(1) George, who has just taken his Ph.D. in chemistry, finds it extremely difficult to get a job. He is not very robust in health, which cuts down the number of jobs he might be able to do satisfactorily. His wife has to go out to work to keep them, which itself causes a great deal of strain, since they have small children and there are severe problems about looking after them. The results of all this, especially on the children, are damaging. An older chemist, who knows about this situation, says that he can get George a decently paid job in a certain laboratory, which pursues research into chemical and biological warfare. George says that he cannot accept this, since he is opposed to chemical and biological warfare. The older man replies that he is not too keen on it himself, come to that, but after all George's refusal is not going to make the job or the laboratory go away; what is

A CRITIQUE OF UTILITARIANISM By Bernard Williams from "A Critique of Utilitarianism" in *Utilitarianism: For and Against*, edited by J. J. C. Smart and Bernard Williams. Reprinted by permission of Cambridge University Press.

more, he happens to know that if George refuses the job, it will certainly go to a contemporary of George's who is not inhibited by any such scruples and is likely if appointed to push along the research with greater zeal than George would. Indeed, it is not merely concern for George and his family, but (to speak frankly and in confidence) some alarm about this other man's excess of zeal, which has led the older man to offer to use his influence to get George the job.... George's wife, to whom he is deeply attached, has views (the details of which need not concern us) from which it follows that at least there is nothing particularly wrong with research into CBW. What should he do?

(2) Jim finds himself in the central square of a small South American town. Tied up against the wall are a row of twenty Indians, most terrified, a few defiant, in front of them several armed men in uniform. A heavy man in a sweat-stained khaki shirt turns out to be the captain in charge and, after a good deal of questioning of Jim which establishes that he got there by accident while on a botanical expedition, explains that the Indians are a random group of the inhabitants who, after recent acts of protest against the government, are just about to be killed to remind other possible protestors of the advantages of not protesting. However, since Jim is an honoured visitor from another land, the captain is happy to offer him a guest's privilege of killing one of the Indians himself. If Jim accepts, then as a special mark of the occasion, the other Indians will be let off. Of course, if Jim refuses, then there is no special occasion, and Pedro here will do what he was about to do when Jim arrived, and kill them all. Jim, with some desperate recollection of schoolboy fiction, wonders whether if he got hold of a gun, he could hold the captain, Pedro and the rest of the soldiers to threat, but it is quite clear from the set-up that nothing of that kind is going to work: any attempt at that sort of thing will mean that all the Indians will be killed, and himself. The men against the wall, and the other villagers, understand the situation, and are obviously begging him to accept. What should he do?

To these dilemmas, it seems to me that utilitarianism replies, in the first case, that George should accept the job, and in the second, that Jim should kill the Indian. Not only does utilitarianism give these answers but, if the situations are essentially as described and there are no further special factors, it regards them, it seems to me, as *obviously* the right answers. But many of us would certainly wonder whether, in (1), that could possibly be the right answer at all; and in the case of (2), even one who came to think that perhaps that was the answer, might well wonder whether it was obviously the answer. Nor is it just a question of the rightness or obviousness of these answers. It is also a question of what sort of considerations come into finding the answer. A feature of utilitarianism is that it cuts out a kind of consideration which for some others makes a difference to what they feel about such cases: a consideration involving the idea, as we might first and very simply put it, that each of us is specially responsible for what *he* does, rather than for what other people do. This is an idea closely connected with the value of integrity. It is often suspected that utilitarianism, at least in its direct forms, makes integrity as a value more or less unintelligible. I shall try to show that this suspicion is correct....

... I want to consider now two types of effect that are often invoked by utilitarians, and which might be invoked in connexion with these imaginary cases. The attitude or tone involved in invoking these effects may sometimes seem peculiar;

but that sort of peculiarity soon becomes familiar in utilitarian discussions, and indeed it can be something of an achievement to retain a sense of it.

First, there is the psychological effect on the agent. Our descriptions of these situations have not so far taken account of how George or Jim will be after they have taken the one course or the other; and it might be said that if they take the course which seemed at first the utilitarian one, the effects on them will be in fact bad enough and extensive enough to cancel out the initial utilitarian advantages of that course. Now there is one version of this effect in which, for a utilitarian, some confusion must be involved, namely that in which the agent feels bad, his subsequent conduct and relations are crippled and so on, *because he thinks that he has done the wrong thing*—for if the balance of outcomes was as it appeared to be *before* invoking this effect, then he has not (from the utilitarian point of view) done the wrong thing. So that version of the effect, for a rational and utilitarian agent, could not possibly make any difference to the assessment of right and wrong. However, perhaps he is not a thoroughly rational agent, and is disposed to have bad feelings, whichever he decided to do. Now such feelings, which are from a strictly utilitarian point of view irrational—nothing, a utilitarian can point out, is advanced by having them—cannot, consistently, have any great weight in a utilitarian calculation. I shall consider in a moment an argument to suggest that they should have no weight at all in it. But short of that, the utilitarian could reasonably say that such feelings should not be encouraged, even if we accept their existence, and that to give them a lot of weight is to encourage them. Or, at the very best, even if they are straightforwardly and without any discount to be put into the calculation, their weight must be small: they are after all (and at best) one man's feelings.

That consideration might seem to have particular force in Jim's case. In George's case, his feelings represent a larger proportion of what is to be weighed, and are more commensurate in character with other items in the calculation. In Jim's case, however, his feelings might seem to be of very little weight compared with other things that are at stake. There is a powerful and recognizable appeal that can be made on this point: as that a refusal by Jim to do what he has been invited to do would be a kind of self-indulgent squea-mishness. That is an appeal which can be made by other than utilitarians—indeed, there are some uses of it which cannot be consistently made by utilitarians, as when it essentially involves the idea that there is something dishonourable about such self-indulgence. But in some versions it is a familiar, and it must be said a powerful, weapon of utilitarianism. One must be clear, though, about what it can and cannot accomplish. The most it can do, so far as I can see, is to invite one to consider how seriously, and for what reasons, one feels that what one is invited to do is (in these circumstances) wrong, and in particular, to consider that question from the utilitarian point of view. When the agent is not seeing the situation from a utilitarian point of view, the appeal cannot force him to do so; and if he does come round to seeing it from a utilitarian point of view, there is virtually nothing left for the appeal to do. If he does not see it from a utilitarian point of view, he will not see his resistance to the invitation, and the unpleasant feelings he associates with accepting it, *just* as disagreeable experiences of his; they figure rather as emotional expressions of a thought that to accept would be wrong. He may be asked, as by the appeal, to consider whether he is right, and indeed whether he is fully serious, in thinking that. But the assertion of the appeal, that he is being self-indulgently squeamish, will not itself answer that question, or even help to answer it, since it essentially tells him to regard his feelings just as unpleasant experiences of his, and he cannot, by doing that, answer the question they pose when they are precisely not so regarded, but are regarded as indications of what he thinks is right and wrong. If he does come round fully to the utilitarian point of view then of course he will regard these feelings just as unpleasant experiences of his. And once Jim—at least—has come to see them in that light, there is nothing left for the appeal to do, since *of course* his feelings, so regarded, are of virtually no weight at all in relation to the other things at stake. The "squeamishness" appeal is not an argument which adds in a hitherto neglected consideration. Rather, it is an invitation to consider the situation, and one's own feelings, from a utilitarian point of view.

The reason why the squeamishness appeal can be very unsettling, and one can be unnerved by the suggestion of self-indulgence in going against utilitarian considerations, is not that we are utilitarians who are uncertain what utilitarian value to attach to our moral feelings, but that we are partially at least not utilitarians, and cannot regard our moral feelings merely as objects of utilitarian value. Because our moral relation to the world is partly given by such feelings, and by a sense of what we can or cannot "live with," to come to regard those feelings from a purely utilitarian point of view, that is to say, as happenings outside one's moral self, is to lose a sense of one's moral identity; to lose, in the most literal way, one's integrity....

Integrity

The [two] situations have in common that if the agent does not do a certain disagreeable thing, someone else will, and in Jim's situation at least the result, the state of affairs after the other man has acted, if he does, will be worse than after Jim has acted, if Jim does. The same, on a smaller scale, is true of George's case. I have already suggested that it is inherent in consequentialism that it offers a strong doctrine of negative responsibility: if I know that if I do X, O_1 will eventuate, and if I refrain from doing X, O_2 will, and that O_2 is worse than O_1, then I am responsible for O_2 if I refrain voluntarily from doing X. "You could have prevented it," as will be said, and truly, to Jim, if he refuses, by the relatives of the other Indians.... [But] what occurs if Jim refrains from action is not solely twenty Indians dead, but *Pedro's killing twenty Indians....* That may be enough for us to speak, in some sense, of Jim's responsibility for that outcome, if it occurs; but it is certainly not enough, it is worth noticing, for us to speak of Jim's *making* those things happen. For granted this way of their coming about, he could have made them happen only by making Pedro shoot, and there is no acceptable sense in which his refusal makes Pedro shoot. If the captain had said on Jim's refusal, "you leave me with no alternative," he would have been lying, like most who use that phrase. While the deaths, and the killing, may be the outcome of Jim's refusal, it is misleading to think, in such a case, of Jim having an *effect* on the world through the medium (as it happens) of Pedro's acts; for this is to leave Pedro out of the picture in his essential role of one who has intentions and projects, projects for realizing which Jim's refusal would leave an opportunity. Instead of thinking in terms of supposed effects of Jim's projects on Pedro, it is more revealing to think in terms of the effects of Pedro's projects on Jim's decision....

Utilitarianism would do well ... to acknowledge the evident fact that among the things that make people happy is not only making other people happy, but being taken up or involved in any of a vast range of projects, or—if we waive the evangelical and moralizing associations of the word—commitments. One can be committed to such things as a person, a cause, an institution, a career, one's own genius, or the pursuit of danger.

Now none of these is itself the *pursuit of happiness*: by an exceedingly ancient platitude, it is not at all clear that there could be anything which was just that, or at least anything that had the slightest chance of being successful. Happiness, rather, requires being involved in, or at least content with, something else. It is not impossible for utilitarianism to accept that point: it does not have to be saddled with a naïve and absurd philosophy of mind about the relation between desire and happiness. What it does have to say is that if such commitments are worthwhile, then pursuing the projects that flow from them, and realizing some of those projects, will make the person for whom they are worthwhile, happy. It may be that to claim that is still wrong: it may well be that a commitment can make sense to a man (can make sense of his life) without his supposing that it will make him *happy*. But that is not the present point; let us grant to utilitarianism that all worthwhile human projects must conduce, one way or another, to happiness. The point is that even if that is true, it does not follow, nor could it possibly be true, that those projects are themselves projects of pursuing happiness. One has to believe in, or at least want, or quite minimally, be content with, other things, for there to be anywhere that happiness can come from.

Utilitarianism, then, should be willing to agree that its general aim of maximizing happiness does not imply that what everyone is doing is just pursuing happiness. On the contrary, people have to be pursuing other things. What those other things may be, utilitarianism, sticking to its professed empirical stance, should be prepared just to find out. No doubt some possible projects it will want to discourage, on the grounds that their being pursued involves a negative balance of happiness to others: though even there, the unblinking accountant's eye of the strict utilitarian will have something to put in the positive column, the satisfactions of the destructive agent. Beyond that, there will be a vast variety of generally beneficent or at least harmless projects; and some no doubt, will take the form not just of tastes or fancies, but of what I have called "commitments." It may even be that the utilitarian researcher will find that many of those with commitments, who have really identified themselves with objects outside themselves, who are thoroughly involved with other persons, or institutions, or activities or causes, are actually happier than those whose projects and wants are not like that. If so, that is an important piece of utilitarian empirical lore.

When I say "happier" here, I have in mind the sort of consideration which any utilitarian would be committed to accepting: as for instance that such people are less likely to have a breakdown or commit suicide. Of course that is not all that is actually involved, but the point in this argument is to use to the maximum degree utilitarian notions, in order to locate a breaking point in utilitarian thought. In appealing to this strictly utilitarian notion, I am being more consistent with utilitarianism than Smart is. In his struggles with the problem of the brain-electrode man, Smart ... commends the idea that "happy" is a partly evaluative term, in the sense that we call "happiness" those kinds of satisfaction which, as things are, we approve of. But *by what standard* is this surplus element of approval supposed, from a utilitarian point of view, to be allocated? There is no source for it, on a strictly utilitarian view, except further degrees of satisfaction, but there are none of those available, or the problem would not arise. Nor does it help to appeal to the fact that we dislike in prospect things which we like when we get there, for from a utilitarian point of view it would seem that the original dislike was merely irrational or based on an error. Smart's argument at this point seems to be embarrassed by a well-known utilitarian uneasiness, which comes from a feeling that it is not respectable to ignore the "deep," while not having anywhere left in human life to locate it.

On a utilitarian view ... [t]he determination to an indefinite degree of my decisions by other people's projects is just another aspect of my unlimited responsibility to act for the best in a causal framework formed to a considerable extent by their projects.

The decision so determined is, for utilitarianism, the right decision. But what if it conflicts with some project of mine? This, the utilitarian will say, has already been dealt with: the satisfaction to you of fulfilling your project, and any satisfaction to others of your so doing, have already been through the calculating device and have been found inadequate. Now in the case of many sorts of projects, that is a perfectly reasonable sort of answer. But in the case of projects of the sort I have called "commitments," those with which one is more deeply and extensively involved and identified, this cannot just by itself be an adequate answer, and there may be no adequate answer at all. For, to take the extreme sort of case, how can a man, as a utilitarian agent, come to regard as one satisfaction among others, and a dispensable one, a project or attitude round which he has built his life, just because someone else's projects have so structured the causal scene that that is how the utilitarian sum comes out?

The point here is not, as utilitarians may hasten to say, that if the project or attitude is that central to his life, then to abandon it will be very disagreeable to him and great loss of utility will be involved.... On the contrary, once he is prepared to look at it like that, the argument in any serious case is over anyway. The point is that he is identified with his actions as flowing from projects and attitudes which in some cases he takes seriously at the deepest level, as what his life is about (or, in some cases, this section of his life—seriousness is not necessarily the same as persistence). It is absurd to demand of such a man, when the sums come in from the utility network which the projects of others have in part determined, that he should just step aside from his own project and decision and acknowledge the decision which utilitarian calculation requires. It is to alienate him in a real sense from his actions and the source of his action in his own convictions. It is to make him into a channel between the input of everyone's projects, including his own, and an output of optimific decision; but this is to neglect the extent to which *his* actions and *his* decisions have to be seen as the actions and decisions which flow from the projects and attitudes with which he is most closely identified. It is thus, in the most literal sense, an attack on his integrity.

[T]he immediate point of all this is to draw one particular contrast with utilitarianism: that to reach a grounded decision ... should not be regarded as a matter of just discontinuing one's reactions, impulses and deeply held projects in the face of the pattern of utilities, nor yet merely adding them in—but in the first instance of trying to understand them.

Of course, time and circumstances are unlikely to make a grounded decision, in Jim's case at least, possible. Very often, we just act, as a possibly confused result of the situation in which we are engaged. That, I suspect, is very often an exceedingly good thing.

STUDY QUESTIONS

1. What are Williams's main objections to utilitarianism?
2. Williams brings two cases that pose difficulties for consequentialists. Discuss both cases. Do you think George's refusal to take the job is right? Could it be construed as right on utilitarian grounds? Explain.
3. What does Williams mean by "deeply held projects"? Why should they count for more than utility?

The Experience Machine

Robert Nozick

Robert Nozick (1936–2000) was a professor of philosophy at Harvard University. His books include *Anarchy, State and Utopia* (1974), *Philosophical Explanations* (1981), and *Invariances: The Structure of the Objective World*, published posthumously in 2001.

John Stuart Mill said that actions are right when they promote happiness and wrong when they promote the opposite of happiness. In this passage, Robert Nozick offers what seems to be a powerful counterexample to Mill's theory. Suppose you could exchange your current life for a vastly more pleasurable one. All you have to do is report to a lab where technicians will connect you to machines which will induce in you pleasurable fantasies and offer you "a lifetime of bliss." Nozick suggests that our unwillingness to accept the invitation shows that we value something other than pleasure and happiness.

There are also substantial puzzles when we ask what matters other than how *people's* experiences feel "from the inside." Suppose there were an experience machine that would give you any experience you desired. Superduper neuropsychologists could stimulate your brain so that you would think and feel you were writing a great novel, or making a friend, or reading an interesting book. All the time you would be floating in a tank, with electrodes attached to your brain. Should you plug into this machine for life, preprogramming your life's experiences? If you are worried about missing out on desirable experiences, we can suppose that business enterprises have researched thoroughly the lives of many others. You can pick and choose from their large library or smorgasbord of such experiences, selecting your life's experiences for, say, the next two years. After two years have passed, you will have ten minutes or ten hours out of the tank, to select the experiences of your *next* two years. Of course, while in the tank you won't know that you're there; you'll think it's all actually happening. Others can also plug in to have the experiences they want, so there's no need to stay unplugged to serve them. (Ignore problems such as who will service the machines if everyone plugs in.) Would you plug in? *What else can matter to us, other than how our lives feel from the inside?* Nor should you refrain because of the few moments of distress between the moment you've decided and the moment you're plugged. What's a few moments of distress compared to a lifetime of bliss (if that's what you choose), and why feel any distress at all if your decision *is* the best one?

What does matter to us in addition to our experiences? First, we want to *do* certain things, and not just have the experience of doing them. In the case of certain experiences, it is only because first we want to do the actions that we want the experiences of doing them or thinking we've done them. (But *why* do we want to do the activities rather than merely to experience them?) A second reason for not plugging in is that we want to *be* a certain way, to be a certain sort of person. Someone floating in a tank is an indeterminate blob. There is no answer to the question of what a person is like who has long been in the tank. Is he courageous, kind, intelligent, witty, loving? It's not merely that it's difficult to tell; there's no way he is. Plugging into the machine is a kind of suicide. It will seem to some, trapped by a picture, that nothing about what we are like can matter except as it gets reflected in our experiences. But should it be surprising that what *we are* is important to us? Why should we be concerned only with how our time is filled, but not with what we are?

Thirdly, plugging into an experience machine limits us to a man-made reality, to a world no deeper or more important than that which people can construct. There is no *actual* contact with any deeper reality, though the experience of it can be simulated. Many persons desire to leave themselves open to such contact and to a plumbing of deeper significance.[1] This clarifies the intensity of the conflict over psychoactive drugs, which some view as mere local experience machines, and others view as avenues to a deeper reality; what some view as equivalent to surrender to the experience machine, others view as following one of the reasons *not* to surrender!

---

[1] Traditional religious views differ on the *point* of contact with a transcendent reality. Some say that contact yields eternal bliss or Nirvana, but they have not distinguished this sufficiently from merely a *very* long run on the experience machine. Others think it is intrinsically desirable to do the will of a higher being which created us all, though presumably no one would think this if we discovered we had been created as an object of amusement by some superpowerful child from another galaxy or dimension. Still others imagine an eventual merging with a higher reality, leaving unclear its desirability, or where that merging leaves *us*.

We learn that something matters to us in addition to experience by imagining an experience machine and then realizing that we would not use it. We can continue to imagine a sequence of machines each designed to fill lacks suggested for the earlier machines. For example, since the experience machine doesn't meet our desire to *be* a certain way, imagine a transformation machine which transforms us into whatever sort of person we'd like to be (compatible with our staying us). Surely one would not use the transformation machine to become as one would wish, and thereupon plug into the experience machine![2] So something matters in addition to one's experiences *and* what one is like. Nor is the reason merely that one's experiences are unconnected with what one is like. For the experience machine might be limited to provide only experiences possible to the sort of person plugged in. Is it that we want to make a difference in the world?

Consider then the result machine, which produces in the world any result you would produce and injects your vector input into any joint activity. We shall not pursue here the fascinating details of these or other machines. What is most disturbing about them is their living of our lives for us. Is it misguided to search for *particular* additional functions beyond the competence of machines to do for us? Perhaps what we desire is to live (an active verb) ourselves, in contact with reality. (And this, machines cannot do *for* us.) Without elaborating on the implications of this, which I believe connect surprisingly with issues about free will and causal accounts of knowledge, we need merely note the intricacy of the question of what matters *for people* other than their experiences. Until one finds a satisfactory answer, and determines that this answer does not *also* apply to animals, one cannot reasonably claim that only the felt experiences of animals limit what we may do to them.

STUDY QUESTIONS

1. Nozick suggests that plugging into the machine is a kind of suicide. Is he right?
2. Mill famously said, "Better to be Socrates dissatisfied than a fool satisfied." Does this kind of qualification protect his version of utilitarianism from Nozick's critique?

---

[2] Some wouldn't use the transformation machine at all; it seems like *cheating*. But the one-time use of the transformation machine would not remove all challenges; there would still be obstacles for the new us to overcome, a new plateau from which to strive even higher. And is this plateau any the less earned or deserved than that provided by genetic endowment and early childhood environment? But if the transformation machine could be used indefinitely often, so that we could accomplish anything by pushing a button to transform ourselves into someone who could do it easily, there would remain no limits we *need* to strain against or try to transcend. Would there be anything left to *do*? Do some theological views place God outside of time because an omniscient omnipotent being couldn't fill up his days?

The Ones Who Walk Away from Omelas

Ursula K. Le Guin

Ursula K. Le Guin (b. 1929) is the author of numerous short stories, novels, and poetry compilations. She is most famous for her science fiction writing, of which *The Left Hand of Darkness* (1969) is the most widely acclaimed. Other works include her *Wizard of Earthsea* fantasy series, *Four Ways to Forgiveness* (1995), and most recently, *Lavinia* (2008).

Ursula Le Guin tells of a highly civilized place called Omelas. Its inhabitants are sophisticated and, by most standards, they are happy. Moreover, they are considerate and decent to one another—with one exception. That exception is a necessary condition for the general welfare. But some citizens cannot reconcile themselves to it. These walk away from Omelas never to return. Le Guin's parable bears on fundamental ethical dilemmas, but most particularly it raises serious questions about the adequacy of utilitarianism as an ethical philosophy.

With a clamor of bells that set the swallows soaring, the Festival of Summer came to the city. Omelas, bright-towered by the sea. The rigging of the boats in harbor sparkled with flags. In the streets between houses with red roofs and painted walls, between old moss-grown gardens and under avenues of trees, past great parks and public buildings, processions moved. Some were decorous: old people in long stiff robes of mauve and grey, grave master workmen, quiet, merry women carrying their babies and chatting as they walked. In other streets the music beat faster, a shimmering of gong and tambourine, and the people went dancing, the procession was a dance. Children dodged in and out, their high calls rising like the swallows' crossing flights over the music and the singing. All the processions wound towards the north side of the city, where on the great water-meadow called the Green Fields boys and girls, naked in the bright air, with mud-stained feet and ankles and long, lithe arms, exercised their restive horses before the race. The horses wore no gear at all but a halter without bit. Their manes were braided with streamers of silver, gold, and green. They flared their nostrils and pranced and boasted to one another; they were vastly excited, the horse being the only animal who has adopted our ceremonies as his own. Far off to the north and west the mountains stood up half encircling Omelas on her bay. The air of morning was so clear that the snow still crowning the Eighteen Peaks burned with white-gold fire across the miles of sunlit air, under the dark blue of the sky. There was just enough wind to make the banners that marked the racecourse snap and flutter now and then. In the silence of the broad green meadows one could hear the music winding through the city streets, farther and nearer and ever approaching, a cheerful faint sweetness of the air that from time to time trembled and gathered together and broke out into the great joyous clanging of the bells.

Joyous! How is one to tell about joy? How describe the citizens of Omelas?

They were not simple folk, you see, though they were happy. But we do not say the words of cheer much any more. All smiles have become archaic. Given a description such as this one tends to make certain assumptions. Given a description such as this one tends to look next for the King, mounted on a splendid stallion and surrounded by his noble knights, or perhaps in a golden litter borne by greatmuscled slaves. But there was no king. They did not use swords, or keep slaves. They were not barbarians. I do not know the rules and laws of their society, but I suspect that they were singularly few. As they did without monarchy and slavery, so they also got on without the stock exchange, the advertisement, the secret police, and the bomb. Yet I repeat that these were not simple folk, not dulcet shepherds, noble savages, bland utopians. They were not less complex than us. The trouble is that we have a bad habit, encouraged by pedants and sophisticates, of considering happiness as something rather stupid. Only pain is intellectual, only evil interesting. This is the treason of the artist: a refusal to admit the banality of evil and the terrible boredom of pain. If you can't lick 'em, join 'em. If it hurts, repeat it. But to praise despair is to condemn delight, to embrace violence is to lose hold of everything else. We have almost lost hold; we can no longer describe a happy man, nor make any celebration of joy. How can I tell you about the people of Omelas? They were not naïve and happy children—though their children were, in fact, happy. They were mature, intelligent, passionate adults whose lives were not wretched. O miracle! But I wish I could describe it better. I wish I could convince you. Omelas sounds in my words like a city in a fairy tale, long ago and far away, once upon a time. Perhaps it would be best if you imagined it as your own fancy bids, assuming it will rise to the occasion, for certainly I cannot suit you all. For instance, how about technology? I think that there would be no cars or helicopters in and above the streets; this follows from the fact that the people of Omelas are happy people. Happiness is based on a just discrimination of what is necessary, what is neither necessary nor destructive, and what is destructive. In the middle category, however—that of the unnecessary but undestructive, that of comfort, luxury, exuberance, etc.—they could perfectly well have central heating, subway trains, washing machines, and all kinds of marvelous devices not yet invented here, floating lightsources, fuelless power, a cure for the common cold. Or they could have none of that: it doesn't matter. As you like it. I incline to think that people from towns up and down the coast have been coming in to Omelas during the last days before the Festival on very fast little trains and double-decked trams and that the train station of Omelas is actually the handsomest building in town, though plainer than the magnificent Farmers' Market. But even granted trains, I fear that Omelas so far strikes some of you as goody-goody. Smiles, bells, parades, horses, bleh. If so, please add an orgy. If an orgy would help, don't hesitate. Let us not, however, have temples from which issue beautiful nude priests and priestesses already half in ecstasy and ready to copulate with any man or woman, lover or stranger, who desires union with the deep godhead of the blood, although that was my first idea. But really it would be better not to have any temples in Omelas—at least, not manned temples. Religion yes, clergy no. Surely the beautiful nudes can just wander about, offering themselves like divine soufflés to the hunger of the needy and the rapture of the flesh. Let them join the processions. Let tambourines be struck above the copulations, and the glory of desire be proclaimed upon the gongs, and (a not unimportant point) let the offspring of these delightful rituals be beloved and looked after by all. One thing I know there is none of in Omelas is guilt. But what else should there be? I thought at first there were no drugs, but that is puritanical. For those who like it, the faint insistent sweetness of *drooz* may perfume the ways of the city, *drooz*, which first brings a great lightness and brilliance to the mind and limbs, and then after some hours a dreamy languor, and wonderful visions at last of the very arcana and inmost secrets of the Universe, as well as exciting the pleasure of sex beyond all belief; and it is not habit-forming. For more modest tastes I think there ought to be beer. What else, what else belongs in the joyous city? The sense of victory, surely, the celebration of courage. But as we did without clergy, let us do without soldiers. The joy built upon successful slaughter is not the right kind of joy; it will not do; it is fearful and it is trivial. A boundless and generous contentment, a magnanimous triumph felt not against some outer enemy but in communion with the finest and fairest in the souls of all men everywhere and the splendor of the world's summer: this is what swells the hearts of the people of Omelas, and the victory they celebrate is that of life. I really don't think many of them need to take *drooz*.

Most of the processions have reached the Green Fields by now. A marvelous smell of cooking goes forth from the red and blue tents of the provisioners. The faces of small children are amiably sticky; in the benign grey beard of a man a couple of crumbs of rich pastry are entangled. The youths and girls have mounted their horses and are beginning to group around the starting line of the course. An old woman, small, fat, and laughing, is passing out flowers from a basket, and tall young men wear her flowers in their shining hair. A child of nine or ten sits at the edge of the crowd, alone, playing on a wooden flute. People pause to listen, and they smile, but they do not speak to him, for he never ceases playing and never sees them, his dark eyes wholly rapt in the sweet, thin magic of the tune.

He finishes, and slowly lowers his hands holding the wooden flute.

As if that little private silence were the signal, all at once a trumpet sounds from the pavilion near the starting line: imperious, melancholy, piercing. The horses rear on their slender legs, and some of them neigh in answer. Sober-faced, the young riders stroke the horses' necks and soothe them, whispering, "Quiet, quiet, there my beauty, my hope...." They begin to form in rank along the starting line. The crowds along the racecourse are like a field of grass and flowers in the wind. The Festival of Summer has begun.

Do you believe? Do you accept the festival, the city, the joy? No? Then let me describe one more thing.

In a basement under one of the beautiful public buildings of Omelas, or perhaps in the cellar of one of its spacious private homes, there is a room. It has one locked door, and no window. A little light seeps in dustily between cracks in the boards, secondhand from a cobwebbed window somewhere across the cellar. In one corner of the little room a couple of mops, with stiff, clotted, foul-smelling heads, stand near a rusty bucket. The floor is dirt, a little damp to the touch, as cellar dirt usually is. The room is about three paces long and two wide: a mere broom closet or disused tool room. In the room a child is sitting. It could be a boy or a girl. It looks about six, but actually is nearly ten. It is feeble-minded. Perhaps it was born defective, or perhaps it has become imbecile through fear, malnutrition, and neglect. It picks its nose and occasionally fumbles vaguely with its toes or genitals, as it sits hunched in the corner farthest from the bucket and the two mops. It is afraid of the mops. It finds them horrible. It shuts its eyes, but it knows the mops are still standing there; and the door is locked; and nobody will come. The door is always locked; and nobody ever comes, except that sometimes—the child has no understanding of time or interval—sometimes the door rattles terribly and opens, and a person, or several people, are there. One of them may come in and kick the child to make it stand up. The others never come close, but peer in at it with frightened, disgusted eyes. The food bowl and the water jug are hastily filled, the door is locked, the eyes disappear. The people at the door never say anything, but the child, who has not always lived in the tool room, and can remember sunlight and its mother's voice, sometimes speaks. "I will be good," it says. "Please let me out. I will be good!" They never answer. The child used to scream for help at night, and cry a good deal, but now it only makes a kind of whining, "eh-haa, eh-haa," and it speaks less and less often. It is so thin there are no calves to its legs; its belly protrudes; it lives on a half-bowl of corn meal and grease a day. It is naked. Its buttocks and thighs are a mass of festered sores, as it sits in its own excrement continually.

They all know it is there, all the people of Omelas. Some of them have come to see it, others are content merely to know it is there. They all know that it has to be there. Some of them understand why, and some do not, but they all understand that their happiness, the beauty of their city, the tenderness of their friendships, the health of their children, the wisdom of their scholars, the skill of their makers, even the abundance of their harvest and the kindly weathers of their skies, depend wholly on this child's abominable misery.

This is usually explained when they are between eight and twelve, whenever they seem capable of understanding; and most of those who come to see the child are young people, though often enough an adult comes, or comes back, to see the child. No matter how well the matter has been explained to them, these young spectators are always shocked and sickened at the sight. They feel disgust, which they had thought themselves superior to. They feel anger, outrage, impotence, despite all the explanations. They would like to do something for the child. But there is nothing they can do. If the child were brought up into the sunlight out of that vile place, if it were cleaned and fed and comforted, that would be a good thing, indeed; but if it were done, in that day and hour all the prosperity and beauty and delight of Omelas would wither and be destroyed. Those are the terms. To exchange all the goodness and grace of every life in Omelas for that single, small improvement: to throw away the happiness of thousands for the chance of the happiness of one: that would be to let guilt within the walls indeed.

The terms are strict and absolute; there may not even be a kind word spoken to the child.

Often the young people go home in tears, or in a tearless rage, when they have seen the child and faced this terrible paradox. They may brood over it for weeks or years. But as time goes on they begin to realize that even if the child could be released, it would not get much good of its freedom: a little vague pleasure of warmth and food, no doubt, but little more. It is too degraded and imbecile to know any real joy. It has been afraid too long ever to be free of fear. Its habits are too uncouth for it to respond to humane treatment. Indeed, after so long it would probably be wretched without walls about it to protect it, and darkness for its eyes, and its own excrement to sit in. Their tears at the bitter injustice dry when they begin to perceive the terrible justice of reality and to accept it. Yet it is their tears and anger, the trying of their generosity and the acceptance of their helplessness, which are perhaps the true source of the splendor of their lives. Theirs is no vapid, irresponsible happiness. They know that they, like the child, are not free. They know compassion. It is the existence of the child, and their knowledge of its existence, that makes possible the nobility of their architecture, the poignancy of their music, the profundity of their science. It is because of the child that they are so gentle with children. They know that if the wretched one were not there snivelling in the dark, the other one, the flute-player, could make no joyful music as the young riders line up in their beauty for the race in the sunlight of the first morning of summer.

Now do you believe in them? Are they not more credible? But there is one more thing to tell, and this is quite incredible.

At times one of the adolescent girls or boys who go to see the child does not go home to weep or rage, does not, in fact, go home at all. Sometimes also a man or woman much older falls silent for a day or two, and then leaves home. These people go out into the street, and walk down the street alone. They keep walking, and walk straight out of the city of Omelas, through the beautiful gates. They keep walking across the farmlands of Omelas. Each one goes alone, youth or girl, man or woman. Night falls; the traveler must pass down village streets, between the houses with yellow-lit windows, and on out into the darkness of the fields. Each alone, they go west or north, toward the mountains. They go on. They leave Omelas, they walk ahead into the darkness, and they do not come back. The place they go towards is a place even less imaginable to most of us than the city of happiness. I cannot describe it at all. It is possible that it does not exist. But they seem to know where they are going, the ones who walk away from Omelas.

STUDY QUESTIONS

1. Ursula Le Guin makes a point of saying that the price of Omelas's happiness is the misery of one child. Some social theorists believe that the fortunate existence of those who live in the more developed nations is achieved at the cost of much misery in undeveloped nations. If so, Le Guin's Omelas is a parable to our own situation. To what extent is the analogy apt, if at all?

2. Le Guin tells us that the citizens of Omelas are fully aware of the suffering of the child, but she makes a point of saying that those who stay in Omelas do not feel guilty. Is it possible to feel guilty constantly about the misery of others? Explain and give examples.

3. If you were a citizen of Omelas, would you stay or walk away? Explain and justify your decision.

Good Will, Duty, and the Categorical Imperative

Immanuel Kant

Immanuel Kant (1724–1804) is considered to be one of the greatest philosophers of all time. He lived in Königsberg, in East Prussia, and was a professor at the university there. Kant made significant and highly original contributions to esthetics, jurisprudence, and the philosophy of religion as well as to ethics and epistemology. His best-known works are the *Critique of Pure Reason* (1781) and the *Groundwork of the Metaphysics of Morals* (1785).

Human beings have desires and appetites. They are also rational, capable of knowing what is right, and capable of willing to do it. They can therefore exercise their wills in the rational control of desire for the purpose of right action. This is what persons of moral worth do. According to Immanuel Kant, to possess moral worth is more important than to possess intelligence, humor, strength, or any other talent of the mind or body. These talents are valuable, but moral worth has *absolute* value, commanding not mere admiration but reverence and respect. Human beings who do right merely because it pleases them are not yet intrinsically moral. For had it pleased them they would have done wrong. To act morally is to act from no other motive than the motive of doing what is right. This kind of motive has nothing to do with anything as subjective as pleasure. To do right out of principle is to recognize an objective right that imposes an obligation on any rational being. Moral persons act in such a way that they could will that the principles of their actions should be universal laws for everyone else as well. This is one test of a moral act: Is it the kind of act that everyone should perform? Kant illustrates how this test can be applied to determine whether a given principle is moral and objective or merely subjective. For example, I may wish to break a promise, but that cannot be moral since I cannot will that promise-breaking be a universal practice.

Universal principles impose *categorical* imperatives. An imperative is a demand that I act in a certain fashion. For example, if I want to buy a house, it is imperative that I learn something about houses. But "Learn about houses!" is a *hypothetical* imperative since it is *conditional* on my wanting to buy a house. A *categorical* imperative is unconditional. An example is "Keep your promises." Thus an imperative is not preceded by any condition, such as "if you want a good reputation." Hypothetical imperatives are "prudential": "If you want security, buy theft insurance." Categorical imperatives are moral: "Do not lie!" Kant argues that the categorical imperative presupposes the absolute worth of all rational beings as ends in themselves. Thus another formulation of the categorical imperative is: "Act in such a way that you treat humanity ... as an end and never simply as a means." Kant calls the domain of beings that are to be treated in this way the "kingdom of ends."

Everyone must admit that if a law is to be morally valid, i.e., is to be valid as a ground of obligation, then it must carry with it absolute necessity. He must admit that the command, "Thou shalt not lie," does not hold only for men, as if other rational beings had no need to abide by it, and so with all the other moral laws properly so called. And he must concede that the ground of obligation here must therefore be sought not in the nature of man nor in the circumstances of the world in which man is placed, but must be sought a priori solely in the concepts of pure reason; he must grant that every other precept which is founded on principles of mere experience—even a precept that may in certain respects be universal—insofar as it rests in the least on empirical grounds—perhaps only in its motive—can indeed be called a practical rule, but never a moral law.

Thus not only are moral laws together with their principles essentially different from every kind of practical cognition in which there is anything empirical, but all moral philosophy rests entirely on its pure part. When applied to man, it does not in the least borrow from acquaintance with him (anthropology) but gives a priori laws to him as a rational being. To be sure, these laws require, furthermore, a power of judgment sharpened by experience, partly in order to distinguish in what cases they are applicable, and partly to gain for them access to the human will as well as influence for putting them into practice. For man is affected by so many inclinations that, even though he is indeed capable of the idea of a pure practical reason, he is not so easily able to make that idea effective *in concreto* in the conduct of his life.

A metaphysics of morals is thus indispensably necessary, not merely because of motives of speculation regarding the source of practical principles which are present a priori in our reason, but because morals themselves are liable to all kinds of corruption as long as the guide and supreme norm for correctly estimating them are missing. For in the case of what is to be morally good, that it conforms to the moral law is not enough; it must also be done for the sake of the moral law. Otherwise that conformity is only very contingent and uncertain, since the non-moral ground may now and then produce actions that conform with the law but quite often produces actions that are contrary to the law. Now the moral law in its purity and genuineness (which is of the utmost concern in the practical realm) can be sought nowhere but in a pure philosophy. Therefore, pure philosophy (metaphysics) must precede; without it there can be no moral philosophy at all. That philosophy which mixes pure principles with empirical ones does not deserve the name of philosophy (for philosophy is distinguished from ordinary rational knowledge by its treatment in a separate science of what the latter comprehends only confusedly). Still less does it deserve the name of moral philosophy, since by this very confusion it spoils even the purity of morals and counteracts its own end....

There is no possibility of thinking of anything at all in the world, or even out of it, which can be regarded as good without qualification, except a *good will*. Intelligence, wit, judgment, and whatever talents of the mind one might want to name are doubtless in many respects good and desirable, as are such qualities of temperament as courage, resolution, perseverance. But they can also become extremely bad and harmful if the will, which is to make use of these gifts of nature and which in its special constitution is called character, is not good. The same holds with gifts of fortune; power, riches, honor, even health, and that complete well-being and contentment with one's condition which is called happiness make for pride and often hereby even arrogance, unless there is a good will to correct their influence on the mind and herewith also to rectify the whole principle of action and make it universally conformable to its end. The sight of a being who is not graced by any touch of a pure and good will but who yet enjoys an uninterrupted prosperity can never delight a rational and impartial spectator. Thus a good will seems to constitute the indispensable condition of being even worthy of happiness.

Some qualities are even conducive to this good will itself and can facilitate its work. Nevertheless, they have no intrinsic unconditional worth; but they always presuppose, rather, a good will, which restricts the high esteem in which they are otherwise rightly held, and does not permit them to be regarded as absolutely good. Moderation in emotions and passions, self-control, and calm deliberation are not only good in many respects but even seem to constitute part of the intrinsic worth of a person. But they are far from being rightly called good without qualification (however unconditionally they were commended by the ancients). For without the principles of a good will, they can become extremely bad; the coolness of a villain makes him not only much more dangerous but also immediately more abominable in our eyes than he would have been regarded by us without it.

A good will is good not because of what it effects or accomplishes, nor because of its fitness to attain some proposed end; it is good only through its willing, i.e., it is good in itself. When it is considered in itself, then it is to be esteemed very much higher than anything which it might, ever bring about merely in order to favor some inclination, or even the sum total of all inclinations. Even if, by some especially unfortunate fate or by the niggardly provision of stepmotherly nature, this will should be wholly lacking in the power to accomplish its purpose; if with the greatest effort it should yet achieve nothing, and only the good will should remain (not, to be sure, as a mere wish but as the summoning of all the means in our power), yet would it, like a jewel, still shine by its own light as something which has its full value in itself. Its usefulness or fruitlessness can neither augment nor diminish this value. Its usefulness would be, as it were, only the setting to enable us to handle it in ordinary dealings or to attract to it the attention of those who are not yet experts, but not to recommend it to real experts or to determine its value....

Thus the moral worth of an action does not lie in the effect expected from it nor in any principle of action that needs to borrow its motive from this expected effect. For all these effects (agreeableness of one's condition and even the furtherance of other people's happiness) could have been brought about also through other causes and would not have required the will of a rational being, in which the highest and unconditioned good can alone be found. Therefore, the pre-eminent good which is called moral can consist in nothing but the representation of the law in itself, and such a representation can admittedly be found only in a rational being insofar as this representation, and not some expected effect, is the determining ground of the will. This good is already present in the person who acts according to this representation, and such good need not be awaited merely from the effect.

But what sort of law can that be the thought of which must determine the will without reference to any expected effect, so that the will can be called absolutely good without qualification? Since I have deprived the will of every impulse that might arise for it from obeying any particular law, there is nothing left to serve the will as principle except the universal conformity of its actions to law as such, i.e., I should never act except in such a way that I can also will that my maxim should become a universal law. Here mere conformity to law as such (without having as its basis any law determining particular actions) serves the will as principle and must so serve it if duty is not to be a vain delusion and a chimerical concept. The ordinary reason of mankind in its practical judgments agrees completely with this, and always has in view the aforementioned principle.

For example, take this question. When I am in distress, may I make a promise with the intention of not keeping it? I readily distinguish here the two meanings which the question may have; whether making a false promise conforms with prudence or with duty. Doubtless the former can often be the case. Indeed I clearly see that escape from some present difficulty by means of such a promise is not enough. In addition I must carefully consider whether from this lie there may later arise far greater inconvenience for me than from what I now try to escape. Furthermore, the consequences of my false promise are not easy to forsee, even with all my supposed cunning; loss of confidence in me might prove to be far more disadvantageous than the misfortune which I now try to avoid. The more prudent way might be to act according to a universal maxim and to make it a habit not to promise anything without intending to keep it. But that such a maxim is, nevertheless, always based on nothing but a fear of consequences becomes clear to me at once. To be truthful from duty is, however, quite different from being truthful from fear of disadvantageous consequences; in the first case the concept of the action itself contains a law for me, while in the second I must first look around elsewhere to see what are the results for me that might be connected with the action. For to deviate from the principle of duty is quite certainly bad; but to abandon my maxim of prudence can often be very advantageous for me, though to abide by it is certainly safer. The most direct and infallible way, however, to answer the question as to whether a lying promise accords with duty is to ask myself whether I would really be content if my maxim (of extricating myself from difficulty by means of a false promise) were to hold as a universal law for myself as well as for others, and could I really say to myself that everyone may promise falsely when he finds himself in a difficulty from which he can find no other way to extricate himself. Then I immediately become aware that I can indeed will the lie but can not at all will a universal law to lie. For by such a law there would really be no promises at all, since in vain would my willing future actions be professed to other people who would not believe what I professed, or if they over-hastily did believe, then they would pay me back in like coin. Therefore, my maxim would necessarily destroy itself just as soon as it was made a universal law.

Therefore, I need no far-reaching acuteness to discern what I have to do in order that my will may be morally good. Inexperienced in the course of the world and incapable of being prepared for all its contingencies, I only ask myself whether I can also will that my maxim should become a universal law. If not, then the maxim must be rejected, not because of any disadvantage accruing to me or even to others, but because it cannot be fitting as a principle in a possible legislation of universal law, and reason exacts from me immediate respect for such legislation. Indeed I have as yet no insight into the grounds of such respect (which the philosopher may investigate). But I at least understand that respect is an estimation of a worth that far outweighs any worth of what is recommended by inclination, and that the necessity of acting from pure respect for the practical law is what constitutes duty, to which every other motive must give way because duty is the condition of a will good in itself, whose worth is above all else....

Everything in nature works according to laws. Only a rational being has the power to act according to his conception of laws, i.e., according to principles, and thereby has he a will. Since the derivation of actions from laws requires reason, the will is nothing but practical reason. If reason infallibly determines the will, then in the case of such a being actions which are recognized to be objectively necessary are also subjectively necessary, i.e., the will is a faculty of choosing only that which reason, independently of inclination, recognizes as being practically necessary, i.e., as good. But if reason of itself does not sufficiently determine the will, and if the will submits also to subjective conditions (certain incentives) which do not always agree with objective conditions; in a word, if the will does not in itself completely accord with reason (as is actually the case with men), then actions which are recognized as objectively necessary are subjectively contingent, and the determination of such a will according to objective laws is necessitation. That is to say that the relation of objective laws to a will not thoroughly good is represented as the determination of the will of a rational being by principles of reason which the will does not necessarily follow because of its own nature.

The representation of an objective principle insofar as it necessitates the will is called a command (of reason), and the formula of the command is called an imperative....

Now all imperatives command either hypothetically or categorically. The former represent the practical necessity of a possible action as a means for attaining something else that one wants (or may possibly want). The categorical imperative would be one which represented an action as objectively necessary in itself, without reference to another end.

Every practical law represents a possible action as good and hence as necessary for a subject who is practically determinable by reason; therefore all imperatives are formulas for determining an action which is necessary according to the principle of a will that is good in some way. Now if the action would be good merely as a means to something else, so is the imperative hypothetical. But if the action is represented as good in itself, and hence as necessary in a will which of itself conforms to reason as the principle of the will, then the imperative is categorical....

If I think of a hypothetical imperative in general, I do not know beforehand what it will contain until its condition is given. But if I think of a categorical imperative, I know immediately what it contains. For since, besides the law, the imperative contains only the necessity that the maxim should accord with this law, while the law contains no condition to restrict it, there remains nothing but the universality of a law as such with which the maxim of the action should conform. This conformity alone is properly what is represented as necessary by the imperative.

Hence there is only one categorical imperative and it is this: Act only according to that maxim whereby you can at the same time will that it should become a universal law.

Now if all imperatives of duty can be derived from this one imperative as their principle, then there can at least be shown what is understood by the concept of duty and what it means, even though there is left undecided whether what is called duty may not be an empty concept.

The universality of law according to which effects are produced constitutes what is properly called nature in the most general sense (as to form), i.e., the existence of things as far as determined by universal laws. Accordingly, the universal imperative of duty may be expressed thus: Act as if the maxim of your action were to become through your will a universal law of nature.

We shall now enumerate some duties, following the usual division of them into duties to ourselves and to others and into perfect and imperfect duties.

1. A man reduced to despair by a series of misfortunes feels sick of life but is still so far in possession of his reason that he can ask himself whether taking his own life would not be contrary to his duty to himself. Now he asks whether the maxim of his action could become a universal law of nature. But his maxim is this: from self-love I make as my principle to shorten my life when its continued duration threatens more evil than it promises satisfaction. There only remains the question as to whether this principle of self-love can become a universal law of nature. One sees at once a contradiction in a system of nature whose law would destroy life by means of the very same feeling that acts so as to stimulate the furtherance of life, and hence there could be no existence as a system of nature. Therefore, such a maxim cannot possibly hold as a universal law of nature and is, consequently, wholly opposed to the supreme principle of all duty.

2. Another man in need finds himself forced to borrow money. He knows well that he won't be able to repay it, but he sees also that he will not get any loan unless he firmly promises to repay it within a fixed time. He wants to make such a promise, but he still has conscience enough to ask himself whether it is not permissible and is contrary to duty to get out of difficulty in this way. Suppose, however, that he decides to do so. The maxim of his action would then be expressed as follows: when I believe myself to be in need of money, I will borrow money and promise to pay it back, although I know that I can never do so. Now this principle of self-love or personal advantage may perhaps be quite compatible with one's entire future welfare, but the question is now whether it is right.[14] I then transform the requirement of self-love into a universal law and put the question thus: how would things stand if my maxim were to become a universal law? He then sees at once that such a maxim could never hold as a universal law of nature and be consistent with itself, but must necessarily be self-contradictory. For the universality of a law which says that anyone believing himself to be in difficulty could promise whatever he pleases with the intention of not keeping it would make promising itself and the end to be attained thereby quite impossible, inasmuch as no one would believe what was promised him but would merely laugh at all such utterances as being vain pretenses.

3. A third finds in himself a talent whose cultivation could make him a man useful in many respects. But he finds himself in comfortable circumstances and prefers to indulge in pleasure rather than to bother himself about broadening and improving his fortunate natural aptitudes. But he asks himself further whether his maxim of neglecting his natural gifts, besides agreeing of itself with his propensity to indulgence, might agree also with what is called duty. He then sees that a system of nature could indeed always subsist according to such a universal law, even

though every man (like South Sea Islanders) should let his talents rust and resolve to devote his life entirely to idleness, indulgence, propagation, and, in a word, to enjoyment. But he cannot possibly will that this should become a universal law of nature or be implanted in us as such a law by a natural instinct. For as a rational being he necessarily wills that all his faculties should be developed, inasmuch as they are given him for all sorts of possible purposes.

4. A fourth man finds things going well for himself but sees others (whom he could help) struggling with great hardships; and he thinks: what does it matter to me? Let everybody be as happy as Heaven wills or as he can make himself; I shall take nothing from him nor even envy him; but I have no desire to contribute anything to his well-being or to his assistance when in need. If such a way of thinking were to become a universal law of nature, the human race admittedly could very well subsist and doubtless could subsist even better than when everyone prates about sympathy and benevolence and even on occasion exerts himself to practice them but, on the other hand, also cheats when he can, betrays the rights of man, or otherwise violates them. But even though it is possible that a universal law of nature could subsist in accordance with that maxim, still it is impossible to will that such a principle should hold everywhere as a law of nature. For a will which resolved in this way would contradict itself, inasmuch as cases might often arise in which one would have need of the love and sympathy of others and in which he would deprive himself, by such a law of nature springing from his own will, of all hope of the aid he wants for himself....

We have thus at least shown that if duty is a concept which is to have significance and real legislative authority for our actions, then such duty can be expressed only in categorical imperatives but not at all in hypothetical ones. We have also— and this is already a great deal—exhibited clearly and definitely for every application what is the content of the categorical imperative, which must contain the principle of all duty (if there is such a thing at all). But we have not yet advanced far enough to prove a priori that there actually is an imperative of this kind, that there is a practical law which of itself commands absolutely and without any incentives, and that following this law is duty....

Now I say that man, and in general every rational being, exists as an end in himself and not merely as a means to be arbitrarily used by this or that will. He must in all his actions, whether directed to himself or to other rational beings, always be regarded at the same time as an end. All the objects of inclinations have only a conditioned value; for if there were not these inclinations and the needs founded on them, then their object would be without value. But the inclinations themselves, being sources of needs, are so far from having an absolute value such as to render them desirable for their own sake that the universal wish of every rational being must be, rather, to be wholly free from them. Accordingly, the value of any object obtainable by our action is always conditioned, Beings whose existence depends not on our will but on nature have, nevertheless, if they are not rational beings, only a relative value as means and are therefore called things. On the other hand, rational beings are called persons inasmuch as their nature already marks them out as ends in themselves, i.e., as something which is not to be used merely as means and hence there is imposed thereby a limit on all arbitrary use of such beings, which are thus objects of respect. Persons are, therefore, not merely subjective ends, whose existence as an effect of our actions has a value for us; but such beings are objective ends, i.e., exist as ends in themselves. Such an end is one for which there can be substituted no other end to which such beings should serve merely as means, for otherwise nothing at all of absolute value would be found anywhere. But if all value were conditioned and hence contingent, then no supreme practical principle could be found for reason at all.

If then there is to be a supreme practical principle and, as far as the human will is concerned, a categorical imperative, then it must be such that from the conception of what is necessarily an end for everyone because this end is an end in itself it constitutes an objective principle of the will and can hence serve as a practical law. The ground of such a principle is this: rational nature exists as an end in itself. In this way man necessarily thinks of his own existence; thus far is it a subjective principle of human actions. But in this way also does every other rational being think of his existence on the same rational ground that holds also for me; hence it is at the same time an objective principle, from which, as a supreme practical ground, all laws of the will must be able to be derived. The practical imperative will therefore be the following: Act in such a way that you treat humanity, whether in your own person or in the person of another, always at the same time as an end and never simply as a means....

The concept of every rational being as one who must regard himself as legislating universal law by all his will's maxims, so that he may judge himself and his actions from this point of view, leads to another very fruitful concept, which depends on the aforementioned one, viz., that of a kingdom of ends.

By "kingdom" I understand a systematic union of different rational beings through common laws. Now laws determine ends as regards their universal validity; therefore, if one abstracts from the personal differences of rational beings and also from all content of their private ends, then it will be possible to think of a whole of all ends in systematic connection (a whole both of rational beings as ends in themselves and also of the particular ends which each may set for himself); that is, one can think of a kingdom of ends that is possible on the aforesaid principles.

For all rational beings stand under the law that each of them should treat himself and all others never merely as means but always at the same time as an end in himself. Hereby arises a systematic union of rational beings through common objective laws, i.e., a kingdom that may be called a kingdom of ends (certainly only an ideal), inasmuch as these laws have in view the very relation of such beings to one another as ends and means.

A rational being belongs to the kingdom of ends as a member when he legislates in it universal laws while also being himself subject to these laws. He belongs to it as sovereign, when as legislator he is himself subject to the will of no other.

A rational being must always regard himself as legislator in a kingdom of ends rendered possible by freedom of the will, whether as member or as sovereign. The position of the latter can be maintained not merely through the maxims of his will but only if he is a completely independent being without needs and with unlimited power adequate to his will.

Hence morality consists in the relation of all action to that legislation whereby alone a kingdom of ends is possible. This legislation must be found in every rational being and must be able to arise from his will, whose principle then is never to act on any maxim except such as can also be a universal law and hence such as the will can thereby regard itself as at the same time the legislator of universal law. If now the maxims do not by their very nature already necessarily conform with this objective principle of rational beings as legislating universal laws, then the necessity of acting on that principle is called practical necessitation, i.e., duty. Duty does not apply to the sovereign in the kingdom of ends, but it does apply to every member and to each in the same degree.

The practical necessity of acting according to this principle, i.e., duty, does not rest at all on feelings, impulses, and inclinations, but only on the relation of rational beings to one another, a relation in which the will of a rational being must always be regarded at the same time as legislative, because otherwise he could not be thought of as an end in himself. Reason, therefore, relates every maxim of the will as legislating universal laws to every other will and also to every action toward oneself; it does so not on account of any other practical motive or future advantage but rather from the idea of the dignity of a rational being who obeys no law except what he at the same time enacts himself.

In the kingdom of ends everything has either a price or a dignity. Whatever has a price can be replaced by something else as its equivalent; on the other hand, whatever is above all price, and therefore admits of no equivalent, has a dignity.

Whatever has reference to general human inclinations and needs has a market price; whatever, without presupposing any need, accords with a certain taste, i.e., a delight in the mere unpurposive play of our mental powers, has an affective price; but that which constitutes the condition under which alone something can be an end in itself has not merely a relative worth, i.e., a price, but has an intrinsic worth, i.e., dignity.

Now morality is the condition under which alone a rational being can be an end in himself, for only thereby can he be a legislating member in the kingdom of ends. Hence morality and humanity, insofar as it is capable of morality, alone have dignity. Skill and diligence in work have a market price; wit, lively imagination, and humor have an affective price; but fidelity to promises and benevolence based on principles (not on instinct) have intrinsic worth. Neither nature nor art contain anything which in default of these could be put in their place; for their worth consists, not in the effects which arise from them, nor in the advantage and profit which they provide, but in mental dispositions, i.e., in the maxims of the will which are ready in this way to manifest themselves in action, even if they are not favored with success. Such actions also need no recommendation from any subjective disposition or taste so as to meet with immediate favor and delight; there is no need of any immediate propensity or feeling toward them. They exhibit the will performing them as an object of immediate respect; and nothing but reason is required to impose them upon the will, which is not to be cajoled into them, since in the case of duties such cajoling would be a contradiction. This estimation, therefore, lets the worth of such a disposition be recognized as dignity and puts it infinitely beyond all price, with which it cannot in the least be brought into competition or comparison without, as it were, violating its sanctity.

What then is it that entitles the morally good disposition, or virtue, to make such lofty claims? It is nothing less than the share which such a disposition affords the rational being of legislating universal laws, so that he is fit to be a member in a possible kingdom of ends, for which his own nature has already determined him as an end in himself and therefore as a legislator in the kingdom of ends. Thereby is he free as regards all laws of nature, and he obeys only those laws which he gives to himself. Accordingly, his maxims can belong to a universal legislation to which he at the same time subjects himself. For nothing can have any worth other than what the law determines. But the legislation itself which determines all worth must for that very reason have dignity, i.e., unconditional and incomparable worth; and the word "respect" alone provides a suitable expression for the esteem which a rational being must have for it. Hence autonomy is the ground of the dignity of human nature and of every rational nature.

STUDY QUESTIONS

1. Why does Kant say that the good will is good without qualification?
2. For Kant, animals are not ends in themselves because they cannot reason. So, says Kant, they have no moral rights. Does this seem right to you?
3. How does Kant distinguish between hypothetical and categorical imperatives? What kind of imperatives do "prudential" concerns impose?
4. What does Kant mean by dignity? Intrinsic worth? Autonomy? How are these concepts related?
5. How does our autonomy make it possible for us to "participate" in the giving of universal law?
6. Describe an imaginary moral dilemma. Formulate a maxim for each alternative course of action, and subject it to the test of universality. Which course of action do you think Kant would support? Why?
7. What in your opinion is Kant's greatest contribution to moral philosophy? What are two of the most serious objections that can be raised against his position?

The Holocaust and Moral Philosophy

Fred Sommers

Fred Sommers (b. 1923) is Harry Austryn Wolfson Professor of Philosophy Emeritus at Brandeis University. He is author of numerous articles and several books, including this anthology.

Fred Sommers raises the question why moral philosophy failed to inhibit the mass acts of cruelty and murder that were perpetrated by so many "ordinary" people who participated in the Holocaust. He contrasts the German tradition that grounds morality in reason with the British tradition

---

THE HOLOCAUST AND MORAL PHILOSOPHY Used by permission of the author.

that grounds morality in sentiments. The rationalist tradition focuses on persons and our duties to them. The sentimentalist tradition focuses on all beings that can feel pain or pleasure and directly prohibits cruelty to all sentient beings. Sommers points out that the exclusion of sentient nonpersons from the domain of beings that are under the protection of morality led to the exclusion (on religious and racial grounds) of many beings as nonpersons. And he argues that a morality based on human sentiments that prohibits cruelty to any sentient being is the superior and less dangerous morality.

At the end of World War II, a horrified world learned about the Holocaust, and many a devout Christian was shocked into awareness of the historic role the Church had played in fostering deadly hatred of the Jewish people. John XXIII, who was pope from 1958 to 1963, prayed thus for forgiveness: "We realize now that many, many centuries of blindness dimmed our eyes, that our brows are branded with the mark of Cain. Forgive us the curse which we unjustly laid on the name of the Jews. Forgive us that with this curse, we crucified Thee a second time."

The curse to which the Pope referred is that Jews were demonized as children of the devil, responsible for the death of Jesus. That belief, which had been spread in the first millennium by Christians embittered by the stubborn refusal of most Jews to convert to Christianity, had fostered hatred of the Jews in ordinary folk. As a result of many centuries of continuous defamation by the morally dominant institutions of Western Europe, Jews became a pariah people. Many vicious lies about Jews were circulated and remained entrenched in the popular mind, even when—as often happened—the Church and civil authorities sought to discredit them. By the twentieth century, anti-Semitism was no longer primarily religious in character. New canards were disseminated, among them the belief that Jews were plotting to rule the world.

A contrite Church has been conscientiously purging its doctrines of anti-Semitic beliefs that had for so long licensed so many people to mistreat Jews. These efforts may well succeed in giving to Jews the religious mantle of protection the Church had so long withheld from them. However, what has gone unnoticed is the enabling role that secular moral philosophy had played in making Europe's Jews persona non grata.

It is now known that large numbers of ordinary Germans actively participated in the Holocaust. Many more passively accepted the ongoing atrocities and did little to prevent them. By contrast, people in countries like Italy, Bulgaria, and Denmark refused to cooperate in the destruction of their Jewish communities, and many took grave risks to save their Jews. We face the question of how so many otherwise decent Germans could have found it acceptable to acquiesce and even cooperate in the callously cruel persecution and systematic murder of a hapless and helpless civilian population. Unless we are to conclude that moral philosophy is not in any meaningful sense a practical civilizing influence on a culture and people, we must seek to understand how the prevailing conception of morality left it open to so many average Germans to behave as they did to Europe's Jews and Gypsies. We need, in other words, to identify the defect in popular German moral philosophy that so signally failed to inhibit the mass acts of cruelty and systematic killings that were part of the "final solution."

We get a whiff of something perversely wrong with the prevailing concept of decency in mid-twentieth-century Germany when we hear Heinrich Himmler, the Nazi SS leader in charge of carrying out the exterminationist policy, addressing the SS generals who were organizing the murders. Himmler speaks with the full confidence that his elite audience will understand and agree with him when he calls them decent fellows engaged in a glorious mission.

> I want to talk to you quite frankly on a very grave matter, the extermination of the Jewish race. Most of you must know what it means when 100 corpses are lying side by side, or 500 or 1,000. To have stuck it out and at the same time to have remained a decent fellow … is a page of glory in our history which has never been written and is never to be written.

A year later Himmler boasted that the SS was wiping out the Jews "without our leaders and their men suffering any damage in the minds and in their souls." The philosopher Jonathan Bennett calls Himmler's morality "bad," but since it was the morality of so many Germans, the imputation is that German morality itself was radically defective. What was its flaw?

The Domain of Moral Patients

In approaching this question we do well to bear in mind the difference between doing wrong and wronging. You can do wrong by damaging a tree, but you do not thereby wrong the tree. Adopting a term first used by Geoffrey Warnock, we call any being that a moral agent can wrong a "moral patient." According to the central (Kantian) tradition in German moral thinking, the domain of moral patients includes all and only moral agents, excluding many nonrational beings as nonpersons or "things." Nonrational beings cannot be wronged; they are not "ends" to whom we owe respect. This view of the moral domain comports with Kant's view of moral philosophy: "All moral philosophy rests wholly on its pure part. When applied to man it does not borrow the least thing from the knowledge of man himself (anthropology), but gives laws to him as a rational being."

Contrast this rationalist approach to morality with the approach of David Hume and later philosophers who grounded ethics on the moral sentiments. In the moral philosophies of Hume, William Shaftsbury, Adam Smith, and the utilitarian philosophers who came after Kant, compassion and feelings of benevolence are at the very ground of moral obligation, determining the members of the moral domain. Any sentient being can be wronged. According to the utilitarian Jeremy Bentham, the question is not "can they think?" but "can they suffer?"

It was this "anthropological" approach to ethics that Kant dubbed "impure." On the other hand, and in its favor, an empirical morality grounded in moral sentiments regards cruelty or brutality to any sentient being as the very paradigm of indecent, inadmissible behavior; a culture and population steeped in such an ethics cannot trespass the bounds of compassion without regarding such actions as morally reprehensible.

According to Kant, animals are not in the domain of moral patients and we have no direct duty to be kind to them. We do have an indirect duty to refrain from acts of cruelty to animals because such behavior on our part could corrupt our character, and this could affect the way we behave to rational beings to whom we do owe respect. According to this influential moral philosophy, cruelty to creatures who are not in the elect circle of beings that belong to "the kingdom of ends" is not directly prohibited; it is however to be avoided because of its potentially brutalizing effects on us as moral agents. An incorruptible (divine) being could be cruel to animals without violating any moral precepts.

This rationalist moral theory is consistent with the central view that sentiment must ever be at the service of moral duty but must not itself be the reason for our adherence to duty. The denigration of sentiment and the austere devotion to duty when sentiment pulls you in the opposite direction is appealed to by Himmler when he speaks of the glory of overcoming one's feelings of compunction in carrying out the duties imposed by a policy of genocidal extermination.

A moral philosophy that does not directly proscribe cruelty to nonpersons opened a hole in the moral ozone with consequences that would surely have horrified Kant. Two flaws soon surfaced. First, in the century after Kant published his *Critique of Practical Reason*, many in Germany were offering their own ideas on which beings possessed the "dignity" that confers on them the moral status of "ends in themselves." The temptation soon arose of circumscribing the moral domain still further by excluding certain "unworthy" rational beings from its protection. In the late nineteenth century, for example, religious and racial criteria for demarcating the moral domain were increasingly being proposed. Just here the millennial belief that Jews are children of Satan came into play, and the exclusion of Jews from the domain of moral patients was on its way to becoming a salient feature of modern anti-Semitism. By the time of the Nazis, Jews had been relegated to the status of nonpersons. Nazis regularly referred to them as vermin. If Jews are like insects, killing them is not a crime against humanity. Indeed a prime method of killing Jews made use of a pesticide, toxic to human beings as well as to insects.

Second, Kant's warning that cruelty to nonpersons could corrupt the character of the moral agent proved unpersuasive and ineffectual. Himmler was not alone in believing that a moral person could be brutal and cruel without suffering corrupting effects. One could still be a decent fellow after all. And nothing in Kant's central moral theory directly proscribes causing suffering to a nonperson.

It is instructive to see how Kant's principled exclusion of sentient nonpersons from the domain of moral patients could, in practice, lead some nineteenth-century moralists to identify the Jews as being outside the moral pale. Some said that Jews were not morally protected because they were inveterately immoral. Even as Kant was working out his system of a pure ethics for and by rational moral agents, Fredric Trougart Harmann was giving "moral" reasons for excluding Jews from the moral domain. "Man is always a man; he is always entitled to expect help from his brother ... *unless* a nation has attracted to itself by its moral vices, the absolute contempt of mankind and unless it deliberately opposes all enlightenment of heart and mind. Is this not the case with the Jews?" Kant himself believed that Judaism was not a moral religion because the Jewish morality of obedience to "externally imposed" laws was incompatible with the precepts of moral "freedom" demanded by a "pure" morality. He held that Jews would be fully worthy of the rights of Christians only when they renounced their stubborn loyalty to the Torah and Talmudic law: "The Euthanasia of Judaism can only be achieved by a pure moral religion, and the abandonment of all legal regulation."

The commonly held opinion that Judaism was an immoral, impure, and superseded religion and that Jews were too legalistic to be deserving of the rights that naturally belonged to Christians was to tempt many an enlightened German to take the path of treating Jews as pariahs, beyond the protections of morality. The nineteenth century made continuous "progress" along these lines. In the hands of a secular young Hegelian like Bruno Bauer we see the claim that Jews are egotistical historical anomalies who had themselves put up the barriers to counting them worthy of moral consideration: "The [Old Testament] Laws had fenced the Jews off from the influences of history." To this is added the claim that Jews are racially apart and dangerous. "The Jewish race is in reality a different blood from that of the Christian people of Europe.... With this ... goes that alienation to which the race was doomed not just since the fall of Jerusalem but since the very beginning of its existence." The religious Hegelian Constantin Frantz stressed the historically alien and unassimilable character of the Jews: "Jews always remain Jews and are thereby in their innermost being excluded from Christian history."

By the second half of the nineteenth century, the social and religious demarcations were rapidly being transposed to a sharper demarcation of race. That Christianity was racially different from Judaism had already been suggested by the eminent German philosopher Johann Fichte, who introduced the potent idea of "the Aryan Christ," proposing a reading of the gospel of St. John that suggested that Christ himself was not of Jewish descent. He jokingly said that the only way to allow Jews civil rights was "to cut off all their heads one night and to substitute other heads without a single Jewish thought in them."

Richard Wagner's glorifications of the German people helped to inspire the Nazis to exalt the "Aryan Race," imbuing many Germans with feelings of deep repugnance to other, "inferior" races, while liberating them from a great many "moral taboos" in their treatment of them. Hitler succeeded in persuading many of his countrymen that Slavs, Negroes, and Gypsies were simply not morally considerable, but he reserved for the Jews his most pitiless revulsion. They became the archenemy. Again the denigration of sentiment in moral judgments had paved the way for action. As Nazi leader Joseph Goebbels wrote in his diary for 27 March 1942, "In such matters there is no room for sentiment. This is a war of life or death between the Aryan race and the Jewish virus." Sentimental misgivings are inappropriate when it comes to exterminating a virus.

Back in the 1940s and 1950s, people asked whether what had happened in Germany could happen in Britain or America. I have been arguing that the answer is: not if the moral philosophies of John Locke, David Hume, and John Stuart Mill, some version of which is tacitly accepted by most Britains and Americans, have any kind of practical influence on the way Anglo-Americans actually behave. A people steeped in the sentimentalist moral philosophy regards all sentient beings as moral patients. Such a people would view an openly cruel leader as unacceptably immoral. No such leader could have had a strong following in England or America. By contrast, the central tradition of moral philosophy in mid-twentieth-century Germany was unique in its depreciation of moral sentiments. Duty and respect, not kindness and compassion, were at its center. This formal approach to ethics and duty had left room for racial criteria in demarcating the domain of moral patients, leaving those outside unprotected. Far from reinforcing the forces of decency, a purist rationalism had dangerously weakened them.

What happened in Germany could not have happened in any country that gives benevolence and human compassion a foundational role in its moral philosophy. Nor, I believe, could it happen again in Germany. Man's shocking inhumanity to man keeps forcing many painful lessons on us. One lesson, now implicitly absorbed by most Germans though not yet learned in many other parts of the world, is that a moral theory that does not absolutely, "directly," and foundationally anathematize cruelty must be ruled out of court.

Study Questions

1. Discuss the contrasting approaches of David Hume and Immanuel Kant to moral philosophy. Show how each sets different boundaries to the domain of beings that can be wronged.
2. Why, according to Sommers, is Hume's "anthropological" approach to moral theory superior to Kant's rationalist approach?
3. Reviewing Kant's influence on German morals, Sommers says, "Far from reinforcing the forces of decency, a purist rationalism had dangerously weakened them." Does he make a convincing case for this contention? Why not? Does a "purist rationalism" still constitute a danger to society? Explain.

A Critique of Kantianism

Richard Taylor

Richard Taylor (1919–2003) was a professor of philosophy at the University of Rochester, Brown, and Columbia, among other places. He was the author of numerous books and articles, including *Good and Evil* (1970), *Virtue, Ethics* (1991), and *Understanding Marriage* (2004). He was also an expert on bees.

Taylor criticizes Kant's moral philosophy for being too abstract and intellectual. We ordinarily think of a person of goodwill as someone with a kindly and sympathetic nature. Not so for Kant. His person of goodwill acts from respect for the moral law. To Kant, acts done solely out of kindness and sympathy have no moral worth. Taylor recommends a moral system less abstract and metaphysical and more compatible with human nature.

From *Good and Evil: A New Direction* by Richard Taylor (Amherst, NY: Prometheus Books, 2000), pp. 147–156. © 2000 by Richard Taylor. All rights reserved. Reprinted with permission of the publisher.

Kantian Morality

It is not my intention to give any detailed exposition of Kant's ethical system. I propose instead to discuss certain of Kant's basic ideas in order to illustrate a certain approach to ethics that I think is essentially wrong. For this I could have chosen the ideas of some other modern moralist, but I prefer to illustrate my points by Kant's thought. I am doing this first because of his great fame and the reverence with which many philosophers still regard him, and secondly because it would be difficult to find any modern thinker who has carried to such an extreme the philosophical presuppositions that I am eager to repudiate. I shall, thus, use some of Kant's ideas to show how the basic ideas of morality, born originally of our practical needs as social beings and having to do originally with our practical relations with each other, can, under the influence of philosophy, become so detached from the world that they become pure abstractions, having no longer anything to do with morality insofar as this is a practical concern. Philosophical or metaphysical morals thereby ceases to have much connection with the morality that is an abiding practical concern and becomes, instead, a purely intellectual thing, something to contemplate and appreciate, much as one would appreciate a geometrical demonstration. Its vocabulary, which is the very vocabulary of everyday morals, no longer has the same meaning, but instead represents a realm of pure abstractions. Intellectually satisfying as this might be, it is nevertheless highly dangerous, for it leads men to suppose that the problems of ethics are essentially intellectual problems, that they are simply philosophical questions in need of philosophical answers. The result is that the eyes of the moralist are directed away from the world, in which moral problems are the most important problems there are, and toward a really nonexistent realm, a realm of ideas rather than things. The image of philosophical moralists, who are quite lacking in any knowledge of the world and whose ideas about it are of the childish sort learned in a Sunday school, is a familiar one. These are moralists whose dialectic is penetrating and whose reasoning is clear—he grapple with many philosophical problems of morality and have many subtle answers to philosophical difficulties—but who has little appreciation of the pain and sorrow of the world beyond the knowledge that it is there.

Duty and Law

Laws, as practical rules of human invention, find no place in Kant's metaphysical morals. The Moral Law that replaces them is sundered from any practical human concerns, for it seemed to Kant that our moral obligations are not only quite different things but, more often than not, are actually opposed to each other. Obligations, which were originally only relations between people arising from mutual undertakings for mutual advantage, similarly disappear from the Kantian morality, to be replaced by an abstract sort of *moral* obligation that has no connection whatsoever with any earthly good. Duties—which were originally and are still imposed by rulers on subjects, masters on servants, employers on workmen, and so on, in return for certain compensations, privileges, and rights—are replaced by Kant with Duty in the abstract. This abstract Duty is deemed by him to be the sole proper motive of moral conduct; yet, it is not a duty *to* anyone, or a duty to do any particular thing. The notion of duty to sovereign or master has always been well understood, and Christians understand the idea of duty God. In such cases duty consists simply of compliance with commands. But in Kant's system, duties are sundered from particular commands, and Duty becomes something singular and metaphysical. We are, according to this system, to do always what Duty requires, for no other reason than that Duty does require it. Beyond a few heterogeneous examples for illustration, we never learn from Kant just what this is, save only that it is the obligation to act from respect for the Moral Law. You must cling to life, for example, and give no thought to suicide—not because any lawgiver or God has commanded it, not because things might work out all right for you if you stick it out a little longer, but just because Duty requires it. You must also help others in distress; not, again, because any man or God has admonished you to, not just because they need you, or because you cares for them, or because you wants to see their baneful condition improved—indeed, it is best that you have no such feelings at all—but just because it is your Duty.

The Good Will

It is in such terms that Kant defined the *good will*, declaring it to be the only thing in the universe that is unqualifiedly good. Now we normally think of a person of good will as one who loves others, one whose happiness is sympathetically bound up with theirs, one who has a keen and constant desire to abolish suffering and make the lot of neighbors more tolerable than it might be without a helping hand. Not so for Kant. Indeed, he dismisses the actions of such persons, "so sympathetically constituted that . . . they find an inner satisfaction in spreading joy, and rejoice in the contentment of others which they have made possible," as devoid of any moral worth. Human conduct, to have any genuine moral worth, must not spring from any such amiable feelings as these; these are, after all, nothing but human feelings; they are not *moral* incentives. To have genuine moral worth, according to this moralist, our actions must spring from the sense of Duty and nothing else. And you act dutifully if you act, not from love or concern for others, but from respect for the Moral Law.

The Categorical Imperative

The Moral Law assumed, in Kant's thought, the form of an imperative, or command. But unlike any command that was ever before heard on earth, this one issues from no commander! Like a question that no one ever asks, or an assertion that no one ever affirms, it is a command that no God or man ever promulgates. It is promulgated by Reason. Nor is this the humble rationality of living, mortal beings it is Reason itself, again in the abstract. And unlike what one would ordinarily think of as a command, this one has no definite content. It is simply the form, Kant says, not of any actual laws, but of The Law, which is again, of course, something abstract. It has, unlike any other imperative of which one has ever heard, no purpose or end. It is not the means to the achievement of anything; and it has no relation to what anyone wants. For this reason Kant called it the Categorical Imperative, a command that is supposed to command absolutely and for its own sake. The Categorical Imperative does not bid us to act in a manner calculated to advance human well-being, for the weal and woe of human beings has for Kant no necessary connection with morality. It does not bid us to act as we would want others to act, for what people want has no more bearing on morals than what they happen to feel. This Imperative does not, in fact, bid us to do anything at all, nor, indeed, even to have any generous or sympathetic motive, but only to honor some maxim or rational principle of conduct. We are, whatever we do, to act in such a manner that we could, consistently with reason, will this maxim to be a universal Law, even a Law of Nature, binding on all rational beings. Kant does not ask us to consider how other rational beings, thus bound, might feel about our maxims, for again, how anyone happens to feel about anything has no bearing on morality anyway. It is Reason that counts. It is not the living and suffering human beings who manage sometimes to be reasonable but most of the time are not. It is not our needs and wants, or any human desires, or any practical human goods. To act immorally is to act contrary to Reason; it is to commit a sort of metaphysical blunder in the relationship between one's behavior and some generalized motive. Human needs and feelings have so little to do with this that they are not even allowed into the picture. If someone reaches forth to help the sick, the troubled, or the dying, this must not be done from any motive of compassion or sentiment of love. Such love, as a feeling, is dismissed by Kant as "pathological," because it is not prompted by that rational respect for Duty that filled Kant with such awe. Indeed, Kant thought that such human feelings as love and compassion should not even be allowed to cooperate in the performance of Duty, for we must act solely *from* Duty, and not merely *in accordance* with it. Such feelings as love, sympathy, and friendship are therefore regarded by Kant as positively dangerous. They incline us to do from sheer goodness of heart what should be done only from Reason and respect for the Moral Law. To be genuinely moral, you must tear yourself away from your inclinations as a loving human being, drown the sympathetic promptings of your heart, scorn any fruits of his efforts, think last of all of the feelings, needs, desires, and inclinations either of yourself or of others and, perhaps detesting what you have to do, do it anyway—solely from respect for the Law.

Rational Nature as an End

This Moral Law is otherwise represented by Kant as respect for Rational Nature, something that again, of course, exists only in the abstract but is, presumably, somehow exemplified in humanity and, Kant thought, in God. Indeed, it is the only thing in us that Kant considered worthy of a philosopher's attention. Because we are deemed to embody this Rational Nature, human nature is declared to be an End in Itself, to possess an absolute Worth, or Dignity. This kind of absolute End is not like ordinary ends or goals, something relative to the aims or purposes of any creature. It is not anything anyone wants or would be moved to try to achieve. It is, like so many of Kant's abstractions, an absolute end. And the Worth that he supposes Rational Nature to possess is no worth *for* or *to* anything; it, too, is an abstract or absolute Worth. Kant peoples a veritable utopia, which he of course does not imagine as existing, with these Ends in Themselves, and calls it the Kingdom of Ends. Ends in Themselves are, thus, not to be thought of as those men that live and toil on earth; they are not suffering, rejoicing, fumbling, living, and dying human beings; they are not beings that anyone has ever seen, or would be apt to recognize as human if he did see them, or apt to like very much if he did recognize them. They are abstract things, reifications of Rational Nature, fabricated by Kant and now called Rational Beings or Ends in Themselves. Their purpose, unlike that of any creature under the sun, is not to sorrow and rejoice, not to love and hate, not to beget offspring, not to grow old and die, and not to get on as best they can to such destinies as the world has allotted them. Their purpose is just to *legislate*—to legislate morally and rationally for this rational Kingdom of Ends.

The Significance of Kant

Kant's system thus represents the rational, logical conclusion of the natural or true morality that was begotten by the Greeks, of the absolute distinction that they drew, and that people still want to draw. This is the distinction between what *is*, or the realm of observation and science, and what *ought* to be, or the realm of obligation and morals. No one has ever suggested that Kant was irrational, and although it is doubtful that his ideas have ever had much impact on human behavior, they have had a profound impact on philosophy, which has always prized reason and abstraction and tended to scorn fact. Kant's metaphysical system of morals rests on notions that are still a part of the fabric of our intellectual culture and inheritance. His greatest merit is that he was consistent. He showed us what sort of metaphysic of morals we must have—if we suppose that morality has any metaphysic, or any logic and method of its own. He showed what morality must be if we suppose it to be something rational and at the same time nonempirical or divorced from psychology, anthropology, or any science. That general conception of morals is, of course, still common in philosophy, and still permeates judicial thought, where it expresses itself in the ideas of guilt and desert. A man is thought to be "deserving" of punishment if he did, and could have avoided doing, something "wrong." Our basic moral presuppositions, in short, are still very much the same as Kant's, and Kant shows where they lead. We still assume, as he did, a basic dichotomy between what in fact *is* and what morally *ought* to be, between what the Greeks called convention and nature. Like the Greeks, and like Kant, we still feel a desperate need to *know* what, by nature or by some natural or rational moral principle, *ought* to be. Kant was entirely right in insisting that no knowledge of what in fact is—no knowledge of human nature, of history, of anthropology, or psychology—can yield this knowledge. But Kant did not consider, and many philosophical minds still think it somehow perverse to consider, that there may be no such knowledge—and not merely because no one has managed to attain it, but because there may really be nothing there to know in the first place. There may be no such thing as a true morality. Perhaps the basic facts of morality are, as Protagoras thought, conventions; that is, the practical formulas, some workable and some not, for enabling us to achieve whatever ideals and aspirations happen to move them. In the Kantian scheme, such considerations have nothing to do with morality which is concerned, not with what is, but with what morally ought to be, with what is in his strange sense commanded. According to the Protagorean scheme, on the other hand, such considerations exhaust the whole subject of morals. Here we are, human beings, possessed of needs, feelings, capacities, and aims that are for the most part not of our creation but are simply part of our endowment as human beings. These are the grist, the data, and the subject matter of morals. The problem is how we get from where we are to where we want to go. It is on our answer to this question that our whole happiness and our worth as human beings depends. Our problem is not whether our answers accord with nature or even with truth. Our problem is to find those answers that do in fact work, whose fruits are sunlight, warmth, and satisfaction in our lives as we live them.

STUDY QUESTIONS

1. Why, in Taylor's view, is Kant so highly esteemed by other philosophers? What are Taylor's basic objections to Kant's theory of ethics?
2. Taylor suggests that ethical knowledge may be impossible. What then is the task of moral philosophy?
3. Compose a debate between a supporter of Kant and someone who agrees with Taylor. Give each side its best arguments.

CHAPTER 5 | VIRTUE

Several acorns fall from a tree. One is eaten by a squirrel. Another decays on the ground. A third grows into an oak tree. We say that the third acorn's fate is appropriate to it, that it succeeds where the other two fail. In our view, the acorn's goal or purpose is to become an oak tree, as if its self-fulfillment depends on achieving this goal. Yet we are aware that to speak of a goal here is grossly anthropomorphic. The acorn is not a conscious being trying to achieve the happy outcome of development. Nor do we feel that this happy outcome is really more natural than the outcome of rotting or being eaten. Indeed, since only a tiny minority of acorns become oak trees, the unhappy outcomes are more natural than the happy one.

All the same, our intuition that becoming an oak tree is the appropriate career for an acorn is sound. Any organic matter—a leaf, for example—can rot on the ground; any nut can serve as squirrel fodder. But only the acorn can grow into an oak tree. The Greeks defined the function or natural purpose of a thing as an activity that is specific to it—an activity that it alone performs or one that it performs better than anything else can. In this sense we think that the third acorn's career is the "happy" or proper one. The metaphor of a happy outcome for the acorn leans heavily on the Greek meaning of happiness (*eudaimonia*) as a well-functioning, self-fulfilling activity.

A biologist could tell us quite a bit about the special characteristics that enable the acorn to perform its function. The Greeks called such characteristics "excellences" or "virtues." In the broad sense a virtue is any trait or capacity that enables an object to perform its appropriate function. More commonly, "virtue" refers to a special kind of excellence that only human beings possess or lack. In this narrow sense the virtues are *moral* excellences that contribute to a life of human fulfillment. And in this sense we speak of the virtues in contrast to vices. A question now arises: What goal is appropriate for human beings? There are in fact rival conceptions of human fulfillment; some of them are represented by the selections in this chapter.

The Greeks confronted this question with their characteristic simplicity and boldness. Human beings, says Aristotle, are rational animals. They are also social animals. They naturally fulfill themselves in functioning as rational and social beings. Given such conceptions of human purpose, such virtues as temperance, magnanimity, and courage come to the fore as traits that allow people to lead graceful lives in a political community.

But political arrangements change from era to era and after the demise of the Greek city states, even wealthy individuals, living in large imperial communities, had very little power to effect radical reforms. Changing and perfecting one's community is no longer the ideal it was for Plato and Aristotle.

Stoic ethics, here represented by the first-century philospher Epictetus, showed how any individual, whatever his social position or material circumstance, can lead a life of virtue and dignity. For Aristotle, moderation is the essence of virtue; for the Stoics, it is integrity and emotional detachment from those things you do not control.

James Stockdale, an American soldier who spent eight years as a prisoner of war in Vietnam, argues for the continued relevance of stoic virtue to contemporary life. He says that when he was captured by the Vietcong, "I entered the world of Epictetus and it's a world that few of us, whether we know it or not, are ever far away from." His captors had absolute power over him, but "I came to realize... that if you don't lose your integrity ... you can't be hurt."

Saint Augustine conceives of the life appropriate to a human being rather differently. Human beings are rational and social beings, but that they are creatures of God is even more important: human purpose and happiness are found in following God. While the Greeks—with their secular conception of the good life—primarily emphasize such "cardinal virtues" as wisdom, courage, and temperance, Augustine—with his Christian conception of the good life—gives priority to such other virtues as charity, humility, and faith. The modern philosopher is less ready to state a conception of the good life for all human beings at all times. Alasdair MacIntyre's conception of human fulfillment is historical. He argues that social context and tradition are always crucial in defining moral obligations: "There is no way to possess the virtues except as part of a tradition in which we inherit them."

Moral philosophers distinguish between two general approaches to their subject. Virtue ethics (Plato and Aristotle are models) focuses on *what kind of person to be*, or the virtues we should possess. An action- or duty-based approach to ethics (Kant and Mill are models) focuses more on *what we should be doing*, or the actions we should engage in. Bernard Mayo is among a growing number of philosophers who are unhappy with the modern emphasis on duty and action. James Rachels sees the merits of virtue ethics, but opposes the suggestion that moral philosophy should return to an exclusively virtue-based approach.

Several articles in Chapter Five give a good idea of the kind of investigations into particular virtues that modern philosophers pursue. Adam Smith gives a careful account of the virtues of beneficence and justice and of the feelings (moral sentiments) that attend the exercise of these virtues. Charles Darwin suggests that filial morality is a product of natural selection.

Evolutionary psychology provides an exciting new perspective on the virtues and the moral sentiments by asking how they have originated in us as a species. Even in this newest approach, the virtues are still regarded in the traditional Aristotelian light: as vital to the flourishing and adaptive well-being of individuals and human societies.

Happiness and the Virtues

Aristotle

TRANSLATED BY J. A. K. THOMSON

Aristotle (384–322 B.C.) is one of the greatest philosophers of all time. He was the son of a Macedonian physician, the personal tutor of Alexander the Great, and a student of Plato. He wrote on a wide range of subjects, including logic (which he founded as a science), metaphysics, biology, ethics, politics, and literature. During the Middle Ages, the authority of his teachings in all matters of secular philosophy was undisputed. It would be difficult to exaggerate his influence on the development of Western culture.

Aristotle defines happiness as functioning well. The function of a thing is its special kind of activity, what it can do better than anything else. Thus, the function of human beings is the exercise of their capacity to reason. A capacity that enables a thing or a being to function well is a virtue. Reason plays a part in all of the specified human virtues. Courageous persons, for example, use reason to control fear; temperate persons use it to control their appetites. Properly employed, reason directs us to a course of moderation between extremes (for example, between the excesses of fear and folly, or gluttony and abstemiousness). Aristotle gives some general rules for pursuing the course of virtuous moderation: (1) avoid the extreme that more strongly opposes the virtue, (2) guard against excessive hedonism, and (3) attend to your characteristic faults. These are not hard-and-fast rules, but rough-and-ready guides.

Aristotle worked out in detail the means, excesses, and deficiencies for many of the virtues he considered important. W. T. Jones, a historian of philosophy, conveniently summarizes Aristotle's views on the moral virtues in the following table.

From *The Ethics of Aristotle*, trans. by J. A. K. Thomson, revised with notes and appendices by Hugh Tredennick, introduction and bibliography by Jonathan Barnes (Penguin Classics 1955, Revised edition 1976). Translation copyright 1953 by J. A. K. Thomson. Revised translation copyright © Hugh Tredennick, 1976. Introduction and bibliography copyright © Jonathan Barnes, 1976. Reproduced by permission of Penguin Books, Ltd.

Activity	Vice (excess)	Virtue (mean)	Vice (deficit)
Facing death	Too much fear (i.e., cowardice)	Right amount of fear (i.e., courage)	Too little fear (i.e., foolhardiness)
Bodily actions (eating, drinking, sex, etc.)	Profligacy	Temperance	No name for this state, but it may be called "insensitivity"
Giving money	Prodigality	Liberality	Illiberality
Large-scale giving	Vulgarity	Magnificence	Meanness
Claiming honors	Vanity	Pride	Humility
Social intercourse	Obsequiousness	Friendliness	Sulkiness
According honors	Injustice	Justice	Injustice
Retribution for wrongdoing	Injustice	Justice	Injustice

Source: W. T. Jones, The Classical Mind (New York: Harcourt, Brace & World, 1952, 1969), p. 268.

Book I

Every rational activity aims at some end or good. One end (like one activity) may be subordinate to another.

i.

Every art and every investigation, and similarly every action and pursuit, is considered to aim at some good. Hence the Good has been rightly defined as "that at which all things aim." Clearly, however, there is some difference between the ends at which they aim: some are activities and others [are] results distinct from the activities. Where there are ends distinct from the actions, the results are by nature superior to the activities. Since there are many actions, arts and sciences, it follows that their ends are many too—the end of medical science is health; of military science, victory; of economic science, wealth. In the case of all skills of this kind that come under a single "faculty"—as a skill in making bridles or any other part of a horse's trappings comes under horsemanship, while this and every kind of military action comes under military science, so in the same way other skills are subordinate to yet others—in all these the ends of the directive arts are to be preferred in every case to those of the subordinate ones, because it is for the sake of the former that the latter are pursued also. It makes no difference whether the ends of the actions are the activities themselves or something apart from them, as in the case of the sciences we have mentioned.

If, then, our activities have some end which we want for its own sake, and for the sake of which we want all the other ends—if we do not choose everything for the sake of something else (for this will involve an infinite progression, so that our aim will be pointless and ineffectual)—it is clear that this must be the Good, that is the supreme good. Does it not follow, then, that a knowledge of the Good is of great importance to us for the conduct of our lives? Are we not more likely to achieve our aim if we have a target? If this is so, we must try to describe at least in outline what the Good really is, and by which of the sciences or faculties it is studied....

iv.

[W]hat is the highest of all practical goods? Well, so far as the name goes there is pretty general agreement. "It is happiness," say both ordinary and cultured people; and they identify happiness with living well or doing well. But when it comes to saying in what happiness consists, opinions differ, and the account given by the generality of mankind is not at all like that of the wise. The former take it to be something obvious and familiar, like pleasure or money or eminence, and there are various other views; and often the same person actually changes his opinion: when he falls ill he says that it is health, and when he is hard up that it is money. Conscious of their own ignorance, most people are impressed by anyone who pontificates and says something that is over their heads. Some, however, have held the view that over and above these particular goods there is another which is good in itself and the cause of whatever goodness there is in all these others. It would no doubt be rather futile to examine all these opinions; enough if we consider those which are most prevalent or seem to have something to be said for them....

The three types of life. Neither pleasure nor public honour seems to be an adequate end; the contemplative life will be considered later.

life of enjoyment, political, & the contemplative

v.

... To judge by their lives, the masses and the most vulgar seem—not unreasonably—to believe that the Good or happiness is pleasure. Accordingly they ask for nothing better than the life of enjoyment. (Broadly speaking, there are three main types of life: the one just mentioned, the political, and thirdly the contemplative.) The utter servility of the masses comes out in their preference for a bovine existence; still, their view obtains consideration from the fact that many of those who are in positions of power share the tastes of Sardanapalus. Cultured people, however, and men of affairs identify the Good with honour, because this is (broadly speaking) the goal of political life. Yet it appears to be too superficial to be the required answer. Honour is felt to depend more on those who confer than on him who receives it; and we feel instinctively that the Good is something proper to its possessor and not easily taken from him. Again, people seem to seek honour in order to convince themselves of their own goodness; at any rate it is by intelligent men, and in a community where they are known, and for their goodness, that they seek to be honoured; so evidently in their view goodness is superior to honour. One might even be inclined to suppose that goodness rather than honour is the end pursued in public life. But even this appears to be somewhat deficient as an end, because the possession of goodness is thought to be compatible even with being asleep, or with leading a life of inactivity, and also with incurring the most atrocious suffering and misfortune; and nobody would call such a life happy—unless he was defending a paradox. So much for these views: they have been fully treated in current discussions. The third type of life is the contemplative, and this we shall examine later.

As for the life of the business man, it does not give him much freedom of action. Besides, wealth is obviously not the good that we are seeking, because it serves only as a means; i.e. for getting something else. Hence the earlier suggestions might be supposed to be more likely ends, because they are appreciated on their own account; but evidently they too are inadequate, and many attacks on them have been published....

What is the Good for man? It must be the ultimate end or object of human life: something that is in itself completely satisfying. Happiness fits this description.

vii.

Let us now turn back again to the good which is the object of our search, and ask what it can possibly be; because it appears to vary with the action or art. It is one thing in medicine and another in strategy, and similarly in all the other sciences. What, then, is the good of each particular one? Surely it is that for the sake of which everything else is done. In medicine this is health; in strategy, victory; in architecture, a building—different things in different arts, but in every action and pursuit it is the *end*, since it is for the sake of this that everything else is done. Consequently if there is any one thing that is the end of all actions, this will be the practical good—or goods, if there are more than one. Thus while changing its ground the argument has reached the same conclusion as before.

We must try, however, to make our meaning still clearer. Since there are evidently more ends than one, and of these we choose some (e.g. wealth or musical instruments or tools generally) as means to something else, it is clear that not all of them are final ends, whereas the supreme good is obviously something final. So if there is only one final end, this will be the good of which we are in search; and if there are more than one, it will be the most final of these. Now we call an object pursued for its own sake more final than one pursued because of something else, and one which is never choosable because of another more final than those which are choosable because of it as well as for their own sakes; and that which is always choosable for its own sake and never because of something else we call final without any qualification.

Well, happiness more than anything else is thought to be just such an end, because we always choose it for itself, and never for any other reason. It is different with honour, pleasure, intelligence and good qualities generally. We do choose them partly for themselves (because we should choose each one of them irrespectively of any consequences); but we choose them also for the sake of our happiness, in the belief that they will be instrumental in promoting it. On the other hand nobody chooses happiness for *their* sake, or in general for any other reason.

The same conclusion seems to follow from another consideration. It is a generally accepted view that the perfect good is self-sufficient. By self-sufficient we mean not what is sufficient for oneself alone living a solitary life, but something that includes parents, wife and children, friends and fellow-citizens in general; for man is by nature a social being. (We must set some limit to these, for if we extend the application to grandparents and grandchildren and friends of friends it will proceed to infinity; but we must consider this point later.) A self-sufficient thing, then, we take to be one which by itself makes life desirable and in no way deficient; and we believe that happiness is such a thing. What is more, we regard it as the most desirable of all things, not reckoned as one item among many; if it were so reckoned, happiness would obviously be more desirable by the addition of even the least good, because the addition makes the sum of goods greater, and the greater of two goods is always more desirable. Happiness, then, is found to be something perfect and self-sufficient, being the end to which our actions are directed.

But what is happiness? If we consider what the function of man is, we find that happiness is a virtuous activity of the soul.

But presumably to say that happiness is the supreme good seems a platitude, and some more distinctive account of it is still required. This might perhaps be achieved by grasping what is the function of man. If we take a flautist or a sculptor or any artist—or in general any class of men who have a specific function or activity—his goodness and proficiency is considered to lie in the performance of that function; and the same will be true of man, assuming that man has a function. But is it likely that whereas joiners and shoemakers have certain functions or activities, man as such has none, but has been left by nature a functionless being? Just as we can see that eye and hand and foot and every one of our members has some function, should we not assume that in like manner a human being has a function over and above these particular functions? What, then, can this possibly be? Clearly life is a thing shared also by plants, and we are looking for man's *proper* function; so we must exclude from our definition the life that consists in nutrition and growth. Next in order would be a sort of sentient life; but this too we see is shared by horses and cattle and animals of all kinds. There remains, then, a practical life of the rational part. (This has two aspects: one amenable to reason, the other possessing it and initiating thought.) As this life also has two meanings, we must lay down that we intend here life determined by activity, because this is accepted as the stricter sense. Now if the function of man is an activity of the soul in accordance with, or implying, a rational principle; and if we hold that the function of an individual and of a good individual of the same kind—e.g. of a harpist and of a good harpist, and so on generally— is generically the same, the latter's distinctive excellence being attached to the name of the function (because the function of the harpist is to play the harp, but that of the good harpist is to play it well); and if we assume that the function of man is a kind of life, viz., an activity or series of actions of the soul, implying a rational principle; and if the function of a good man is to perform these well and rightly; and if every function is performed well when performed in accordance with its proper excellence: if all this is so, the conclusion is that the good for man is an activity of soul in accordance with virtue, or if there are more kinds of virtue than one, in accordance with the best and most perfect kind.

There is a further qualification: in a complete lifetime. One swallow does not make a summer; neither does one day. Similarly neither can one day, or a brief space of time, make a man blessed and happy....

How is happiness acquired?

ix.

... Is happiness something that can be learnt, or acquired by habituation, or culti-vated in some other way, or does it come to us by a sort of divine dispensation, or even by chance? Well, in the first place, if anything is a gift of the gods to men, it is reasonable that happiness should be such a gift, especially since of all human possessions it is the best. This point, however, would perhaps be considered more appropriately by another branch of study. Yet even if happiness is not sent by a divine power, but is acquired by moral goodness and by some kind of study or training, it seems clearly to be one of our most divine possessions; for the crown and end of goodness is surely of all things the best: something divine and blissful. Also on this view happiness will be something widely shared; for it can attach, through some form of study or application, to anyone who is not handicapped by some incapacity for goodness. And, assuming that it is better to win happiness by the means described than by chance, it is reasonable that this should in fact be so, since it is natural for nature's effects to be the finest possible, and similarly for the effects of art and of any [other] cause, especially those of the best kind. That the most important and finest thing of all should be left to chance would be a gross disharmony.

The problem also receives some light from our definition, for in it happiness has been described as a kind of virtuous activity of soul; whereas all the other goods either are necessary pre-conditions of happiness or naturally contribute to it and serve as its instruments. This will agree with what we said at the outset: we suggested that the end of political science is the highest good; and the chief concern of this science is to endue the citizens with certain qualities, namely virtue and the readiness to do fine deeds....

Book II

Any excellence enables its possessor to function; therefore this is true of human excellence, i.e. virtue.   Virtue enables humans 2 function

vi.

... [A]ny kind of excellence renders that of which it is the excellence *good*, and makes it perform its function *well*. For example, the excellence of the eye makes both the eye and its function good (because it is through the excellence of the eye that we see well). Similarly the excellence of a horse makes him both a fine horse and good at running and carrying his rider and facing the enemy. If this rule holds good for all cases, then *human* excellence will be the disposition that makes one a good man and causes him to perform his function well. We have already explained how this will be; but it will also become clear in another way if we consider what is the specific nature of virtue....

By virtue I mean *moral virtue* since it is this that is concerned with feelings and actions, and these involve excess, deficiency and a mean. It is possible, for example, to feel fear, confidence, desire, anger, pity, and pleasure and pain generally, too much or too little; and both of these are wrong. But to have these feelings at the right times on the right grounds towards the right people for the right motive and in the right way is to feel them to an intermediate, that is to the best, degree; and this is the mark of virtue. Similarly there are excess and deficiency and a mean in the case of actions. But it is in the field of actions and feelings that virtue operates; and in them excess and deficiency are failings, whereas the mean is praised and recognized as a success: and these are both marks of virtue. Virtue, then, is a mean condition, inasmuch as it aims at hitting the mean....

The doctrine of the mean applied to particular virtues.

vii.

But a generalization of this kind is not enough; we must apply it to particular cases....

In the field of Fear and Confidence the mean is Courage; and of those who go to extremes the man who exceeds in fearlessness has no name to describe him (there are many nameless cases), the one who exceeds in confidence is called Rash, and the one who shows an excess of fear and a deficiency of confidence is called Cowardly. In the field of Pleasures and Pains—not in all, especially not in all pains—the mean is Temperance, the excess Licentiousness; cases of defective response to pleasures scarcely occur, and therefore people of this sort too have no name to describe them, but let us class them as Insensible. In the field of Giving and Receiving Money the mean is Liberality, the excess and deficiency are Prodigality and Illiberality; but these show excess and deficiency in contrary ways to one another: the prodigal man goes too far in spending and not far enough in getting, while the illiberal man goes too far in getting money and not far enough in spending it. This present account is in outline and summary, which is all that we need at this stage; we shall give a more accurate analysis later.

But there are other dispositions too that are concerned with money. There is a mean called Magnificence (because the magnificent is not the same as the liberal man: the one deals in large and the other in small outlays); the excess is Tastelessness and Vulgarity, the deficiency Pettiness. These are different from the extremes between which liberality lies; how they differ will be discussed later. In the field of Public Honour and Dishonour the mean is Magnanimity, the excess is called a sort of Vanity, and the deficiency Pusillanimity. And just as liberality differs, as we said, from magnificence in being concerned with small outlays, so there is a state related to Magnanimity in the same way, being concerned with small honours, while magnanimity is concerned with great ones; because it is possible to aspire to [small] honours in the right way, or to a greater or less degree than is right. The man who goes too far in his aspirations is called Ambitious, the one who falls short, Unambitious; the one who is a mean between them has no name. This is true also of the corresponding dispositions, except that the ambitious man's is called Ambitiousness. This is why the extremes lay claim to the intermediate territory. We ourselves sometimes call the intermediate man ambitious and sometimes unambitious; that is, we sometimes commend the ambitious and sometimes the unambitious. Why it is that we do this will be explained in our later remarks. Meanwhile let us continue our discussion of the remaining virtues and vices, following the method already laid down.

In the field of Anger, too, there is excess, deficiency and the mean. They do not really possess names, but we may call the intermediate man Patient and the mean Patience; and of the extremes the one who exceeds can be Irascible and his vice Irascibility, while the one who is deficient can be Spiritless and the deficiency Lack of Spirit.

There are also three other means which, though different, somewhat resemble each other. They are all concerned with what we do and say in social intercourse, but they differ in this respect, that one is concerned with truthfulness in such intercourse, the other two with pleasantness—one with pleasantness in entertainment, the other with pleasantness in every department of life. We must therefore say something about these too, in order that we may better discern that in all things the mean is to be commended, while the extremes are neither commendable nor right, but reprehensible. Most of these too have no names; but, as in the other cases, we must try to coin names for them in the interest of clarity and to make it easy to follow the argument.

Well, then, as regards Truth the intermediate man may be called Truthful and the mean Truthfulness; pretension that goes too far may be Boastfulness and the man who is disposed to it a Boaster, while that which is deficient may be called Irony and its exponent Ironical. As for Pleasantness in Social Entertainment, the intermediate man is Witty, and the disposition Wit; the excess is Buffoonery and the indulger in it a Buffoon; the man who is deficient is a kind of Boor and his disposition Boorishness. In the rest of the sphere of the Pleasant—life in general— the person who is pleasant in the right way is Friendly and the mean is Friendliness; the person who goes too far, if he has no motive, is Obsequious; if his motive is self-interest, he is a Flatterer. The man who is deficient and is unpleasant in all circumstances is Cantankerous and Ill-tempered.

There are mean states also in the sphere of feelings and emotions. Modesty is not a virtue, but the modest man too is praised. Here too one person is called intermediate and another excessive—like the Shy man who is overawed at anything. The man who feels too little shame or none at all is Shameless, and the intermediate man is Modest.

Righteous Indignation is a mean between Envy and Spite, and they are all concerned with feelings of pain or pleasure at the experiences of our neighbours. The man who feels righteous indignation is distressed at instances of undeserved good fortune, but the envious man goes further and is distressed at *any* good fortune, while the spiteful man is so far from feeling distress that he actually rejoices....

Summing up of the foregoing discussion, together with three practical rules for good conduct.

ix.

We have now said enough to show that moral virtue is a mean, and in what sense it is so: that it is a mean between two vices, one of excess and the other of deficiency, and that it is such because it aims at hitting the mean point in feelings and actions. For this reason it is a difficult business to be good; because in any given case it is difficult to find the midpoint—for instance, not everyone can find the centre of a circle; only the man who knows how. So too it is easy to get angry—anyone can do that—or to give and spend money; but to feel or act towards the right person to the right extent at the right time for the right reason in the right way—that is not easy, and it is not everyone that can do it. Hence to do these things well is a rare, laudable and fine achievement.

For this reason anyone who is aiming at the mean should (1) keep away from that extreme which is more contrary to the mean, just as Calypso advises:

Far from this surf and surge keep thou thy ship.

For one of the extremes is always more erroneous than the other; and since it is extremely difficult to hit the mean, we must take the next best course, as they say, and choose the lesser of the evils; and this will be most readily done in the way that we are suggesting. (2) We must notice the errors into which we ourselves are liable to fall (because we all have different natural tendencies—we shall find out what ours are from the pleasure and pain that they give us), and we must drag ourselves in the contrary direction; for we shall arrive at the mean by pressing well away from our failing—just like somebody straightening a warped piece of wood. (3) In every situation one must guard especially against pleasure and pleasant things, because we are not impartial judges of pleasure. So we should adopt the same attitude towards it as the Trojan elders did towards Helen, and constantly repeat their pronouncement; because if in this way we relieve ourselves of the attraction, we shall be less likely to go wrong.

To sum up: by following these rules we shall have the best chance of hitting the mean. But this is presumably difficult, especially in particular cases; because it is not easy to determine what is the right way to be angry, and with whom, and on what grounds, and for how long. Indeed we sometimes praise those who show deficiency, and call them patient, and sometimes those who display temper, calling them manly. However, the man who deviates only a little from the right degree, either in excess or in deficiency, is not censured—only the one who goes too far, because he is noticeable. Yet it is not easy to define by rule for how long, and how much, a man may go wrong before he incurs blame; no easier than it is to define any other object of perception. Such questions of degree occur in particular cases, and the decision lies with our perception.

This much, then, is clear: in all our conduct it is the mean that is to be commended. But one should incline sometimes towards excess and sometimes towards deficiency, because in this way we shall most easily hit upon the mean, that is, the right course.

Book X

Recapitulaton: The nature of happiness

vi.

[I]t remains for us to give an outline account of happiness, since we hold it to be the end of human conduct. It may make our treatment of the subject more concise if we recapitulate what has been said already.

We said, then, that happiness is not a *state*, since if it were it might belong even to a man who slept all through his life, passing a vegetable existence; or to a victim of the greatest misfortunes. So if this is unacceptable, and we ought rather to refer happiness to some activity, as we said earlier; and if activities are either necessary and to be chosen for the sake of something else, or to be chosen for themselves: clearly we must class happiness as one of those to be chosen for themselves, and not as one of the other kind, because it does not need anything else: it is self-sufficient. The activities that are to be chosen for themselves are those from which nothing is required beyond the exercise of the activity; and such a description is thought to fit actions that accord with goodness; because the doing of fine and good actions is one of the things that are to be chosen for themselves.

Happiness must be distinguished from amusement.

Pleasant amusements are also thought to belong to this class, because they are not chosen as means to something else: in fact their effects are more harmful than beneficial, since they make people neglect their bodies and their property. However, most of those who are regarded as happy have recourse to such occupations, and that is why those who show some dexterity in them are highly esteemed at the courts of tyrants; they make themselves agreeable by providing the sort of entertainment that their patrons want, and such persons are in demand. So these amusements are thought to be conducive to happiness, because men in positions of power devote their leisure to them. But what people of this kind do is probably no evidence, because virtue and intelligence, which are the sources of serious activities, do not depend upon positions of power; and if these persons, never having tasted pure and refined pleasure, have recourse to physical pleasures, that is no reason why the latter should be regarded as worthier of choice. Children, too, believe that the things they prize are the most important; so it is natural that just as different things seem valuable to children and adults, so they should seem different also to good and bad men. Thus, as we have often said, it is the things that seem valuable and pleasant to the good man that are really such. But to each individual it is the activity in accordance with his own disposition that is most desirable, and therefore to the good man virtuous activity is most desirable. It follows that happiness does not consist in amusement. Indeed it would be paradoxical if the end were amusement; if we toiled and suffered all our lives long to amuse ourselves. For we choose practically everything for the sake of something else, except happiness, because it is the end. To spend effort and toil for the sake of amusement seems silly and unduly childish; but on the other hand the maxim of Anacharsis, "Play to work harder," seems to be on the right lines, because amusement is a form of relaxation, and people need relaxation because they cannot exert themselves continuously. Therefore relaxation is not an end, because it is taken for the sake of the activity. But the happy life seems to be lived in accordance with goodness, and such a life implies seriousness and does not consist in amusing oneself. Also we maintain that serious things are better than those that are merely comical and amusing, and that the activity of a man, or part of a man, is always more serious in proportion as it is better. Therefore the activity of the better part is superior, and *eo ipso* more conducive to happiness.

Anybody can enjoy bodily pleasures—a slave no less than the best of men— but nobody attributes a part in happiness to a slave, unless he also attributes to him a life of his own. Therefore happiness does not consist in occupations of this kind, but in activities in accordance with virtue, as we have said before.

Happiness and contemplation.

vii.

If happiness is an activity in accordance with virtue, it is reasonable to assume that it is in accordance with the highest virtue, and this will be the virtue of the best part of us. Whether this is the intellect or something else that we regard as naturally ruling and guiding us, and possessing insight into things noble and divine—either as being actually divine itself or as being more divine than any other part of us—it is the activity of this part, in accordance with the virtue proper to it, that will be perfect happiness.

We have already said that it is a contemplative activity. This may be regarded as consonant both with our earlier arguments and with the truth. For contemplation is both the highest form of activity (since the intellect is the highest thing in us, and the objects that it apprehends are the highest things that can be known), and also it is the most continuous, because we are more capable of continuous contemplation than we are of any practical activity. Also we assume that happiness must contain an admixture of pleasure; now activity in accordance with [philosophic] wisdom is admittedly the most pleasant of the virtuous activities; at any rate philosophy is held to entail pleasures that are marvellous in purity and permanence; and it stands to reason that those who possess knowledge pass their time more pleasantly than those who are still in pursuit of it. Again, the quality that we call self-sufficiency will belong in the highest degree to the contemplative activity. The wise man, no less than the just one and all the rest, requires the necessaries of life; but, given an adequate supply of these, the just man also needs people with and towards whom he can perform just actions, and similarly with the temperate man, the brave man, and each of the others; but the wise man can practise contemplation by himself, and the wiser he is, the more he can do it. No doubt he does it better with the help of fellowworkers; but for all that he is the most self-sufficient of men. Again, contemplation would seem to be the only activity that is appreciated for its own sake; because nothing is gained from it except the act of contemplation, whereas from practical activities we expect to gain something more or less over and above the action.

Since happiness is thought to imply leisure, it must be an intellectual, not a practical activity.

Also it is commonly believed that happiness depends on leisure; because we occupy ourselves so that we may have leisure, just as we make war in order that we may live at peace. Now the exercise of the practical virtues takes place in politics or in warfare, and these professions seem to have no place for leisure. This is certainly true of the military profession, for nobody chooses to make war or provokes it for the sake of making war; a man would be regarded as a blood-thirsty monster if he made his friends into enemies in order to bring about battles and slaughter. The politician's profession also makes leisure impossible, since besides the business of politics it aims at securing positions of power and honour, or the happiness of the politician himself and of his fellow-citizens—a happiness separate from politics, and one which we clearly pursue as separate.

If, then, politics and warfare, although pre-eminent in nobility and grandeur among practical activities in accordance with goodness, are incompatible with leisure and, not being desirable in themselves, are directed towards some other end, whereas the activity of the intellect is considered to excel in seriousness, taking as it does the form of contemplation, and to aim at no other end beyond itself, and to possess a pleasure peculiar to itself, which intensifies its activity; and if it is evident that self-sufficiency and leisuredness and such freedom from fatigue as is humanly possible, together with all the other attributes assigned to the supremely happy man, are those that accord with this activity; then this activity will be the perfect happiness for man—provided that it is allowed a full span of life; for nothing that pertains to happiness is incomplete.

Life on this plane is not too high for the divine element in human nature.

But such a life will be too high for human attainment; for any man who lives it will do so not as a human being but in virtue of something divine within him, and in proportion as this divine element is superior to the composite being, so will its activity be superior to that of the other kind of virtue. So if the intellect is divine compared with man, the life of the intellect must be divine compared with the life of a human being. And we ought not to listen to those who warn us that "man should think the thoughts of man," or "mortal thoughts fit mortal minds"; but we ought, so far as in us lies, to put on immortality, and do all that we can to live in conformity with the highest that is in us; for even if it is small in bulk, in power and preciousness it far excels all the rest. Indeed it would seem that this is the true self of the individual, since it is the authoritative and better part of him; so it would be an odd thing if a man chose to live someone else's life instead of his own. Moreover, what we said above will apply here too: that what is best and most pleasant for any given creature is that which is proper to it. Therefore for man, too, the best and most pleasant life is the life of the intellect, since the intellect is in the fullest sense the man. So this life will also be the happiest.

STUDY QUESTIONS

1. How, according to Aristotle, does reason determine right action? How is this related to the general principle that virtuous action is a mean between extremes?
2. In Aristotle's view, what is happiness, and how does it relate to virtue?
3. Of two extremes, one is usually worse, being "more opposed to the mean." Aristotle proposes that we take special care to avoid that extreme. Give an example (not found in Aristotle) of a person in a situation that falls under Aristotle's rule. Show how to apply the rule.
4. In the typical situation where we must choose an action guided by Aristotle's principles, do we have several choices, all falling within the range of the mean between two extremes, or does the principle of the mean determine a particular course of action? Supply an example of your own.

Virtue and the Human Soul

Saint Augustine

> Saint Augustine (A.D. 354–430), born in North Africa, is recognized as one of the very greatest Christian philosophers. His best known works are his *Confessions* (A.D. 400) and *The City of God* (A.D. 427).

> Augustine defines happiness as the enjoyment of the chief good. The chief good is not something that can be lost by accident or misfortune, for then we cannot enjoy it confidently. Such a good must therefore be of the soul and not the body. Augustine concludes that the chief good is the possession of virtue. The virtuous Christian follows God, avoiding sin and obeying his will.

Happiness is in the enjoyment of man's chief good. Two conditions of the chief good: 1st, Nothing is better than it; 2nd, it cannot be lost against the will

How then, according to reason, ought man to live? We all certainly desire to live happily; and there is no human being but assents to this statement almost before it is made. But the title happy cannot, in my opinion, belong either to him who has not what he loves, whatever it may be, or to him who has what he loves if it is hurtful, or to him who does not love what he has, although it is good in perfection. For one who seeks what he cannot obtain suffers torture, and one who has got what is not desirable is cheated, and one who does not seek for what is worth seeking for is diseased. Now in all these cases the mind cannot but be unhappy, and happiness and unhappiness cannot reside at the same time in one man; so in none of these cases can the man be happy. I find, then, a fourth case, where the happy life exists,—when that which is man's chief good is both loved and possessed. For what do we call enjoyment but having at hand the object of love? And no one can be happy who does not enjoy what is man's chief good, nor is there any one who enjoys this who is not happy. We must then have at hand our chief good, if we think of living happily.

We must now inquire what is man's chief good, which of course cannot be anything inferior to man himself. For whoever follows after what is inferior to himself, becomes himself inferior. But every man is bound to follow what is best. Wherefore man's chief good is not inferior to man. Is it then something similar to man himself? It must be so, if there is nothing above man which he is capable of enjoying. But if we find something which is both superior to man, and can be possessed by the man who loves it, who can doubt that in seeking for happiness man should endeavour to reach that which is more excellent than the being who makes

---

OF THE MORALS OF THE CATHOLIC CHURCH By Saint Augustine from *The Works of Aurelius Augustine*, edited by M. Dods (T. & T. Clark, Edinburgh, 1892).

the endeavour? For if happiness consists in the enjoyment of a good than which there is nothing better, which we call the chief good, how can a man be properly called happy who has not yet attained to his chief good? or how can that be the chief good beyond which something better remains for us to arrive at? Such, then, being the chief good, it must be something which cannot be lost against the will. For no one can feel confident regarding a good which he knows can be taken from him, although he wishes to keep and cherish it. But if a man feels no confidence regarding the good which he enjoys, how can he be happy while in such fear of losing it?

Man—what?

Let us then see what is better than man. This must necessarily be hard to find, unless we first ask and examine what man is. I am not now called upon to give a definition of man. The question here seems to me to be,—since almost all agree, or at least, which is enough, those I have now to do with are of the same opinion with me, that we are made up of soul and body,—What is man? Is he both of these? or is he the body only, or the soul only? For although the things are two, soul and body, and although neither without the other could be called man (for the body would not be man without the soul, nor again would the soul be man if there were not a body animated by it), still it is possible that one of these may be held to be man, and may be called so. What then do we call man? Is he soul and body, as in a double harness, or like a centaur? Or do we mean the body only, as being in the service of the soul which rules it, as the word lamp denotes not the light and the case together, but only the case, though on account of the light? Or do we mean only mind, and that on account of the body which it rules, as horseman means not the man and the horse, but the man only, and that as employed in ruling the horse? This dispute is not easy to settle; or, if the proof is plain, the statement requires time. This is an expenditure of time and strength which we need not incur. For whether the name man belongs to both, or only to the soul, the chief good of man is not the chief good of the body; but what is the chief good either of both soul and body, or of the soul only, that is man's chief good.

Man's chief good is not the chief good of the body only, but the chief good of the soul

Now if we ask what is the chief good of the body, reason obliges us to admit that it is that by means of which the body comes to be in its best state. But of all the things which invigorate the body, there is nothing better or greater than the soul. The chief good of the body, then, is not bodily pleasure, not absence of pain, not strength, not beauty, not swiftness, or whatever else is usually reckoned among the goods of the body, but simply the soul. For all the things mentioned the soul supplies to the body by its presence, and, what is above them all, life. Hence I conclude that the soul is not the chief good of man, whether we give the name of man to soul and body together, or to the soul alone. For as, according to reason, the chief good of the body is that which is better than the body, and from which the body receives vigour and life, so whether the soul itself is man, or soul and body both, we must discover whether there is anything which goes before the soul itself, in following which the soul comes to the perfection of good of which it is capable in its own kind. If such a thing can be found, all uncertainty must be at an end, and we must pronounce this to be really and truly the chief good of man.

If, again, the body is man, it must be admitted that the soul is the chief good of man. But clearly, when we treat of morals—when we inquire what manner of life must be held in order to obtain happiness—it is not the body to which the precepts are addressed, it is not bodily discipline which we discuss. In short, the observance of good customs belongs to that part of us which inquires and learns, which are the prerogatives of the soul; so, when we speak of attaining to virtue, the question does not regard the body. But if it follows, as it does, that the body which is ruled over by a soul possessed of virtue is ruled both better and more honourably, and is in its greatest perfection in consequence of the perfection of the soul which rightfully governs it, that which gives perfection to the soul will be man's chief good, though we call the body man. For if my coachman, in obedience to me, feeds and drives the horses he has charge of in the most satisfactory manner, himself enjoying the more of my bounty in proportion to his good conduct, can any one deny that the good condition of the horses, as well as that of the coachman, is due to me? So the question seems to me to be not, whether soul and body is man, or the soul only, or body only, but what gives perfection to the soul; for when this is obtained, a man cannot but be either perfect, or at least much better than in the absence of this one thing.

Virtue gives perfection to the soul; the soul obtains virtue by following God; following God is the happy life

No one will question that virtue gives perfection to the soul. But it is a very proper subject of inquiry whether this virtue can exist by itself or only in the soul. Here again arises a profound discussion, needing lengthy treatment; but perhaps my summary will serve the purpose. God will, I trust, assist me, so that, notwithstanding our feebleness, we may give instruction on these great matters briefly as well as intelligibly. In either case, whether virtue can exist by itself without the soul, or can exist only in the soul, undoubtedly in the pursuit of virtue the soul follows after something, and this must be either the soul itself, or virtue, or something else. But if the soul follows after itself in the pursuit of virtue, it follows after a foolish thing; for before obtaining virtue it is foolish. Now the height of a follower's desire is to reach that which he follows after. So the soul must either not wish to reach what it follows after, which is utterly absurd and unreasonable, or, in following after itself while foolish, it reaches the folly which it flees from. But if it follows after virtue in the desire to reach it, how can it follow what does not exist? or how can it desire to reach what it already possesses? Either, therefore, virtue exists beyond the soul, or if we are not allowed to give the name of virtue except to the habit and disposition of the wise soul, which can exist only in the soul, we must allow that the soul follows after something else in order that virtue may be produced in itself; for neither by following after nothing, nor by following after folly, can the soul, according to my reasoning, attain to wisdom.

This something else, then, by following after which the soul becomes possessed of virtue and wisdom, is either a wise man or God. But we have said already that it must be something that we cannot lose against our will. No one can think it necessary to ask whether a wise man, supposing we are content to follow after him, can be taken from us in spite of our unwillingness or our persistence. God then remains, in following after whom we live well, and in reaching whom we live both well and happily.

STUDY QUESTIONS

1. What does Augustine mean by happiness? How does this conception of happiness differ from others with which you are acquainted?
2. What does Augustine mean by "following God"? How does he argue that happiness consists in following God?
3. What does the idea of virtue as primarily theological imply for morality in general?

The Art of Living

Epictetus

Epictetus (ca. A.D. 55–135) is preeminent among the ancient Roman Stoic philosophers. He was born a slave, but his master, impressed with his intellectual abilities, sent him to Rome to be formally educated. He was eventually freed and became a brilliant, popular teacher. In A.D. 94 he was banished to northwestern Greece, where he established a school of philosophy. His most famous student was the young Marcus Aurelius, who would later become ruler of the Roman Empire. Epictetus was known not only for his intellectual brilliance but also for his personal simplicity and kindness.

Epictetus's manual (also called the *Enchiridion*) summarizes his ethical teachings. The manual was much used by Roman soldiers, but its fame as a guide to life and inner composure extends to the present day. It has proved especially useful to people in exceptionally difficult situations. (See the reading by James Stockdale that follows this one.) Stoic philosophy was popular in the time of the great empires, when ordinary people living in large imperial civilizations had to cope with a social and political reality over which they had little or no control. Epictetus tells us that regardless of circumstances, human beings are capable of dignity and self-control. If we can't change the externals, we can work on changing ourselves. Essential to his ethical teaching are the techniques that enable us (1) to differentiate between what is in our own power to control and what is not, and (2) to use this knowledge in achieving a more tranquil, dignified existence.

---

1. Some things are up to us and some are not up to us. Our opinions are up to us, and our impulses, desires, aversions—in short, whatever is our own doing. Our bodies are not up to us, nor are our possessions, our reputations, or our public offices, or, that is, whatever is not our own doing. The things that are up to us are by nature free, unhindered, and unimpeded; the things that are not up to us are weak, enslaved, hindered, not our own. So remember, if you think that things naturally enslaved are free or that things not your own are your own, you will be thwarted, miserable, and upset, and will blame both gods and men. But if you think that only what is yours is yours, and that what is not your own is, just as it is, not your own, then no one will ever coerce you, no one will hinder you, you will blame no one, you will not accuse anyone, you will not do a single thing unwillingly, you will have no enemies, and no one will harm you, because you will not be harmed at all.

As you aim for such great goals, remember that you must not undertake them by acting moderately, but must let some things go completely and postpone others for the time being. But if you want both those great goals and also to hold public office and to be rich, then you may perhaps not get even the latter just because you aim at the former too; and you certainly will fail to get the former, which are the only things that yield freedom and happiness.

From the start, then, work on saying to each harsh appearance, "You are an appearance, and not at all the thing that has the appearance." Then examine it and assess it by these yardsticks that you have, and first and foremost by whether it concerns the things that are up to us or the things that are not up to us. And if it is about one of the things that is not up to us, be ready to say, "You are nothing in relation to me."

2. Remember, what a desire proposes is that you gain what you desire, and what an aversion proposes is that you not fall into what you are averse to. Someone who fails to get what he desires is *un*fortunate, while someone who falls into what he is averse to has met *mis*fortune. So if you are averse only to what is against nature among the things that are up to you, then you will never fall into anything that you are averse to; but if you are averse to illness or death or poverty, you will meet misfortune. So detach your aversion from everything not up to us, and transfer it to what is against nature among the things that are up to us. And for the time being eliminate desire completely, since if you desire something that is not up to us, you are bound to be unfortunate, and at the same time none of the things that are up to us, which it would be good to desire, will be available to you. Make use only of impulse and its contrary, rejection, though with reservation, lightly, and without straining.

3. In the case of everything attractive or useful or that you are fond of, remember to say just what sort of thing it is, beginning with the least little things. If you are fond of a jug, say "I am fond of a jug!" For then when it is broken you will not be upset. If you kiss your child or your wife, say that you are kissing a human being; for when it dies you will not be upset.

4. When you are about to undertake some action, remind yourself what sort of action it is. If you are going out for a bath, put before your mind what happens at baths—there are people who splash, people who jostle, people who are insulting,

people who steal. And you will undertake the action more securely if from the start you say of it; "I want to take a bath and to keep my choices in accord with nature"; and likewise for each action. For that way if something happens to interfere with your bathing you will be ready to say, "Oh, well, I wanted not only this but also to keep my choices in accord with nature, and I cannot do that if I am annoyed with things that happen."

5. What upsets people is not things themselves but their judgments about the things. For example, death is nothing dreadful (or else it would have appeared dreadful to Socrates), but instead the judgment about death that it is dreadful—*that* is what is dreadful. So when we are thwarted or upset or distressed, let us never blame someone else but rather ourselves, that is, our own judgments. An uneducated person accuses others when he is doing badly; a partly educated person accuses himself, an educated person accuses neither someone else nor himself....

7. On a voyage when your boat has anchored, if you want to get fresh water you may pick up a small shellfish and a vegetable by the way, but you must keep your mind fixed on the boat and look around frequently in case the captain calls. If he calls you must let all those other things go so that you will not be tied up and thrown on the ship like livestock. That is how it is in life too: if you are given a wife and a child instead of a vegetable and a small shellfish, that will not hinder you; but if the captain calls, let all those things go and run to the boat without turning back; and if you are old, do not even go very far from the boat, so that when the call comes you are not left behind.

8. Do not seek to have events happen as you want them to, but instead want them to happen as they do happen, and your life will go well.

9. Illness interferes with the body, not with one's faculty of choice, unless that faculty of choice wishes it to. Lameness interferes with the limb, not with one's faculty of choice. Say this at each thing that happens to you, since you will find that it interferes with something else, not with you.

10. At each thing that happens to you, remember to turn to yourself and ask what capacity you have for dealing with it. If you see a beautiful boy or woman, you will find the capacity of self-control for that. If hardship comes to you, you will find endurance. If it is abuse, you will find patience. And if you become used to this, you will not be carried away by appearances....

15. Remember, you must behave as you do at a banquet. Something is passed around and comes to you: reach out your hand politely and take some. It goes by: do not hold it back. It has not arrived yet: do not stretch your desire out toward it, but wait until it comes to you. In the same way toward your children, in the same way toward your wife, in the same way toward public office, in the same way toward wealth, and you will be fit to share a banquet with the gods. But if when things are set in front of you, you do not take them but despise them, then you will not only share a banquet with the gods but also be a ruler along with them. For by acting in this way Diogenes and Heraclitus and people like them were deservedly gods and were deservedly called gods....

17. Remember that you are an actor in a play, which is as the playwright wants it to be: short if he wants it short, long if he wants it long. If he wants you to play a

beggar, play even this part skillfully, or a cripple, or a public official, or a private citizen. What is yours is to play the assigned part well. But to choose it belongs to someone else.

18. When a raven gives all unfavorable sign by croaking, do not be carried away by the appearance, but immediately draw a distinction to yourself and say, "None of these signs is for me, but only for my petty body or my petty property or my petty judgments or children or wife. For all signs are favorable if I wish, since it is up to me to be benefited by whichever of them turns out correct."

19. You can be invincible if you do not enter any contest in which victory is not up to you. See that you are not carried away by the appearance, in thinking that someone is happy when you see him honored ahead of you or very powerful or otherwise having a good reputation. For if the really good things are up to us, neither envy nor jealousy has a place, and you yourself will want neither to be a general or a magistrate or a consul, but to be free. And there is one road to this: despising what is not up to us.

20. Remember that what is insulting is not the person who abuses you or hits you, but the judgment about them that they *are* insulting. So when someone irritates you be aware that what irritates you is your own belief. Most importantly, therefore, try not to be carried away by appearance, since if you once gain time and delay you will control yourself more easily.

21. Let death and exile and everything that is terrible appear before your eyes every day, especially death; and you will never have anything contemptible in your thoughts or crave anything excessively.

22. If you crave philosophy prepare yourself on the spot to be ridiculed, to be jeered at by many people who will say, "Here he is again, all of a sudden turned philosopher on us!" and "Where did he get that high brow?" But don't *you* put on a high brow, but hold fast to the things that appear best to you, as someone assigned by god to this place. And remember that if you hold to these views, those who previously ridiculed you will later be impressed with you, but if you are defeated by them you will be doubly ridiculed.

30. Appropriate actions are in general measured by relationships. He is a father: that entails taking care of him, yielding to him in everything, putting up with him when he abuses you or strikes you. "But he is a bad father." Does nature then determine that you have a good father? No, only that you have a father. "My brother has done me wrong." Then keep your place in relation to him; do not consider his action, but instead consider what you can do to bring your own faculty of choice into accord with nature. Another person will not do you harm unless you wish it; you will be harmed at just that time at which you take yourself to be harmed. In this way, then, you will discover the appropriate actions to expect from a neighbor, from a citizen, from a general, if you are in the habit of looking at relationships.

31. The most important aspect of piety toward the gods is certainly both to have correct beliefs about them, as beings that arrange the universe well and justly, and to set yourself to obey them and acquiesce in everything that happens and to follow it willingly, as something brought to completion by the best judgment. For in this way you will never blame the gods or accuse them of neglecting you. And this piety is impossible unless you detach the good and the bad from what is not

up to us and attach it exclusively to what is up to us, because if you think that any of what is not up to us is good or bad, then when you fail to get what you want and fall into what you do not want, you will be bound to blame and hate those who cause this....

STUDY QUESTIONS

1. Epictetus claims that his Stoic teachings protect and enhance the dignity of those who apply them. How does he argue for this claim? Do you think he is right? Explain.
2. Epictetus says, "What upsets people is not things themselves, but their judgment about the things." Explain his meaning and why you agree or disagree with him.
3. Epictetus warns against the dangers posed by one's desires. What dangers does he have in mind? What solutions does he propose?

The World of Epictetus

James Stockdale

James Stockdale (1923–2005) spent ten years in Vietnam, two as a combat naval aviator and eight as a prisoner of war, including four years in solitary confinement. He received the Congressional Medal of Honor and, after retiring from the navy, served as president of the War College. He was a Senior Fellow at the Hoover Institution on War, Revolution and Peace. His books include *In Love and War* (1984), *A Vietnam Experience: Ten Years of Reflection* (1985), and *Courage Under Fire: Testing Epictetus's Doctrines in a Laboratory of Human Behavior* (1993).

James Stockdale was a senior naval wing commander when he was shot down over North Vietnam in 1965. This reading tells of the resources Stockdale found in himself in order to survive the ordeal with his sense of self-respect intact. Not all his fellow prisoners were as internally resourceful. Stockdale reports that he owed a great deal to a classical education that gave him an invaluable perspective on his situation. He learned from literature and from the Bible (Job especially) that life is not fair. The *Enchiridion* of Epictetus taught him to concern himself only with what was within his power. As a prisoner, he was physically powerless and had to learn to control and strengthen his will. He learned that integrity was far more valuable than sleep or food if these were obtained from his captors at the

THE WORLD OF EPICTETUS By Vice Admiral James Bond Stockdale, USN. Reprinted from the *Atlantic Monthly*, April 1978. By permission of the author.

price of loss of self-respect. He learned that persons of little learning or philosophy were more vulnerable to brainwashing and the weakness that leads to treasonable betrayal of fellow prisoners. As a result, Stockdale recommends training in history and philosophy for professional soldiers. "In stress situations, the fundamentals, the hardcore classical subjects, are what serve best."

In 1965 I was a forty-one-year-old commander, the senior pilot of Air Wing 16, flying combat missions in the area just south of Hanoi from the aircraft carrier *Oriskany*. By September of that year I had grown quite accustomed to briefing dozens of pilots and leading them on daily air strikes; I had flown nearly 200 missions myself and knew the countryside of North Vietnam like the back of my hand. On the ninth of that month I led about thirty-five airplanes to the Thanh Hoa Bridge, just west of that city. That bridge was tough; we had been bouncing 500-pounders off it for weeks.

The September 9 raid held special meaning for *Oriskany* pilots because of a special bomb load we had improvised; we were going in with our biggest, the 2000-pounders, hung not only on our attack planes but on our F-8 fighter-bombers as well. This increase in bridge-busting capability came from the innovative brain of a major flying with my Marine fighter squadron. He had figured out how we could jury-rig some switches, hang the big bombs, pump out some of the fuel to stay within takeoff weight limits, and then top off our tanks from our airborne refuelers while en route to the target. Although the pilot had to throw several switches in sequence to get rid of his bombs, a procedure requiring above-average cockpit agility, we routinely operated on the premise that all pilots of Air Wing 16 were above average. I test-flew the new load on a mission, thought it over, and approved it; that's the way we did business.

Our spirit was up. That morning, the *Oriskany* Air Wing was finally going to drop the bridge that was becoming a North Vietnamese symbol of resistance. You can imagine our dismay when we crossed the coast and the weather scout I had sent on ahead radioed back that ceiling and visibility were zero-zero in the bridge area. In the tiny cockpit of my A-4 at the front of the pack, I pushed the button on the throttle, spoke into the radio mike in my oxygen mask, and told the formation to split up and proceed in pairs to the secondary targets I had specified in my contingency briefing. What a letdown.

The adrenaline stopped flowing as my wingman and I broke left and down and started sauntering along toward our "milk run" target: boxcars on a railroad siding between Vinh and Thanh Hoa, where the flak was light. Descending through 10,000 feet, I unsnapped my oxygen mask and let it dangle, giving my pinched face a rest—no reason to stay uncomfortable on this run.

As I glided toward that easy target, I'm sure I felt totally self-satisfied. I had the top combat job that a Navy commander can hold and I was in tune with my environment. I was confident—I knew airplanes and flying inside out. I was comfortable with the people I worked with and I knew the trade so well that I often improvised variations in accepted procedures and encouraged others to do so under my watchful eye. I was on top. I thought I had found every key to success and had no doubt that my Academy and test-pilot schooling had provided me with every-thing I needed in life.

I passed down the middle of those boxcars and smiled as I saw the results of my instinctive timing. A neat pattern—perfection. I was just pulling out of my dive low to the ground when I heard a noise I hadn't expected—the *boom boom boom* of a 57-millimeter gun—and then I saw it just behind my wingtip. I was hit—all the red lights came on, my control system was going out—and I could barely keep that plane from flying into the ground while I got that damned oxygen mask up to my mouth so I could tell my wingman that I was about to eject. What rotten luck. And on a "milk run"!

The descent in the chute was quiet except for occasional rifle shots from the streets below. My mind was clear, and I said to myself, "five years." I knew we were making a mess of the war in Southeast Asia, but I didn't think it would last longer than that; I was also naive about the resources I would need in order to sur-vive a lengthy period of captivity.

The Durants have said that culture is a thin and fragile veneer that superim-poses itself on mankind. For the first time I was on my own, without the veneer. I was to spend years searching through and refining my bag of memories, looking for useful tools, things of value. The values were there, but they were all mixed up with technology, bureaucracy, and expediency, and had to be brought up into the open.

Education should take care to illuminate values, not bury them amongst the trivia. Are our students getting the message that without personal integrity intellec-tual skills are worthless?

Integrity is one of those words which many people keep in that desk drawer labeled "too hard." It's not a topic for the dinner table or the cocktail party. You can't buy or sell it. When supported with education, a person's integrity can give him something to rely on when his perspective seems to blur, when rules and prin-ciples seem to waver, and when he's faced with hard choices of right or wrong. It's something to keep him on the right track, something to keep him afloat when he's drowning; if only for practical reasons, it is an attribute that should be kept at the very top of a young person's consciousness.

The importance of the latter point is highlighted in prison camps, where every-day human nature, stripped bare, can be studied under a magnifying glass in accel-erated time. Lessons spotlighted and absorbed in that laboratory sharpen one's eye for their abstruse but highly relevant applications in the "real time" world of now.

In the five years since I've been out of prison, I've participated several times in the process of selecting senior naval officers for promotion or important command assignments. I doubt that the experience is significantly different from that of execu-tives who sit on "selection boards" in any large hierarchy. The system must be for-mal, objective, and fair; if you've seen one, you've probably seen them all. Navy selection board proceedings go something like this.

The first time you know the identity of the other members of the board is when you walk into a boardroom at eight o'clock on an appointed morning. The first order of business is to stand, raise your right hand, put your left hand on the Bible, and swear to make the best judgment you can, on the basis of merit, without prejudice. You're sworn to confidentiality regarding all board members' remarks during the proceedings. Board members are chosen for their experience and understanding; they often have knowledge of the particular individuals under consideration. They must feel free to speak their minds. They read and grade dozens of dossiers, and each candidate is discussed extensively. At voting time, a member casts his vote by selecting and pushing a "percent confidence" button, visible only to himself, on a console attached to his chair. When the last member pushes his button, a totalizer displays the numerical average "confidence" of the board. No one knows who voted what.

I'm always impressed by the fact that every effort is made to be fair to the candidate. Some are clearly out, some are clearly in; the borderline cases are the tough ones. You go over and over those in the "middle pile" and usually you vote and revote until late at night. In all the boards I've sat on, no inference or statement in a "jacket" is as sure to portend a low confidence score on the vote as evidence of a lack of directness or rectitude of a candidate in his dealings with others. Any hint of moral turpitude really turns people off. When the crunch comes, they prefer to work with forthright plodders rather than with devious geniuses. I don't believe that this preference is unique to the military. In any hierarchy where people's fates are decided by committees or boards, those who lose credibility with their peers and who cause their superiors to doubt their directness, honesty, or integrity are dead. Recovery isn't possible.

The linkage of men's ethics, reputations, and fates can be studied in even more vivid detail in prison camp. In that brutally controlled environment a perceptive enemy can get his hooks into the slightest chink in a man's ethical armor and accelerate his downfall. Given the right opening, the right moral weakness, a certain susceptibility on the part of the prisoner, a clever extortionist can drive his victim into a downhill slide that will ruin his image, self-respect, and life in a very short time.

There are some uncharted aspects to this, some traits of susceptibility which I don't think psychologists yet have words for. I am thinking of the tragedy that can befall a person who has such a need for love or attention that he will sell his soul for it. I use tragedy with the rigorous definition Aristotle applied to it: the story of a good man with a flaw who comes to an unjustified bad end. This is a rather delicate point and one that I want to emphasize. We had very very few collaborators in prison, and comparatively few Aristotelian tragedies, but the story and fate of one of these good men with a flaw might be instructive.

He was handsome, smart, articulate, and smooth. He was almost sincere. He was obsessed with success. When the going got tough, he decided expediency was preferable to principle.

This man was a classical opportunist. He befriended and worked for the enemy to the detriment of his fellow Americans. He made a tacit deal; moreover, he accepted favors (a violation of the code of conduct). In time, out of fear and shame, he withdrew; we could not get him to communicate with the American prisoner organization.

I couldn't learn what made the man tick. One of my best friends in prison, one of the wisest persons I have ever known, had once been in a squadron with this fellow. In prisoners' code I tapped a question to my philosophical friend: "What in the world is going on with that fink?"

"You're going to be surprised at what I have to say," he meticulously tapped back. "In a squadron he pushes himself forward and dominates the scene. He's a continual fountain of information. He's the person everybody relies on for inside dope. He works like mad; often flies more hops than others. It drives him crazy if he's not liked. He tends to grovel and ingratiate himself before others. I didn't realize he was really pathetic until I was sitting around with him and his wife one night when he was spinning his yarns of delusions of grandeur, telling of his great successes and his pending ascension to the top. His wife knew him better than anybody else; she shook her head with genuine sympathy and said to him: 'Gee, you're just a phony.'"

In prison, this man had somehow reached the point where he was willing to sell his soul just to satisfy this need, this immaturity. The only way he could get the attention that he demanded from authority was to grovel and ingratiate himself before the enemy. As a soldier he was a miserable failure, but he had not crossed the boundary of willful treason; he was not written off as an irrevocable loss, as were the two patent collaborators with whom the Vietnamese soon arranged that he live.

As we American POWs built our civilization, and wrote our own laws (which we leaders obliged all to memorize), we also codified certain principles which formed the backbone of our policies and attitudes. I codified the principles of compassion, rehabilitation, and forgiveness with the slogan: "It is neither American nor Christian to nag a repentant sinner to his grave." (Some didn't like it, thought it seemed soft on finks.) And so, we really gave this man a chance. Over time, our efforts worked. After five years of self-indulgence he got himself together and started to communicate with the prisoner organization. I sent the message "Are you on the team or not?"; he replied, "Yes," and came back. He told the Vietnamese that he didn't want to play their dirty games anymore. He wanted to get away from those willful collaborators and he came back and he was accepted, after a fashion.

I wish that were the end of the story. Although he came back, joined us, and even became a leader of sorts, he never totally won himself back. No matter how forgiving we were, he was conscious that many resented him—not so much because he was weak but because he had broken what we might call a gentleman's code. In all of those years when he, a senior officer, had willingly participated in making tape recordings of anti-American material, he had deeply offended the sensibilities of the American prisoners who were forced to listen to him. To most of us it wasn't the rhetoric of the war or the goodness or the badness of this or that issue that counted. The object of our highest value was the well-being of our fellow prisoners. He had broken that code and hurt some of those people. Some thought that as an informer he had indirectly hurt them physically. I don't believe that. What indisputably hurt them was his not having the sensitivity to realize the damage his opportunistic conduct would do to the morale of a bunch of Middle American guys with Middle American attitudes which they naturally cherished. He should have known that in those solitary cells where his tapes were piped were idealistic, direct, patriotic fellows who would be crushed and embarrassed to have him, a senior man in excellent physical shape, so obviously not under torture, telling the world that the war was wrong. Even if he believed what he said, which he did not, he should have had the common decency to keep his mouth shut. You can sit and think anything you want, but when you insensitively cut down those who want to love and help you, you cross a line. He seemed to sense that he could never truly be one of us.

And yet he was likable—particularly back in civilization after release—when tension was off, and making a deal did not seem so important. He exuded charm and "hail fellow" sophistication. He wanted so to be liked by all those men he had once discarded in his search for new friends, new deals, new fields to conquer in Hanoi. The tragedy of his life was obvious to us all. Tears were shed by some of his old prison mates when he was killed in an accident that strongly resembled suicide some months later. The Greek drama had run its course. He was right out of Aristotle's book, a good man with a flaw who had come to an unjustified bad end. The flaw was insecurity: the need to ingratiate himself, the need for love and adulation at any price.

He reminded me of Paul Newman in *The Hustler*. Newman couldn't stand success. He knew how to make a deal. He was handsome, he was smart, he was attractive to everybody; but he had to have adulation, and therein lay the seed of tragedy. Playing high-stakes pool against old Minnesota Fats (Jackie Gleason), Newman was well in the lead, and getting more full of himself by the hour. George C. Scott, the pool bettor, whispered to his partner: "I'm going to keep betting on Minnesota Fats; this other guy [Newman] is a born loser—he's all skill and no character." And he was right, a born loser—I think that's the message.

How can we educate to avoid these casualties? Can we by means of education prevent this kind of tragedy? What we prisoners were in was a one-way leverage game in which the other side had all the mechanical advantage. I suppose you could say that we all live in a leverage world to some degree; we all experience people trying to use us in one way or another. The difference in Hanoi was the degradation of the ends (to be used as propaganda agents of an enemy, or as informers on your fellow Americans), and the power of the means (total environmental control including solitary confinement, restraint by means of leg-irons and handcuffs, and torture). Extortionists always go down the same track: the imposition of guilt and fear for having disobeyed their rules, followed in turn by punishment, apology, confession, and atonement (their payoff). Our captors would go to great lengths to get a man to compromise his own code, even if only slightly, and then they would hold that in their bag, and the next time get him to go a little further.

Some people are psychologically, if not physically, at home in extortion environments. They are tough people who instinctively avoid getting sucked into the undertows. They never kid themselves or their friends; if they miss the mark they admit it. But there's another category of person who gets tripped up. He makes a small compromise, perhaps rationalizes it, and then makes another one; and then he gets depressed, full of shame, lonesome, loses his willpower and self-respect, and comes to a tragic end. Somewhere along the line he realizes that he has turned a corner that he didn't mean to turn. All too late he realizes that he has been worshiping the wrong gods and discovers the wisdom of the ages: life is not fair.

In sorting out the story after our release, we found that most of us had come to combat constant mental and physical pressure in much the same way. We discovered that when a person is alone in a cell and sees the door open only once or twice a day for a bowl of soup, he realizes after a period of weeks in isolation and darkness that he has to build some sort of ritual into his life if he wants to avoid becoming an animal. Ritual fills a need in a hard life and it's easy to see how formal church ritual grew. For almost all of us, this ritual was built around prayer, exercise, and clandestine communication. The prayers I said during those days were prayers of quality with ideas of substance. We found that over the course of time our minds had a tremendous capacity for invention and introspection, but had the weakness of being an integral part of our bodies. I remembered Descartes and how in his philosophy he separated mind and body. One time I cursed my body for the way it decayed my mind. I had decided that I would become a Gandhi. I would have to be carried around on a pallet and in that state I could not be used by my captors for propaganda purposes. After about ten days of fasting, I found that I had become so depressed that soon I would risk going into interrogation ready to spill my guts just looking for a friend. I tapped to the guy next door and I said, "Gosh, how I wish Descartes could have been right, but he's wrong." He was a little slow to reply; I reviewed Descartes's deduction with him and explained how I had discovered that body and mind are inseparable.

On the positive side, I discovered the tremendous file-cabinet volume of the human mind. You can memorize an incredible amount of material and you can draw the past out of your memory with remarkable recall by easing slowly toward the event you seek and not crowding the mind too closely. You'll try to remember who was at your birthday party when you were five years old, and you can get it, but only after months of effort. You can break the locks and find the answers, but you need time and solitude to learn how to use this marvelous device in your head which is the greatest computer on earth.

Of course many of the things we recalled from the past were utterly useless as sources of strength or practicality. For instance, events brought back from cocktail parties or insincere social contacts were almost repugnant because of their emptiness, their utter lack of value. More often than not, the locks worth picking had been on old schoolroom doors. School days can be thought of as a time when one is filling the important stacks of one's memory library. For me, the golden doors were labeled history and the classics. The historical perspective which enabled a man to take himself away from all the agitation, not necessarily to see a rosy lining, but to see the real nature of the situation he faced, was truly a thing of value.

Here's how this historical perspective helped me see the reality of my own situation and thus cope better with it. I learned from a Vietnamese prisoner that the same cells we occupied had in years before been lived in by many of the leaders of the Hanoi government. From my history lessons I recalled that when metropolitan France permitted communists in the government in 1936, the communists who occupied cells in Vietnam were set free. I marveled at the cycle of history, all within my memory, which prompted Hitler's rise in Germany, then led to the rise of the Popular Front in France, and finally vacated this cell of mine halfway around the world ("Perhaps Pham Van Dong lived here"). I came to understand what tough people these were. I was willing to fight them to the death, but I grew to realize that hatred was an indulgence, a very inefficient emotion. I remember thinking,

"If you were committed to beating the dealer in a gambling casino, would *hating* him help your game?" In a pidgin English propaganda book the guard gave me, speeches by these old communists about their prison experiences stressed how they learned to beat down the enemy by being united. It seemed comforting to know that we were united against the communist administration of Hoa Lo prison just as the Vietnamese communists had united against the French administration of Hoa Lo in the thirties. Prisoners are prisoners, and there's only one way to beat administrations. We resolved to do it better in the sixties than they had in the thirties. You don't base system-beating on any thought of political idealism; you do it as a competitive thing, as an expression of self-respect.

Education in the classics teaches you that all organizations since the beginning of time have used the power of guilt; that cycles are repetitive; and that this is the way of the world. It's a naive person who comes in and says, "Let's see, what's good and what's bad?" That's a quagmire. You can get out of that quagmire only by recalling how wise men before you accommodated the same dilemmas. And I believe a good classical education and an understanding of history can best determine the rules you should live by. They also give you the power to analyze reasons for these rules and guide you as to how to apply them to your own situation. In a broader sense, all my education helped me. Naval Academy discipline and body contact sports helped me. But the education which I found myself using most was what I got in graduate school. The messages of history and philosophy I used were simple.

The first one is this business about life not being fair. That is a very important lesson and I learned it from a wonderful man named Philip Rhinelander. As a lieutenant commander in the Navy studying political science at Stanford University in 1961, I went over to philosophy corner one day and an older gentleman said, "Can I help you?" I said, "Yes, I'd like to take some courses in philosophy." I told him I'd been in college for six years and had never had a course in philosophy. He couldn't believe it. I told him that I was a naval officer and he said, "Well, I used to be in the Navy. Sit down." Philip Rhinelander became a great influence in my life.

He had been a Harvard lawyer and had pleaded cases before the Supreme Court and then gone to war as a reserve officer. When he came back he took his doctorate at Harvard. He was also a music composer, had been director of general education at Harvard, dean of the School of Humanities and Sciences at Stanford, and by the time I met him had by choice returned to teaching in the classroom. He said, "The course I'm teaching is my personal two-term favorite—The Problem of Good and Evil—and we're starting our second term." He said the message of his course was from the Book of Job. The number one problem in this world is that people are not able to accommodate the lesson in the book.

He recounted the story of Job. It starts out by establishing that Job was the most honorable of men. Then he lost all his goods. He also lost his reputation, which is what really hurt. His wife was badgering him to admit his sins, but he knew he had made no errors. He was not a patient man and demanded to speak to the Lord. When the Lord appeared in the whirlwind, he said, "Now, Job, you have to shape up! Life is not fair." That's my interpretation and that's the way the book ended for hundreds of years. I agree with those of the opinion that the happy ending was spliced on many years later. If you read it, you'll note that the meter changes. People couldn't live with the original message. Here was a good man who came to unexplained grief, and the Lord told him: "That's the way it is. Don't challenge me. This is my world and you either live in it as I designed it or get out."

This was a great comfort to me in prison. It answered the question "Why me?" I cast aside any thoughts of being punished for past actions. Sometimes I shared the message with fellow prisoners as I tapped through the walls to them, but I learned to be selective. It's a strong message which upsets some people.

Rhinelander also passed on to me another piece of classical information which I found of great value. On the day of our last session together he said, "You're a military man, let me give you a book to remember me by. It's a book of military ethics." He handed it to me, and I bade him goodbye with great emotion. I took the book home and that night started to read it. It was the *Enchiridion* of the philosopher Epictetus, his "manual" for the Roman field soldier.

As I began to read, I thought to myself in disbelief, "Does Rhinelander think I'm going to draw lessons for my life from this thing? I'm a fighter pilot. I'm a technical man. I'm a test pilot. I know how to get people to do technical work. I play golf; I drink martinis. I know how to get ahead in my profession. And what does he hand me? A book that says in part, 'It's better to die in hunger, exempt from guilt and fear, than to live in affluence and with perturbation.'" I remembered this later in prison because perturbation was what I was living with. When I ejected from the airplane on that September morn in 1965, I had left the land of technology. I had entered the world of Epictetus, and it's a world that few of us, whether we know it or not, are ever far away from.

In Palo Alto, I had read this book, not with contentment, but with annoyance. Statement after statement: "Men are disturbed not by things, but by the view that they take of them." "Do not be concerned with things which are beyond your power." "Demand not that events should happen as you wish, but wish them to happen as they do happen and you will go on well." This is stoicism. It's not the last word, but it's a viewpoint that comes in handy in many circumstances, and it surely did for me. Particularly this line: "Lameness is an impediment to the body but not to the will." That was significant for me because I wasn't able to stand up and support myself on my badly broken leg for the first couple of years I was in solitary confinement.

Other statements of Epictetus took on added meaning in the light of extortions which often began with our captors' callous pleas: "If you are just reasonable with us we will compensate you. You get your meals, you get to sleep, you won't be pestered, you might even get a cellmate." The catch was that by being "reasonable with us" our enemies meant being their informers, their propagandists. The old stoic had said, "If I can get the things I need with the preservation of my honor and fidelity and self-respect, show me the way and I will get them. But, if you require me to lose my own proper good, that you may gain what is no good, consider how unreasonable and foolish you are." To love our fellow prisoners was within our power. To betray, to propagandize, to disillusion conscientious and patriotic shipmates and destroy their morale so that they in turn would be destroyed was to lose one's proper good.

What attributes serve you well in the extortion environment? We learned there, above all else, that the best defense is to keep your conscience clean. When we did something we were ashamed of, and our captors realized we were ashamed of it, we were in trouble. A little white lie is where extortion and ultimately blackmail start. In 1965, I was crippled and I was alone. I realized that they had all the power. I couldn't see how I was ever going to get out with my honor and self-respect. The one thing I came to realize was that if you don't lose integrity you can't be had and you can't be hurt. Compromises multiply and build up when you're working against a skilled extortionist or a good manipulator. You can't be had if you don't take that first shortcut, or "meet them halfway," as they say, or look for that tacit "deal," or make that first compromise.

Bob North, a political science professor at Stanford, taught me a course called Comparative Marxist Thought. This was not an anti-communist course. It was the study of dogma and thought patterns. We read no criticism of Marxism, only primary sources. All year we read the works of Marx and Lenin. In Hanoi, I understood more about Marxist theory than my interrogator did. I was able to say to that interrogator, "That's not what Lenin said; you're a deviationist."

One of the things North talked about was brainwashing. A psychologist who studied the Korean prisoner situation, which somewhat paralleled ours, concluded that three categories of prisoners were involved there. The first was the redneck Marine sergeant from Tennessee who had an eighth-grade education. He would get in that interrogation room and they would say that the Spanish-American War was started by the bomb within the *Maine*, which might be true, and he would answer, "B.S." They would show him something about racial unrest in Detroit. "B.S." There was no way they could get to him; his mind was made up. He was a straight guy, red, white, and blue, and everything else was B.S.! He didn't give it a second thought. Not much of a historian, perhaps, but a good security risk.

In the next category were the sophisticates. They were the fellows who could be told these same things about the horrors of American history and our social problems, but had heard it all before, knew both sides of every story, and thought we were on the right track. They weren't ashamed that we had robber barons at a certain time in our history; they were aware of the skeletons in most civilizations' closets. They could not be emotionally involved and so they were good security risks.

The ones who were in trouble were the high school graduates who had enough sense to pick up the innuendo, and yet not enough education to accommodate it properly. Not many of them fell, but most of the men that got entangled started from that background.

The psychologist's point is possibly oversimplistic, but I think his message has some validity. A little knowledge is a dangerous thing.

Generally speaking, I think education is a tremendous defense; the broader, the better. After I was shot down my wife, Sybil, found a clipping glued in the front of my collegiate dictionary: "Education is an ornament in prosperity and a refuge in adversity." She certainly agrees with me on that. Most of us prisoners found that the so-called practical academic exercises in how to do things, which I'm told are proliferating, were useless. I'm not saying that we should base education on training people to be in prison, but I am saying that in stress situations, the fundamentals, the hardcore classical subjects, are what serve best.

Theatrics also helped sustain me. My mother had been a drama coach when I was young and I was in many of her plays. In prison I learned how to manufacture a personality and live it, crawl into it, and hold that role without deviation. During interrogations, I'd check the responses I got to different kinds of behavior. They'd get worried when I did things irrationally. And so, every so often, I would play that "irrational" role and come completely unglued. When I could tell that pressure to make a public exhibition of me was building, I'd stand up, tip the table over, attempt to throw the chair through the window, and say, "No way, Goddammit! I'm not doing that! Now, come over here and fight!" This was a risky ploy, because if they thought you were acting, they would slam you into the ropes and make you scream in pain like a baby. You could watch their faces and read their minds. They had expected me to behave like a stoic. But a man would be a fool to make their job easy by being conventional and predictable. I could feel the tide turn in my favor at that magic moment when their anger turned to pleading: "Calm down, now calm down." The payoff would come when they decided that the risk of my going haywire in front of some touring American professor on a "fact-finding" mission was too great. More important, they had reason to believe that I would tell the truth—namely, that I had been in solitary confinement for four years and tortured fifteen times—without fear of future consequences. So theatrical training proved helpful to me.

Can you educate for leadership? I think you can, but the communists would probably say no. One day in an argument with an interrogator, I said, "You are so proud of being a party member, what are the criteria?" He said in a flurry of anger, "There are only four: you have to be seventeen years old, you have to be selfless, you have to be smart enough to understand the theory, and you've got to be a person who innately influences others." He stressed that fourth one. I think psychologists would say that leadership is innate, and there is truth in that. But, I also think you can learn some leadership traits that naturally accrue from a good education: compassion is a necessity for leaders, as are spontaneity, bravery, self-discipline, honesty, and above all, integrity.

I remember being disappointed about a month after I was back when one of my young friends, a prison mate, came running up after a reunion at the Naval Academy. He said with glee, "This is really great, you won't believe how this country has advanced. They've practically done away with plebe year at the Academy, and they've got computers in the basement of Bancroft Hall." I thought, "My God, if there was anything that helped us get through those eight years, it was plebe year, and if anything screwed up that war, it was computers!"

STUDY QUESTIONS

1. In his years of confinement and torment, Stockdale relied upon the Stoic philosophy of Epictetus. Is Stoicism primarily a philosophy for critical and extreme situations? If so, why? If not, how does it apply in ordinary life?
2. How does Stockdale define personal integrity? Does this conform to your idea of personal integrity? How did readings in history and philosophy help Stockdale retain his dignity and integrity under great stress?

3. Discuss the case of the officer who betrayed his fellow prisoners. Stockdale attributes this to a character fault. Could a proper moral education of the kind Stockdale advocates have prevented it?
4. What does Stockdale's essay tell us about the importance or unimportance of a formal training in ethics? Is great fiction more valuable for moral development? Explain.

Virtue or Duty?

Bernard Mayo

> Bernard Mayo (1920–2000) was an English philosopher. He is the author of *Ethics and the Moral Life* (1958) and *The Philosophy of Right and Wrong: An Introduction to Ethical Theory* (1986).
>
> Bernard Mayo points out that the classical philosophers did not lay down principles of moral behavior but concentrated instead on the character of the moral person. He claims that classical moral theory is superior to a modern (Kantian) ethics of duty. "The basic moral question, for Aristotle, is not, What shall I do? but, What shall I be?" The morality of "doing" is logically simple: we determine what we ought to do by seeing whether it maximizes happiness (utilitarianism) or is universalizable (Kantianism). The morality of "being" has another kind of simplicity, which Mayo calls the unity of character. Persons of character, heroes or saints, do not merely give us principles to follow; more importantly, they provide an example for us to follow. An ethics of character is more flexible than an ethics of rules. We can find more than one good way to follow a good personal example.

The philosophy of moral principles, which is characteristic of Kant and the post-Kantian era, is something of which hardly a trace exists in Plato.... Plato says nothing about rules or principles or laws, except when he is talking politics. Instead he talks about virtues and vices, and about certain types of human character. The key word in Platonic ethics is Virtue; the key word in Kantian ethics is Duty. And modern ethics is a set of footnotes, not to Plato, but to Kant....

Attention to the novelists can be a welcome correction to a tendency of philosophical ethics of the last generation or two to lose contact with the ordinary life of man which is just what the novelists, in their own way, are concerned with. Of course there are writers who can be called in to illustrate problems about Duty (Graham Greene is a good example). But there are more who perhaps never mention

VIRTUE OR DUTY? From *Ethics and the Moral Life* by Bernard Mayo. Reprinted by permission of Macmillan Press, Ltd.

the words duty, obligation or principle. Yet they are all concerned—Jane Austen, for instance, entirely and absolutely—with the moral qualities or defects of their heroes and heroines and other characters. This points to a radical one-sidedness in the philosophers' account of morality in terms of principles: it takes little or no account of qualities, of what people *are*. It is just here that the old-fashioned word Virtue used to have a place; and it is just here that the work of Plato and Aristotle can be instructive. Justice, for Plato, though it is closely connected with acting according to law, does not *mean* acting according to law: it is a quality of character, and a just action is one such as a just man would do. Telling the truth, for Aristotle, is not, as it was for Kant, fulfilling an obligation; again it is a quality of character, or, rather, a whole range of qualities of character, some of which may actually be defects, such as tactlessness, boastfulness, and so on—a point which can be brought out, in terms of principles, only with the greatest complexity and artificiality, but quite simply and naturally in terms of character.

If we wish to enquire about Aristotle's moral views, it is no use looking for a set of principles. Of course we can find *some* principles to which he must have subscribed— for instance, that one ought not to commit adultery. But what we find much more prominently is a set of character-traits, a list of certain types of person—the courageous man, and the niggardly man, the boaster, the lavish spender and so on. The basic moral question, for Aristotle, is not, What shall I do? but, What shall I be?

These contrasts between doing and being, negative and positive, and modern as against Greek morality were noted by John Stuart Mill; I quote from the *Essay on Liberty*:

> Christian morality (so-called) has all the characters of a reaction; it is, in great part, a protest against Paganism. Its ideal is negative rather than positive, passive rather than active; Innocence rather than Nobleness; Abstinence from Evil, rather than energetic Pursuit of the Good; in its precepts (as has been well said) "Thou shalt not" predominates unduly over "Thou shalt...." Whatever exists of magnanimity, high-mindedness, personal dignity, even the sense of honour, is derived from the purely human, not the religious part of our education, and never could have grown out of a standard of ethics in which the only worth, professedly recognised, is that of obedience.

Of course, there are connections between being and doing. It is obvious that a man cannot just *be*; he can only be what he is by doing what he does; his moral qualities are ascribed to him because of his actions, which are said to manifest those qualities. But the point is that an ethics of Being must include this obvious fact, that Being involves Doing; whereas an ethics of Doing, such as I have been examining, may easily overlook it. As I have suggested, a morality of principles is concerned only with what people do or fail to do, since that is what rules are for. And as far as this sort of ethics goes, people might well have no moral qualities at all except the possession of principles and the will (and capacity) to act accordingly.

When we speak of a moral quality such as courage, and say that a certain action was courageous, we are not merely saying something about the action. We are referring, not so much to what is done, as to the kind of person by whom we take it to have been done. We connect, by means of imputed motives and intentions, with the character of the agent as courageous. This explains, incidentally, why both Kantians and Utilitarians encounter, in their different ways, such difficulties in dealing with motives, which their principles, on the face of it, have no room for. A Utilitarian, for example, can only praise a courageous action in some such way as this: the action is of a sort such as a person of courage is likely to perform, and courage is a quality of character the cultivation of which is likely to increase rather than diminish the sum total of human happiness. But Aristotelians have no need of such circumlocution. For them a courageous action just is one which proceeds from and manifests a certain type of character, and is praised because such a character trait is good, or better than others, or is a virtue. An evaluative criterion is sufficient: there is no need to look for an imperative criterion as well, or rather instead, according to which it is not the character which is good, but the cultivation of the character which is right....

No doubt the fundamental moral question is just "What ought I to do?" And according to the philosophy of moral principles, the answer (which must be an imperative "Do this") must be derived from a conjunction of premises consisting (in the simplest case) firstly of a rule, or universal imperative, enjoining (or forbidding) all actions of a certain type in situations of a certain type, and, secondly, a statement to the effect that this is a situation of that type, falling under that rule. In practice the emphasis may be on supplying only one of these premises, the other being assumed or taken for granted: one may answer the question "What ought I to do?" either by quoting a rule which I am to adopt, or by showing that my case is legislated for by a rule which I do adopt. To take a previous example of moral perplexity, if I am in doubt whether to tell the truth about his condition to a dying man, my doubt may be resolved by showing that the case comes under a rule about the avoidance of unnecessary suffering, which I am assumed to accept. But if the case is without precedent in my moral career, my problem may be soluble only by adopting a new principle about what I am to do now and in the future about cases of this kind.

This second possibility offers a connection with moral ideas. Suppose my perplexity is not merely an unprecedented situation which I could cope with by adopting a new rule. Suppose the new rule is thoroughly inconsistent with my existing moral code. This may happen, for instance, if the moral code is one to which I only pay lip-service; if ... its authority is not yet internalised, or if it has ceased to be so; it is ready for rejection, but its final rejection awaits a moral crisis such as we are assuming to occur. What I now need is not a rule for deciding how to act in this situation and others of its kind. I need a whole set of rules, a complete morality, new principles to live by.

Now according to the philosophy of moral character, there is another way of answering the fundamental question "What ought I to do?" Instead of quoting a rule, we quote a quality of character, a virtue: we say "Be brave," or "Be patient" or "Be lenient." We may even say "Be a man": if I am in doubt, say, whether to take a risk, and someone says "Be a man," meaning a morally sound man, in this case a man of sufficient courage. (Compare the very different ideal invoked in "Be a gentleman." I shall not discuss whether this is a *moral* ideal.) Here, too, we have the extreme cases, where a man's moral perplexity extends not merely to a particular situation but to his whole way of living. And now the question "What ought I to do?" turns into the question "What ought I to be?"—as, indeed, it was treated in the first place. ("Be brave.") It is answered, not by quoting a rule or a set of rules, but by describing a quality of character or a type of person. And here the ethics of character gains a practical simplicity which offsets the greater logical simplicity of the ethics of principles. We do not have to give a list of characteristics or virtues, as we might list a set of principles. We can give a unity to our answer.

Of course we can in theory give a unity to our principles: this is implied by speaking of a *set* of principles. But if such a set is to be a system and not merely aggregate, the unity we are looking for is a logical one, namely the possibility that some principles are deductible from others, and ultimately from one. But the attempt to construct a deductive moral system is notoriously difficult, and in any case ill-founded. Why should we expect that all rules of conduct should be ultimately reducible to a few?

Saints and Heroes

But when we are asked "What shall I be?" we can readily give a unity to our answer, though not a logical unity. It is the unity of character. A person's character is not merely a list of dispositions; it has the organic unity of something that is more than the sum of its parts. And we can say, in answer to our morally perplexed questioner, not only "Be this" and "Be that," but also "Be like So-and-So"—where So-and-So is either an ideal type of character, or else an actual person taken as representative of the ideal, an exemplar. Examples of the first are Plato's "just man" in the Republic; Aristotle's man of practical wisdom, in the Nicomachean Ethics; Augustine's citizen of the City of God; the good Communist; the American way of life (which is a collective expression for a type of character). Examples of the second kind, the exemplar, are Socrates, Christ, Buddha, St. Francis, the heroes of epic writers and of novelists. Indeed the idea of the Hero, as well as the idea of the Saint, are very much the expression of this attitude to morality. Heroes and saints are not merely people who did things. They are people whom we are expected, and expect ourselves, to imitate. And imitating them means not merely doing what they did; it means being like them. Their status is not in the least like that of legislators whose laws we admire; for the character of a legislator is irrelevant to our judgment about his legislation. The heroes and saints did not merely give us principles to live by (though some of them did that as well): they gave us examples to follow.

Kant, as we should expect, emphatically rejects this attitude as "fatal to morality." According to him, examples serve only to render *visible* an instance of the moral principle, and thereby to demonstrate its practical feasibility. But every exemplar, such as Christ himself, must be judged by the independent criterion of the moral law, before we are entitled to recognize him as worthy of imitation. I am not suggesting that the subordination of exemplars to principles is incorrect, but that it is one-sided and fails to do justice to a large area of moral experience.

Imitation can be more or less successful. And this suggests another defect of the ethics of principles. It has no room for ideals, except the ideal of a perfect set of principles (which, as a matter of fact, is intelligible only in terms of an ideal character or way of life), and the ideal of perfect conscientiousness (which is itself a character-trait). This results, of course, from the "black-or-white" nature of moral verdicts based on rules. There are no degrees by which we approach or recede from the attainment of a certain quality or virtue; if there were not, the word "ideal" would have no meaning. Heroes and saints are not people whom we try to be *just* like, since we know that is impossible. It is precisely because it is impossible for ordinary human beings to achieve the same qualities as the saints, and in the same degree, that we do set them apart from the rest of humanity. It is enough if we try to be a little like them....

STUDY QUESTIONS

1. Morality, says Mayo, involves "being" as well as "doing." What does he mean by "being" and "doing"? What sort of moral theory concentrates on being? On doing?
2. Philosophers of virtue or moral character tell us how to develop ourselves as moral persons. They answer the question "What ought I to do?" by telling us what to be. How does that work?
3. Mayo says that the moral content of literature emphasizes character and virtue more than duty and obligation. Is he right about this? Explain. If he is, then is a moral philosophy of duty necessarily inadequate? Explain.

Tradition and the Virtues

Alasdair MacIntyre

Alasdair MacIntyre (b. 1929) is senior research professor of philosophy at Notre Dame University. He has written many books, including *After Virtue* (1981), *First Principles, Final Ends, and Contemporary Philosophical Issues* (1990), *Dependent Rational Animals* (1999), and *Edith Stein: A Philosophical Prologue* (2005).

Alasdair MacIntyre's perspective on virtue is historical and "particularist." "[We] all approach our own circumstances as bearers of a particular social identity." Each of us "inhabits a role" in our social environment: we are citizens of a country; a son, daughter, parent, aunt, and so forth, in a family. Such roles provide a "moral starting point." What is good for a person also must be good for one who inhabits the particular role. "As such, I inherit from the past of my family, my city, my tribe, my nation, a variety of debts, inheritances, rightful expectations and obligations."

Ideally, each human life is a unity. The meaning and ethical worth of any person's act can be understood only as a part of the life story of that

TRADITION AND THE VIRTUES From *After Virtue* by Alasdair MacIntyre. Second Edition 1984. The University of Notre Dame Press, Notre dame, IN. Copyright 1981, 1984 by Alasdaire McIntyre. Used by permission of the publisher.

person. But a person's history only makes sense in terms of the social and historical contexts that define his or her roles, expectations, and obligations.

Because virtue is best understood in terms of the way one lives one's roles in a narrative, the background of which is richly historical and traditional, the *teaching* of virtue is best accomplished through stories. "Man is ... essentially a story-telling animal," and moral education is realized primarily through narrative means. "Deprive children of stories and you leave them unscripted, anxious stutterers in their actions as in their words."

MacIntyre criticizes most modern approaches to ethics for neglecting history and tradition by attending exclusively to principles that apply universally to all individuals regardless of social role. He warns that the insistence on evaluating all acts and projects in terms of abstract universal principles is dangerous. On the other hand, a virtuous respect for particular traditions is conducive to a decent and balanced life. MacIntyre therefore urges that we should recognize and promote a special virtue: "the virtue of having an adequate sense of the traditions to which one belongs or which confront one."

Any contemporary attempt to envisage each human life as a whole, as a unity, whose character provides the virtues with an adequate *telos* encounters two different kinds of obstacle, one social and one philosophical. The social obstacles derive from the way in which modernity partitions each human life into a variety of segments, each with its own norms and modes of behavior. So work is divided from leisure, private life from public, the corporate from the personal. So both childhood and old age have been wrenched away from the rest of human life and made over into distinct realms. And all these separations have been achieved so that it is the distinctiveness of each and not the unity of the life of the individual who passes through those parts in terms of which we are taught to think and to feel.

The philosophical obstacles derive from two distinct tendencies, one chiefly, though not only, domesticated in analytical philosophy and one at home in both sociological theory and in existentialism. The former is the tendency to think atomistically about human action and to analyze complex actions and transactions in terms of simple components. Hence the recurrence in more than one context of the notion of a "basic action." That particular actions derive their character as parts of larger wholes is a point of view alien to our dominant ways of thinking and yet one which is necessary at least to consider if we are to begin to understand how a life may be more than a sequence of individual actions and episodes.

Equally the unity of a human life becomes invisible to us when a sharp separation is made either between the individual and the roles he or she plays ... or between the different role ... enactments of an individual life so that the life comes to appear as nothing but a series of unconnected episodes—a liquidation of the self....

[T]he liquidation of the self into a set of demarcated areas of role-playing allows no scope for the exercise of dispositions which could genuinely be accounted virtues in any sense remotely Aristotelian. For a virtue is not a disposition that makes for success only in one particular type of situation. What are spoken of as the virtues of a good committee man or of a good administrator or of a gambler or a pool hustler are professional skills professionally deployed in those situations where they can be effective, not virtues. Someone who genuinely possesses a virtue can be expected to manifest it in very different types of situation, many of them situations where the practice of a virtue cannot be expected to be effective in the way that we expect a professional skill to be. Hector exhibited one and the same courage in his parting from Andromache and on the battlefield with Achilles; Eleanor Marx exhibited one and the same compassion in her relationship with her father, in her work with trade unionists and in her entanglement with Aveling. And the unity of a virtue in someone's life is intelligible only as a characteristic of a unitary life, a life that can be conceived and evaluated as a whole. Hence just as in the discussion of the changes in and fragmentation of morality which accompanied the rise of modernity in the earlier parts of this book, each stage in the emergence of the characteristically modern views of the moral judgment was accompanied by a corresponding stage in the emergence of the characteristically modern conceptions of selfhood; so now, in defining the particular pre-modern concept of the virtues with which I have been preoccupied, it has become necessary to say something of the concomitant concept of selfhood, a concept of a self whose unity resides in the unity of a narrative which links birth to life to death as narrative beginning to middle to end.

Such a conception of the self is perhaps less unfamiliar than it may appear at first sight. Just because it has played a key part in the cultures which are historically predecessors of our own, it would not be surprising if it turned out to be still an unacknowledged presence in many of our ways of thinking and acting. Hence it is not inappropriate to begin by scrutinizing some of our most taken-for-granted, but clearly correct, conceptual insights about human actions and selfhood in order to show how natural it is to think of the self in a narrative mode.

It is a conceptual commonplace, both for philosophers and for ordinary agents, that one and the same segment of human behavior may be correctly characterized in a number of different ways. To the question "What is he doing?" the answers may with equal truth and appropriateness be "Digging," "Gardening," "Taking exercise," "Preparing for winter" or "Pleasing his wife." Some of these answers will characterize the agent's intentions, other unintended consequences of his actions, and of these unintended consequences some may be such that the agent is aware of them and others not. What is important to notice immediately is that any answer to the questions of how we are to understand or to explain a given segment of behavior will presuppose some prior answer to the question of how these different correct answers to the question "What is he doing?" are related to each other. For if someone's primary intention is to put the garden in order before the winter and it is only incidentally the case that in so doing he is taking exercise and pleasing his wife, we have one type of behavior to be explained; but if the agent's primary intention is to please his wife by taking exercise, we have quite another type of behavior to be explained and we will have to look in a different direction for understanding and explanation.

In the first place the episode has been situated in an annual cycle of domestic activity, and the behavior embodies an intention which presupposes a particular type of household-cum-garden setting with the peculiar narrative history of that setting in which this segment of behavior now becomes an episode. In the second instance the episode has been situated in the narrative history of a marriage, a very different, even if related, social setting. We cannot, that is to say, characterize behavior independently of intentions, and we cannot characterize intentions independently of the settings which make those intentions intelligible both to agents themselves and to others.

I use the word "setting" here as a relatively inclusive term. A social setting may be an institution, it may be what I have called a practice, or it may be a milieu of some other human kind. But it is central to the notion of a setting as I am going to understand it that a setting has a history, a history within which the histories of individual agents not only are, but have to be, situated, just because without the setting and its changes through time the history of the individual agent and his changes through time will be unintelligible. Of course one and the same piece of behavior may belong to more than one setting. There are at least two different ways in which this may be so. In my earlier example the agent's activity may be part of the history both of the cycle of household activity and of his marriage, two histories which have happened to intersect. The household may have its own history stretching back through hundreds of years, as do the histories of some European farms, where the farm has had a life of its own, even though different families have in different periods inhabited it; and the marriage will certainly have its own history, a history which itself presupposes that a particular point has been reached in the history of the institution of marriage. If we are to relate some particular segment of behavior in any precise way to an agent's intentions and thus to the settings which that agent inhabits, we shall have to understand in a precise way how the variety of correct characterizations of the agent's behavior relate to each other first by identifying which characteristics refer us to an intention and which do not and then by classifying further the items in both categories.

Where intentions are concerned, we need to know which intention or intentions were primary, that is to say, of which it is the case that, had the agent intended otherwise, he would not have performed that action. Thus if we know that a man is gardening with the self-avowed purposes of healthful exercise and of pleasing his wife, we do not yet know how to understand what he is doing until we know the answer to such questions as whether he would continue gardening if he continued to believe that gardening was healthful exercise, but discovered that his gardening no longer pleased his wife, *and* whether he would continue gardening, if he ceased to believe that gardening was healthful exercise, but continued to believe that it pleased his wife, *and* whether he would continue gardening if he changed his beliefs on both points. That is to say, we need to know both what certain of his beliefs are and which of them are causally effective; and, that is to say, we need to know whether certain contrary-to-fact hypothetical statements are true or false. And until we know this, we shall not know how to characterize correctly what the agent is doing....

Consider what the argument so far implies about the interrelationships of the intentional, the social and the historical. We identify a particular action only by invoking two kinds of context, implicitly if not explicitly. We place the agent's intentions, I have suggested, in causal and temporal order with reference to their role in his or her history; and we also place them with reference to their role in the history of the setting or settings to which they belong. In doing this, in determining what causal efficacy the agent's intentions had in one or more directions, and how his short-term intentions succeeded or failed to be constitutive of long-term intentions, we ourselves write a further part of these histories. Narrative history of a certain kind turns out to be the basic and essential genre for the characterization of human action....

At the beginning of this chapter I argued that in successfully identifying and understanding what someone else is doing we always move towards having a particular episode in the context of a set of narrative histories, histories both of the individuals concerned and of the settings in which they act and suffer. It is now becoming clear that we render the actions of others intelligible in this way because action itself has a basically historical character. It is because we all live out narratives in our lives and because we understand our own lives in terms of the narratives that we live out that the form of narrative is appropriate for understanding the actions of others. Stories are lived before they are told—except in the case of fiction....

A central thesis then begins to emerge: man is in his actions and practice, as well as in his fictions, essentially a story-telling animal. He is not essentially, but becomes through his history, a teller of stories that aspire to truth. But the key question for men is not about their own authorship; I can only answer the question "What am I to do?" if I can answer the prior question "Of what story or stories do I find myself a part?" We enter human society, that is, with one or more imputed characters—roles into which we have been drafted—and we have to learn what they are in order to be able to understand how others respond to us and how our responses to them are apt to be construed. It is through hearing stories about wicked stepmothers, lost children, good but misguided kings, wolves that suckle twin boys, youngest sons who receive no inheritance but must make their own way in the world and eldest sons who waste their inheritance on riotous living and go into exile to live with the swine, that children learn or mislearn both what a child and what a parent is, what the cast of characters may be in the drama into which they have been born and what the ways of the world are. Deprive children of stories and you leave them unscripted, anxious stutterers in their actions as in their words. Hence there is no way to give us an understanding of any society, including our own, except through the stock of stories which constitute its initial dramatic resources. Mythology, in its original sense, is at the heart of things. Vico was right and so was Joyce. And so too of course is that moral tradition from heroic society to its medieval heirs according to which the telling of stories has a key part in educating us into the virtues.

To be the subject of a narrative that runs from one's birth to one's death is, I remarked earlier, to be accountable for the actions and experiences which compose a narratable life. It is, that is, to be open to being asked to give a certain kind of account of what one did or what happened to one or what one witnessed at any earlier point in one's life than the time at which the question is posed. Of course someone may have forgotten or suffered brain damage or simply not attended sufficiently at the relevant time to be able to give the relevant account. But to say of someone under some one description ("The prisoner of the Chateau d'If") that he is the same person as someone characterized quite differently ("The Count of Monte Cristo") is precisely to say that it makes sense to ask him to give an intelligible narrative account enabling us to understand how he could at different times and different places be one and the same person and yet be so differently characterized. Thus personal identity is just that identity presupposed by the unity of the character which the unity of a narrative requires. Without such unity there would not be subjects of whom stories could be told.

The other aspect of narrative selfhood is correlative: I am not only accountable, I am one who can always ask others for an account, who can put others to the question. I am part of their story, as they are part of mine. The narrative of any one life is part of an interlocking set of narratives. Moreover this asking for and giving of accounts itself plays an important part in constituting narratives. Asking you what you did and why, saying what I did and why, pondering the differences between your account of what I did and my account of what I did, and *vice versa*, these are essential constituents of all but the very simplest and barest of narratives. Thus without the accountability of the self those trains of events that constitute all but the simplest and barest of narratives could not occur; and without that same accountability narratives would lack that continuity required to make both them and the actions that constitute them intelligible....

It is now possible to return to the question from which this enquiry into the nature of human action and identity started: In what does the unity of an individual life consist? The answer is that its unity is the unity of a narrative embodied in a single life. To ask "What is the good for me?" is to ask how best I might live out that unity and bring it to completion. To ask "What is the good for man?" is to ask what all answers to the former question must have in common. But now it is important to emphasize that it is the systematic asking of these two questions and the attempt to answer them in deed as well as in word which provide the moral life with its unity. The unity of a human life is the unity of a narrative quest. Quests sometimes fail, are frustrated, abandoned or dissipated into distractions; and human lives may in all these ways also fail. But the only criteria for success or failure in a human life as a whole are the criteria of success or failure in a narrated or to-be-narrated quest. A quest for what?

Two key features of the medieval conception of a quest need to be recalled. The first is that without some at least partly determinate conception of the final *telos* there could not be any beginning to a quest. Some conception of the good for man is required. Whence is such a conception to be drawn? Precisely from those questions which led us to attempt to transcend that limited conception of the virtues which is available in and through practices. It is in looking for a conception of *the* good which will enable us to order other goods, for a conception of *the* good which will enable us to extend our understanding of the purpose and content of the virtues, for a conception of *the* good which will enable us to understand the place of integrity and constancy in life, that we initially define the kind of life which is a quest for the good. But secondly it is clear the medieval conception of a quest is not at all that of a search for something already adequately characterized, as miners search for gold or geologists for oil. It is in the course of the quest and only through encountering and coping with the various particular harms, dangers, temptations and distractions which provide any quest with its episodes and incidents that the goal of the quest is finally to be understood. A quest is always an education both as to the character of that which is sought and in self-knowledge.

The virtues therefore are to be understood as those dispositions which will not only sustain practices and enable us to achieve the goods internal to practices, but which will also sustain us in the relevant kind of quest for the good, by enabling us to overcome the harms, dangers, temptations and distractions which we encounter, and which will furnish us with increasing self-knowledge and increasing knowledge of the good. The catalogue of the virtues will therefore include the virtues required to sustain the kind of households and the kind of political communities in which men and women can seek for the good together and the virtues necessary for philosophical enquiry about the character of the good. We have then arrived at a provisional conclusion about the good life for man: the good life for man is the life spent in seeking for the good life for man, and the virtues necessary for the seeking are those which will enable us to understand what more and what else the good life for man is. We have also completed the second stage in our account of the virtues, by situating them in relation to the good life for man and not only in relation to practices. But our enquiry requires a third stage.

For I am never able to seek for the good or exercise the virtues only *qua* individual. This is partly because what it is to live the good life concretely varies from circumstance to circumstance even when it is one and the same conception of the good life and one and the same set of virtues which are being embodied in a human life. What the good life is for a fifth-century Athenian general will not be the same as what it was for a medieval nun or a seventeenth-century farmer. But it is not just that different individuals live in different social circumstances; it is also that we all approach our own circumstances as bearers of a particular social identity. I am someone's son or daughter, someone else's cousin or uncle; I am a citizen of this or that city, a member of this or that guild or profession; I belong to this clan, that tribe, this nation. Hence what is good for me has to be the good for one who inhabits these roles. As such, I inherit from the past of my family, my city, my tribe, my nation, a variety of debts, inheritances, rightful expectations and obligations. These constitute the given of my life, my moral starting point. This is in part what gives my life its own moral particularity.

This thought is likely to appear alien and even surprising from the standpoint of modern individualism. From the standpoint of individualism I am what I myself choose to be. I can always, if I wish to, put in question what are taken to be the merely contingent social features of my existence. I may biologically be my father's son; but I cannot be held responsible for what he did unless I choose implicitly or explicitly to assume such responsibility. I may legally be a citizen of a certain country; but I cannot be held responsible for what my country does or has done unless I choose implicitly or explicitly to assume such responsibility. Such individualism is expressed by those modern Americans who deny any responsibility for the effects of slavery upon black Americans, saying "I never owned any slaves." It is more subtly the standpoint of those other modern Americans who accept a nicely calculated responsibility for such effects measured precisely by the benefits they themselves as individuals have indirectly received from slavery. In both cases "being an American" is not in itself taken to be part of the moral identity of the individual. And of course there is nothing peculiar to modern Americans in this attitude: the Englishman who says, "*I* never did any wrong to Ireland; why bring up that old history as though it had something to do with *me?*" or the young German who believes that being born after 1945 means that what Nazis did to Jews has no moral relevance to his relationship to his Jewish contemporaries, exhibit the same attitude, that according to which the self is detachable from its social and historical roles and statuses. And the self so detached is of course a self very much at home in either Sartre's or Goffman's perspective, a self that can have no history. The contrast with the narrative view of the self is clear. For the story of my life is always embedded in the story of those communities from which I derive my identity. I am born with a past; and to try to cut myself off from that past, in the individualist mode, is to deform my present relationships. The possession of an historical identity and the possession of a social identity coincide. Notice that rebellion against my identity is always one possible mode of expressing it.

Notice also that the fact that the self has to find its moral identity in and through its membership in communities such as those of the family, the neighborhood, the city and the tribe does not entail that the self has to accept the moral *limitations* of the particularity of those forms of community. Without those moral particularities to begin from there would never be anywhere to begin; but it is in moving forward from such particularity that the search for the good, for the universal, consists. Yet particularity can never be simply left behind or obliterated. The notion of escaping from it into a realm of entirely universal maxims which belong to man as such, whether in its eighteenth-century Kantian form or in the presentation of some modern analytical moral philosophies, is an illusion and an illusion with painful consequences. When men and women identify what are in fact their partial and particular causes too easily and too completely with the cause of some universal principle, they usually behave worse than they would otherwise do.

What I am, therefore, is in key part what I inherit, a specific past that is present to some degree in my present. I find myself part of a history and that is generally to say, whether I like it or not, whether I recognize it or not, one of the bearers of a tradition. It was important when I characterized the concept of a practice to notice that practices always have histories and that at any given moment what a practice is depends on a mode of understanding it which has been transmitted often through many generations. And thus; insofar as the virtues sustain the relationships required for practices, they have to sustain relationships to the past—and to the future—as well as in the present. But the traditions through which particular practices are transmitted and reshaped never exist in isolation for larger social traditions. What constitutes such traditions?

We are apt to be misled here by the ideological uses to which the concept of a tradition has been put by conservative political theorists. Characteristically such theorists have followed Burke in contrasting tradition with reason and the stability of tradition with conflict. Both contrasts obfuscate. For all reasoning takes place within the context of some traditional mode of thought, transcending through criticism and invention the limitations of what had hitherto been reasoned in that tradition; this is as true of modern physics as of medieval logic. Moreover when a tradition is in good order it is always partially constituted by an argument about the goods the pursuit of which gives to that tradition its particular point and purpose.

So when an institution—a university, say, or a farm, or a hospital—is the bearer of a tradition of practice or practices, its common life will be partly, but in a centrally important way, constituted by a continuous argument as to what a university is and ought to be or what good farming is or what good medicine is. Traditions, when vital, embody continuities of conflict. Indeed when a tradition becomes Burkean, it is always dying or dead....

A living tradition then is an historically extended, socially embodied argument, and an argument precisely in part about the goods which constitute that tradition. Within a tradition the pursuit of goods extends through generations, sometimes through many generations. Hence the individual's search for his or her good is generally and characteristically conducted within a context defined by those traditions of which the individual's life is a part, and this is true both of those goods which are internal to practices and of the goods of a single life. Once again the narrative phenomenon of embedding is crucial: the history of a practice in our time is generally and characteristically embedded in and made intelligible in terms of the larger and longer history of the tradition through which the practice in its present form was conveyed to us; the history of each of our own lives is generally and characteristically embedded in and made intelligible in terms of the larger and longer histories of a number of traditions. I have to say "generally and characteristically" rather than "always," for traditions decay, disintegrate and disappear. What then sustains and strengthens traditions? What weakens and destroys them?

The answer in key part is: the exercise or the lack of exercise of the relevant virtues. The virtues find their point and purpose not only in sustaining those relationships necessary if the variety of goods internal to practices are to be achieved and not only in sustaining the form of an individual life in which that individual may seek out his or her good as the good of his or her whole life, but also in sustaining those traditions which provide both practices and individual lives with their necessary historical context. Lack of justice, lack of truthfulness, lack of courage, lack of the relevant intellectual virtues—these corrupt traditions, just as they do those institutions and practices which derive their life from the traditions of which they are the contemporary embodiments. To recognize this is of course also to recognize the existence of an additional virtue, one whose importance is perhaps most obvious when it is least present, the virtue of having an adequate sense of the traditions to which one belongs or which confront one....

STUDY QUESTIONS

1. What roles do history and tradition play in MacIntyre's moral philosophy? Choose a specific moral question, and describe how MacIntyre approaches it. Then choose another moral philosopher whom you have studied and illustrate the difference in approach.

2. Discuss and explain: "I can only answer the question 'What am I to do?' if I can answer the prior question 'Of what story or stories do I find myself a part?'"

3. "I am someone's son or daughter ... I belong to this clan, that tribe, this nation. Hence, what is good for me has to be the good for one who inhabits these roles." Do you agree that the virtues are largely determined by social role? Explain.
4. What does MacIntyre find wrong with "modern individualism"? How is individualism at odds with a life of virtue? How does it conflict with tradition? In what ways is individualism morally irresponsible?
5. What does MacIntyre mean by a "living tradition"? How do the virtues sustain traditions?

The Ethics of Virtue

James Rachels

A biographical sketch of James Rachels is found on page 151.

Virtue ethics centers on what kind of person one should be, and its focus is on character traits. Action ethics centers on right and wrong, and its focus is on obligations, rules, and actions. James Rachels surveys virtue-based theories of morality of the kind exemplified by Aristotle, contrasting them with action- or duty-based theories, of the kind exemplified by Mill or Kant. He considers the suggestion that moral philosophers should return to an exclusively virtue-based approach. After examining that proposal in some detail, he rejects it. According to Rachels, a purely virtue-based morality must always be incomplete, since it could not by itself explain why certain character traits are morally good. Unless lying were against the rules, a trait like honesty would not *be* a virtue, but showing that lying is wrong is beyond the compass of virtue ethics. Rachels concludes that a combined approach, incorporating both virtue and duty ethics, is needed for an adequate moral philosophy.

The concepts of obligation, and duty—moral obligation and moral duty, that is to say—and of what is morally right and wrong, and of the moral sense of "ought," ought to be jettisoned.... It would be a great improvement if, instead of "morally wrong," one always named a genus such as "untruthful," "unchaste," "unjust."

G. E. M. Anscombe
Modern Moral Philosophy (1958)

The Ethics of Virtue and the Ethics of Right Action

In thinking about any subject it makes a great deal of difference what questions we begin with. In Aristotle's *Nicomachean Ethics* (ca. 325 B.C.), the central questions are about *character*. Aristotle begins by asking "What is the good of man?" and his answer is that "The good of man is an activity of the soul in conformity with virtue." To understand ethics, therefore, we must understand what makes someone a virtuous person, and Aristotle, with a keen eye for the details, devotes much space to discussing such particular virtues as courage, self-control, generosity, and truthfulness. The good man is the man of virtuous character, he says, and so the virtues are taken to be the subject-matter of ethics.

Although this way of thinking is closely identified with Aristotle, it was not unique to him—it was also the approach taken by Socrates, Plato, and a host of other ancient thinkers. They all approached the subject by asking: *What traits of character make one a good person?* and as a result "the virtues" occupied center stage in all of their discussions.

As time passed, however, this way of thinking about ethics came to be neglected. With the coming of Christianity a new set of ideas was introduced. The Christians, like the Jews, were monotheists who viewed God as a lawgiver, and for them righteous living meant obedience to the divine commandments. The Greeks had viewed reason as the source of practical wisdom—the virtuous life was, for them, inseparable from the life of reason. But St. Augustine, the fourth-century Christian thinker who was to be enormously influential, distrusted reason and taught that moral goodness depends on subordinating oneself to the will of God. Therefore, when the medieval philosophers discussed the virtues, it was in the context of Divine Law. The "theological virtues"—faith, hope, charity, and, of course, *obedience*—came to have a central place.

After the Renaissance, moral philosophy began to be secularized once again, but philosophers did not return to the Greek way of thinking. Instead, the Divine Law was replaced by its secular equivalent, something called the *Moral Law*. The Moral Law, which was said to spring from human reason rather than divine fiat, was conceived to be a system of rules specifying which actions are right. Our duty as moral agents, it was said, is to follow its directives. Thus modern moral philosophers approached their subject by asking a fundamentally different question than the one that had been asked by the ancients. Instead of asking: *What traits of character make one a good person?* they began by asking: *What is the right thing to do?* This led them in a different direction. They went on to develop theories, not of virtue, but of rightness and obligation:

- Each person ought to do whatever will best promote his or her own interests. (Ethical Egoism)
- We ought to do whatever will promote the greatest happiness for the greatest number. (Utilitarianism)
- Our duty is to follow rules that we could consistently will to be universal laws—that is, rules that we would be willing to have followed by all people in all circumstances. (Kant's theory)
- The right thing to do is to follow the rules that rational, self-interested people can agree to establish for their mutual benefit. (The Social Contract Theory)

And these are the familiar theories that have dominated modern moral philosophy from the seventeenth century on.

Should We Return to the Ethics of Virtue?

Recently a number of philosophers have advanced a radical idea: they have suggested that modern moral philosophy is bankrupt and that, in order to salvage the subject, we should return to Aristotle's way of thinking....

This idea was first put forth in 1958 when the distinguished British philosopher G. E. M. Anscombe published an article called "Modern Moral Philosophy" in the academic journal *Philosophy*. In that article she suggested that modern moral philosophy is misguided because it rests on the incoherent notion of a "law" without a lawgiver. The very concepts of obligation, duty, and rightness, on which modern moral philosophers have concentrated their attention, are inextricably linked to this nonsensical idea. Therefore, she concluded, we should stop thinking about obligation, duty, and rightness. We should abandon the whole project that modern philosophers have pursued and return instead to Aristotle's approach. This means that the concept of virtue should once again take center stage.

In the wake of Anscombe's article a flood of books and essays appeared discussing the virtues, and "virtue theory" soon became a major option in contemporary moral philosophy. There is, however, no settled body of doctrine on which all these philosophers agree. Compared to such theories as Utilitarianism, virtue theory is still in a relatively undeveloped state. Yet the virtue theorists are united in believing that modern moral philosophy has been on the wrong track and that a radical reorientation of the subject is needed.

In what follows we shall first take a look at what the theory of virtue is like. Then we shall consider some of the reasons that have been given for thinking that the ethics of virtue is superior to other, more modern ways of approaching the subject. And at the end we will consider whether a "return to the ethics of virtue" is really a viable option.

The Virtues

A theory of virtue should have several components. First, there should be an explanation of what a virtue *is*. Second, there should be a list specifying which character traits are virtues. Third, there should be an explanation of what these virtues consist in. Fourth, there should be an explanation of why these qualities are good ones for a person to have. Finally, the theory should tell us whether the virtues are the same for all people or whether they differ from person to person or from culture to culture.

What Is Virtue?

The first question that must be asked is: *What is a virtue?* Aristotle suggested one possible answer. He said that a virtue is a trait of character that is manifested in habitual actions. The virtue of honesty is not possessed by someone who tells the truth only occasionally or whenever it is to his own advantage. The honest person is truthful as a matter of principle; his actions "spring from a firm and unchangeable character."

This is a start, but it is not enough. It does not distinguish virtues from vices, for vices are also traits of character manifested in habitual action. Edmund L. Pincoffs, a philosopher at the University of Texas, has made a suggestion that takes care of this problem. Pincoffs suggests that virtues and vices are qualities that we refer to in deciding whether someone is to be sought or avoided. "Some sorts of persons we prefer; others we avoid," he says. "The properties on our list [of virtues and vices] can serve as reasons for preference or avoidance."

We seek out people for different purposes, and this makes a difference to the virtues that are relevant. In looking for an auto mechanic, we want someone who is skillful, honest, and conscientious; in looking for a teacher, we want someone who is knowledgeable, articulate, and patient. Thus the virtues associated with auto repair are different from the virtues associated with teaching. But we also assess people *as people*, in a more general way: and so we have the concept, not just of a good mechanic or a good teacher, but of a good person. The moral virtues are the virtues of persons as such.

Taking our cue from Pincoffs, then, we may define a virtue as *a trait of character, manifested in habitual action, that it is good for a person to have.*

What Are the Virtues?

What, then, *are* the virtues? Which traits of character should be fostered in human beings? There is no short answer, but the following is a partial list:

benevolence	fairness	reasonableness
civility	friendliness	self-confidence
compassion	generosity	self-control
conscientiousness	honesty	self-discipline
cooperativeness	industriousness	self-reliance
courage	justice	tactfulness
courteousness	loyalty	thoughtfulness
dependability	moderation	tolerance

The list could be expanded, of course, with other traits added. But this is a reasonable start.

What Do These Virtues Consist In?

It is one thing to say, in a general way, that we should be conscientious and compassionate; it is another thing to try to say exactly what these character traits consist in. Each of the virtues has its own distinctive features and raises its own distinctive problems. There isn't enough space here to consider all the items on our list, but we may examine four of them briefly.

1. *Courage.* According to Aristotle, virtues are means poised between extremes; a virtue is "the mean by reference to two vices: the one of excess and the other of deficiency." Courage is a mean between the extremes of cowardice and foolhardiness—it is cowardly to run away from all danger; yet it is foolhardy to risk too much.

Courage is sometimes said to be a military virtue because it is so obviously needed to accomplish the soldier's task. Soldiers do battle; battles are fraught with danger; and so without courage the battle will be lost. But soldiers are not the only ones who need courage. Courage is needed by anyone who faces danger—and at different times this includes all of us. A scholar who spends his timid and safe life studying medieval literature might seem the very opposite of a soldier. Yet even he might become ill and need courage to face a dangerous operation. As Peter Geach (a contemporary British philosopher) puts it:

> Courage is what we all need in the end, and it is constantly needed in the ordinary course of life: by women who are with child, by all of us because our bodies are vulnerable, by coalminers and fishermen and steel-workers and lorry-drivers.

So long as we consider only "the ordinary course of life," the nature of courage seems unproblematic. But unusual circumstances present more troublesome types of cases. Consider a Nazi soldier, for example, who fights valiantly—he faces great risk without flinching—but he does so in an evil cause. Is he courageous? Geach holds that, contrary to appearances, the Nazi soldier does not really possess the virtue of courage at all. "Courage in an unworthy cause," he says, "is no virtue; still less is courage in an evil cause. Indeed I prefer not to call this non-virtuous facing of danger 'courage.'"

It is easy to see Geach's point. Calling the Nazi soldier "courageous" seems to praise his performance, and we should not want to praise it. Instead we would rather he behaved differently. Yet neither does it seem quite right to say that he is *not* courageous—after all, look at how he behaves in the face of danger. To get around this problem perhaps we should just say that he displays *two* qualities of character, one that is admirable (steadfastness in facing danger) and one that is not (a willingness to defend a despicable regime). He is courageous all right, and courage is an admirable thing; but because his courage is deployed in an evil cause, his behavior is *on the whole* wicked.

2. *Generosity.* Generosity is the willingness to expend one's resources to help others. Aristotle says that, like courage, it is also a mean between extremes: it stands somewhere between stinginess and extravagance. The stingy person gives too little, the extravagant person gives too much. But how much is enough?

The answer will depend to some extent on what general ethical view we accept. Jesus, another important ancient teacher, said that we must give all we have to help the poor. The possession of riches, while the poor starve, was in his view unacceptable. This was regarded by those who heard him as a hard teaching and it was generally rejected. It is still rejected by most people today, even by those who consider themselves to be his followers.

The modern utilitarians are, in this regard at least, Jesus' moral descendants. They hold that in every circumstance it is one's duty to do whatever will have the best overall consequences for everyone concerned. This means that we should be generous with our money until the point has been reached at which further giving would be more harmful to us than it would be helpful to others.

Why do people resist this idea? Partly it may be a matter of selfishness; we do not want to make ourselves poor by giving away what we have. But there is also the problem that adopting such a policy would prevent us from living normal lives.

Not only money but time is involved. Our lives consist in projects and relationships that require a considerable investment of both. An ideal of "generosity" that demands spending our money and time as Jesus and the utilitarians recommend would require that we abandon our everyday lives and live very differently.

A reasonable interpretation of the demands of generosity might, therefore, be something like this: we should be as generous with our resources as is consistent with conducting our ordinary lives in a minimally satisfying way. Even this, though, will leave us with some awkward questions. Some people's "ordinary lives" are quite extravagant—think of a rich person whose everyday life includes luxuries without which he would feel deprived. The virtue of generosity, it would seem, cannot exist in the context of a life that is too sumptuous, especially when there are others about whose basic needs are unmet. To make this a "reasonable" interpretation of the demands of generosity, we need a conception of ordinary life that is itself not too extravagant.

3. *Honesty.* The honest person is, first of all, someone who does not lie. But is that enough? There are other ways of misleading people than by lying. Geach tells the story of St. Athanasius, who "was rowing on a river when the persecutors came rowing in the opposite direction: 'Where is the traitor Athanasius?' 'Not far away,' the Saint gaily replied, and rowed past them unsuspected."

Geach approves of Athanasius's deception even though he thinks it would have been wrong to tell an outright lie. Lying, Geach thinks, is always forbidden: a person possessing the virtue of honesty will not even consider it. Indeed, on his view that is what the virtues are: they are dispositions of character that simply *rule out* actions that are incompatible with them. Honest people will not lie, and so they will have to find other ways to deal with difficult situations. Athanasius was clever enough to do so. He told the truth, even if it was a deceptive truth.

Of course, it is hard to see why Athanasius's deception was not also dishonest. What nonarbitrary principle would approve of misleading people by one means but not by another? But whatever we think about this, the larger question is whether virtue requires adherence to absolute rules. Concerning honesty, we may distinguish two views of the matter:

1. That an honest person will never lie

and

2. That an honest person will never lie except in rare circumstances when there are compelling reasons why it must be done.

There is no obvious reason why the first view must be accepted. On the contrary, there is reason to favor the second. To see why, we need only to consider why lying is a bad thing in the first place. The explanation might go like this:

Our ability to live together in communities depends on our capacities of communication. We talk to one another, read one another's writing, exchange information and opinions, express our desires to one another, make promises, ask and answer questions, and much more. Without these sorts of interchanges, social living would be impossible. But in order for these interchanges to be successful, we must be able to assume that there are certain rules in force: we must be able to rely on one another to speak honestly.

Moreover, when we accept someone's word we make ourselves vulnerable to harm in a special way. By accepting what they say and modifying our beliefs accordingly, we place our welfare in their hands. If they speak truthfully, all is well. But if they lie, we end up with false beliefs; and if we act on those beliefs, we end up doing foolish things. It is *their fault*: we trusted them, and they let us down. This explains why being given the lie is distinctively offensive. It is at bottom a violation of trust. (It also explains, incidentally, why lies and "deceptive truths" may seem morally indistinguishable. Both may violate trust in the same fashion.)

None of this, however, implies that honesty is the *only* important value or that we have an obligation to deal honestly with *everyone* who comes along, regardless of who they are and what they are up to. Self-preservation is also an important matter, especially protecting ourselves from those who would harm us unjustly. When this comes into conflict with the rule against lying it is not unreasonable to think it takes priority. Suppose St. Athanasius had told the persecutors "I don't know him," and as a result they went off on a wild goose chase. Later, could they sensibly complain that he had violated their trust? Wouldn't they have forfeited any right they might have had to the truth from him when they set out unjustly to persecute him?

4. *Loyalty to family and friends.* At the beginning of Plato's dialogue *Euthyphro* Socrates learns that Euthyphro, whom he has encountered near the entrance to the court, has come there to prosecute his father for murder. Socrates expresses surprise at this and wonders whether it is proper for a son to bring charges against his father. Euthyphro sees no impropriety, however: for him, a murder is a murder. Unfortunately, the question is left unresolved as their discussion moves on to other matters.

The idea that there is something morally special about family and friends is, of course, familiar. We do not treat our family and friends as we would treat strangers. We are bound to them by love and affection and we do things for them that we would not do for just anybody. But this is not merely a matter of our being nicer to people we like. The nature of our relationships with family and friends is different from our relationships with other people, and part of the difference is that our *duties and responsibilities* are different. This seems to be an integral part of what friendship is. How could I be your friend and yet have no duty to treat you with special consideration?

If we needed proof that humans are essentially social creatures, the existence of friendship would supply all we could want. As Aristotle said, "No one would choose to live without friends, even if he had all other goods":

> How could prosperity be safeguarded and preserved without friends? The greater it is the greater are the risks it brings with it. Also, in poverty and all other kinds of misfortune men believe that their only refuge consists in their friends. Friends help young men avoid error; to older people they give the care and help needed to supplement the failing powers of action which infirmity brings.

Friends give help, to be sure, but the benefits of friendship go far beyond material assistance. Psychologically, we would be lost without friends. Our triumphs seem hollow unless we have friends to share them with, and our failures are made bearable by their understanding. Even our self-esteem depends in large measure on the assurances of friends: by returning our affection, they confirm our worthiness as human beings.

If we need friends, we need no less the qualities of character that enable us to *be* a friend. Near the top of the list is loyalty. Friends can be counted on. They stick by one another even when the going is hard, and even when, objectively speaking, the friend might deserve to be abandoned. They make allowances for one another; they forgive offenses and they refrain from harsh judgments. There are limits, of course: sometimes a friend will be the only one who can tell us hard truths about ourselves. But criticism is acceptable from friends because we know that, even if they scold us privately, they will not embarrass us in front of others.

None of this is to say that we do not have duties to other people, even to strangers. But they are different duties, associated with different virtues. Generalized beneficence is a virtue, and it may demand a great deal, but it does not require for strangers the same level of concern that we have for friends. Justice is another such virtue; it requires impartial treatment for all. But because friends are loyal, the demands of justice apply less certainly between them.

That is why Socrates is surprised to learn that Euthyphro is prosecuting his father. The relationship that we have with members of our family may be even closer than that of friendship; and so, as much as we might admire his passion for justice, we still may be startled that Euthyphro could take the same attitude toward his father that he would take toward someone else who had committed the same crime. It seems inconsistent with the proper regard of a son. The point is still recognized by the law today. In the United States, as well as in some other countries, a wife cannot be compelled to testify in court against her husband, and vice versa.

Why Are the Virtues Important?

We said that virtues are traits of character that are good for people to have. This only raises the further question of *why* the virtues are desirable. Why is it a good thing for a person to be courageous, generous, honest, or loyal? The answer, of course, may vary depending on the particular virtue in question. Thus:

- Courage is a good thing because life is full of dangers and without courage we would be unable to cope with them.
- Generosity is desirable because some people will inevitably be worse off than others and they will need help.
- Honesty is needed because without it relations between people would go wrong in myriad ways.
- Loyalty is essential to friendship—friends stick by one another, even when they are tempted to turn away.

Looking at this list suggests that each virtue is valuable for a different reason. However, Aristotle believed it is possible to give a more general answer to our question: he thought that the virtuous person will fare better in life. The point is not that the virtuous will be richer—that is obviously not so, or at least it is not always so. The point is that the virtues are needed to conduct our lives well.

To see what Aristotle is getting at, consider the kinds of creatures we are and the kinds of lives we lead. On the most general level, we are rational and social beings who both want and need the company of other people. So we live in communities among friends, family, and fellow citizens. In this setting, such qualities as loyalty, fairness, and honesty are needed for interacting with all those other people successfully. (Imagine the difficulties that would be experienced by someone who habitually manifested the opposite qualities in his or her social life.) On a more individual level, our separate lives might include working at a particular kind of job and having particular sorts of interests. Other virtues may be necessary for successfully doing that job or pursuing those interests—perseverance and industriousness might be important. Again, it is part of our common human condition that we must sometimes face danger or temptation; and so courage and self-control are needed. The upshot is that, despite their differences, the virtues all have the same general sort of value: they are all qualities needed for successful human living....

Societies provide systems of values, institutions, and ways of life within which individual lives are fashioned. The traits of character that are needed to occupy these roles will differ, and so the traits needed to live successfully will differ. Thus the virtues will be different. In light of all this, why shouldn't we just say that which qualities are virtues will depend on the ways of life that are created and sustained by particular societies?

To this it may be countered that *there are some virtues that will be needed by all people in all times.* This was Aristotle's view, and he was probably right. Aristotle believed that we all have a great deal in common, despite our differences. "One may observe," he said, "in one's travels to distant countries the feelings of recognition and affiliation that link every human being to every other human being." Even in the most disparate societies, people face the same basic problems and have the same basic needs. Thus:

- Everyone needs courage, because no one (not even the scholar) is so safe that danger may not sometimes arise.
- In every society there will be property to be managed, and decisions to be made about who gets what, and in every society there will be some people who are worse off than others; so generosity is always to be prized.
- Honesty in speech is always a virtue because no society can exist without communication among its members.
- Everyone needs friends, and to have friends one must be a friend; so everyone needs loyalty.

This sort of list could—and in Aristotle's hands it does—go on and on.

To summarize, then, it may be true that in different societies the virtues are given somewhat different interpretations, and different sorts of actions are counted as satisfying them; and it may be true that some people, because they lead particular sorts of lives in particular sorts of circumstances, will have occasion to need some virtues more than others. But it cannot be right to say simply that whether any particular character trait is a virtue is never anything more than a matter of social convention. The major virtues are mandated not by social convention but by basic facts about our common human condition.

Some Advantages of Virtue Ethics

As we noted above, some philosophers believe that an emphasis on the virtues is superior to other ways of thinking about ethics. Why? A number of reasons have been suggested. Here are three of them.

1. *Moral motivation*. First, virtue ethics is appealing because it provides a natural and attractive account of moral motivation. The other theories seem deficient on this score. Consider the following example.

You are in the hospital recovering from a long illness. You are bored and restless, and so you are delighted when Smith arrives to visit. You have a good time chatting with him; his visit is just the tonic you needed. After a while you tell Smith how much you appreciate his coming: he really is a fine fellow and a good friend to take the trouble to come all the way across town to see you. But Smith demurs; he protests that he is merely doing his duty. At first you think Smith is only being modest, but the more you talk, the clearer it becomes that he is speaking the literal truth. He is not visiting you because he wants to, or because he likes you, but only because he thinks it is his duty to "do the right thing," and on this occasion he has decided it is his duty to visit you—perhaps because he knows of no one else who is more in need of cheering up or no one easier to get to.

This example was suggested by Michael Stocker in an influential article that appeared in the *Journal of Philosophy* in 1976. Stocker comments that surely you would be very disappointed to learn Smith's motive; now his visit seems cold and calculating and it loses all value to you. You thought he was your friend, but now you learn otherwise. Stocker says about Smith's behavior: "Surely there is something lacking here—and lacking in moral merit or value."

Of course, there is nothing wrong with what Smith *did*. The problem is his *motive*. We value friendship, love, and respect; and we want our relationships with people to be based on mutual regard. Acting from an abstract sense of duty, or from a desire to "do the right thing," is not the same. We would not want to live in a community of people who acted only from such motives, nor would we want to *be* such a person. Therefore, the argument goes, theories of ethics that emphasize only right action will never provide a completely satisfactory account of the moral life. For that, we need a theory that emphasizes personal qualities such as friendship, love, and loyalty—in other words, a theory of the virtues.

2. *Doubts about the "ideal" of impartiality*. A dominant theme of modern moral philosophy has been impartiality—the idea that all persons are morally equal, and that in deciding what to do we should treat everyone's interests as equally important. (Of the four theories of "right action" listed above, only Ethical Egoism, a theory with few adherents, denies this.) John Stuart Mill put the point well when he wrote that "Utilitarianism requires [the moral agent] to be as strictly impartial as a benevolent and disinterested spectator." The book you are now reading also treats impartiality as a fundamental moral requirement: in the first chapter impartiality was included as a part of the "minimum conception" of morality.

It may be doubted, though, whether impartiality is really such an important feature of the moral life. Consider one's relationships with family and friends. Are we really impartial where their interests are concerned? And should we be? A mother loves her children and cares for them in a way that she does not care for other children. She is partial to them through and through. But is there anything wrong with that? Isn't it exactly the way a mother *should* be? Again, we love our friends and we are willing to do things for them that we would not do for just any-one. Is there anything wrong with *that?* On the contrary, it seems that the love of family and friends is an inescapable feature of the morally good life. Any theory that emphasizes impartiality will have a difficult time accounting for this.

A moral theory that emphasizes the virtues, however, can account for all this very comfortably. Some virtues are partial and some are not. Love and friendship involve partiality toward loved ones and friends; beneficence toward people in gen-eral is also a virtue, but it is a virtue of a different kind. What is needed, on this view, is not some general requirement of impartiality, but an understanding of the nature of these different virtues and how they relate to one another.

3. *Virtue ethics and feminism.* Finally, we may notice a connection between the ethics of virtue and some concerns voiced by feminist thinkers. Feminists have ar-gued that modern moral philosophy incorporates a subtle male bias. It isn't just that the most renowned philosophers have all been men, or that many of them have been guilty of sexist prejudice in what they have said about women. The bias is more systematic, deeper, and more interesting than that.

To see the bias, we need first to notice that social life has traditionally been di-vided into public and private realms, with men in charge of public affairs and women assigned responsibility for life's more personal and private dimensions. Men have dominated political and economic life, while women have been consigned to home and hearth. *Why* there has been this division would, in a different context, be a matter of some interest. Perhaps it is due to some inherent difference between men and women that suits them for the different roles. Or it may be merely a mat-ter of social custom. But for present purposes, the cause of this arrangement need not concern us. It is enough to note that it has existed for a long time.

The public and private realms each have their own distinctive concerns. In pol-itics and business, one's relations with other people are frequently impersonal and contractual. Often the relationship is adversarial—they have interests that conflict with our own. So we negotiate; we bargain and make deals. Moreover, in public life our decisions may affect large numbers of people whom we do not even know. So we may try to calculate, in an impersonal way, which decisions will have the best overall outcome for the most people.

In the world of home and hearth, however, things are different. It is a smaller-scale environment. In it, we are dealing mainly with family and friends, with whom our relationships are more personal and intimate. Bargaining and calculating play a much smaller role. Relations of love and caring are paramount.

Now with this in mind, think again about the theories of "right action" that have dominated modern moral philosophy—theories produced by male philoso-phers whose sensibilities were shaped by their own distinctive sorts of experience. The influence of that experience is plain. Their theories emphasize impersonal duty, contracts, the harmonization of competing interests, and the calculation of costs and benefits. The concerns that accompany private life—the realm in which women traditionally dominate—are almost wholly absent. The theory of virtue may be seen as a corrective to this imbalance. It can make a place for the virtues of private life as well as the rather different virtues that are required by public life.

It is no accident that feminist philosophers are among those who are now most actively promoting the idea of a return to the ethics of virtue.

The Incompleteness of Virtue Ethics

The preceding arguments make an impressive case for two general points: first, that an adequate philosophical theory of ethics must provide an understanding of moral character; and second, that modern moral philosophers have failed to do this. Not only have they neglected the topic; what is more, their neglect has led them some-times to embrace doctrines that *distort* the nature of moral character. Suppose we accept these conclusions. Where do we go from here?

One way of proceeding would be to develop a theory that combines the best features of the right action approach with insights drawn from the virtues approach—we might try to improve utilitarianism, Kantianism, and the like by adding to them a better account of moral character. Our total theory would then include an account of the virtues, but that account would be offered only as a sup-plement to a theory of right action. This sounds sensible, and if such a project could be carried out successfully, there would obviously be much to be said in its favor.

Some virtue theorists, however, have suggested that we should proceed differently They have argued that the ethics of virtue should be considered as an *alternative* to the other sorts of theories—as an independent theory of ethics that is complete in itself. We might call this "radical virtue ethics." Is this a viable view?

Virtue and Conduct

As we have seen, theories that emphasize right action seem incomplete because they neglect the question of character. Virtue theory remedies this problem by making the question of character its central concern. But as a result, virtue theory runs the risk of being incomplete in the opposite way. Moral problems are frequently pro-blems about what we should *do*. It is not obvious how, according to virtue theory, we should we go about deciding what to do. What can this approach tell us about the assessment, not of character, but of action?

The answer will depend on the spirit in which virtue theory is offered. If a the-ory of the virtues is offered only as a supplement to a theory of right action, then when the assessment of action is at issue the resources of the total theory will be brought into play and some version of utilitarian or Kantian policies (for example) will be recommended. On the other hand, if the theory of virtue is offered as an independent theory intended to be complete in itself, more drastic steps must be taken. Either the theory will have to jettison the notion of "right action" altogether or it will have to give some account of the notion derived from the conception of virtuous character.

Although it sounds at first like a crazy idea, some philosophers have in fact argued that we should simply get rid of such concepts as "morally right action." Anscombe says that "it would be a great improvement" if we stopped using such notions altogether. We could still assess conduct as better or worse, she says, but we would do so in other terms. Instead of saying that an action was "morally wrong" we would simply say that it was "untruthful" or "unjust"—terms derived from the vocabulary of virtue. On her view, we need not say anything more than this to explain why an action is to be rejected.

But it is not really necessary for radical virtue theorists to jettison such notions as "morally right." Such notions can be retained but given a new interpretation within the virtue framework. This might be done as follows. First, it could be said that actions are to be assessed as right or wrong in the familiar way, by reference to the reasons that can be given for or against them: we ought to do those actions that have the best reasons in their favor. However, *the reasons cited will all be reasons that are connected with the virtues*—the reasons in favor of doing an act will be that it is honest, or generous, or fair, and the like; while the reasons against doing it will be that it is dishonest, or stingy, or unfair, and the like. This analysis could be summed up by saying that our duty is to act virtuously—the "right thing to do," in other words, is whatever a virtuous person would do.

The Problem of Incompleteness

We have now sketched the radical virtue theorist's way of understanding what we ought to do. Is that understanding sufficient? The principal problem for the theory is the problem of incompleteness.

First, consider what it would mean in the case of a typical virtue—the virtue of honesty. Suppose a person is tempted to lie, perhaps because lying offers some advantage in a particular situation. The reason he or she should not lie, according to the radical virtue ethics approach, is simply because doing so would be dishonest. This sounds reasonable enough. But what does it mean to be honest? Isn't an honest person simply one who follows such rules as "Do not lie"? It is hard to see what honesty consists in if it is not the disposition to follow such rules.

But we cannot avoid asking *why* such rules are important. Why shouldn't a person lie, especially when there is some advantage to be gained from it? Plainly we need an answer that goes beyond the simple observation that doing so would be incompatible with having a particular character trait; we need an explanation of why it is better to have this trait than its opposite. Possible answers might be that a policy of truth-telling is on the whole to one's own advantage; or that it promotes the general welfare; or that it is needed by people who must live together relying on one another. The first explanation looks suspiciously like Ethical Egoism; the second is utilitarian; and the third recalls contractarian ways of thinking. In any case, giving any explanation at all seems to take us beyond the limits of unsupplemented virtue theory.

Second, it is difficult to see how unsupplemented virtue theory could handle cases of moral *conflict*. Suppose you must choose between A and B, when it would be dishonest but kind to do A, and honest but unkind to do B. (An example might be telling the truth in circumstances that would be hurtful to someone.) Honesty and kindness are both virtues, and so there are reasons both for and against each alternative. But you must do one or the other—you must either tell the truth, and be unkind, or not tell the truth, and be dishonest. So which should you do? The admonition to act virtuously does not, by itself, offer much help. It only leaves you wondering which virtue takes precedence. It seems that we need some more general guidance, beyond that which radical virtue theory can offer, to resolve such conflicts.

Is There a Virtue That Matches Every Morally Good Reason for Doing Something?

The problem of incompleteness points toward a more general theoretical difficulty for the radical virtue ethics approach. As we have seen, according to this approach the reasons for or against doing an action must always be associated with one or more virtues. Thus radical virtue ethics is committed to the idea that *for any good reason that may be given in favor of doing an action, there is a corresponding virtue that consists in the disposition to accept and act on that reason.* But this does not appear to be true.

Suppose, for example, that you are a legislator and you must decide how to allocate funds for medical research—there isn't enough money for everything, and you must decide whether to invest resources in AIDS research or in some other worthy project. And suppose you decide it is best in these circumstances to do what will benefit the most people. Is there a virtue that matches the disposition to do this? If there is, perhaps it should be called "acting like a utilitarian." Or, to return to our example of moral conflicts—is there a virtue connected with every principle that can be invoked to resolve conflicts between the other virtues? If there is, perhaps it is the "virtue" of wisdom—which is to say, the ability to figure out and do what is on the whole best. But this gives away the game. If we posit such "virtues" only to make all moral decision making fit into the preferred framework, we will have saved radical virtue ethics, but at the cost of abandoning its central idea.

Conclusion

For these reasons, it seems best to regard the theory of virtue as part of an overall theory of ethics rather than as a complete theory in itself. The total theory would include an account of all the considerations that figure in practical decision making, together with their underlying rationale. The question, then, will be whether such a total view can accommodate *both* an adequate conception of right action *and* a related conception of virtuous character in a way that does justice to both.

I can see no reason why this is not possible. Our overall theory might begin by taking human welfare—or the welfare of all sentient creatures, for that matter—as the surpassingly important value. We might say that, from a moral point of view, we should want a society in which all people can lead happy and satisfying lives. We could then go on to consider both the question of what sorts of actions and social policies would contribute to this goal *and* the question of what qualities of character are needed to create and sustain individual lives. An inquiry into the nature of virtue could profitably be conducted from within the perspective that such a larger view would provide. Each could illuminate the other; and if each part of the overall theory has to be adjusted a bit here and there to accommodate the other, so much the better for truth.

Study Questions

1. Rachels gives a partial list of virtues. Add several others to his list, and justify your additions.
2. Why does Rachels think it is incorrect to say that all virtues depend on ways of life that are created and sustained by particular societies? Contrast Rachels's view with that of Alasdair MacIntyre, who holds that the virtues are best understood in terms of the particular traditions that inform our lives.
3. Do you agree with Peter Geach that no one possessing the virtue of honesty would even consider lying? Why does Geach think that? Why do you think Rachels rejects this view?
4. Why is generosity a virtue? How do we justify being more generous to our friends and relations than to strangers who may be more needy than those close to us?
5. Why does Aristotle think that the virtues are important? What does Rachels mean when he says that the major virtues are mandated by the fact of our common human condition?
6. What, according to Rachels, are the advantages of virtue ethics? Where do virtue ethics fall short?
7. Rachels conceives of a "complete" moral theory that would combine virtue ethics with an ethics of right action. Explain.

Of Justice and Beneficence

Adam Smith

Adam Smith (1723–1790) was a Scottish moral philosopher educated at Glasgow and Oxford. He is most famous as the author of *The Wealth of Nations* (1776) and *The Theory of Moral Sentiments* (1759), from which the following excerpt is taken.

Adam Smith was among a group of moral philosophers who paid a great deal of attention to the moral feelings, or "sentiments," that are associated with specific virtues. Smith focuses on the two major virtues of beneficence and justice. The desire to be helpful to others, our approval of those who are unselfish and cooperative, the general craving for such approval, and the common disapproval of those who fail to act sympathetically—such sentiments and feelings motivate us to be generous and benevolent. Our efforts to be just and to refrain from interfering with the liberties of our neighbors are motivated by other feelings; mainly we seek to avoid the indignation and sanctions that society imposes on those of us who hurt, harm, or otherwise intrude on the rightful property or activities of others.

OF JUSTICE AND BENEFICENCE From *The Theory of Moral Sentiments* (1759).

Injustice is punishable; nonbenevolence is not. Justice is enforceable and, in that sense, is not a matter of our free will; benevolence is freely bestowed and voluntary. Unlike injustice, the lack of benevolence is merely blamable. Unlike benevolence, which is voluntary and so praiseworthy, justice that is not optional (in the sense that we have no right to act unjustly) is not especially praiseworthy.

Smith discusses those who never show the slightest sympathy for others but manage nevertheless to stay within the formal bounds of justice by not doing active harm. He contends that, apart from subjecting them to social disapproval, it would not be just for us to interfere with their freedom to be selfish and unhelpful. On the other hand, the benevolent persons who hope for rewards have no actual right to them. They will, however, be approved of and liked, and even when that does not happen, they will be rewarded by the feeling that they have rendered themselves worthy of the favorable regard of others.

Section II

Of Justice and Beneficence

Chap. I
Comparison of those two virtues

1. Actions of a beneficent tendency, which proceed from proper motives, seem alone to require reward; because such alone are the approved objects of gratitude, or excite the sympathetic gratitude of the spectator.

2. Actions of a hurtful tendency, which proceed from improper motives, seem alone to deserve punishment; because such alone are the approved objects of resentment, or excite the sympathetic resentment of the spectator.

3. Beneficence is always free, it cannot be extorted by force, the mere want of it exposes to no punishment; because the mere want of beneficence tends to do no real positive evil. It may disappoint of the good which might reasonably have been expected, and upon that account it may justly excite dislike and disapprobation: it cannot, however, provoke any resentment which mankind will go along with. The man who does not recompense his benefactor, when he has it in his power, and when his benefactor needs his assistance, is, no doubt, guilty of the blackest ingratitude. The heart of every impartial spectator rejects all fellow-feeling with the selfishness of his motives, and he is the proper object of the highest disapprobation. But still he does no positive hurt to any body. He only does not do that good which in propriety he ought to have done. He is the object of hatred, a passion which is naturally excited by impropriety of sentiment and behaviour; not of resentment....

5. There is, however, another virtue, of which the observance is not left to the freedom of our own wills, which may be extorted by force, and of which the violation exposes to resentment, and consequently to punishment. This virtue is justice: the violation of justice is injury: it does real and positive hurt to some particular

persons, from motives which are naturally disapproved of. It is, therefore, the proper object of resentment, and of punishment, which is the natural consequence of resentment. As mankind go along with, and approve of the violence employed to avenge the hurt which is done by injustice, so they much more go along with, and approve of, that which is employed to prevent and beat off the injury, and to restrain the offender from hurting his neighbours. The person himself who meditates an injustice is sensible of this, and feels that force may, with the utmost propriety, be made use of, both by the person whom he is about to injure, and by others, either to obstruct the execution of his crime, or to punish him when he has executed it. And upon this is founded that remarkable distinction between justice and all the other social virtues ... that we feel ourselves to be under a stricter obligation to act according to justice, than agreeably to friendship, charity, or generosity; that the practice of these last mentioned virtues seems to be left in some measure to our own choice, but that, somehow or other, we feel ourselves to be in a peculiar manner tied, bound, and obliged to the observation of justice. We feel, that is to say, that force may, with the utmost propriety, and with the approbation of all mankind, be made use of to constrain us to observe the rules of the one, but not to follow the precepts of the other.

6. We must always, however, carefully distinguish what is only blamable, or the proper object of disapprobation, from what force may be employed either to punish or to prevent. That seems blamable which falls short of that ordinary degree of proper beneficence which experience teaches us to expect of every body; and on the contrary, that seems praise-worthy which goes beyond it. The ordinary degree itself seems neither blamable nor praise-worthy. A father, a son, a brother, who behaves to the correspondent relation neither better nor worse than the greater part of men commonly do, seems properly to deserve neither praise nor blame. He who surprises us by extraordinary and unexpected, though still proper and suitable kindness, or on the contrary by extraordinary and unexpected, as well as unsuitable unkindness, seems praise-worthy in the one case, and blamable in the other.

7. Even the most ordinary degree of kindness or beneficence, however, cannot, among equals, be extorted by force. Among equals each individual is naturally, and antecedent to the institution of civil government, regarded as having a right both to defend himself from injuries, and to exact a certain degree of punishment for those which have been done to him. Every generous spectator not only approves of his conduct when he does this, but enters so far into his sentiments as often to be willing to assist him. When one man attacks, or robs, or attempts to murder another, all the neighbours take the alarm, and think that they do right when they run, either to revenge the person who has been injured, or to defend him who is in danger of being so. But when a father fails in the ordinary degree of parental affection towards a son; when a son seems to want that filial reverence which might be expected to his father; when brothers are without the usual degree of brotherly affection; when a man shuts his breast against compassion, and refuses to relieve the misery of his fellow-creatures, when he can with the greatest ease; in all these cases, though every body blames the conduct, nobody imagines that those who might have reason, perhaps, to expect more kindness, have any right to extort it by force. The sufferer can only complain, and the spectator can intermeddle no other way than by advice and persuasion. Upon all such occasions,

for equals to use force against one another, would be thought the highest degree of insolence and presumption.

8. A superior may, indeed, sometimes, with universal approbation, oblige those under his jurisdiction to behave, in this respect, with a certain degree of propriety to one another. The laws of all civilized nations oblige parents to maintain their children, and children to maintain their parents, and impose upon men many other duties of beneficence. The civil magistrate is entrusted with the power not only of preserving the public peace by restraining injustice, but of promoting the prosperity of the commonwealth, by establishing good discipline, and by discouraging every sort of vice and impropriety; he may prescribe rules, therefore, which not only prohibit mutual injuries among fellow-citizens, but command mutual good offices to a certain degree. When the sovereign commands what is merely indifferent, and what, antecedent to his orders, might have been omitted without any blame, it becomes not only blamable but punishable to disobey him. When he commands, therefore, what, antecedent to any such order, could not have been omitted without the greatest blame, it surely becomes much more punishable to be wanting in obedience. Of all the duties of a law-giver, however, this, perhaps, is that which it requires the greatest delicacy and reserve to execute with propriety and judgment. To neglect it altogether exposes the commonwealth to many gross disorders and shocking enormities, and to push it too far is destructive of all liberty, security, and justice.

9. Though the mere want of beneficence seems to merit no punishment from equals, the greater exertions of that virtue appear to deserve the highest reward. By being productive of the greatest good, they are the natural and approved objects of the liveliest gratitude. Though the breach of justice, on the contrary, exposes to punishment, the observance of the rules of that virtue seems scarce to deserve any reward. There is, no doubt, a propriety in the practice of justice, and it merits, upon that account, all the approbation which is due to propriety. But as it does no real positive good, it is entitled to very little gratitude. Mere justice is, upon most occasions, but a negative virtue, and only hinders us from hurting our neighbour. The man who barely abstains from violating either the person, or the estate, or the reputation of his neighbours, has surely very little positive merit. He fulfils, however, all the rules of what is peculiarly called justice, and does every thing which his equals can with propriety force him to do, or which they can punish him for not doing. We may often fulfil all the rules of justice by sitting still and doing nothing.

10. As every man doth, so shall it be done to him, and retaliation seems to be the great law which is dictated to us by Nature. Beneficence and generosity we think due to the generous and beneficent. Those whose hearts never open to the feelings of humanity, should, we think, be shut out, in the same manner, from the affections of all their fellow-creatures, and be allowed to live in the midst of society, as in a great desert where there is nobody to care for them, or to inquire after them. The violator of the laws of justice ought to be made to feel himself that evil which he has done to another; and since no regard to the sufferings of his brethren is capable of restraining him, he ought to be over-awed by the fear of his own. The man who is barely innocent, who only observes the laws of justice with regard to others, and merely abstains from hurting his neighbours, can merit only

that his neighbours in their turn should respect his innocence, and that the same laws should be religiously observed with regard to him.

Chap. II
Of the sense of Justice, of Remorse, and of the consciousness of Merit

1. There can be no proper motive for hurting our neighbour, there can be no incitement to do evil to another, which mankind will go along with, except just indignation for evil which that other has done to us. To disturb his happiness merely because it stands in the way of our own, to take from him what is of real use to him merely because it may be of equal or of more use to us, or to indulge, in this manner, at the expence of other people, the natural preference which every man has for his own happiness above that of other people, is what no impartial spectator can go along with. Every man is, no doubt, by nature, first and principally recommended to his own care; and as he is fitter to take care of himself than of any other person, it is fit and right that it should be so. Every man, therefore, is much more deeply interested in whatever immediately concerns himself, than in what concerns any other man: and to hear, perhaps, of the death of another person, with whom we have no particular connexion, will give us less concern, will spoil our stomach, or break our rest much less than a very insignificant disaster which has befallen ourselves. But though the ruin of our neighbour may affect us much less than a very small misfortune of our own, we must not ruin him to prevent that small misfortune, nor even to prevent our own ruin. We must, here, as in all other cases, view ourselves not so much according to that light in which we may naturally appear to ourselves, as according to that in which we naturally appear to others. Though every man may, according to the proverb, be the whole world to himself, to the rest of mankind he is a most insignificant part of it. Though his own happiness may be of more importance to him than that of all the world besides, to every other person it is of no more consequence than that of any other man. Though it may be true, therefore, that every individual, in his own breast, naturally prefers himself to all mankind, yet he dares not look mankind in the face, and avow that he acts according to this principle. He feels that in this preference they can never go along with him, and that how natural soever it may be to him, it must always appear excessive and extravagant to them. When he views himself in the light in which he is conscious that others will view him, he sees that to them he is but one of the multitude in no respect better than any other in it. If he would act so as that the impartial spectator may enter into the principles of his conduct, which is what of all things he has the greatest desire to do, he must, upon this, as upon all other occasions, humble the arrogance of his self-love, and bring it down to something which other men can go along with. They will indulge it so far as to allow him to be more anxious about, and to pursue with more earnest assiduity, his own happiness than that of any other person. Thus far, whenever they place themselves in his situation, they will readily go along with him. In the race for wealth, and honours, and preferments, he may run as hard as he can, and strain every nerve and every muscle, in order to outstrip all his competitors. But if he should justle, or throw down any of them, the indulgence of the spectators is entirely at an end. It is a

violation of fair play, which they cannot admit of. This man is to them, in every respect, as good as he: they do not enter into that self-love by which he prefers himself so much to this other, and cannot go along with the motive from which he hurt him. They readily, therefore, sympathize with the natural resentment of the injured, and the offender becomes the object of their hatred and indignation. He is sensible that he becomes so, and feels that those sentiments are ready to burst out from all sides against him.

2. As the greater and more irreparable the evil that is done, the resentment of the sufferer runs naturally the higher; so does likewise the sympathetic indignation of the spectator, as well as the sense of guilt in the agent. Death is the greatest evil which one man can inflict upon another, and excites the highest degree of resentment in those who are immediately connected with the slain. Murder, therefore, is the most atrocious of all crimes which affect individuals only, in the sight both of mankind, and of the person who has committed it. To be deprived of that which we are possessed of, is a greater evil than to be disappointed of what we have only the expectation. Breach of property, therefore, theft and robbery, which take from us what we are possessed of, are greater crimes than breach of contract, which only disappoints us of what we expected. The most sacred laws of justice, therefore, those whose violation seems to call loudest for vengeance and punishment, are the laws which guard the life and person of our neighbour; the next are those which guard his property and possessions; and last of all come those which guard what are called his personal rights, or what is due to him from the promises of others.

3. The violator of the more sacred laws of justice can never reflect on the sentiments which mankind must entertain with regard to him, without feeling all the agonies of shame, and horror, and consternation. When his passion is gratified, and he begins coolly to reflect on his past conduct, he can enter into none of the motives which influenced it. They appear now as detestable to him as they did always to other people. By sympathizing with the hatred and abhorrence which other men must entertain for him, he becomes in some measure the object of his own hatred and abhorrence. The situation of the person, who suffered by his injustice, now calls upon his pity. He is grieved at the thought of it; regrets the unhappy effects of his own conduct, and feels at the same time that they have rendered him the proper object of the resentment and indignation of mankind, and of what is the natural consequence of resentment, vengeance and punishment. The thought of this perpetually haunts him, and fills him with terror and amazement. He dares no longer look society in the face, but imagines himself as it were rejected, and thrown out from the affections of all mankind. He cannot hope for the consolation of sympathy in this his greatest and most dreadful distress. The remembrance of his crimes has shut out all fellow-feeling with him from the hearts of his fellow-creatures. The sentiments which they entertain with regard to him, are the very thing which he is most afraid of. Every thing seems hostile, and he would be glad to fly to some inhospitable desert, where he might never more behold the face of a human creature, nor read in the countenance of mankind the condemnation of his crimes. But solitude is still more dreadful than society. His own thoughts can present him with nothing but what is black, unfortunate, and disastrous, the melancholy forebodings of incomprehensible misery and ruin. The horror of solitude drives him back into

society, and he comes again into the presence of mankind, astonished to appear before them, loaded with shame and distracted with fear, in order to supplicate some little protection from the countenance of those very judges, who he knows have already all unanimously condemned him. Such is the nature of that sentiment, which is properly called remorse; of all the sentiments which can enter the human breast the most dreadful. It is made up of shame from the sense of the impropriety of past conduct; of grief for the effects of it; of pity for those who suffer by it; and of the dread and terror of punishment from the consciousness of the justly provoked resentment of all rational creatures.

4. The opposite behaviour naturally inspires the opposite sentiment. The man who, not from frivolous fancy, but from proper motives, has performed a generous action, when he looks forward to those whom he has served, feels himself to be the natural object of their love and gratitude, and, by sympathy with them, of the esteem and approbation of all mankind. And when he looks backward to the motive from which he acted, and surveys it in the light in which the indifferent spectator will survey it, he still continues to enter into it, and applauds himself by sympathy with the approbation of this supposed impartial judge. In both these points of view his own conduct appears to him every way agreeable. His mind, at the thought of it, is filled with cheerfulness, serenity, and composure. He is in friendship and harmony with all mankind, and looks upon his fellow-creatures with confidence and benevolent satisfaction, secure that he has rendered himself worthy of their most favourable regards. In the combination of all these sentiments consists the consciousness of merit, or of deserved reward.

STUDY QUESTIONS

1. In the reading that follows this one, Charles Darwin addresses the evolutionary value of the moral sentiments and the virtues. What did Adam Smith, who lived before the theory of evolution was developed, think of the origin and social significance of the moral sentiments?

2. Benevolence has to do with doing good, justice with refraining from doing harm. Can these two principles be collapsed into one? If they cannot, which do you consider more important? Is there any hint in Smith of the primacy of one over the other?

3. Injustice, says Smith, arouses resentment in the sufferer, sympathetic indignation in the spectator, and feelings of guilt in the perpetrator. Are these the reasons we should punish injustice? Or is there an independent reason and justification?

4. Smith writes as if the moral sentiments were fairly constant in all societies and times. Do you get the impression from reading Smith that the moral sentiments were stronger in his day than in ours? If so, what would this imply? If not, why not?

5. Smith's focus on moral sentiments as essential to morality is in contrast with Immanuel Kant's focus on the rational will to act from duty. Discuss these different approaches to moral behavior. What relative weight do you think moral philosophers should be giving to the sentiments and to reason?

The Origin of the Moral Sense

Charles Darwin

Charles Darwin (1809–1882), one of the seminal thinkers of the modern era, developed the theory of evolution. His two greatest works are *The Origin of Species* (1859) and *The Descent of Man* (1871).

Approaching morality "from the side of natural history," Charles Darwin proposes to see what light the study of lower animals throws on the origin of the human sense of right and wrong. He contends that any animal "endowed with well-marked social instincts" is latently moral, and if it became conscious of its own behavior, "would inevitably acquire a moral sense or conscience." Moreover, once it acquired language, "the common opinion how each member ought to act for the public good, would naturally become in a paramount degree the guide to action."

What morality would be for a conscious social animal—that is, what its conscience would dictate—would depend on the social organization of its species. If humans lived in bee-fashion, it would be moral for mothers to strive to kill their fertile daughters and for "worker bee" people to kill their brothers, all such action being accompanied by feelings of rightness.

Our actual development dictates all kinds of social behavior, among them mutual defense against outside enemies and mutual cooperation and organization in acquiring adequate sustenance. All of these modes of behavior would be enhanced, and were in fact enhanced by the evolution of instinctive sympathy and the aversion to suffer social disapproval of asocial behavior. This development in us, says Darwin (perhaps mischievously), might even culminate in a Kantian declaration not to violate "the dignity of humanity."

I fully subscribe to the judgment of those writers who maintain that of all the differences between man and the lower animals, the moral sense or conscience is by far the most important. This sense, as Mackintosh remarks, has a rightful supremacy over every other principle of human action; it is summed up in that short but imperious word *ought*, so full of high significance. It is the most noble of all the attributes of man, leading him without a moment's hesitation to risk his life for that of a fellow-creature; or after due deliberation, impelled simply by the deep feeling of right or duty, to sacrifice it in some great cause. Immanuel Kant exclaims, "Duty! Wondrous thought, that workest neither by fond insinuation, flattery, nor

THE ORIGIN OF THE MORAL SENSE From *The Descent of Man*, 3rd ed. (John Murray: London, 1875), 97–111. First published in 1871.

by any threat, but merely by holding up thy naked law in the soul, and so extorting for thyself always reverence, if not always obedience; before whom all appetites are dumb, however secretly they rebel; whence thy original?"

This great question has been discussed by many writers of consummate ability: and my sole excuse for touching on it, is the impossibility of here passing it over; and because, as far as I know, no one has approached it exclusively from the side of natural history. The investigation possesses, also, some independent interest, as an attempt to see how far the study of the lower animals throws light on one of the highest psychical faculties of man.

The following proposition seems to me in a high degree probable—namely, that any animal whatever, endowed with well-marked social instincts, the parental and filial affections being here included, would inevitably acquire a moral sense or conscience, as soon as its intellectual powers had become as well, or nearly as well developed, as in man. For, *firstly*, the social instincts lead an animal to take pleasure in the society of its fellows, to feel a certain amount of sympathy with them, and to perform various services for them. The services may be of a definite and evidently instinctive nature; or there may be only a wish and readiness, as with most of the higher social animals, to aid their fellows in certain general ways. But these feelings and services are by no means extended to all the individuals of the same species, only to those of the same association. *Secondly*, as soon as the mental faculties had become highly developed, images of all past actions and motives would be incessantly passing through the brain of each individual; and that feeling of dissatisfaction, or even misery, which invariably results, as we shall hereafter see, from any unsatisfied instinct, would arise, as often as it was perceived that the enduring and always present social instinct had yielded to some other instinct, at the time stronger, but neither enduring in its nature, nor leaving behind it a very vivid impression. It is clear that many instinctive desires, such as that of hunger, are in their nature of short duration; and after being satisfied, are not readily or vividly recalled. *Thirdly*, after the power of language had been acquired, and the wishes of the community could be expressed, the common opinion how each member ought to act for the public good, would naturally become in a paramount degree the guide to action. But it should be borne in mind that however great weight we may attribute to public opinion, our regard for the approbation and disapprobation of our fellows depends on sympathy, which, as we shall see, forms an essential part of the social instinct, and is indeed its foundation-stone. *Lastly*, habit in the individual would ultimately play a very important part in guiding the conduct of each member; for the social instinct, together with sympathy, is, like any other instinct, greatly strengthened by habit, and so consequently would be obedience to the wishes and judgment of the community. These several subordinate propositions must now be discussed, and some of them at considerable length.

It may be well first to premise that I do not wish to maintain that any strictly social animal, if its intellectual faculties were to become as active and as highly developed as in man, would acquire exactly the same moral sense as ours. In the same manner as various animals have some sense of beauty, though they admire widely different objects, so they might have a sense of right and wrong, though led by it to follow widely different lines of conduct. If, for instance, to take an extreme case, men were reared under precisely the same conditions as hive-bees, there can hardly be a doubt that our unmarried females would, like the worker-bees, think it a sacred duty to kill their brothers, and mothers would strive to kill their fertile daughters; and no one would think of interfering. Nevertheless, the bee, or any other social animal, would gain in our supposed case, as it appears to me, some feeling of right or wrong, or a conscience. For each individual would have an inward sense of possessing certain stronger or more enduring instincts, and others less strong or enduring; so that there would often be a struggle as to which impulse should be followed; and satisfaction, dissatisfaction, or even misery would be felt, as past impressions were compared during their incessant passage through the mind. In this case an inward monitor would tell the animal that it would have been better to have followed the one impulse rather than the other. The one course ought to have been followed, and the other ought not; the one would have been right and the other wrong; but to these terms I shall recur.

Sociability

Animals of many kinds are social; we find even distinct species living together; for example, some American monkeys; and united flocks of rooks, jackdaws, and starlings. Man shews the same feeling in his strong love for the dog, which the dog returns with interest. Every one must have noticed how miserable horses, dogs, sheep, &c., are when separated from their companions, and what strong mutual affection the two former kinds, at least, shew on their reunion. It is curious to speculate on the feelings of a dog, who will rest peacefully for hours in a room with his master or any of the family, without the least notice being taken of him; but if left for a short time by himself, barks or howls dismally. We will confine our attention to the higher social animals; and pass over insects, although some of these are social, and aid one another in many important ways. The most common mutual service in the higher animals is to warn one another of danger by means of the united senses of all.... Social animals perform many little services for each other: horses nibble, and cows lick each other, on any spot which itches: monkeys search each other for external parasites; and Brehm states that after a troop of the *Cercopithecus griseo-viridis* has rushed through a thorny brake, each monkey stretches itself on a branch, and another monkey sitting by, "conscientiously" examines its fur, and extracts every thorn or burr.

Animals also render more important services to one another: thus wolves and some other beasts of prey hunt in packs, and aid one another in attacking their victims. Pelicans fish in concert. The Hamadryas baboons turn over stones to find insects, &c.; and when they come to a large one, as many as can stand round, turn it over together and share the booty. Social animals mutually defend each other....

Besides love and sympathy, animals exhibit other qualities connected with the social instincts, which in us would be called moral; and I agree with Agassiz that dogs possess something very like a conscience.

Dogs possess some power of self-command, and this does not appear to be wholly the result of fear. As Braubach remarks, they will refrain from stealing food in the absence of their master. They have long been accepted as the very type of fidelity and obedience. But the elephant is likewise very faithful to his driver or keeper, and probably considers him as the leader of the herd....

All animals living in a body, which defend themselves or attack their enemies in concert, must indeed be in some degree faithful to one another; and those that follow a leader must be in some degree obedient....

It has often been assumed that animals were in the first place rendered social, and that they feel as a consequence uncomfortable when separated from each other, and comfortable whilst together; but it is a more probable view that these sensations were first developed, in order that those animals which would profit by living in society, should be induced to live together, in the same manner as the sense of hunger and the pleasure of eating were, no doubt, first acquired in order to induce animals to eat. The feeling of pleasure from society is probably an extension of the parental or filial affections, since the social instinct seems to be developed by the young remaining for a long time with their parents; and this extension may be attributed in part to habit, but chiefly to natural selection. With those animals which were benefited by living in close association, the individuals which took the greatest pleasure in society would best escape various dangers; whilst those that cared least for their comrades, and lived solitary, would perish in greater numbers. With respect to the origin of the parental and filial affections, which apparently lie at the base of the social instincts, we know not the steps by which they have been gained; but we may infer that it has been to a large extent through natural selection....

Man a Social Animal

Every one will admit that man is a social being. We see this in his dislike of solitude, and in his wish for society beyond that of his own family.... As man is a social animal, it is almost certain that he would inherit a tendency to be faithful to his comrades, and obedient to the leader of his tribe; for these qualities are common to most social animals. He would consequently possess some capacity for self-command. He would from an inherited tendency be willing to defend, in concert with others, his fellow-men; and would be ready to aid them in any way, which did not too greatly interfere with his own welfare or his own strong desires.

The social animals which stand at the bottom of the scale are guided almost exclusively, and those which stand higher in the scale are largely guided, by special instincts in the aid which they give to the members of the same community; but they are likewise in part impelled by mutual love and sympathy, assisted apparently by some amount of reason. Although man, as just remarked, has no special instincts to tell him how to aid his fellow-men, he still has the impulse, and with his improved intellectual faculties would naturally be much guided in this respect by reason and experience. Instinctive sympathy would also cause him to value highly the approbation of his fellows.... Consequently man would be influenced in the highest degree by the wishes, approbation, and blame of his fellow-men, as expressed by their gestures and language. Thus the social instincts, which must have been acquired by man in a very rude state, and probably even by his early ape-like progenitors, still give the impulse to some of his best actions; but his actions are in a higher degree determined by the expressed wishes and judgment of his fellow-men, and unfortunately very often by his own strong selfish desires. But as love, sympathy and self-command become strengthened by habit, and as the power of reasoning becomes clearer, so that man can value justly the judgments of his fellows, he will feel

himself impelled, apart from any transitory pleasure or pain, to certain lines of conduct. He might then declare—not that any barbarian or uncultivated man could
thus think—I am the supreme judge of my own conduct, and in the words of
Kant, I will not in my own person violate the dignity of humanity.

STUDY QUESTIONS

1. Alluding to Immanuel Kant and our reverence for duty, Darwin asks how duty
    originated: "Whence thy original?" Imagine Kant attending a lecture by Darwin and
    hearing his answer. How might Kant have reacted to Darwin's approach to morality?
2. Darwin puts the idea of man as a social animal in evolutionary perspective. Moral
    sentiments like love and sympathy evolved in us as our species fought for survival. How
    does the study of morality "from the side of natural history" affect our view of the
    nature of the moral sentiments?
3. What does "having a conscience" mean? How in Darwin's view did human conscience
    evolve? Why does Darwin say that dogs have something like a conscience?
4. Darwin notes that we often feel impelled to be helpful to others, quite apart from the
    immediate feelings of pleasure that such conduct may give us. How does he account for
    this kind of unselfish impulse?

The Parable of the Sadhu

Bowen McCoy

> Bowen McCoy is a retired executive from Morgan Stanley where he worked
> for twenty-eight years. He is now a philanthropist business advisor and
> teacher of business ethics.
>
> In 1996 McCoy, along with a small group of hikers from around the
> world, were close to reaching a mountain summit in the Himalayas. But
> along the trail, at an altitude of about 15,500 feet, one of them discovers
> a shivering, barefoot Indian holy man—a sadhu—lying on the ice. Each of
> the hikers does something to help the man, but neither the group nor any
> of the individuals within it assume full responsibility. The man's fate re-
> mains unknown. How much do we owe one another? How good do we
> have to be? And what is the relationship between personal and corporate
> goodness? These are a few of the questions McCoy considers.

Last year, as the first participant in the new six-month sabbatical program that
Morgan Stanley has adopted, I enjoyed a rare opportunity to collect my thoughts
as well as do some traveling. I spent the first three months in Nepal, walking 600
miles through 200 villages in the Himalayas and climbing some 120,000 vertical

feet. My sole Western companion on the trip was an anthropologist who shed light on the cultural patterns of the villages that we passed through.

During the Nepal hike, something occurred that has had a powerful impact on my thinking about corporate ethics. Although some might argue that the experience has no relevance to business, it was a situation in which a basic ethical dilemma suddenly intruded into the lives of a group of individuals. How the group responded holds a lesson for all organizations, no matter how defined.

The Sadhu

The Nepal experience was more rugged than I had anticipated. Most commercial treks last two or three weeks and cover a quarter of the distance we traveled.

My friend Stephen, the anthropologist, and I were halfway through the 60-day Himalayan part of the trip when we reached the high point, an 18,000-foot pass over a crest that we'd have to traverse to reach the village of Muklinath, an ancient holy place for pilgrims.

Six years earlier, I had suffered pulmonary edema, an acute form of altitude sickness, at 16,500 feet in the vicinity of Everest base camp—so we were understandably concerned about what would happen at 18,000 feet. Moreover, the Himalayas were having their wettest spring in 20 years; hip-deep powder and ice had already driven us off one ridge. If we failed to cross the pass, I feared that the last half of our once-in-a-lifetime trip would be ruined.

The night before we would try the pass, we camped in a hut at 14,500 feet. In the photos taken at that camp, my face appears wan. The last village we'd passed through was a sturdy two-day walk below us, and I was tired.

During the late afternoon, four backpackers from New Zealand joined us, and we spent most of the night awake, anticipating the climb. Below, we could see the fires of two other parties, which turned out to be two Swiss couples and a Japanese hiking club.

To get over the steep part of the climb before the sun melted the steps cut in the ice, we departed at 3:30 A.M. The New Zealanders left first, followed by Stephen and myself, our porters and Sherpas, and then the Swiss. The Japanese lingered in their camp. The sky was clear, and we were confident that no spring storm would erupt that day to close the pass.

At 15,500 feet, it looked to me as if Stephen were shuffling and staggering a bit, which are symptoms of altitude sickness. (The initial stage of altitude sickness brings a headache and nausea. As the condition worsens, a climber may encounter difficult breathing, disorientation, aphasia, and paralysis. I felt strong—my adrenaline was flowing—but I was very concerned about my ultimate ability to get across. A couple of our porters were also suffering from the height, and Pasang, our Sherpa sirdar (leader), was worried.

Just after daybreak, while we rested at 15,500 feet, one of the New Zealanders, who had gone ahead, came staggering down toward us with a body slung across his shoulders. He dumped the almost naked, barefoot body of an Indian holy man—a sadhu—at my feet. He had found the pilgrim lying on the ice, shivering and suffering from hypothermia. I cradled the sadhu's head and laid him out on the rocks. The New Zealander was angry. He wanted to get across the pass before the bright sun melted the snow. He said, "Look, I've done what I can. You have porters and Sherpa guides. You care for him. We're going on!" He turned and went back up the mountain to join his friends.

I took a carotid pulse and found that the sadhu was still alive. We figured he had probably visited the holy shrines at Muklinath and was on his way home. It was fruitless to question why he had chosen this desperately high route instead of the safe, heavily traveled caravan route through the Kali Gandaki gorge. Or why he was shoeless and almost naked, or how long he had been lying in the pass. The answers weren't going to solve our problem.

Stephen and the four Swiss began stripping off their outer clothing and opening their packs. The sadhu was soon clothed from head to foot. He was not able to walk, but he was very much alive. I looked down the mountain and spotted the Japanese climbers, marching up with a horse.

Without a great deal of thought, I told Stephen and Pasang that I was concerned about withstanding the heights to come and wanted to get over the pass. I took off after several of our porters who had gone ahead.

On the steep part of the ascent where, if the ice steps had given way, I would have slid down about 3,000 feet, I felt vertigo. I stopped for a breather, allowing the Swiss to catch up with me. I inquired about the sadhu and Stephen. They said that the sadhu was fine and that Stephen was just behind them. I set off again for the summit.

Stephen arrived at the summit an hour after I did. Still exhilarated by victory, I ran down the slope to congratulate him. He was suffering from altitude sickness—walking 15 steps, then stopping, walking 15 steps, then stopping. Pasang accompanied him all the way up. When I reached them, Stephen glared at me and said: "How do you feel about contributing to the death of a fellow man?"

I did not completely comprehend what he meant. "Is the sadhu dead?" I inquired.

"No," replied Stephen, "but he surely will be!"

After I had gone, followed not long after by the Swiss, Stephen had remained with the sadhu. When the Japanese had arrived, Stephen had asked to use their horse to transport the sadhu down to the hut. They had refused. He had then asked Pasang to have a group of our porters carry the sadhu. Pasang had resisted the idea, saying that the porters would have to exert all their energy to get themselves over the pass. He believed they could not carry a man down 1,000 feet to the hut, re-climb the slope, and get across safely before the snow melted. Pasang had pressed Stephen not to delay any longer.

The Sherpas had carried the sadhu down to a rock in the sun at about 15,000 feet and pointed out the hut another 500 feet below. The Japanese had given him food and drink. When they had last seen him, he was listlessly throwing rocks at the Japanese party's dog, which had frightened him.

We do not know if the sadhu lived or died.

For many of the following days and evenings, Stephen and I discussed and debated our behavior toward the sadhu. Stephen is a committed Quaker with deep moral vision. He said, "I feel that what happened with the sadhu is a good example of the breakdown between the individual ethic and the corporate ethic. No one person was willing to assume ultimate responsibility for the sadhu. Each was willing to do his bit just so long as it was not too inconvenient. When it got to be a bother, everyone just passed the buck to someone else and took off. Jesus was relevant to a more individualistic stage of society, but how do we interpret his teaching today in a world filled with large, impersonal organizations and groups?"

I defended the larger group, saying, "Look, we all cared. We all gave aid and comfort. Everyone did his bit.

The New Zealander carried him down below the snow line. I took his pulse and suggested we treat him for hypothermia. You and the Swiss gave him clothing and got him warmed up. The Japanese gave him food and water. The Sherpas carried him down to the sun and pointed out the easy trail toward the hut. He was well enough to throw rocks at a dog. What more could we do?"

"You have just described the typical affluent Westerner's response to a problem. Throwing money—in this case, food and sweaters—at it, but not solving the fundamentals!" Stephen retorted.

"What would satisfy you?" I said. "Here we are, a group of New Zealanders, Swiss, Americans, and Japanese who have never met before and who are at the apex of one of the most powerful experiences of our lives. Some years the pass is so bad no one gets over it. What right does an almost naked pilgrim who chooses the wrong trail have to disrupt our lives? Even the Sherpas had no interest in risking the trip to help him beyond a certain point."

Stephen calmly rebutted, "I wonder what the Sherpas would have done if the sadhu had been a well-dressed Nepali, or what the Japanese would have done if the sadhu had been a well-dressed Asian, or what you would have done, Buzz, if the sadhu had been a well-dressed Western woman?"

"Where, in your opinion," I asked, "is the limit of our responsibility in a situation like this? We had our own well-being to worry about. Our Sherpa guides were unwilling to jeopardize us or the porters for the sadhu. No one else on the mountain was willing to commit himself beyond certain self-imposed limits."

Stephen said, "As individual Christians or people with a Western ethical tradition, we can fulfill our obligations in such a situation only if one, the sadhu dies in our care; two, the sadhu demonstrates to us that he can undertake the two-day walk down to the village; or three, we carry the sadhu for two days down to the village and persuade someone there to care for him."

"Leaving the sadhu in the sun with food and clothing—where he demonstrated hand-eye coordination by throwing a rock at a dog—comes close to fulfilling items one and two," I answered. "And it wouldn't have made sense to take him to the village where the people appeared to be far less caring than the Sherpas, so the third condition is impractical. Are you really saying that, no matter what the implications, we should, at the drop of a hat, have changed our entire plan?"

The Individual Versus the Group Ethic

Despite my arguments, I felt and continue to feel guilt about the sadhu. I had literally walked through a classic moral dilemma without fully thinking through the consequences. My excuses for my actions include a high adrenaline flow, a superordinate goal, and a once-in-a-lifetime opportunity—common factors in corporate situations, especially stressful ones.

Real moral dilemmas are ambiguous, and many of us hike right through them, unaware that they exist. When, usually after the fact, someone makes an issue of one, we tend to resent his or her bringing it up. Often, when the full import of what we have done (or not done) hits us, we dig into a defensive position from which it is very difficult to emerge. In rare circumstances, we may contemplate what we have done from inside a prison.

Had we mountaineers been free of stress caused by the effort and the high altitude, we might have treated the sadhu differently. Yet isn't stress the real test of personal and corporate values? The instant decisions that executives make under pressure reveal the most about personal and corporate character.

Among the many questions that occur to me when I ponder my experience with the sadhu are: What are the practical limits of moral imagination and vision? Is there a collective or institutional ethic that differs from the ethics of the individual? At what level of effort or commitment can one discharge one's ethical responsibilities?

Not every ethical dilemma has a right solution. Reasonable people often disagree; otherwise there would be no dilemma. In a business context, however, it is essential that managers agree on a process for dealing with dilemmas.

Our experience with the sadhu offers an interesting parallel to business situations. An immediate response was mandatory. Failure to act was a decision in itself. Up on the mountain we could not resign and submit our résumés to a headhunter. In contrast to philosophy, business involves action and implementation—getting things done. Managers must come up with answers based on what they see and what they allow to influence their decision-making processes. On the mountain, none of us but Stephen realized the true dimensions of the situation we were facing.

One of our problems was that as a group we had no process for developing a consensus. We had no sense of purpose or plan. The difficulties of dealing with the sadhu were so complex that no one person could handle them. Because the group did not have a set of preconditions that could guide its action to an acceptable resolution, we reacted instinctively as individuals. The cross-cultural nature of the group added a further layer of complexity. We had no leader with whom we could all identify and in whose purpose we believed. Only Stephen was willing to take charge, but he could not gain adequate support from the group to care for the sadhu.

Some organizations do have values that transcend the personal values of their managers. Such values, which go beyond profitability, are usually revealed when the organization is under stress. People throughout the organization generally accept its values, which, because they are not presented as a rigid list of commandments, may be somewhat ambiguous. The stories people tell, rather than printed materials, transmit the organization's conceptions of what is proper behavior.

For 20 years, I have been exposed at senior levels to a variety of corporations and organizations. It is amazing how quickly an outsider can sense the tone and style of an organization and, with that, the degree of tolerated openness and freedom to challenge management.

Organizations that do not have a heritage of mutually accepted, shared values tend to become unhinged during stress, with each individual bailing out for himself or herself. In the great takeover battles we have witnessed during past years, companies that had strong cultures drew the wagons around them and fought it out, while other companies saw executives—supported by golden parachutes—bail out of the struggles.

Because corporations and their members are interdependent, for the corporation to be strong the members need to share a preconceived notion of correct behavior, a "business ethic," and think of it as a positive force, not a constraint.

As an investment banker, I am continually warned by well-meaning lawyers, clients, and associates to be wary of conflicts of interest. Yet if I were to run away from every difficult situation, I wouldn't be an effective investment banker. I have to feel my way through conflicts. An effective manager can't run from risk either; he or she has to confront risk. To feel "safe" in doing that, managers need the guidelines of an agreed-upon process and set of values within the organization.

After my three months in 'Nepal, I spent three months as an executive-in-residence at both the Stanford Business School and the University of California at Berkeley's Center for Ethics and Social Policy of the Graduate Theological Union. Those six months away from my job gave me time to assimilate 20 years of business experience. My thoughts turned often to the meaning of the leadership role in any large organization. Students at the seminary thought of themselves as antibusiness. But when I questioned them, they agreed that they distrusted all large organizations, including the church. They perceived all large organizations as impersonal and opposed to individual values and needs. Yet we all know of organizations in which people's values and beliefs are respected and their expressions encouraged. What makes the difference? Can we identify the difference and, as a result, manage more effectively?

The word *ethics* turns off many and confuses more. Yet the notions of shared values and an agreed-upon process for dealing with adversity and change—what many people mean when they talk about corporate culture—seem to be at the heart of the ethical issue. People who are in touch with their own core beliefs and the beliefs of others and who are sustained by them can be more comfortable living on the cutting edge. At times, taking a tough line or a decisive stand in a muddle of ambiguity is the only ethical thing to do. If a manager is indecisive about a problem and spends time trying to figure out the "good" thing to do, the enterprise may be lost.

Business ethics, then, has to do with the authenticity and integrity of the enterprise. To be ethical is to follow the business as well as the cultural goals of the corporation, its owners, its employees, and its customers. Those who cannot serve the corporate vision are not authentic businesspeople and, therefore, are not ethical in the business sense.

At this stage of my own business experience, I have a strong interest in organizational behavior. Sociologists are keenly studying what they call corporate stories, legends, and heroes as a way organizations have of transmitting value systems. Corporations such as Arco have even hired consultants to perform an audit of their corporate culture. In a company, a leader is a person who understands, interprets, and manages the corporate value system. Effective managers, therefore, are action-oriented people who resolve conflict, are tolerant of ambiguity, stress, and change, and have a strong sense of purpose for themselves and their organizations.

If all this is true, I wonder about the role of the professional manager who moves from company to company. How can he or she quickly absorb the values and culture of different organizations? Or is there, indeed, an art of management that is totally transportable? Assuming that such fungible managers do exist, is it proper for them to manipulate the values of others?

What would have happened had Stephen and I carried the sadhu for two days back to the village and become involved with the villagers in his care? In four trips to Nepal, my most interesting experience occurred in 1975 when I lived in a Sherpa home in the Khumbu for five days while recovering from altitude sickness. The high point of Stephen's trip was an invitation to participate in a family funeral ceremony in Manang. Neither experience had to do with climbing the high passes of the Himalayas. Why were we so reluctant to try the lower path, the ambiguous trail? Perhaps because we did not have a leader who could reveal the greater purpose of the trip to us.

Why didn't Stephen, with his moral vision, opt to take the sadhu under his personal care? The answer is partly because Stephen was hard-stressed physically himself and partly because, without some support system that encompassed our involuntary and episodic community on the mountain, it was beyond his individual capacity to do so.

I see the current interest in corporate culture and corporate value systems as a positive response to pessimism such as Stephen's about the decline of the role of the individual in large organizations. Individuals who operate from a thoughtful set of personal values provide the foundation for a corporate culture. A corporate tradition that encourages freedom of inquiry, supports personal values, and reinforces a focused sense of direction can fulfill the need to combine individuality with the prosperity and success of the group. Without such corporate support, the individual is lost.

That is the lesson of the sadhu. In a complex corporate situation, the individual requires and deserves the support of the group. When people cannot find such support in their organizations, they don't know how to act. If such support is forthcoming, a person has a stake in the success of the group and can add much to the process of establishing and maintaining a corporate culture. Management's challenge is to be sensitive to individual needs, to shape them, and to direct and focus them for the benefit of the group as a whole.

For each of us the sadhu lives. Should we stop what we are doing and comfort him; or should we keep trudging up toward the high pass? Should I pause to help the derelict I pass on the street each night as I walk by the Yale Club en route to Grand Central Station? Am I his brother? What is the nature of our responsibility if we consider ourselves to be ethical persons? Perhaps it is to change the values of the group so that it can, with all its resources, take the other road.

When Do We Take a Stand?

I wrote about my experiences purposely to present an ambiguous situation. I never found out if the sadhu lived or died. I can attest, though, that the sadhu lives on in his story. He lives in the ethics classes I teach each year at business schools and churches. He lives in the classrooms of numerous business schools, where professors have taught the case to tens of thousands of students. He lives in several casebooks on ethics and on an educational video. And he lives in organizations such as the American Red Cross and AT&T, which use his story in their ethics training.

As I reflect on the sadhu now, 15 years after the fact, I first have to wonder, What actually happened on that Himalayan slope? When I first wrote about the event, I reported the experience in as much detail as I could remember, but I shaped it to the needs of a good classroom discussion. After years of reading my story, viewing it on vide, and hearing others discuss it, I'm not sure I myself know what actually occurred on the mountainside that day!

I've also heard a wide variety of responses to the story. The sadhu, for example, may not have wanted our help at all—he may have been intentionally bringing on his own death as a way to holiness. Why had he taken the dangerous way over the pass instead of the caravan route through the gorge? Hindu businesspeople have told me that in trying to assist the sadhu, we were being typically arrogant Westerners imposing our cultural values on the world.

I've learned that each year along the pass, a few Nepali porters are left to freeze to death outside the tents of the unthinking tourists who hired them. A few years asgo, a French group even left one of their own, a young French woman, to die there. The difficult pass seems to demonstrate a perverse version of Fresham's law of currency: The bad practices of previous travelers have driven out the values that new travelers might have followed if they were at home. Perhaps that helps to explain why our porters behaved as they did and why it was so difficult for Stephen or anyone else to establish a different approach on the spot.

Our Sherpa sirdar, Pasang, was focused on his responsibility for bringing us up the mountain safe and sound. (His livelihood and status in the Sherpa ethnic group depended on our safe return.) We were weak, our party was split, the porters were well on their way to the top with all our gear and food, and a storm would have separated us irrevocably from our logistical base.

The fact was, we had no plan for dealing with the contingency of the sadhu. There was nothing we could do to unite our multicultural group in the little time we had. An ethical dilemma had come upon us unexpectedly, an element of drama that may explain why the sadhu's story has continued to attract students.

I am often asked for help in teaching the story. I usually advise keeping the details as ambiguous as possible. A true ethical dilemma requires a decision between two hard choices. In the case of the sadhu, we had to decide how much to sacrifice ourselves to take care of a stranger. And given the constraints of our trek, we had to make a group decision, not an individual one. If a large majority of students in a class ends of thinking I'm a bad person because of my decision on the mountain, the instructor may not have been given the case its due. The same is true if the majority sees no problem with the choices we made.

Any class's response depends on its setting, whether it's a business school, a church, or a corporation. I've found that younger students are more likely to see the issue as black-and-white, whereas older ones tend to see shades of gray. Some have seen a conflict between the different ethical approaches that we followed at the time. Stephen felt he had to do everything he could to save the sadhu's life, in accordance with his Christian ethic of compassion. I had a utilitarian response: do the greatest good for the greatest number. Give a burst of aid to minimize the sadhu's exposure, then continue on our way.

The basic question of the case remains, When do we take a stand? When do we allow a "sadhu" to intrude into our daily lives? Few of us can afford the time or effort to take care of every needy person we encounter. How much must we give of ourselves? And how do we prepare our organizations and institutions so they will respond appropriately in a crisis? How do we influence them if we do not agree with their points of view?

We cannot quit our jobs over every ethical dilemma, but if we continually ignore our sense of values, who do we become? As a journalist asked at a recent conference on ethics, "Which ditch are we willing to die in?" For each of us, the answer is a bit different. How we act in response to that question defines better than anything else who we ware, just as, in a collective sense, our acts define our institutions. In effect, the sadhu is always there, ready to remind us of the tensions between our own goals and the claims of strangers.

STUDY QUESTIONS

1. McCoy says, "If a large majority of students in a class ends up thinking I'm a bad person because of my decision on the mountain, the instructor may not have given the case its due. The same is true if the majority sees no problem with the choices we made." Do you agree that the case is an irresolvable dilemma or do you see a clear right and wrong?
2. Stephen subscribes to a Christian ethic; McCoy is a utilitarian. Does this difference explain their different judgments about what they should do?
3. McCoy concludes, "For each of us the sadhu lives." What does he mean and do you agree?

VICE

CHAPTER **6**

What is vice? The question has both Christian and pagan answers. The philosophers of antiquity, from Plato to Plutarch, saw vice as a defect that we may overcome by education and discipline, including self-discipline. Virtuous persons are free of vice; their lives are ordered and rational. Plutarch's analysis of vice and virtue is fairly representative of the views of most educated thinkers in the pre-Christian era. Base persons are not controlled by reason; they are prone to impulse, discontented, ridden with anxiety. Plutarch was influenced as much by the Stoic and Epicurean philosophers as he was by Plato and Aristotle. The popular connotations of the word *epicurean* distort the doctrine; the Epicureans were far more concerned with the problem of avoiding pain and frustration than with the pursuit of pleasure and satisfaction. For both Stoics and Epicureans, contentment and inner tranquility, not pleasure, is the essence of the good life. Conversely, a vice is a character defect that promotes inner tensions and chaos as well as outer deeds that are base or ignoble.

Why are some people so susceptible to vice? The pagans attribute vice to improper development. Aristotle and Plato, in somewhat different ways, stress the *learned* character of the virtues. Virtue is a product of an education that includes self-discipline as well as discipline by parents and teachers. Persons of vice, then, have failed to shape a better character for themselves and are responsible for what they are.

The great pagan philosophers thought of virtue as the disposition to do what is right and the developed disinclination to do what is wrong. The Christian philosophers did not disagree with this, but their conception of vice is more highly seasoned. For Augustine and Jonathan Edwards, to do wrong is to *sin*, to rebel against God: the sinner defies God by transgressing his law. Augustine argues that the impulse to sin is not simply a drive to satisfy desires. As he sees it, sin needs no motive beyond the perverse desire to sin. The desire to do evil is an endowment of Adam and Eve, the original sinners. Since the Fall, people have loved sin for its own sake; sin is, as it were, its own reward. According to Augustine, the pagan view that humans are fully able to control vice and develop the virtues by education and self-discipline is unduly optimistic. He maintains that we cannot achieve salvation or happiness without God's grace.

The question of human perfectability is important whether or not one views it in theological terms. Is it altogether utopian to hope for a day when cruelty and gratuitous malice are things of the past? If Augustine is right, this change will take a miracle.

Sin construed as defiance and rebellion against the powers of good is a more dramatic affair than character defect due to improper education. Jonathan Edwards's harrowing description of the consequences suffered by those who rebel against God exemplifies a "fire-and-brimstone" style of preaching that was in vogue in early New England and for which Edwards remains famous to this day. (According to Jonathan Bennett, *infamous* would be a more suitable term. See Bennett's article in Chapter One.)

Recognizing a strong tendency to evil in humans, most Christian philosophers consider persons who have base desires to be virtuous provided they do not "consent" to those desires. Pagan thinkers from Plato to Plutarch are more suspicious of those who are strongly tempted to do wrong. They find the idea of a virtuous person beset by base desires and constantly, if successfully, overcoming them, decidedly odd. Both viewpoints have strengths. Surely the pagans were not realistic in thinking of virtue as freedom from even the temptation to do wrong. It would seem that the very merit of doing what is right is due at least in part to the existence of a temptation to do what is wrong, a temptation we resist. If the temptation to vice is absent altogether, we are less praiseworthy for remaining virtuous. On the other hand, we do think of people as virtuous if they are not even tempted to do what is base. The two intuitions conflict, yet each is persuasive. This usually shows that more analysis is needed.

Modern philosophers tend to reject the Augustinian thesis that something in humans is ineradicably corrupt. Immanuel Kant and Joseph Butler do so explicitly. Butler argues that all vice is due to self-deception stemming from a false regard for oneself. He denies that anyone loves sin.

> Vice in general consists in having an unreasonable and too great regard to ourselves, in comparison of others. Robbery and murder is never from the love of injustice or cruelty, but to gratify some other passion, to gain some supposed advantage: and it is false selfishness alone, whether cool or passionate, which makes a man resolutely pursue that end, be it ever so much to the injury of another.

Kant, too, denies the existence of any impulse to evil that is not connected with a desire to satisfy oneself in some way. "We have ... no direct inclination towards evil as evil, but only an indirect one." If Kant and Butler are right, the evil we do is always inadvertent: it is not what we are after.

Most traditional philosophers agree that we need a uniform account of vice and virtue. We have already seen that Augustine and other Christian thinkers find the common denominator of vice in the defiance of God. Butler finds it in the element of self-deception that permits people to do what they want without admitting to themselves that an action is wrong and self-debasing. Kant, we saw, finds the unity of virtue in the will. The very first philosopher to propose a unified theory of the virtues and vices was Plato, who identified virtue with knowledge and vice with ignorance. Ever since then, philosophers have been hard at work trying to give meaningful substance to what seems right about these identifications.

Vice

Plutarch

TRANSLATED BY FRANK COLE BABBITT

Plutarch (A.D. c. 46–c. 120) was a Greek moralist and biographer. His *Lives* is a classic in the genre of short biography. Plutarch's philosophy was neo-Platonic, and he was a sharp critic of Epicureanism.

Plutarch contrasts persons of virtue with persons of vice, claiming that the former can achieve equanimity even in poverty. He depicts the latter as ill and peevish, incapable of truly enjoying even the external things they covet. Plutarch points out that we cannot rid ourselves of vice the way we rid ourselves of bad company. Vicious persons must live in constant proximity to their unpleasant selves.

1. Clothes are supposed to make a man warm, not of course by warming him themselves in the sense of adding their warmth to him, because each garment by itself is cold, and for this reason very often persons who feel hot and feverish keep changing from one set of clothes to another; but the warmth which a man gives off from his own person the clothing, closely applied to the body, confines and enwraps, and does not allow it, when thus imprisoned in the body, to be dissipated again. Now the same condition existing in human affairs deceives most people, who think that, if they surround themselves with vast houses, and get together a mass of slaves and money, they shall live pleasantly. But a pleasant and happy life comes not from external things, but, on the contrary, man draws on his own character as a source from which to add the element of pleasure and joy to the things which surround him.

> Bright with a blazing fire a house looks far more cheerful, and wealth is pleasanter, and repute and power more resplendent, if with them goes the gladness which springs from the heart; and so too men bear poverty, exile, and old age lightly and gently in proportion to the serenity and mildness of their character.

2. As perfumes make coarse and ragged garments fragrant, but the body of Anchises gave off a noisome exudation,

> Damping the linen robe adown his back,

so every occupation and manner of life, if attended by virtue, is untroubled and delightful, while, on the other hand, any admixture of vice renders those things

Reprinted by permission of the publishers and the Trustees of the Loeb Classical Library from PLUTARCH: MORALIA ~ VOLUME II, Loeb Classical Library Volume 222, translated by F. C. Babbitt, Cambridge, Mass.: Harvard University Press, 1928. The Loeb Classical Library® is a registered trademark of the President and Fellows of Harvard College.

which to others seem splendid, precious, and imposing, only troublesome, sickening, and unwelcome to their possessors.

> This man is happy deemed 'mid public throng,
> But when he opens his door he's thrice a wretch;
> His wife controls, commands, and always fights.

Yet it is not difficult for any man to get rid of a bad wife if he be a real man and not a slave; but against his own vice it is not possible to draw up a writing of divorcement and forthwith to be rid of troubles and to be at peace, having arranged to be by himself. No, his vice, a settled tenant of his very vitals always, both at night and by day,

> Burns, but without e'er a brand, and consigns to an eld all untimely.

For in travelling vice is a troublesome companion because of arrogance, at dinner an expensive companion owing to gluttony, and a distressing bedfellow, since by anxieties, cares and jealousies it drives out and destroys sleep. For what slumber there may be is a sleep and repose for the body only, but for the soul terrors, dreams, and agitations, because of superstition.

> When grief o'ertakes me as I close my eyes,
> I'm murdered by my dreams.

says one man. In such a state do envy, fear, temper, and licentiousness put a man. For by day vice, looking outside of itself and conforming its attitude to others, is abashed and veils its emotions, and does not give itself up completely to its impulses, but oftentimes resists them and struggles against them; but in the hours of slumber, when it has escaped from opinion and law, and got away as far as possible from feeling fear or shame, it sets every desire stirring, and awakens its depravity and licentiousness. It "attempts incest," as Plato says, partakes of forbidden meats, abstains from nothing which it wishes to do, but revels in lawlessness so far as it can, with images and visions which end in no pleasure or accomplishment of desire, but have only the power to stir to fierce activity the emotional and morbid propensities.

3. Where, then, is the pleasure in vice, if in no part of it is to be found freedom from care and grief, or contentment or tranquility or calm? For a well-balanced and healthy condition of the body gives room for engendering the pleasures of the flesh; but in the soul lasting joy and gladness cannot possibly be engendered, unless it provide itself first with cheerfulness, fearlessness, and courageousness as a basis to rest upon, or as a calm tranquillity that no billows disturb; otherwise, even though some hope or delectation lure us with a smile, anxiety suddenly breaks forth, like a hidden rock appearing in fair weather, and the soul is overwhelmed and confounded.

4. Heap up gold, amass silver, build stately promenades, fill your house with slaves and the city with your debtors; unless you lay level the emotions of your soul, put a stop to your insatiate desires, and quit yourself of fears and anxieties, you are but decanting wine for a man in a fever, offering honey to a bilious man, and preparing tidbits and dainties for sufferers from colic or dysentery, who cannot retain them or be strengthened by them, but are only brought nearer to death thereby. Does not your observation of sick persons teach you that they dislike and reject and decline the finest and costliest viands which their attendants offer and try

to force upon them; and then later, when their whole condition has changed, and good breathing, wholesome blood, and normal temperature have returned to their bodies, they get up and have joy and satisfaction in eating plain bread with cheese and cress? It is such a condition that reason creates in the soul. You will be contented with your lot if you learn what the honourable and good is. You will be luxurious in poverty, and live like a king, and you will find no less satisfaction in the care-free life of a private citizen than in the life connected with high military or civic office. If you become a philosopher, you will live not unpleasantly, but you will learn to subsist pleasantly anywhere and with any resources. Wealth will give you gladness for the good you will do to many, poverty for your freedom from many cares, repute for the honours you will enjoy, and obscurity for the certainty that you shall not be envied.

STUDY QUESTIONS

1. Plutarch seems to deny that vice contains any real pleasure or satisfaction. Do you agree? Why or why not?
2. Do you agree with his claim that persons given over to vice are poor company for everyone, including themselves? Explain.
3. Plutarch associates vice with a troubled nature, and virtue with a contented, serene nature. Are these correlations realistic? Explain.
4. Plutarch claims that the person of vice is subject to the ills of poverty, while the person of virtue transcends them. Does this claim have merit? Why or why not? In your opinion, what effect does economic circumstance have on a virtuous or a vicious nature?

The Depths of Vice

Saint Augustine

TRANSLATED BY JOHN K. RYAN

A biographical sketch of Saint Augustine is found on page 264.

Augustine, writing about his sixteenth year, describes the time he and his friends stole some pears for which they had no use. He ponders the motive and concludes that the perverse desire to defy God's will, an expression of humanity's corrupted nature, was itself the motive. Augustine is now disgusted with his past self, but confesses that he was once ready to sin whenever someone urged, "Let's go! Let's do it!"

I wish to bring back to mind my past foulness and the carnal corruptions of my soul. This is not because I love them, but that I may love you, my God. Out of love for your love I do this. In the bitterness of my remembrance, I tread again my most evil ways, so that you may grow sweet to me, O sweetness that never fails, O sweetness happy and enduring, which gathers me together again from that disordered state in which I lay in shattered pieces, wherein, turned away from you, the one, I spent myself upon the many. For in my youth, I burned to get my fill of hellish things. I dared to run wild in different darksome ways of love. My comeliness wasted away. I stank in your eyes, but I was pleasing to myself and I desired to be pleasing to the eyes of men....

The Stolen Fruit

Surely, Lord, your law punishes theft, as does that law written on the hearts of men, which not even iniquity itself blots out. What thief puts up with another thief with a calm mind? Not even a rich thief will pardon one who steals from him because of want. But I willed to commit theft, and I did so, not because I was driven to it by any need, unless it were by poverty of justice, and dislike of it, and by a glut of evildoing. For I stole a thing of which I had plenty of my own and of much better quality. Nor did I wish to enjoy that thing which I desired to gain by theft, but rather to enjoy the actual theft and the sin of theft.

In a garden nearby to our vineyard there was a pear tree, loaded with fruit that was desirable neither in appearance nor in taste. Late one night—to which hour, according to our pestilential custom, we had kept our street games—a group of very bad youngsters set out to shake down and rob this tree. We took great loads of fruit from it, not for our own eating, but rather to throw it to the pigs; even if we did eat a little of it, we did this to do what pleased us for the reason that it was forbidden....

When there is discussion concerning a crime and why it was committed, it is usually held that there appeared possibility that the appetites would obtain some of these goods, which we have termed lower, or there was fear of losing them. These things are beautiful and fitting, but in comparison with the higher goods, which bring happiness, they are mean and base. A man commits murder: why did he do so? He coveted his victim's wife or his property; or he wanted to rob him to get money to live on; or he feared to be deprived of some such thing by the other; or he had been injured, and burned for revenge. Would anyone commit murder without reason and out of delight in murder itself? Who can believe such a thing? Of a certain senseless and utterly cruel man it was said that he was evil and cruel without reason. Nevertheless, a reason has been given, for he himself said, "I don't want to let my hand or will get out of practice through disuse." Why did he want that? Why so? It was to the end that after he had seized the city by the practice of crime, he would attain to honors, power, and wealth, and be free from fear of the law and from trouble due to lack of wealth or from a guilty conscience. Therefore, not even Catiline himself loved his crimes, but something else, for sake of which he committed them.

The Anatomy of Evil

What was it that I, a wretch, loved in you, my act of theft, my deed of crime done by night, done in the sixteenth year of my age? You were not beautiful, for you were but an act of thievery. In truth, are you anything at all, that I may speak to you? The fruit we stole was beautiful, for it was your creation, O most beautiful of all beings, creator of all things, God the good, God the supreme good and my true good. Beautiful was the fruit, but it was not what my unhappy soul desired. I had an abundance of better pears, but those pears I gathered solely that I might steal. The fruit I gathered I threw away, devouring in it only iniquity, and that I rejoiced to enjoy. For if I put any of that fruit into my mouth, my sin was its seasoning. But now, O Lord my God, I seek out what was in that theft to give me delight, and lo, there is no loveliness in it. I do not say such loveliness as there is in justice and prudence, or in man's mind, and memory, and senses, and vigorous life, nor that with which the stars are beautiful and glorious in their courses, or the land and the sea filled with their living kinds, which by new births replace those that die, nor even that flawed and shadowy beauty found in the vices that deceive us.

For pride imitates loftiness of mind, while you are the one God, highest above all things. What does ambition seek, except honor and glory, while you alone are to be honored above all else and are glorious forever? The cruelty of the mighty desires to be feared: but who is to be feared except the one God, and from his power what can be seized and stolen away, and when, or where, or how, or by whom? The caresses of the wanton call for love; but there is naught more caressing than your charity, nor is anything to be loved more wholesomely than your truth, which is beautiful and bright above all things. Curiosity pretends to be a desire for knowledge, while you know all things in the highest degree. Ignorance itself and folly are cloaked over the names of simplicity and innocence, because nothing more simple than you can be found. What is more innocent than you, whereas to evil men their own works are hostile? Sloth seeks rest as it were, but what sure rest is there apart from the Lord? Luxury of life desires to be called plenty and abundance; you are the fullness and the unfailing plenty of incorruptible pleasure. Prodigality casts but the shadow of liberality, while you are the most affluent giver of all good things. Avarice desires to possess many things, and you possess all things. Envy contends for excellence: what is more excellent than you? Anger seeks vengeance: who takes vengeance with more justice than you? Fear shrinks back at sudden and unusual things threatening what it loves, and is on watch for its own safety. But for you what is unusual or what is sudden? Or who can separate you from what you love? Where, except with you, is there firm security? Sadness wastes away over things now lost in which desire once took delight. It did not want this to happen, whereas from you nothing can be taken away.

Thus the soul commits fornication when it is turned away from you and, apart from you, seeks such pure, clean things as it does not find except when it returns to you. In a perverse way, all men imitate you who put themselves far from you, and rise up in rebellion against you. Even by such imitation of you they prove that you are the creator of all nature, and that therefore there is no place where they can depart entirely from you.

What, therefore did I love in that theft of mine, in what manner did I perversely or viciously imitate my Lord? Did it please me to go against your law, at least by trickery, for I could not do so with might? Did it please me that as a captive I should imitate a deformed liberty, by doing with impunity things illicit bearing a shadowy likeness of your omnipotence? Behold, your servant flees from his Lord and follows after a shadow! O rottenness! O monstrous life and deepest death! Could a thing give pleasure which could not be done lawfully, and which was done for no other reason but because it was unlawful? ...

Evil Communications

What was my state of mind? Truly and clearly, it was most base, and woe was it to me who had it. Yet, what was it? Who understands his sins? It was like a thing of laughter, which reached down as it were into our hearts, that we were tricking those who did not know what we were doing and would most strenuously resent it. Why, then, did even the fact that I did not do it alone give me pleasure? Is it because no one can laugh readily when he is alone? No one indeed does laugh readily when alone. However, individual men, when alone and when no one else is about, are sometimes overcome by laughter if something very funny affects their senses or strikes their mind. But that deed I would not have done alone; alone I would never have done it.

Behold, the living record of my soul lies before you, my God. By myself I would not have committed that theft in which what pleased me was not what I stole but the fact that I stole. This would have pleased me not at all if I had done it alone; nor by myself would I have done it at all. O friendship too unfriendly! Unfathomable seducer of the mind, greed to do harm for fun and sport, desire for another's injury, arising not from desire for my own gain or for vengeance, but merely when someone says, "Let's go! Let's do it!" and it is shameful not to be shameless!

A Soul in Waste

Who can untie this most twisted and intricate mass of knots? It is a filthy thing: I do not wish to think about it; I do not wish to look upon it. I desire you, O justice and innocence, beautiful and comely to all virtuous eyes, and I desire this unto a satiety that can never be satiated. With you there is true rest and life untroubled. He who enters into you enters into the joy of his Lord, and he shall have no fear, and he shall possess his soul most happily in him who is the supreme good. I fell away from you, my God, and I went astray, too far astray from you, the support of my youth, and I became to myself a land of want.

STUDY QUESTIONS

1. Do you agree with Augustine that we often pursue vice for its own sake? Why or why not?
2. Explain what Augustine means when he says, "In a perverse way, all men imitate [God] who put themselves far from [him], and rise up in rebellion against [him]."
3. Do you agree with Augustine's implicit claim that a crime such as theft is worse when committed for the thrill of it rather than for material gain? Explain.
4. People sometimes say that evil will be greatly mitigated when human nature changes for the better. Do you believe that human beings have evolved morally? Can we reasonably expect that they may become significantly more moral than they now are? What would Augustine say?

Sinners in the Hands of an Angry God

Jonathan Edwards

Jonathan Edwards (1703–1758) was a prominent New England Congregationalist minister and theologian during the Great Awakening, a religious revival movement of the 1730s. Edwards's ideas were taken very seriously in his day and helped to revitalize American Protestantism. His works include *A Faithful Narrative of the Surprising Word of God in the Conversion of Many Hundreds of Souls* (1737) and *A Careful and Strict Enquiry into the Freedom of the Will* (1754).

Jonathan Edwards preached the Calvinist doctrine that evil is innate in the human soul. No one, no matter how "strict, sober or religious," could count on escaping eternal damnation. Good *actions* were insufficient: "Nothing that you ever have done, nothing that you can do [will] induce God to spare you." God's mercy is obtainable only through *faith*.

Edwards's call for a personal experience of conversion as proof of genuine faith (and freedom from sin or vice) has been a central feature of a number of religious movements. The following excerpt is from a sermon by Edwards that was so vivid and frightening that several listeners became hysterical. Some even fainted.

The God that holds you over the pit of hell much as one holds a spider or some loathsome insect over the fire, abhors you, and is dreadfully provoked; his wrath towards you burns like fire; he looks upon you as worthy of nothing else but to be cast into the fire; he is of purer eyes than to bear to have you in his sight; you are ten thousand times so abominable in his eyes as the most hateful and venomous serpent is in ours. You have offended him infinitely more than ever a stubborn rebel did his prince: and yet it is nothing but his hand that holds you from falling into the fire every moment. 'Tis ascribed to nothing else, that you did not go to hell the last night; that you was suffered to awake again in this world after you closed your eyes to sleep; and there is no other reason to be given why you have not dropped into hell since you arose in the morning, but that God's hand has held you up. There is no other reason to be given why you have not gone to hell since you have sat here in the house of God, provoking his pure eyes by your sinful wicked manner of attending his solemn worship. Yea, there is nothing else that is to be given as a reason why you do not this very moment drop down into hell.

SINNERS IN THE HANDS OF AN ANGRY GOD From "Children in the Hands of an Angry God," a sermon preached in Enfield, CT, July 1742, by Jonathan Edwards.

O sinner! Consider the fearful danger you are in. 'Tis a great furnace of wrath, a wide and bottomless pit, full of the fire of wrath, that you are held over in the hand of that God whose wrath is provoked and incensed as much against you as against many of the damned in hell. You hang by a slender thread, with the flames of divine wrath flashing about it, and ready every moment to singe it and burn it asunder; and you have no interest in any Mediator, and nothing to lay hold of to save yourself, nothing to keep off the flames of wrath, nothing of your own, nothing that you ever have done, nothing that you can do, to induce God to spare you one moment....

It is *everlasting* wrath. It would be dreadful to suffer this fierceness and wrath of Almighty God one moment; but you must suffer it to all eternity: there will be no end to this exquisite, horrible misery. When you look forward you shall see a long forever, a boundless duration before you, which will swallow up your thoughts and amaze your soul; and you will absolutely despair of ever having any deliverance, any end, any mitigation, any rest at all; you will know certainly that you must wear out long ages, millions of millions of ages, in wrestling and conflicting with this almighty, merciless vengeance; and then when you have so done, when so many ages have actually been spent by you in this manner, you will know that all is but a point to what remains. So that your punishment will indeed be infinite. Oh, who can express what the state of a soul in such circumstances is! All that we can possibly say about it gives but a very feeble, faint representation of it: it is inexpressible and inconceivable, for "who knows the power of God's anger?"

How dreadful is the state of those that are daily and hourly in danger of this great wrath and infinite misery! But this is the dismal case of every soul in this congregation that has not been born again, however moral and strict, sober and religious, they may otherwise be. Oh, that you would consider it, whether you be young or old! There is reason to think that there are many in this congregation now hearing this discourse, that will actually be the subjects of this very misery to all eternity. We know not who they are, or in what seats they sit, or what thoughts they now have. It may be they are now at ease and hear all these things without much disturbance, and are now flattering themselves that they are not the persons, promising themselves that they shall escape. If we knew that there was one person, and but one, in the whole congregation, that was to be the subject of this misery, what an awful thing it would be to think of! If we knew who it was, what an awful sight would it be to see such a person! How might all the rest of the congregation lift up a lamentable and bitter cry over him! But alas! instead of one, how many is it likely will remember this discourse in hell! And it would be a wonder, if some that are now present should not be in hell in a very short time, before this year is out. And it would be no wonder if some persons that now sit here in some seats of this meetinghouse in health, and quiet and secure, should be there before tomorrow morning. Those of you that finally continue in a natural condition, that shall keep out of hell longest, will be there in a little time! Your damnation does not slumber; it will come swiftly and, in all probability, very suddenly upon many of you. You have reason to wonder that you are not already in hell. 'Tis doubtless the case of some that heretofore you have seen and known, that never deserved hell more than you and that heretofore appeared as likely to have been now alive as you. Their case is past all hope; they are crying in extreme misery and perfect despair.

But here you are in the land of the living and in the house of God, and have an opportunity to obtain salvation. What would not those poor, damned, hopeless souls give for one day's such opportunity as you now enjoy!

And now you have an extraordinary opportunity, a day wherein Christ has flung the door of mercy wide open, and stands in the door calling and crying with a loud voice to poor sinners; a day wherein many are flocking to him and pressing into the Kingdom of God. Many are daily coming from the east, west, north, and south; many that were very likely in the same miserable condition that you are in, are in now a happy state, with their hearts filled with love to him that has loved them and washed them from their sins in his own blood, and rejoicing in hope of the glory of God. How awful is it to be left behind at such a day! To see so many others feasting, while you are pining and perishing! To see so many rejoicing and singing for joy of heart, while you have cause to mourn for sorrow of heart and howl for vexation of spirit! How can you rest for one moment in such a condition? Are not your souls as precious as the souls of the people at Suffield,[1] where they are flocking from day to day to Christ?

STUDY QUESTIONS

1. Reread the exchange between Jonathan Bennett and Philip Hallie (Chapter One), noting Bennett's harsh judgment of Edwards that Hallie does not share. Where do you stand?
2. Getting someone to avoid vice is a problem. Strong medicine may be called for. Edwards used the threat of divine judgment. What alternative incentives are available? Discuss the general problem of how we may induce someone to change for the better.
3. The Calvinist doctrine of the "total depravity" of humankind holds that, because of the original sin of Adam and Eve, we are all innately prone to do evil acts rather than good ones. Do you believe there is some truth in this doctrine? Why or why not? How, in your view, does a belief in original sin affect one's approach to moral education?

---

[1] Edwards delivered this sermon in Enfield, Connecticut; Suffield was a nearby town.

The Hypocrites

Dante Alighieri

TRANSLATED BY JOHN CIARDI

Dante Alighieri (1265–1321) is the Florentine author of the *Divine Comedy,* which is regarded as one of the supreme literary works of all time. It recounts the poet's journey through hell (the *Inferno*), purgatory (the

---

Purgatorio), and finally heaven (the *Paradiso*), and describes the fate of human souls after death.

Dante intended the *Divine Comedy* as an allegory. In a letter to his patron he wrote, "[I]ts subject is: 'Man, as by good or ill deserts, in the exercise of his free choice, becomes liable to rewarding or punishing justice.'" The *Inferno* is also meant as an allegorical description of the state of sinners' souls while they are still alive. Thus, hypocrites, even while alive, may appear to be "all dazzle, golden and fair," but on the inside they are heavy, leaden, and tormented. For Dante, the internal effects of sin are as punishing as the torments of hell.

About us now in the depth of the pit we found
  a painted people, weary and defeated.
  Slowly, in pain, they paced it round and round

All wore great cloaks cut to as ample a size
  as those worn by the Benedictines of Cluny.[1]
  The enormous hoods were drawn over their eyes.

The outside is all dazzle, golden and fair;
  the inside, lead, so heavy that Frederick's capes,[2]
  compared to these, would seem as light as air.

O weary mantle for eternity!
  We turned to the left again along their course,
  listening to their moans of misery,

but they moved so slowly down that barren strip,
  tired by their burden, that our company
  was changed at every movement of the hip.[3]

And walking thus, I said: "As we go on,
  may it please you to look about among these people
  for any whose name or history may be known."

And one who understood Tuscan cried to us there
  as we hurried past: "I pray you check your speed,
  you who run so fast through the sick air:

it may be I am one who will fit your case."
  And at his words my Master turned and said:
  "Wait now, then go with him at his own pace."

---

[1] *the Benedictines of Cluny:* The habit of these monks was especially ample and elegant. St. Bernard once wrote ironically to a nephew who had entered this monastery: "If length of sleeves and amplitude of hood made for holiness, what could hold me back from following [your lead]."

[2] *Frederick's capes:* Frederick II executed persons found guilty of treason by fastening them into a sort of leaden shell. The doomed man was then placed in a cauldron over a fire and the lead was melted around him.

[3] *our company was changed, etc.:* Another tremendous Dantean figure. Sense: "They moved so slowly that at every step (movement of the hip) we found ourselves beside new sinners."

I waited there, and saw along that track
    two souls who seemed in haste to be with me;
    but the narrow way and their burden held them back.

When they had reached me down that narrow way
    they stared at me in silence and amazement,
    then turned to one another. I heard one say:

"This one seems, by the motion of his throat,
    to be alive; and if they are dead, how is it
    they are allowed to shed the leaden coat?"

And then to me "O Tuscan, come so far
    to the college of the sorry hypocrites,
    do not disdain to tell us who you are."

And I: "I was born and raised a Florentine
    on the green and lovely banks of Arno's waters,
    I go with the body that was always mine.

But who are *you*, who sighing as you go
    distill in floods of tears that drown your cheeks?
    What punishment is this that glitters so?"

"These burnished robes are of thick lead," said one,
    "and are hung on us like counterweights, so heavy
    that we, their weary fulcrums, creak and groan.

Jovial Friars and Bolognese were we.[4]
    We were chosen jointly by your Florentines[5]
    to keep the peace, an office usually

held by a single man; near the Gardingo[6]
    one still may see the sort of peace we kept.
    I was called Catalano, he, Loderingo."

I began: "O Friars, your evil ... "—and then I saw
    a figure crucified upon the ground[7]
    by three great stakes, and I fell still in awe.

---

[4] *Jovial Friars:* A nickname given to the military monks of the order of the Glorious Virgin Mary founded at Bologna in 1261. Their original aim was to serve as peacemakers, enforcers of order, and protectors of the weak, but their observance of their rules became so scandalously lax, and their management of worldly affairs so self-seeking, that the order was disbanded by Papal decree.

[5] *We were chosen jointly ... to keep the peace:* Catalano del Malavolti (c. 1210–1285), a Guelph, and Loderingo degli Andolo (c. 1210–1293), a Ghibelline, were both Bolognese and, as brothers of the Jovial Friars, both had served as *podestà* (the chief officer charged with keeping the peace) of many cities for varying terms. In 1266 they were jointly appointed to the office of *podestà* of Florence on the theory that a bipartisan administration by men of God would bring peace to the city. Their tenure of office was marked by great violence, however; and they were forced to leave in a matter of months. Modern scholarship has established the fact that they served as instruments of Clement IV's policy in Florence, working at his orders to overthrow the Ghibellines under the guise of an impartial administration.

[6] *Gardingo:* The site of the palace of the Ghibelline family degli Uberti. In the riots resulting from the maladministration of the two Jovial Friars, the Ghibellines were forced out of the city and the Uberti palace was razed.

[7] *a figure crucified upon the ground:* Caiaphas. His words were: "It is expedient that one man shall die for the people and that the whole nation perish not." (*John* xi, 50.)

When he saw me there, he began to puff great sighs
    into his beard, convulsing all his body;
    and Friar Catalano, following my eyes,

said to me: "That one nailed across the road
    counselled the Pharisees that it was fitting
    one man be tortured for the public good.

Naked he lies fixed there, as you see,
    in the path of all who pass; there he must feel
    the weight of all through all eternity.

His father-in-law and the others of the Council[8]
    which was a seed of wrath to all the Jews,
    are similarly staked for the same evil."

Then I saw Virgil marvel for a while[9]
    over that soul so ignominiously
    stretched on the cross in Hell's eternal exile.

Then, turning, he asked the Friar: "If your law permit,
    can you tell us if somewhere along the right
    there is some gap in the stone wall of the pit

through which we two may climb to the next brink
    without the need of summoning the Black Angels
    and forcing them to raise us from this sink?"

He: "Nearer than you hope, there is a bridge
    that runs from the great circle of the scarp
    and crosses every ditch from ridge to ridge,

except that in this it is broken; but with care
    you can mount the ruins which lie along the slope
    and make a heap on the bottom." My Guide stood there

motionless for a while with a dark look.
    At last he said: "He lied about this business,
    who spears the sinners yonder with his hook."[10]

And the Friar: "Once at Bologna I heard the wise
    discussing the Devil's sins; among them I heard
    that he is a liar and the father of lies."

When the sinner had finished speaking, I saw the face
    of my sweet Master darken a bit with anger:[11]
    he set off at a great stride from that place,

---

[8] *his father-in-law and the others:* Annas, father-in-law of Caiaphas, was the first before whom Jesus was led upon his arrest. (*John* xviii, 13.) He had Jesus bound and delivered to Caiaphas.

[9] *I saw Virgil marvel:* Caiaphas had not been there on Virgil's first descent into Hell.

[10] *he lied ... who spears the sinners yonder:* Malacoda.

[11] *darken a bit:* The original is *turbato un poco d'ira*. A bit of anger befits the righteous indignation of Human Reason, but immoderate anger would be out of character. One of the sublimities of Dante's writing is the way in which even the smallest details reinforce the great concepts.

and I turned from that weighted hypocrite
to follow in the prints of his dear feet.

STUDY QUESTIONS

1. Why is hypocrisy a vice?
2. What forms of hypocrisy are most damaging?
3. Do hypocrites deceive themselves as well as others? Explain.
4. Is Dante right about the psychological and spiritual effects of hypocrisy? Why or why not? Does hypocrisy weigh people down and make them "weary and defeated"? Explain.
5. Can a hypocrite be happy? Why or why not?

Self-Deception

Samuel Johnson

Samuel Johnson (1709–1784), immortalized by his famous biographer, James Boswell, was one of the most prominent figures of eighteenth-century English intellectual life. He wrote essays, novels, biographies, political tracts, a dictionary, and poetry, all in a scintillating style.

Johnson examines the devices of self-deceivers. One device they use is to congratulate themselves on a single act of generosity, thereby conferring on themselves the attribute "compassionate" or "generous," even though the vast majority of their actions are mean and self-serving. Or they may praise goodness verbally, and thereby deceive themselves into thinking they are good. Still another device is to appear virtuous by dwelling on the evils of others. Self-deceivers will try to keep their distance from people who truly know what they are like, preferring the company of those who won't expose them to themselves. And they avoid "self-communion."

One sophism by which men persuade themselves that they have those virtues which they really want, is formed by the substitution of single acts for habits. A miser who once relieved a friend from the danger of a prison, suffers his imagination to dwell for ever upon his own heroick generosity; he yields his heart up to indignation at those who are blind to merit, or insensible to misery, and who can please themselves with the enjoyment of that wealth, which they never permit others to partake. From any censures of the world, or reproaches of his conscience, he has an

SELF-DECEPTION From *The Works of Samuel Johnson*, vol. 1, "The Rambler" no. 29 (June 23, 1750).

appeal to action and to knowledge; and though his whole life is a course of rapacity and avarice, he concludes himself to be tender and liberal, because he has once performed an act of liberality and tenderness.

As a glass which magnifies objects by the approach of one end to the eye, lessens them by the application of the other, so vices are extenuated by the inversion of that fallacy, by which virtues are augmented. Those faults which we cannot conceal from our own notice, are considered, however frequent, not as habitual corruptions, or settled practices, but as casual failures, and single lapses. A man who has, from year to year, set his country to sale, either for the gratification of his ambition or resentment, confesses that the heat of party now and then betrays the severest virtue to measures that cannot be seriously defended. He that spends his days and nights in riot and debauchery, owns that his passions oftentimes overpower his resolution. But each comforts himself that his faults are not without precedent, for the best and the wisest men have given way to the violence of sudden temptations.

There are men who always confound the praise of goodness with the practice, and who believe themselves mild and moderate, charitable and faithful, because they have exerted their eloquence in commendation of mildness, fidelity, and other virtues. This is an error almost universal among those that converse much with dependents, with such whose fear or interest disposes them to a seeming reverence for any declamation, however enthusiastick, and submission to any boast, however arrogant. Having none to recall their attention to their lives, they rate themselves by the goodness of their opinions, and forget how much more easily men may shew their virtue in their talk than in their actions.

The tribe is likewise very numerous of those who regulate their lives, not by the standard of religion, but the measure of other men's virtue; who lull their own remorse with the remembrance of crimes more atrocious than their own, and seem to believe that they are not bad while another can be found worse.

For escaping these and a thousand other deceits, many expedients have been proposed. Some have recommended the frequent consultation of a wise friend, admitted to intimacy, and encouraged to sincerity. But this appears a remedy by no means adapted to general use: for in order to secure the virtue of one, it presupposes more virtue in two than will generally be found. In the first, such a desire of rectitude and amendment, as may incline him to hear his own accusation from the mouth of him whom he esteems, and by whom, therefore, he will always hope that his faults are not discovered; and in the second such zeal and honesty, as will make him content for his friend's advantage to lose his kindness.

A long life may be passed without finding a friend in whose understanding and virtue we can equally confide, and whose opinion we can value at once for its justness and sincerity. A weak man, however honest, is not qualified to judge. A man of the world, however penetrating, is not fit to counsel. Friends are often chosen for similitude of manners, and therefore each palliates the other's failings, because they are his own. Friends are tender and unwilling to give pain, or they are interested, and fearful to offend.

These objections have inclined others to advise, that he who would know himself, should consult his enemies, remember the reproaches that are vented to his face, and listen for the censures that are uttered in private. For his great business is to know his faults, and those malignity will discover, and resentment will reveal.

But this precept may be often frustrated; for it seldom happens that rivals or opponents are suffered to come near enough to know our conduct with so much exactness as that conscience should allow and reflect the accusation. The charge of an enemy is often totally false, and commonly so mingled with falsehood, that the mind takes advantage from the failure of one part to discredit the rest, and never suffers any disturbance afterward from such partial reports.

Yet it seems that enemies have been always found by experience the most faithful monitors; for adversity has ever been considered as the state in which a man most easily becomes acquainted with himself, and this effect it must produce by withdrawing flatterers, whose business it is to hide our weaknesses from us, or by giving loose to malice, and licence to reproach; or at least by cutting of those pleasures which called us away from meditation on our conduct, and repressing that pride which too easily persuades us, that we merit whatever we enjoy.

Part of these benefits it is in every man's power to procure himself, by assigning proper portions of his life to the examination of the rest, and by putting himself frequently in such a situation by retirement and abstraction, as may weaken the influence of external objects. By this practice he may obtain the solitude of adversity without its melancholy, its instructions without its censures, and its sensibility without its perturbations.

The necessity of setting the world at a distance from us, when we are to take a survey of ourselves, has sent many from high stations to the severities of a monastick life; and indeed, every man deeply engaged in business, if all regard to another state be not extinguished, must have the conviction, tho', perhaps, not the resolution of Valdesso, who, when he solicited Charles the Fifth to dismiss him, being asked, whether he retired upon disgust, answered that he laid down his commission, for no other reason but because "there ought to be some time for sober reflection between the life of a soldier and his death."

There are few conditions which do not entangle us with sublunary hopes and fears, from which it is necessary to be at intervals disencumbered, that we may place ourselves in his presence who views effects in their causes, and actions in their motives; that we may, as Chillingworth expresses it, consider things as if there were no other beings in the world but God and ourselves; or, to use language yet more awful, "may commune with our own hearts, and be still."

STUDY QUESTIONS

1. Self-deceivers are sometimes virtuous. How, in Johnson's opinion, does this aid in self-deception?
2. What part does self-deception play in our choice of friends?
3. Why does Johnson say that we should consult not our friends but our enemies if we want to learn about ourselves? Do you think he is right? Explain.
4. What techniques of self-deception does Johnson mention? What others can you think of?

Upon Self-Deceit

Joseph Butler

Joseph Butler (1692–1752) was an English moral philosopher and theologian. In 1738, he was made a bishop of the Church of England. Butler's *Fifteen Sermons*, from which the present selection is taken, are still admired for their style, acumen, and good sense.

Butler cites the example of King David to show how easily even good persons can deceive themselves. King David committed an injustice without condemning himself, but was morally outraged on hearing that someone else had done a similar thing. Butler points out the difficulty of living by the ancient dictum "Know thyself." Self-deception often works in the service of self-regard. We want something and make ourselves believe we do right in acquiring it when, in fact, we do wrong. Moreover, we retain a good opinion of ourselves by avoiding the company of those who would condemn us. Self-deceit is especially prevalent in the undefined areas of moral behavior where moral duties are not *explicit*. There self-deceivers can be ungenerous and spiteful, and still remain within the letter of the law, comfortably at peace with their conscience. Butler argues that self-deception is a very grave moral defect because it enables us to do evil in a self-righteous manner. Self-deception undermines the whole principle of good and so is worse than open, unhypocritical wickedness.

And Nathan said to David, Thou art the man. *2 Samuel 12.7*

These words are the application of Nathan's parable to David, upon occasion of his adultery with Bathsheba, and the murder of Uriah her husband. The parable, which is related in the most beautiful simplicity, is this: *There were two men in one city; the one rich, and the other poor. The rich man had exceeding many flocks and herds: but the poor man had nothing, save one little ewe lamb, which he had bought and nourished up: and it grew up together with him, and with his children: it did eat of his own meat, and drank of his own cup, and lay in his bosom, and was unto him as a daughter. And there came a traveller unto the rich man, and he spared to take of his own flock and of his own herd, to dress for the wayfaring man that was come unto him; but took the poor man's lamb, and dressed it for the man that was come to him. And David's anger was greatly kindled against the man; and he said to Nathan, As the Lord liveth, the man that hath done this thing shall surely die: and he shall restore the lamb fourfold, because he did this thing, and because he had not pity.* David passes sentence, not only that there should be a fourfold

UPON SELF-DECEIT From *Fifteen Sermons upon Human Nature* by Joseph Butler (1726).

restitution made; but he proceeds to the rigour of justice, *the man that hath done this thing shall die:* and this judgment is pronounced with the utmost indignation against such an act of inhumanity; *As the Lord liveth, he shall surely die: and his anger was greatly kindled against the man.* And the Prophet answered, *Thou art the man.* He had been guilty of much greater inhumanity, with the utmost deliberation, thought, and contrivance. Near a year must have passed, between the time of the commission of his crimes, and the time of the Prophet's coming to him; and it does not appear from the story, that he had in all this while the least remorse or contrition.

Nothing is more strange than our self-partiality

There is not any thing, relating to men and characters, more surprising and unaccountable, than this partiality to themselves, which is observable in many; as there is nothing of more melancholy reflection, respecting morality, virtue, and religion. Hence it is that many men seem perfect strangers to their own characters. They think, and reason, and judge quite differently upon any matter relating to themselves, from what they do in cases of others where they are not interested. Hence it is one hears people exposing follies, which they themselves are eminent for; and talking with great severity against particular vices, which, if all the world be not mistaken, they themselves are notoriously guilty of. This self-ignorance and self-partiality may be in all different degrees. It is a lower degree of it which David himself refers to in these words, *Who can tell how oft he offendeth? O cleanse thou me from my secret faults.* This is the ground of that advice of Elihu to Job: *Surely it is meet to be said unto God,—That which I see not, teach thou me; if I have done iniquity, I will do no more.* And Solomon saw this thing in a very strong light, when he said, *He that trusteth his own heart is a fool.*

Hence the 'Know thyself' of the ancients

This likewise was the reason why that precept, *Know thyself*, was so frequently inculcated by the philosophers of old. For if it were not for that partial and fond regard to ourselves, it would certainly be no great difficulty to know our own character, what passes within, the bent and bias of our mind; much less would there be any difficulty in judging rightly of our own actions. But from this partiality it frequently comes to pass, that the observation of many men's being themselves last of all acquainted with what falls out in their own families, may be applied to a nearer home, to what passes within their own breasts.

Usual temper: (a) absence of mistrust: (b) assumption that all is right: (c) disregard of precept, when against ourselves

There is plainly, in the generality of mankind, an absence of doubt or distrust, in a very great measure, as to their moral character and behaviour; and likewise a disposition to take for granted, that all is right and well with them in these respects. The former is owing to their not reflecting, not exercising their judgment upon themselves; the latter, to self-love. I am not speaking of that extravagance, which is sometimes to be met with; instances of persons declaring in words at length, that they never were in the wrong, nor had ever any diffidence to the justness of their conduct, in their whole lives. No, these people are too far gone to have anything said to them. The thing before us is indeed of this kind, but in a lower degree, and confined to the moral character; somewhat of which we almost all of us have, without reflecting upon it. Now consider how long, and how grossly, a person of the best understanding might be imposed upon by one of whom he had not any suspicion, and in whom he placed an entire confidence; especially if there were friendship and real kindness in the case: surely this holds even stronger with respect to that self we are all so fond of. Hence arises in men a disregard of reproof and instruction, rules of conduct and moral discipline, which occasionally come in their way: a disregard, I say, of these; not in every respect, but in this single one, namely, as what may be of service to them in particular towards mending their own hearts and tempers, and making them better men. It never in earnest comes into their thoughts, whether such admonitions may not relate, and be of service to themselves; and this quite distinct from a positive persuasion to the contrary, a persuasion from reflection that they are innocent and blameless in those respects. Thus we may invert the observation which is somewhere made upon Brutus, that he never read, but in order to make himself a better man. It scarce comes into the thoughts of the generality of mankind, that this use is to be made of moral reflections which they meet with; that this use, I say, is to be made of them by themselves, for every body observes and wonders that it is not done by others.

Also exclusive self-interest

Further, there are instances of persons having so fixed and steady an eye upon their own interest, whatever they place it in, and the interest of those whom they consider as themselves, as in a manner to regard nothing else; their views are almost confined to this alone. Now we cannot be acquainted with, or in any propriety of speech be said to know any thing, but what we attend to. If therefore they attend only to one side, they really will not, cannot see or know what is to be alleged on the other. Though a man hath the best eyes in the world, he cannot see any way but that which he turns them. Thus these persons, without passing over the least, the most minute thing, which can possibly be urged in favour of themselves, shall overlook entirely the plainest and most obvious things on the other side.

They inquire only to justify

And whilst they are under the power of this temper, thought and consideration upon the matter before them has scarce any tendency to set them right: because they are engaged; and their deliberation concerning an action to be done, or reflection upon it afterwards, is not to see whether it be right, but to find out reasons to justify or palliate it; palliate it, not to others, but to themselves.

With self-ignorance, perhaps, only in the favourite propensity

In some there is to be observed a general ignorance of themselves, and wrong way of thinking and judging in every thing relating to themselves; their fortune, reputation, every thing in which self can come in: and this perhaps attended with the rightest judgment in all other matters. In others this partiality is not so general, has not taken hold of the whole man, but is confined to some particular favourite passion, interest, or pursuit; suppose ambition, covetousness, or any other. And these persons may probably judge and determine what is perfectly just and proper, even in things in which they themselves are concerned, if these things have no relation to their particular favourite passion or pursuit. Hence arises that amazing incongruity, and seeming inconsistency of character, from whence slight observers take it for granted, that the whole is hypocritical and false; not being able otherwise to reconcile the several parts: whereas in truth there is real honesty, so far as it goes. There is such a thing as men's being honest to such a degree, and in such respects, but no further. And this, as it is true, so it is absolutely necessary to be taken notice of, and allowed them; such general and undistinguishing censure of their whole character, as designing and false, being one main thing which confirms them in their self-deceit. They know that the whole censure is not true; and so take for granted that no part of it is.

The judgment is perverted through the passions

But to go on with the explanation of the thing itself: Vice in general consists in having an unreasonable and too great regard to ourselves, in comparison of others. Robbery and murder is never from the love of injustice or cruelty, but to gratify some other passion, to gain some supposed advantage: and it is false selfishness alone, whether cool or passionate, which makes a man resolutely pursue that end, be it ever so much to the injury of another. But whereas, in common and ordinary wickedness, this unreasonableness, this partiality and selfishness, relates only, or chiefly, to the temper and passions in the characters we are now considering, it reaches to the understanding, and influences the very judgment. And, besides that general want of distrust and diffidence concerning our own character, there are, you see, two things, which may thus prejudice and darken the understanding itself: that overfondness for ourselves, which we are all so liable to; and also being under the power of any particular passion or appetite, or engaged in any particular pursuit. And these, especially the last of the two, may be in so great a degree, as to influence our judgment, even of other persons and their behaviour. Thus a man, whose temper is former to ambition or covetousness, shall even approve of them sometimes in others....

Frequent difficulty of defining: enhanced by vice

It is to be observed then, that as there are express determinate acts of wickedness, such as murder, adultery, theft: so, on the other hand, there are numberless cases in which the vice and wickedness cannot be exactly defined; but consists in a certain general temper and course of action, or in the neglect of some duty, suppose charity or any other, whose bounds and degrees are not fixed. This is the very province of self-deceit and self-partiality: here it governs without check or control. For what commandment is there broken? Is there a transgression where there is no law? A vice which cannot be defined?

Whoever will consider the whole commerce of human life, will see that a great part, perhaps the greatest part, of the intercourse amongst mankind, cannot be reduced to fixed determinate rules. Yet in these cases there is a right and a wrong: a merciful, a liberal, a kind and compassionate behaviour, which surely is our duty; and an unmerciful contracted spirit, an hard and oppressive course of behaviour, which is most certainly immoral and vicious. But who can define precisely, wherein that contracted spirit and hard usage of others consist, as murder and theft may be defined? There is not a word in our language, which expresses more detestable wickedness than *oppression:* yet the nature of this vice cannot be so exactly stated, nor the bounds of it so determinately marked, as that we shall be able to say in all instances, where rigid right and justice ends, and oppression begins. In these cases there is great latitude left, for every one to determine for, and consequently to deceive himself. It is chiefly in these cases that self-deceit comes in; as every one must see that there is much larger scope for it here, than in express, single, determinate acts of wickedness....

It is safer to be wicked in the ordinary way, than from this corruption lying at the root

Upon the whole it is manifest, that there is such a thing as this self-partiality and self-deceit: that in some persons it is to a degree which would be thought incredible, were not the instances before our eyes; of which the behaviour of David is perhaps the highest possible one, in a single particular case; for there is not the least appearance, that it reached his general character: that we are almost all of us influenced by it in some degree, and in some respects: that therefore every one ought to have an eye to and beware of it. And all that I have further to add upon this subject is, that either there is a difference between right and wrong, or there is not: religion is true, or it is not. If it be not, there is no reason for any concern about it: but if it be true, it requires real fairness of mind and honesty of heart. And, if people will be wicked, they had better of the two be so from the common vicious passions without such refinements, than from this deep and calm source of delusion; which undermines the whole principle of good; darkens that light, that *candle of the Lord within*, which is to direct our steps; and corrupts conscience, which is the guide of life.

Study Questions

1. What does Butler mean when he says that many people are strangers to their own character? Do you agree with his belief that we succeed in deceiving ourselves? Is there not a part of us that knows the truth? Explain.
2. Do you agree that the injunction "Know thyself" should be a fundamental moral rule?
3. According to Butler, vice results from our having an unreasonably high regard for ourselves in comparison with others. Do you think he is right? Why or why not?
4. What does Butler mean when he says that being "wicked in the ordinary way" is safer than being deeply self-deluded?
5. Why is self-deception most prevalent where the vice is undefined?

Jealousy, Envy, and Spite

Immanuel Kant

TRANSLATED BY LOUIS ENFIELD

A biographical sketch of Immanuel Kant is found on page 230.

In this selection, excerpted from his lectures on ethics, Immanuel Kant gives readers an account of the vices of jealousy, envy, spite, ingratitude, and malice. When we compare ourselves with those who are morally or materially better than us, we may become jealous of what they possess; then we may either attempt to depreciate that possession or try to emulate the owners by acquiring those same moral qualities or material objects. *Grudge* is the displeasure we feel when someone else has what we lack. Grudge becomes *envy* when we begrudge others their happiness. If we possess a good we do not need, but take pleasure in refusing to give it to someone who needs it, then we are *spiteful*. Another vice, *ingratitude*, has its origin in the resentment of another's superiority. In the extreme, ungrateful persons hate their benefactors. Kant calls the extremes of envy and ingratitude "devilish vices." A third devilish vice is *malice*—the gratuitous desire to see others fail. Malicious persons enjoy the misery of others. Kant denies that people are directly inclined to be "devilish." In this respect he differs from Augustine.

There are two methods by which men arrive at an opinion of their worth: by comparing themselves with the idea of perfection and by comparing themselves with others. The first of these methods is sound; the second is not, and it frequently even leads to a result diametrically opposed to the first. The idea of perfection is a proper standard, and if we measure our worth by it, we find that we fall short of it and feel that we must exert ourselves to come nearer to it; but if we compare ourselves with others, much depends upon who those others are and how they are constituted, and we can easily believe ourselves to be of great worth if those with whom we set up comparison are rogues. Men love to compare themselves with others, for by that method they can always arrive at a result favourable to themselves. They choose as a rule the worst and not the best of the class with which they set up comparison; in this way their own excellence shines out. If they choose those of greater worth the result of the comparison is, of course, unfavourable to them.

When I compare myself with another who is better than I, there are but two ways by which I can bridge the gap between us. I can either do my best to attain to his perfections, or else I can seek to depreciate his good qualities. I either increase

JEALOUSY, ENVY, AND SPITE from "Jealousy, Envy, and Grudge" from *Lectures on Ethics* by Immanuel Kant. Translated by Louis Enfield, Routledge, 1963. Reprinted by permission of the publisher.

my own worth, or else I diminish his so that I can always regard myself as superior to him. It is easier to depreciate another than to emulate him, and men prefer the easier course. They adopt it, and this is the origin of jealousy. When a man compares himself with another and finds that the other has many more good points, he becomes jealous of each and every good point he discovers in the other, and tries to depreciate it so that his own good points may stand out. This kind of jealousy may be called grudging. The other species of the genus jealousy, which makes us try to add to our good points so as to compare well with another, may be called emulating jealousy. The jealousy of emulation is, as we have stated, more difficult than the jealousy of grudge and so is much the less frequent of the two.

Parents ought not, therefore, when teaching their children to be good, to urge them to model themselves on other children and try to emulate them, for by so doing they simply make them jealous. If I tell my son, "Look, how good and industrious John is," the result will be that my son will bear John a grudge. He will think to himself that, but for John, he himself would be the best, because there would be no comparison. By setting up John as a pattern for imitation I anger my son, make him feel a grudge against this so-called paragon, and I instil jealousy in him. My son might, of course, try to emulate John, but not finding it easy, he will bear John ill-will. Besides, just as I can say to my son, "Look, how good John is," so can he reply: "Yes, he is better than I, but are there not many who are far worse? Why do you compare me with those who are better? Why not with those who are worse than I?" Goodness must, therefore, be commended to children in and for itself. Whether other children are better or worse has no bearing on the point. If the comparison were in the child's favour, he would lose all ground of impulse to improve his own conduct. To ask our children to model themselves on others is to adopt a faulty method of upbringing, and as time goes on the fault will strike its roots deep. It is jealousy that parents are training and presupposing in their children when they set other children before them as patterns. Otherwise, the children would be quite indifferent to the qualities of others. They will find it easier to belittle the good qualities of their patterns than to emulate them, so they will choose the easier path and learn to show a grudging disposition. It is true that jealousy is natural, but that is no excuse for cultivating it. It is only a motive, a reserve in case of need. While the maxims of reason are still undeveloped in us, the proper course is to use reason to keep it within bounds. For jealousy is only one of the many motives, such as ambition, which are implanted in us because we are designed for a life of activity. But so soon as reason is enthroned, we must cease to seek perfection in emulation of others and must covet it in and for itself. Motives must abdicate and let reason bear rule in their place.

Persons of the same station and occupation in life are particularly prone to be jealous of each other. Many business-men are jealous of each other; so are many scholars, particularly in the same line of scholarship; and women are liable to be jealous of each other regarding men.

Grudge is the displeasure we feel when another has an advantage; his advantage makes us feel unduly small and we grudge it him. But to grudge a man his share of happiness is envy. To be envious is to desire the failure and unhappiness of another not for the purpose of advancing our own success and happiness but because we might then ourselves be perfect and happy as we are. An envious man is not happy unless all around him are unhappy; his aim is to stand alone in the enjoyment of his happiness. Such is envy, and we shall learn below that it is satanic. Grudge, although it too should not be countenanced, is natural. Even a good-natured person may at times be grudging. Such a one may, for instance, begrudge those around him their jollity when he himself happens to be sorrowful; for it is hard to bear one's sorrow when all around are joyful. When I see everybody enjoying a good meal and I alone must content myself with inferior fare, it upsets me and I feel a grudge; but if we are all in the same boat I am content. We find the thought of death bearable, because we know that all must die; but if everybody were immortal and I alone had to die, I should feel aggrieved. It is not things themselves that affect us, but things in their relation to ourselves. We are grudging because others are happier than we. But when a good-natured man feels happy and cheerful, he wishes that every one else in the world were as happy as he and shared his joy; he begrudges no one his happiness.

When a man would not grant to another even that for which he himself has no need, he is spiteful. Spite is a maliciousness of spirit which is not the same thing as envy. I may not feel inclined to give to another something which belongs to me, even though I myself have no use for it, but it does not follow that I grudge him his own possessions, that I want to be the only one who has anything and wish him to have nothing at all. There is a deal of grudge in human nature which could develop into envy but which is not itself envy. We feel pleasure in gossiping about the minor misadventures of other people; we are not averse, although we may express no pleasure thereat, to hearing of the fall of some rich man; we may enjoy in stormy weather, when comfortably seated in our warm, cosy parlour, speaking of those at sea, for it heightens our own feeling of comfort and happiness; there is grudge in all this, but it is not envy.

The three vices which are the essence of vileness and wickedness are ingratitude, envy, and malice. When these reach their full degree they are devilish.

Men are shamed by favours. If I receive a favour, I am placed under an obligation to the giver; he has a call upon me because I am indebted to him. We all blush to be obliged. Noble-minded men accordingly refuse to accept favours in order not to put themselves under an obligation. But this attitude predisposes the mind to ingratitude. If the man who adopts it is noble-minded, well and good; but if he be proud and selfish and has perchance received a favour, the feeling that he is beholden to his benefactor hurts his pride and, being selfish, he cannot accommodate himself to the idea that he owes his benefactor anything. He becomes defiant and ungrateful. His ingratitude might even conceivably assume such dimensions that he cannot bear his benefactor and becomes his enemy. Such ingratitude is of the devil; it is out of all keeping with human nature. It is inhuman to hate and persecute one from whom we have reaped a benefit, and if such conduct were the rule it would cause untold harm. Men would then be afraid to do good to anyone lest they should receive evil in return for their good. They would become misanthropic.

The second devilish vice is envy. Envy is in the highest degree detestable. The envious man does not merely want to be happy; he wants to be the only happy person in the world; he is really contented only when he sees nothing but misery around him. Such an intolerable creature would gladly destroy every source of joy and happiness in the world.

Malice is the third kind of viciousness which is of the devil. It consists in taking a direct pleasure in the misfortunes of others. Men prone to this vice will seek, for instance, to make mischief between husband and wife, or between friends, and then enjoy the misery they have produced. In these matters we should make it a rule never to repeat to a person anything that we may have heard to his disadvantage from another, unless our silence would injure him. Otherwise we start an enmity and disturb his peace of mind, which our silence would have avoided, and in addition we break faith with our informant. The defence against such mischief-makers is upright conduct. Not by words but by our lives we should confute them. As Socrates said: We ought so to conduct ourselves that people will not credit anything spoken in disparagement of us.

These three vices—ingratitude *(ingratitudo qualificata)*, envy, and malice—are devilish because they imply a direct inclination to evil. There are in man certain indirect tendencies to wickedness which are human and not unnatural. The miser wants everything for himself, but it is no satisfaction to him to see that his neighbour is destitute. The evilness of a vice may thus be either direct or indirect. In these three vices it is direct.

We may ask whether there is in the human mind an immediate inclination to wickedness, an inclination to the devilish vices. Heaven stands for the acme of happiness, hell for all that is bad, and the earth stands midway between these two extremes; and just as goodness which transcends anything which might be expected of a human being is spoken of as being angelic, so also do we speak of devilish wickedness when the wickedness oversteps the limits of human nature and becomes inhuman. We may take it for granted that the human mind has no immediate inclination to wickedness, but is only indirectly wicked. Man cannot be so ungrateful that he simply must hate his neighbour; he may be too proud to show his gratitude and so avoid him, but he wishes him well. Again, our pleasure in the misfortune of another is not direct. We may rejoice, for example, in a man's misfortunes, because he was haughty, rich and selfish; for man loves to preserve equality. We have thus no direct inclination towards evil as evil, but only an indirect one. But how are we to explain the fact that even young children have the spirit of mischief strongly developed? For a joke, a boy will stick a pin in an unsuspecting playmate, but it is only for fun. He has no thought of the pain the other must feel on all such occasions. In the same spirit he will torture animals; twisting the cat's tail or the dog's. Such tendencies must be nipped in the bud, for it is easy to see where they will lead. They are, in fact, something animal, something of the beast of prey which is in us all, which we cannot overcome, and the source of which we cannot explain. There certainly are in human nature characteristics for which we can assign no reason. There are animals too who steal anything that comes their way, though it is quite useless to them; and it seems as if man has retained this animal tendency in his nature.

Ingratitude calls for some further observations here. To help a man in distress is charity; to help him in less urgent needs is benevolence; to help him in the amenities of life is courtesy. We may be the recipients of a charity which has not cost the giver much and our gratitude is commensurate with the degree of good-will which moved him to the action. We are grateful not only for what we have received but also for the good intention which prompted it, and the greater the effort it has cost our benefactor, the greater our gratitude.

Gratitude may be either from duty or from inclination. If an act of kindness does not greatly move us, but if we nevertheless feel that it is right and proper that we should show gratitude, our gratitude is merely prompted by a sense of duty. Our heart is not grateful, but we have principles of gratitude. If however, our heart goes out to our benefactor, we are grateful from inclination. There is a weakness of the understanding which we often have cause to recognize. It consists in taking the conditions of our understanding as conditions of the thing understood. We can estimate force only in terms of the obstacles it overcomes. Similarly, we can only estimate the degree of good-will in terms of the obstacles it has to surmount. In consequence we cannot comprehend the love and goodwill of a being for whom there are no obstacles. If God has been good to me, I am liable to think that after all it has cost God no trouble, and that gratitude to God would be mere fawning on my part. Such thoughts are not at all unnatural. It is easy to fear God, but not nearly so easy to love God from inclination because of our consciousness that God is a being whose goodness is unbounded but to whom it is no trouble to shower kindness upon us. This is not to say that such should be our mental attitude; merely that when we examine our hearts, we find that this is how we actually think. It also explains why to many races God appeared to be a jealous God, seeing that it cost Him nothing to be more bountiful with His goodness; it explains why many nations thought that their gods were sparing of their benefits and that they required propitiating with prayers and sacrifices. This is the attitude of man's heart; but when we call reason to our aid we see that God's goodness must be of a high order if He is to be good to a being so unworthy of His goodness. This solves our difficulty. The gratitude we owe to God is not gratitude from inclination, but from duty, for God is not a creature like ourselves, and can be no object of our inclinations.

We ought not to accept favours unless we are either forced to do so by dire necessity or have implicit confidence in our benefactor (for he ceases to be our friend and becomes our benefactor) that he will not regard it as placing us under an obligation to him. To accept favours indiscriminately and to be constantly seeking them is ignoble and the sign of a mean soul which does not mind placing itself under obligations. Unless we are driven by such dire necessity that it compels us to sacrifice our own worth, or unless we are convinced that our benefactor will not account it to us as a debt, we ought rather to suffer deprivation than accept favours, for a favour is a debt which can never be extinguished. For even if I repay my benefactor tenfold, I am still not even with him, because he has done me a kindness which he did not owe. He was the first in the field, and even if I return his gift tenfold I do so only as repayment. He will always be the one who was the first to show kindness and I can never be beforehand with him.

The man who bestows favours can do so either in order to make the recipient indebted to him or as an expression of his duty. If he makes the recipient feel a sense of indebtedness, he wounds his pride and diminishes his sense of gratitude. If he wishes to avoid this he must regard the favours he bestows as the discharge of a duty he owes to mankind, and he must not give the recipient the impression that it is a debt to be repaid. On the other hand, the recipient of the favour must still consider himself under an obligation to his benefactor and must be grateful to him. Under these conditions there can be benefactors and beneficiaries. A right-thinking man will not accept kindnesses, let alone favours. A grateful disposition is a touching thing and brings tears to our eyes on the stage, but a generous disposition is lovelier still. Ingratitude we detest to a surprising degree; even though we are not ourselves the victims of it, it angers us to such an extent that we feel inclined to intervene. But this is due to the fact that ingratitude decreases generosity.

Envy does not consist in wishing to be more happy than others—that is grudge—but in wishing to be the only one to be happy. It is this feeling which makes envy so evil. Why should not others be happy along with me? Envy shows itself also in relation to things which are scarce. Thus the Dutch, who as a nation are rather envious, once valued tulips at several hundreds of florins apiece. A rich merchant, who had one of the finest and rarest specimens, heard that another had a similar specimen. He thereupon bought it from him for 2,000 florins and trampled it underfoot, saying that he had no use for it, as he already possessed a specimen, and that he only wished that no one else should share that distinction with him. So it is also in the matter of happiness.

Malice is different. A malicious man is pleased when others suffer, he can laugh when others weep. An act which willfully brings unhappiness is cruel; when it produces physical pain it is bloodthirsty. Inhumanity is all these together, just as humanity consists in sympathy and pity, since these differentiate man from the beasts. It is difficult to explain what gives rise to a cruel disposition. It may arise when a man considers another so evilly disposed that he hates him. A man who believes himself hated by another, hates him in return, although the former may have good reason to hate him. For if a man is hated because he is selfish and has other vices, and he knows that he is hated for these reasons, he hates those who hate him although these latter do him no injustice. Thus kings who know that they are hated by their subjects become even more cruel. Equally, when a man has done a good deed to another, he knows that the other loves him, and so he loves him in return, knowing that he himself is loved. Just as love is reciprocated, so also is hate. We must for our own sakes guard against being hated by others lest we be affected by that hatred and reciprocate it. The hater is more disturbed by his hatred than is the hated.

Study Questions

1. How does Kant distinguish spite from envy? Why is the extreme of envy "devilish"?
2. We sometimes say to a friend, "I envy you." Can we envy people without begrudging their happiness? Explain. How does Kant view this?
3. Why does Kant advise us to compare ourselves with the ideal of perfection? What vices are associated with comparing ourselves with others?
4. What are the three devilish vices, and what is devilish about them? Does Kant believe that the devilish vices are natural? Why or why not? What is their origin?
5. What does Kant think is wrong about accepting favors? Do you think Kant demands too much of the average person? Is his doctrine too austere? Explain

How Much Land Does a Man Need?
A Parable on Greed

Leo Tolstoy

Leo Tolstoy (1828–1910) is widely considered to be one of the greatest writers of the Western tradition. His works include classics such as *War and Peace* (1869) and *Anna Karenina* (1878). He was born into Russia's nobility but frequently found himself at odds with Russian high society. Near the end of his life, he freed his serfs, gave away most of his earthly possessions, and tried to live simply and without luxury.

James Joyce called Tolstoy's short story "How Much Land Does a Man Need?" (1880) "the greatest story that the literature of the world knows." It is a morality tale about the dangers of greed.

I

An elder sister came to visit her younger sister in the country. The elder was married to a tradesman in town, the younger to a peasant in the village. As the sisters sat over their tea talking, the elder began to boast of the advantages of town life: saying how comfortably they lived there, how well they dressed, what fine clothes her children wore, what good things they ate and drank, and how she went to the theatre, promenades, and entertainments.

The younger sister was piqued, and in turn disparaged the life of a tradesman, and stood up for that of a peasant.

"I would not change my way of life for yours," said she. "We may live roughly, but at least we are free from anxiety. You live in better style than we do, but though you often earn more than you need, you are very likely to lose all you have. You know the proverb, 'Loss and gain are brothers twain.' It often happens that people who are wealthy one day are begging their bread the next. Our way is safer. Though a peasant's life is not a fat one, it is a long one. We shall never grow rich, but we shall always have enough to eat."

The elder sister said sneeringly:

"Enough? Yes, if you like to share with the pigs and the calves! What do you know of elegance or manners! However much your good man may slave, you will die as you are living-on a dung heap-and your children the same."

"Well, what of that?" replied the younger. "Of course our work is rough and coarse. But, on the other hand, it is sure; and we need not bow to any one. But you, in your towns, are surrounded by temptations; today all may be right, but tomorrow the Evil One may tempt your husband with cards, wine, or women, and all will go to ruin. Don't such things happen often enough?"

Pahom, the master of the house, was lying on the top of the oven, and he listened to the women's chatter.

"It is perfectly true," thought he. "Busy as we are from childhood tilling Mother Earth, we peasants have no time to let any nonsense settle in our heads. Our only trouble is that we haven't land enough. If I had plenty of land, I shouldn't fear the Devil himself!"

The women finished their tea, chatted a while about dress, and then cleared away the tea-things and lay down to sleep. But the Devil had been sitting behind the oven, and had heard all that was said. He was pleased that the peasant's wife had led her husband into boasting, and that he had said that if he had plenty of land he would not fear the Devil himself.

"All right," thought the Devil. "We will have a tussle. I'll give you land enough; and by means of that land I will get you into my power."

II

Close to the village there lived a lady, a small landowner, who had an estate of about three hundred acres. She had always lived on good terms with the peasants, until she engaged as her steward an old soldier, who took to burdening the people with fines. However careful Pahom tried to be, it happened again and again that now a horse of his got among the lady's oats, now a cow strayed into her garden, now his calves found their way into her meadows-and he always had to pay a fine.

Pahom paid, but grumbled, and, going home in a temper, was rough with his family. All through that summer Pahom had much trouble because of this steward; and he was even glad when winter came and the cattle had to be stabled. Though he grudged the fodder when they could no longer graze on the pasture-land, at least he was free from anxiety about them.

In the winter the news got about that the lady was going to sell her land, and that the keeper of the inn on the high road was bargaining for it. When the peasants heard this they were very much alarmed.

"Well," thought they, "if the innkeeper gets the land he will worry us with fines worse than the lady's steward. We all depend on that estate."

So the peasants went on behalf of their Commune, and asked the lady not to sell the land to the innkeeper; offering her a better price for it themselves. The lady agreed to let them have it. Then the peasants tried to arrange for the Commune to buy the whole estate, so that it might be held by all in common. They met twice to discuss it, but could not settle the matter; the Evil One sowed discord among them, and they could not agree. So they decided to buy the land individually, each according to his means; and the lady agreed to this plan as she had to the other.

Presently Pahom heard that a neighbor of his was buying fifty acres, and that the lady had consented to accept one half in cash and to wait a year for the other half. Pahom felt envious.

"Look at that," thought he, "the land is all being sold, and I shall get none of it." So he spoke to his wife.

"Other people are buying," said he, "and we must also buy twenty acres or so. Life is becoming impossible. That steward is simply crushing us with his fines."

So they put their heads together and considered how they could manage to buy it. They had one hundred roubles laid by. They sold a colt, and one half of their bees; hired out one of their sons as a laborer, and took his wages in advance; borrowed the rest from a brother-in-law, and so scraped together half the purchase money.

Having done this, Pahom chose out a farm of forty acres, some of it wooded, and went to the lady to bargain for it. They came to an agreement, and he shook hands with her upon it, and paid her a deposit in advance. Then they went to town and signed the deeds; he paying half the price down, and undertaking to pay the remainder within two years.

So now Pahom had land of his own. He borrowed seed, and sowed it on the land he had bought. The harvest was a good one, and within a year he had managed to pay off his debts both to the lady and to his brother-in-law. So he became a landowner, ploughing and sowing his own land, making hay on his own land, cutting his own trees, and feeding his cattle on his own pasture. When he went out to plough his fields, or to look at his growing corn, or at his grass meadows, his heart would fill with joy. The grass that grew and the flowers that bloomed there, seemed to him unlike any that grew elsewhere. Formerly, when he had passed by that land, it had appeared the same as any other land, but now it seemed quite different.

III

So Pahom was well contented, and everything would have been right if the neighboring peasants would only not have trespassed on his cornfields and meadows. He appealed to them most civilly, but they still went on: now the Communal herdsmen would let the village cows stray into his meadows; then horses from the night pasture would get among his corn. Pahom turned them out again and again, and forgave their owners, and for a long time he forbore from prosecuting any one. But at last he lost patience and complained to the District Court. He knew it was the peasants' want of land, and no evil intent on their part, that caused the trouble; but he thought:

"I cannot go on overlooking it, or they will destroy all I have. They must be taught a lesson."

So he had them up, gave them one lesson, and then another, and two or three of the peasants were fined. After a time Pahom's neighbours began to bear him a grudge for this, and would now and then let their cattle on his land on purpose. One peasant even got into Pahom's wood at night and cut down five young lime trees for their bark. Pahom passing through the wood one day noticed something white. He came nearer, and saw the stripped trunks lying on the ground, and close by stood the stumps, where the tree had been. Pahom was furious.

"If he had only cut one here and there it would have been bad enough," thought Pahom, "but the rascal has actually cut down a whole clump. If I could only find out who did this, I would pay him out."

He racked his brains as to who it could be. Finally he decided: "It must be Simon-no one else could have done it." Se he went to Simon's homestead to have a look around, but he found nothing, and only had an angry scene. However' he now felt more certain than ever that Simon had done it, and he lodged a complaint. Simon was summoned. The case was tried, and re-tried, and at the end of it all

Simon was acquitted, there being no evidence against him. Pahom felt still more aggrieved, and let his anger loose upon the Elder and the Judges.

"You let thieves grease your palms," said he. "If you were honest folk yourselves, you would not let a thief go free."

So Pahom quarrelled with the Judges and with his neighbors. Threats to burn his building began to be uttered. So though Pahom had more land, his place in the Commune was much worse than before.

About this time a rumor got about that many people were moving to new parts.

"There's no need for me to leave my land," thought Pahom. "But some of the others might leave our village, and then there would be more room for us. I would take over their land myself, and make my estate a bit bigger. I could then live more at ease. As it is, I am still too cramped to be comfortable."

One day Pahom was sitting at home, when a peasant passing through the village, happened to call in. He was allowed to stay the night, and supper was given him. Pahom had a talk with this peasant and asked him where he came from. The stranger answered that he came from beyond the Volga, where he had been working. One word led to another, and the man went on to say that many people were settling in those parts. He told how some people from his village had settled there. They had joined the Commune, and had had twenty-five acres per man granted them. The land was so good, he said, that the rye sown on it grew as high as a horse, and so thick that five cuts of a sickle made a sheaf. One peasant, he said, had brought nothing with him but his bare hands, and now he had six horses and two cows of his own.

Pahom's heart kindled with desire. He thought:

"Why should I suffer in this narrow hole, if one can live so well elsewhere? I will sell my land and my homestead here, and with the money I will start afresh over there and get everything new. In this crowded place one is always having trouble. But I must first go and find out all about it myself."

Towards summer he got ready and started. He went down the Volga on a steamer to Samara, then walked another three hundred miles on foot, and at last reached the place. It was just as the stranger had said. The peasants had plenty of land: every man had twenty-five acres of Communal land given him for his use, and any one who had money could buy, besides, at fifty-cents an acre as much good freehold land as he wanted.

Having found out all he wished to know, Pahom returned home as autumn came on, and began selling off his belongings. He sold his land at a profit, sold his homestead and all his cattle, and withdrew from membership of the Commune. He only waited till the spring, and then started with his family for the new settlement.

IV

As soon as Pahom and his family arrived at their new abode, he applied for admission into the Commune of a large village. He stood treat to the Elders, and obtained the necessary documents. Five shares of Communal land were given him for his own and his sons' use: that is to say—125 acres (not altogether, but in different fields) besides the use of the Communal pasture. Pahom put up the buildings he needed, and bought cattle. Of the Communal land alone he had three times as much as at his former home, and the land was good corn-land. He was ten times better off than he had been. He had plenty of arable land and pasturage, and could keep as many head of cattle as he liked.

At first, in the bustle of building and settling down, Pahom was pleased with it all, but when he got used to it he began to think that even here he had not enough land. The first year, he sowed wheat on his share of the Communal land, and had a good crop. He wanted to go on sowing wheat, but had not enough Communal land for the purpose, and what he had already used was not available; for in those parts wheat is only sown on virgin soil or on fallow land. It is sown for one or two years, and then the land lies fallow till it is again overgrown with prairie grass. There were many who wanted such land, and there was not enough for all; so that people quarrelled about it. Those who were better off, wanted it for growing wheat, and those who were poor, wanted it to let to dealers, so that they might raise money to pay their taxes. Pahom wanted to sow more wheat; so he rented land from a dealer for a year. He sowed much wheat and had a fine crop, but the land was too far from the village—the wheat had to be carted more than ten miles. After a time Pahom noticed that some peasant-dealers were living on separate farms, and were growing wealthy; and he thought:

"If I were to buy some freehold land, and have a homestead on it, it would be a different thing, altogether. Then it would all be nice and compact."

The question of buying freehold land recurred to him again and again.

He went on in the same way for three years; renting land and sowing wheat. The seasons turned out well and the crops were good, so that he began to lay money by. He might have gone on living contentedly, but he grew tired of having to rent other people's land every year, and having to scramble for it. Wherever there was good land to be had, the peasants would rush for it and it was taken up at once, so that unless you were sharp about it you got none. It happened in the third year that he and a dealer together rented a piece of pasture land from some peasants; and they had already ploughed it up, when there was some dispute, and the peasants went to law about it, and things fell out so that the labor was all lost.

"If it were my own land," thought Pahom, "I should be independent, and there would not be all this unpleasantness."

So Pahom began looking out for land which he could buy; and he came across a peasant who had bought thirteen hundred acres, but having got into difficulties was willing to sell again cheap. Pahom bargained and haggled with him, and at last they settled the price at 1,500 roubles, part in cash and part to be paid later. They had all but clinched the matter, when a passing dealer happened to stop at Pahom's one day to get a feed for his horse, He drank tea with Pahom, and they had a talk. The dealer said that he was just returning from the land of the Bashkirs, far away, where he had bought thirteen thousand acres of land all for 1,000 roubles. Pahom questioned him further, and the tradesman said:

"All one need do is to make friends with the chiefs. I gave away about one hundred roubles' worth of dressing-gowns and carpets, besides a case of tea, and I gave wine to those who would drink it; and I got the land for less than two cents an acre." And he showed Pahom the title-deeds, saying:

"The land lies near a river, and the whole prairie is virgin soil."

Pahom plied him with questions, and the tradesman said:

"There is more land there than you could cover if you walked a year, and it all belongs to the Bashkirs. They are as simple as sheep, and land can be got almost for nothing."

"There now," thought Pahom, "with my one thousand roubles, why should I get only thirteen hundred acres, and saddle myself with a debt besides. If I take it out there, I can get more than ten times as much for the money."

V

Pahom inquired how to get to the place, and as soon as the tradesman had left him, he prepared to go there himself. He left his wife to look after the homestead, and started on his journey taking his man with him. They stopped at a town on their way, and bought a case of tea, some wine, and other presents, as the tradesman had advised. On and on they went until they had gone more than three hundred miles, and on the seventh day they came to a place where the Bashkirs had pitched their tents. It was all just as the tradesman had said. The people lived on the steppes, by a river, in felt-covered tents. They neither tilled the ground, nor ate bread. Their cattle and horses grazed in herds on the steppe. The colts were tethered behind the tents, and the mares were driven to them twice a day. The mares were milked, and from the milk kumiss was made. It was the women who prepared kumiss, and they also made cheese. As far as the men were concerned, drinking kumiss and tea, eating mutton, and playing on their pipes, was all they cared about. They were all stout and merry, and all the summer long they never thought of doing any work. They were quite ignorant, and knew no Russian, but were good-natured enough.

As soon as they saw Pahom, they came out of their tents and gathered round their visitor. An interpreter was found, and Pahom told them he had come about some land. The Bashkirs seemed very glad; they took Pahom and led him into one of the best tents, where they made him sit on some down cushions placed on a carpet, while they sat round him. They gave him tea and kumiss, and had a sheep killed, and gave him mutton to eat. Pahom took presents out of his cart and distributed them among the Bashkirs, and divided amongst them the tea. The Bashkirs were delighted. They talked a great deal among themselves, and then told the interpreter to translate.

"They wish to tell you," said the interpreter, "that they like you, and that it is our custom to do all we can to please a guest and to repay him for his gifts. You have given us presents, now tell us which of the things we possess please you best, that we may present them to you."

"What pleases me best here," answered Pahom, "is your land. Our land is crowded, and the soil is exhausted; but you have plenty of land and it is good land. I never saw the like of it."

The interpreter translated. The Bashkirs talked among themselves for a while. Pahom could not understand what they were saying, but saw that they were much amused, and that they shouted and laughed. Then they were silent and looked at Pahom while the interpreter said:

"They wish me to tell you that in return for your presents they will gladly give you as much land as you want. You have only to point it out with your hand and it is yours."

The Bashkirs talked again for a while and began to dispute. Pahom asked what they were disputing about, and the interpreter told him that some of them thought they ought to ask their Chief about the land and not act in his absence, while others thought there was no need to wait for his return.

VI

While the Bashkirs were disputing, a man in a large fox-fur cap appeared on the scene. They all became silent and rose to their feet. The interpreter said, "This is our Chief himself."

Pahom immediately fetched the best dressing-gown and five pounds of tea, and offered these to the Chief. The Chief accepted them, and seated himself in the place of honour. The Bashkirs at once began telling him something. The Chief listened for a while, then made a sign with his head for them to be silent, and addressing himself to Pahom, said in Russian:

"Well, let it be so. Choose whatever piece of land you like; we have plenty of it."

"How can I take as much as I like?" thought Pahom. "I must get a deed to make it secure, or else they may say, 'It is yours,' and afterwards may take it away again."

"Thank you for your kind words," he said aloud. "You have much land, and I only want a little. But I should like to be sure which bit is mine. Could it not be measured and made over to me? Life and death are in God's hands. You good people give it to me, but your children might wish to take it away again."

"You are quite right," said the Chief. "We will make it over to you."

"I heard that a dealer had been here," continued Pahom, "and that you gave him a little land, too, and signed title-deeds to that effect. I should like to have it done in the same way."

The Chief understood.

"Yes," replied he, "that can be done quite easily. We have a scribe, and we will go to town with you and have the deed properly sealed."

"And what will be the price?" asked Pahom.

"Our price is always the same: one thousand roubles a day."

Pahom did not understand.

"A day? What measure is that? How many acres would that be?"

"We do not know how to reckon it out," said the Chief. "We sell it by the day. As much as you can go round on your feet in a day is yours, and the price is one thousand roubles a day."

Pahom was surprised.

"But in a day you can get round a large tract of land," he said.

The Chief laughed.

"It will all be yours!" said he. "But there is one condition: If you don't return on the same day to the spot whence you started, your money is lost."

"But how am I to mark the way that I have gone?"

"Why, we shall go to any spot you like, and stay there. You must start from that spot and make your round, taking a spade with you. Wherever you think necessary, make a mark. At every turning, dig a hole and pile up the turf; then afterwards we will go round with a plough from hole to hole. You may make as large a circuit as you please, but before the sun sets you must return to the place you started from. All the land you cover will be yours."

Pahom was delighted. It-was decided to start early next morning. They talked a while, and after drinking some more kumiss and eating some more mutton, they had tea again, and then the night came on. They gave Pahom a feather-bed to sleep on, and the Bashkirs dispersed for the night, promising to assemble the next morning at daybreak and ride out before sunrise to the appointed spot.

VII

Pahom lay on the feather-bed, but could not sleep. He kept thinking about the land. "What a large tract I will mark off!" thought he. "I can easily go thirty-five miles in a day. The days are long now, and within a circuit of thirty-five miles what a lot of land there will be! I will sell the poorer land, or let it to peasants, but I'll pick out the best and farm it. I will buy two ox-teams, and hire two more laborers. About a hundred and fifty acres shall be plough-land, and I will pasture cattle on the rest."

Pahom lay awake all night, and dozed off only just before dawn. Hardly were his eyes closed when he had a dream. He thought he was lying in that same tent, and heard somebody chuckling outside. He wondered who it could be, and rose and went out, and he saw the Bashkir Chief sitting in front of the tent holding his side and rolling about with laughter. Going nearer to the Chief, Pahom asked: "What are you laughing at?" But he saw that it was no longer the Chief, but the dealer who had recently stopped at his house and had told him about the land. Just as Pahom was going to ask, "Have you been here long?" he saw that it was not the dealer, but the peasant who had come up from the Volga, long ago, to Pahom's old home. Then he saw that it was not the peasant either, but the Devil himself with hoofs and horns, sitting there and chuckling, and before him lay a man barefoot, prostrate on the ground, with only trousers and a shirt on. And Pahom dreamt that he looked more attentively to see what sort of a man it was lying there, and he saw that the man was dead, and that it was himself! He awoke horror-struck.

"What things one does dream," thought he.

Looking round he saw through the open door that the dawn was breaking.

"It's time to wake them up," thought he. "We ought to be starting."

He got up, roused his man (who was sleeping in his cart), bade him harness; and went to call the Bashkirs.

"It's time to go to the steppe to measure the land," he said.

The Bashkirs rose and assembled, and the Chief came, too. Then they began drinking kumiss again, and offered Pahom some tea, but he would not wait.

"If we are to go, let us go. It is high time," said he.

VIII

The Bashkirs got ready and they all started: some mounted on horses, and some in carts. Pahom drove in his own small cart with his servant, and took a spade with him. When they reached the steppe, the morning red was beginning to kindle. They ascended a hillock (called by the Bashkirs a shikhan) and dismounting from their carts and their horses, gathered in one spot. The Chief came up to Pahom and stretched out his arm towards the plain:

"See," said he, "all this, as far as your eye can reach, is ours. You may have any part of it you like."

Pahom's eyes glistened: it was all virgin soil, as flat as the palm of your hand, as black as the seed of a poppy, and in the hollows different kinds of grasses grew breast high.

The Chief took off his fox-fur cap, placed it on the ground and said:

"This will be the mark. Start from here, and return here again. All the land you go round shall be yours."

Pahom took out his money and put it on the cap. Then he took off his outer coat, remaining in his sleeveless under coat. He unfastened his girdle and tied it tight below his stomach, put a little bag of bread into the breast of his coat, and tying a flask of water to his girdle, he drew up the tops of his boots, took the spade from his man, and stood ready to start. He considered for some moments which way he had better go—it was tempting everywhere.

"No matter," he concluded, "I will go towards the rising sun."

He turned his face to the east, stretched himself, and waited for the sun to appear above the rim.

"I must lose no time," he thought, "and it is easier walking while it is still cool."

The sun's rays had hardly flashed above the horizon, before Pahom, carrying the spade over his shoulder, went down into the steppe.

Pahom started walking neither slowly nor quickly. After having gone a thousand yards he stopped, dug a hole and placed pieces of turf one on another to make it more visible. Then he went on; and now that he had walked off his stiffness he quickened his pace. After a while he dug another hole.

Pahom looked back. The hillock could be distinctly seen in the sunlight, with the people on it, and the glittering tires of the cartwheels. At a rough guess Pahom concluded that he had walked three miles. It was growing warmer; he took off his under-coat, flung it across his shoulder, and went on again. It had grown quite warm now; he looked at the sun, it was time to think of breakfast.

"The first shift is done, but there are four in a day, and it is too soon yet to turn. But I will just take off my boots," said he to himself.

He sat down, took off his boots, stuck them into his girdle, and went on. It was easy walking now.

"I will go on for another three miles," thought he, "and then turn to the left. The spot is so fine, that it would be a pity to lose it. The further one goes, the better the land seems."

He went straight on a for a while, and when he looked round, the hillock was scarcely visible and the people on it looked like black ants, and he could just see something glistening there in the sun.

"Ah," thought Pahom, "I have gone far enough in this direction, it is time to turn. Besides I am in a regular sweat, and very thirsty."

He stopped, dug a large hole, and heaped up pieces of turf. Next he untied his flask, had a drink, and then turned sharply to the left. He went on and on; the grass was high, and it was very hot.

Pahom began to grow tired: he looked at the sun and saw that it was noon.

"Well," he thought, "I must have a rest."

He sat down, and ate some bread and drank some water; but he did not lie down, thinking that if he did he might fall asleep. After sitting a little while, he went on again. At first he walked easily: the food had strengthened him; but it had become terribly hot, and he felt sleepy; still he went on, thinking: "An hour to suffer, a life-time to live."

He went a long way in this direction also, and was about to turn to the left again, when he perceived a damp hollow: "It would be a pity to leave that out," he thought. "Flax would do well there." So he went on past the hollow, and dug a hole on the other side of it before he turned the corner. Pahom looked towards the hillock. The heat made the air hazy: it seemed to be quivering, and through the haze the people on the hillock could scarcely be seen.

"Ah!" thought Pahom, "I have made the sides too long; I must make this one shorter." And he went along the third side, stepping faster. He looked at the sun: it was nearly half way to the horizon, and he had not yet done two miles of the third side of the square. He was still ten miles from the goal.

"No," he thought, "though it will make my land lopsided, I must hurry back in a straight line now. I might go too far, and as it is I have a great deal of land."

So Pahom hurriedly dug a hole, and turned straight towards the hillock.

IX

Pahom went straight towards the hillock, but he now walked with difficulty. He was done up with the heat, his bare feet were cut and bruised, and his legs began to fail. He longed to rest, but it was impossible if he meant to get back before sunset. The sun waits for no man, and it was sinking lower and lower.

"Oh dear," he thought, "if only I have not blundered trying for too much! What if I am too late?"

He looked towards the hillock and at the sun. He was still far from his goal, and the sun was already near the rim. Pahom walked on and on; it was very hard walking, but he went quicker and quicker. He pressed on, but was still far from the place. He began running, threw away his coat, his boots, his flask, and his cap, and kept only the spade which he used as a support.

"What shall I do," he thought again, "I have grasped too much, and ruined the whole affair. I can't get there before the sun sets."

And this fear made him still more breathless. Pahom went on running, his soaking shirt and trousers stuck to him, and his mouth was parched. His breast was working like a blacksmith's bellows, his heart was beating like a hammer, and his legs were giving way as if they did not belong to him. Pahom was seized with terror lest he should die of the strain.

Though afraid of death, he could not stop. "After having run all that way they will call me a fool if I stop now," thought he. And he ran on and on, and drew near and heard the Bashkirs yelling and shouting to him, and their cries inflamed his heart still more. He gathered his last strength and ran on.

The sun was close to the rim, and cloaked in mist looked large, and red as blood. Now, yes now, it was about to set! The sun was quite low, but he was also quite near his aim. Pahom could already see the people on the hillock waving their arms to hurry him up. He could see the fox-fur cap on the ground, and the money on it, and the Chief sitting on the ground holding his sides. And Pahom remembered his dream.

"There is plenty of land," thought he, "but will God let me live on it? I have lost my life, I have lost my life! I shall never reach that spot!"

Pahom looked at the sun, which had reached the earth: one side of it had already disappeared. With all his remaining strength he rushed on, bending his body forward so that his legs could hardly follow fast enough to keep him from falling. Just as he reached the hillock it suddenly grew dark. He looked up—the sun had already set. He gave a cry: "All my labor has been in vain," thought he, and was about to stop, but he heard the Bashkirs still shouting, and remembered that though to him, from below, the sun seemed to have set, they on the hillock could still see it. He took a long breath and ran up the hillock. It was still light there. He reached the top and saw the cap. Before it sat the Chief laughing and holding his sides. Again Pahom remembered his dream, and he uttered a cry: his legs gave way beneath him, he fell forward and reached the cap with his hands.

"Ah, what a fine fellow!" exclaimed the Chief. "He has gained much land!"

Pahom's servant came running up and tried to raise him, but he saw that blood was flowing from his mouth. Pahom was dead!

The Bashkirs clicked their tongues to show their pity.

His servant picked up the spade and dug a grave long enough for Pahom to lie in, and buried him in it. Six feet from his head to his heels was all he needed.

STUDY QUESTIONS

1. What lessons does Pahom's unhealthy greed hold for today's society?
2. Some might call Pahom extremely ambitious. Do you agree? What separates ambition from greed?
3. Tolstoy was sympathetic to communism and was sometimes referred to as "Comrade Count." His story could be discounted for its harsh denunciation of private property. On the other hand, many would say that this tale carries a universal message that transcends politics. Would you agree?

7 | Morality and Social Policy

One striking development in contemporary moral philosophy is the increasing attention we pay to specific practical questions in social ethics. Is abortion right or wrong? Are physicians ever authorized to give lethal injections to dying, pain-ridden patients who request their own deaths? Do animals have moral rights? The practical ethics movement originated in the late sixties when philosophers began to participate in national debates on such issues as free speech, civil disobedience, capital punishment, euthanasia, and abortion. The recent interest in applying ethical theory to practical social problems is not a novel development, for philosophers since Plato and Aristotle continuously have concerned themselves with questions of everyday morality. The period between 1940 and 1970 is something of a historical exception. During those post–World War II decades, Western philosophy became increasingly analytical and methodologically rigorous. Clarification and theory were of primary concern; applied ethics was secondary. Although this interest in theory and method has not waned, in the past few decades philosophers have reentered the arena of applied ethics in force.

The essays in Chapter Seven deal primarily with questions of social policy. Here morality is somewhat impersonal since, in the main, our actions are not directed to persons with whom we are acquainted. Nevertheless, as the controversy over abortion shows, the issues strike home in a very personal way. The controversy turns on how to interpret fundamental moral principles. Consider the argument offered by those who oppose abortion:

1. It is wrong to kill an innocent human being.
2. The fetus is an innocent human being.
   ... It is wrong to kill the fetus.

The conclusion follows logically from the two premises. The question then is whether to accept the premises, and that, in turn, depends on how we should interpret them. John Noonan presents arguments for accepting both premises. Most defenders of a woman's right to choose challenge (1) or (2). Mary Anne Warren offers criteria for being a *person*, and she argues that only those human beings who are also persons qualify for an overriding right to life. According to Warren, because fetuses and brain-dead human beings lack the attributes of personhood, the prohibition against the destruction of human life does not apply. Judith Jarvis Thomson goes further, contending that in circumstances where one's liberty is threatened, even persons may be destroyed to free oneself. Thomson argues that in an unwanted pregnancy the mother's liberty is compromised and she may take drastic measures to regain it.

Though arguments like these are made with the aim of influencing social policy, they demand of us a very personal response. Even the debate on whether and how much to sacrifice for famine relief shows that there is clearly a personal side to the ethical question of what to do about the multitudes whom we shall never know, but who need our help. Peter Singer maintains that readers themselves have a serious moral obligation to do all they can to fight world hunger.

John Arthur claims that even if Singer is right about the overall utility of famine relief, it still is not our duty to do without luxuries in order to help distant strangers. Common morality does not make such demands on ordinary human beings, and common morality is reasonable in this respect since "morality is not for angels." The Kenyan economist James Shikwati casts doubt on the overall value of foreign aid to the poor. He accuses westerners of "devastating" Africa with their goodness. In their admirable desire to improve the lives of Africans, Shikwati claims that European and American charities have unwittingly encouraged and enriched corrupt leaders and undermined local economies.

Most of the authors in this chapter believe that animals deserve some moral consideration. They differ on how much and on what grounds. James Rachels and Peter Singer do not believe that killing and eating animals is morally justifiable. As utilitarians concerned to diminish suffering, both defend the view that vegetarianism is the only correct moral policy. Michael Pollan and Roger Scruton reject this conclusion as too extreme.

Famine, Affluence, and Morality

Peter Singer

A biographical sketch of Peter Singer is found on page 176.

Peter Singer describes the mass starvation in many parts of the world and argues that affluent people are morally obligated to contribute part of their time and income toward alleviating hunger. He assumes that passivity, when people are able to act to prevent evil, is morally wrong. Nowadays we can help people over great distances; instant communication and air travel have transformed the world into a "global village." If, says Singer, bystanders see a child drowning in a shallow pond, they ought to save that child even if it means muddying their clothes. Failure to do so is gross moral negligence. Singer compares the citizens of the affluent West to these bystanders.

As I write this, in November 1971, people are dying in East Bengal from lack of food, shelter, and medical care. The suffering and death that are occurring there now are not inevitable, not unavoidable in any fatalistic sense of the term. Constant poverty, a cyclone, and a civil war have turned at least nine million people into destitute refugees; nevertheless, it is not beyond the capacity of the richer nations to give enough assistance to reduce any further suffering to very small proportions. The decisions and actions of human beings can prevent this kind of suffering. Unfortunately, human beings have not made the necessary decisions. At the individual level, people have, with very few exceptions, not responded to the situation in any significant way. Generally speaking, people have not given large sums to relief funds; they have not written to their parliamentary representatives demanding increased government assistance; they have not demonstrated in the streets, held symbolic fasts, or done anything else directed toward providing the refugees with the means to satisfy their essential needs. At the government level, no government has given the sort of massive aid that would enable the refugees to survive for more than a few days. Britain, for instance, has given rather more than most countries. It has, to date, given £14,750,000. For comparative purposes, Britain's share of the nonrecoverable development costs of the Anglo-French Concorde project is already in excess of £275,000,000, and on present estimates will reach £400,000,000. The implication is that the British government values a supersonic transport more than thirty times as highly as it values the lives of the nine million refugees. Australia is another country which, on a per capita basis, is

FAMINE, AFFLUENCE, AND MORALITY By Peter Singer from *Philosophy and Public Affairs*, vol. 1, no. 3 (Spring 1972), pp. 229–243. Copyright © 1972 by Princeton University Press, Philosophy and Public Affairs. Reprinted by permission of Blackwell Publishing.

well up in the "aid to Bengal" table. Australia's aid, however, amounts to less than one-twelfth of the cost of Sydney's new opera house. The total amount given, from all sources, now stands at about £65,000,000. The estimated cost of keeping the refugees alive for one year is £464,000,000. Most of the refugees have now been in the camps for more than six months. The World Bank has said that India needs a minimum of £300,000,000 in assistance from other countries before the end of the year. It seems obvious that assistance on this scale will not be forthcoming. India will be forced to choose between letting the refugees starve or diverting funds from her own development program, which will mean that more of her own people will starve in the future.[1]

These are the essential facts about the present situation in Bengal. So far as it concerns us here, there is nothing unique about this situation except its magnitude. The Bengal emergency is just the latest and most acute of a series of major emergencies in various parts of the world, arising both from natural and from man-made causes. There are also many parts of the world in which people die from malnutrition and lack of food independent of any special emergency. I take Bengal as my example only because it is the present concern, and because the size of the problem has ensured that it has been given adequate publicity. Neither individuals nor governments can claim to be unaware of what is happening there.

What are the moral implications of a situation like this? In what follows, I shall argue that the way people in relatively affluent countries react to a situation like that in Bengal cannot be justified; indeed, the whole way we look at moral issues—our moral conceptual scheme—needs to be altered, and with it, the way of life that has come to be taken for granted in our society.

In arguing for this conclusion I will not, of course, claim to be morally neutral. I shall, however, try to argue for the moral position that I take, so that anyone who accepts certain assumptions, to be made explicit, will, I hope, accept my conclusion.

I begin with the assumption that suffering and death from lack of food, shelter, and medical care are bad. I think most people will agree about this, although one may reach the same view by different routes. I shall not argue for this view. People can hold all sorts of eccentric positions, and perhaps from some of them it would not follow that death by starvation is in itself bad. It is difficult, perhaps impossible, to refute such positions, and so for brevity I will henceforth take this assumption as accepted. Those who disagree need read no further.

My next point is this: if it is in our power to prevent something bad from happening, without thereby sacrificing anything of comparable moral importance, we ought, morally, to do it. By "without sacrificing anything of comparable moral importance" I mean without causing anything else comparably bad to happen, or doing something that is wrong in itself, or failing to promote some moral good, comparable in significance to the bad thing that we can prevent. This principle seems almost as uncontroversial as the last one. It requires us only to prevent what is bad, and not to promote what is good, and it requires this of us only when we can do it without

---

[1] There was also a third possibility: that India would go to war to enable the refugees to return to their lands. Since I wrote this paper, India has taken this way out. The situation is no longer that described above, but this does not affect my argument, as the next paragraph indicates.

sacrificing anything that is, from the moral point of view, comparably important. I could even, as far as the application of my argument to the Bengal emergency is concerned, qualify the point so as to make it: if it is in our power to prevent something very bad from happening, without thereby sacrificing anything morally significant, we ought, morally, to do it. An application of this principle would be as follows: if I am walking past a shallow pond and see a child drowning in it, I ought to wade in and pull the child out. This will mean getting my clothes muddy, but this is insignificant, while the death of the child would presumably be a very bad thing.

The uncontroversial appearance of the principle just stated is deceptive. If it were acted upon, even in its qualified form, our lives, our society, and our world would be fundamentally changed. For the principle takes, firstly, no account of proximity or distance. It makes no moral difference whether the person I can help is a neighbor's child ten yards from me or a Bengali whose name I shall never know, ten thousand miles away. Secondly, the principle makes no distinction between cases in which I am the only person who could possibly do anything and cases in which I am just one among millions in the same position.

I do not think I need to say much in defense of the refusal to take proximity and distance into account. The fact that a person is physically near to us, so that we have personal contact with him, may make it more likely that we *shall* assist him, but this does not show that we *ought* to help him rather than another who happens to be further away. If we accept any principle of impartiality, uni-versalizability, equality, or whatever, we cannot discriminate against someone merely because he is far away from us (or we are far away from him). Admittedly, it is possible that we are in a better position to judge what needs to be done to help a person near to us than one far away, and perhaps also to provide the assistance we judge to be necessary. If this were the case, it would be a reason for helping those near to us first. This may once have been a justification for being more concerned with the poor in one's own town than with famine victims in India. Unfortunately for those who like to keep their moral responsibilities limited, instant communication and swift transportation have changed the situation. From the moral point of view, the development of the world into a "global village" has made an important, though still unrecognized, difference to our moral situation. Expert observers and supervisors, sent out by famine relief organizations or permanently stationed in the famine-prone areas, can direct our aid to a refugee in Bengal almost as effectively as we could get it to someone in our own block. There would seem, therefore, to be no possible justification for discriminating on geographical grounds.

There may be a greater need to defend the second implication of my principle—that the fact that there are millions of other people in the same position, in respect to the Bengali refugees, as I am, does not make the situation significantly different from a situation in which I am the only person who can prevent something very bad from occurring. Again, of course, I admit that there is a psychological difference between the cases; one feels less guilty about doing nothing if one can point to others, similarly placed, who have also done nothing. Yet this can make no real difference to our moral obligations. Should I consider that I am less obliged to pull the drowning child out of the pond if on looking around I see other people, no further away than I am, who have also noticed the child but are doing nothing? One has only to ask this question to see the absurdity of the view that numbers lessen obligation. It is a view that is an ideal excuse for inactivity; unfortunately most of the major evils—poverty, overpopulation, pollution—are problems in which everyone is almost equally involved.

The view that numbers do make a difference can be made plausible if stated in this way: if everyone in circumstances like mine gave £5 to the Bengal Relief Fund, there would be enough to provide food, shelter, and medical care for the refugees; there is no reason why I should give more than anyone else in the same circumstances as I am; therefore I have no obligation to give more than £5. Each premise in this argument is true, and the argument looks sound. It may convince us, unless we notice that it is based on a hypothetical premise, although the conclusion is not stated hypothetically. The argument would be sound if the conclusion were: if everyone in circumstances like mine were to give £5, I would have no obligation to give more than £5. If the conclusion were so stated, however, it would be obvious that the argument has no bearing on a situation in which it is not the case that everyone else gives £5. This, of course, is the actual situation. It is more or less certain that not everyone in circumstances like mine will give £5. So there will not be enough to provide the needed food, shelter, and medical care. Therefore by giving more than £5 I will prevent more suffering than I would if I gave just £5.

It might be thought that this argument has an absurd consequence. Since the situation appears to be that very few people are likely to give substantial amounts, it follows that I and everyone else in similar circumstances ought to give as much as possible, that is, at least up to the point at which by giving more one would begin to cause serious suffering for oneself and one's dependents—perhaps even beyond this point to the point of marginal utility, at which by giving more one would cause oneself and one's dependents as much suffering as one would prevent in Bengal. If everyone does this, however, there will be more than can be used for the benefit of the refugees, and some of the sacrifice will have been unnecessary. Thus, if everyone does what he ought to do, the result will not be as good as it would be if everyone did a little less than he ought to do, or if only some do all that they ought to do.

The paradox here arises only if we assume that the actions in question—sending money to the relief funds—are performed more or less simultaneously, and are also unexpected. For if it is to be expected that everyone is going to contribute something, then clearly each is not obliged to give as much as he would have been obliged to had others not been giving too. And if everyone is not acting more or less simultaneously, then those giving later will know how much more is needed, and will have no obligation to give more than is necessary to reach this amount. To say this is not to deny the principle that people in the same circumstances have the same obligations, but to point out that the fact that others have given, or may be expected to give, is a relevant circumstance: those giving after it has become known that many others are giving and those giving before are not in the same circumstances. So the seemingly absurd consequence of the principle I have put forward can occur only if people are in error about the actual circumstances—that is, if they think they are giving when others are not, but in fact they are giving when others are. The result of everyone doing what he really ought to do cannot be worse than the result of everyone doing less than he ought to do, although the result of everyone doing what he reasonably believes he ought to do could be.

If my argument so far has been sound, neither our distance from a preventable evil nor the number of other people who, in respect to that evil, are in the same situation as we are, lessens our obligation to mitigate or prevent that evil. I shall therefore take as established the principle I asserted earlier. As I have already said, I need to assert it only in its qualified form: if it is in our power to prevent something very bad from happening, without thereby sacrificing anything else morally significant, we ought, morally, to do it.

The outcome of this argument is that our traditional moral categories are upset. The traditional distinction between duty and charity cannot be drawn, or at least, not in the place we normally draw it. Giving money to the Bengal Relief Fund is regarded as an act of charity in our society. The bodies which collect money are known as "charities." These organizations see themselves in this way—if you send them a check, you will be thanked for your "generosity." Because giving money is regarded as an act of charity, it is not thought that there is anything wrong with not giving. The charitable man may be praised, but the man who is not charitable is not condemned. People do not feel in any way ashamed or guilty about spending money on new clothes or a new car instead of giving it to famine relief. (Indeed, the alternative does not occur to them.) This way of looking at the matter cannot be justified. When we buy new clothes not to keep ourselves warm but to look "well-dressed" we are not providing for any important need. We would not be sacrificing anything significant if we were to continue to wear our old clothes, and give the money to famine relief. By doing so, we would be preventing another person from starving. It follows from what I have said earlier that we ought to give money away, rather than spend it on clothes which we do not need to keep us warm. To do so is not charitable, or generous. Nor is it the kind of act which philosophers and theologians have called "supererogatory"—an act which it would be good to do, but not wrong not to do. On the contrary, we ought to give the money away, and it is wrong not to do so.

I am not maintaining that there are no acts which are charitable, or that there are no acts which it would be good to do but not wrong not to do. It may be possible to redraw the distinction between duty and charity in some other place. All I am arguing here is that the present way of drawing the distinction, which makes it an act of charity for a man living at the level of affluence which most people in the "developed nations" enjoy to give money to save someone else from starvation, cannot be supported. It is beyond the scope of my argument to consider whether the distinction should be redrawn or abolished altogether. There would be many other possible ways of drawing the distinction—for instance, one might decide that it is good to make other people as happy as possible, but not wrong not to do so.

Despite the limited nature of the revision in our moral conceptual scheme which I am proposing, the revision would, given the extent of both affluence and famine in the world today, have radical implications. These implications may lead to further objections, distinct from those I have already considered. I shall discuss two of these.

One objection to the position I have taken might be simply that it is too drastic a revision of our moral scheme. People do not ordinarily judge in the way I have suggested they should. Most people reserve their moral condemnation for those who violate some moral norm, such as the norm against taking another person's property. They do not condemn those who indulge in luxury instead of giving to famine relief.

But given that I did not set out to present a morally neutral description of the way people make moral judgments, the way people do in fact judge has nothing to do with the validity of my conclusion. My conclusion follows from the principle which I advanced earlier, and unless that principle is rejected, or the arguments shown to be unsound, I think the conclusion must stand, however strange it appears....

The second objection to my attack on the present distinction between duty and charity is one which has from time to time been made against utilitarianism. It follows from some forms of utilitarian theory that we all ought, morally, to be working full time to increase the balance of happiness over misery. The position I have taken here would not lead to this conclusion in all circumstances, for if there were no bad occurrences that we could prevent without sacrificing something of comparable moral importance, my argument would have no application. Given the present conditions in many parts of the world, however, it does follow from my argument that we ought, morally, to be working full time to relieve great suffering of the sort that occurs as a result of famine or other disasters. Of course, mitigating circumstances can be adduced—for instance, that if we wear ourselves out through overwork, we shall be less effective than we would otherwise have been. Nevertheless, when all considerations of this sort have been taken into account, the conclusion remains: we ought to be preventing as much suffering as we can without sacrificing something else of comparable moral importance. This conclusion is one which we may be reluctant to face. I cannot see, though, why it should be regarded as a criticism of the position for which I have argued, rather than a criticism of our ordinary standards of behavior. Since most people are self-interested to some degree, very few of us are likely to do everything that we ought to do. It would, however, hardly be honest to take this as evidence that it is not the case that we ought to do it....

The conclusion reached earlier [raises] the question of just how much we all ought to be giving away. One possibility, which has already been mentioned, is that we ought to give until we reach the level of marginal utility—that is, the level at which, by giving more, I would cause as much suffering to myself or my dependents as I would relieve by my gift. This would mean, of course, that one would reduce oneself to very near the material circumstances of a Bengali refugee. It will be recalled that earlier I put forward both a strong and a moderate version of the principle of preventing bad occurrences. The strong version, which required us to prevent bad things from happening unless in doing so we would be sacrificing something of a comparable moral significance, does seem to require reducing ourselves to the level of marginal utility. I should also say that the strong version seems to me to be the correct one. I proposed the more moderate version—that we should prevent bad occurrences unless, to do so, we had to sacrifice something morally significant—only in order to show that even on this surely undeniable principle a great change in our way of life is required. On the more moderate principle, it may not follow that we ought to reduce ourselves to the level of marginal utility, for one might hold that to reduce oneself and one's family to this level is to cause something significantly bad to happen. Whether this is so I shall not discuss, since, as I have said, I can see no good reason for holding the moderate version of the principle rather than the strong version. Even if we accepted the principle only in its moderate form, however, it should be clear that we would have to give away enough to ensure that the consumer society, dependent as it is on people spending on trivia rather than giving to famine relief, would slow down and perhaps disappear entirely. There are several reasons why this would be desirable in itself. The value and necessity of economic growth are now being questioned not only by conservationists, but by economists as well.[2] There is no doubt, too, that the consumer society has had a distorting effect on the goals and purposes of its members. Yet looking at the matter purely from the point of view of overseas aid, there must be a limit to the extent to which we should deliberately slow down our economy; for it might be the case that if we gave away, say, forty percent of our Gross National Product, we would slow down the economy so much that in absolute terms we would be giving less than if we gave twenty-five percent of the much larger GNP that we would have if we limited our contribution to this smaller percentage.

I mention this only as an indication of the sort of factor that one would have to take into account in working out an ideal. Since Western societies generally consider one percent of the GNP an acceptable level for overseas aid, the matter is entirely academic. Nor does it affect the question of how much an individual should give in a society in which very few are giving substantial amounts.

It is sometimes said, though less often now than it used to be, that philosophers have no special role to play in public affairs, since most public issues depend primarily on an assessment of facts. On questions of fact, it is said, philosophers as such have no special expertise, and so it has been possible to engage in philosophy without committing oneself to any position on major public issues. No doubt there are some issues of social policy and foreign policy about which it can truly be said that a really expert assessment of the facts is required before taking sides or acting, but the issue of famine is surely not one of these. The facts about the existence of suffering are beyond dispute. Nor, I think, is it disputed that we can do something about it, either through orthodox methods of famine relief or through population control or both. This is therefore an issue on which philosophers are competent to take a position. The issue is one which faces everyone who has more money than he needs to support himself and his dependents, or who is in a position to take some sort of political action. These categories must include practically every teacher and student of philosophy in the universities of the Western world. If philosophy is to deal with matters that are relevant to both teachers and students, this is an issue that philosophers should discuss.

Discussion, though, is not enough. What is the point of relating philosophy to public (and personal) affairs if we do not take our conclusions seriously? In this instance, taking our conclusion seriously means acting upon it. The philosopher will not find it any easier than anyone else to alter his attitudes and way of life to the extent that, if I am right, is involved in doing everything that we ought to be doing. At the very least, though, one can make a start. The philosopher who does so will have to sacrifice some of the benefits of the consumer society, but he can find compensation in the satisfaction of a way of life in which theory and practice, if not yet in harmony, are at least coming together.

---

[2] See, for instance, John Kenneth Galbraith, *The New Industrial State* (Boston, 1967); and E. J. Mishan, *The Costs of Economic Growth* (London, 1967).

STUDY QUESTIONS

1. Do you accept Singer's conclusion that you *personally* have a serious moral obligation to do something about world hunger? If so, what part of his argument do you find most convincing, and why? If not, where do you think his argument goes wrong?
2. Briefly outline Singer's argument. Name two of the strongest objections you can raise against his position. How do you think he would reply to them?
3. If Singer is right, then what we regard as charity is really moral duty. Does this set too high a standard for most people to follow? Explain.
4. For utilitarians like Singer the *consequences* of an action determine its moral character. The consequences of not sending food to starving people are the same as sending them poisoned food: in both cases the people die. Are you guilty of the moral equivalent of murder? Why or why not?

World Hunger and Moral Obligation: The Case against Singer

John Arthur

A biographical sketch of John Arthur is found on page 200.

John Arthur criticizes what he calls Singer's "greater moral evil rule," according to which we ought to sacrifice our own interests if that will result in a greater net welfare to others. (For example, we should all do without luxuries to help those who are starving in Ethiopia.) Singer's premise is the equality of interests: like amounts of suffering or happiness are of equal moral significance no matter who is experiencing them.

Arthur objects that Singer ignores the part of our common moral code that recognizes rights and deserts as determinants of duty. We have rights to our own lives, to our body parts, to the fruits of our labor—and these qualify our obligations to help others. Arthur denies that others have the *right* to our property whenever our property can reduce their misery without undue sacrifice on our part. "We are ... entitled to invoke our own rights as justification for not giving to distant strangers." On the other hand, our moral code does recognize that our *own* children do have rights against us for food and protection.

Rights are one kind of entitlement that qualifies the duty of benevolence. Another is *desert*. We deserve the fruits of our labors. Our common morality does encourage benevolence, "especially when it's a friend or someone we are close to geographically, and when the cost is not significant. But it also gives weight to rights and desert, so that we are not usually obligated to give to strangers."

But perhaps Singer can be seen as advocating a reasonable *reform* of our present moral code. Perhaps we, who are in fortunate circumstances, should ignore our current entitlements and *change* our ways. Arthur argues that a call for reform is unreasonable and morally suspect. Moral codes are not made for angels, but for human beings with their subjective biases in favor of those close to them. Moreover, ignoring rights and deserts suggests a lack of respect for other persons. So Arthur concludes that our present moral code (that Singer judges to be overly selfish) *is* morally reasonable and in need of no reform in the direction suggested by Singer.

Introduction

My guess is that everyone who reads these words is wealthy by comparison with the poorest millions of people on our planet. Not only do we have plenty of money for food, clothing, housing, and other necessities, but a fair amount is left over for far less important purchases like phonograph records, fancy clothes, trips, intoxicants, movies, and so on. And what's more we don't usually give a thought to whether or not we ought to spend our money on such luxuries rather than to give it to those who need it more; we just assume it's ours to do with as we please.

Peter Singer, "Famine, Affluence, and Morality" argues that our assumption is wrong, that we should not buy luxuries when others are in severe need. But [is he] correct? ...

He first argues that two general moral principles are widely accepted, and then that those principles imply an obligation to eliminate starvation.

The first principle is simply that "suffering and death from lack of food, shelter and medical care are bad." Some may be inclined to think that the mere existence of such an evil in itself places an obligation on others, but that is, of course, the problem which Singer addresses. I take it that he is not begging the question in this obvious way and will argue from the existence of evil to the obligation of others to eliminate it. But how, exactly, does he establish this? The second principle, he thinks, shows the connection, but it is here that controversy arises.

This principle, which I will call the greater moral evil rule, is as follows:

> If it is in our power to prevent something bad from happening, without thereby sacrificing anything of comparable moral importance, we ought, morally, to do it.[1]

In other words, people are entitled to keep their earnings only if there is no way for them to prevent a greater evil by giving them away. Providing others with food,

---

[1] Singer also offers a "weak" version of this principle which, it seems to me, is *too* weak. It requires giving aid only if the gift is of *no* moral significance to the giver. But since even minor embarrassment or small amounts of happiness are not completely without moral importance, this weak principle implies little or no obligation to aid, even to the drowning child.

clothing, and housing would generally be of more importance than buying luxuries, so the greater moral evil rule now requires substantial redistribution of wealth.

Certainly there are few, if any, of us who live by that rule, although that hardly shows we are *justified* in our way of life; we often fail to live up to our own standards. Why does Singer think our shared morality requires that we follow the greater moral evil rule? What arguments does he give for it?

He begins with an analogy. Suppose you came across a child drowning in a shallow pond. Certainly we feel it would be wrong not to help. Even if saving the child meant we must dirty our clothes, we would emphasize that those clothes are not of comparable significance to the child's life. The greater moral evil rule thus seems a natural way of capturing why we think it would be wrong not to help.

But the argument for the greater moral evil rule is not limited to Singer's claim that it explains our feelings about the drowning child or that it appears "uncontroversial." Moral equality also enters the picture. Besides the Jeffersonian idea that we share certain rights equally, most of us are also attracted to another type of equality, namely that like amounts of suffering (or happiness) are of equal significance, no matter who is experiencing them. I cannot reasonably say that, while my pain is no more severe than yours, I am somehow special and it's more important that mine be alleviated. Objectivity requires us to admit the opposite, that no one has a unique status which warrants such special pleading. So equality demands equal consideration of interests as well as respect for certain rights.

But if we fail to give to famine relief and instead purchase a new car when the old one will do, or buy fancy clothes for a friend when his or her old ones are perfectly good, are we not assuming that the relatively minor enjoyment we or our friends may get is as important as another person's life? And that is a form of prejudice; we are acting as if people were not equal in the sense that their interests deserve equal consideration. We are giving special consideration to ourselves or to our group, rather like a racist does. Equal consideration of interests thus leads naturally to the greater moral evil rule.

Rights and Desert

Equality, in the sense of giving equal consideration to equally serious needs, is part of our moral code. And so we are led, quite rightly I think, to the conclusion that we should prevent harm to others if in doing so we do not sacrifice anything of comparable moral importance. But there is also another side to the coin, one which Singer ignore[s].... This can be expressed rather awkwardly by the notion of entitlements. These fall into two broad categories, rights and desert. A few examples will show what I mean.

All of us could help others by giving away or allowing others to use our bodies. While your life may be shortened by the loss of a kidney or less enjoyable if lived with only one eye, those costs are probably not comparable to the loss experienced by a person who will die without any kidney or who is totally blind. We can even imagine persons who will actually be harmed in some way by your not granting sexual favors to them. Perhaps the absence of a sexual partner would cause psychological harm or even rape. Now suppose that you can prevent this evil without sacrificing anything of comparable importance. Obviously such relations may not be pleasant, but according to the greater moral evil rule that is not enough; to be justified in refusing, you must show that the unpleasantness you would experience is of equal importance to the harm you are preventing. Otherwise, the rule says you must consent.

If anything is clear, however, it is that our code does not *require* such heroism; you are entitled to keep your second eye and kidney and not bestow sexual favors on anyone who may be harmed without them. The reason for this is often expressed in terms of rights; it's your body, you have a right to it, and that weighs against whatever duty you have to help. To sacrifice a kidney for a stranger is to do more than is required, it's heroic.

Moral rights are normally divided into two categories. Negative rights are rights of noninterference. The right to life, for example, is a right not to be killed. Property rights, the right to privacy, and the right to exercise religious freedom are also negative, requiring only that people leave others alone and not interfere.

Positive rights, however, are rights of recipience. By not putting their children up for adoption, parents give them various positive rights, including rights to be fed, clothed, and housed. If I agree to share in a business venture, my promise creates a right of recipience, so that when I back out of the deal, I've violated your right.

Negative rights also differ from positive in that the former are natural; the ones you have depend on what you are. If lower animals lack rights to life or liberty it is because there is a relevant difference between them and us. But the positive rights you may have are not natural; they arise because others have promised, agreed, or contracted to give you something.

Normally, then, a duty to help a stranger in need is not the result of a right he has. Such a right would be positive, and since no contract or promise was made, no such right exists. An exception to this would be a lifeguard who contracts to watch out for someone's children. The parent whose child drowns would in this case be doubly wronged. First, the lifeguard should not have cruelly or thoughtlessly ignored the child's interests, and second, he ought not to have violated the rights of the parents that he helped. Here, unlike Singer's case, we can say there are rights at stake. Other bystanders also act wrongly by cruelly ignoring the child, but unlike the lifeguard they do not violate anybody's rights. Moral rights are one factor to be weighed, but we also have other obligations; I am not claiming that rights are all we need to consider. That view, like the greater moral evil rule, trades simplicity for accuracy. In fact, our code expects us to help people in need as well as to respect negative and positive rights. But we are also entitled to invoke our own rights as justification for not giving to distant strangers or when the cost to us is substantial, as when we give up an eye or kidney....

Desert is a second form of entitlement. Suppose, for example, an industrious farmer manages through hard work to produce a surplus of food for the winter while a lazy neighbor spends his summer fishing. Must our industrious farmer ignore his hard work and give the surplus away because his neighbor or his family will suffer? What again seems clear is that we have more than one factor to weigh. Not only should we compare the consequences of his keeping it with his giving it away; we also should weigh the fact that one farmer deserves the food, he earned it through his hard work. Perhaps his deserving the product of his labor is out-weighed by the greater need of his lazy neighbor, or perhaps it isn't, but being outweighed is in any case not the same as weighing nothing!

Desert can be negative, too. The fact that the Nazi war criminal did what he did means he deserves punishment, that we have a reason to send him to jail. Other considerations, for example the fact that nobody will be deterred by his suf-fering, or that he is old and harmless, may weigh against punishment and so we may let him go; but again that does not mean he doesn't still deserve to be punished.

Our moral code gives weight to both the greater moral evil principle and entitle-ments. The former emphasizes equality, claiming that from an objective point of view all comparable suffering, whoever its victim, is equally significant. It encourages us to take an impartial look at all the various effects of our actions; it is thus forward-looking. When we consider matters of entitlement, however, our attention is directed to the past. Whether we have rights to money, property, eyes, or whatever, depends on how we came to possess them. If they were acquired by theft rather than from birth or through gift exchange, then the right is suspect. Desert, like rights, is also backward-looking, emphasizing past effort or past transgressions which now warrant reward or punishment.

Our commonly shared morality thus requires that we ignore neither conse-quences nor entitlements, neither the future results of our action nor relevant events in the past. It encourages people to help others in need, especially when it's a friend or someone we are close to geographically, and when the cost is not significant. But it also gives weight to rights and desert, so that we are not usually obligated to give to strangers....

But unless we are moral relativists, the mere fact that entitlements are an important part of our moral code does not in itself justify such a role. Singer ... can perhaps best be seen as a moral reformer advocating the rejection of rules which provide for distribution according to rights and desert. Certainly the fact that in the past our moral code condemned suicide and racial mixing while condon-ing slavery should not convince us that a more enlightened moral code, one which we would want to support, would take such positions. Rules which define accept-able behavior are continually changing, and we must allow for the replacement of inferior ones.

Why should we not view entitlements as examples of inferior rules we are bet-ter off without? What could justify our practice of evaluating actions by looking backward to rights and desert instead of just to their consequences? One answer is that more fundamental values than rights and desert are at stake, namely fairness, justice, and respect. Failure to reward those who earn good grades or promotions is wrong because it's *unfair*; ignoring past guilt shows a lack of regard for *justice*; and failure to respect rights to life, privacy, or religious choice suggests a lack of *respect for other persons*.

Some people may be persuaded by those remarks, feeling that entitlements are now on an acceptably firm foundation. But an advocate of equality may well want to question why fairness, justice, and respect for persons should matter. But since it is no more obvious that preventing suffering matters than that fairness, respect, and justice do, we again seem to have reached an impasse....

The lesson to be learned here is a general one: The moral code it is rational for us to support must be practical; it must actually work. This means, among other things, that it must be able to gain the support of almost everyone.

But the code must be practical in other respects as well.... [It] is wrong to ignore the possibilities of altruism, but it is also important that a code not assume people are more unselfish than they are. Rules that would work only for angels are not the ones it is rational to support for humans. Second, an ideal code cannot assume we are more objective than we are; we often tend to rationalize when our own interests are at stake, and a rational person will also keep that in mind when choosing a moral code. Finally, it is not rational to support a code which assumes we have perfect knowledge. We are often mistaken about the consequences of what we do, and a workable code must take that into account as well....

It seems to me, then, that a reasonable code would require people to help when there is no substantial cost to themselves, that is, when what they are sacrificing would not mean *significant* reduction in their own or their families' level of happiness. Since most people's savings accounts and nearly everybody's second kidney are not insignificant, entitlements would in those cases outweigh another's need. But if what is at stake is trivial, as dirtying one's clothes would normally be, then an ideal moral code would not allow rights to override the greater evil that can be prevented. Despite our code's unclear and sometimes schizophrenic posture, it seems to me that these judgments are not that different from our current moral attitudes. We tend to blame people who waste money on trivia when they could help others in need, yet not to expect people to make large sacrifices to distant strangers. An ideal moral code thus might not be a great deal different from our own.

STUDY QUESTIONS

1. What is Singer's "greater moral evil rule," and why does Arthur object to it?
2. What is the status of the common moral code in Arthur's moral system? How does Arthur deploy the moral code to undermine Singer's general position that utilitarian considerations override parochial loyalties and interests?
3. How does Arthur classify rights? Why is the child's right to parental protection and food a "positive right"? How does Arthur's conception of rights preclude the view that needy but distant strangers have the right to our benevolence?
4. Arthur says, "Our commonly shared morality ... requires that we ignore neither consequences nor entitlements." Is it fair to say that Singer ignores entitlements? Explain.

"For Heaven's Sake, Please Stop the Aid!"

James Shikwati

James Shikwati (b. 1970) is the founder and Executive Director of the Inter Region Economic Network, a nonprofit independent public policy research and educational organization in Nairobi, Kenya, that promotes market-based responses to contemporary social-economic and environmental problems.

Shikwati is sharply impatient with moral theorists like Peter Singer who call on affluent citizens of developed countries to increase the aid they currently send to third world countries. While he acknowledges the good intentions of donors, Shikwati is persuaded that the aid does not help African nations overcome poverty, but instead keeps them mired in it. The current system keeps developing African countries poor, dependent on their corrupt rulers, and permanently beholden to the developed world. When the West sends its billions of dollars of food and mountains of clothes, African farmers and small businesses lose their livelihoods. In the long run, sending aid with no system of accountability in place and no demands for corrupt leaders to reform does more harm than good.

This interview appeared in the German magazine *Der Spiegel* in the summer of 2005, soon after a group of world leaders held a summit in Scotland that focused on relieving poverty in Africa.

SPIEGEL: Mr. Shikwati, the G8 summit at Gleneagles is about to beef up the development aid for Africa …

SHIKWATI: … for God's sake, please just stop.

SPIEGEL: Stop? The industrialized nations of the West want to eliminate hunger and poverty.

SHIKWATI: Such intentions have been damaging our continent for the past 40 years. If the industrial nations really want to help the Africans, they should finally terminate this awful aid. The countries that have collected the most development aid are also the ones that are in the worst shape. Despite the billions that have poured into Africa, the continent remains poor.

SPIEGEL: Do you have an explanation for this paradox?

SHIKWATI: Huge bureaucracies are financed (with the aid money), corruption and complacency are promoted, Africans are taught to be beggars and not to be independent. In addition, development aid weakens the local markets everywhere and dampens the spirit of entrepreneurship that we so desperately need. As absurd as it may sound: Development aid is one of the reasons for Africa's problems. If the West were to cancel these payments, normal Africans wouldn't even notice. Only the functionaries would be hard hit. Which is why they maintain that the world would stop turning without this development aid.

SPIEGEL: Even in a country like Kenya, people are starving to death each year. Someone has got to help them.

SHIKWATI: But it has to be the Kenyans themselves who help these people. When there's a drought in a region of Kenya, our corrupt politicians reflexively cry out for more help. This call then reaches the United Nations World Food Program—which is a massive agency of *apparatchiks* who are in the absurd situation of, on the one hand, being dedicated to the fight against hunger while, on the other hand, being faced with unemployment were hunger actually eliminated. It's only natural that they willingly accept the plea for more help. And it's not uncommon that they demand a little more money than the respective African government originally requested. They then forward that request to their headquarters, and before long, several thousands tons of corn are shipped to Africa....

SPIEGEL: ... corn that predominantly comes from highly subsidized European and American farmers....

SHIKWATI: ... and at some point, this corn ends up in the harbor of Mombasa. A portion of the corn often goes directly into the hands of unscrupulous politicians who then pass it on to their own tribe to boost their next election campaign. Another portion of the shipment ends up on the black market where the corn is dumped at extremely low prices. Local farmers may as well put down their hoes right away; no one can compete with the UN's World Food Program. And because the farmers go under in the face of this pressure, Kenya would have no reserves to draw on if there actually were a famine next year. It's a simple but fatal cycle.

SPIEGEL: If the World Food Program didn't do anything, the people would starve.

SHIKWATI: I don't think so. In such a case, the Kenyans, for a change, would be forced to initiate trade relations with Uganda or Tanzania, and buy their food there. This type of trade is vital for Africa. It would force us to improve our own infrastructure, while making national borders—drawn by the Europeans by the way—more permeable. It would also force us to establish laws favoring market economy.

SPIEGEL: Would Africa actually be able to solve these problems on its own?

SHIKWATI: Of course. Hunger should not be a problem in most of the countries south of the Sahara. In addition, there are vast natural resources: oil, gold, diamonds. Africa is always only portrayed as a continent of suffering, but most figures are vastly exaggerated. In the industrial nations, there's a sense that Africa would go under without development aid. But believe me, Africa existed before you Europeans came along. And we didn't do all that poorly either.

SPIEGEL: But AIDS didn't exist at that time.

SHIKWATI: If one were to believe all the horrifying reports, then all Kenyans should actually be dead by now. But now, tests are being carried out everywhere, and it turns out that the figures were vastly exaggerated. It's not three million Kenyans that are infected. All of the sudden, it's only about one million. Malaria is just as much of a problem, but people rarely talk about that.

SPIEGEL: And why's that?

SHIKWATI: AIDS is big business, maybe Africa's biggest business. There's nothing else that can generate as much aid money as shocking figures on AIDS. AIDS is a political disease here, and we should be very skeptical.

SPIEGEL: The Americans and Europeans have frozen funds previously pledged to Kenya. The country is too corrupt, they say.

SHIKWATI: I am afraid, though, that the money will still be transfered before long. After all, it has to go somewhere. Unfortunately, the Europeans' devastating urge to do good can no longer be countered with reason. It makes no sense whatsoever that directly after the new Kenyan government was elected—a leadership change that ended the dictatorship of Daniel arap Moi—the faucets were suddenly opened and streams of money poured into the country.

SPIEGEL: Such aid is usually earmarked for a specific objective, though.

SHIKWATI: That doesn't change anything. Millions of dollars earmarked for the fight against AIDS are still stashed away in Kenyan bank accounts and have not been spent. Our politicians were overwhelmed with money, and they try to siphon off as much as possible. The late tyrant of the Central African Republic, Jean Bedel Bokassa, cynically summed it up by saying: "The French government pays for everything in our country. We ask the French for money. We get it, and then we waste it."

SPIEGEL: In the West, there are many compassionate citizens wanting to help Africa. Each year, they donate money and pack their old clothes into collection bags …

SHIKWATI: … and they flood our markets with that stuff We can buy these donated clothes cheaply at our so-called Mitumba markets. There are Germans who spend a few dollars to get used Bayern Munich or Werder Bremen jerseys, in other words, clothes that that some German kids sent to Africa for a good cause. After buying these jerseys, they auction them off at Ebay and send them back to Germany—for three times the price. That's insanity.…

SPIEGEL: …and hopefully an exception.

SHIKWATI: Why do we get these mountains of clothes? No one is freezing here. Instead, our tailors lose their livelihoods. They're in the same position as our farmers. No one in the low-wage world of Africa can be cost-efficient enough to keep pace with donated products. In 1997, 137,000 workers were employed in Nigeria's textile industry. By 2003, the figure had dropped to 57,000. The results are the same in all other areas where overwhelming helpfulness and fragile African markets collide.

SPIEGEL: Following World War II, Germany only managed to get back on its feet because the Americans poured money into the country through the Marshall Plan. Wouldn't that qualify as successful development aid?

SHIKWATI: In Germany's case, only the destroyed infrastructure had to be repaired. Despite the economic crisis of the Weimar Republic, Germany was a highly industrialized country before the war. The damages created by the tsunami in Thailand can also be fixed with a little money and some reconstruction aid. Africa, however, must take the first steps into modernity on its own. There must be a change in mentality. We have to stop perceiving ourselves as beggars. These days, Africans only perceive themselves as victims. On the other hand, no one can really picture an African as a businessman. In order to change the current situation, it would be helpful if the aid organizations were to pull out.

SPIEGEL: If they did that, many jobs would be immediately lost.…

SHIKWATI: … jobs that were created artificially in the first place and that distort reality. Jobs with foreign aid organizations are, of course, quite popular, and they can be very selective in choosing the best people. When an aid organization needs a driver, dozens apply for the job. And because it's unacceptable that the aid worker's chauffeur only speaks his own tribal language, an applicant is needed who also speaks English fluently—and, ideally, one who is also well mannered. So you end up with some African biochemist driving an aid worker around, distributing European food, and forcing local farmers out of their jobs. That's just crazy!

SPIEGEL: The German government takes pride in precisely monitoring the recipients of its funds.

SHIKWATI: And what's the result? A disaster. The German government threw money right at Rwanda's president Paul Kagame. This is a man who has the deaths of a million people on his conscience—people that his army killed in the neighboring country of Congo.

SPIEGEL: What are the Germans supposed to do?

SHIKWATI: If they really want to fight poverty, they should completely halt development aid and give Africa the opportunity to ensure its own survival. Currently, Africa is like a child that immediately cries for its babysitter when something goes wrong. Africa should stand on its own two feet.

STUDY QUESTIONS

1. Shikwati points out that Africa is especially vulnerable to the harm done by well-meaning moralists who urge the West to help the poor. He calls for a halt in the implementation of Western development policies. Do you think he makes a valid case for his position?
2. How might someone like Peter Singer respond to Shikwati's argument?
3. Shikwati argues that the current policies of aid initiate a fatal cycle in which local farmers go under and Africans have no food reserves of their own. But, as the interviewer for *Der Spiegel* argues, if the international famine relief programs did nothing, then people would starve. What reasonable course of actions seems to you to be just and effective?
4. What fault does Shikwati find with the efforts being mounted by the Western governments and health agencies to help African governments deal with the AIDS epidemic? In what sense is AIDS "big business"? Do you agree with his criticism?

An Almost Absolute Value in History

John T. Noonan, Jr.

John Noonan (b. 1926) has served on the Ninth Circuit Court since 1986. Before that he was a professor of law at the University of California at Berkeley and at the University of Notre Dame. His many books include *The Scholastic Analysis of Usury and Contraception: A History of Its Treatment by the Catholic Theologians and Canonists* (1957). His most recent work is *A Church That Can and Cannot Change: The Development of Catholic Moral Teaching* (2005).

According to Noonan the question of abortion turns on the question of when an individual human life begins. Noonan's answer is consistent with the answer given by Christian theologians as well as biologists: Life conceived by human parents is human from the moment of conception. Noonan's second principle is that human life at any stage is protected. "A being with a human genetic code is man." He therefore rejects "viability" as the necessary condition for being protected. He denies that one can be more or less human. And he rejects appeals to feelings. For it may be true that we do not feel much sympathy with the fetus in its earliest stages, but that is irrelevant. The only exceptions to the prohibition against abortion turn on threats to the mother's life.

AN ALMOST ABSOLUTE VALUE IN HISTORY Reprinted by permission of the publisher from THE MORALITY OF ABORTION: LEGAL AND HISTORICAL PERSPECTIVES by John T. Noonan, Jr., pp. 51–59, Cambridge, Mass: Harvard University Press, Copyright © 1970 by the President and Fellows of Harvard College.

The most fundamental question involved in the long history of thought on abortion is: How do you determine the humanity of a being? To phrase the question that way is to put in comprehensive humanistic terms what the theologians either dealt with as an explicitly theological question under the heading of "ensoulment" or dealt with implicitly in their treatment of abortion. The Christian position as it originated did not depend on a narrow theological or philosophical concept. It had no relation to theories of infant baptism. It appealed to no special theory of instantaneous ensoulment. It took the world's view on ensoulment as that view changed from Aristotle to Zacchia. There was, indeed, theological influence affecting the theory of ensoulment finally adopted, and, of course, ensoulment itself was a theological concept, so that the position was always explained in theological terms. But the theological notion of ensoulment could easily be translated into humanistic language by substituting "human" for "rational soul"; the problem of knowing when a man is a man is common to theology and humanism.

If one steps outside the specific categories used by the theologians, the answer they gave can be analyzed as a refusal to discriminate among human beings on the basis of their varying potentialities. Once conceived, the being was recognized as man because he had man's potential. The criterion for humanity, thus, was simple and all-embracing: if you are conceived by human parents, you are human.

The strength of this position may be tested by a review of some of the other distinctions offered in the contemporary controversy over legalizing abortion. Perhaps the most popular distinction is in terms of viability. Before an age of so many months, the fetus is not viable, that is, it cannot be removed from the mother's womb and live apart from her. To that extent, the life of the fetus is absolutely dependent on the life of the mother. This dependence is made the basis of denying recognition to its humanity.

There are difficulties with this distinction. One is that the perfection of artificial incubation may make the fetus viable at any time: it may be removed and artificially sustained. Experiments with animals already show that such a procedure is possible. This hypothetical extreme case relates to an actual difficulty: there is considerable elasticity to the idea of viability. Mere length of life is not an exact measure. The viability of the fetus depends on the extent of its anatomical and functional development. The weight and length of the fetus are better guides to the state of its development than age, but weight and length vary. Moreover, different racial groups have different ages at which their fetuses are viable. Some evidence, for example, suggests that Negro fetuses mature more quickly than white fetuses. If viability is the norm, the standard would vary with race and with many individual circumstances.

The most important objection to this approach is that dependence is not ended by viability. The fetus is still absolutely dependent on someone's care in order to continue existence; indeed a child of one or three or even five years of age is absolutely dependent on another's care for existence; uncared for, the older fetus or the younger child will die as surely as the early fetus detached from the mother. The unsubstantial lessening in dependence at viability does not seem to signify any special acquisition of humanity.

A second distinction has been attempted in terms of experience. A being who has had experience, has lived and suffered, who possesses memories, is more human than one who has not. Humanity depends on formation by experience. The fetus is thus "unformed" in the most basic human sense.

This distinction is not serviceable for the embryo which is already experiencing and reacting. The embryo is responsive to touch after eight weeks and at least at that point is experiencing. At an earlier stage the zygote is certainly alive and responding to its environment. The distinction may also be challenged by the rare case where aphasia has erased adult memory: has it erased humanity? More fundamentally, this distinction leaves even the older fetus or the younger child to be treated as an unformed inhuman thing. Finally, it is not clear why experience as such confers humanity. It could be argued that certain central experiences such as loving or learning are necessary to make a man human. But then human beings who have failed to love or to learn might be excluded from the class called man.

A third distinction is made by appeal to the sentiments of adults. If a fetus dies, the grief of the parents is not the grief they would have for a living child. The fetus is an unnamed "it" till birth, and is not perceived as personality until at least the fourth month of existence when movements in the womb manifest a vigorous presence demanding joyful recognition by the parents.

Yet feeling is notoriously an unsure guide to the humanity of others. Many groups of humans have had difficulty in feeling that persons of another tongue, color, religion, sex, are as human as they. Apart from reactions to alien groups, we mourn the loss of a ten-year-old boy more than the loss of his one-day-old brother or his 90-year-old grandfather. The difference felt and the grief expressed vary with the potentialities extinguished, or the experience wiped out; they do not seem to point to any substantial difference in the humanity of baby, boy, or grandfather.

Distinctions are also made in terms of sensation by the parents. The embryo is felt within the womb only after about the fourth month. The embryo is seen only at birth. What can be neither seen nor felt is different from what is tangible. If the fetus cannot be seen or touched at all, it cannot be perceived as man.

Yet experience shows that sight is even more untrustworthy than feeling in determining humanity. By sight, color became an appropriate index for saying who was a man, and the evil of racial discrimination was given foundation. Nor can touch provide the test; a being confined by sickness, "out of touch" with others, does not thereby seem to lose his humanity. To the extent that touch still has appeal as a criterion, it appears to be a survival of the old English idea of "quickening"—a possible mistranslation of the Latin *animatus* used in the canon law. To that extent touch as a criterion seems to be dependent on the Aristotelian notion of ensoulment, and to fall when this notion is discarded.

Finally, a distinction is sought in social visibility. The fetus is not socially perceived as human. It cannot communicate with others. Thus, both subjectively and objectively, it is not a member of society. As moral rules are rules for the behavior of members of society to each other, they cannot be made for behavior toward what is not yet a member. Excluded from the society of men, the fetus is excluded from the humanity of men.

By force of the argument from the consequences, this distinction is to be rejected. It is more subtle than that founded on an appeal to physical sensation, but it is equally dangerous in its implications. If humanity depends on social recognition, individuals or whole groups may be dehumanized by being denied any status in their society. Such a fate is fictionally portrayed in *1984* and has actually been the lot of many men in many societies. In the Roman empire, for example, condemnation to slavery meant the practical denial of most human rights; in the Chinese Communist world, landlords have been classified as enemies of the people and so treated as nonpersons by the state. Humanity does not depend on social recognition, though often the failure of society to recognize the prisoner, the alien, the heterodox as human has led to the destruction of human beings. Anyone conceived by a man and a woman is human. Recognition of this condition by society follows a real event in the objective order, however imperfect and halting the recognition. Any attempt to limit humanity to exclude some group runs the risk of furnishing authority and precedent for excluding other groups in the name of the consciousness or perception of the controlling group in the society.

A philosopher may reject the appeal to the humanity of the fetus because he views "humanity" as a secular view of the soul and because he doubts the existence of anything real and objective which can be identified as humanity. One answer to such a philosopher is to ask how he reasons about moral questions without supposing that there is a sense in which he and the others of whom he speaks are human. Whatever group is taken as the society which determines who may be killed is thereby taken as human. A second answer is to ask if he does not believe that there is a right and wrong way of deciding moral questions. If there is such a difference, experience may be appealed to: to decide who is human on the basis of the sentiment of a given society has led to consequences which rational men would characterize as monstrous.

The rejection of the attempted distinctions based on viability and visibility, experience and feeling, may be buttressed by the following considerations: Moral judgments often rest on distinctions, but if the distinctions are not to appear arbitrary fiat, they should relate to some real difference in probabilities. There is a kind of continuity in all life, but the earlier stages of the elements of human life possess tiny probabilities of development. Consider for example, the spermatozoa in any normal ejaculate: There are about 200,000,000 in any single ejaculate, of which one has a chance of developing into a zygote. Consider the oocytes which may become ova: there are 100,000 to 1,000,000 oocytes in a female infant, of which a maximum of 390 are ovulated. But once spermatozoon and ovum meet and the conceptus is formed, such studies as have been made show that roughly in only 20 percent of the cases will spontaneous abortion occur. In other words, the chances are about 4 out of 5 that this new being will develop. At this stage in the life of the being there is a sharp shift in probabilities, an immense jump in potentialities. To make a distinction between the rights of spermatozoa and the rights of the fertilized ovum is to respond to an enormous shift in possibilities. For about twenty days after conception the egg may split to form twins or combine with another egg to form a chimera, but the probability of either event happening is very small.

It may be asked, What does a change in biological probabilities have to do with establishing humanity? The argument from probabilities is not aimed at establishing humanity but at establishing an objective discontinuity which may be taken into account in moral discourse. As life itself is a matter of probabilities, as most moral reasoning is an estimate of probabilities, so it seems in accord with the structure of reality and the nature of moral thought to found a moral judgment on the change in probabilities at conception. The appeal to probabilities is the most commonsensical of arguments, to a greater or smaller degree all of us base our actions on probabilities, and in morals, as in law, prudence and negligence are often measured by the account one has taken of the probabilities. If the chance is 200,000,000 to 1 that the movement in the bushes into which you shoot is a man's, I doubt if many persons would hold you careless in shooting; but if the chances are 4 out of 5 that the movement is a human being's, few would acquit you of blame. Would the argument be different if only one out of ten children conceived came to term? Of course this argument would be different. This argument is an appeal to probabilities that actually exist, not to any and all states of affairs which may be imagined.

The probabilities as they do exist do not show the humanity of the embryo in the sense of a demonstration in logic any more than the probabilities of the movement in the bush being a man demonstrate beyond all doubt that the being is a man. The appeal is a "buttressing" consideration, showing the plausibility of the standard adopted. The argument focuses on the decisional factor in any moral judgment and assumes that part of the business of a moralist is drawing lines. One evidence of the nonarbitrary character of the line drawn is the difference of probabilities on either side of it. If a spermatozoon is destroyed, one destroys a being which had a chance of far less than 1 in 200 million of developing into a reasonable being, possessed of the genetic code, a heart and other organs, and capable of pain. If a fetus is destroyed, one destroys a being already possessed of the genetic code, organs, and sensitivity to pain, and one which had an 80 percent chance of developing further into a baby outside the womb who, in time, would reason.

The positive argument for conception as the decisive moment of humanization is that at conception the new being receives the genetic code. It is this genetic information which determines his characteristics, which is the biological carrier of the possibility of human wisdom, which makes him a self-evolving being. A being with a human genetic code is man.

This review of current controversy over the humanity of the fetus emphasizes what a fundamental question the theologians resolved in asserting the inviolability of the fetus. To regard the fetus as possessed of equal rights with other humans was not, however, to decide every case where abortion might be employed. It did decide the case where the argument was that the fetus should be aborted for its own good. To say a being was human was to say it had a destiny to decide for itself which could not be taken from it by another man's decision. But human beings with equal rights often come in conflict with each other, and some decision must be made as whose claims are to prevail. Cases of conflict involving the fetus are different only in two respects: the total inability of the fetus to speak for itself and the fact that the right of the fetus regularly at stake is the right to life itself.

The approach taken by the theologians to these conflicts was articulated in terms of "direct" and "indirect." Again, to look at what they were doing from outside their categories, they may be said to have been drawing lines or "balancing values." "Direct" and "indirect" are spatial metaphors; "line-drawing" is another. "To weigh" or "to balance" values is a metaphor of a more complicated mathematical sort hinting at the process which goes on in moral judgments. All the metaphors suggest that, in the moral judgments made, comparisons were necessary, that no value completely controlled. The principle of double effect was no doctrine fallen from heaven, but a method of analysis appropriate where two relative values were being compared. In Catholic moral theology, as it developed, life even of the innocent was not taken as an absolute. Judgments on acts affecting life issued from a process of weighing. In the weighing, the fetus was always given a value greater than zero, always a value separate and independent from its parents. This valuation was crucial and fundamental in all Christian thought on the subject and marked it off from any approach which considered that only the parents' interests needed to be considered.

Even with the fetus weighed as human, one interest could be weighed as equal or superior: that of the mother in her own life. The casuists between 1450 and 1895 were willing to weigh this interest as superior. Since 1895, that interest was given decisive weight only in the two special cases of the cancerous uterus and the ectopic pregnancy. In both of these cases the fetus itself had little chance of survival even if the abortion were not performed. As the balance was once struck in favor of the mother whenever her life was endangered, it could be so struck again. The balance reached between 1895 and 1930 attempted prudentially and pastorally to forestall a multitude of exceptions for interests less than life.

The perception of the humanity of the fetus and the weighing of fetal rights against other human rights constituted the work of the moral analysts. But what spirit animated their abstract judgments? For the Christian community it was the injunction of Scripture to love your neighbor as yourself. The fetus as human was a neighbor; his life had parity with one's own. The commandment gave life to what otherwise would have been only rational calculation.

The commandment could be put in humanistic as well as theological terms: Do not injure your fellow man without reason. In these terms, once the humanity of the fetus is perceived, abortion is never right except in self-defense. When life must be taken to save life, reason alone cannot say that a mother must prefer a child's life to her own. With this exception, now of great rarity, abortion violates the rational humanist tenet of the equality of human lives.

For Christians the commandment to love had received a special imprint in that the exemplar proposed of love was the love of the Lord for his disciples. In the light given by this example, self-sacrifice carried to the point of death seemed in the extreme situations not without meaning. In the less extreme cases, preference for one's own interests to the life of another seemed to express cruelty or selfishness irreconcilable with the demands of love.

STUDY QUESTIONS

1. Many philosophers disagree with Noonan's position that being human is in and of itself a sufficient condition for having an inviolable right to life. They point to brain-dead human beings and ask whether that right applies to them. They argue that the necessary condition for such a right must come some time after conception, perhaps even after birth. Take sides in this dispute.
2. Noonan's argument seems insensitive to considerations that victims of rape should be exceptions to the rule. How would Noonan react to the charge of insensitivity?
3. What role does religion play in Noonan's position? Is a religious standpoint indispensable for holding a strong "right-to-life" point of view?

On the Moral and Legal Status of Abortion

Mary Anne Warren

Mary Anne Warren (b. 1946) recently retired from her professorship in the philosophy department at San Francisco State University. She has written numerous articles in the area of ethics, particularly on abortion, and is the author of *The Nature of Woman: An Encyclopedia and Guide to the Literature* (1980), *Gendercide: The Implications of Sex Selection* (1985), and *Moral Status: Obligations to Persons and Other Living Things* (1997).

Warren distinguishes between being human in the biological sense and being human in the moral sense. She acknowledges that human life begins with conception, but argues that we can only wrong human beings who are also *persons*. To be a person is to have sensitivity to pain, some capacity to reason, some capacity to communicate and some self-awareness. Since the fetus has none of these attributes, it is not a person possessed of a serious right to life. Warren notes that newborn infants also fall short of being persons; nevertheless, a neonate may not be killed, even when the mother does not want the burden of caring for it, for others may now want to take over its nurture. Warren does say that unwanted, defective infants may be destroyed, for they are not persons and there is no prima facie obligation to keep them alive.

The question which we must answer in order to produce a satisfactory solution to the problem of the moral status of abortion is this: How are we to define the moral community, the set of beings with full and equal moral rights, such that we can decide whether a human fetus is a member of this community or not? What sort of entity, exactly, has the inalienable rights to life, liberty, and the pursuit of happiness? Jefferson attributed these rights to all *men*, and it may or may not be fair to suggest that he intended to attribute them *only* to men. Perhaps he ought to have attributed them to all human beings. If so, then we arrive, first, at Noonan's problem of defining what makes a being human, and, second, at the equally vital question which Noonan does not consider; namely, What reason is there for identifying the moral community with the set of all human beings, in whatever way we have chosen to define that term?

1. On the Definition of "Human"

One reason why this vital second question is so frequently overlooked in the debate over the moral status of abortion is that the term "human" has two distinct, but not often distinguished, senses. This fact results in a slide of meaning, which serves to conceal the fallaciousness of the traditional argument that since (1) it is wrong to kill innocent human beings, and (2) fetuses are innocent human beings, then (3) it is wrong to kill fetuses. For if "human" is used in the same sense in both (1) and (2) then, whichever of the two senses is meant, one of these premises is question-begging. And if it is used in two different senses then of course the conclusion doesn't follow.

Thus, (1) is a self-evident moral truth,[1] and avoids begging the question about abortion, only if "human being" is used to mean something like "a full-fledged member of the moral community." (It may or may not also be meant to refer exclusively to members of the species *Homo sapiens*.) We may call this the *moral* sense of "human." It is not to be confused with what we will call the *genetic* sense, i.e., the sense in which *any* member of the species is a human being, and no member of any other species could be. If (1) is acceptable only if the moral sense is intended, (2) is non-question-begging only if what is intended is the genetic sense.

In "Deciding Who Is Human," Noonan argues for the classification of fetuses with human beings by pointing to the presence of the full genetic code, and the potential capacity for rational thought.[2] It is clear that what he needs to show, for his version of the traditional argument to be valid, is that fetuses are human in the moral sense, the sense in which it is analytically true that all human beings have full moral rights. But, in the absence of any argument showing that whatever is genetically human is also morally human, and he gives none, nothing more than genetic humanity can be demonstrated by the presence of the human genetic code. And, as we will see, the *potential* capacity for rational thought can at most show that an entity has the potential for *becoming* human in the moral sense.

2. Defining the Moral Community

Can it be established that genetic humanity is sufficient for moral humanity? I think that there are very good reasons for not defining the moral community in this way. I would like to suggest an alternative way of defining the moral community, which I will argue for only to the extent of explaining why it is, or should be, self-evident. The suggestion is simply that the moral community consists of all and *only people*, rather than all and only human beings;[3] and probably the best way of demonstrating its self-evidence is by considering the concept of person-hood, to see what sorts of entity are and are not persons, and what the decision that a being is or is not a person implies about its moral rights.

What characteristics entitle an entity to be considered a person? This is obviously not the place to attempt a complete analysis of the concept of personhood,

---

[1] Of course, the principle that it is (always) wrong to kill innocent human beings is in need of many other modifications, e.g., that it may be permissible to do so to save a greater number of other innocent human beings, but we may safely ignore these complications here.

[2] John Noonan, "Deciding Who Is Human," *Natural Law Forum*, 13 (1968), 135.

[3] From here on, we will use "human" to mean genetically human, since the moral sense seems closely connected to, and perhaps derived from, the assumption that genetic humanity is sufficient for membership in the moral community.

but we do not need such a fully adequate analysis just to determine whether and why a fetus is or isn't a person. All we need is a rough and approximate list of the most basic criteria of personhood, and some idea of which, or how many, of these an entity must satisfy in order to properly be considered a person.

In searching for such criteria, it is useful to look beyond the set of people with whom we are acquainted, and ask how we would decide whether a totally alien being was a person or not. (For we have no right to assume that genetic humanity is necessary for personhood.) Imagine a space traveler who lands on an unknown planet and encounters a race of beings utterly unlike any he has ever seen or heard of. If he wants to be sure of behaving morally toward these beings, he has to somehow decide whether they are people, and hence have full moral rights, or whether they are the sort of thing which he need not feel guilty about treating as, for example, a source of food.

How should he go about making this decision? If he has some anthropological background, he might look for such things as religion, art, and the manufacturing of tools, weapons, or shelters, since these factors have been used to distinguish our human from our prehuman ancestors, in what seems to be closer to the moral than the genetic sense of "human." And no doubt he would be right to consider the presence of such factors as good evidence that the alien beings were people, and morally human. It would, however, be overly anthropocentric of him to take the absence of these things as adequate evidence that they were not, since we can imagine people who have progressed beyond, or evolved without ever developing, these cultural characteristics.

I suggest that the traits which are most central to the concept of personhood, or humanity in the moral sense, are, very roughly, the following:

1. consciousness (of objects and events external and/or internal to the being), and in particular the capacity to feel pain;
2. reasoning (the *developed* capacity to solve new and relatively complex problems);
3. self-motivated activity (activity which is relatively independent of either genetic or direct external control);
4. the capacity to communicate, by whatever means, messages of an indefinite variety of types, that is, not just with an indefinite number of possible contents, but on indefinitely many possible topics;
5. the presence of self-concepts, and self-awareness, either individual or racial, or both.

Admittedly, there are apt to be a great many problems involved in formulating precise definitions of these criteria, let alone in developing universally valid behavioral criteria for deciding when they apply. But I will assume that both we and our explorer know approximately what (1)–(5) mean, and that he is also able to determine whether or not they apply. How, then, should he use his findings to decide whether or not the alien beings are people? We needn't suppose that an entity must have *all* of these attributes to be properly considered a person; (1) and (2) alone may well be sufficient for personhood, and quite probably (1)–(3) are sufficient. Neither do we need to insist that any one of these criteria is *necessary* for personhood, although once again (1) and (2) look like fairly good candidates for necessary conditions, as does (3), if "activity" is construed so as to include the activity of reasoning.

All we need to claim, to demonstrate that a fetus is not a person, is that any being which satisfies *none* of (1)–(5) is certainly not a person. I consider this claim to be so obvious that I think anyone who denied it, and claimed that a being which satisfied none of (1)–(5) was a person all the same, would thereby demonstrate that he had no notion at all of what a person is—perhaps because he had confused the concept of a person with that of genetic humanity. If the opponents of abortion were to deny the appropriateness of these five criteria, I do not know what further arguments would convince them. We would probably have to admit that our conceptual schemes were indeed irreconcilably different, and that our dispute could not be settled objectively.

I do not expect this to happen, however, since I think that the concept of a person is one which is very nearly universal (to people), and that it is common to both proabortionists and antiabortionists, even though neither group has fully realized the relevance of this concept to the resolution of their dispute. Furthermore, I think that on reflection even the antiabortionists ought to agree not only that (1)–(5) are central to the concept of personhood, but also that it is a part of this concept that all and only people have full moral rights. The concept of a person is in part a moral concept; once we have admitted that x is a person we have recognized, even if we have not agreed to respect, x's right to be treated as a member of the moral community. It is true that the claim that x is a *human being* is more commonly voiced as part of an appeal to treat x decently than is the claim that x is a person, but this is either because "human being" is here used in the sense which implies personhood, or because the genetic and moral senses of "human" have been confused.

Now if (1)–(5) are indeed the primary criteria of personhood, then it is clear that genetic humanity is neither necessary nor sufficient for establishing that an entity is a person. Some human beings are not people, and there may well be people who are not human beings. A man or woman whose consciousness has been permanently obliterated but who remains alive is a human being which is no longer a person; defective human beings, with no appreciable mental capacity, are not and presumably never will be people; and a fetus is a human being which is not yet a person, and which therefore cannot coherently be said to have full moral rights. Citizens of the next century should be prepared to recognize highly advanced, self-aware robots or computers, should such be developed, and intelligent inhabitants of other worlds, should such be found, as people in the fullest sense, and to respect their moral rights. But to ascribe full moral rights to an entity which is not a person is as absurd as to ascribe moral obligations and responsibilities to such an entity.

3. Fetal Development and the Right to Life

Two problems arise in the application of these suggestions for the definition of the moral community to the determination of the precise moral status of a human fetus. Given that the paradigm example of a person is a normal adult human being, then (1) How like this paradigm, in particular how far advanced since conception, does a human being need to be before it begins to have a right to life by virtue, not of being fully a person as of yet, but of being *like* a person? and (2) To what extent, if any, does the fact that a fetus has the *potential* for becoming a person endow it with some of the same rights? Each of these questions requires some comment.

In answering the first question, we need not attempt a detailed consideration of the moral rights of organisms which are not developed enough, aware enough, intelligent enough, etc., to be considered people, but which resemble people in some respects. It does seem reasonable to suggest that the more like a person, in the relevant respects, a being is, the stronger is the case for regarding it as having a right to life, and indeed the stronger its right to life is. Thus we ought to take seriously the suggestion that, insofar as "the human individual develops biologically in a continuous fashion ... the rights of a human person might develop in the same way."[4] But we must keep in mind that the attributes which are relevant in determining whether or not an entity is enough like a person to be regarded as having some of the same moral rights are no different from those which are relevant to determining whether or not it is fully a person—that is, are no different from (1)–(5)—and that being genetically human, or having recognizably human facial and other physical features, or detectable brain activity, or the capacity to survive outside the uterus, are simply not among these relevant attributes.

Thus it is clear that even though a seven- or eight-month fetus has features which make it apt to arouse in us almost the same powerful protective instinct as is commonly aroused by a small infant, nevertheless it is not significantly more personlike than is a very small embryo. It is *somewhat* more personlike; it can apparently feel and respond to pain, and it may even have a rudimentary form of consciousness, insofar as its brain is quite active. Nevertheless, it seems safe to say that it is not fully conscious, in the way that an infant of a few months is, and that it cannot reason, or communicate messages of indefinitely many sorts, does not engage in self-motivated activity, and has no self-awareness. Thus, in the *relevant* respects, a fetus, even a fully developed one, is considerably less personlike than is the average mature mammal, indeed the average fish. And I think that a rational person must conclude that if the right to life of a fetus is to be based upon its resemblance to a person, then it cannot be said to have any more right to life than, let us say, a newborn guppy (which also seems to be capable of feeling pain), and that a right of that magnitude could never override a woman's right to obtain an abortion, at any stage of her pregnancy.

There may, of course, be other arguments in favor of placing legal limits upon the stage of pregnancy in which an abortion may be performed. Given the relative safety of the new techniques of artificially inducing labor during the third trimester, the danger to the woman's life or health is no longer such an argument. Neither is the fact that people tend to respond to the thought of abortion in the later stages of pregnancy with emotional repulsion, since mere emotional responses cannot take the place of moral reasoning in determining what ought to be permitted. Nor, finally, is the frequently heard argument that legalizing abortion, especially late in the pregnancy, may erode the level of respect for human life, leading, perhaps, to an increase in unjustified euthanasia and other crimes. For this threat, if it is a

---

[4] Thomas L. Hayes, "A Biological View," *Commonweal*, 85 (March 17, 1967), 677–78; quoted by Daniel Callahan, in *Abortion: Law, Choice and Morality* (London: Macmillan & Co., 1970).

threat, can be better met by educating people to the kinds of moral distinctions which we are making here than by limiting access to abortion (which limitation may, in its disregard for the rights of women, be just as damaging to the level of respect for human rights).

Thus, since the fact that even a fully developed fetus is not personlike enough to have any significant right to life on the basis of its personlikeness shows that no legal restrictions upon the stage of pregnancy in which an abortion may be performed can be justified on the grounds that we should protect the rights of the older fetus, and since there is no other apparent justification for such restrictions, we may conclude that they are entirely unjustified. Whether or not it would be *indecent* (whatever that means) for a woman in her seventh month to obtain an abortion just to avoid having to postpone a trip to Europe, it would not, in itself, be *immoral*, and therefore it ought to be permitted.

4. Potential Personhood and the Right to Life

We have seen that a fetus does not resemble a person in any way which can support the claim that it has even some of the same rights. But what about its *potential*, the fact that if nurtured and allowed to develop naturally it will very probably become a person? Doesn't that alone give it at least some right to life? It is hard to deny that the fact that an entity is a potential person is a strong prima facie reason for not destroying it; but we need not conclude from this that a potential person has a right to life, by virtue of that potential. It may be that our feeling that it is better, other things being equal, not to destroy a potential person is better explained by the fact that potential people are still (felt to be) an invaluable resource, not to be lightly squandered. Surely, if every speck of dust were a potential person, we would be much less apt to conclude that every potential person has a right to become actual.

Still, we do not need to insist that a potential person has no right to life whatever. There may well be something immoral, and not just imprudent, about wantonly destroying potential people, when doing so isn't necessary to protect anyone's rights. But even if a potential person does have some prima facie right to life, such a right could not possibly outweigh the right of a woman to obtain an abortion, since the rights of any actual person invariably outweigh those of any potential person, whenever the two conflict. Since this may not be immediately obvious in the case of a human fetus, let us look at another case.

Suppose that our space explorer falls into the hands of an alien culture, whose scientists decide to create a few hundred thousand or more human beings, by breaking his body into its component cells, and using these to create fully developed human beings, with, of course, his genetic code. We may imagine that each of these newly created men will have all of the original man's abilities, skills, knowledge, and so on, and also have an individual self-concept, in short that each of them will be a bona fide (though hardly unique) person. Imagine that the whole project will take only seconds, and that its chances of success are extremely high, and that our explorer knows all of this, and also knows that these people will be treated fairly. I maintain that in such a situation he would have every right to escape if he could, and thus to deprive all of these potential people of their potential lives; for his right to life outweighs all of theirs together, in spite of the fact that they are all genetically human, all innocent, and all have a very high probability of becoming people very soon, if only he refrains from acting.

Indeed, I think he would have a right to escape even if it were not his life which the alien scientists planned to take, but only a year of his freedom, or, indeed, only a day. Nor would he be obligated to stay if he had gotten captured (thus bringing all these people-potentials into existence) because of his own carelessness, or even if he had done so deliberately, knowing the consequences. Regardless of how he got captured, he is not morally obligated to remain in captivity for *any* period of time for the sake of permitting any number of potential people to come into actuality, so great is the margin by which one actual person's right to liberty outweighs whatever right to life even a hundred thousand potential people have. And it seems reasonable to conclude that the rights of a woman will outweigh by a similar margin whatever right to life a fetus may have by virtue of its potential personhood.

Thus, neither a fetus's resemblance to a person, nor its potential for becoming a person provides any basis whatever for the claim that it has any significant right to life. Consequently, a woman's right to protect her health, happiness, freedom, and even her life,[5] by terminating an unwanted pregnancy, will always override whatever right to life it may be appropriate to ascribe to a fetus, even a fully developed one. And thus, in the absence of any overwhelming social need for every possible child, the laws which restrict the right to obtain an abortion, or limit the period of pregnancy during which an abortion may be performed, are a wholly unjustified violation of a woman's most basic moral and constitutional rights.[6]

Postscript on Infanticide

Since the publication of this article, many people have written to point out that my argument appears to justify not only abortion, but infanticide as well. For a newborn infant is not significantly more personlike than an advanced fetus, and consequently it would seem that if the destruction of the latter is permissible so too must be that of the former. Inasmuch as most people, regardless of how they feel about the morality of abortion, consider infanticide a form of murder, this might appear to represent a serious flaw in my argument.

Now, if I am right in holding that it is only people who have a full-fledged right to life, and who can be murdered, and if the criteria of personhood are as I have described them, then it obviously follows that killing a newborn infant isn't murder. It does *not* follow, however, that infanticide is permissible, for two reasons. In the first place, it would be wrong, at least in this country and in this period of history, and other things being equal, to kill a newborn infant, because even if its parents do not want it and would not suffer from its destruction, there are other people who would like to have it, and would, in all probability, be deprived of a great deal of pleasure by its destruction. Thus, infanticide is wrong for reasons analogous to those which make it wrong to wantonly destroy natural resources, or great works of art.

---

[5] That is, insofar as the death rate, for the woman, is higher for childbirth than for early abortion.

[6] My thanks to the following people, who were kind enough to read and criticize an earlier version of this paper: Herbert Gold, Gene Glass, Anne Lauterbach, Judith Thomson, Mary Mothersill, and Timothy Binkley.

Secondly, most people, at least in this country, value infants and would much prefer that they be preserved, even if foster parents are not immediately available. Most of us would rather be taxed to support orphanages than allow unwanted infants to be destroyed. So long as there are people who want an infant preserved, and who are willing and able to provide the means of caring for it, under reasonably humane conditions, it is *ceteris paribus*, wrong to destroy it.

But, it might be replied, if this argument shows that infanticide is wrong, at least at this time and in this country, doesn't it also show that abortion is wrong? After all, many people value fetuses, are disturbed by their destruction, and would much prefer that they be preserved, even at some cost to themselves. Furthermore, as a potential source of pleasure to some foster family, a fetus is just as valuable as an infant. There is, however, a crucial difference between the two cases: so long as the fetus is unborn, its preservation, contrary to the wishes of the pregnant woman, violates her rights to freedom, happiness, and self-determination. Her rights override the rights of those who would like the fetus preserved, just as if someone's life or limb is threatened by a wild animal, his right to protect himself by destroying the animal overrides the rights of those who would prefer that the animal not be harmed.

The minute the infant is born, however, its preservation no longer violates any of its mother's rights, even if she wants it destroyed, because she is free to put it up for adoption. Consequently, while the moment of birth does not mark any sharp discontinuity in the degree to which an infant possesses the right to life, it does mark the end of its mother's right to determine its fate. Indeed, if abortion could be performed without killing the fetus, she would never possess the right to have the fetus destroyed, for the same reasons that she has no right to have an infant destroyed.

On the other hand, it follows from my argument that when an unwanted or defective infant is born into a society which cannot afford and/or is not willing to care for it, then its destruction is permissible. This conclusion will, no doubt, strike many people as heartless and immoral; but remember that the very existence of people who feel this way, and who are willing and able to provide care for unwanted infants, is reason enough to conclude that they should be preserved.

STUDY QUESTIONS

1. Discuss the distinction between being human and being a person. Do you agree that being a person is a necessary condition for having a right to life? Obviously Noonan disagrees. What could his arguments be?

2. Suppose you are a doctor in an intensive care unit for neonates. Legal considerations aside, do you apply Warren's position on defective infants in your practice? Why or why not?

A Defense of Abortion

Judith Jarvis Thomson

Judith Jarvis Thomson (b. 1929) is a professor emeritus of philosophy at the Massachusetts Institute of Technology. She has written numerous articles on ethics and metaphysics and is the author *of Acts and Other Events* (1977), *Rights, Restitution, and Risk* (1986), and *The Realm of Rights* (1990).

In her defense of abortion, Thomson accepts, for the sake of argument, that the fetus is an innocent human being with a right to live. Her strategy is to show that killing an innocent human being is not always wrong. She asks you to imagine yourself waking up one morning and finding that you have been kidnapped, taken to a hospital, and attached to the circulatory system of a famous violinist who will die if you unplug yourself. Apparently, a group of music lovers canvassed local medical records and determined that you alone have the right blood type. Thomson argues that you have the right to unhook yourself even if this will cause the violinist's death. According to Thomson, you might allow the violinist to use your kidneys out of kindness, but you are certainly not *obligated* to do so and may rightfully pull the plug on him. To the objection that in pregnancy the mother in some sense invites the fetus to use her body, Thomson replies that this is more like the negligence of opening a window that permits easy intrusion by an unwanted visitor. You still have the right to cast out the intruder. Thomson concedes that abortion is sometimes a selfish act, but denies that we must refrain from selfishness; an act may be "self-centered, callous, indecent, but not unjust." No law requires anyone to be even a "Minimally Decent Samaritan." Yet prohibiting abortion forces women to be Good Samaritans.

Thomson's argument does not give blanket permission for abortions. Some cases require minimal decency and entail no right to abort. She considers this consequence a merit of her argument. Finally, the right to abort is not the right to kill: If a fetus can be saved once it is taken from its mother's body then she has no right to demand its death.

Most opposition to abortion relies on the premise that the fetus is a human being, a person, from the moment of conception. The premise is argued for, but, as I think, not well. Take, for example, the most common argument. We are asked to notice that the development of a human being from conception through birth into

A DEFENSE OF ABORTION. From *Philosophy and Public Affairs*, vol. 1, no. 1, pp. 47–50; 54–66 (Fall 1971). Copyright © by Princeton University Press. Reprinted by permission of Blackwell Publishing.

I am very much indebted to James Thomson for discussion, criticism, and many helpful suggestions.

childhood is continuous; then it is said that to draw a line, to choose a point in this development and say "before this point the thing is not a person, after this point it is a person" is to make an arbitrary choice, a choice for which in the nature of things no good reason can be given. It is concluded that the fetus is, or anyway that we had better say it is, a person from the moment of conception. But this conclusion does not follow. Similar things might be said about the development of an acorn into an oak tree, and it does not follow that acorns are oak trees, or that we had better say they are. Arguments of this form are sometimes called "slippery slope arguments"—the phrase is perhaps self-explanatory—and it is dismaying that opponents of abortion rely on them so heavily and uncritically.

I am inclined to agree, however, that the prospects for "drawing a line" in the development of the fetus look dim. I am inclined to think also that we shall probably have to agree that the fetus has already become a human person well before birth. Indeed, it comes as a surprise when one first learns how early in its life it begins to acquire human characteristics. By the tenth week, for example, it already has a face, arms and legs, fingers and toes; it has internal organs, and brain activity is detectable.[1] On the other hand, I think that the premise is false, that the fetus is not a person from the moment of conception. A newly fertilized ovum, a newly implanted clump of cells, is no more a person than an acorn is an oak tree. But I shall not discuss any of this. For it seems to me to be of great interest to ask what happens if, for the sake of argument, we allow the premise. How, precisely, are we supposed to get from there to the conclusion that abortion is morally impermissible? Opponents of abortion commonly spend most of their time establishing that the fetus is a person, and hardly any time explaining the step from there to the impermissibility of abortion. Perhaps they think the step too simple and obvious to require much comment. Or perhaps instead they are simply being economical in argument. Many of those who defend abortion rely on the premise that the fetus is not a person, but only a bit of tissue that will become a person at birth; and why pay out more arguments than you have to? Whatever the explanation, I suggest that the step they take is neither easy nor obvious, that it calls for closer examination than it is commonly given, and that when we do give it this closer examination we shall feel inclined to reject it.

I propose, then, that we grant that the fetus is a person from the moment of conception. How does the argument go from here? Something like this, I take it. Every person has a right to life. So the fetus has a right to life. No doubt the mother has a right to decide what shall happen in and to her body; everyone would grant that. But surely a person's right to life is stronger and more stringent than the mother's right to decide what happens in and to her body, and so outweighs it. So the fetus may not be killed; an abortion may not be performed.

It sounds plausible. But now let me ask you to imagine this. You wake up in the morning and find yourself back to back in bed with an unconscious violinist.

---

[1] Daniel Callahan, *Abortion: Law, Choice and Morality* (New York, 1970), p. 373. This book gives a fascinating survey of the available information on abortion. The Jewish tradition is surveyed in David M. Feldman, *Birth Control in Jewish Law* (New York, 1968), Part 5, the Catholic tradition in John T. Noonan, Jr., "An Almost Absolute Value in History," in *The Morality of Abortion*, ed. John T. Noonan, Jr. (Cambridge, Mass., 1970).

A famous unconscious violinist. He has been found to have a fatal kidney ailment, and the Society of Music Lovers has canvassed all the available medical records and found that you alone have the right blood type to help. They have therefore kidnapped you, and last night the violinist's circulatory system was plugged into yours, so that your kidneys can be used to extract poisons from his blood as well as your own. The director of the hospital now tells you, "Look, we're sorry the Society of Music Lovers did this to you—we would never have permitted it if we had known. But still, they did it, and the violinist now is plugged into you. To unplug you would be to kill him. But never mind, it's only for nine months. By then he will have recovered from his ailment, and can safely be unplugged from you." Is it morally incumbent on you to accede to this situation? No doubt it would be very nice of you if you did, a great kindness. But do you *have* to accede to it? What if it were not nine months, but nine years? Or longer still? What if the director of the hospital says, "Tough luck, I agree, but you've now got to stay in bed, with the violinist plugged into you, for the rest of your life. Because remember this. All persons have a right to life, and violinists are persons. Granted you have a right to decide what happens in and to your body, but a person's right to life outweighs your right to decide what happens in and to your body. So you cannot ever be unplugged from him." I imagine you would regard this as outrageous, which suggests that something really is wrong with that plausible-sounding argument I mentioned a moment ago.

In this case, of course, you were kidnapped; you didn't volunteer for this operation that plugged the violinist into your kidneys. Can those who oppose abortion on the ground I mentioned make an exception for a pregnancy due to rape? Certainly. They can say that persons have a right to life only if they didn't come into existence because of rape; or they can say that all persons have a right to life, but that some have less of a right to life than others, in particular, that those who came into existence because of rape have less. But these statements have a rather unpleasant sound. Surely the question of whether you have a right to life at all, or how much of it you have, shouldn't turn on the question of whether or not you are the product of a rape. And in fact the people who oppose abortion on the ground I mentioned do not make this distinction, and hence do not make an exception in case of rape.

Nor do they make an exception for a case in which the mother has to spend the nine months of her pregnancy in bed. They would agree that would be a great pity, and hard on the mother; but all the same, all persons have a right to life, the fetus is a person, and so on. I suspect, in fact, that they would not make an exception for a case in which, miraculously enough, the pregnancy went on for nine years, or even the rest of the mother's life.

Some won't even make an exception for a case in which continuation of the pregnancy is likely to shorten the mother's life; they regard abortion as impermissible even to save the mother's life. Such cases are nowadays very rare, and many opponents of abortion do not accept this extreme view. All the same, it is a good place to begin: a number of points of interest come out in respect to it.

1. Let us call the view that abortion is impermissible even to save the mother's life "the extreme view." I want to suggest first that it does not issue from the argument I mentioned earlier without the addition of some fairly powerful premises.

Suppose a woman has become pregnant, and now learns that she has a cardiac condition such that she will die if she carries the baby to term. What may be done for her? The fetus, being a person, has a right to life, but as the mother is a person too, so she has a right to life. Presumably they have an equal right to life. How is it supposed to come out that an abortion may not be performed? If mother and child have an equal right to life, shouldn't we perhaps flip a coin? Or should we add to the mother's right to life her right to decide what happens in and to her body, which everybody seems to be ready to grant—the sum of her rights now outweighing the fetus' right to life?

The most familiar argument here is the following. We are told that performing the abortion would be directly killing[2] the child, whereas doing nothing would not be killing the mother, but only letting her die. Moreover, in killing the child, one would be killing an innocent person, for the child has committed no crime, and is not aiming at his mother's death. And then there are a variety of ways in which this might be continued. (1) But as directly killing an innocent person is always and absolutely impermissible, an abortion may not be performed. Or, (2) as directly killing an innocent person is murder, and murder is always and absolutely impermissible, an abortion may not be performed.[3] Or, (3) as one's duty to refrain from directly killing an innocent person is more stringent than one's duty to keep a person from dying, an abortion may not be performed. Or, (4) if one's only options are directly killing an innocent person or letting a person die, one must prefer letting the person die, and thus an abortion may not be performed.[4]

Some people seem to have thought that these are not further premises which must be added if the conclusion is to be reached, but that they follow from the very fact that an innocent person has a right to life.[5] But this seems to me to be a mistake, and perhaps the simplest way to show this is to bring out that while we must certainly grant that innocent persons have a right to life, the theses in (1) through (4) are all false. Take (2), for example. If directly killing an innocent person

---

[2] The term "direct" in the arguments I refer to is a technical one. Roughly, what is meant by "direct killing" is either killing as an end in itself, or killing as a means of some end, for example, the end of saving someone else's life. See footnote 5, for an example of its use.

[3] Cf. *Encyclical Letter of Pope Pius XI on Christian Marriage*, St. Paul Editions (Boston, n.d.), p. 32: "however much we may pity the mother whose health and even life is gravely imperiled in the performance of the duty allotted to her by nature, nevertheless what could ever be a sufficient reason for excusing in any way the direct murder of the innocent? This is precisely what we are dealing with here." Noonan *(The Morality of Abortion*, p. 43) reads this as follows: "What cause can ever avail to excuse in any way the direct killing of the innocent? For it is a question of that."

[4] The thesis in (4) is in an interesting way weaker than those in (1), (2), and (3): they rule out abortion even in cases in which both mother *and* child will die if the abortion is not performed. By contrast, one who held the view expressed in (4) could consistently say that one needn't prefer letting two persons die to killing one.

[5] Cf the following passage from Pius XII, *Address to the Italian Catholic Society of Midwives:* "The baby in the maternal breast has the right to life immediately from God.—Hence there is no man, no human authority, no science, no medical, eugenic, social, economic or moral 'indication' which can establish or grant a valid juridical ground for a direct deliberate disposition of an innocent human life, that is a disposition which looks to its destruction either as an end or as a means to another end perhaps in itself not illicit.—The baby, still not born, is a man in the same degree and for the same reason as the mother" (quoted in Noonan, *The Morality of Abortion*, p. 45).

is murder, and thus is impermissible, then the mother's directly killing the innocent person inside her is murder, and thus is impermissible. But it cannot seriously be thought to be murder if the mother performs an abortion on herself to save her life. It cannot seriously be said that she *must* refrain, that she *must* sit passively by and wait for her death. Let us look again at the case of you and the violinist. There you are, in bed with the violinist, and the director of the hospital says to you, "It's all most distressing, and I deeply sympathize, but you see this is putting an additional strain on your kidneys, and you'll be dead within the month. But you *have* to stay where you are all the same. Because unplugging you would be directly killing an innocent violinist, and that's murder, and that's impermissible." If anything in the world is true, it is that you do not commit murder, you do not do what is impermissible, if you reach around to your back and unplug yourself from that violinist to save your life.

The main focus of attention in writings on abortion has been on what a third party may or may not do in answer to a request from a woman for an abortion. This is in a way understandable. Things being as they are, there isn't much a woman can safely do to abort herself. So the question asked is what a third party may do, and what the mother may do, if it is mentioned at all, is deduced, almost as an afterthought, from what it is concluded that third parties may do. But it seems to me that to treat the matter in this way is to refuse to grant to the mother that very status of person which is so firmly insisted on for the fetus. For we cannot simply read off what a person may do from what a third party may do. Suppose you find yourself trapped in a tiny house with a growing child. I mean a very tiny house, and a rapidly growing child—you are already up against the wall of the house and in a few minutes you'll be crushed to death. The child on the other hand won't be crushed to death; if nothing is done to stop him from growing he'll be hurt, but in the end he'll simply burst open the house and walk out a free man. Now I could well understand it if a bystander were to say, "There's nothing we can do for you. We cannot choose between your life and his, we cannot be the ones to decide who is to live, we cannot intervene." But it cannot be concluded that you too can do nothing, that you cannot attack it to save your life. However innocent the child may be, you do not have to wait passively while it crushes you to death. Perhaps a pregnant woman is vaguely felt to have the status of house, to which we don't allow the right of self-defense. But if the woman houses the child, it should be remembered that she is a person who houses it.

I should perhaps stop to say explicitly that I am not claiming that people have a right to do anything whatever to save their lives. I think, rather, that there are drastic limits to the right of self-defense. If someone threatens you with death unless you torture someone else to death, I think you have not the right, even to save your life, to do so. But the case under consideration here is very different. In our case there are only two people involved, one whose life is threatened, and one who threatens it. Both are innocent: the one who is threatened is not threatened because of any fault, the one who threatens does not threaten because of any fault. For this reason we may feel that we bystanders cannot intervene. But the person threatened can.

In sum, a woman surely can defend her life against the threat to it posed by the unborn child, even if doing so involves its death. And this shows not merely that the theses in (1) through (4) are false; it shows also that the extreme view of abortion is false, and so we need not canvass any other possible ways of arriving at it from the argument I mentioned at the outset.

2. The extreme view could of course be weakened to say that while abortion is permissible to save the mother's life, it may not be performed by a third party, but only by the mother herself. But this cannot be right either. For what we have to keep in mind is that the mother and the unborn child are not like two tenants in a small house which has, by an unfortunate mistake, been rented to both: the mother *owns* the house. The fact that she does add to the offensiveness of deducing that the mother can do nothing from the supposition that third parties can do nothing. But it does more than this: it casts a bright light on the supposition that third parties can do nothing. Certainly it lets us see that a third party who says "I cannot choose between you" is fooling himself if he thinks this is impartiality. If Jones has found and fastened on a certain coat, which he needs to keep him from freezing, but which Smith also needs to keep him from freezing, then it is not impartiality that says "I cannot choose between you" when Smith owns the coat. Women have said again and again "This body is *my* body!" and they have reason to feel angry, reason to feel that it has been like shouting into the wind. Smith, after all, is hardly likely to bless us if we say to him, "Of course it's your coat, anybody would grant that it is. But no one may choose between you and Jones who is to have it."

We should really ask what it is that says "no one may choose" in the face of the fact that the body that houses the child is the mother's body. It may be simply a failure to appreciate this fact. But it may be something more interesting, namely the sense that one has a right to refuse to lay hands on people, even where it would be just and fair to do so, even where justice seems to require that somebody do so. Thus justice might call for somebody to get Smith's coat back from Jones, and yet you have a right to refuse to be the one to lay hands on Jones, a right to refuse to do physical violence to him. This, I think, must be granted. But then what should be said is not "no one may choose," but only " *I* cannot choose," and indeed not even this, but "*I* will not *act*," leaving it open that somebody else can or should, and in particular that anyone in a position of authority, with the job of securing people's rights, both can and should. So this is no difficulty. I have not been arguing that any given third party must accede to the mother's request that he perform an abortion to save her life, but only that he may.

I suppose that in some views of human life the mother's body is only on loan to her, the loan not being one which gives her any prior claim to it. One who held this view might well think it impartiality to say "I cannot choose." But I shall simply ignore this possibility. My own view is that if a human being has any just, prior claim to anything at all, he has a just, prior claim to his own body. And perhaps this needn't be argued for here anyway, since, as I mentioned, the arguments against abortion we are looking at do grant that the woman has a right to decide what happens in and to her body.

But although they do grant it, I have tried to show that they do not take seriously what is done in granting it. I suggest the same thing will reappear even more clearly when we turn away from cases in which the mother's life is at stake, and attend, as I propose we now do, to the vastly more common cases in which a woman wants an abortion for some less weighty reason than preserving her own life.

3. Where the mother's life is not at stake, the argument I mentioned at the out-set seems to have a much stronger pull. "Everyone has a right to life, so the unborn person has a right to life." And isn't the child's right to life weightier than anything other than the mother's own right to life, which she might put forward as ground for an abortion?

This argument treats the right to life as if it were unproblematic. It is not, and this seems to me to be precisely the source of the mistake.

For we should now, at long last, ask what it comes to, to have a right to life. In some views having a right to life includes having a right to be given at least the bare minimum one needs for continued life. But suppose that what in fact *is* the bare minimum a man needs for continued life is something he has no right at all to be given? If I am sick unto death, and the only thing that will save my life is the touch of Henry Fonda's cool hand on my fevered brow, then all the same, I have no right to be given the touch of Henry Fonda's cool hand on my fevered brow. It would be frightfully nice of him to fly in from the West Coast to provide it. It would be less nice, though no doubt well meant, if my friends flew out to the West Coast and carried Henry Fonda back with them. But I have no right at all against anybody that he should do this for me. Or again, to return to the story I told earlier, the fact that for continued life that violinist needs the continued use of your kidneys does not establish that he has a right to be given the continued use of your kidneys. He certainly has no right against you that *you* should give him continued use of your kidneys. For nobody has any right to use your kidneys unless you give him such a right; and nobody has the right against you that you shall give him this right—if you do allow him to go on using your kidneys, this is a kindness on your part, and not something he can claim from you as his due. Nor has he any right against anybody else that *they* should give him continued use of your kidneys. Certainly he had no right against the Society of Music Lovers that they should plug him into you in the first place. And if you now start to unplug your-self, having learned that you will otherwise have to spend nine years in bed with him, there is nobody in the world who must try to prevent you, in order to see to it that he is given something he has a right to be given.

Some people are rather stricter about the right to life. In their view, it does not include the right to be given anything, but amounts to, and only to, the right not to be killed by anybody. But here a related difficulty arises. If everybody must refrain from killing that violinist, then everybody must refrain from doing a great many different sorts of things. Everybody must refrain from slitting his throat, everybody must refrain from shooting him—and everybody must refrain from unplugging you from him. But does he have a right against everybody that they shall refrain from unplugging you from him? To refrain from doing this is to allow him to continue to use your kidneys. It could be argued that he has a right against us that *we* should allow him to continue to use your kidneys. That is, while he had no right against us that we should give him the use of your kidneys, it might be argued that he anyway has a right against us that we shall not now intervene and deprive him of the use of your kidneys. I shall come back to third-party interventions later. But certainly the violinist has no right against you that *you* shall allow him to continue to use your kidneys. As I said, if you do allow him to use them, it is a kindness on your part, and not something you owe him.

The difficulty I point to here is not peculiar to the right to life. It reappears in connection with all the other natural rights; and it is something which an adequate account of rights must deal with. For present purposes it is enough just to draw attention to it. But I would stress that I am not arguing that people do not have a right to life—quite to the contrary, it seems to me that the primary control we must place on the acceptability of an account of rights is that it should turn out in that account to be a truth that all persons have a right to life. I am arguing only that having a right to life does not guarantee having either a right to be given the use of or a right to be allowed continued use of another person's body—even if one needs it for life itself. So the right to life will not serve the opponents of abortion in the very simple and clear way in which they seem to have thought it would.

4. There is another way to bring out the difficulty. In the most ordinary sort of case, to deprive someone of what he has a right to is to treat him unjustly. Suppose a boy and his small brother are jointly given a box of chocolates for Christmas. If the older boy takes the box and refuses to give his brother any of the chocolates, he is unjust to him, for the brother has been given a right to half of them. But suppose that, having learned that otherwise it means nine years in bed with that violinist, you unplug yourself from him. You surely are not being unjust to him, for you gave him no right to use your kidneys, and no one else can have given him any such right. But we have to notice that, in unplugging yourself, you are killing him; and violinists, like everybody else, have a right to life, and thus in the view we were considering just now, the right not to be killed. So here you do what he supposedly has a right you shall not do, but you do not act unjustly to him in doing it.

The emendation which may be made at this point is this: the right to life consists not in the right not to be killed, but rather in the right not to be killed unjustly. This runs a risk of circularity, but never mind: it would enable us to square the fact that the violinist has a right to life with the fact that you do not act unjustly toward him in unplugging yourself, thereby killing him. For if you do not kill him unjustly, you do not violate his right to life, and so it is no wonder you do him no injustice.

But if this emendation is accepted, the gap in the argument against abortion stares us plainly in the face: it is by no means enough to show that the fetus is a person, and to remind us that all persons have a right to life—we need to be shown also that killing the fetus violates its right to life, i.e., that abortion is unjust killing. And is it?

I suppose we may take it as a datum that in a case of pregnancy due to rape the mother has not given the unborn person a right to the use of her body for food and shelter. Indeed, in what pregnancy could it be supposed that the mother has given the unborn person such a right? It is not as if there were unborn persons drifting about the world, to whom a woman who wants a child says "I invite you in."

But it might be argued that there are other ways one can have acquired a right to the use of another person's body than by having been invited to use it by that person. Suppose a woman voluntarily indulges in intercourse, knowing of the chance it will issue in pregnancy, and then she does become pregnant; is she not in part responsible for the presence, in fact the very existence, of the unborn person inside her? No doubt she did not invite it in. But doesn't her partial responsibility for its being there itself give it a right to the use of her body?[6] If so, then her aborting it would be more like the boy's taking away the chocolates, and less like your unplugging yourself from the violinist—doing so would be depriving it of what it does have a right to, and thus would be doing it an injustice.

And then, too, it might be asked whether or not she can kill it even to save her own life: If she voluntarily called it into existence, how can she now kill it, even in self-defense?

The first thing to be said about this is that it is something new. Opponents of abortion have been so concerned to make out the independence of the fetus, in order to establish that it has a right to life, just as its mother does, that they have tended to overlook the possible support they might gain from making out that the fetus is *dependent* on the mother, in order to establish that she has a special kind of responsibility for it, a responsibility that gives it rights against her which are not possessed by any independent person—such as an ailing violinist who is a stranger to her.

On the other hand, this argument would give the unborn person a right to its mother's body only if her pregnancy resulted from a voluntary act, undertaken in full knowledge of the chance a pregnancy might result from it. It would leave out entirely the unborn person whose existence is due to rape. Pending the availability of some further argument, then, we would be left with the conclusion that unborn persons whose existence is due to rape have no right to the use of their mothers' bodies, and thus that aborting them is not depriving them of anything they have a right to and hence is not unjust killing.

And we should also notice that it is not at all plain that this argument really does go even as far as it purports to. For there are cases and cases, and the details make a difference. If the room is stuffy, and I therefore open a window to air it, and a burglar climbs in, it would be absurd to say, "Ah, now he can stay, she's given him a right to the use of her house—for she is partially responsible for his presence there, having voluntarily done what enabled him to get in, in full knowledge that there are such things as burglars, and that burglars burgle." It would be still more absurd to say this if I had had bars installed outside my windows, precisely to prevent burglars from getting in, and a burglar got in only because of a defect in the bars. It remains equally absurd if we imagine it is not a burglar who climbs in, but an innocent person who blunders or falls in. Again, suppose it were like this: people-seeds drift about in the air like pollen, and if you open your windows, one may drift in and take root in your carpets or upholstery. You don't want children, so you fix up your windows with fine mesh screens, the very best you can buy. As can happen, however, and on very, very rare occasions does happen, one of the screens is defective; and a seed drifts in and takes root. Does the person-plant who now develops have a right to the use of your house? Surely not—despite the fact that you voluntarily opened your windows, you knowingly kept carpets and

---

[6] The need for discussion of this argument was brought home to me by members of the Society for Ethical and Legal Philosophy, to whom this paper was originally presented.

upholstered furniture, and you knew that screens were sometimes defective. Someone may argue that you are responsible for its rooting, that it does have a right to your house, because after all you *could* have lived out your life with bare floors and furniture, or with sealed windows and doors. But this won't do—for by the same token anyone can avoid a pregnancy due to rape by having a hysterectomy, or anyway by never leaving home without a (reliable!) army.

It seems to me that the argument we are looking at can establish at most that there are *some* cases in which the unborn person has a right to the use of its mother's body, and therefore *some* cases in which abortion is unjust killing. There is room for much discussion and argument as to precisely which, if any. But I think we should sidestep this issue and leave it open, for at any rate the argument certainly does not establish that all abortion is unjust killing.

5. There is room for yet another argument here, however. We surely must all grant that there may be cases in which it would be morally indecent to detach a person from your body at the cost of his life. Suppose you learn that what the violinist needs is not nine years of your life, but only one hour: all you need to do to save his life is to spend one hour in that bed with him. Suppose also that letting him use your kidneys for that one hour would not affect your health in the slightest. Admittedly you were kidnapped. Admittedly you did not give anyone permission to plug him into you. Nevertheless it seems to me plain you *ought* to allow him to use your kidneys for that hour—it would be indecent to refuse.

Again, suppose pregnancy lasted only one hour, and constituted no threat to life or health. And suppose that a woman becomes pregnant as a result of rape. Admittedly she did not voluntarily do anything to bring about the existence of a child. Admittedly she did nothing at all which would give the unborn person a right to the use of her body. All the same it might well be said, as in the newly emended violinist story, that she *ought* to allow it to remain for that hour—that it would be indecent in her to refuse.

Now some people are inclined to use the term "right" in such a way that it follows from the fact that you ought to allow a person to use your body for the hour he needs, that he has a right to use your body for the hour he needs, even though he has not been given that right by any person or act. They may say that it follows also that if you refuse, you act unjustly toward him. This use of the term is perhaps so common that it cannot be called wrong; nevertheless it seems to me to be an unfortunate loosening of what we would do better to keep a tight rein on. Suppose that box of chocolates I mentioned earlier had not been given to both boys jointly, but was given only to the older boy. There he sits, stolidly eating his way through the box, his small brother watching enviously. Here we are likely to say "You ought not to be so mean. You ought to give your brother some of those chocolates." My own view is that it just does not follow from the truth of this that the brother has any right to any of the chocolates. If the boy refuses to give his brother any, he is greedy, stingy, callous—but not unjust. I suppose that the people I have in mind will say it does follow that the brother has a right to some of the chocolates, and thus that the boy does act unjustly if he refuses to give his brother any. But the effect of saying this is to obscure what we should keep distinct, namely the difference between the boy's refusal in this case and the boy's refusal in the earlier case, in which the box was given to both boys jointly, and in which the small brother thus had what was from any point of view clear title to half.

A further objection to so using the term "right" that from the fact that A ought to do a thing for B, it follows that B has a right against A that A do it for him, is that it is going to make the question of whether or not a man has a right to a thing turn on how easy it is to provide him with it; and this seems not merely unfortunate, but morally unacceptable. Take the case of Henry Fonda again. I said earlier that I had no right to the touch of his cool hand on my fevered brow, even though I needed it to save my life. I said it would be frightfully nice of him to fly in from the West Coast to provide me with it, but that I had no right against him that he should do so. But suppose he isn't on the West Coast. Suppose he has only to walk across the room, place a hand briefly on my brow—and lo, my life is saved. Then surely he ought to do it, it would be indecent to refuse. Is it to be said "Ah, well, it follows that in this case she has a right to the touch of his hand on her brow, and so it would be an injustice in him to refuse"? So that I have a right to it when it is easy for him to provide it, though no right when it's hard? It's rather a shocking idea that anyone's rights should fade away and disappear as it gets harder and harder to accord them to him.

So my own view is that even though you ought to let the violinist use your kidneys for the one hour he needs, we should not conclude that he has a right to do so—we should say that if you refuse, you are, like the boy who owns all the chocolates and will give none away, self-centered and callous, indecent in fact, but not unjust. And similarly, that even supposing a case in which a woman pregnant due to rape ought to allow the unborn person to use her body for the hour he needs, we should conclude that she is self-centered, callous, indecent, but not unjust, if she refuses. The complaints are no less grave; they are just different. However, there is no need to insist on this point. If anyone does wish to deduce "he has a right" from "you ought," then all the same he must surely grant that there are cases in which it is not morally required of you that you allow that violinist to use your kidneys, and in which he does not have a right to use them, and in which you do not do him an injustice if you refuse. And so also for mother and unborn child. Except in such cases as the unborn person has a right to demand it—and we were leaving open the possibility that there may be such cases—nobody is morally *required* to make large sacrifices, of health, of all other interests and concerns, of all other duties and commitments, for nine years, or even for nine months, in order to keep another person alive.

6. We have in fact to distinguish between two kinds of Samaritan: the Good Samaritan and what we might call the Minimally Decent Samaritan. The story of the Good Samaritan, you will remember, goes like this:

> A certain man went down from Jerusalem to Jericho, and fell among thieves, which stripped him of his raiment, and wounded him, and departed, leaving him half dead.
>
> And by chance there came down a certain priest that way; and when he saw him, he passed by on the other side.
>
> And likewise a Levite, when he was at the place, came and looked on him, and passed by on the other side.
>
> But a certain Samaritan, as he journeyed, came where he was; and when he saw him he had compassion on him.

And went to him, and bound up his wounds, pouring in oil and wine, and set him on his own beast, and brought him to an inn, and took care of him.

And on the morrow, when he departed, he took out two pence, and gave them to the host, and said unto him, "Take care of him; and whatsoever thou spendest more, when I come again, I will repay thee."

(Luke 10:30–35)

The Good Samaritan went out of his way, at some cost to himself, to help one in need of it. We are not told what the options were, that is, whether or not the priest and the Levite could have helped by doing less than the Good Samaritan did, but assuming they could have, then the fact they did nothing at all shows they were not even Minimally Decent Samaritans, not because they were not Samaritans, but because they were not even minimally decent.

These things are a matter of degree, of course, but there is a difference, and it comes out perhaps most clearly in the story of Kitty Genovese, who, as you will remember, was murdered while thirty-eight people watched or listened, and did nothing at all to help her. A Good Samaritan would have rushed out to give direct assistance against the murderer. Or perhaps we had better allow that it would have been a Splendid Samaritan who did this, on the ground that it would have involved a risk of death for himself. But the thirty-eight not only did not do this, they did not even trouble to pick up a phone to call the police. Minimally Decent Samaritanism would call for doing at least that, and their not having done it was monstrous.

After telling the story of the Good Samaritan, Jesus said "Go, and do thou likewise." Perhaps he meant that we are morally required to act as the Good Samaritan did. Perhaps he was urging people to do more than is morally required of them. At all events it seems plain that it was not morally required of any of the thirty-eight that he rush out to give direct assistance at the risk of his own life, and that it is not morally required of anyone that he give long stretches of his life—nine years or nine months—to sustaining the life of a person who has no special right (we were leaving open the possibility of this) to demand it.

Indeed, with one rather striking class of exceptions, no one in any country in the world is *legally* required to do anywhere near as much as this for anyone else. The class of exceptions is obvious. My main concern here is not the state of the law in respect to abortion, but it is worth drawing attention to the fact that in no state in this country is any man compelled by law to be even a Minimally Decent Samaritan to any person; there is no law under which charges could be brought against the thirty-eight who stood by while Kitty Genovese died. By contrast, in most states in this country women are compelled by law to be not merely Minimally Decent Samaritans, but Good Samaritans to unborn persons inside them. This doesn't by itself settle anything one way or the other, because it may well be argued that there should be laws in this country—as there are in many European countries—compelling at least Minimally Decent Samaritanism.[7] But it does show that there is a gross injustice in the existing state of the law. And it

---

[7] For a discussion of the difficulties involved, and a survey of the European experience with such laws, see *The Good Samaritan and the Law*, ed. James M. Ratcliffe (New York, 1966).

shows also that the groups currently working against liberalization of abortion laws, in fact working toward having it declared unconstitutional for a state to permit abortion, had better start working for the adoption of Good Samaritan laws generally, or earn the charge that they are acting in bad faith.

I should think, myself, that Minimally Decent Samaritan laws would be one thing, Good Samaritan laws quite another, and in fact highly improper. But we are not here concerned with the law. What we should ask is not whether anybody should be compelled by law to be a Good Samaritan, but whether we must accede to a situation in which somebody is being compelled—by nature, perhaps—to be a Good Samaritan. We have, in other words, to look now at third-party interventions. I have been arguing that no person is morally required to make large sacrifices to sustain the life of another who has no right to demand them, and this even where the sacrifices do not include life itself; we are not morally required to be Good Samaritans or anyway Very Good Samaritans to one another. But what if a man cannot extricate himself from such a situation? What if he appeals to us to extricate him? It seems to me plain that there are cases in which we can, cases in which a Good Samaritan would extricate him. There you are, you were kidnapped, and nine years in bed with that violinist lie ahead of you. You have your own life to lead. You are sorry, but you simply cannot see giving up so much of your life to the sustaining of his. You cannot extricate yourself, and ask us to do so. I should have thought of that—in light of his having no right to the use of your body—it was obvious that we do not have to accede to your being forced to give up so much. We can do what you ask. There is no injustice to the violinist in our doing so.

7. Following the lead of the opponents of abortion, I have throughout been speaking of the fetus merely as a person, and what I have been asking is whether or not the argument we began with, which proceeds only from the fetus' being a person, really does establish its conclusion. I have argued that it does not.

But of course there are arguments and arguments, and it may be said that I have simply fastened on the wrong one. It may be said that what is important is not merely the fact that the fetus is a person, but that it is a person for whom the woman has a special kind of responsibility issuing from the fact that she is its mother. And it might be argued that all my analogies are therefore irrelevant—for you do not have that special kind of responsibility for that violinist, Henry Fonda does not have that special kind of responsibility for me. And our attention might be drawn to the fact that men and women both *are* compelled by law to provide support for their children.

I have in effect dealt (briefly) with this argument in section 4 above; but a (still briefer) recapitulation now may be in order. Surely we do not have any such "special responsibility" for a person unless we have assumed it, explicitly or implicitly. If a set of parents do not try to prevent pregnancy, do not obtain an abortion, and then at the time of birth of the child do not put it out for adoption, but rather take it home with them, then they have assumed responsibility for it, they have given it rights, and they cannot *now* withdraw support from it at the cost of its life because they now find it difficult to go on providing for it. But if they have taken all reasonable precautions against having a child, they do not simply by virtue of their biological relationship to the child who comes into existence have a special responsibility for it. They may wish to assume responsibility for it, or they may not wish to. And I am suggesting that if assuming responsibility for it would require large sacrifices, then they may refuse. A Good Samaritan would not refuse—or anyway, a Splendid Samaritan, if the sacrifices that had to be made were enormous. But then so would a Good Samaritan assume responsibility for that violinist; so would Henry Fonda, if he is a Good Samaritan, fly in from the West Coast and assume responsibility for me.

8. My argument will be found unsatisfactory on two counts by many of those who want to regard abortion as morally permissible. First, while I do argue that abortion is not permissible, I do not argue that it is always permissible. There may well be cases in which carrying the child to term requires only Minimally Decent Samaritanisms of the mother, and this is a standard we must not fall below. I am inclined to think it a merit of my account precisely that it does *not* give a general yes or a general no. It allows for and supports our sense that, for example, a sick and desperately frightened fourteen-year-old schoolgirl, pregnant due to rape, may *of course* choose abortion, and that any law which rules this out is an insane law. And it also allows for and supports our sense that in other cases resort to abortion is even positively indecent. It would be indecent in the woman to request an abortion, and indecent in a doctor to perform it, if she is in her seventh month, and wants the abortion just to avoid the nuisance of postponing a trip abroad. The very fact that the arguments I have been drawing attention to treat all cases of abortion, or even all cases of abortion in which the mother's life is not at stake as morally on a par ought to have made them suspect at the outset.

Secondly, while I am arguing for the permissibility of abortion in some cases, I am not arguing for the right to secure the death of the unborn child. It is easy to confuse these two things in that up to a certain point in the life of the fetus it is not able to survive outside the mother's body; hence removing it from her body guarantees its death. But they are importantly different. I have argued that you are not morally required to spend nine months in bed, sustaining the life of that violinist; but to say this is by no means to say that if, when you unplug yourself, there is a miracle and he survives, you then have a right to turn round and slit his throat. You may detach yourself even if this costs him his life; you have no right to be guaranteed his death, by some other means, if unplugging yourself does not kill him. There are some people who will feel dissatisfied by this feature of my argument. A woman may be utterly devastated by the thought of a child, a bit of herself, put out for adoption and never seen or heard of again. She may therefore want not merely that the child be detached from her, but more, that it die. Some opponents of abortion are inclined to regard this as beneath contempt—thereby showing insensitivity to what is surely a powerful source of despair. All the same, I agree that the desire for the child's death is not one which anybody may gratify, should it turn out to be possible to detach the child alive.

At this place, however, it should be remembered that we have only been pretending throughout that the fetus is a human being from the moment of conception. A very early abortion is surely not the killing of a person, and so is not dealt with by anything I have said here.

STUDY QUESTIONS

1. What moral responsibility, if any, does a pregnant woman have for the fetus? What is the basis for such a responsibility? Does it make a difference whether the pregnancy is wanted? Imposed?
2. Thomson distinguishes among Good Samaritans, Splendid Samaritans, and Minimally Decent Samaritans. Which are we obligated to be? How does the distinction between being a Good Samaritan and a Minimally Decent Samaritan apply to the woman with an unwanted pregnancy?

Why Abortion Is Immoral

Don Marquis

> Don Marquis is a professor of philosophy at the University of Kansas. He has written several articles, including "Leaving Therapy to Chance: An Impasse in the Ethics of Randomized Clinical Trials" (*The Hastings Center Report*, 1983); "Why Abortion Is Immoral" (*The Journal of Philosophy*, 1989); and "An Ethical Problem Concerning Recent Therapeutic Research on Breast Cancer" (*Hypatia: A Journal of Feminist Philosophy*, 1989).
>
> Don Marquis argues that we cannot address the issue of a fetal right to life without a clear understanding of why it is wrong to kill adult human beings. He rejects many secondary reasons against killing (e.g., loved ones would suffer from our loss) and fixes on the reason he considers *primary:* If someone killed you, he would be depriving you of all the activities, projects, experiences, and enjoyments that could constitute your future and to which you have an "inalienable" right. According to this argument, abortion is equally wrong on these grounds: it, too, deprives the fetus of its potential future. Preventing pregnancy by contraception, however, does not fall under this prohibition. In acts of contraception, one is not depriving any particular being of its potential future because no such being actually exists. Nor, says Marquis, does his argument taken by itself prohibit euthanasia or mercy killing where a future is not desired or is worse than valueless.

The view that abortion is, with rare exceptions, seriously immoral has received little support in the recent philosophical literature. No doubt most philosophers affiliated with secular institutions of higher education believe that the antiabortion position is

---

Don Marquis, "Why Abortion Is Immoral," *Journal of Philosophy*, vol. 86, April 1989, pp. 183–202. Some notes have been omitted. Reprinted by permission of author and the *Journal of Philosophy*.

either a symptom of irrational religious dogma or a conclusion generated by seriously confused philosophical argument. The purpose of this essay is to undermine this general belief. This essay sets out an argument that purports to show, as well as any argument in ethics can show, that abortion is, except possibly in rare cases, seriously immoral, that it is in the same moral category as killing an innocent adult human being.

The argument is based on a major assumption. Many of the most insightful and careful writers on the ethics of abortion—such as Joel Feinberg, Michael Tooley, Mary Anne Warren, H. Tristram Engelhardt, Jr., L. W. Sumner, John T. Noonan, Jr., and Philip Devine[1]—believe that whether or not abortion is morally permissible stands or falls on whether or not a fetus is the sort of being whose life it is seriously wrong to end. The argument of this essay will assume, but not argue, that they are correct.

Also, this essay will neglect issues of great importance to a complete ethics of abortion. Some antiabortionists will allow that certain abortions, such as abortion before implantation or abortion when the life of a woman is threatened by a pregnancy or abortion after rape, may be morally permissible. This essay will not explore the casuistry of these hard cases. The purpose of this essay is to develop a general argument for the claim that the overwhelming majority of deliberate abortions are seriously immoral....

A necessary condition of resolving the abortion controversy is a more theoretical account of the wrongness of killing. After all, if we merely believe, but do not understand, why killing adult human beings such as ourselves is wrong, how could we conceivably show that abortion is either immoral or permissible?

In order to develop such an account, we can start from the following un-problematic assumption concerning our own case: it is wrong to kill *us*. Why is it wrong? Some answers can be easily eliminated. It might be said that what makes killing us wrong is that a killing brutalizes the one who kills. But the brutalization consists of being inured to the performance of an act that is hideously immoral; hence, the brutalization does not explain the immorality. It might be said that what makes killing us wrong is the great loss others would experience due to our absence. Although such hubris is understandable, such an explanation does not account for the wrongness of killing hermits, or those whose lives are relatively independent and whose friends find it easy to make new friends.

A more obvious answer is better. What primarily makes killing wrong is neither its effect on the murderer nor its effect on the victim's friends and relatives, but its effect on the victim. The loss of one's life is one of the greatest losses one can suffer. The loss of one's life deprives one of all the experiences, activities, projects, and

---

[1] Feinberg, "Abortion," in *Matters of Life and Death: New Introductory Essays in Moral Philosophy,* Tom Regan, ed. (New York: Random House, 1986), pp. 256–293; Tooley, "Abortion and Infanticide," *Philosophy and Public Affairs,* II, 1 (1972): 37–65, Tooley, *Abortion and Infanticide* (New York: Oxford, 1984); Warren, "On the Moral and Legal Status of Abortion," *The Monist,* I.VII, 1 (1973): 43–61; Engelhardt, "The Ontology of Abortion," *Ethics,* I.XXXIV, 3 (1974): 217–234; Sumner, *Abortion and Moral Theory* (Princeton: University Press, 1981); Noonan, "An Almost Absolute Value in History," in *The Morality of Abortion: Legal and Historical Perspectives,* Noonan, ed. (Cambridge: Harvard, 1970); and Devine, *The Ethics of Homicide* (Ithaca: Cornell, 1978).

enjoyments that would otherwise have constituted one's future. Therefore, killing someone is wrong, primarily because the killing inflicts (one of) the greatest possible losses on the victim. To describe this as the loss of life can be misleading, however. The change in my biological state does not by itself make killing me wrong. The effect of the loss of my biological life is the loss to me of all those activities, projects, experiences, and enjoyments which would otherwise have constituted my future personal life. These activities, projects, experiences, and enjoyments are either valuable for their own sakes or are means to something else that is valuable for its own sake. Some parts of my future are not valued by me now, but will come to be valued by me as I grow older and as my values and capacities change. When I am killed, I am deprived both of what I now value which would have been part of my future personal life, but also what I would come to value. Therefore, when I die, I am deprived of all of the value of my future. Inflicting this loss on me is ultimately what makes killing me wrong. This being the case, it would seem that what makes killing *any* adult human being prima facie seriously wrong is the loss of his or her future....

The view that what makes killing wrong is the loss to the victim of the value of the victim's future gains additional support when some of its implications are examined. In the first place, it is incompatible with the view that it is wrong to kill only beings who are biologically human. It is possible that there exists a different species from another planet whose members have a future like ours. Since having a future like that is what makes killing someone wrong, this theory entails that it would be wrong to kill members of such a species. Hence, this theory is opposed to the claim that only life that is biologically human has great moral worth, a claim which many antiabortionists have seemed to adopt. This opposition, which this theory has in common with personhood theories, seems to be a merit of the theory.

In the second place, the claim that the loss of one's future is the wrong-making feature of one's being killed entails the possibility that the futures of some actual nonhuman mammals on our own planet are sufficiently like ours that it is seriously wrong to kill them also. Whether some animals do have the same right to life as human beings depends on adding to the account of the wrongness of killing some additional account of just what it is about my future or the futures of other adult human beings which makes it wrong to kill us. No such additional account will be offered in this essay. Undoubtedly, the provision of such an account would be a very difficult matter. Undoubtedly, any such account would be quite controversial. Hence, it surely should not reflect badly on this sketch of an elementary theory of the wrongness of killing that it is indeterminate with respect to some very difficult issues regarding animal rights.

In the third place, the claim that the loss of one's future is the wrong-making feature of one's being killed does not entail, as sanctity of human life theories do, that active euthanasia is wrong. Persons who are severely and incurably ill, who face a future of pain and despair, and who wish to die will not have suffered a loss if they are killed. It is, strictly speaking, the value of a human's future which makes killing wrong in this theory. This being so, killing does not necessarily wrong some persons who are sick and dying. Of course, there may be other reasons for a prohibition of active euthanasia, but that is another matter. Sanctity-of-human-life theories seem to hold that active euthanasia is seriously wrong even in an individual case where there seems to be good reason for it independently of public policy considerations. This consequence is most implausible, and it is a plus for the claim that the loss of a future of value is what makes killing wrong that it does not share this consequence.

In the fourth place, the account of the wrongness of killing defended in this essay does straightforwardly entail that it is prima facie seriously wrong to kill children and infants, for we do presume that they have futures of value. Since we do believe that it is wrong to kill defenseless little babies, it is important that a theory of the wrongness of killing easily account for this. Personhood theories of the wrongness of killing, on the other hand, cannot straightforwardly account for the wrongness of killing infants and young children.[2] Hence, such theories must add special ad hoc accounts of the wrongness of killing the young. The plausibility of such ad hoc theories seems to be a function of how desperately one wants such theories to work. The claim that the primary wrong-making feature of a killing is the loss to the victim of the value of its future accounts for the wrongness of killing young children and infants directly; it makes the wrongness of such acts as obvious as we actually think it is....

The claim that the primary wrong-making feature of a killing is the loss to the victim of the value of its future has obvious consequences for the ethics of abortion. The future of a standard fetus includes a set of experiences, projects, activities, and such which are identical with the futures of adult human beings and are identical with the futures of young children. Since the reason that is sufficient to explain why it is wrong to kill human beings after the time of birth is a reason that also applies to fetuses, it follows that abortion is prima facie seriously morally wrong.

This argument does not rely on the invalid inference that, since it is wrong to kill persons, it is wrong to kill potential persons also. The category that is morally central to this analysis is the category of having a valuable future like ours; it is not the category of personhood. The argument to the conclusion that abortion is prima facie seriously morally wrong proceeded independently of the notion of person or potential person or any equivalent....

Of course, this value of a future-like-ours argument, if sound, shows only that abortion is prima facie wrong, not that it is wrong in any and all circumstances. Since the loss of the future to a standard fetus, if killed, is, however, at least as great a loss as the loss of the future to a standard adult human being who is killed, abortion, like ordinary killing, could be justified only by the most compelling reasons. The loss of one's life is almost the greatest misfortune that can happen to one. Presumably abortion could be justified in some circumstances, only if the loss consequent on failing to abort would be at least as great. Accordingly, morally permissible abortions will be rare indeed unless, perhaps, they occur so early in pregnancy that a fetus is not yet definitely an individual. Hence, this argument should be taken as showing that abortion is presumptively very seriously wrong, where the presumption is very strong—as strong as the presumption that killing another adult human being is wrong.

How complete an account of the wrongness of killing does the value of a future-like-ours account have to be in order that the wrongness of abortion is a consequence? This account does not have to be an account of the necessary

---

[2] Feinberg, Tooley, Warren, and Engelhardt have all dealt with this problem.

conditions for the wrongness of killing. Some persons in nursing homes may lack valuable human futures, yet it may be wrong to kill them for other reasons. Furthermore, this account does not obviously have to be the sole reason killing is wrong where the victim did have a valuable future. This analysis claims only that, for any killing where the victim did have a valuable future like ours, having that future by itself is sufficient to create the strong presumption that the killing is seriously wrong....

In this essay, it has been argued that the correct ethic of the wrongness of killing can be extended to fetal life and used to show that there is a strong presumption that any abortion is morally impermissible. If the ethic of killing adopted here entails, however, that contraception is also seriously immoral, then there would appear to be a difficulty with the analysis of this essay.

But this analysis does not entail that contraception is wrong. Of course, contraception prevents the actualization of a possible future of value. Hence, it follows from the claim that futures of value should be maximized that contraception is prima facie immoral. This obligation to maximize does not exist, however; furthermore, nothing in the ethics of killing in this paper entails that it does. The ethics of killing in this essay would entail that contraception is wrong only if something were denied a human future of value by contraception. Nothing at all is denied such a future by contraception, however.

Candidates for a subject of harm by contraception fall into four categories: (1) some sperm or other, (2) some ovum or other, (3) a sperm and an ovum separately, and (4) a sperm and an ovum together. Assigning the harm to some sperm [or ovum] is utterly arbitrary.... One might attempt to avoid these problems by insisting that contraception deprives both the sperm and the ovum separately of a valuable future like ours. On this alternative, too many futures are lost. Contraception was supposed to be wrong, because it deprived us of one future of value, not two. One might attempt to avoid this problem by holding that contraception deprives the combination of sperm and ovum of a valuable future like ours. But here the definite article misleads. At the time of contraception, there are hundreds of millions of sperm, one (released) ovum and millions of possible combinations of all of these. There is no actual combination at all. Is the subject of the loss to be a merely possible combination? Which one? This alternative does not yield an actual subject of harm either. Accordingly, the immorality of contraception is not entailed by the loss of a future-like-ours argument simply because there is no nonarbitrarily identifiable subject of the loss in the case of contraception.

The purpose of this essay has been to set out an argument for the serious presumptive wrongness of abortion subject to the assumption that the moral permissibility of abortion stands or falls on the moral status of the fetus. Since a fetus possesses a property, the possession of which in adult human beings is sufficient to make killing an adult human being wrong, abortion is wrong. This way of dealing with the problem of abortion seems superior to other approaches to the ethics of abortion, because it rests on an ethics of killing which is close to self-evident, because the crucial morally relevant property clearly applies to fetuses, and because the argument avoids the usual equivocations on "human life," "human being," or "person." The argument rests neither on religious claims nor on Papal dogma. It is not subject to the objection of "speciesism." Its soundness is compatible with the moral permissibility of euthanasia and contraception. It deals with our intuitions concerning young children.

Finally, this analysis can be viewed as resolving a standard problem—indeed, *the* standard problem—concerning the ethics of abortion. Clearly, it is wrong to kill adult human beings. Clearly, it is not wrong to end the life of some arbitrarily chosen single human cell. Fetuses seem to be like arbitrarily chosen human cells in some respects and like adult humans in other respects. The problem of the ethics of abortion is the problem of determining the fetal property that settles this moral controversy. The thesis of this essay is that the problem of the ethics of abortion, so understood, is solvable.

STUDY QUESTIONS

1. Explain and critique Marquis' position on the wrongness of killing.
2. What are the implications of Marquis' argument against abortion for issues such euthanasia and animal rights?
3. When could abortion be justified according to Marquis?

On Duties to Animals

Immanuel Kant

A biographical sketch of Immanuel Kant is found on page 230.

According to Kant, we have no "direct duties" to animals because they lack personal attributes such as rationality, self-consciousness, and free will. Animals exist solely "as means to an end." Their inferior mental and spiritual capacities place them outside the moral community. Nevertheless, Kant argues, treating animals humanely is an "indirect duty" to humanity because, "such actions help to support us in our own duties towards human beings." If we practice kindness to animals, we are more likely to practice it with our fellow human beings.

Baumgarten speaks of duties towards beings which are beneath us and beings which are above us. But so far as animals are concerned, we have no direct duties. Animals are not self-conscious and are there merely as a means to an end. That end is man. We can ask, "Why do animals exist?" But to ask, "Why does man exist?" is a meaningless question. Our duties towards animals are merely indirect duties

Immanuel Kant, "Our Duties to Animals" from *Lectures on Ethics*, trans. Louis Infield (Harper & Row, 1963), pp. 239–241. Reprinted with permission of Routledge Publishing.

towards humanity. Animal nature has analogies to human nature, and by doing our duties to animals in respect of manifestations which correspond to manifestations of human nature, we indirectly do our duty towards humanity. Thus, if a dog has served his master long and faithfully, his service, on the analogy of human service, deserves reward, and when the dog has grown too old to serve, his master ought to keep him until he dies. Such action helps to support us in our duties towards human beings, where they are bounden duties. If then any acts of animals are analogous to human acts and spring from the same principles, we have duties towards the animals because thus we cultivate the corresponding duties towards human beings. If a man shoots his dog because the animal is no longer capable of service, he does not fail in his duty to the dog, for the dog cannot judge, but his act is inhuman and damages in himself that humanity which it is his duty to show towards mankind. If he is not to stifle his human feelings, he must practise kindness towards animals, for he who is cruel to animals becomes hard also in his dealings with men. We can judge the heart of a man by his treatment of animals. Hogarth[1] depicts this in his engravings. He shows how cruelty grows and develops. He shows the child's cruelty to animals, pinching the tail of a dog or a cat; he then depicts the grown man in his cart running over a child; and lastly, the culmination of cruelty in murder. He thus brings home to us in a terrible fashion the rewards of cruelty, and this should be an impressive lesson to children. The more we come in contact with animals and observe their behaviour, the more we love them, for we see how great is their care for their young. It is then difficult for us to be cruel in thought even to a wolf. Leibnitz used a tiny worm for purposes of observation, and then carefully replaced it with its leaf on the tree so that it should not come to harm through any act of his. He would have been sorry—a natural feeling for a humane man—to destroy such a creature for no reason. Tender feelings towards dumb animals develop humane feelings towards mankind. In England butchers and doctors do not sit on a jury because they are accustomed to the sight of death and hardened. Vivisectionists who use living animals for their experiments, certainly act cruelly, although their aim is praiseworthy, and they can justify their cruelty, since animals must be regarded as man's instruments; but any such cruelty for sport cannot be justified. A master who turns out his ass or his dog because the animal can no longer earn it keep manifests a small mind. The Greeks' ideas in this respect were high-minded, as can be seen from the fable of the ass and the bell of ingratitude. Our duties towards animals, then, are indirect duties towards mankind.

Study Questions

1. Explain the distinction between direct and indirect duties. In what way do our indirect duties to animals "support us in our duties to human beings"?
2. Does Kant's view afford animals sufficient protection from human cruelty?
3. Many human beings lack rationality and free will (infants and the mentally impaired, for example). Does it follow from Kant's argument that they too are there as "merely as means to an end?"

---

[1] Hogarth's four engravings, 'The Stages of Cruelty', 1751.

A Moral Defense of Vegetarianism

James Rachels

A biographical sketch of James Rachels is found on page 151.

Arguing for vegetarianism, James Rachels criticizes Immanuel Kant's belief that animals do not have moral standing. Rachels points out that cruelty, even to animals, cannot be right, and he describes the atrocities committed against the average animal that ends as food on the table. He argues that to eat meat is to support a cruel system of meat production. Rachels likens the meat eater who says, "If I don't eat it, someone else will," to the slave owner who says, "If I don't buy these slaves, someone else will." Both slavery and meat production are morally wrong; both become unprofitable when the consumer rejects them as criminal.

... One of my conclusions will be that it is morally wrong for us to eat meat. Many readers will find this implausible and even faintly ridiculous, as I once did. After all, meat eating is a normal, well-established part of our daily routines; people have always eaten meat; and many find it difficult even to conceive of what an alternate diet would be like. So it is not easy to take seriously the possibility that it might be wrong. Moreover, vegetarianism is commonly associated with Eastern religions whose tenets we do not accept, and with extravagant, unfounded claims about health. A quick perusal of vegetarian literature might confirm the impression that it is all a crackpot business: tracts have titles like "Victory Through Vegetables" and promise that if one will only keep to a meat-less diet one will have perfect health and be filled with wisdom. Of course we can ignore this kind of nonsense. However, there are other arguments for vegetarianism that must be taken seriously....

I

The wrongness of cruelty to animals is often explained in terms of its effects on human beings. The idea seems to be that the animals' interests are not *themselves* morally important or worthy of protection, but, since cruelty to animals often has bad consequences for *humans*, it is wrong to make animals suffer. In legal writing, for example, cruelty to animals is included among the "victimless crimes," and the problem of justifying legal prohibitions is seen as comparable to justifying the prohibition of other behavior, such as homosexuality or the distribution of pornography,

A MORAL DEFENSE OF VEGETARIANISM By James Rachels from *World Hunger and Moral Obligation*, edited by William Aiken and Hugh La Follette (Prentice-Hall, 1977). Reprinted by permission of the author.

where no one (no human) is obviously hurt. Thus, Louis Schwartz says that, in prohibiting the torturing of animals:

> It is not the mistreated dog who is the ultimate object of concern.... Our concern is for the feelings of other human beings, a large portion of whom, although accustomed to the slaughter of animals for food, readily identify themselves with a tortured dog or horse and respond with great sensitivity to its sufferings.[1]

Philosophers also adopt this attitude. Kant, for example, held that we have no direct duties to nonhuman animals. "The Categorical Imperative," the ultimate principle of morality, applies only to our dealings with humans:

> The practical imperative, therefore, is the following: Act so that you treat humanity, whether in your own person or in that of another, always as an end and never as a means only.[2]

And of other animals, Kant says:

> But so far as animals are concerned, we have no direct duties. Animals are not self-conscious, and are there merely as means to an end. That end is man.[3]

He adds that we should not be cruel to animals only because "He who is cruel to animals becomes hard also in his dealings with men."[4]

Surely this is unacceptable. Cruelty to animals ought to be opposed, not only because of the ancillary effects on humans, but because of the direct effects on the animals themselves. Animals that are tortured *suffer*, just as tortured humans suffer, and *that* is the primary reason why it is wrong. We object to torturing humans on a number of grounds, but the main one is that the victims suffer so. Insofar as nonhuman animals also suffer, we have the *same* reason to oppose torturing them, and it is indefensible to take the one suffering but not the other as grounds for objection.

Although cruelty to animals is wrong, it does not follow that we are never justified in inflicting pain on an animal. Sometimes we are justified in doing this, just as we are sometimes justified in inflicting pain on humans. It does follow, however, that there must be a *good reason* for causing the suffering, and if the suffering is great, the justifying reason must be correspondingly powerful. As an example, consider the treatment of the civet cat, a highly intelligent and sociable animal. Civet cats are trapped and placed in small cages inside darkened sheds, where the temperature is kept up to 110°F by fires.[5] They are confined in this way until they finally die. What justifies this extraordinary mistreatment? These animals have the misfortune to produce a substance that is useful in the manufacture of perfume. Musk, which is scraped from their genitals once a day for as long as they can survive,

---

[1] Louis B. Schwartz, "Morals Offenses and the Model Penal Code," *Columbia Law Review*, 63 (1963); reprinted in Joel Feinberg and Hyman Gross, eds., *Philosophy of Law* (Encino, Calif: Dickenson Publishing Company, Inc., 1975), p. 156.

[2] Immanuel Kant, *Foundations of the Metaphysics of Morals*, trans. Lewis White Beck (Indianapolis: The Bobbs-Merrill Co., Inc., 1959), p. 47.

[3] Immanuel Kant, *Lectures on Ethics*, trans. Louis Infield (New York: Harper Torchbooks, 1963), p. 239.

[4] Ibid., p. 240.

[5] Muriel the Lady Dowding, "Furs and Cosmetics: Too High a Price?" in Stanley and Rosling Godlovitch and John Harris, eds., *Animals, Men and Morals* (New York: Taplinger Publishing Co., Inc., 1972), p. 36.

makes the scent of perfume last a bit longer after each application. (The heat increases their "production" of musk.) Here Kant's rule—"Animals are merely means to an end; that end is man"—is applied with a vengeance. To promote one of the most trivial interests we have, thousands of animals are tormented for their whole lives.

It is usually easy to persuade people that this use of animals is not justified, and that we have a moral duty not to support such cruelties by consuming their products. The argument is simple: Causing suffering is not justified unless there is a good reason; the production of perfume made with musk causes considerable suffering; our enjoyment of this product is not a good enough reason to justify causing that suffering; therefore, the use of animals in this way is wrong. At least my experience has been that, once people learn the facts about musk production, they come to regard using such products as morally objectionable. They are surprised to discover, however, that an exactly analogous argument can be given in connection with the use of animals as food. Animals that are raised and slaughtered for food also suffer, and our enjoyment of the way they taste is not a sufficient justification for mistreating them.

Most people radically underestimate the amount of suffering that is caused to animals who are raised and slaughtered for food.[6] They think, in a vague way, that slaughterhouses are cruel, and perhaps even that methods of slaughter ought to be made more humane. But after all, the visit to the slaughterhouse is a relatively brief episode in the animal's life; and beyond that, people imagine that the animals are treated well enough. Nothing could be further from the truth. Today the production of meat is Big Business, and the helpless animals are treated more as machines in a factory than as living creatures.

Veal calves, for example, spend their lives in pens too small to allow them to turn around or even to lie down comfortably—exercise toughens the muscles, which reduces the "quality" of the meat, and besides, allowing the animals adequate living space would be prohibitively expensive. In these pens the calves cannot perform such basic actions as grooming themselves, which they naturally desire to do, because there is not room for them to twist their heads around. It is clear that the calves miss their mothers, and like human infants they want something to suck: they can be seen trying vainly to suck the sides of their stalls. In order to keep their meat pale and tasty, they are fed a liquid diet deficient in both iron and roughage. Naturally they develop cravings for these things, because they need them. The calf's craving for iron is so strong that, if it is allowed to turn around, it will lick at its own urine, although calves normally find this repugnant. The tiny stall, which prevents the animal from turning, solves this "problem." The craving for roughage is especially strong since without it the animal cannot form a cud to chew. It cannot be given any straw for bedding, since the animal would be driven to eat it, and that would spoil the meat. For these animals the slaughterhouse is not an unpleasant end

---

[6] By far the best account of these cruelties is to be found in Chapter 3 of Peter Singer's *Animal Liberation* (New York Review of Books, 1975). I have drawn on Singer's work for the factual material in the following two paragraphs. *Animal Liberation* should also be consulted for a thorough treatment of matters to which I can refer here only sketchily.

to an otherwise contented life. As terrifying as the process of slaughter is, for them it may actually be regarded as a merciful release.

Similar stories can be told about the treatment of other animals on which we dine. In order to "produce" animals by the millions, it is necessary to keep them crowded together in small spaces. Chickens are commonly kept eight or ten to a space smaller than a newspaper page. Unable to walk around or even stretch their wings—much less build a nest—the birds become vicious and attack one another. The problem is sometimes exacerbated because the birds are so crowded that, unable to move, their feet literally grow around the wire floors of the cages anchoring them to the spot. An "anchored" bird cannot escape attack no matter now desperate it becomes. Mutilation of the animals is an efficient solution. To minimize the damage they can do to one another, the birds' beaks are cut off. The mutilation is painful, but probably not as painful as other sorts of mutilations that are routinely practiced. Cows are castrated, not to prevent the unnatural "vices" to which overcrowded chickens are prone, but because castrated cows put on more weight, and there is less danger of meat being "tainted" by male hormones.

> In Britain an anesthetic must be used, unless the animal is very young, but in America anesthetics are not in general use. The procedure is to pin the animal down, take a knife and slit the scrotum, exposing the testicles. You then grab each testicle in turn and pull on it, breaking the cord that attaches it; on older animals it may be necessary to cut the cord.[7]

It must be emphasized that the treatment I am describing—and I have hardly scratched the surface here—is not out of the ordinary. It is typical of the way that animals raised for food are treated, now that meat production is Big Business. As Peter Singer puts it, these are the sorts of things that happened to your dinner when it was still an animal.

What accounts for such cruelties? As for the meat producers, there is no reason to think they are unusually cruel men. They simply accept the common attitude expressed by Kant: "Animals are merely means to an end; that end is man." The cruel practices are adopted not because they are cruel but because they are efficient, given that one's only concern is to produce meat (and eggs) for humans as cheaply as possible. But clearly this use of animals is immoral if anything is. Since we can nourish ourselves very well without eating them, our *only reason* for doing all this to the animals is our enjoyment of the way they taste. And this will not even come close to justifying the cruelty.

II

Does this mean that we should stop eating meat? Such a conclusion will be hard for many people to accept. It is tempting to say: "What is objectionable is not *eating* the animals, but only making them suffer. Perhaps we ought to protest the way they are treated, and even work for better treatment of them. But it doesn't follow that we must stop eating them." This sounds plausible until you realize that it would be impossible to treat the animals decently and still produce meat in

---

[7] Singer, *Animal Liberation*, p. 152.

sufficient quantities to make it a normal part of our diets. As I have already remarked, cruel methods are used in the meat-production industry because such methods are economical; they enable the producers to market a product that people can afford. Humanely produced chicken, beef, and pork would be so expensive that only the very rich could afford them. (*Some* of the cruelties could be eliminated without too much expense—the cows could be given an anesthetic before castration, for example, even though this alone would mean a slight increase in the cost of beef. But others, such as overcrowding, could not be eliminated without really prohibitive cost.) So to work for better treatment for the animals would be to work for a situation in which most of us would *have* to adopt a vegetarian diet.

Still, there remains the interesting theoretical question: *If* meat could be produced humanely, without mistreating the animals prior to killing them painlessly, would there be anything wrong with it? The question is only of theoretical interest because the actual choice we face in the supermarket is whether to buy the remains of animals that are *not* treated humanely. Still, the question has some interest, and I want to make two comments about it.

First, it is a vexing issue whether animals have a "right to life" that is violated when we kill them for trivial purposes; but we should not simply assume until proven otherwise that they *don't* have a right.[8] We assume that humans have a right to life—It would be wrong to murder a normal, healthy human even if it were done painlessly—and it is hard to think of any plausible rationale for granting this right to humans that does not also apply to other animals. Other animals live in communities, as do humans; they communicate with one another, and have ongoing social relationships, killing them disrupts lives that are perhaps not as complex, emotionally and intellectually, as our own, but that are nevertheless quite complicated. They suffer, and are capable of happiness as well as fear and distress, as we are. So what could be the rational basis for saying that we have a right to life, but that they don't? Or even more pointedly, what could be the rational basis for saying that a severely retarded human, who is inferior in every important respect to an intelligent animal, has a right to life but that the animal doesn't? Philosophers often treat such questions as "puzzles," assuming that there must be answers even if we are not clever enough to find them. I am suggesting that, on the contrary, there may not be any acceptable answers to these questions. If it seems, intuitively, that there *must* be some difference between us and the other animals which confers on us, but not them, right to life, perhaps this intuition is mistaken. At the very least, the difficulty of answering such questions should make us hesitant about asserting that it is all right to kill animals, as long as we don't make them suffer, unless we are also willing to take seriously the possibility that it is all right to kill people, so long as we don't make them suffer.

Second, it is important to see the slaughter of animals for food as part of a larger pattern that characterizes our whole relationship with the nonhuman world.

---

[8] It is controversial among philosophers whether animals can have any rights at all. See various essays collected in Part IV of Tom Regan and Peter Singer, eds., *Animal Rights and Human Obligations* (Englewood Cliffs, N.J.: Prentice-Hall, 1976). My own defense of animal rights is given in "Do Animals Have a Right to Liberty?" pp. 205–223, and in "A reply to Van De Veer," pp. 230–32.

Animals are wrenched from their natural homes to be made objects of our entertainment in zoos, circuses, and rodeos. They are used in laboratories, not only for experiments that are themselves morally questionable,[9] but also in testing everything from shampoo to chemical weapons. They are killed so that their heads can be used as wall decorations, or their skins as ornamental clothing or rugs. Indeed, simply killing them for the fun of it is thought to be "sport."[10] This pattern of cruel exploitation flows naturally from the Kantian attitude that animals are nothing more than things to be used for our purposes. It is this whole attitude that must be opposed, and not merely its manifestation in our willingness to hurt the animals we eat. Once one rejects this attitude, and no longer regards the animals as disposable at one's whim, one ceases to think it all right to kill them, even painlessly, just for a snack.

But now let me return to the more immediate practical issue. The meat at the supermarket was not produced by humane methods. The animals whose flesh this meat once was were abused in ways similar to the ones I have described. Millions of other animals are being treated in these ways now, and their flesh will soon appear in the markets. Should one support such practices by purchasing and consuming its products?

It is discouraging to realize that no animals will actually be helped simply by one person ceasing to eat meat. One consumer's behavior, by itself, cannot have a noticeable impact on an industry as vast as the meat business. However, it is important to see one's behavior in a wider context. There are already millions of vegetarians, and because they don't eat meat there *is* less cruelty than there otherwise would be. The question is whether one ought to side with that group, or with the carnivores whose practices cause the suffering. Compare the position of someone thinking about whether to buy slaves in the year 1820. He might reason as follows: "The whole practice of slavery is immoral, but I cannot help any of the poor slaves by keeping clear of it. If I don't buy these slaves, someone else will. One person's decision just can't by itself have any impact on such a vast business. So I may as well use slaves like everyone else." The first thing we notice is that this fellow was too pessimistic about the possibilities of a successful movement; but beyond that, there is something else wrong with his reasoning. If one really thinks that a social practice is immoral, that *in itself* sufficient grounds for a refusal to participate. In 1848 Thoreau remarked that even if someone did not want to devote himself to the abolition movement, and actively oppose slavery, "... it is his duty, at least, to wash his hands of it, and, if he gives it no thought longer, not to give it practically his support."[11] In the case of slavery, this seems clear. If it seems less clear in the case of the cruel exploitation of nonhuman animals, perhaps it is because the Kantian attitude is so deeply entrenched in us....

---

[9] See Singer, Animal Liberation, Chap. 2.

[10] It is sometimes said, in defense of "non-slob" hunting: "Killing for pleasure is wrong, but killing for food is all right." This won't do, since for those of us who are able to nourish ourselves without killing animals, killing them for food is a form of killing for pleasure, namely the pleasures of the palate.

[11] Henry David Thoreau, *Civil Disobedience* (1848).

STUDY QUESTIONS

1. You may choose to (a) be a vegetarian, (b) be a meat eater, or (c) pick holes in Rachels's arguments. Assuming that you have not done either (a) or (c), justify (b).
2. If I kill my neighbor's dog, I wrong my neighbor. Do I also wrong his dog? Discuss the view that animals have a right to life.
3. What, in your opinion, is Rachels's strongest argument for becoming a vegetarian? What other steps might we take to address the problem of commercial cruelty to animals?
4. Can we reasonably believe that animals feel pain? Why or why not?

Down on the Factory Farm

Peter Singer

A biographical sketch of Peter Singer is found on page 176.

The title of Singer's piece is ironic. The factory farm of today is not the pastoral farmyard of yesterday. In former times, most human beings had contact with the animals they raised for food. Often, they lived together on farms where the animals were accorded some consideration and could enjoy a natural and healthy existence before being slaughtered. The advent of the industrial era brought with it enormous changes to the way in which animals are raised and slaughtered for food in the United States. Singer argues that today's industrialized farm more closely resembles a mechanized assembly line than the farms of yore. In this process of modernization, the livestock industry and, tangentially, consumers of such meat and dairy products, has degraded the status of the animals raised simply to parts of a great machine with no moral status. Singer describes in detail the fate of chickens and veal calves in a vast automated system that gives little or no regard to their well-being.

For most humans, especially those in modern urban and suburban communities, the most direct form of contact with nonhuman animals is at meal time: we eat them. This simple fact is the key to our attitudes to other animals, and also the key to what each one of us can do about changing these attitudes. The use and abuse of animals raised for food far exceeds, in sheer numbers of animals affected, any other kind of mistreatment. Hundreds of millions of cattle, pigs, and sheep are raised and slaughtered in the United States alone each year; and for poultry the figure is a staggering 3 billion. (That means that about 5,000 birds—mostly chickens—will have been slaughtered in the time it takes you to read this page.) It is here, on our dinner table and in our neighborhood supermarket or butcher's shop, that we are brought into direct touch with the most extensive exploitation of other species that has ever existed.

In general, we are ignorant of the abuse of living creatures that lies behind the food we eat. Consider the images conjured up by the word "farm": a house, a barn, a flock of hens, overseen by a strutting rooster, scratching around the farmyard, a herd of cows being brought in from the fields for milking, and perhaps a sow rooting around in the orchard with a litter of squealing piglets running excitedly behind her.

Very few farms were ever as idyllic as that traditional image would have us believe. Yet we still think of a farm as a pleasant place, far removed from our own industrial, profit-conscious city life. Of those few who think about the lives of animals on farms, not many know much of modern methods of animal raising. Some people wonder whether animals are slaughtered painlessly, and anyone who has followed a truckload of cattle must know that farm animals are transported in very crowded conditions; but few suspect that transportation and slaughter are anything more than the brief and inevitable conclusion of a life of ease and contentment, a life that contains the natural pleasures of animal existence without the hardships that wild animals must endure in the struggle for survival.

These comfortable assumptions bear little relation to the realities of modern farming. For a start, farming is no longer controlled by simple country folk. It is a business, and big business at that. In the last thirty years the entry of large corporations and assembly-line methods of production have turned farming into "agribusiness."...

The first animal to be removed from the relatively natural conditions of the traditional farms and subjected to the full stress of modern intensive farming was the chicken. Chickens have the misfortune of being useful to humans in two ways: for their flesh and for their eggs. There are now standard mass-production techniques for obtaining both these products.

Agribusiness enthusiasts consider the rise of the chicken industry to be one of the great success stories of farming. At the end of World War II chicken for the table was still relatively rare. It came mainly from small independent farmers or from the unwanted males produced by egg-laying flocks. Today "broilers"—as table chickens are now usually called—are produced literally by the million from the highly automated factory-like plants of the large corporations that own or control 98 percent of all broiler production in the United States.[1]

The essential step in turning the chicken from a farmyard bird into a manufactured item was confining them indoors. A broiler producer today gets a load of 10,000, 50,000, or even more day-old chicks from the hatcheries, and puts them straight into a long, windowless shed—usually on the floor, although some producers use tiers of cages in order to get more birds into the same size shed. Inside the shed, every aspect of the birds' environment is controlled to make them grow faster on less feed. Food and water are fed automatically from hoppers suspended from the roof. The lighting is adjusted according to advice from agricultural researchers: for instance, there may be bright light 24 hours a day for the first week or two, to encourage the chicks to gain quickly; then the lights may be dimmed slightly and made to go off and on every two hours, in the belief that the chickens are readier to eat after a period of sleep; finally there comes a point, around six weeks of age, when the birds have grown so much that they are becoming crowded, and the lights will then be made very dim at all times. The point of this dim lighting is to reduce the effects of crowding. Toward the end of the eight- or nine-week life of the chicken, there may be as little as half a square foot of space per chicken—or less than the area of a sheet of quarto paper for a three and one-half-pound bird. Under these conditions with normal lighting the stress of crowding and the absence of natural outlets for the bird's energies lead to outbreaks of fighting; with birds pecking at each other's feathers and sometimes killing and eating one another. Very dim lighting has been found to reduce this and so the birds are likely to live out their last weeks in near-darkness.

Feather-pecking and cannibalism are, in the broiler producer's language, "vices." They are not natural vices, however—they are the result of the stress and crowding to which the modern broilerman subjects his birds. Chickens are highly social animals, and in the farmyard they develop a hierarchy, sometimes called a "pecking order." Every bird yields, at the food trough or elsewhere, to those above it in rank, and takes precedence over those below. There may be a few confrontations before the order is firmly established but more often than not a show of force, rather than actual physical contact, is enough to put a chicken in its place. As Konrad Lorenz, a renowned figure in the field of animal behavior, wrote in the days when flocks were still small:

> Do animals thus know each other among themselves? They certainly do.... Every poultry farmer knows that... there exists a very definite order, in which each bird is afraid of those that are above her in rank. After some few disputes, which need not necessarily come to blows, each bird knows which of the others she has to fear and which must show respect to her. Not only physical strength, but also personal courage; energy, and even the self-assurance of every individual bird are decisive in the maintenance of the pecking order.[2]

Other studies have shown that a flock of up to 90 chickens can maintain a stable social order, each bird knowing its place; but 10,000 birds crowded together in a single shed is obviously a different matter.[3] The birds cannot establish a social order, and as a result they fight frequently with each other. Quite apart from the inability of the individual bird to recognize so many other birds, the mere fact of extreme crowding probably contributes to irritability and excitability in chickens, as it does in humans and other animals. This is something farming magazines are aware of, and they frequently warn their readers:

> Feather-pecking and cannibalism have increased to a formidable extent of late years, due, no doubt, to the changes in technique and the swing towards completely intensive management of laying flocks and table poultry.... The most common faults in management which may lead to vice are boredom, overcrowding in badly ventilated houses.... Lack of feeding space, unbalanced food or shortage of water, and heavy infestation with insect pests.[4]

Clearly the farmer must stop "vices," because they cost him money; but although he may know that overcrowding is the root cause, he cannot do anything about this, since in the competitive state of the industry, eliminating overcrowding could mean eliminating his profit margin at the same time. He would have fewer birds to sell, but would have had to pay the same outlay for his building, for the automatic feeding equipment, for the fuel used to heat and ventilate the building, and for labor. So the farmer limits his efforts to reducing the consequences of the stress that costs him money. The unnatural way in which he keeps his birds causes the vices; but to control them the poultryman must make the conditions still more unnatural. Very dim lighting is one way of doing this. A more drastic step, though one now almost universally used in the industry, is "de-beaking." This involves inserting the chick's head in a guillotine-like device which cuts off part of its beak. Alternatively the operation may be done with a hot knife. Some poultrymen claim that this operation is painless, but an expert British Government committee under zoologist Professor F. W. Rogers Brambell appointed to look into aspects of intensive farming found otherwise:

> ... between the horn and the bone is a thin layer of highly sensitive soft tissue, resembling the "quick" of the human nail. The hot knife used in de-beaking cuts through this complex of horn, bone and sensitive tissue, causing severe pain.[5]

De-beaking, which is routinely performed in anticipation of cannibalism by most poultrymen, does greatly reduce the amount of damage a chicken can do to other chickens. It also, in the words of the Brambell Committee, "deprives the bird of what is in effect its most versatile member" while it obviously does nothing to reduce the stress and overcrowding that lead to this unnatural cannibalism in the first place....

"A hen," Samuel Butler once wrote, "is only an egg's way of making another egg." Butler, no doubt, was being humorous; but when Fred C. Haley, president of a Georgia poultry firm that controls the lives of 225,000 laying hens, describes the hen as "an egg producing machine" his words have more serious implications. To emphasize his businesslike attitude Haley adds: "The object of producing eggs is to make money. When we forget this objective, we have forgotten what it is all about."[6]

Nor is this only an American attitude. A British farming magazine has told its readers:

> The modern layer is, after all, only a very efficient converting machine, changing the raw material—feedingstuffs—into the finished product—the egg—less, of course, maintenance requirements.[7]

Remarks of this kind can regularly be found in the egg industry trade journals throughout the United States and Europe, and they express an attitude that is common in the industry. As may be anticipated, their consequences for the laying hens are not good.

Laying hens go through many of the same procedures as broilers, but there are some differences. Like broilers, layers have to be de-beaked, to prevent the cannibalism that would otherwise occur in their crowded conditions; but because they live much longer than broilers, they often go through this operation twice. So we find a poultry specialist at the New Jersey College of Agriculture advising poultrymen to de-beak their chicks when they are between one and two weeks old because there is, he says, less stress on the chicks at this time than if the operation is done earlier, and in addition "there are fewer culls in the laying flock as a result of improper de-beaking." In either case, the article continues, the birds must be de-beaked again when they are ready to begin laying, at around twenty weeks of age.[8]

Laying hens get no more individual attention than broilers. Alan Hainsworth, owner of a poultry farm in upstate New York, told an inquiring local reporter that four hours a day is all he needs for the care of his 36,000 laying hens, while his wife looks after the 20,000 pullets (as the younger birds not yet ready to lay are called): "It takes her about 15 minutes a day. All she checks is their automatic feeders, water cups and any deaths during the night."

This kind of care does not make for a happy flock as the reporter's description shows:

> Walk into the pullet house and the reaction is immediate—complete pandemonium. The squawking is loud and intense as some 20,000 birds shove to the farthest side of their cages in fear of the human intruders.[9]

Julius Goldman's Egg City, 50 miles northwest of Los Angeles, is one of the world's largest egg producing units, consisting of 2 million hens divided into block long buildings containing 90,000 hens each, five birds to a 16- by 18-inch cage. When the *National Geographic* magazine did an enthusiastic survey of new farming methods, Ben Shames, Egg City's executive vice-president, explained to its reporter the methods used to look after so many birds:

> We keep track of the food eaten and the eggs collected in 2 rows of cages among the 110 rows in each building. When production drops to the uneconomic point, all 90,000 birds are sold to processors for potpies or chicken soup. It doesn't pay to keep track of every row in the house, let alone individual hens; with 2 million birds on hand you have to rely on statistical samplings.[10]

Nearly all the big egg producers now keep their laying hens in cages. Originally there was only one bird to a cage; and the idea was that the farmer could then tell which birds were not laying enough eggs to give an economic return on their food. Those birds were then killed. Then it was found that more birds could be housed and costs per bird reduced if two birds were put in each cage. That was only the first step, and as we have seen, there is no longer any question of keeping a tally of each bird's eggs. The advantages of cages for the egg producer now consist in the greater number of birds that can be housed, warmed, fed, and watered in one building, and in the greater use that can be made of labor-saving automatic equipment.

The cages are stacked in tiers, with food and water troughs running along the rows, filled automatically from a central supply. They have sloping wire floors. The slope—usually a gradient of 1 in 5—makes it more difficult for the birds to stand comfortably, but it causes the eggs to roll to the front of the cage where they can easily be collected by hand or, in the more modern plants, carried by conveyor belt to a packing plant.

When a reporter from the *New York Daily News* wanted to see a typical modern egg farm, he visited Frenchtown Poultry Farm, in New Jersey, where he found that

> Each 18 by 24 inch cage on the Frenchtown farm contains nine hens who seemed jammed into them by some unseen hand. They barely have enough room to turn around in the cages.
>
> "Really, you should have no more than eight birds in a cage that size," conceded Oscar Grossman, the farm's lessor. "But sometimes you have to do things to get the most out of your stock."[11]

Actually, if Mr. Grossman had put only eight birds in his cages they would still have been grossly over-crowded; at nine to a cage they have only one-third square foot per bird.

In 1968 the farm magazine *American Agriculturalist* advised its readers in an article headed "Bird Squeezing" that it had been found possible to stock at one-third square foot per bird by putting four birds in a 12- by 16-inch cage. This was apparently a novel step at the time; the steady increase in densities over the years is indicated by the fact that a 1974 issue of the same magazine describing the Lannsdale Poultry Farm, near Rochester, New York, mentions the same housing density without any suggestion that it is unusual.[12] In reading egg industry magazines I have found numerous reports of similar high densities, and scarcely any that are substantially lower. My own visits to poultry farms in the United States have shown the same pattern. The highest reported density that I have read about is at the Hainsworth farm in Mt. Morris, New York, where four hens are squeezed into cages 12 inches by 12 inches, or just one square foot—and the reporter adds: "Some hold five birds when Hainsworth has more birds than room."[13] This means one-fourth, and sometimes one-fifth, square foot per bird. At this stocking rate a *single sheet of quarto paper represents the living area of two to three hens.*

Under the conditions standard on modern egg farms in the United States and other "developed nations" every natural instinct the birds have is frustrated. They cannot walk around, scratch the ground, dustbathe, build a nest, or stretch their wings. They are not part of a flock. They cannot keep out of each other's way and weaker birds have no escape from the attacks of stronger ones, already maddened by the unnatural conditions....

Intensive production of pigs and cattle is now also common; but of all the forms of intensive farming now practiced, the quality veal industry ranks as the most morally repugnant, comparable only with barbarities like the force-feeding of geese through a funnel that produces the deformed livers made into pate de foie gras. The essence of veal raising is the feeding of a high-protein food (that should be used to reduce malnutrition in poorer parts of the world) to confined, anemic calves in a manner that will produce a tender, pale-colored flesh that will be served to gourmets in expensive restaurants. Fortunately this industry does not compare in size with poultry, beef, or pig production; nevertheless it is worth our attention because it represents an extreme, both in the degree of exploitation to which it subjects its animals and in its absurd inefficiency as a method of providing people with nourishment.

Veal is the flesh of a young calf, and the term was originally reserved for calves killed before they had been weaned from their mothers. The flesh of these very young animals was paler and more tender than that of a calf that had begun to eat grass; but there was not much of it since calves begin to eat grass when they are a few weeks old and still very small. So there was little money in veal, and the small amount available came from the unwanted male calves produced by the dairy industry. These males were a nuisance to the dairy farmers, since the dairy breeds do not make good beef cattle. Therefore they were sold as quickly as possible. A day or two after being born they were trucked to market where, hungry and frightened by the strange surroundings and the absence of their mothers, they were sold for immediate delivery to the slaughterhouse.

Once this was the main source of veal in the United States. Now, using methods first developed in Holland, farmers have found a way to keep the calf longer without the flesh becoming darker in color or less tender. This means that the veal calf, when sold, may weigh as much as 325 pounds, instead of the 90-odd pounds that newborn calves weigh. Because veal fetches a premium price, this has made rearing veal calves a profitable occupation.

The trick depends on keeping the calf in highly unnatural conditions. If the calf were left to grow up outside, its playful nature would lead it to romp around the fields. Soon it would begin to develop muscles, which would make its flesh tough. At the same time it would eat grass and its flesh would lose the pale color that the flesh of newborn calves has. So the specialist veal producer takes his calves straight from the auction ring to a confinement unit. Here, in a converted barn or purpose-built shed, he will have rows of wooden stalls. Each stall will be 1 foot 10 inches wide and 4 feet 6 inches long. It will have a slatted wooden floor, raised above the concrete floor of the shed. The calves will be tethered by a chain around the neck to prevent them from turning around in their stalls. (The chain may be removed when the calves grow too big to turn around in such narrow stalls.) The stall will have no straw or other bedding, since the calf might eat it, spoiling the paleness of his flesh.

Here the calves will live for the next thirteen to fifteen weeks. They will leave their stalls only to be taken out to slaughter. They are fed a totally liquid diet, based on non-fat milk powder with added vitamins, minerals, and growth-promoting drugs....

The narrow stalls and their slatted wooden floors are a serious source of discomfort for the calves. The inability to turn around is frustrating. When he lies down, the calf must lie hunched up, sitting almost on top of his legs rather than having them out to one side as he would do if he had more room. A stall too narrow to turn around in is also too narrow to groom comfortably in; and calves have an innate desire to twist their heads around and groom themselves with their tongues. A wooden floor without any bedding is hard and uncomfortable; it is rough on the calves' knees as they get up and lie down. In addition, animals with hooves are uncomfortable on slatted floors. A slatted floor is like a cattle grid, which cattle will always avoid, except that the slats are closer together. The spaces, however, must still be large enough to allow manure to fall or be washed through, and this means that they are large enough to make the calves uncomfortable.[14]

The special nature of the veal calf has other implications that show the industry's lack of genuine concern for the animals' welfare. Obviously the calves sorely miss their mothers. They also miss something to suck on. The urge to suck is strong in a baby calf, as it is in a baby human. These calves have no teat to suck on, nor do they have any substitute. From their first day in confinement—which may well be only the third or fourth day of their lives—they drink from a plastic bucket. Attempts have been made to feed calves through artificial teats, but the problems of keeping the teats clean and sterile are apparently too great for the farmer to try to overcome. It is common to see calves frantically trying to suck some part of their stalls, although there is usually nothing suitable; and if you offer a veal calf your finger he will immediately begin to suck on it, as a human baby sucks its thumb.

Later on the calf develops a desire to ruminate—that is, to take in roughage and chew the cud. But roughage is strictly forbidden and so, again, the calf may resort to vain attempts to chew the sides of its stall. Digestive disorders, including stomach ulcers, are common in veal calves, as are chronically loose bowel movements.

As if this were not enough, there is the fact that the calf is deliberately kept anemic. As one veal producers' journal has said,

> Color of veal is one of the primary factors involved in obtaining "topdollar" returns from the fancy veal market… "light color" veal is a premium item much in demand at better clubs, hotels and restaurants. "Light color" or pink veal is partly associated with the amount of iron in the muscle of the calves.[15]

So veal feeds are deliberately kept low in iron. A normal calf would obtain iron from grass or other forms of roughage, but since a veal calf is not allowed this he becomes anemic. Pale pink flesh is in fact anemic flesh. The demand for flesh of this color is a matter of snob appeal. The color does not affect the taste and it certainly does not make the flesh more nourishing—rather the opposite.

Calves kept in this manner are unhappy and unhealthy animals. Despite the fact that the veal producer selects only the strongest, healthiest calves to begin with, uses a medicated feed as a routine measure, and gives additional injections at the slightest sign of illness, digestive, respiratory and infectious diseases are widespread. It is common for a veal producer to find that one in ten of a batch of calves do not survive the fifteen weeks of confinement. Ten percent mortality over such a short period would be disastrous for anyone raising calves for beef, but the veal producer can tolerate this loss because of the high price restaurants are prepared to pay for his product. If the reader will recall that this whole laborious, wasteful, and painful process exists for the sole purpose of pandering to would-be gourmets who insist on pale, soft veal, no further comment should be needed.

NOTES

1. Harrison Wellford, *Sowing the Wind: The Politics of Food, Safety and Agribusiness* (New York: Grossman Press, 1971), p. 104.
2. K. Lorenz, *King Solomon's Ring* (London: Methuen, 1964), p. 147.
3. Ian Duncan, "Can the Psychologist Measure Stress?" *New Scientist*, October 18, 1973.
4. *The Smallholder*, January 6, 1962; quoted by Ruth Harrison, *Animal Machines* (London: Vincent Stuart, 1964), p. 18.

5. *Report of the Technical Committee to Enquire into the Welfare of Animals Kept Under Intensive Livestock Husbandry Systems* (London: Her Majesty's Stationery Office, 1965), para. 97.

6. *Poultry Tribune*, January 1974.

7. *Farmer and Stockbreeder*, January 30, 1962; quoted by Ruth Harrison, *Animal Machines*, p. 50.

8. *American Agriculturist*, July 1966.

9. *Upstate*, August 5, 1973, report by Mary Rita Kiereck.

10. *National Geographic*, February 1970.

11. *New York Daily News*, September 1, 1971.

12. *American Agriculturist*, August 1968, April 1974.

13. *Upstate*, August 5, 1973.

14. Ruth Harrison, *Animal Machines*, p. 72.

15. *The Wall Street Journal*, published by Provimi, Inc., Watertown, Wisconsin, November 1973.

STUDY QUESTIONS

1. How much of our current indifference to the plight of the billions of creatures being processed in the factory farms is due to our ignorance of the realities of farm factory systems? How much is due to our alienation from the animals that we no longer see in their natural state? What, if anything, could be done to increase our awareness?

2. Why does Singer find the veal industry especially repugnant? Do you agree with his assessment?

3. Do you think societies that permit factory farming are grossly remiss in their duties to animals—directly or indirectly? Should they be blamed for callousness and cruelty?

An Animal's Place

Michael Pollan

Michael Pollan (b. 1955) is Knight Professor of Journalism at the Graduate School and director of the Knight Program in Science and Environmental Journalism at the University of California at Berkeley. He is a contributing writer at *The New York Times Magazine* and the author of several books, including *The Botany of Desire: A Plant's-Eye View of the World* (2001) and *In Defense of Food: An Eater's Manifesto* (2008).

AN ANIMAL'S PLACE. Reprinted by permission of Michael Pollan. This essay originally appeared in *The New York Times Magazine*, November 10, 2002.

Pollan agrees with Peter Singer that factory farming is morally indefensible, but he defends the practice of eating meat as long as the animals are treated humanely. Pollan describes some economically successful farms that maintain a traditional farm life for animals raised for the slaughter, with space and fresh air and what Pollan calls the "ability to express their creaturely natures." To eat the produce of such farms, Pollan asserts, is not immoral—both human beings and animals benefit.

To achieve the reform of the factory farms, Pollan advocates forcing the farms to allow the public to see how their animals are being raised and slaughtered. "Who could stand the sight?" Though meat would be far more expensive, it is the price we would pay for granting animals the "respect they deserve."

The first time I opened Peter Singer's *Animal Liberation*, I was dining alone at the Palm, trying to enjoy a ribeye steak cooked medium rare. If this sounds like a good recipe for cognitive dissonance (if not indigestion), that was sort of the idea....

Even in 1975, when *Animal Liberation* was first published, Singer, an Australian philosopher now teaching at Princeton, was confident that he had the wind of history at his back. The recent civil rights past was prologue, as one liberation movement followed on the heels of another. Slowly but surely, the white man's circle of moral consideration was expanded to admit first blacks, then women, then homosexuals. In each case, a group once thought to be so different from the prevailing "we" as to be undeserving of civil rights was, after a struggle, admitted to the club. Now it was animals' turn.

That animal liberation is the logical next step in the forward march of moral progress is no longer the fringe idea it was back in 1975. A growing and increasingly influential movement of philosophers, ethicists, law professors, and activists are convinced that the great moral struggle of our time will be for the rights of animals.

So far the movement has scored some of its biggest victories in Europe. Earlier this year, Germany became the first nation to grant animals a constitutional right: the words "and animals" were added to a provision obliging the state to respect and protect the dignity of human beings. The farming of animals for fur was recently banned in England. In several European nations, sows may no longer be confined to crates nor laying hens to "battery cages"—stacked wired cages so small the birds cannot stretch their wings. The Swiss are amending their laws to change the status of animals from "things" to "beings."

Though animals are still very much "things" in the eyes of American law, change is in the air. Thirty-seven states have recently passed laws making some forms of animal cruelty a crime, 21 of them by ballot initiative. Following protests by activists, McDonald's and Burger King forced significant improvements in the way the U.S. meat industry slaughters animals. Agribusiness and the cosmetics and apparel industries are all struggling to defuse mounting public concerns over animal welfare.

Once thought of as a left-wing concern, the movement now cuts across ideological lines. Perhaps the most eloquent recent plea on behalf of animals, a new book called *Dominion* was written by a former speechwriter for President Bush. And once outlandish ideas are finding their way into mainstream opinion. A recent Zogby poll found that 51 percent of Americans believe that primates are entitled to the same rights as human children.

What is going on here? A certain amount of cultural confusion, for one thing. For at the same time many people seem eager to extend the circle of our moral consideration to animals, in our factory farms and laboratories we are inflicting more suffering on more animals than at any time in history. One by one, science is dismantling our claims to uniqueness as a species, discovering that such things as culture, tool making, language and even possibly self-consciousness are not the exclusive domain of Homo sapiens. Yet most of the animals we kill lead lives organized very much in the spirit of Descartes, who famously claimed that animals were mere machines, incapable of thought or feeling. There's a schizoid quality to our relationship with animals, in which sentiment and brutality exist side by side. Half the dogs in America will receive Christmas presents this year, yet few of us pause to consider the miserable life of the pig—an animal easily as intelligent as a dog—that becomes the Christmas ham.

We tolerate this disconnect because the life of the pig has moved out of view. When's the last time you saw a pig? (Babe doesn't count.) Except for our pets, real animals—animals living and dying—no longer figure in our everyday lives. Meat comes from the grocery store, where it is cut and packaged to look as little like parts of animals as possible. The disappearance of animals from our lives has opened a space in which there's no reality check, either on the sentiment or the brutality. This is pretty much where we live now, with respect to animals, and it is a space in which the Peter Singers and Frank Perdues of the world can evidently thrive equally well....

Singer's argument is disarmingly simple and, if you accept its premises, difficult to refute. Take the premise of equality, which most people readily accept. Yet what do we really mean by it? People are not, as a matter of fact, equal at all—some are smarter than others, better looking, more gifted. "Equality is a moral idea," Singer points out, "not an assertion of fact." The moral idea is that everyone's interests ought to receive equal consideration, regardless of "what abilities they may possess." Fair enough; many philosophers have gone this far. But fewer have taken the next logical step. "If possessing a higher degree of intelligence does not entitle one human to use another for his or her own ends, how can it entitle humans to exploit nonhumans for the same purpose?"

This is the nub of Singer's argument, and right around here I began scribbling objections in the margin. But humans differ from animals in morally significant ways. Yes they do, Singer acknowledges, which is why we shouldn't treat pigs and children alike. Equal consideration of interests is not the same as equal treatment, he points out: children have an interest in being educated; pigs, in rooting around in the dirt. But where their interests are the same, the principle of equality demands they receive the same consideration. And the one all-important interest that we share with pigs, as with all sentient creatures, is an interest in avoiding pain.

Here Singer quotes a famous passage from Jeremy Bentham, the eighteenth-century utilitarian philosopher, that is the wellspring of the animal rights movement. Bentham was writing in 1789, soon after the French colonies freed black slaves, granting them fundamental rights. "The day may come," he speculates, "when the rest of the animal creation may acquire those rights." Bentham then asks what characteristic entitles any being to moral consideration. "Is it the faculty of reason or perhaps the faculty of discourse?" Obviously not, since "a full-grown horse or dog is beyond comparison a more rational, as well as a more conversable animal, than an infant." He concludes: "The question is not, Can they reason? nor, Can they talk? but, Can they suffer?"

Bentham here is playing a powerful card philosophers call the "argument from marginal cases," or AMC for short. It goes like this: there are humans—infants, the severely retarded, the demented—whose mental function cannot match that of a chimpanzee. Even though these people cannot reciprocate our moral attentions, we nevertheless include them in the circle of our moral consideration. So on what basis do we exclude the chimpanzee?

Because he's a chimp, I furiously scribbled in the margin, and they're human! For Singer that's not good enough. To exclude the chimp from moral consideration simply because he's not human is no different from excluding the slave simply because he's not white. In the same way we'd call that exclusion racist, the animal rightist contends that it is speciesist to discriminate against the chimpanzee solely because he's not human.

But the differences between blacks and whites are trivial compared with the differences between my son and a chimp. Singer counters by asking us to imagine a hypothetical society that discriminates against people on the basis of something nontrivial—say, intelligence. If that scheme offends our sense of equality, then why is the fact that animals lack certain human characteristics any more just as a basis for discrimination? Either we do not owe any justice to the severely retarded, he concludes, or we do owe it to animals with higher capabilities.

This is where I put down my fork. If I believe in equality, and equality is based on interests rather than characteristics, then either I have to take the interests of the steer I'm eating into account or concede that I am a speciesist. For the time being, I decided to plead guilty as charged. I finished my steak.

But Singer had planted a troubling notion, and in the days afterward, it grew and grew, watered by the other animal-rights thinkers I began reading: the philosophers Tom Regan and James Rachels; the legal theorist Steven M. Wise; the writers Joy Williams and Matthew Scully. I didn't think I minded being a speciesist, but could it be, as several of these writers suggest, that we will someday come to regard speciesism as an evil comparable to racism? Will history someday judge us as harshly as it judges the Germans who went about their ordinary lives in the shadow of Treblinka? Precisely that question was recently posed by J. M. Coetzee, the South African novelist, in a lecture delivered at Princeton; he answered it in the affirmative. If animal rightists are right, "a crime of stupefying proportions" (in Coetzee's words) is going on all around us every day, just beneath our notice.

It's an idea almost impossible to entertain seriously, much less to accept, and in the weeks following my restaurant face-off between Singer and the steak, I found myself marshaling whatever mental power I could muster to try to refute it. Yet Singer and his allies managed to trump almost all my objections.

My first line of defense was obvious. Animals kill one another all the time. Why treat animals more ethically than they treat one another? (Ben Franklin tried this one long before me: during a fishing trip, he wondered, "If you eat one another, I don't see why we may not eat you." He admits, however, that the ratio-nale didn't occur to him until the fish were in the frying pan, smelling "admirably well." The advantage of being a "reasonable creature," Franklin remarks, is that you can find a reason for whatever you want to do.) To the "they do it, too" defense, the animal rightist has a devastating reply: do you really want to base your morality on the natural order? Murder and rape are natural, too. Besides, humans don't need to kill other creatures in order to survive; animals do. (Though if my cat, Otis, is any guide, animals sometimes kill for sheer pleasure.)

This suggests another defense. Wouldn't life in the wild be worse for these farm animals? "Defenders of slavery imposed on black Africans often made a similar point," Singer retorts. "The life of freedom is to be preferred."

But domesticated animals can't survive in the wild; in fact, without us they wouldn't exist at all. Or as one nineteenth-century political philosopher put it, "The pig has a stronger interest than anyone in the demand for bacon. If all the world were Jewish, there would be no pigs at all." But it turns out that this would be fine by the animal rightists: for if pigs don't exist, they can't be wronged.

Animals on factory farms have never known any other life. Singer replies that "animals feel a need to exercise, stretch their limbs or wings, groom themselves and turn around, whether or not they have ever lived in conditions that permit this." The measure of their suffering is not their prior experiences but the unremitting daily frustration of their instincts.

OK, the suffering of animals is a legitimate problem, but the world is full of problems, and surely human problems must come first! Sounds good, and yet all the animal people are asking me to do is to stop eating meat and wearing animal furs and hides. There's no reason I can't devote myself to solving humankind's pro-blems while being a vegetarian who wears synthetics.

But doesn't the fact that we could choose to forgo meat for moral reasons point to a crucial moral difference between animals and humans? As Kant pointed out, the human being is the only moral animal, the only one even capable of entertain-ing a concept of "rights." What's wrong with reserving moral consideration for those able to reciprocate it? Right here is where you run smack into the AMC: the moral status of the retarded, the insane, the infant, and the Alzheimer's patient. Such "marginal cases," in the detestable argot of modern moral philosophy, cannot participate in moral decision making any more than a monkey can, yet we never-theless grant them rights.

That's right, I respond, for the simple reason that they're one of us. And all of us have been, and will probably once again be, marginal cases ourselves. What's more, these people have fathers and mothers, daughters and sons, which makes our interest in their welfare deeper than our interest in the welfare of even the most brilliant ape.

Alas, none of these arguments evade the charge of speciesism; the racist, too, claims that it's natural to give special consideration to one's own kind. A utilitarian like Singer would agree, however, that the feelings of relatives do count for some-thing. Yet the principle of equal consideration of interests demands that, given the choice between performing a painful medical experiment on a severely retarded orphan and on a normal ape, we must sacrifice the child. Why? Because the ape has a greater capacity for pain.

Here in a nutshell is the problem with the AMC: it can be used to help the animals, but just as often it winds up hurting the marginal cases. Giving up our speciesism will bring us to a moral cliff from which we may not be prepared to jump, even when logic is pushing us.

And yet this isn't the moral choice I am being asked to make. (Too bad; it would be so much easier!) In everyday life, the choice is not between babies and chimps but between the pork and the tofu. Even if we reject the "hard utilitarianism" of a Peter Singer, there remains the question of whether we owe animals that can feel pain any moral consideration, and this seems impossible to deny. And if we do owe them moral consideration, how can we justify eating them?

This is why killing animals for meat (and clothing) poses the most difficult animal rights challenge. In the case of animal testing, all but the most radical animal rightists are willing to balance the human benefit against the cost to the animals. That's because the unique qualities of human consciousness carry weight in the utilitarian calculus: human pain counts for more than that of a mouse, since our pain is amplified by emotions like dread; similarly, our deaths are worse than an animal's because we understand what death is in a way they don't. So the argument over animal testing is really in the details: is this particular procedure or test really necessary to save human lives? (Very often it's not, in which case we probably shouldn't do it.) But if humans no longer need to eat meat or wear skins, then what exactly are we putting on the human side of the scale to outweigh the interests of the animal?

I suspect that this is finally why the animal people managed to throw me on the defensive. It's one thing to choose between the chimp and the retarded child or to accept the sacrifice of all those pigs surgeons practiced on to develop heart-bypass surgery. But what happens when the choice is between "a lifetime of suffering for a nonhuman animal and the gastronomic preference of a human being?" You look away—or you stop eating animals. And if you don't want to do either? Then you have to try to determine if the animals you're eating have really endured "a lifetime of suffering."

Whether our interest in eating animals outweighs their interest in not being eaten (assuming for the moment that is their interest) turns on the vexed question of animal suffering. Vexed, because it is impossible to know what really goes on in the mind of a cow or a pig or even an ape. Strictly speaking, this is true of other humans, too, but since humans are all basically wired the same way, we have excellent reason to assume that other people's experience of pain feels much like our own. Can we say that about animals? Yes and no.

I have yet to find anyone who still subscribes to Descartes's belief that animals cannot feel pain because they lack a soul. The general consensus among scientists and philosophers is that when it comes to pain, the higher animals are wired much like we are for the same evolutionary reasons, so we should take the writhings of the kicked dog at face value. Indeed, the very premise of a great deal of animal testing—the reason it has value—is that animals' experience of physical and even some psychological pain closely resembles our own....

Which brings us—reluctantly, necessarily—to the American factory farm, the place where all such distinctions turn to dust. It's not easy to draw lines between pain and suffering in a modern egg or confinement hog operation. These are places where the subtleties of moral philosophy and animal cognition mean less than nothing, where everything we've learned about animals at least since Darwin has been simply... set aside. To visit a modern CAFO (Confined Animal Feeding Operation) is to enter a world that, for all its technological sophistication, is still designed according to Cartesian principles: animals are machines incapable of feeling pain. Since no thinking person can possibly believe this any more, industrial animal agriculture depends on a suspension of disbelief on the part of the people who operate it and a willingness to avert your eyes on the part of everyone else.

From everything I've read, egg and hog operations are the worst. Beef cattle in America at least still live outdoors, albeit standing ankle deep in their own waste eating a diet that makes them sick. And broiler chickens, although they do get their beaks snipped off with a hot knife to keep them from cannibalizing one another under the stress of their confinement, at least don't spend their eight-week lives in cages too small to ever stretch a wing. That fate is reserved for the American laying hen, who passes her brief span piled together with a half-dozen other hens in a wire cage whose floor a single page of this magazine could carpet. Every natural instinct of this animal is thwarted, leading to a range of behavioral "vices" that can include cannibalizing her cagemates and rubbing her body against the wire mesh until it is featherless and bleeding. Pain? Suffering? Madness? The operative suspension of disbelief depends on more neutral descriptors, like "vices" and "stress." Whatever you want to call what's going on in those cages, the 10 percent or so of hens that can't bear it and simply die is built into the cost of production. And when the output of the others begins to ebb, the hens will be "force-molted"—starved of food and water and light for several days in order to stimulate a final bout of egg laying before their life's work is done.

Simply reciting these facts, most of which are drawn from poultry-trade magazines, makes me sound like one of those animal people, doesn't it? I don't mean to, but this is what can happen when... you look. It certainly wasn't my intention to ruin anyone's breakfast. But now that I probably have spoiled the eggs, I do want to say one thing about the bacon, mention a single practice (by no means the worst) in modern hog production that points to the compound madness of an impeccable industrial logic.

Piglets in confinement operations are weaned from their mothers 10 days after birth (compared with 13 weeks in nature) because they gain weight faster on their hormone- and antibiotic-fortified feed. This premature weaning leaves the pigs with a lifelong craving to suck and chew, a desire they gratify in confinement by biting the tail of the animal in front of them. A normal pig would fight off his molester, but a demoralized pig has stopped caring. "Learned helplessness" is the psychological term, and it's not uncommon in confinement operations, where tens of thousands of hogs spend their entire lives ignorant of sunshine or earth or straw, crowded together beneath a metal roof upon metal slats suspended over a manure pit. So it's not surprising that an animal as sensitive and intelligent as a pig would get depressed, and a depressed pig will allow his tail to be chewed on to the point of infection. Sick pigs, being underper-forming "production units," are clubbed to death on the spot. The U.S.D.A.'s recommended solution to the problem is called "tail docking." Using a pair of pliers (and no anesthetic), most but not all of the tail is snipped off Why the little stump? Because the whole point of the exercise is not to remove the object of tail-biting so much as to render it more sensitive. Now, a bite on the tail is so painful that even the most demoralized pig will mount a struggle to avoid it.

Much of this description is drawn from *Dominion*, Matthew Scully's recent book in which he offers a harrowing description of a North Carolina hog operation. Scully, a Christian conservative, has no patience for lefty rights talk, arguing instead that while God did give man "dominion" over animals ("Every moving thing that liveth shall be meat for you"), he also admonished us to show them mercy. "We are called to treat them with kindness, not because they have rights or power or some claim to equality but... because they stand unequal and powerless before us."

Scully calls the contemporary factory farm "our own worst nightmare" and, to his credit, doesn't shrink from naming the root cause of this evil: unfettered capitalism. (Perhaps this explains why he resigned from the Bush administration just before his book's publication.) A tension has always existed between the capitalist imperative to maximize efficiency and the moral imperatives of religion or community, which have historically served as a counterweight to the moral blindness of the market. This is one of "the cultural contradictions of capitalism"—the tendency of the economic impulse to erode the moral underpinnings of society. Mercy toward animals is one such casualty.

More than any other institution, the American industrial animal farm offers a nightmarish glimpse of what capitalism can look like in the absence of moral or regulatory constraint. Here in these places life itself is redefined—as protein production—and with it suffering. That venerable word becomes "stress," an economic problem in search of a cost-effective solution, like tail-docking or beak-clipping or, in the industry's latest plan, by simply engineering the "stress gene" out of pigs and chickens. "Our own worst nightmare," such a place may well be; it is also real life for the billions of animals unlucky enough to have been born beneath these grim steel roofs, into the brief, pitiless life of a "production unit" in the days before the suffering gene was found.

Vegetarianism doesn't seem an unreasonable response to such an evil. Who would want to be made complicit in the agony of these animals by eating them? You want to throw something against the walls of those infernal sheds, whether it's the Bible, a new constitutional right or a whole platoon of animal rightists bent on breaking in and liberating the inmates. In the shadow of these factory farms, Coetzee's notion of a "stupefying crime" doesn't seem far-fetched at all.

But before you swear off meat entirely, let me describe a very different sort of animal farm. It is typical of nothing, and yet its very existence puts the whole moral question of animal agriculture in a different light. Polyface Farm occupies 550 acres of rolling grassland and forest in the Shenandoah Valley of Virginia. Here, Joel Salatin and his family raise six different food animals—cattle, pigs, chickens, rabbits, turkeys and sheep—in an intricate dance of symbiosis designed to allow each species, in Salatin's words, "to fully express its physiological distinctiveness."

What this means in practice is that Salatin's chickens live like chickens; his cows, like cows; pigs, pigs. As in nature, where birds tend to follow herbivores, once Salatin's cows have finished grazing a pasture, he moves them out and tows in his "eggmobile," a portable chicken coop that houses several hundred laying hens—roughly the natural size of a flock. The hens fan out over the pasture, eating the short grass and picking insect larvae out of the cowpats—all the while spreading the cow manure and eliminating the farm's parasite problem. A diet of grubs and grass makes for exceptionally tasty eggs and contented chickens, and their nitrogenous manure feeds the pasture. A few weeks later, the chickens move out, and the sheep come in, dining on the lush new growth, as well as on the weed species (nettles, nightshade) that the cattle and chickens won't touch.

Meanwhile, the pigs are in the barn turning the compost. All winter long, while the cattle were indoors, Salatin layered their manure with straw, wood chips—and corn. By March, this steaming compost layer cake stands three feet high, and the pigs, whose powerful snouts can sniff out and retrieve the fermented corn at the bottom, get to spend a few happy weeks rooting through the pile, aerating it as they work. All you can see of these pigs, intently nosing out the tasty alcoholic morsels, are their upturned pink hams and corkscrew tails churning the air. The finished compost will go to feed the grass; the grass, the cattle; the cattle, the chickens; and eventually all of these animals will feed us.

I thought a lot about vegetarianism and animal rights during the day I spent on Joel Salatin's extraordinary farm. So much of what I'd read, so much of what I'd accepted, looked very different from here. To many animal rightists, even Polyface Farm is a death camp. But to look at these animals is to see this for the sentimental conceit it is. In the same way that we can probably recognize animal suffering when we see it, animal happiness is unmistakable, too, and here I was seeing it in abundance.

For any animal, happiness seems to consist in the opportunity to express its creaturely character—its essential pigness or wolfness or chickenness. Aristotle speaks of each creature's "characteristic form of life." For domesticated species, the good life, if we can call it that, cannot be achieved apart from humans—apart from our farms and, therefore, our meat eating. This, it seems to me, is where animal rightists betray a profound ignorance about the workings of nature. To think of domestication as a form of enslavement or even exploitation is to misconstrue the whole relationship, to project a human idea of power onto what is, in fact, an instance of mutualism between species. Domestication is an evolutionary, rather than a political, development. It is certainly not a regime humans imposed on animals some 10,000 years ago.

Rather, domestication happened when a small handful of especially opportunistic species discovered through Darwinian trial and error that they were more likely to survive and prosper in an alliance with humans than on their own. Humans provided the animals with food and protection, in exchange for which the animals provided the humans their milk and eggs and—yes—their flesh. Both parties were transformed by the relationship: animals grew tame and lost their ability to fend for themselves (evolution tends to edit out unneeded traits), and the humans gave up their hunter-gatherer ways for the settled life of agriculturists. (Humans changed biologically, too, evolving such new traits as a tolerance for lactose as adults.)

From the animals' point of view, the bargain with humanity has been a great success, at least until our own time. Cows, pigs, dogs, cats and chickens have thrived, while their wild ancestors have languished. (There are 10,000 wolves in North America, 50,000,000 dogs.) Nor does their loss of autonomy seem to trouble these creatures. It is wrong, the rightists say, to treat animals as "means" rather than "ends," yet the happiness of a working animal like the dog consists precisely in serving as a "means." Liberation is the last thing such a creature wants: To say of one of Joel Salatin's caged chickens that "the life of freedom is to be preferred" betrays an ignorance about chicken preferences—which on this farm are heavily focused on not getting their heads bitten off by weasels.

But haven't these chickens simply traded one predator for another—weasels for humans? True enough, and for the chickens this is probably not a bad deal. For brief as it is, the life expectancy of a farm animal would be considerably briefer in the world beyond the pasture fence or chicken coop. A sheep farmer told me that a bear will eat a lactating ewe alive, starting with her udders. "As a rule," he explained, "animals don't get 'good deaths' surrounded by their loved ones."

The very existence of predation—animals eating animals—is the cause of much anguished hand-wringing in animal rights circles. "It must be admitted," Singer writes, "that the existence of carnivorous animals does pose one problem for the ethics of Animal Liberation, and that is whether we should do anything about it." Some animal rightists train their dogs and cats to become vegetarians. (Note: cats will require nutritional supplements to stay healthy.) Matthew Scully calls predation "the intrinsic evil in nature's design... among the hardest of all things to fathom." Really? A deep Puritan streak pervades animal rights activists, an abiding discomfort not only with our animality, but with the animals' animality too.

However it may appear to us, predation is not a matter of morality or politics; it, also, is a matter of symbiosis. Hard as the wolf may be on the deer he eats, the herd depends on him for its well-being; without predators to cull the herd, deer overrun their habitat and starve. In many places, human hunters have taken over the predator's ecological role. Chickens also depend for their continued well-being on their human predators—not individual chickens, but chickens as a species. The surest way to achieve the extinction of the chicken would be to grant chickens a "right to life."

Yet here's the rub: the animal rightist is not concerned with species, only individuals. Tom Regan, author of *The Case for Animal Rights*, bluntly asserts that because "species are not individuals... the rights view does not recognize the moral rights of species to anything, including survival." Singer concurs, insisting that only sentient individuals have interests. But surely a species can have interests—in its survival, say—just as a nation or community or a corporation can. The animal rights movement's exclusive concern with individual animals makes perfect sense given its roots in a culture of liberal individualism, but does it make any sense in nature?

In 1611 Juan da Goma (aka Juan the Disoriented) made accidental landfall on Wrightson Island, a six-square-mile rock in the Indian Ocean. The island's sole distinction is as the only known home of the Arcania tree and the bird that nests in it, the Wrightson giant sea sparrow. Da Goma and his crew stayed a week, much of that time spent in a failed bid to recapture the ship's escaped goat—who happened to be pregnant. Nearly four centuries later, Wrightson Island is home to 380 goats that have consumed virtually every scrap of vegetation in their reach. The youngest Arcania tree on the island is more than 300 years old, and only 52 sea sparrows remain. In the animal rights view, any one of those goats have at least as much right to life as the last Wrightson sparrow on earth, and the trees, because they are not sentient, warrant no moral consideration whatsoever. (In the mid-80s a British environmental group set out to shoot the goats, but was forced to cancel the expedition after the Mammal Liberation Front bombed its offices.)

The story of Wrightson Island (recounted by the biologist David Ehrenfeld in *Beginning Again*) suggests at the very least that a human morality based on individual rights makes for an awkward fit when applied to the natural world. This should come as no surprise: morality is an artifact of human culture, devised to help us negotiate social relations. It's very good for that. But just as we recognize that nature doesn't provide an adequate guide for human social conduct, isn't it anthropocentric to assume that our moral system offers an adequate guide for nature? We may require a different set of ethics to guide our dealings with the natural world, one as well suited to the particular needs of plants and animals and habitats (where sentience counts for little) as rights suit us humans today.

To contemplate such questions from the vantage of a farm is to appreciate just how parochial and urban an ideology animal rights really is. It could thrive only in a world where people have lost contact with the natural world, where animals no longer pose a threat to us and human mastery of nature seems absolute. "In our normal life," Singer writes, "there is no serious clash of interests between human and nonhuman animals." Such a statement assumes a decidedly urbanized "normal life," one that certainly no farmer would recognize.

The farmer would point out that even vegans have a "serious clash of interests" with other animals. The grain that the vegan eats is harvested with a combine that shreds field mice, while the farmer's tractor crushes woodchucks in their burrows, and his pesticides drop songbirds from the sky. Steve Davis, an animal scientist at Oregon State University, has estimated that if America were to adopt a strictly vegetarian diet, the total number of animals killed every year would actually increase, as animal pasture gave way to row crops. Davis contends that if our goal is to kill as few animals as possible, then people should eat the largest possible animal that can live on the least intensively cultivated land: grass-fed beef for everybody. It would appear that killing animals is unavoidable no matter what we choose to eat.

When I talked to Joel Salatin about the vegetarian utopia, he pointed out that it would also condemn him and his neighbors to importing their food from distant places, since the Shenandoah Valley receives too little rainfall to grow many row crops. Much the same would hold true where I live, in New England. We get plenty of rain, but the hilliness of the land has dictated an agriculture based on animals since the time of the Pilgrims. The world is full of places where the best, if not the only, way to obtain food from the land is by grazing animals on it—especially ruminants, which alone can transform grass into protein and whose presence can actually improve the health of the land.

The vegetarian utopia would make us even more dependent than we already are on an industrialized national food chain. That food chain would in turn be even more dependent than it already is on fossil fuels and chemical fertilizer, since food would need to travel farther and manure would be in short supply. Indeed, it is doubtful that you can build a more sustainable agriculture without animals to cycle nutrients and support local food production. If our concern is for the health of nature —rather than, say, the internal consistency of our moral code or the condition of our souls—then eating animals may sometimes be the most ethical thing to do.

There is, too, the fact that we humans have been eating animals as long as we have lived on this earth. Humans may not need to eat meat in order to survive, yet doing so is part of our evolutionary heritage, reflected in the design of our teeth and the structure of our digestion. Eating meat helped make us what we are, in a social and biological sense. Under the pressure of the hunt, the human brain grew in size and complexity, and around the fire where the meat was cooked, human culture first flourished. Granting rights to animals may lift us up from the brutal world of predation, but it will entail the sacrifice of part of our identity—our own animality.

Surely this is one of the odder paradoxes of animal rights doctrine. It asks us to recognize all that we share with animals and then demands that we act toward them in a most unanimalistic way. Whether or not this is a good idea, we should at least acknowledge that our desire to eat meat is not a trivial matter, no mere "gastronomic preference." We might as well call sex—also now technically unnecessary—a mere "recreational preference." Whatever else it is, our meat eating is something very deep indeed.

Are any of these good enough reasons to eat animals? I'm mindful of Ben Franklin's definition of the reasonable creature as one who can come up with reasons for whatever he wants to do. So I decided I would track down Peter Singer and ask him what he thought. In an e-mail message, I described Poly-face and asked him about the implications for his position of the Good Farm—one where animals got to live according to their nature and to all appearances did not suffer.

"I agree with you that it is better for these animals to have lived and died than not to have lived at all," Singer wrote back. Since the utilitarian is concerned exclusively with the sum of happiness and suffering and the slaughter of an animal that doesn't comprehend that death need not involve suffering, the Good Farm adds to the total of animal happiness, provided you replace the slaughtered animal with a new one. However, he added, this line of thinking doesn't obviate the wrongness of killing an animal that "has a sense of its own existence over time and can have preferences for its own future." In other words, it's OK to eat the chicken, but he's not so sure about the pig. Yet, he wrote, "I would not be sufficiently confident of my arguments to condemn someone who purchased meat from one of these farms."

Singer went on to express serious doubts that such farms could be practical on a large scale, since the pressures of the marketplace will lead their owners to cut costs and corners at the expense of the animals. He suggested, too, that killing animals is not conducive to treating them with respect. Also, since humanely raised food will be more expensive, only the well-to-do can afford morally defensible animal protein. These are important considerations, but they don't alter my essential point: what's wrong with animal agriculture—with eating animals—is the practice, not the principle.

What this suggests to me is that people who care should be working not for animal rights but animal welfare—to ensure that farm animals don't suffer and that their deaths are swift and painless. In fact, the decent-life-merciful-death line is how Jeremy Bentham justified his own meat eating. Yes, the philosophical father of animal rights was himself a carnivore. In a passage rather less frequently quoted by animal rightists, Bentham defended eating animals on the grounds that "we are the better for it, and they are never the worse.... The death they suffer in our hands commonly is, and always may be, a speedier and, by that means, a less painful one than that which would await them in the inevitable course of nature."

My guess is that Bentham never looked too closely at what happens in a slaughterhouse, but the argument suggests that, in theory at least, a utilitarian can justify the killing of humanely treated animals—for meat or, presumably, for clothing....

No doubt the sight of some of these places would turn many people into vegetarians. Many others would look elsewhere for their meat, to farmers like Salatin. There are more of them than I would have imagined. Despite the relentless consolidation of the American meat industry, there has been a revival of small farms where animals still live their "characteristic form of life." I'm thinking of the ranches where cattle still spend their lives on grass, the poultry farms where chickens still go outside, and the hog farms where pigs live as they did 50 years ago—in contact with the sun, the earth and the gaze of a farmer....

The industrialization—and dehumanization—of American animal farming is a relatively new, evitable and local phenomenon: no other country raises and slaughters its food animals quite as intensively or as brutally as we do. Were the walls of our meat industry to become transparent, literally or even figuratively, we would not long continue to do it this way. Tail-docking and sow crates and beak-clipping would disappear overnight, and the days of slaughtering 400 head of cattle an hour would come to an end. For who could stand the sight? Yes, meat would get more expensive. We'd probably eat less of it, too, but maybe when we did eat animals, we'd eat them with the consciousness, ceremony, and respect they deserve.

STUDY QUESTIONS

1. What is "speciesism"? Are people who believe it is right to eat the meat of animals speciesist? Where does Pollan stand on this question?
2. Pollan believes that the meat from certain farms may be eaten. As matters stand now, do you believe that it is right to eat meat at a restaurant without knowing that the animals were treated humanely?
3. What "bargain" was struck between man and domestic animals that Pollan appeals to in arguing for the morality of killing animals for food? How might James Rachels or Peter Singer respond?

The Case Against Animal Rights

Roger Scruton

Roger Scruton (b. 1944) taught philosophy for many years at Birbeck College (London). He has held visiting posts at many other institutions, including Princeton, Stanford, and Cambridge. He is the author of more than twenty books, including *An Intelligent Person's Guide to Philosophy*

Roger Scruton, "The Moral Status of Animals," *Animal Rights and Wrongs*, p. 51–56, 79–83.

(1996), *Death-Devoted Heart: Sex and the Sacred* (2003), and *Culture Counts: Faith and Feeling in a World Besieged* (2007).

Roger Scruton takes a Kantian approach to the question of the moral status of animals. Though we can behave wrongly to animals, we cannot, strictly speaking, wrong them. Animals lack rationality and self-awareness and therefore are not the sort of beings to whom we can meaningfully attribute rights. If animals did have rights, they would be in the moral domain and so, like human beings, they would also have duties and deserve punishments for failure to fulfill their obligations. "Any morality which really attributed rights to animals would therefore constitute a gross and callous abuse of them." Although animals have no rights, human beings do have some obligations to treat them humanely. Humane treatment, says Scruton, falls "under the broader principle of charity."

Scruton's Kantian approach to animals does run into the problem of how to account for the moral rights of nonrational human beings such as infants or the severely retarded. Do these human beings fall outside the moral community? Scruton argues for "extending the shield" to all members of the human species, including the severely mentally impaired. "It is part of human virtue to acknowledge human life as sacrosanct... it is [also] a sign of piety. And... virtue and piety are cornerstones of moral thinking."

... I shall use the term 'animal' to mean those animals that lack the distinguishing features of the moral being—rationality, self-consciousness, personality, and so on. If there are non-human animals who are rational and self-conscious, then they, like us, are persons, and should be described and treated accordingly. If *all* animals are persons, then there is no longer a problem as to how we should treat them. They would be full members of the moral community, with rights and duties like the rest of us. But it is precisely because there are animals who are not persons that the moral problem exists. And to treat these non-personal animals as persons is not to grant to them a privilege nor to raise their chances of contentment. It is to ignore what they essentially are and so to fall out of relation with them altogether.

The concept of the person belongs to the ongoing dialogue which binds the moral community. Creatures who are by nature incapable of entering into this dialogue have neither rights nor duties nor personality. If animals had rights, then we should require their consent before taking them into captivity, training them, domesticating them or in any way putting them to our uses. But there is no conceivable process whereby this consent could be delivered or withheld. Furthermore, a creature with rights is duty-bound to respect the rights of others. The fox would be duty-bound to respect the right to life of the chicken and whole species would be condemned out of hand as criminal by nature. Any law which compelled persons to respect the rights of non-human species would weigh so heavily on the predators as to drive them to extinction in a short while. Any morality which really attributed rights to animals would therefore constitute a gross and callous abuse of them.

Those considerations are obvious, but by no means trivial. For they point to a deep difficulty in the path of any attempt to treat animals as our equals. By ascribing rights to animals, and so promoting them to full membership of the moral community, we tie them in obligations that they can neither fulfil nor comprehend. Not only is this senseless cruelty in itself; it effectively destroys all possibility of cordial and beneficial relations between us and them. Only by refraining from personalising animals do we behave towards them in ways that they can understand. And even the most sentimental animal lovers know this, and confer 'rights' on their favourites in a manner so selective and arbitrary as to show that they are not really dealing with the ordinary moral concept. When a dog savages a sheep no one believes that the dog, rather than its owner, should be sued for damages. Sei Shonagon, in *The Pillow Book*, tells of a dog breaching some rule of court etiquette and being horribly beaten, as the law requires. The scene is most disturbing to the modern reader. Yet surely, if dogs have rights, punishment is what they must expect when they disregard their duties.

But the point does not concern rights only. It concerns the deep and impassable difference between personal relations, founded on dialogue, criticism and the sense of justice, and animal relations, founded on affections and needs. The moral problem of animals arises because they cannot enter into relations of the first kind, while we are so much bound by those relations that they seem to tie us even to creatures who cannot themselves be bound by them.

Defenders of 'animal liberation' have made much of the fact that animals suffer as we do: they feel pain, hunger, cold and fear and therefore, as Singer puts it, have 'interests' which form, or ought to form, part of the moral equation. While this is true, it is only part of the truth. There is more to morality than the avoidance of suffering: to live by no other standard than this one is to avoid life, to forgo risk and adventure, and to sink into a state of cringing morbidity. Moreover, while our sympathies ought to be—and unavoidably will be—extended to the animals, they should not be indiscriminate. Although animals have no rights, we still have duties and responsibilities towards them, or towards some of them. These will cut across the utilitarian equation, distinguishing the animals who are close to us and who have a claim on our protection from those towards whom our duties fall under the broader rule of charity.

This is important for two reasons. Firstly, we relate to animals in three distinct situations, which define three distinct kinds of responsibility: as pets, as domestic animals reared for human purposes and as wild creatures. Secondly, the situation of animals is radically and often irreversibly changed as soon as human beings take an interest in them. Pets and other domestic animals are usually entirely dependent on human care for their survival and well-being; and wild animals, too, are increasingly dependent on human measures to protect their food supplies and habitats.

Some shadow version of the moral law therefore emerges in our dealings with animals. I cannot blithely count the interests of my dog as on a par with the interests of any other dog, wild or domesticated, even though they have an equal capacity for suffering and an equal need for help. My dog has a special claim on me, not wholly dissimilar from the claim of my child. I caused it to be dependent on me precisely by leading it to expect that I would cater for its needs.

The situation is further complicated by the distinction between species. Dogs form life-long attachments and a dog brought up by one person may be incapable of living comfortably with another. A horse may be bought or sold many times, with little or no distress, provided it is properly cared for by each of its owners. Sheep maintained in flocks are every bit as dependent on human care as dogs and horses; but they do not notice it and regard their shepherds and guardians as little more than aspects of the environment, which rise like the sun in the morning and depart like the sun at night.…

It will be said that *natura non fecit saltus*—that nature makes no leaps—and therefore that between the moral being and the cognitive animal there ought to be a continuum, with a grey area in which it simply cannot be determined whether rights, duties and so on are to be imputed on the basis of what we observe. The existence of this continuum is precisely what motivates people who advocate animal 'rights' or who recommend at least that we extend to animals the protection offered by the moral law. To behave in any other way is to make an absolute division, where in fact there is only a gradual transition and a difference of degree.

Two points should be made in answer to this argument. First, the distinguishing features of the moral being—including rationality and self-consciousness—belong to another *system* of behaviour from that which characterises the merely cognitive animal. The transition from the one behavioural system to the other is as absolute a transition as that from vegetable to sentient life, or that from sentience to appetite. This is confirmed by all the other concepts which seem to pile in irresistibly behind the ideas of rationality and personhood—concepts which suggest a distinct form of mental life, unknown to the lower animals.

The second point is this. It is true that we arrive at the rational from the merely animal by the route of behaviour, and that there are degrees of complexity both before and after the transition. But we are dealing here, in Hegel's phrase, with a 'transition from quantity to quality'. Something wholly new emerges as a result of a process which merely adapts what is old. An analogy may help to understand the point. An array of dots on a canvas may look like an array of dots and nothing more. But suddenly, with the addition of just one more dot, a face appears. And this face has a character, a meaning and an identity which no array of dots could ever have. In a similar way, at a certain level of complexity, the behaviour of an animal becomes the expression of a self-conscious person. And this transition is well likened to the emergence of a face, a look, a gaze. Another subject now stands before me, seeing me, not as an animal sees me, but I to I.…

But this brings me to a vexed question, much emphasised by Regan and Singer, the question of 'marginal humans,' as Regan describes them. Even if we grant a distinction between moral beings and other animals, and recognise the importance of rationality, self-consciousness and moral dialogue in defining it, we must admit that many human beings do not lie on the moral side of the dividing line. For example, infants are *not yet* members of the moral community; senile and brain-damaged people are *no longer* members; congenital idiots *never will be* members. Are we to say that they have no rights? Or are we to say that, since they differ in no fundamental respect from animals, that we ought in consistency to treat other animals as we treat these 'marginal' humans? Whichever line we take, the hope of making an absolute moral distinction between human and animal life collapses.

It seems to me that we should clearly distinguish the case of 'pre-moral' infants, from those of the 'post-moral' and 'non-moral' human adults. The former are *potential* moral beings, who will naturally develop, in the conditions of society, into full members of the moral community. Our attitude towards them depends on this fact; and indeed, it is only because we look on them as incipiently rational that we eventually elicit the behaviour that justifies our treatment. Just as an acorn is, by its nature, the seed of an oak tree, so is an infant, by its nature, a potential rational being. And it is only by treating it as such that we enable it to realise this potential and so to become what it essentially is.

The other cases of 'marginal humans' are more problematic. And this is instinctively recognised by all who have to deal with them. Infanticide is an inexcusable crime; but the killing of a human vegetable, however much we shrink from it, may often strike us as understandable, even excusable. Although the law may treat this act as murder, we ourselves, and especially those upon whom the burden falls to protect and nurture this unfortunate creature, will seldom see it in such a light. On the other hand, to imagine that we can simply dispose of mental cripples is to display not only a callousness towards the individual, but also a cold and calculating attitude to the human species and the human form. It is part of human virtue to acknowledge human life as sacrosanct, to recoil from treating other humans, however hopeless their life may seem to us, as merely disposable and to look for the signs of personality wherever the human eye seems able to meet and return our gaze. This is not part of virtue only; it is a sign of piety. And... virtue and piety are cornerstones of moral thinking.

There is a further point to be made. Our world makes sense to us because we divide it into kinds, distinguishing animals and plants by species and instantly recognising the individual as an example of the universal. This recog-nitional expertise is essential to survival and especially to the survival of the hunter-gatherer. And it is essential also to the moral life. I relate to you as a human being and accord to you the privileges attached to the kind. It is in the nature of human beings that, in normal conditions they become members of a moral community, governed by duty and protected by rights. Abnormality in this respect does not cancel membership. It merely compels us to adjust our response. Infants and imbeciles belong to the same kind as you or me: the kind whose normal instances are also moral beings. It is this that causes us to extend to them the shield that we consciously extend to each other and which is built collectively through our moral dialogue.

It is not just that dogs and bears do not belong to the moral community. They have no potential for membership. They are not *the kind of thing* that can settle disputes, that can exert sovereignty over its life and respect the sovereignty of others, that can respond to the call of duty or take responsibility on a matter of trust. Moreover, it should be noted that we do not accord to infants and imbeciles the same rights as we accord to normal adults: in many of our dealings with them we assume the right to bypass their consent. Their disabilities have moral consequences. And although infants cause us no difficulties, since we curtail their rights only in order to enhance them, imbeciles cause us real moral problems.

Much more needs to be said about these difficult cases; for our purposes it is enough, however, to recognise that the difficulty arises not because we make no distinction between moral beings and animals, but precisely because we do make such a distinction, and on very good grounds. It is precisely this that lands us with such an intractable problem, when our instinctive reverence for human beings is thwarted by their inability to respond to it. Our difficulties over 'marginal humans' do not cast doubt on the moral distinction between people and animals; on the contrary, they confirm it.

Study Questions

1. Describe Scruton's concept of a "person." How do persons differ from animals?
2. How does Scruton deal with the problem of "marginal humans"? What role does the concept of belonging to a species play in his arguments? Do you find his arguments reasonable?
3. Scruton ends his remarks on the moral status of animals with the following statement: "Our difficulties over 'marginal humans' do not cast doubt on the moral distinction between people and animals; on the contrary, they confirm it." Comment on this assertion. Do you agree with it? Why or why not?

The Case for Affirmative Action

Barbara Bergman

> Barbara Bergman (b. 1927), a professor emeritus of economics at American University, has written widely on the economics of the labor market. She is the author of *In Defense of Affirmative Action* (1997); *Saving Our Children from Poverty: What the United States Can Learn from France* (1996); and *America's Child Care Problem: The Way Out* (2002).
>
> Bergman takes a critical look at the claim that affirmative action hurts those it intends to help. Using real life examples and quantitative evidence, she argues that though affirmative action has some drawbacks, the positives far outweigh the negatives.

According to its opponents, affirmative action makes blacks lazy and unambitious, ruins the reputations of blacks who could make it on their own, and makes blacks angry at whites and whites angry at blacks. It has even been claimed that affirmative action promotes the popularity of anti-Semitic demagogues in the black community.

Supreme Court Justice Clarence Thomas, in the *Adarand* case, said:

> So-called "benign" discrimination teaches many that because of chronic and apparently immutable handicaps, minorities cannot compete with them without their patronizing indulgence. Inevitably, such programs engender attitudes of superiority or, alternatively,

From *In Defense of Affirmative Action*. New York: Basic Books, Inc., 1996 © 1966 by Basic Books, Inc. Reprinted by permission of the publisher.

provoke resentment among those who believe that they have been wronged by the Government's use of race. These programs stamp minorities with a badge of inferiority and may cause them to develop dependencies or to adopt an attitude that they are "entitled" to preferences.

Just as all potent medications have side effects, affirmative action may well have some results that are bad for blacks or bad for women. To fight a war, you generally have to suffer some casualties; the war may also corrupt some of your own soldiers. As always, the issue is the balance of good and bad: are the bad effects of affirmative action so pervasive and so harmful that they outweigh whatever good might be accomplished?

Affirmative Action and White Behavior

Imagine you are an African American, recently hired for a job that you are perfectly competent to do well. When you start work, however, you find that some of your white colleagues resent your presence, shun you, and do nothing to help you learn the ropes. They do not explain their surly attitude to you, and you do not confront them. What caused this conduct? Were they simply ill disposed to accept an African American coworker? Or might affirmative action be responsible for their behavior, as some claim? Would those white workers have treated you well if the company did not have an affirmative action plan? In other words, did the company's affirmative action plan transform your otherwise congenial and fair-thinking white coworkers into mean-tempered bathers of their black colleague's abilities?

Nobody knows how often black workers who are put into all-white work groups receive hostile treatment, because such information has not been collected systematically. That kind of behavior is probably far from rare. It can make life miserable for the new black employee, sometimes causing him or her to quit or fail. The motive behind at least some hostile behavior is to maintain the segregation that some white workers prefer.

It is not unusual for women placed in previously all-male job crews to be received with hostility out of similar motives. Margaret S. Coleman, who was taken on in a crafts job at a New York telephone company, said this of her experience:

> People don't have a real understanding of the stress involved in being the woman who integrates a job. This stress is incredibly wearing and exhausting. She is in a situation where there is a wall of humanity antagonistically looking at every blemish, and the first sign of weakness is exploited to the max. I wonder how many men would make it if they would see such hate in the eyes of their assessors!

Sometimes the hostility takes the form of sexual harassment.

There has been no research on the treatment of black employees in workplaces with and without affirmative action plans. Lacking research of this type, we cannot reliably distinguish instances of previously benign whites being turned ugly by affirmative action from those in which the whites were not benign to begin with. Thus, we have to conclude that this apparently potent accusation against affirmative action is not based on substantial information. It has been created by some of affirmative action's detractors, with a few anecdotes and some "common sense" serving as raw material. Affirmative action may sometimes be hurtful in the way these detractors claim, but we do not know how often. Pending some definitive research, some anecdotes and some common sense can testify for the defense of affirmative action as well.

I witnessed an incident in which a new African American employee, hired through an affirmative action program, had to face surly coworkers. It occurred when the University of Maryland Economics Department hired its first black secretary while I was a professor there. The three white secretaries who were to be her coworkers campaigned hard against the hiring of this black woman, on the grounds of lack of competence. They never made it clear how they knew she was not competent, but they were quite certain on this point. Our chair was a considerate and gentlemanly older man, but not an enthusiast for racial integration. He took the white secretaries' opposition seriously and did not like to go against them. He quizzed our black candidate's two former employers for twenty minutes each in a vain attempt to find some negative information about her. Without the pressure of affirmative action, she would certainly never have been hired: his reluctance, plus the white secretaries' all-out opposition, would have been decisive. But our chair was a team player when it came to dealing with the university administration, so the black candidate was hired.

Our white secretaries were not haters. I suspect they feared damage to their self-image if they belonged to a work group that included a black person. After she came aboard, their conduct for a time was rather poor. They talked to her as little as possible and did not invite her to join their lunch group. The black secretary tolerated their behavior with seeming serenity and held her peace, since the job was a relatively good one for her and she wanted to keep it. In the matter of competence, our new secretary was not the best, but neither was she the worst. The white secretaries were really decent people, and after a month or so they relented. Perhaps they also realized that she was there to stay, and that nothing could be accomplished by continuing their hostility, which I would guess was hard on their consciences. Thereafter, the four of them worked together normally.

Where was the balance of the good and the bad in this incident? The biggest plus was that a black woman got a job that would not otherwise have been offered to her. The opposition to her appointment shows that race did handicap her, and our affirmative action program redressed that. Our department made a small contribution to the achievement of an integrated society.

Students and staff who came into our department's office saw a work group that was integrated by race, a relatively rare sight at that time.

On the bad side, our black secretary had to suffer being labeled incompetent, although she later was able to remove the label by demonstrating normal competence. She herself was clearly willing to bear the label if doing so was the price of getting and keeping the job. Given the opposition to hiring a black for the job, it is not clear that she would have been spared that label even if the affirmative action program had been kept a secret from the white secretaries, or if she had been hired in the absence of an affirmative action plan, assuming that to be possible. In this case, the good clearly outweighed the bad.

A similar case in the Economics Department at Harvard turned out less happily. Until the early 1980s, the Economics Department, like almost all other Harvard departments, had never had a black person or a woman as a tenured professor. Probably under some pressure, or in response to some incentive from the Harvard administration, the department looked around and found an African

American whom it was willing to hire for a tenured professorship. He was Glen Loury, a very bright theoretician and full professor at the University at Michigan, with a Ph.D. from MIT. Apparently, Loury never was made to feel at home in the Harvard Economics Department and deeply resented that. He transferred to another Harvard department and eventually, after some unrelated difficulties, went to another university. In a letter published in the *New York Times*, Loury testified to his own injury by affirmative action; he has since campaigned against it. We have to believe Loury's word that he was made miserable. However, his diagnosis that it was affirmative action that motivated the actions that constituted his colleagues' unwelcoming behavior may not be as firmly based as his report of his own misery Even in this case, the good outcomes for Loury of affirmative action may have outweighed the bad: his hiring by Harvard gave him a prominent platform for his views he would not otherwise have had.

The suspicion of their peers that they are not competent must be particularly galling to those women and blacks who feel (correctly or not) that they were chosen on the basis of their perceived merit and would have been chosen even in the absence of an affirmative action plan. Such people, who may themselves have come to believe the argument that affirmative action inevitably means the hiring of incompetent people, feel that the affirmative action program has ruined their career by causing them to be labeled incompetent. But the affirmative action plan from hell that turns otherwise congenial colleagues into suspicious nasties has not been documented in a real-life case and may be a myth.

If hostilities and suspicions toward competent black colleagues are generated by affirmative action, they may be temporary. In some cases, such as that of the black secretary hired by the University of Maryland Economics Department, the hostility may diminish as white coworkers come to know blacks as individuals, something that might never occur in the absence of affirmative action. In other cases, the hostility may prove intractable. However, intractable hostility itself testifies to the need for affirmative action programs if there is to be integration.

Sleeping Her Way to the Top

In the days before affirmative action for women, any woman who achieved any kind of success in the workplace was likely to be the subject of remarks that she had "slept her way to the top." In those days, sexual harassment was common, as it remains today. The people who made such remarks were not deploring the demands for sexual favors by those with power to promote. Those demands were an accepted fact of life. Rather, those who made those remarks were maligning both the morals and the competence of any woman who advanced.

Such abusive remarks undoubtedly made life and work more difficult for the women subjected to them. The people who made them were not friendly to women's success in the workplace, or even neutral about it. Many men—and women also—held sexist attitudes, were jealous, and intended the remarks to be damaging and hurtful. They were looking for a way to tear down competent women, destroy respect for them, reduce any authority they might have, and make them fail in their jobs. Now affirmative action has been seized on as a way to disparage women and blacks who get promoted, with similar motives.

When people make remarks about women "sleeping their way to the top" or claim that all or most blacks hired through affirmative action are incompetent, they are expressing their resistance to change and trying to ensure the failure of the beneficiaries of affirmative action. This kind of behavior, assuming that it is wide-spread, certainly reduces the benefits of affirmative action to its intended beneficiaries. In the absence of affirmative action, blacks and women would be spared some ill-natured comments, but they would also be likely to be doing less interesting work, at lower pay and with less chance at promotion. The sentiments and behavior of people who make such comments are exactly what make affirmative action necessary in the first place. Their misbehavior is not valid argument that nothing should be done to counter the effect of their prejudices.

The Four Sons Who Were Not Ashamed

In 1991, the *Washington Post* ran a story about a successful small bank in Washington, D.C. In the picture that accompanies the story, two of the bank's tellers, a black woman and a white woman, stand in their cubicles. Above them, posed on a balcony leading to the suite of executive offices, are the president of the bank and its four vice presidents, all white men. The five white executives on the balcony are revealed in the accompanying story to be a father and his four sons. The four sons look in the picture as if they were posing for the photographer quite proudly, although they knew that the picture and the facts of their family relationship would be in the newspaper. They apparently had little or no fear that they would be disgraced by having their filial relationship to the bank's president revealed to hundreds of thousands of people. Like the alumni children who receive special admission to Harvard, Yale, and Princeton, they probably had never been anxious that people might make hurtful speculations about whether they deserved the slots they occupied or were competent to fill them. They had no worry about accusations that the special hiring plan their dad used to staff the highest executive positions in the bank was unfair to those who might otherwise have had their jobs.

We do not hear warnings to rich and well-connected people that they should refrain from using their influence to get their children into exclusive schools or hired for good jobs. Nobody writes books telling rich people that if they persist in this behavior they will create doubts about the talents of all of the rich children and about whether they deserve their college degrees and jobs. Luckily for the rich and their children, people almost never think to be hateful to them.

Affirmative Action and Laziness

The opponents of affirmative action claim, again without evidence, that affirmative action makes its beneficiaries lazy. In the words of Shelby Steele, "Affirmative action ... offers entitlements, rather than development to blacks. A preference is not a training program; it teaches no skills, instills no values. It only makes a color a passport. ... [T]he worst aspect of racial preferences is that they encourage dependency on entitlements, rather than on our own initiative. Glen Loury asserts that affirmative action discourages the acquisition of skills. In his analysis, anything that helps an unskilled worker get a job in an unskilled occupation decreases that worker's interest in learning a skill and going into a skilled occupation.

These claims are not even mildly plausible. The opposite is far more plausible. Affirmative action should make training more attractive rather than less. Why should a black person aspire to go to business school if he or she has a very low chance of getting a job in management? Many of the jobs that have been reserved for white men and that affirmative action programs try to open up have good on-the-job training opportunities. Shelby Steele's evidence for his theory is a story about a black graduate school colleague who told Steele that he planned not to exert himself too much after he got his Ph.D. degree. The man was true to his promise, says Steele, and got a job as a college administrator. As any college professor will testify, college administrators do have pleasant and easy duties, high pay, high status, good parking spots, and lots of perks like all-expenses-paid travel to nice places. One reason their jobs have been made so nice is that most college administrators are, of course, white men. Steele's contempt for his black colleague's alleged loss of energy and low aspirations does not appear to extend to those white men.

Loury's worry seems to be something like this: if you give a black person who had been excluded from a truck driver's job for reasons of race a fairer chance to get a truck-driving job, he or she will be more likely to pass up a chance to become a lawyer. He seems to think that is a good reason not to fight discrimination in fields like trucking. Loury's argument, to the extent it works at all, works equally well against any improvement in the chances for an unskilled person—black or white—to make a decent living. By that logic, we should tax the wages of lower-paid unskilled workers extra heavily so they will be motivated to acquire skills. Affirmative action seeks to reduce the unfair exclusion of blacks and women from both skilled and unskilled occupations, so there is no reason to think it should make the latter occupations relatively more attractive. (Perhaps the reader is beginning to wonder about the appropriateness of Loury's appointment to the Economics Department at Harvard. But the reader should be informed that silly theories are no disqualification there, as long as they are expressed mathematically.)

Exploring How Blacks Feel about Affirmative Action

The opponents of affirmative action, particularly those who warn blacks that affirmative action will put them at grave disadvantage, have dominated the public discussion of the issue. In an attempt to see what some young blacks think about affirmative action, Sandra Tangri and I asked a group of fifty-two black college students to tell us how they thought affirmative action might affect them.

We first asked the students to imagine themselves working in a job they had gotten without the benefit of affirmative action, a job in which they were doing well. Then their company decides to start an affirmative action plan. The students were asked to agree or disagree with a series of statements about the effect on them of that affirmative action plan. Their responses, given in table 6.1, show that some would worry about possible negative effects: about 20 percent of the students expressed anxiety about being typed as not competent because of the existence of the affirmative action plan (statement 6). However, a large majority would favor their employer starting such a plan. Seventy-five percent agreed with a statement favoring the affirmative action plan (statement 9). Only 4 percent disagreed; the rest apparently were undecided.

The purpose of this questionnaire is to find out how African Americans feel about *affirmative action*. You are asked to think about how affirmative action would be likely to help you or hurt you in various job situations.

Situation I: In this case, you have a job in a company that has never had an affirmative action plan. You got your job because you were clearly the best applicant. There are very few African Americans at your level or above—only you and one other person. You have been doing well, and seem to be well liked. The company wants to increase the number of African American employees, and has decided to start an affirmative action plan. What would you think about that?

	disagree	agree	undecided
1. I would be worried about the plan's effect on me.	58%	27%	15%
2. I think they could probably find quite a few really good African American applicants.	8	79	13
3. I would be glad that there will be more African Americans around.	0	92	8
4. I would be worried that they night hire African Americans who wouldn't work out.	60	17	23
5. Since there are plenty of mediocre whites on the payroll, I wouldn't be worried about a few mediocre blacks.	42	33	25
6. I would fear that some white coworkers would think, I had been hired through affirmative action, and couldn't do the job. My chances for respect would go down.	60	19	21
7. If even one mediocre African American were hired, my future would be threatened.	83	6	11
8. I'd be glad to help the company find promising African Americans to hire.	4	88	8
9. On the whole, I would favor establishing the affirmative action plan.	4	75	21

Data are from a survey conducted by the author and Sandra Tangri.

The students were next invited to put themselves in the place of someone applying for a job at a company with an affirmative action plan (see table 6.2). Only 11 percent said they would pass up a job offered through an affirmative action plan (statement 9); another 6 percent were undecided. Only 12 percent would give up a job gained thanks to affirmative action for one that did not involve affirmative action but was somewhat less advantageous (statement 8).

| TABLE 6.2 | OPINIONS OF BLACK STUDENTS REGARDING THE EFFECTS OF AFFIRMATIVE ACTION ON BLACK JOB APPLICANTS |

The purpose of this questionnaire is to find out how African Americans feel about *affirmative action*. You are asked to think about how affirmative action would be likely to help you or hurt you in various job situations.

Situation II: In this case, you are looking for a job. You answer an advertisement and are told about a job that sounds quite good. You feel confident that you could do well at it. You are offered the job. You find out that the company has very few African American employees and has recently instituted an affirmative action plan. You guess that the plan might have played a part in your being offered the job. What would your reaction be to this offer?

	disagree	agree	undecided
1. I would welcome the chance for such a job, to show what I could do.	0%	89%	11%
2. I would rather be considered only on merit, even if that lowered my chance for an offer.	46	21	33
3. I would accept the job, if it was the best offer I could expect.	6	71	23
4. I would take the job, but I would worry that my white coworkers would think I was unqualified.	56	21	23
5. The people doing the hiring have not judged African American applicants fairly in the past, and that's why the company has so few of them.	11	56	33
6. I would expect that most of the white employees would treat me fairly, and accept me if I do good work.	35	42	23
7. If even a few of my white coworkers doubted my abilities, that would make things very hard for me on the job.	52	27	21
8. If I had another offer in a company where affirmative action wasn't an issue, I would take the other offer, even if it weren't quite as good as the one I could get through affirmative action.	61	12	27
9. I would probably pass up any job offered because of affirmative action, no matter how good.	83	11	6

Data are from a survey conducted by the author and Sandra Tangri.

By a majority of 64 percent to 12 percent, the students thought that affirmative action did more good than harm; 24 percent said they believed it made no difference. However, 82 percent thought that its abolition would make it harder for African Americans to get jobs. Only one of the fifty-two students who participated claimed to have personal knowledge of anybody who had been hurt through affirmative action, and 46 percent said they knew of people who had been helped.

Affirmative Action and Anger

One claim made against affirmative action is that the program's very existence is taken by blacks to be an admission on the part of the white community that it has victimized blacks. This evidence of their victimization supposedly makes blacks angry and therefore susceptible to the rhetoric of extremists such as the anti-Semitic demagogue Louis Farrakhan. Shelby Steele, the leading exponent of this chain of reasoning, goes on to argue that the presence of angry anti-Semites in the black community creates a vicious circle by deceiving the white community into thinking that it needs to continue affirmative action to prevent even more anger from developing.

There obviously is a great deal of black anger in this country, but the connection that Steele draws between affirmative action and black anti-Semitism, and his general point about the connections between oppression, remedies for oppression, and anger, are, when examined, quite implausible. First, blacks' discovery that they were oppressed did not have to wait for the appearance of affirmative action programs. The people who took part in the civil rights agitations of the 1950s and 1960s knew the score, and black people continue to be aware of oppression simply through living their lives. The frequency of gross police misconduct toward African Americans is known to everybody. The humiliating treatment that even well-dressed blacks receive in stores and in their own workplaces perennially demonstrates to blacks that some whites, including some whites in influential positions, are racists.

Second, when a problem is perceived, are we all supposed to just forget it? Are we to adopt the principle that we must never do anything about any problems we see because the people we are trying to help will get angry that the problem has not yet been fixed and will then act irrationally? That principle would condemn us to total immobility in all arenas, not just that of racial unfairness. One could more plausibly argue that oppression that is allowed to continue with no attempt at a remedy produces more anger than openly acknowledged oppression for which a remedy is being attempted.

Affirmative action does arouse anger among some whites, and this reaction does hurt blacks. Some of that white anger is whipped up by the foes of affirmative action, who then proceed to say that white anger is another bad effect of affirmative action. But some of the anger comes from whites who think, correctly or not, that they have been passed over for jobs or promotions because of affirmative action. Unfortunately, any advance, through any method, that gives a black a job that a white wanted and might have had may arouse resentment in the white person displaced, especially if he or she thinks that blacks are not good enough to deserve access to such jobs. If we were to avoid any degree of white resentment, we could accomplish nothing.

STUDY QUESTIONS

1. Some have argued that affirmative action programs reduce incentives for women and minorities to work hard and to gain more qualifications. How does Bergman reply? Does she make her case?
2. Do you believe that affirmative action programs place a stigma on women and minority groups? What does Bergman say?
3. Bergman argues that the children of the rich and well-connected have often benefited from a type of preferential treatment in society. Why not provide some balance by using affirmative action to benefit a historically disadvantaged group? Do you agree with Bergman's analysis?

What Is Wrong with Affirmative Action?

Shelby Steele

Shelby Steele (1946) is the Robert J. and Marion E. Oster Senior Fellow at the Hoover Institution at Stanford University. He is the author of *White Guilt: How Blacks and Whites Together Destroyed the Promise of the Civil Rights Era* (2006); *A Dream Deferred: The Second Betrayal of Black Freedom in America* (1999); and *The Content of Our Character: A New Vision of Race in America* (1990).

In a few short years, when my two children will be applying to college, the affirmative action policies by which most universities offer black students some form of preferential treatment will present me with a dilemma. I am a middle-class black, a college professor, far from wealthy, but also well-removed from the kind of deprivation that would qualify my children for the label "disadvantaged." Both of them have endured racial insensitivity from whites. They have been called names, have suffered slights, and have experienced firsthand the peculiar malevolence that racism brings out in people. Yet, they have never experienced racial discrimination, have never been stopped by their race on any path they have chosen to follow. Still, their society now tells them that if they will only designate themselves as black on their college applications, they will likely do better in the college lottery than if they conceal this fact. I think there is something of a Faustian bargain in this.

Of course, many blacks and a considerable number of whites would say that I was sanctimoniously making affirmative action into a test of character. They would say that this small preference is the meagerest recompense for centuries of unrelieved oppression. And to these arguments other very obvious facts must be added.

From Shelby Steele, *The Content of Our Character*, pp. 111–125. © 1990 St. Martin's Press.

In America, many marginally competent or flatly incompetent whites are hired everyday—some because their white skin suits the conscious or unconscious racial preference of their employer. The white children of alumni are often grand-fathered into elite universities in what can only be seen as a residual benefit of historic white privilege. Worse, white incompetence is always an individual matter, while for blacks it is often confirmation of ugly stereotypes. The Peter Principle was not conceived with only blacks in mind. Given that unfairness cuts both ways, doesn't it only balance the scales of history that my children now receive a slight preference over whites? Doesn't this repay, in a small way, the systematic denial under which their grandfather lived out his days?

So, in theory, affirmative action certainly has all the moral symmetry that fairness requires—the injustice of historical and even contemporary white advantage is offset with black advantage; preference replaces prejudice, inclusion answers exclusion. It is reformist and corrective, even repentant and redemptive. And I would never sneer at these good intentions. Born in the late forties in Chicago, I started my education (a charitable term in this case) in a segregated school and suffered all the indignities that come to blacks in a segregated society. My father, born in the South, only made it to the third grade before the white man's fields took permanent priority over his formal education. And though he educated himself into an advanced reader with an almost professorial authority, he could only drive a truck for a living and never earned more than ninety dollars a week in his entire life. So, yes, it is crucial to my sense of citizenship, to my ability to identify with the spirit and the interests of America, to know that this country, however imperfectly, recognizes its past sins and wishes to correct them.

Yet good intentions, because of the opportunity for innocence they offer us, are very seductive and can blind us to the effects they generate when implemented. In our society, affirmative action is, among other things, a testament to white goodwill and to black power, and in the midst of these heavy investments, its effects can be hard to see. But after twenty years of implementation, I think affirmative action has shown itself to be more bad than good and that blacks—whom I will focus on in this essay—now stand to lose more from it than they gain.

In talking with affirmative action administrators and with blacks and whites in general, it is clear that supporters of affirmative action focus on its good intentions while detractors emphasize its negative effects. Proponents talk about "diversity" and "pluralism"; opponents speak of "reverse discrimination," the unfairness of quotas and set-asides. It was virtually impossible to find people outside either camp. The closest I came was a white male manager at a large computer company who said, "I think it amounts to reverse discrimination, but I'll put up with a little of that for a little more diversity." I'll live with a little of the effect to gain a little of the intention, he seemed to be saying. But this only makes him a halfhearted supporter of affirmative action. I think many people who don't really like affirmative action support it to one degree or another anyway.

I believe they do this because of what happened to white and black Americans in the crucible of the sixties when whites were confronted with their racial guilt and blacks tasted their first real power. In this stormy time white absolution and black power coalesced into virtual mandates for society. Affirmative action became a meeting ground for these mandates in the law, and in the late sixties and early seventies it underwent a remarkable escalation of its mission from simple anti-discrimination enforcement to social engineering by means of quotas, goals, time-tables, set-asides, and other forms of preferential treatment.

Legally, this was achieved through a series of executive orders and EEOC guide-lines that allowed racial imbalances in the workplace to stand as proof of racial discrimination. Once it could be assumed that discrimination explained racial imbalances, it became easy to justify group remedies to presumed discrimination, rather than the normal case-by-case redress for proven discrimination. Preferential treatment through quotas, goals, and so on is designed to correct imbalances based on the assumption that they always indicate discrimination. This expansion of what constitutes discrimination allowed affirmative action to escalate into the business of social engineering in the name of anti-discrimination, to push society toward statistically proportionate racial representation, without any obligation of proving actual discrimination.

What accounted for this shift, I believe, was the white mandate to achieve a new racial innocence and the black mandate to gain power. Even though blacks had made great advances during the sixties without quotas, these mandates, which came to a head in the very late sixties, could no longer be satisfied by anything less than racial preferences. I don't think these mandates in themselves were wrong, since whites clearly needed to do better by blacks and blacks needed more real power in society. But, as they came together in affirmative action, their effect was to distort our understanding of racial discrimination in a way that allowed us to offer the remediation of preference on the basis of mere color rather than actual injury. By making black the color of preference, these mandates have reburdened society with the very marriage of color and preference (in reverse) that we set out to eradicate. The old sin is reaffirmed in a new guise.

But the essential problem with this form of affirmative action is the way it leaps over the hard business of developing a formerly oppressed people to the point where they can achieve proportionate representation on their own (given equal opportunity) and goes straight for the proportionate representation. This may satisfy some whites of their innocence and some blacks of their power, but it does very little to truly up-lift blacks.

A white female affirmative action officer at an Ivy League university told me what many supporters of affirmative action now say: "We're after diversity. We ideally want a student body where racial and ethnic groups are represented according to their proportion in society." When affirmative action escalated into social engineering, diversity became a golden word. It grants whites an egalitarian fairness (innocence) and blacks an entitlement to proportionate representation (power). *Diversity* is a term that applies democratic principles to races and cultures rather than to citizens, despite the fact that there is nothing to indicate that real diversity is the same thing as proportionate representation. Too often the result of this on campuses (for example) has been a democracy of colors rather than of people, an artificial diversity that gives the appearance of an educational parity between black and white students that has not yet been achieved in reality. Here again, racial preferences allow society to leapfrog over the difficult problem of developing blacks to parity with whites and into a cosmetic diversity that covers the blemish of disparity—a full six years after admission, only about 26 percent of black students graduate from college.

Racial representation is not the same thing as racial development, yet affirmative action fosters a confusion of these very different needs. Representation can be manufactured; development is always hard-earned. However, it is the music of innocence and power that we hear in affirmative action that causes us to cling to it and to its distracting emphasis on representation. The fact is that after twenty years of racial preferences, the gap between white and black median income is greater than it was in the seventies. None of this is to say that blacks don't need policies that ensure our right to equal opportunity, but what we need more is the development that will let us take advantage of society's efforts to include us.

I think that one of the most troubling effects of racial preferences for blacks is a kind of demoralization, or put another way, an enlargement of self-doubt. Under affirmative action the quality that earns us preferential treatment is an implied inferiority. However this inferiority is explained—and it is easily enough explained by the myriad deprivations that grew out of our oppression—it is still inferiority. There are explanations, and then there is the fact. And the fact must be borne by the individual as a condition apart from the explanation, apart even from the fact that others like himself also bear this condition. In integrated situations where blacks must compete with whites who may be better prepared, these explanations may quickly wear thin and expose the individual to racial as well as personal self-doubt.

All of this is compounded by the cultural myth of black inferiority that blacks have always lived with. What this means in practical terms is that when blacks deliver themselves into integrated situations, they encounter a nasty little reflex in whites, a mindless, atavistic reflex that responds to the color black with alarm. Attributions may follow this alarm if the white cares to indulge them, and if they do, they will most likely he negative—one such attribution is intellectual ineptness. I think this reflex and the attributions that may follow it embarrass most whites today; therefore, it is usually quickly repressed. Nevertheless, on an equally atavistic level, the black will be aware of the reflex his color triggers and will feel a stab of horror at seeing himself reflected in this way. He, too, will do a quick repression, but a lifetime of such stabbings is what constitutes his inner realm of racial doubt.

The effects of this may be a subject for another essay. The point here is that the implication of inferiority that racial preferences engender in both the white and black mind expands rather than contracts this doubt. Even when the black sees no implication of inferiority in racial preferences, he knows that whites do, so that—consciously or unconsciously—the result is virtually the same. The effect of preferential treatment—the lowering of normal standards to increase black representation—puts blacks at war with an expanded realm of debilitating doubt, so that the doubt itself becomes an unrecognized preoccupation that undermines their ability to perform, especially in integrated situations. On largely white campuses, blacks are five times more likely to drop out than whites. Preferential treatment, no matter how it is justified in the light of day, subjects blacks to a midnight of self-doubt, and so often transforms their advantage into a revolving door.

Another liability of affirmative action comes from the fact that it indirectly encourages blacks to exploit their own past victimization as a source of power and privilege. Victimization, like implied inferiority, is what justifies preference, so that to receive the benefits of preferential treatment one must, to some extent, become invested in the view of one's self as a victim. In this way, affirmative action nurtures a victim-focused identity in blacks. The obvious irony here is that we become inadvertently invested in the very condition we are trying to overcome. Racial preferences send us the message that there is more power in our past suffering than our present achievements—none of which could bring us a *preference* over others.

When power itself grows out of suffering, then blacks are encouraged to expand the boundaries of what qualifies as racial oppression, a situation that can lead us to paint our victimization in vivid colors, even as we receive the benefits of preference. The same corporations and institutions that give us preference are also seen as our oppressors. At Stanford University minority students—some of whom enjoy as much as $15,000 a year in financial aid—recently took over the president's office demanding, among other things, more financial aid. The power to be found in victimization, like any power, is intoxicating and can lend itself to the creation of a new class of super-victims who can feel the pea of victimization under twenty mattresses. Preferential treatment rewards us for being underdogs rather than for moving beyond that status—a misplacement of incentives that, along with its deepening of our doubt, is more a yoke than a spur.

But, I think, one of the worst prices that blacks pay for preference has to do with an illusion. I saw this illusion at work recently in the mother of a middle-class black student who was going off to his first semester of college. "They owe us this, so don't think for a minute that you don't belong there." This is the logic by which many blacks, and some whites, justify affirmative action—it is something "owed," a form of reparation. But this logic overlooks a much harder and less digestible reality, that it is impossible to repay blacks living today for the historic suffering of the race. If all blacks were given a million dollars tomorrow morning it would not amount to a dime on the dollar of three centuries of oppression, nor would it obviate the residues of that oppression that we still carry today. The concept of historic reparation grows out of man's need to impose a degree of justice on the world that simply does not exist. Suffering can be endured and overcome, it cannot be repaid. Blacks cannot be repaid for the injustice done to the race, but we can be corrupted by society's guilty gestures of repayment.

Affirmative action is such a gesture. It tells us that racial preferences can do for us what we cannot do for ourselves. The corruption here is in the hidden incentive *not* to do what we believe preferences will do. This is an incentive to be reliant on others just as we are struggling for self-reliance. And it keeps alive the illusion that we can find some deliverance in repayment. The hardest thing for any sufferer to accept is that his suffering excuses him from very little and never has enough currency to restore him. To think otherwise is to prolong the suffering.

Several blacks I spoke with said they were still in favor of affirmative action because of the "subtle" discrimination blacks were subject to once on the job. One photojournalist said, "They have ways of ignoring you." A black female television producer said, "You can't file a lawsuit when your boss doesn't invite you to the insider meetings without mining your career. So we still need affirmative action." Others mentioned the infamous "glass ceiling" through which blacks can see the top positions of authority but never reach them. But I don't think racial preferences are a protection against this subtle discrimination; I think they contribute to it.

In any workplace, racial preferences will always create two-tiered populations composed of preferreds and unpreferreds. This division makes automatic a perception of enhanced competence for the unpreferreds and of questionable competence for the preferreds—the former earned his way, even though others were given preference, while the latter made it by color as much as by competence. Racial preferences implicitly mark whites with an exaggerated superiority just as they mark blacks with an exaggerated inferiority. They not only reinforce America's oldest racial myth but, for blacks, they have the effect of stigmatizing the already stigmatized.

I think that much of the "subtle" discrimination that blacks talk about is often (not always) discrimination against the stigma of questionable competence that affirmative action delivers to blacks. In this sense, preferences scapegoat the very people they seek to help. And it may be that at a certain level employers impose a glass ceiling, but this may not be against the race so much as against the race's reputation for having advanced by color as much as by competence. Affirmative action makes a glass ceiling virtually necessary as a protection against the corruptions of preferential treatment. This ceiling is the point at which corporations shift the emphasis from color to competency and stop playing the affirmative action game. Here preference backfires for blacks and becomes a taint that holds them back. Of course, one could argue that this taint, which is, after all, in the minds of whites, becomes nothing more than an excuse to discriminate against blacks. And certainly the result is the same in either case—blacks don't get past the glass ceiling. But this argument does not get around the fact that racial preferences now taint this color with a new theme of suspicion that makes it even more vulnerable to the impulse in others to discriminate. In this crucial yet gray area of perceived competence, preferences make whites look better than they are and blacks worse, while doing nothing whatever to stop the very real discrimination that blacks may encounter. I don't wish to justify the glass ceiling here, but only to suggest the very subtle ways that affirmative action revives rather than extinguishes the old rationalizations for racial discrimination.

In education, a revolving door; in employment, a glass ceiling.

I believe affirmative action is problematic in our society because it tries to function like a social program. Rather than ask it to ensure equal opportunity we have demanded that it create parity between the races. But preferential treatment does not teach skills, or educate, or instill motivation. It only passes out entitlement by color, a situation that in my profession has created an unrealistically high demand for black professors. The social engineer's assumption is that this high demand will inspire more blacks to earn Ph.D.'s and join the profession. In fact, the number of blacks earning Ph.D.'s has declined in recent years. A Ph.D. must be developed from preschool on. He requires family and community support. He must acquire an entire system of values that enables him to work hard while delaying gratification. There are social programs, I believe, that can (and should) help blacks *develop* in all these areas, but entitlement by color is not a social program; it is a dubious reward for being black....

I would also like to see affirmative action go back to its original purpose of enforcing equal opportunity—a purpose that in itself disallows racial preferences. We cannot be sure that the discriminatory impulse in America has yet been shamed into inction, and I believe affirmative action can make its greatest contribution by ding a rigorous vigilance in this area. It can guard constitutional rather than racial rights, and help institutions evolve standards of merit and selection that are appropriate to the institution's needs yet as free of racial bias as possible (again, with the understanding that racial imbalances arc not always an indication of racial bias). One of the most important things affirmative action can do is to define exactly what racial discrimination is and how it might manifest itself within a specific institution. The impulse to discriminate *is* subtle and cannot be ferreted out unless its many guises are made clear to people. Along with this there should be monitoring of institutions and heavy sanctions brought to bear when actual discrimination is found. This is the sort of affirmative action that America owes to blacks and to itself. It goes after the evil of discrimination itself while preferences only sidestep the evil and grant entitlement to its *presumed* victims.

But if not preferences, then what I think we need social policies that are committed to two goals: the educational and economic development of disadvantaged people, regardless of race, and the eradication from our society—through close monitoring and severe sanctions—of racial, ethnic, or gender discrimination. Preferences will not deliver us to either of these goals, since they tend to benefit those who are not disadvantaged—middle-class white women and middle-class blacks—and attack one form of discrimination with another. Preferences are inexpensive and carry the glamour of good intentions—change the numbers and the good deed is done. To be against them is to be unkind. But I think the unkindest cut is to bestow on children like my own an undeserved advantage while neglecting the development of those disadvantaged children on the East Side of my city who will likely never be in a position to benefit from a preference. Give my children fairness; give disadvantaged children a better shot at development—better elementary and secondary schools, job training, safer neighborhoods, better financial assistance for college, and so on. Fewer blacks go to college today than ten years ago; more black males of college age are in prison or under the control of the criminal justice system than in college. This despite racial preferences.

The mandates of black power and white absolution out of which preferences emerged were not wrong in themselves. What was wrong was that both races focused more on the goals of these mandates than on the means to the goals. Blacks can have no real power without taking responsibility for their own educational and economic development. Whites can have no racial innocence without earning it by eradicating discrimination and helping the disadvantaged to develop. Because we ignored the means, the goals have not been reached, and the real work remains to be done.

STUDY QUESTIONS

1. Steele claims that affirmative action does little to help African Americans and distracts us from resolving the underlying problems that created the inequities. Do you agree?
2. According to Steele, racial preferences are harmful to the intended beneficiaries because they undermine confidence and create self-doubt. Does he make his case?

CHAPTER 8 | THE MEANING OF LIFE

Faced with the knowledge of our own mortality and seeing the misery about us, we ask for meaning. In the popular mind, being "philosophical" is a good thing to be, especially in moments of difficulty. So we look to philosophy, in the old-fashioned sense, to put the human predicament in a perspective that will help us to accept life with composure. The wise, so we hope and sometimes believe, can show us how to mitigate grief and despair by explaining to us the point of our existence, thereby giving us the courage to live our lives with a measure of understanding and dignity.

Two groups of philosophers speak to us in different ways on the meaning of life. Those who believe in a divine providence offer us their ideas on life's purpose and the value of faith. Religion, as Leo Tolstoy testifies, can lift us from the slough of despair. But secular or agnostic thinkers like Bertrand Russell and Albert Camus ask us to face a harsher truth: life, they say, has no final meaning. Camus even calls our existence "absurd." To cope with our despair, the skeptics impart a different teaching, one designed for the nonbeliever and adapted to a world that seems to have no purpose and that is indifferent to our finite existence.

There are varieties of religion. In the Judeo-Christian tradition, God, though all-powerful, infinite, and unknowable, is nevertheless viewed as a person to whom one may direct complaints, petitions, and questions. Before any philosophers in that tradition can offer the consolations of faith, they must first somehow come to terms with "the problem of evil": If an all-powerful God is good and merciful, why do so many innocent people live in pain and misery? The biblical figure Job, a man of faith who suffered terrible losses and afflictions, addresses this question to God himself and is told that no mere mortal creature can possibly fathom the mysteries of creation. "Where were you when I founded the earth?" Chastened, Job realizes that in a world that is beyond humanity's powers to understand, reason is of no help and unquestioning faith an appropriate response.

For others, it is not suffering, but our finitude that prompts them to ask for the meaning and purpose of our existence. Death seems to render life pointless; why

468

strive if it all must end for everyone? The Chinese poet T'ao Ch'ien does not see this as a theoretical question; rather, it is practical and moral: Since we must die, how should we live our finite lives? T'ao Ch'ien tells us of three answers and recommends the third: "Give yourself to the waves of the Great Change." This note of renunciation is heard in many an Eastern religious classic including the Bhagavad Gita, a Hindu classic. The god Krishna there exhorts the despairing Prince Arjuna to practice a detachment to his fate and points out that such detachment will make it easier for him to do the duty that lies ahead.

Moving back to the West and forward in time, we read *My Confession* of the great Russian novelist, Leo Tolstoy. Tolstoy experienced a prolonged period of melancholy and became obsessed with the idea that human life was pointless. Reason seemed to provide no exit from his despair. Finally, inspired by the lives of peasants who rarely question their hard fates, Tolstoy, like Job, found his salvation in an irrational commitment to living "according to God's law." In still more recent times we have the wisdom of the holocaust survivor, Viktor Frankl, who provides an object lesson for finding meaning and dignity in the midst of inescapable suffering.

For most of us, the problem of the meaning of life comes down to the question of how to live in a world that seems indifferent to our wider purposes. That is a practical problem, and the Stoics saw it that way. Our fates, they said, are largely determined and beyond our control. So we face the problem of coping in a dignified manner. According to the Stoics, most of the misery and despair we experience can be avoided if only we change our attitudes. A harsh world owes us no accounts, and the sooner we realize this, the better off we will be. This admonition is reminiscent of T'ao Ch'ien: the Stoics too counsel us to desist from useless attempts at changing the world, turning us instead to the more promising task of changing ourselves to accept life and death more calmly.

In the twentieth century, especially in the West, the breakdown of faith and the turmoil of the Second World War created an atmosphere of disillusionment that exacerbated the problem of the purpose and meaning of life. Modern philosophers are less attracted to the old proposals of renunciation and acceptance, and new attitudes have come to the fore. Camus and Russell believe that those who find consolation in religion are avoiding the brute facts of our arbitrary and finite existence in a world that has *no* creator and *no* ultimate purpose. For Camus, the proper posture to strike in such a predicament is "defiance." We may be doomed and we may be living in a world that offers no answers to our demand for a final purpose; even so, we must not allow ourselves to become ridiculous and acquiescent by giving way to despair. For Russell, the proper posture is pride, in our ability to penetrate nature's secrets, in our ability to make a precarious place in this world and to do in it what we can to dispel ignorance and alleviate suffering.

Thomas Nagel and Joel Feinberg suggest that a world that lacks an overarching purpose should be confronted with an attitude of irony and a large dose of self-deprecating humor. In any case, as Feinberg reminds us, there is nothing in our predicament to cast serious doubt on the importance of fulfilling ourselves by developing our talents and making a difference to those we love.

Substance, Shadow, and Spirit

T'ao Ch'ien

T'ao Ch'ien (365–427), a government official and farmer, is one of the great figures in Chinese literature. His philosophical poetry is said to be very direct, personal, and to have universal human appeal. In T'ao Ch'ien's words, "Those who share my tastes will all get what I am driving at."

The question of life's meaning arises acutely when we ponder evil and suffering. It is also prompted by the realization of our finitude. The poem "Substance, Shadow, and Spirit" expresses three responses of the poet as he faces mortality. Substance concentrates on the material consolations: because we have only a brief time, we should not abjure life's small pleasures. "When wine is offered, don't refuse." Shadow argues for the Confucian doctrine that places human goodness above physical pleasure. "Do good, and your love will outlive you." Spirit, on the other hand, recommends neither the pursuit of pleasure nor moral activism, but rather surrender and detachment. Spirit's philosophy is Taoist: "Give yourself to the waves of the Great Change."

Noble or base, wise or stupid, none but cling tenaciously to life. This is a great delusion. I have put in the strongest terms the complaints of Substance and Shadow and then, to resolve the matter, have made Spirit the spokesman for naturalness. Those who share my tastes will all get what I am driving at.

I

SUBSTANCE TO SHADOW

Earth and heaven endure forever,
Streams and mountains never change.
Plants observe a constant rhythm,
Withered by frost, by dew restored.
But man, most sentient being of all,
In this is not their equal.
He is present here in the world today,
Then leaves abruptly, to return no more.
No one marks there's one man less—
Not even friends and family think of him;
The things that he once used are all that's left

SUBSTANCE, SHADOW, AND SPIRIT From *The Poetry of T'ao Ch'ien*, translated by James Robert Hightower (1970). Reprinted by permission of Oxford University Press.

To catch their eye and move them to grief.
I have no way to transcend change,
That it must be, I no longer doubt.
I hope you will take my advice:
When wine is offered, don't refuse.

II

Shadow to Substance

No use discussing immortality
When just to keep alive is hard enough.
Of course I want to roam in paradise
But it's a long way there and the road is lost.
In all the time since I met up with you
We never differed in our grief and joy.
In shade we may have parted for a time,
But sunshine always brings us close again.
Still this union cannot last forever—
Together we will vanish into darkness.
The body goes; that fame should also end
Is a thought that makes me burn inside.[1]
Do good, and your love will outlive you;
Surely this is worth your every effort.
While it is true, wine may dissolve care
That is not so good a way as this.

III

Spirit's solution

The Great Potter cannot intervene—
All creation thrives of itself.
That Man ranks with Earth and Heaven
Is it not because of me?
Though we belong to different orders,
Being alive, I am joined to you,
Bound together for good or ill
I cannot refuse to tell you what I know:
The Three August Ones were great saints[2]
But where are they living today?
Though P'eng-tsu lasted a long time[3]
He still had to go before he was ready.
Die old or die young, the death is the same.
Wise or stupid, there is no difference.

---

[1] *burn inside*: Confucius has a similar statement in the *Analects*, XV, 19.

[2] *Three August Ones*: These cannot be identified with certainty. Various suggestions have been made by Chinese commentators.

[3] *a long time*: Traditionally, he lived eight hundred years, a record even in China, and he died regretting that he had not lived out his span.

Drunk every day you may forget,
But won't it shorten your life span?
Doing good is always a joyous thing
But no one has to praise you for it.
Too much thinking harms my life;
Just surrender to the cycle of things,
Give yourself to the waves of the Great Change
Neither happy nor yet afraid.
And when it is time to go, then simply go
Without any unnecessary fuss.

STUDY QUESTIONS

1. Explain the different teachings of Substance, Shadow, and Spirit.
2. How does Spirit resolve the conflict between Substance and Shadow? Do you agree with T'ao Ch'ien that the way of the Spirit is indeed the wisest way? Why?
3. Are there teachings comparable to T'ao Ch'ien's in the Western tradition? Specify and discuss.

The Bhagavad Gita

The Bhagavad Gita (The Song of God) is part of a larger epic poem called the Mahabharata. It was written in its present classical Sanskrit form in the period between A.D. 300 and 500. The Bhagavad Gita occupies a place in Hinduism similar to that of the Gospels in Christianity.

Situations of crisis often cause us to reflect on the meaning of life and death. In particular, soldiers getting ready for battle may be led to ask why they are fighting and killing. In this famous epic poem taken from the Mahabharata, the narrator Sanjaya tells of Prince Arjuna's anguished doubts as he stood ready to engage the enemy. Arjuna is addressing his charioteer, who is really the god Krishna in disguise. He tells Krishna that he sees no point in killing those who oppose him. "Now let them kill me, that will be better." When Krishna says that Arjuna speaks from weakness and self-indulgence, Arjuna begins to doubt whether his scruples are sincere. "Is this real compassion that I feel, or only a delusion?" Krishna points out that Arjuna's compunctions come from being too attached to pleasures, sentiments, and purposes from which he should be free. Should Arjuna achieve real "non-attachment" he would not shrink from doing his duty (his dharma), which he now finds so disagreeable. This passage gives expression to the Hindu teaching that enjoins a combination of action and

THE BHAGAVAD GITA From *Bhagavad Gita: The Song of God* translated by Swami Prabhavananda and Christopher Isherwood. Used with permission of the Vedanta Society of Southern California.

renunciation. All Hindus are expected to perform the duties appropriate to their station, at the same time they are to be emotionally detached from the outcome. A soldier is to fight skillfully and valiantly, but he is not to be concerned with the outcome—be it pain and death or glory and wealth.

[T]he prince looked on the array, and in both armies he recognized fathers and grandfathers, teachers, uncles, sons, brothers, grandsons, fathers-in-law, dear friends, and many other familiar faces.

When Kunti's son saw all those ranks of kinsmen he was filled with deep compassion, and he spoke despairingly, as follows:

ARJUNA: Krishna, Krishna,
Now as I look on
These my kinsmen
Arrayed for battle,
My limbs are weakened,
My mouth is parching,
My body trembles,
My hair stands upright,
My skin seems burning,
The bow Gandiva
Slips from my hand,
My brain is whirling
Round and round,
I can stand no longer:
Krishna, I see such
Omens of evil!
What can we hope from
This killing of kinsmen?

What do I want with
Victory, empire,
Or their enjoyment?
O Govinda,
How can I care for
Power or pleasure,
My own life, even,
When all these others,
Teachers, fathers,
Grandfathers, uncles,
Sons and brothers,
Husbands of sisters,
Grandsons and cousins,
For whose sake only
I could enjoy them
Stand here ready
To risk blood and wealth
In war against us?

Knower of all things,
Though they should slay me

How could I harm them?
I cannot wish it:
Never, never,
Not though it won me
The throne of the three worlds;
How much the less for
Earthly lordship!

Krishna, hearing
The prayers of all men,
Tell me how can
We hope to be happy
Slaying the sons
Of Dhritarashtra?
Evil they may be,
Worst of the wicked,
Yet if we kill them
Our sin is greater.
How could we dare spill
The blood that unites us?
Where is joy in
The killing of kinsmen?

Foul their hearts are
With greed, and blinded:
They see no evil
In breaking of blood-bonds,
See no sin
In treason to comrades.
But we, clear-sighted,
Scanning the ruin
Of families scattered,
Should we not shun
This crime, O Krishna?

We know what fate falls
On families broken:
The rites are forgotten,
Vice rots the remnant
Defiling the women,
And from their corruption
Comes mixing of castes:
The curse of confusion
Degrades the victims
And damns the destroyers.

The rice and the water
No longer are offered;
The ancestors also
Must fall dishonoured
From home in heaven.
Such is the crime

Of the killers of kinsmen:
The ancient, the sacred,
Is broken, forgotten.
Such is the doom
Of the lost, without caste-rites:
Darkness and doubting
And hell for ever.

What is the crime
I am planning, O Krishna?
Murder most hateful,
Murder of brothers!
Am I indeed
So greedy for greatness?

Rather than this
Let the evil children
Of Dhritarashtra
Come with their weapons
Against me in battle:
I shall not struggle,
I shall not strike them.
Now let them kill me,
That will be better.

SANJAYA (THE NARRATOR):   Having spoken thus, Arjuna threw aside his arrows and his bow in the midst of the battlefield. He sat down on the seat of the chariot, and his heart was overcome with sorrow. Then his eyes filled with tears, and his heart grieved and was bewildered with pity. And Sri Krishna spoke to him, saying:

SRI KRISHNA: Arjuna, is this hour of battle the time for scruples and fancies? Are they worthy of you, who seek enlightenment? Any brave man who merely hopes for fame or heaven would despise them.

What is this weakness? It is beneath you. Is it for nothing men call you the foe-consumer? Shake off this cowardice, Arjuna. Stand up.

ARJUNA: Bhisma and Drona are noble and ancient, worthy of the deepest reverence. How can I greet them with arrows, in battle? If I kill them, how can I ever enjoy my wealth, or any other pleasure? It will be cursed with bloodguilt. I would much rather spare them, and eat the bread of a beggar.

Which will be worse, to win this war, or to lose it? I scarcely know. Even the sons of Dhritarashtra stand in the enemy ranks. If we kill them, none of us will wish to live.

Is this real compassion that I feel, or only a delusion? My mind gropes about in darkness. I cannot see where my duty lies. Krishna, I beg you, tell me frankly and clearly what I ought to do. I am your disciple. I put myself into your hands. Show me the way.

Not this world's kingdom,
Supreme, unchallenged,
No, nor the throne
Of the gods in heaven,
Could ease this sorrow
That numbs my senses!

SANJAYA: When Arjuna, the foe-consuming, the never-slothful, had spoken thus to Govinda, ruler of the senses, he added: "I will not fight," and was silent....

ARJUNA: But, Krishna, if you consider knowledge of Brahman superior to any sort of action, why are you telling me to do these terrible deeds?

Your statements seem to contradict each other. They confuse my mind. Tell me one definite way of reaching the highest good. I want to learn the truth about renunciation and non-attachment. What is the difference between these two principles?

SRI KRISHNA: The sages tell us that renunciation means the complete giving-up of all actions which are motivated by desire. And they say that non-attachment means abandonment of the fruits of action.

Some philosophers declare that all kinds of action should be given up, because action always contains a certain measure of evil. Others say that acts of sacrifice, almsgiving and austerity should not be given up. Now you shall hear the truth of this matter.

Acts of sacrifice, almsgiving and austerity should not be given up: Their performance is necessary. For sacrifice, almsgiving and austerity are a means of purification to those who rightly understand them. But even these acts must be performed without attachment or regard for their fruits. Such is my final and considered judgment.

Renunciation is said to be of three kinds. If a man, in his ignorance, renounces those actions which the scriptures ordain, his renunciation is inspired by tamas. If he abstains from any action merely because it is disagreeable, or because he fears it will cause him bodily pain, his renunciation is inspired by rajas. He will not obtain any spiritual benefit from such renunciation. But when a man performs an action which is sanctioned by the scriptures, and does it for duty's sake only, renouncing all attachment and desire for its fruits, then his renunciation is inspired by sattwa.

When a man is endowed with spiritual discrimination and illumined by knowledge of the Atman, all his doubts are dispelled. He does not shrink from doing what is disagreeable to him, nor does he long to do what is agreeable. No human being can give up action altogether, but he who gives up the fruits of action is said to be non-attached.

To those who have not yet renounced the ego and its desires, action bears three kinds of fruit— pleasant, unpleasant, and a mixture of both. They will be reaped in due season. But those who have renounced ego and desire will reap no fruit at all, either in this world or in the next....

STUDY QUESTIONS

1. Hinduism teaches the doctrine of duty for duty's sake: the baker is to bake bread, the soldier to fight, the farmer to till the soil; but they are to be indifferent to the fruits of their labor, be it pain or pleasure, glory or disgrace. Some critics have said that this teaching encourages passivity in the face of social injustice. Is this a fair criticism, or does it reflect a basic misunderstanding of Hindu Philosophy? Explain why.

2. Arjuna's scruples about killing seem reasonable. Do you find Krishna's counterarguments as reasonable? Why? Can you mount a better defense of Arjuna's position than he does himself?

3. Compare Arjuna's doubts to Leo Tolstoy's (selection to follow). Contrast the ways each has resolved his dilemma. Is resignation an essential part of a balanced approach to life? Why?

My Confession

Leo Tolstoy

A biographical sketch of Leo Tolstoy is found on page 357.

Leo Tolstoy describes the feeling of pointlessness that governed him for several years. Reason offered no way out. Life seemed meaningless. Art was no help. All causes and enterprises seemed doomed and without purpose. Science seemed to endorse the notion that life was temporary and that all human endeavor would come to naught. Tolstoy tells us how he lived for years "in this madness" but was saved by his love for simple working people who carry "their own lives and ours upon their shoulders." These people inspired Tolstoy by their irrational faith that life itself was to be lived "according to God's law." Death cannot destroy the union with an infinite God. According to Tolstoy, only an irrational faith can give meaning to life. "Without faith one cannot live." Tolstoy came to believe that the lives of the privileged intelligentsia were empty and futile; by contrast, the hard lives of the peasants were full and meaningful.

Although I regarded authorship as a waste of time, I continued to write during those fifteen years. I had tasted of the seduction of authorship, of the seduction of enormous monetary remunerations and applauses for my insignificant labour, and so I submitted to it, as being a means for improving my material condition and for stifling in my soul all questions about the meaning of my life and life in general.

In my writings I advocated, what to me was the only truth, that it was necessary to live in such a way as to derive the greatest comfort for oneself and one's family.

Thus I proceeded to live, but five years ago something very strange began to happen with me: I was overcome by minutes at first of perplexity and then of an arrest of life, as though I did not know how to live or what to do, and I lost myself and was dejected. But that passed, and I continued to live as before. Then those minutes of perplexity were repeated oftener and oftener, and always in one and the same form. These arrests of life found their expression in ever the same questions: "Why? Well, and then?"...

All that happened with me when I was on every side surrounded by what is considered to be complete happiness. I had a good, loving, and beloved wife, good children, and a large estate, which grew and increased without any labour on my part. I was respected by my neighbours and friends, more than ever before, was praised by strangers, and, without any self-deception, could consider my name famous. With all that, I was not deranged or mentally unsound,—on the contrary, I was in full command of my mental and physical powers, such as I had rarely met with in people of my age: physically I could work in a field, mowing, without falling behind a peasant; mentally I could work from eight to ten hours in succession, without experiencing any consequences from the strain. And while in such condition I arrived at the conclusion that I could not live, and, fearing death, I had to use cunning against myself, in order that I might not take my life.

This mental condition expressed itself to me in this form: my life is a stupid, mean trick played on me by somebody. Although I did not recognize that "somebody" as having created me, the form of the conception that some one had played a mean, stupid trick on me by bringing me into the world was the most natural one that presented itself to me.

Involuntarily I imagined that there, somewhere, there was somebody who was now having fun as he looked down upon me and saw me, who had lived for thirty or forty years, learning, developing, growing in body and mind, now that I had become strengthened in mind and had reached that summit of life from which it lay all before me, standing as a complete fool on that summit and seeing clearly that there was nothing in life and never would be. And that was fun to him—

But whether there was or was not that somebody who made fun of me, did not make it easier for me. I could not ascribe any sensible meaning to a single act, or to my whole life. I was only surprised that I had not understood that from the start. All that had long ago been known to everybody. Sooner or later there would come diseases and death (they had come already) to my dear ones and to me, and there would be nothing left but stench and worms. All my affairs, no matter what they might be, would sooner or later be forgotten, and I myself should not exist. So why should I worry about all these things? How could a man fail to see that and live,—that was surprising! A person could live only so long as he was drunk; but the moment he sobered up, he could not help seeing that all that was only a deception, and a stupid deception at that! Really, there was nothing funny and ingenious about it, but only something cruel and stupid.

Long ago has been told the Eastern story about the traveller who in the steppe is overtaken by an infuriated beast. Trying to save himself from the animal, the traveller jumps into a waterless well, but at its bottom he sees a dragon who opens his jaws in order to swallow him. And the unfortunate man does not dare climb out, lest he perish from the infuriated beast, and does not dare jump down to the bottom of the well, lest he be devoured by the dragon, and so clutches the twig of a wild bush growing in a cleft of the well and holds on to it. His hands grow weak and he feels that soon he shall have to surrender to the peril which awaits him at either side; but he still holds on and sees two mice, one white, the other black, in even measure making a circle around the main trunk of the bush to which he is clinging, and nibbling at it on all sides. Now, at any moment, the bush will break and tear off, and he will fall into the dragon's jaws. The traveller sees that and knows that he will inevitably perish; but while he is still clinging, he sees some drops of honey hanging on the leaves of the bush, and so reaches out for them with his tongue and licks the leaves. Just so I hold on to the branch of life, knowing that the dragon of death is waiting inevitably for me, ready to tear me to pieces, and I cannot understand why I have fallen on such suffering. And I try to lick that honey which used to give me pleasure; but now it no longer gives me joy, and the white and the black mouse day and night nibble at the branch to which I am holding on. I clearly see the dragon, and the honey is no longer sweet to me. I see only the inevitable dragon and the mice, and am unable to turn my glance away from them. That is not a fable, but a veritable, indisputable, comprehensible truth.

The former deception of the pleasures of life, which stifled the terror of the dragon, no longer deceives me. No matter how much one should say to me, "You cannot understand the meaning of life, do not think, live!" I am unable to do so, because I have been doing it too long before. Now I cannot help seeing day and night, which run and lead me up to death. I see that alone, because that alone is the truth. Everything else is a lie.

The two drops of honey that have longest turned my eyes away from the cruel truth, the love of family and of authorship, which I have called an art, are no longer sweet to me.

"My family—" I said to myself, "but my family, my wife and children, they are also human beings. They are in precisely the same condition that I am in: they must either live in the lie or see the terrible truth. Why should they live? Why should I love them, why guard, raise, and watch them? Is it for the same despair which is in me, or for dullness of perception? Since I love them, I cannot conceal the truth from them,— every step in cognition leads them up to this truth. And the truth is death."

"Art, poetry?" For a long time, under the influence of the success of human praise, I tried to persuade myself that that was a thing which could be done, even though death should come and destroy everything, my deeds, as well as my memory of them; but soon I came to see that that, too, was a deception. It was clear to me that art was an adornment of life, a decoy of life. But life lost all its attractiveness for me. How, then, could I entrap others? So long as I did not live my own life, and a strange life bore me on its waves; so long as I believed that life had some sense, although I was not able to express it,—the reflections of life of every description in poetry and in the arts afforded me pleasure, and I was delighted to look at life through this little mirror of art; but when I began to look for the meaning of life, when I experienced the necessity of living myself, that little mirror became either useless, superfluous, and ridiculous, or painful to me. I could no longer console myself with what I saw in the mirror, namely, that my situation was stupid and desperate. It was all right for me to rejoice so long as I believed in the depth of my soul that life had some sense. At that time the play of lights—of the comical, the tragical, the touching, the beautiful, the terrible in life—afforded me amusement. But when I knew that life was meaningless and terrible, the play in the little mirror could no longer amuse me. No sweetness of honey could be sweet to me, when I saw the dragon and the mice that were nibbling down my support....

In my search after the question of life I experienced the same feeling which a man who has lost his way in the forest may experience.

He comes to a clearing, climbs a tree, and clearly sees an unlimited space before him; at the same time he sees that there are no houses there, and that there can be none; he goes back to the forest, into the darkness, and he sees darkness, and again there are no houses.

Thus I blundered in this forest of human knowledge, between the clearings of the mathematical and experimental sciences, which disclosed to me clear horizons, but such in the direction of which there could be no house, and between the darkness of the speculative sciences, where I sunk into a deeper darkness, the farther I proceeded, and I convinced myself at last that there was no way out and could not be.

By abandoning myself to the bright side of knowledge I saw that I only turned my eyes away from the question. No matter how enticing and clear the horizons were that were disclosed to me, no matter how enticing it was to bury myself in the infinitude of this knowledge, I comprehended that these sciences were the more clear, the less I needed them, the less they answered my question.

"Well, I know," I said to myself, "all which science wants so persistently to know, but there is no answer to the question about the meaning of my life." But in the speculative sphere I saw that, in spite of the fact that the aim of the knowledge was directed straight to the answer of my question, or because of that fact, there could be no other answer than what I was giving to myself: "What is the meaning of my life?"—"None." Or, "What will come of my life?"—"Nothing." Or, "Why does everything which exists exist, and why do I exist?"—"Because it exists."

Putting the question to the one side of human knowledge, I received an endless quantity of exact answers about what I did not ask: about the chemical composition of the stars, about the movement of the sun toward the constellation of Hercules, about the origin of species and of man, about the forms of infinitely small, imponderable particles of ether; but the answer in this sphere of knowledge to my question what the meaning of my life was, was always: "You are what you call your life; you are a temporal, accidental conglomeration of particles. The interrelation, the change of these particles, produces in you that which you call life. This congeries will last for some time; then the interaction of these particles will cease, and that which you call life and all your questions will come to an end. You are an accidentally cohering globule of something. The globule is fermenting. This fermentation the globule calls its life. The globule falls to pieces, and all fermentation and all questions will come to an end." Thus the clear side of knowledge answers, and it cannot say anything else, if only it strictly follows its principles.

With such an answer it appears that the answer is not a reply to the question. I want to know the meaning of my life, but the fact that it is a particle of the infinite not only gives it no meaning, but even destroys every possible meaning.

Those obscure transactions, which this side of the experimental, exact science has with speculation, when it says that the meaning of life consists in evolution and the cooperation with this evolution, because of their obscurity and inexactness cannot be regarded as answers.

The other side of knowledge, the speculative, so long as it sticks strictly to its fundamental principles in giving a direct answer to the question, everywhere and at all times has answered one and the same: "The world is something infinite and incomprehensible. Human life is an incomprehensible part of this incomprehensible *all*....."

I lived for a long time in this madness, which, not in words, but in deeds, is particularly characteristic of us, the most liberal and learned of men. But, thanks either to my strange, physical love for the real working class, which made me understand it and see that it is not so stupid as we suppose, or to the sincerity of my conviction, which was that I could know nothing and that the best that I could do was to hang myself,—I felt that if I wanted to live and understand the meaning of life, I ought naturally to look for it, not among those who had lost the meaning of life and wanted to kill themselves, but among those billions of departed and living men who had been carrying their own lives and ours upon their shoulders. And I looked around at the enormous masses of deceased and living men,—not learned and wealthy, but simple men,—and I saw something quite different. I saw that all these billions of men that lived or had lived, all, with rare exceptions, did not fit into my subdivisions, and that I could not recognize them as not understanding the question, because they themselves put it and answered it with surprising clearness. Nor could I recognize them as Epicureans, because their lives were composed rather of privations and suffering than of enjoyment. Still less could I recognize them as senselessly living out their meaningless lives, because every act of theirs and death itself was explained by them. They regarded it as the greatest evil to kill themselves. It appeared, then, that all humanity was in possession of a knowledge of the meaning of life, which I did not recognize and which I condemned. It turned out that rational knowledge did not give any meaning to life, excluded life, while the meaning which by billions of people, by all humanity, was ascribed to life was based on some despised, false knowledge.

The rational knowledge in the person of the learned and the wise denied the meaning of life, but the enormous masses of men, all humanity, recognized this meaning in an irrational knowledge. This irrational knowledge was faith, the same that I could not help but reject. That was God as one and three, the creation in six days, devils and angels, and all that which I could not accept so long as I had not lost my senses.

My situation was a terrible one. I knew that I should not find anything on the path of rational knowledge but the negation of life, and there, in faith, nothing but the negation of reason, which was still more impossible than the negation of life. From the rational knowledge it followed that life was an evil and men knew it,—it depended on men whether they should cease living, and yet they lived and continued to live, and I myself lived, though I had known long ago that life was meaningless and an evil. From faith it followed that, in order to understand life, I must renounce reason, for which alone a meaning was needed.

There resulted a contradiction, from which there were two ways out: either what I called rational was not so rational as I had thought; or that which to me appeared irrational was not so irrational as I had thought. And I began to verify the train of thoughts of my rational knowledge.

In verifying the train of thoughts of my rational knowledge, I found that it was quite correct. The deduction that life was nothing was inevitable; but I saw a mistake. The mistake was that I had not reasoned in conformity with the question put by me. The question was, "Why should I live?" that is, "What real, indestructible essence will come from my phantasmal, destructible life? What meaning has my finite existence in this infinite world?" And in order to answer this question, I studied life.

The solutions of all possible questions of life apparently could not satisfy me, because my question, no matter how simple it appeared in the beginning, included the necessity of explaining the finite through the infinite, and vice versa.

I asked, "What is the extra-temporal, extra-causal, extra-spatial meaning of life?" But I gave an answer to the question, "What is the temporal, causal, spatial meaning of my life?" The result was that after a long labour of mind I answered, "None."

In my reflections I constantly equated, nor could I do otherwise, the finite with the finite, the infinite with the infinite, and so from that resulted precisely what had to result: force was force, matter was matter, will was will, infinity was infinity, nothing was nothing,—and nothing else could come from it.

There happened something like what at times takes place in mathematics: you think you are solving an equation, when you have only an identity. The reasoning is correct, but you receive as a result the answer: $a = a$, or $x = x$, or $o = o$. The same happened with my reflection in respect to the question about the meaning of my life. The answers given by all science to that question are only identities.

Indeed, the strictly scientific knowledge, that knowledge which, as Descartes did, begins with a full doubt in everything, rejects all knowledge which has been taken on trust, and builds everything anew on the laws of reason and experience, cannot give any other answer to the question of life than what I received,—an indefinite answer. It only seemed to me at first that science gave me a positive answer,—Schopenhauer's answer: "Life has no meaning, it is an evil." But when I analyzed the matter, I saw that the answer was not a positive one, but that it was only my feeling which expressed it as such. The answer, strictly expressed, as it is expressed by the Brahmins, by Solomon, and by Schopenhauer, is only an indefinite answer, or an identity, $o = o$, life is nothing. Thus the philosophical knowledge does not negate anything, but only answers that the question cannot be solved by it, that for philosophy the solution remains insoluble.

When I saw that, I understood that it was not right for me to look for an answer to my question in rational knowledge, and that the answer given by rational knowledge was only an indication that the answer might be got if the question were differently put, but only when into the discussion of the question should be introduced the question of the relation of the finite to the infinite. I also understood that, no matter how irrational and monstrous the answers might be that faith gave, they had this advantage that they introduced into each answer the relation of the finite to the infinite, without which there could be no answer.

No matter how I may put the question, "How must I live?" the answer is, "According to God's law." "What real result will there be from my life?"—"Eternal torment or eternal bliss." "What is the meaning which is not destroyed by death?"—"The union with infinite God, paradise."

Thus, outside the rational knowledge, which had to me appeared as the only one, I was inevitably led to recognize that all living humanity had a certain other irrational knowledge, faith, which made it possible to live.

All the irrationality of faith remained the same for me, but I could not help recognizing that it alone gave to humanity answers to the questions of life, and, in consequence of them, the possibility of living.

The rational knowledge brought me to the recognition that life was meaning-less,—my life stopped, and I wanted to destroy myself. When I looked around at people, at all humanity, I saw that people lived and asserted that they knew the meaning of life. I looked back at myself: I lived so long as I knew the meaning of life. As to other people, so even to me, did faith give the meaning of life and the possibility of living.

Looking again at the people of other countries, contemporaries of mine and those passed away, I saw again the same. Where life had been, there faith, ever since humanity had existed, had given the possibility of living, and the chief features of faith were everywhere one and the same.

No matter what answers faith may give, its every answer gives to the finite existence of man the sense of the infinite,— a sense which is not destroyed by suf-fering, privation, and death. Consequently in faith alone could we find the meaning and possibility of life. What, then, was faith? I understood that faith was not merely an evidence of things not seen, and so forth, not revelation (that is only the descrip-tion of one of the symptoms of faith), not the relation of man to man (faith has to be defined, and then God, and not first God, and faith through him), not merely an agreement with what a man was told, as faith was generally understood,—that faith was the knowledge of the meaning of human life, in consequence of which man did not destroy himself, but lived. Faith is the power of life. If a man lives he believes in something. If he did not believe that he ought to live for some purpose, he would not live. If he does not see and understand the phantasm of the finite, he believes in that finite; if he understands the phantasm of the finite, he must believe in the infi-nite. Without faith one cannot live....

In order that all humanity may be able to live, in order that they may continue living, giving a meaning to life, they, those billions, must have another, a real knowledge of faith, for not the fact that I, with Solomon and Schopenhauer, did not kill myself convinced me of the existence of faith, but that these billions had lived and had borne us, me and Solomon, on the waves of life.

Then I began to cultivate the acquaintance of the believers from among the poor, the simple and unlettered folk, of pilgrims, monks, dissenters, peasants. The doctrine of these people from among the masses was also the Christian doctrine that the quasi-believers of our circle professed. With the Christian truths were also mixed in very many superstitions, but there was this difference: the superstitions of our circle were quite unnecessary to them, had no connection with their lives, were only a kind of an Epicurean amusement, while the superstitions of the believers from among the labouring classes were to such an extent blended with their life that it would have been impossible to imagine it without these superstitions,—it was a necessary condi-tion of that life. I began to examine closely the lives and beliefs of these people, and the more I examined them, the more did I become convinced that they had the real faith, that their faith was necessary for them, and that it alone gave them a meaning and possibility of life. In contradistinction to what I saw in our circle, where life with-out faith was possible, and where hardly one in a thousand professed to be a believer, among them there was hardly one in a thousand who was not a believer. In contradistinction to what I saw in our circle, where all life passed in idleness, amusements, and tedium of life, I saw that the whole life of these people was passed in hard work, and that they were satisfied with life. In contradistinction to the people of our circle, who struggled and murmured against fate because of their privations and their suffering, these people accepted diseases and sorrows without any perplexity or opposition, but with the calm and firm conviction that it was all for good. In contradistinction to the fact that the more intelligent we are, the less do we understand the meaning of life and the more do we see a kind of a bad joke in our suffering and death, these people live, suffer, and approach death, and suffer in peace and more often in joy. In contradistinction to the fact that a calm death, a death without terror or despair, is the greatest exception in our circle, a restless, insubmissive, joyless death is one of the greatest exceptions among the masses. And of such people, who are deprived of everything which for Solomon and for me constitutes the only good of life, and who withal experience the greatest happiness, there is an enormous number. I cast a broader glance about me. I examined the life of past and present vast masses of men, and I saw people who in like manner had understood the meaning of life, who had known how to live and die, not two, not three, not ten, but hundreds, thousands, millions. All of them, infinitely diversified as to habits, intellect, culture, situation, all equally and quite contrary to my ignorance knew the meaning of life and of death, worked calmly, bore privations and suffering, lived and died, seeing in that not vanity, but good.

I began to love those people. The more I penetrated into their life, the life of the men now living, and the life of men departed, of whom I had read and heard, the more did I love them, and the easier it became for me to live. Thus I lived for about two years, and within me took place a transformation, which had long been working within me, and the germ of which had always been in me. What happened with me was that the life of our circle,—of the rich and the learned,—not only disgusted me, but even lost all its meaning. All our acts, reflections, sciences, arts,—all that appeared to me in a new light. I saw that all that was mere pampering of the appetites, and that no meaning could be found in it; but the life of all the working masses, of all humanity, which created life, presented itself to me in its real significance. I saw that that was life itself and that the meaning given to this life was truth, and I accepted it.

STUDY QUESTIONS

1. If believing in God makes our lives richer and happier, is that a good enough reason for believing? Is it any kind of proof of God's presence in the world? Explain why.
2. Imagine that Tolstoy has just read Thomas Nagel's little essay (selection to follow) on the meaning of life. His reaction to it is very unfavorable. What does he find wrong with it?
3. Both God and the peasants who believe in him inspire Tolstoy and help him out of the "madness" that overcame him when he thought life was pointless. What inspiration does Tolstoy find in the life of the peasants? How is that related to Tolstoy's faith in God?

A Free Man's Worship

Bertrand Russell

Bertrand Russell (1872–1970) was a clearheaded and fearless thinker who greatly influenced philosophy in the twentieth century. He did groundbreaking work in the logic and the philosophy of language. He wrote many books on morals, politics, religion, education, and history. His style was scintillating and effortless. He worked indefatigably for peace and humanitarian causes throughout his long and productive life. When Russell was awarded the Nobel Prize for literature in 1950, the Nobel Committee described him as "one of our time's most brilliant spokesmen of rationality and humanity, and a fearless champion of free speech and free thought in the West." Readers who want to know more about Russell will enjoy his autobiography. An excerpt from it, which appears at the end of this essay, communicates the flavor of Russell's hatred of injustice and his passion for truth.

Tolstoy had denied that science and reason could provide any grounds for a meaningful existence. Bertrand Russell's "free man's worship" accepts Tolstoy's challenge to find meaning within the boundaries of a rational, scientific worldview. At first, science does seem to present us with a world devoid of meaning. "We arise accidentally." We are constantly subject to the brute power of nature and have but a brief span before extinction. However, blind nature has produced a creature "gifted with sight." Our very consciousness of our predicament is liberating and inspiring. Our desire to know, our capacity to judge, to criticize, to imagine: these all confer meaning on our existence. We find meaning in defying and resisting the brute powers and in cultivating knowledge. Contemplating nature, even contemplating our own inevitable extinction, is liberating. For we are exercising that which is unique in us as visionary and thinking creatures. "Such thought makes us free men." Fate itself is "subdued by the mind."

That man is the product of causes which had no prevision of the end they were achieving; that his origin, his growth, his hopes and fears, his loves and his beliefs, are but the outcome of accidental collocations of atoms; that no fire, no heroism, no intensity of thought and feeling, can preserve an individual life beyond the grave; that all the labors of the ages, all the devotion, all the inspiration, all the noonday brightness of human genius, are destined to extinction in the vast death of the solar system, and that the whole temple of man's achievement must inevitably be buried beneath the debris of a universe in ruins—all these things, if not quite beyond dispute, are yet so nearly certain that no philosophy which rejects them can hope to stand. Only within the scaffolding of these truths, only on the firm foundation of unyielding despair, can the soul's habitation henceforth be safely built.

How, in such an alien and inhuman world, can so powerless a creature as man preserve his aspirations untarnished? A strange mystery it is that nature, omnipotent but blind, in the revolutions of her secular hurryings through the abysses of space, has brought forth at last a child, subject still to her power, but gifted with sight, with knowledge of good and evil, with the capacity of judging all the works of his unthinking mother. In spite of death, the mark and seal of the parental control, man is yet free, during his brief years, to examine, to criticize, to know, and in imagination to create. To him alone, in the world with which he is acquainted, this freedom belongs; and in this lies his superiority to the resistless forces that control his outward life.

The savage, like ourselves, feels the oppression of his impotence before the powers of nature; but having in himself nothing that he respects more than power, he is willing to prostrate himself before his gods, without inquiring whether they are worthy of his worship. Pathetic and very terrible is the long history of cruelty and torture, of degradation and human sacrifice, endured in the hope of placating the jealous gods: surely, the trembling believer thinks, when what is most precious has been freely given, their lust for blood must be appeased, and more will not be required. The religion of Moloch—as such creeds may be generically called—is in essence the cringing submission of the slave, who dare not, even in his heart, allow the thought that his master deserves no adulation. Since the independence of ideals is not yet acknowledged, power may be freely worshiped and receive an unlimited respect, despite its wanton infliction of pain.

But gradually, as morality grows bolder, the claim of the ideal world begins to be felt; and worship, if it is not to cease, must be given to gods of another kind than those created by the savage. Some, though they feel the demands of the ideal, will still consciously reject them, still urging that naked power is worthy of worship. Such is the attitude inculcated in God's answer to Job out of the whirlwind: the divine power and knowledge are paraded, but of the divine goodness there is no hint. Such also is the attitude of those who, in our own day, base their morality upon the struggle for survival, maintaining that the survivors are necessarily the fittest. But others, not content with an answer so repugnant to the moral sense, will adopt the position which we have become accustomed to regard as specially religious, maintaining that, in some hidden manner, the world of fact is really harmonious with the world of ideals. Thus man created God, all-powerful and all-good, the mystic unity of what is and what should be.

But the world of fact, after all, is not good; and, in submitting our judgment to it, there is an element of slavishness from which our thoughts must be purged. For in all things it is well to exalt the dignity of man, by freeing him as far as possible from the tyranny of nonhuman power. When we have realized that power is largely bad, that man, with his knowledge of good and evil, is but a helpless atom in a world which has no such knowledge, the choice is again presented to us: Shall we worship force, or shall we worship goodness? Shall our God exist and be evil, or shall he be recognized as the creation of our own conscience?

The answer to this question is very momentous and affects profoundly our whole morality. The worship of force, to which Carlyle and Nietzsche and the creed of militarism have accustomed us, is the result of failure to maintain our own ideals against a hostile universe: it is itself a prostrate submission to evil, a sacrifice of our best to Moloch. If strength indeed is to be respected, let us respect rather the strength of those who refuse that false "recognition of facts" which fails to recognize that facts are often bad. Let us admit that, in the world we know, there are many things that would be better otherwise, and that the ideals to which we do and must adhere are not realized in the realm of matter. Let us preserve our respect for truth, for beauty, for the ideal of perfection which life does not permit us to attain, though none of these things meet with the approval of the unconscious universe. If power is bad, as it seems to be, let us reject it from our hearts. In this lies man's true freedom: in determination to worship only the God created by our own love of the good, to respect only the heaven which inspires the insight of our best moments. In action, in desire, we must submit perpetually to the tyranny of outside forces; but in thought, in aspiration, we are free, free from our fellow men, free from the petty planet on which our bodies impotently crawl, free even, while we live, from the tyranny of death. Let us learn, then, that energy of faith which enables us to live constantly in the vision of the good; and let us descend, in action, into the world of fact, with that vision always before us.

When first the opposition of fact and ideal grows fully visible, a spirit of fiery revolt, of fierce hatred of the gods, seems necessary to the assertion of freedom. To defy with Promethean constancy a hostile universe, to keep its evil always in view, always actively hated, to refuse no pain that the malice of power can invent, appears to be the duty of all who will not bow before the inevitable. But indignation is still a bondage, for it compels our thoughts to be occupied with an evil world; and in the fierceness of desire from which rebellion springs there is a kind of self-assertion which it is necessary for the wise to overcome. Indignation is a submission of our thoughts but not of our desires; the Stoic freedom in which wisdom consists is found in the submission of our desires but not of our thoughts. From the submission of our desires springs the virtue of resignation; from the freedom of our thoughts springs the whole world of art and philosophy, and the vision of beauty by which, at last, we half reconquer the reluctant world. But the vision of beauty is possible only to unfettered contemplation, to thoughts not weighted by the load of eager wishes; and thus freedom comes only to those who no longer ask of life that it shall yield them any of those personal goods that are subject to the mutations of time.

Although the necessity of renunciation is evidence of the existence of evil, yet Christianity, in preaching it, has shown a wisdom exceeding that of the Promethean philosophy of rebellion. It must be admitted that, of the things we desire, some, though they prove impossible, are yet real goods; others, however, as ardently longed for, do not form part of a fully purified ideal. The belief that what must be renounced is bad, though sometimes false, is far less often false than untamed passion supposes; and the creed of religion, by providing a reason for proving that it is never false, has been the means of purifying our hopes by the discovery of many austere truths.

But there is in resignation a further good element: even real goods, when they are unattainable, ought not to be fretfully desired. To every man comes, sooner or later, the great renunciation. For the young, there is nothing unattainable; a good thing desired with the whole force of a passionate will, and yet impossible, is to them not credible. Yet, by death, by illness, by poverty, or by the voice of duty, we must learn, each one of us, that the world was not made for us, and that, however beautiful may be the things we crave, Fate may nevertheless forbid them. It is the part of courage, when misfortune comes, to bear without repining the ruin of our hopes, to turn away our thoughts from vain regrets. This degree of submission to power is not only just and right: it is the very gate of wisdom.

But passive renunciation is not the whole of wisdom; for not by renunciation alone can we build a temple for the worship of our own ideals. Haunting foreshadowings of the temple appear in the realm of imagination, in music, in architecture, in the untroubled kingdom of reason, and in the golden sunset magic of lyrics, where beauty shines and glows, remote from the touch of sorrow, remote from the fear of change, remote from the failures and disenchantments of the world of fact. In the contemplation of these things the vision of heaven will shape itself in our hearts, giving at once a touchstone to judge the world about us and an inspiration by which to fashion to our needs whatever is not incapable of serving as a stone in the sacred temple.

Except for those rare spirits that are born without sin, there is a cavern of darkness to be traversed before that temple can be entered. The gate of the cavern is despair, and its floor is paved with the gravestones of abandoned hopes. There self must die; there the eagerness, the greed of untamed desire, must be slain, for only so can the soul be freed from the empire of Fate. But out of the cavern, the Gate of Renunciation leads again to the daylight of wisdom, by whose radiance a new insight, a new joy, a new tenderness, shine forth to gladden the pilgrim's heart.

When, without the bitterness of impotent rebellion, we have learned both to resign ourselves to the outward rule of Fate and to recognize that the nonhuman world is unworthy of our worship, it becomes possible at last so to transform and refashion the unconscious universe, so to transmute it in the crucible of imagination, that a new image of shining gold replaces the old idol of clay. In all the multiform facts of the world—in the visual shapes of trees and mountains and clouds, in the events of the life of man, even in the very omnipotence of death—the insight of creative idealism can find the reflection of a beauty which its own thoughts first made. In this way mind asserts its subtle mastery over the thoughtless forces of nature. The more evil the material with which it deals, the more thwarting to untrained desire, the greater is its achievement in inducing the reluctant rock to yield up its hidden treasures, the prouder its victory in compelling the opposing forces to swell the pageant of its triumph. Of all the arts, tragedy is the proudest, the most triumphant; for it builds its shining citadel in the very center of the enemy's country, on the very summit of his highest mountain; from its impregnable watchtowers, his camps and arsenals, his columns and forts, are all revealed; within its walls the free life continues, while the legions of death and pain and despair, and all the servile captains of tyrant Fate, afford the burghers of that dauntless city new spectacles of beauty. Happy those sacred ramparts, thrice happy the dwellers on that all-seeing eminence. Honor to those brave warriors who, through countless ages of warfare, have preserved for us the priceless heritage of liberty and have kept undefiled by sacrilegious invaders the home of the unsubdued.

But the beauty of tragedy does but make visible a quality which, in more or less obvious shapes, is present always and everywhere in life. In the spectacle of death, in the endurance of intolerable pain, and in the irrevocableness of a vanished past, there is a sacredness, an overpowering awe, a feeling of the vastness, the depth, the inexhaustible mystery of existence, in which, as by some strange marriage of pain, the sufferer is bound to the world by bonds of sorrow. In these moments of insight, we lose all eagerness of temporary desire, all struggling and striving for petty ends, all care for the little trivial things that, to a superficial view, make up the common life of day by day; we see, surrounding the narrow raft illumined by the flickering light of human comradeship, the dark ocean on whose rolling waves we toss for a brief hour; from the great night without, a chill blast breaks in upon our refuge; all the loneliness of humanity amid hostile forces is concentrated upon the individual soul, which must struggle alone, with what of courage it can command, against the whole weight of a universe that cares nothing for its hopes and fears. Victory, in this struggle with the powers of darkness, is the true baptism into the glorious company of heroes, the true initiation into the overmastering beauty of human existence. From that awful encounter of the soul with the outer world, renunciation, wisdom, and charity are born; and with their birth a new life begins. To take into the inmost shrine of the soul the irresistible forces whose puppets we seem to be—death and change, the irrevocableness of the past, and the powerlessness of man before the blind hurry of the universe from vanity to vanity—to feel these things and know them is to conquer them.

This is the reason why the past has such magical power. The beauty of its motionless and silent pictures is like the enchanted purity of late autumn, when the leaves, though one breath would make them fall, still glow against the sky in golden glory. The past does not change or strive like Duncan, after life's fitful fever it sleeps well; what was eager and grasping, what was petty and transitory, has faded away; the things that were beautiful and eternal shine out of it like stars in the night. Its beauty, to a soul not worthy of it, is unendurable; but to a soul which has conquered Fate it is the key of religion.

The life of man, viewed outwardly, is but a small thing in comparison with the forces of nature. The slave is doomed to worship Time and Fate and Death, because they are greater than anything he finds in himself, and because all his thoughts are of things which they devour. But, great as they are, to think of them greatly, to feel their passionless splendor, is greater still. And such thought makes us free men; we no longer bow before the inevitable in Oriental subjection, but we absorb it and make it a part of ourselves. To abandon the struggle for private happiness, to expel all eagerness of temporary desire, to burn with passion for eternal things—this is emancipation, and this is the free man's worship. And this liberation is effected by contemplation of Fate; for Fate itself is subdued by the mind which leaves nothing to be purged by the purifying fire of time.

United with his fellow men by the strongest of all ties, the tie of a common doom, the free man finds that a new vision is with him always, shedding over every daily task the light of love. The life of man is a long march through the night, surrounded by invisible foes, tortured by weariness and pain, toward a goal that few can hope to reach, and where none may tarry long. One by one, as they march, our comrades vanish from our sight, seized by the silent orders of omnipotent death.

Very brief is the time in which we can help them, in which their happiness or misery is decided. Be it ours to shed sunshine on their path, to lighten their sorrows by the balm of sympathy, to give them the pure joy of a never-tiring affection, to strengthen failing courage, to instill faith in hours of despair. Let us not weigh in grudging scales their merits and demerits, but let us think only of their need—of the sorrows, the difficulties, perhaps the blindnesses, that make the misery of their lives; let us remember that they are fellow sufferers in the same darkness, actors in the same tragedy with ourselves. And so, when their day is over, when their good and their evil have become eternal by the immortality of the past, be it ours to feel that; where they suffered, where they failed, no deed of ours was the cause; but wherever a spark of the divine fire kindled in their hearts, we were ready with encouragement, with sympathy, with brave words in which high courage glowed.

Brief and powerless is man's life; on him and all his race the slow, sure doom falls pitiless and dark. Blind to good and evil, reckless of destruction, omnipotent matter rolls on its relentless way; for man, condemned today to lose his dearest, tomorrow himself to pass through the gate of darkness, it remains only to cherish, ere yet the blow fall, the lofty thoughts that ennoble his little day; disdaining the coward terrors of the slave of Fate, to worship at the shrine that his own hands have built; undismayed by the empire of chance, to preserve a mind free from the wanton tyranny that rules his outward life; proudly defiant of the irresistible forces that tolerate, for a moment, his knowledge and his condemnation, to sustain alone, a weary but unyielding Atlas, the world that his own ideals have fashioned despite the trampling march of unconscious power.

Love, Knowledge, and Pity

Three passions, simple but overwhelmingly strong, have governed my life: the longing for love, the search for knowledge, and unbearable pity for the suffering of mankind. These passions, like great winds, have blown me hither and thither, in a wayward course, over a deep ocean of anguish, reaching to the very verge of despair.

I have sought love, first, because it brings ecstasy—ecstasy so great that I would often have sacrificed all the rest of life for a few hours of this joy. I have sought it, next, because it relieves loneliness—that terrible loneliness in which one shivering consciousness looks over the rim of the world into the cold unfathomable lifeless abyss. I have sought it, finally, because in the union of love I have seen, in a mystic miniature, the prefiguring vision of the heaven that saints and poets have imagined. This is what I sought, and though it might seem too good for human life, this is what—at last—I have found.

With equal passion I have sought knowledge. I have wished to understand the hearts of men. I have wished to know why the stars shine. And I have tried to apprehend the Pythagorean power by which number holds sway above the flux. A little of this, but not much, I have achieved.

Love and knowledge, so far as they were possible, led upward toward the heavens. But always pity brought me back to earth. Echoes of cries of pain reverberate in my heart. Children in famine, victims tortured by oppressors, helpless old people a hated burden to their sons, and the whole world of loneliness, poverty, and pain make a mockery of what human life should be. I long to alleviate the evil, but I cannot, and I too suffer.

This has been my life. I have found it worth living, and would gladly live it again if the chance were offered me.

STUDY QUESTIONS

1. Russell describes the evolution of religions from "the religion of Moloch" to more idealistic and humanitarian forms of worship. Some contemporary cults have rituals reminiscent of ancient, brutal religions. What, in your opinion, is their appeal? Has Russell underestimated the "brute powers" within us? Explain.
2. What does Russell mean when he says: "Of all the arts, tragedy is the proudest, the most triumphant; for it builds its shining citadel in the very center of the enemy's country...."
3. Russell tells us to "burn with passion for eternal things." What are these "eternal things"?
4. If there were a debate between Bertrand Russell and Leo Tolstoy over religion, who do you think would win? Explain.
5. Russell, like Albert Camus (see next essay), speaks of defiance. But he seems more optimistic and upbeat about life, and he does not concede that life is absurd. What in Russell's thinking leads him to reject the fatalistic proposition that life is meaningless? Why does Camus disagree?

The Myth of Sisyphus

Albert Camus

Albert Camus (1913–1960) was born and educated in Algeria. In 1940 he moved to Paris where he became active in French intellectual life. He was editor of *Le Combat*, an underground publication of the French Resistance. He is the author of several important literary works: most notably *The Stranger, The Plague,* and *The Fall.* His philosophical essays include *The Rebel* and *The Myth of Sisyphus.* In 1957 Camus received the Nobel Prize for literature. He died tragically at age 47 in a car accident.

After the grotesque and brutal behavior of the Nazis in Europe in the middle of the twentieth century, many could no longer believe that "God's in His heaven, all's right with the world." Camus, writing at that time, was addressing a public that had lost faith. Many people felt alien in a world

THE MYTH OF SISYPHUS From *The Myth of Sisyphus* by Albert Camus, translated by Justin O'Brien, copyright © 1955, 1983 by Alfred A. Knopf. Used by permission of Alfred A. Knopf, a division of Random House, Inc.

that seemed no longer to offer moral guidance. Camus agreed and sympathized with those who said that life had no meaning. But he rejected despair and asked: Does it follow that life is not worth living? If that did follow, suicide would be reasonable. Camus did not believe he could honestly offer anyone the comfort of a doctrine that attributes meaning to life. But he argued that life's absurdity does not entail suicide. On the contrary, the proper attitude to adopt in the face of absurdity and alienation is defiance. "That revolt gives life its value." To kill oneself is to give in to the absurdity; it is to acquiesce. We must not succumb to meaninglessness. "It is essential to die unreconciled and not of one's own free will."

Absurdity and Suicide

There is but one truly serious philosophical problem, and that is suicide. Judging whether life is or is not worth living amounts to answering the fundamental question of philosophy.... A world that can be explained even with bad reasons is a familiar world. But, on the other hand, in a universe suddenly divested of illusions and lights, man feels an alien, a stranger. His exile is without remedy since he is deprived of the memory of a lost home or the hope of a promised land. This divorce between man and his life, the actor and his setting, is properly the feeling of absurdity. All healthy men having thought of their own suicide, it can be seen, without further explanation, that there is a direct connection between this feeling and the longing for death.

The subject of this essay is precisely this relationship between the absurd and suicide, the exact degree to which suicide is a solution to the absurd. The principle can be established that for a man who does not cheat, what he believes to be true must determine his action. Belief in the absurdity of existence must then dictate his conduct. It is legitimate to wonder, clearly and without false pathos, whether a conclusion of this importance requires forsaking as rapidly as possible an incomprehensible condition.... Hitherto, and it has not been wasted effort, people have played on words and pretended to believe that refusing to grant a meaning to life necessarily leads to declaring that it is not worth living. In truth, there is no necessary common measure between these two judgments. One merely has to refuse to be misled by the confusions, divorces, and inconsistencies previously pointed out. One must brush everything aside and go straight to the real problem. One kills oneself because life is not worth living, that is certainly a truth—yet an unfruitful one because it is a truism. But does that insult to existence, that flat denial in which it is plunged come from the fact that it has no meaning? Does its absurdity require one to escape it through hope or suicide—this is what must be clarified, hunted down, and elucidated while brushing aside all the rest. Does the Absurd dictate death? This problem must be given priority over others, outside all methods of thought and all exercises of the disinterested mind....

Absurd Freedom

I don't know whether this world has a meaning that transcends it. But I know that I do not know that meaning and that it is impossible for me just now to know it.

What can a meaning outside my condition mean to me? I can understand only in human terms. What I touch, what resists me—that is what I understand. And these two certainties—my appetite for the absolute and for unity and the impossibility of reducing this world to a rational and reasonable principle—I also know that I cannot reconcile them. What other truth can I admit without lying, without bringing in a hope I lack and which means nothing within the limits of my condition?

If I were a tree among trees, a cat among animals, this life would have a meaning, or rather this problem would not arise, for I should belong to this world. I should *be* this world to which I am now opposed by my whole consciousness and my whole insistence upon familiarity. This ridiculous reason is what sets me in opposition to all creation. I cannot cross it out with a stroke of the pen. What I believe to be true I must therefore preserve. What seems to me so obvious, even against me, I must support. And what constitutes the basis of that conflict, of that break between the world and my mind, but the awareness of it? If therefore I want to preserve it, I can through a constant awareness, ever revived, ever alert. This is what, for the moment, I must remember. At this moment the absurd, so obvious and yet so hard to win, returns to a man's life and finds its home there. At this moment, too, the mind can leave the arid, dried-up path of lucid effort. That path now emerges in daily life. It encounters the world of the anonymous impersonal pronoun "one," but henceforth man enters in with his revolt and his lucidity. He has forgotten how to hope. This hell of the present is his Kingdom at last. All problems recover their sharp edge. Abstract evidence retreats before the poetry of forms and colors. Spiritual conflicts become embodied and return to the abject and magnificent shelter of man's heart. None of them is settled. But all are transfigured. Is one going to die, escape by the leap, rebuild a mansion of ideas and forms to one's own scale? Is one, on the contrary, going to take up the heartrending and marvelous wager of the absurd? Let's make a final effort in this regard and draw all our conclusions. The body, affection, creation, action, human nobility will then resume their places in this mad world. At last man will again find there the wine of the absurd and the bread of indifference on which he feeds his greatness.

Let us insist again on the method: it is a matter of persisting. At a certain point on his path the absurd man is tempted. History is not lacking in either religions or prophets, even without gods. He is asked to leap. All he can reply is that he doesn't fully understand, that it is not obvious. Indeed, he does not want to do anything but what he fully understands. He is assured that this is the sin of pride, but he does not understand the notion of sin; that perhaps hell is in store, but he has not enough imagination to visualize that strange future; that he is losing immortal life, but that seems to him an idle consideration. An attempt is made to get him to admit his guilt. He feels innocent. To tell the truth, that is all he feels—his irreparable innocence. This is what allows him everything. Hence, what he demands of himself is to live *solely* with what he knows, to accommodate himself to what is, and to bring in nothing that is not certain. He is told that nothing is. But this at least is a certainty. And it is with this that he is concerned: he wants to find out if it is possible to live *without appeal*.

Now I can broach the notion of suicide. It has already been felt what solution might be given. At this point the problem is reversed. It was previously a question of finding out whether or not life had to have a meaning to be lived. It now becomes clear, on the contrary, that it will be lived all the better if it has no meaning. Living an experience, a particular fate, is accepting it fully. Now, no one will live this fate, knowing it to be absurd, unless he does everything to keep before him that absurd brought to light by consciousness. Negating one of the terms of the opposition on which he lives amounts to escaping it. To abolish conscious revolt is to elude the problem. The theme of permanent revolution is thus carried into individual experience. Living is keeping the absurd alive. Keeping it alive is, above all, contemplating it. Unlike Eurydice, the absurd dies only when we turn away from it. One of the only coherent philosophical positions is thus revolt. It is a constant confrontation between man and his own obscurity. It is an insistence upon an impossible transparency. It challenges the world anew every second. Just as danger provided man the unique opportunity of seizing awareness, so metaphysical revolt extends awareness to the whole of experience. It is that constant presence of man in his own eyes. It is not aspiration, for it is devoid of hope. That revolt is the certainty of a crushing fate, without the resignation that ought to accompany it.

This is where it is seen to what a degree absurd experience is remote from suicide. It may be thought that suicide follows revolt—but wrongly. For it does not represent the logical outcome of revolt. It is just the contrary by the consent it presupposes. Suicide, like the leap, is acceptance at its extreme. Everything is over and man returns to his essential history. His future, his unique and dreadful future—he sees and rushes toward it. In its way, suicide settles the absurd. It engulfs the absurd in the same death. But I know that in order to keep alive, the absurd cannot be settled. It escapes suicide to the extent that it is simultaneously awareness and rejection of death. It is, at the extreme limit of the condemned man's last thought, that shoelace that despite everything he sees a few yards away, on the very brink of his dizzying fall. The contrary of suicide, in fact, is the man condemned to death.

That revolt gives life its value. Spread out over the whole length of a life, it restores its majesty to that life. To a man devoid of blinders, there is no finer sight than that of the intelligence at grips with a reality that transcends it. The sight of human pride is unequaled. No disparagement is of any use. That discipline that the mind imposes on itself, that will conjured up out of nothing, that face-to-face struggle have something exceptional about them. To impoverish that reality whose inhumanity constitutes man's majesty is tantamount to impoverishing him himself. I understand then why the doctrines that explain everything to me also debilitate me at the same time. They relieve me of the weight of my own life, and yet I must carry it alone. At this juncture, I cannot conceive that a skeptical metaphysics can be joined to an ethics of renunciation.

Consciousness and revolt, these rejections are the contrary of renunciation. Everything that is indomitable and passionate in a human heart quickens them, on the contrary, with its own life. It is essential to die unreconciled and not of one's own free will. Suicide is a repudiation. The absurd man can only drain everything to the bitter end, and deplete himself. The absurd is his extreme tension, which he maintains constantly by solitary effort, for he knows that in that consciousness and in that day-to-day revolt he gives proof of his only truth, which is defiance.

STUDY QUESTIONS

1. Why does Camus say that the most serious philosophical problem is the problem of suicide? In what sense is life absurd? According to Camus, what is the relationship between "the absurd" and the question of suicide?
2. Explain what Camus means by saying that life "will be lived all the better if it has no meaning" and "Living is keeping the absurd alive." How does he reach these conclusions?
3. Why does Camus think that defiance is the appropriate response to absurdity? Do you agree? Explain.
4. Camus believed that those who deny life's absurdity are fooling themselves. Do you agree that life is absurd? If you do, what do you find most convincing about Camus's argument? If you do not, can you answer Camus's accusation that you are avoiding facing some unpleasant truth about the meaning or meaninglessness of life?
5. Is there any possible world that Camus would *not* find absurd? What sort of world would satisfy his conditions for meaning?
6. Bertrand Russell and Albert Camus are dining together. They have both just read Tolstoy's "My Confession." Write an account of their conversation discussing it.

The Meaning of Life

Thomas Nagel

A biographical sketch of Thomas Nagel is found on page 113.

What is the point of living? We'll be dead anyway in one hundred years. One possible answer is that the point of living can be found within our (mortal) lives. We all have large or small chains of projects, such as working to earn money to feed our families and getting ready to go to bed so that we can sleep because we are tired. Each act has a point and the sum of these constitutes the meaning of life. But may we not ask: what is the point of *life as a whole?*

Looking at life in the larger context, "from the outside," we may ask, "Why does my whole existence matter? The *whole* thing does not seem to matter." Thomas Nagel acknowledges that the demand for ultimate meaning may be legitimate. Many of us need to feel that our lives are important in the large sense. We want to matter "from the outside" and not merely within our own little scheme of things. But our lives probably do not have any such enduring meanings. On the other hand, we cannot help taking ourselves seriously. Our predicament renders us slightly ridiculous, even absurd.

THE MEANING OF LIFE From *What Does It All Mean?: A Very Short Introduction to Philosophy* by Thomas Nagel, copyright © 1987 by Thomas Nagel. Used by permission of Oxford University Press.

Perhaps you have had the thought that nothing really matters, because in two hundred years we'll all be dead. This is a peculiar thought, because it's not clear why the fact that we'll be dead in two hundred years should imply that nothing we do now really matters.

The idea seems to be that we are in some kind of rat race, struggling to achieve our goals and make something of our lives, but that this makes sense only if those achievements will be permanent. But they won't be. Even if you produce a great work of literature which continues to be read thousands of years from now, eventually the solar system will cool or the universe will wind down or collapse, and all trace of your efforts will vanish. In any case, we can't hope for even a fraction of this sort of immortality. If there's any point at all to what we do, we have to find it within our own lives.

Why is there any difficulty in that? You can explain the point of most of the things you do. You work to earn money to support yourself and perhaps your family. You eat because you're hungry, sleep because you're tired, go for a walk or call up a friend because you feel like it, read the newspaper to find out what's going on in the world. If you didn't do any of those things you'd be miserable; so what's the big problem?

The problem is that although there are justifications and explanations for most of the things, big and small, that we do *within* life, none of these explanations explain the point of your life as a whole—the whole of which all these activities, successes and failures, strivings and disappointments are parts. If you think about the whole thing, there seems to be no point to it at all. Looking at it from the outside, it wouldn't matter if you had never existed. And after you have gone out of existence, it won't matter that you did exist.

Of course your existence matters to other people—your parents and others who care about you—but taken as a whole, their lives have no point either, so it ultimately doesn't matter that you matter to them. You matter to them and they matter to you, and that may give your life a feeling of significance, but you're just taking in each other's washing, so to speak. Given that any person exists, he has needs and concerns which make particular things and people within his life matter to him. But the *whole thing* doesn't matter.

But does it matter that it doesn't matter? "So what?" you might say. "It's enough that it matters whether I get to the station before my train leaves, or whether I've remembered to feed the cat. I don't need more than that to keep going." This is a perfectly good reply. But it only works if you really can avoid setting your sights higher, and asking what the point of the whole thing is. For once you do that, you open yourself to the possibility that your life is meaningless.

The thought that you'll be dead in two hundred years is just a way of seeing your life embedded in a larger context, so that the point of smaller things inside it seems not to be enough—seems to leave a larger question unanswered. But what if your life as a whole did have a point in relation to something larger? Would that mean that it wasn't meaningless after all?

There are various ways your life could have a larger meaning. You might be part of a political or social movement which changed the world for the better, to the benefit of future generations. Or you might just help provide a good life for your own children and their descendants. Or your life might be thought to have meaning in a religious context, so that your time on Earth was just a preparation for an eternity in direct contact with God.

About the types of meaning that depend on relations to other people, even people in the distant future, I've already indicated what the problem is. If one's life has a point as a part of something larger, it is still possible to ask about that larger thing, what is the point of *it?* Either there's an answer in terms of something still larger or there isn't. If there is, we simply repeat the question. If there isn't, then our search for a point has come to an end with something which has no point. But if that pointlessness is acceptable for the larger thing of which our life is a part, why shouldn't it be acceptable already for our life taken as a whole? Why isn't it all right for your life to be pointless? And if it isn't acceptable there, why should it be acceptable when we get to the larger context? Why don't we have to go on to ask, "But what is the point of all *that?*" (human history, the succession of the generations, or whatever).

The appeal to a religious meaning to life is a bit different. If you believe that the meaning of your life comes from fulfilling the purpose of God, who loves you, and seeing Him in eternity, then it doesn't seem appropriate to ask, "And what is the point of *that?*" It's supposed to be something which is its own point, and can't have a purpose outside itself. But for this very reason it has its own problems.

The idea of God seems to be the idea of something that can explain everything else, without having to be explained itself. But it's very hard to understand how there could be such a thing. If we ask the question, "Why is the world like this?" and are offered a religious answer, how can we be prevented from asking again, "And why is *that* true?" What kind of answer would bring all of our "Why?" questions to a stop, once and for all? And if they can stop there, why couldn't they have stopped earlier?

The same problem seems to arise if God and His purposes are offered as the ultimate explanation of the value and meaning of our lives. The idea that our lives fulfil God's purpose is supposed to give them their point, in a way that doesn't require or admit of any further point. One isn't supposed to ask, "What is the point of God?" any more than one is supposed to ask, "What is the explanation of God?"

But my problem here, as with the role of God as ultimate explanation, is that I'm not sure I understand the idea. Can there really be something which gives point to everything else by encompassing it, but which couldn't have, or need, any point itself ? Something whose point can't be questioned from outside because there is no outside?

If God is supposed to give our lives a meaning that we can't understand, it's not much of a consolation. God as ultimate justification, like God as ultimate explanation, may be an incomprehensible answer to a question that we can't get rid of. On the other hand, maybe that's the whole point, and I am just failing to understand religious ideas. Perhaps the belief in God is the belief that the universe is intelligible, but not to us.

Leaving that issue aside, let me return to the smaller-scale dimensions of human life. Even if life as a whole is meaningless, perhaps that's nothing to worry about. Perhaps we can recognize it and just go on as before. The trick is to keep your eyes on what's in front of you, and allow justifications to come to an end inside your life, and inside the lives of others to whom you are connected. If you ever ask yourself the question, "But what's the point of being alive at all?"— leading the particular life of a student or bartender or whatever you happen to be—you'll answer, "There's no point. It wouldn't matter if I didn't exist at all, or if I didn't care about anything. But I do. That's all there is to it."

Some people find this attitude perfectly satisfying. Others find it depressing, though unavoidable. Part of the problem is that some of us have an incurable tendency to take ourselves seriously. We want to matter to ourselves "from the outside." If our lives as a whole seem pointless, then a part of us is dissatisfied— the part that is always looking over our shoulders at what we are doing. Many human efforts, particularly those in the service of serious ambitions rather than just comfort and survival, get some of their energy from a sense of importance—a sense that what you are doing is not just important to you, but important in some larger sense: important, period. If we have to give this up, it may threaten to take the wind out of our sails. If life is not real, life is not earnest, and the grave is its goal, perhaps it's ridiculous to take ourselves so seriously. On the other hand, if we can't help taking ourselves so seriously, perhaps we just have to put up with being ridiculous. Life may be not only meaningless but absurd.

STUDY QUESTIONS

1. "We want to matter to ourselves 'from the outside.'" What does Nagel mean by this?
2. Explain Nagel's objections to a religious approach to the question of the meaning of life. How might a person of faith answer Nagel?
3. Contrast Nagel and Camus in the way they approach the question of life's meaning. How does each react to the idea that life may be meaningless and absurd?
4. A, despairingly: "Life does not matter." B, cynically: "If that is true, why should it matter that it does not matter?" What is A's response? Continue the exchange.

Existentialism Is Humanism

Jean-Paul Sartre

TRANSLATED BY BERNARD FRECHTMAN

Jean-Paul Sartre (1905–1980) was a French existentialist and is well known for his novels, plays, and philosophical works. With the outbreak of World War II he served in the French Army and became a leader in the French Resistance. He was awarded the Nobel Prize for literature in 1964, but refused it.

EXISTENTIALISM IS HUMANISM From *Existentialism* by Jean-Paul Sartre. Translated by Bernard Frechtman. Reprinted by permission of the publisher, The Philosophical Library.

Sartre briefly explains existentialism as the doctrine that, in human beings, "existence precedes essence." An inanimate object—Sartre's example is a paper-cutter—is designed by someone who had in mind the object's purpose (essence) and then brought it into being (essence precedes existence). Human beings have no prior essence. We exist first and then determine what sort of beings we shall be (existence precedes essence). This is what Sartre means when he says that "man is nothing else but what he makes of himself." We are always faced with choices; in choosing we make ourselves what we are. Herein lies our dignity and our tragedy, for we can find no excuses for what we are. "The full responsibility of [our] existence rest[s] on [us]." In choosing a particular course of action as the right one to follow, we choose it as right for every other conscious being. With every act we "create an image of man as we think he ought to be." In this sense we create right and wrong. The responsibility is awesome; ethically we are alone and anguished. Sartre is an atheistic existentialist and recognizes no God-given rules. "That is the very starting point of existentialism": Human freedom is unqualified, and so is human responsibility.

What is meant by the term *existentialism?*

Most people who use the word would be rather embarrassed if they had to explain it, since, now that the word is all the rage, even the work of a musician or painter is being called existentialist....It seems that for want of an advance-guard doctrine analogous to surrealism, the kind of people who are eager for scandal and flurry turn to this philosophy which in other respects does not at all serve their purposes in this sphere.

Actually, it is the least scandalous, the most austere of doctrines. It is intended strictly for specialists and philosophers. Yet it can be defined easily. What complicates matters is that there are two kinds of existentialists; first, those who are Christian, among whom I include Jaspers and Gabriel Marcel, both Catholic; and on the other hand, the atheistic existentialists, among whom I class Heidegger, and then the French existentialists and myself. What they have in common is that they think that existence precedes essence, or, if you prefer, that subjectivity must be the starting point.

Just what does that mean? Let us consider some object that is manufactured, for example, a book or a paper-cutter: here is an object which has been made by an artisan whose inspiration came from a concept. He referred to the concept of what a paper-cutter is and likewise to a known method of production, which is part of the concept, something which is, by and large, a routine. Thus, the paper-cutter is at once an object produced in a certain way and, on the other hand, one having a specific use; and one cannot postulate a man who produces a paper-cutter but does not know what it is used for. Therefore, let us say that, for the paper-cutter, essence—that is, the ensemble of both the production routines and the properties which enable it to be both produced and defined— precedes existence. Thus, the presence of the paper-cutter or book in front of me is determined. Therefore, we have here a technical view of the world whereby it can be said that production precedes existence.

When we conceive God as the Creator, He is generally thought of as a superior sort of artisan. Whatever doctrine we may be considering, whether one like that of Descartes or that of Leibnitz, we always grant that will more or less follows understanding or, at the very least, accompanies it, and that when God creates He knows exactly what He is creating. Thus, the concept of man in the mind of God is comparable to the concept of paper-cutter in the mind of the manufacturer, and, following certain techniques and a conception, God produces man, just as the artisan, following a definition and a technique, makes a paper-cutter. Thus, the individual man is the realization of a certain concept in the divine intelligence.

In the eighteenth century, the atheism *of the philosophes* discarded the idea of God, but not so much for the notion that essence precedes existence. To a certain extent, this idea is found everywhere; we find it in Diderot, in Voltaire, and even in Kant. Man has a human nature; this human nature, which is the concept of the human, is found in all men, which means that each man is a particular example of a universal concept, man. In Kant, the result of this universality is that the wild-man, the natural man, as well as the bourgeois, are circumscribed by the same definition and have the same basic qualities. Thus, here too the essence of man precedes the historical existence that we find in nature.

Atheistic existentialism, which I represent, is more coherent. It states that if God does not exist, there is at least one being in whom existence precedes essence, a being who exists before he can be defined by any concept, and that this being is man, or, as Heidegger says, human reality. What is meant here by saying that existence precedes essence? It means that, first of all, man exists, turns up, appears on the scene, and, only afterwards, defines himself. If man, as the existentialist conceives him, is indefinable, it is because at first he is nothing. Only afterward will he be something, and he himself will have made what he will be. Thus, there is no human nature, since there is no God to conceive it. Not only is man what he conceives himself to be, but he is also only what he wills himself to be after this thrust toward existence.

Man is nothing else but what he makes of himself. Such is the first principle of existentialism. It is also what is called subjectivity, the name we are labeled with when charges are brought against us. But what do we mean by this, if not that man has a greater dignity than a stone or table? For we mean that man first exists, that is, that man first of all is the being in the future. Man is at the start a plan which is aware of itself, rather than a patch of moss, a piece of garbage, or a cauliflower; nothing exists prior to this plan; there is nothing in heaven; man will be what he will have planned to be. Not what he will want to be. Because by the word "will" we generally mean a conscious decision, which is subsequent to what we have already made of ourselves. I may want to belong to a political party, write a book, get married; but all that is only a manifestation of an earlier, more spontaneous choice that is called "will." But if existence really does precede essence, man is responsible for what he is. Thus, existentialism's first move is to make every man aware of what he is and to make the full responsibility of his existence rest on him. And when we say that a man is responsible for himself, we do not only mean that he is responsible for his own individuality, but that he is responsible for all men.

The word subjectivism has two meanings, and our opponents play on the two. Subjectivism means, on the one hand, that an individual chooses and makes himself; and, on the other, that it is impossible for man to transcend human subjectivity. The second of these is the essential meaning of existentialism. When we say that man chooses his own self, we mean that every one of us does likewise; but we also mean by that that in making this choice he also chooses all men. In fact, in creating the man that we want to be, there is not a single one of our acts which does not at the same time create an image of man as we think he ought to be. To choose to be this or that is to affirm at the same time the value of what we choose, because we can never choose evil. We always choose the good, and nothing can be good for us without being good for all.

If, on the other hand, existence precedes essence, and if we grant that we exist and fashion our image at one and the same time, the image is valid for everybody and for our whole age. Thus, our responsibility is much greater than we might have supposed, because it involves all mankind. If I am a workingman and choose to join a Christian trade-union rather than be a communist, and if by being a member I want to show that the best thing for man is resignation, that the kingdom of man is not of this world, I am not only involving my own case—I want to be resigned for everyone. As a result, my action has involved all humanity. To take a more individual matter, if I want to marry, to have children; even if this marriage depends solely on my own circumstances or passion or wish, I am involving all humanity in monogamy and not merely myself. Therefore, I am responsible for myself and for everyone else. I am creating a certain image of man of my own choosing. In choosing myself, I choose man.

This helps us understand what the actual content is of such rather grandiloquent words as anguish, forlornness, despair. As you will see, it's all quite simple.

First, what is meant by anguish? The existentialists say at once that man is anguish. What that means is this: the man who involves himself and who realizes that he is not only the person he chooses to be, but also a law-maker who is, at the same time, choosing all mankind as well as himself, cannot help escape the feeling of his total and deep responsibility. Of course, there are many people who are not anxious; but we claim that they are hiding their anxiety, that they are fleeing from it. Certainly, many people believe that when they do something, they themselves are the only ones involved, and when someone says to them, "What if everyone acted that way?" they shrug their shoulders and answer, "Everyone doesn't act that way." But really, one should always ask himself, "What would happen if everybody looked at things that way?" There is no escaping this disturbing thought except by a kind of double-dealing. A man who lies and makes excuses for himself by saying "not everybody does that," is someone with an uneasy conscience, because the act of lying implies that a universal value is conferred upon the lie.

Anguish is evident even when it conceals itself. This is the anguish that Kierkegaard called the anguish of Abraham. You know the story: an angel has ordered Abraham to sacrifice his son; if it really were an angel who has come and said, "You are Abraham, you shall sacrifice your son," everything would be all right. But everyone might first wonder, "Is it really an angel, and am I really Abraham? What proof do I have?"...

Now, I'm not being singled out as an Abraham, and yet at every moment I'm obliged to perform exemplary acts. For every man, everything happens as if all mankind had its eyes fixed on him and were guiding itself by what he does. And every man ought to say to himself, "Am I really the kind of man who has the right to act in such a way that humanity might guide itself by my actions?" And if he does not say that to himself, he is masking his anguish.

There is no question here of the kind of anguish which would lead to quietism, to inaction. It is a matter of a simple sort of anguish that anybody who has had responsibilities is familiar with. For example, when a military officer takes the responsibility for an attack and sends a certain number of men to death, he chooses to do so, and in the main he alone makes the choice. Doubtless, orders come from above, but they are too broad; he interprets them, and on this interpretation depend the lives of ten or fourteen or twenty men. In making a decision he cannot help having a certain anguish. All leaders know this anguish. That doesn't keep them from acting; on the contrary, it is the very condition of their action. For it implies that they envisage a number of possibilities, and when they choose one, they realize that it has value only because it is chosen. We shall see that this kind of anguish, which is the kind that existentialism describes, is explained, in addition, by a direct responsibility to the other men whom it involves. It is not a curtain separating us from action, but is part of action itself.

When we speak of forlornness, a term Heidegger was fond of, we mean only that God does not exist and that we have to face all the consequences of this. The existentialist is strongly opposed to a certain kind of secular ethics which would like to abolish God with the least possible expense. About 1880, some French teachers tried to set up a secular ethics which went something like this: God is a useless and costly hypothesis; we are discarding it; but meanwhile, in order for there to be an ethics, a society, a civilization, it is essential that certain values be taken seriously and that they be considered as having an *a priori* existence. It must be obligatory, *a priori*, to be honest, not to lie, not to beat your wife, to have children, etc., etc. So we're going to try a little device which will make it possible to show that values exist all the same, inscribed in a heaven of ideas, though otherwise God does not exist. In other words—and this, I believe, is the tendency of everything called reformism in France—nothing will be changed if God does not exist. We shall find ourselves with the same norms of honesty, progress, and humanism, and we shall have made of God an outdated hypothesis which will peacefully die off by itself.

The existentialist, on the contrary, thinks it very distressing that God does not exist, because all possibility of finding values in a heaven of ideas disappears along with Him; there can be no longer an *a priori* Good, since there is no infinite and perfect consciousness to think it. Nowhere is it written that the Good exists, that we must be honest, that we must not lie; because the fact is we are on a plane where there are only men. Dostoievsky said, "If God didn't exist, everything would be possible." That is the very starting point of existentialism. Indeed, everything is permissible if God does not exist, and as a result man is forlorn, because neither within him nor without does he find anything to cling to. He can't start making excuses for himself.

If existence really does precede essence, there is no explaining things away by reference to a fixed and given human nature. In other words, there is no determinism, man is free, man is freedom. On the other hand, if God does not exist, we find no values or commands to turn to which legitimize our conduct. So, in the bright realm of values, we have no excuse behind us, no justification before us. We are alone, with no excuses.

That is the idea I shall try to convey when I say that man is condemned to be free. Condemned, because he did not create himself, yet, in other respects is free; because, once thrown into the world, he is responsible for everything he does. The existentialist does not believe in the power of passion. He will never agree that a sweeping passion is a ravaging torrent which fatally leads a man to certain acts and is therefore an excuse. He thinks that man is responsible for his passion.

The existentialist does not think that man is going to help himself by finding in the world some omen by which to orient himself. Because he thinks that man will interpret the omen to suit himself. Therefore, he thinks that man, with no support and no aid, is condemned every moment to invent man. Ponge, in a very fine article, has said, "Man is the future of man." That's exactly it. But if it is taken to mean that this future is recorded in heaven, that God sees it, then it is false, because it would really no longer be a future. If it is taken to mean that, whatever a man may be, there is a future to be forged, a virgin future before him, then this remark is sound. But then we are forlorn.

To give you an example which will enable you to understand forlornness better, I shall cite the case of one of my students who came to see me under the following circumstances: his father was on bad terms with his mother, and, moreover, was inclined to be a collaborationist; his older brother had been killed in the German offensive of 1940, and the young man, with somewhat immature but generous feelings, wanted to avenge him. His mother lived alone with him, very much upset by the half-treason of her husband and the death of her older son; the boy was her only consolation.

The boy was faced with the choice of leaving for England and joining the Free French Forces—that is, leaving his mother behind—or remaining with his mother and helping her carry on. He was fully aware that the woman lived only for him and that his going-off—and perhaps his death—would plunge her into despair. He was also aware that every act that he did for his mother's sake was a sure thing, in the sense that it was helping her to carry on, whereas every effort he made toward going off and fighting was an uncertain move which might run aground and prove completely useless; for example, on his way to England he might, while passing through Spain, be detained indefinitely in a Spanish camp; he might reach England or Algiers and be stuck in an office at a desk job. As a result, he was faced with two very different kinds of action: one, concrete, immediate, but concerning only one individual; the other concerned an incomparably vaster group, a national collectivity, but for that very reason was dubious, and might be interrupted en route. And, at the same time, he was wavering between two kinds of ethics. On the one hand, an ethics of sympathy, of personal devotion; on the other, a broader ethics, but on whose efficacy was more dubious. He had to choose between the two.

Who could help him choose? Christian doctrine? No. Christian doctrine says, "Be charitable, love your neighbor, take the more rugged path, etc., etc." But which is the more rugged path? Whom should he love as a brother? The fighting man or his mother? Which does the greater good, the vague act of fighting in a group, or the concrete one of helping a particular human being to go on living? Who can decide *a priori*? Nobody. No book of ethics can tell him. The Kantian ethics says, "Never treat any person as a means, but as an end." Very well, if I stay with my mother, I'll treat her as an end and not as a means; but by virtue of this very fact,

I'm running the risk of treating the people around me who are fighting, as means; and, conversely, if I go to join those who are fighting, I'll be treating them as an end, and, by doing that, I run the risk of treating my mother as a means.

If values are vague, and if they are always too broad for the concrete and specific case that we are considering, the only thing left for us is to trust our instincts. That's what this young man tried to do; and when I saw him, he said, "In the end, feeling is what counts. I ought to choose whichever pushes me in one direction. If I feel that I love my mother enough to sacrifice everything else for her—my desire for vengeance, for action, for adventure—then I'll stay with her. If, on the contrary, I feel that my love for my mother isn't enough, I'll leave."

But how is the value of a feeling determined? What gives his feeling for his mother value? Precisely the fact that he remained with her. I may say that I like so-and-so well enough to sacrifice a certain amount of money for him, but I may say so only if I've done it. I may say, "I love my mother well enough to remain with her" if I have remained with her. The only way to determine the value of this affection is, precisely, to perform an act which confirms and defines it. But, since I require this affection to justify my act, I find myself caught in a vicious circle....

As for despair, the term has a very simple meaning. It means that we shall confine ourselves to reckoning only with what depends upon our will, or on the ensemble of probabilities which make our action possible. When we want something, we always have to reckon with probabilities. I may be counting on the arrival of a friend. The friend is coming by rail or street-car; this supposes that the train will arrive on schedule, or that the street-car will not jump the track. I am left in the realm of possibility; but possibilities are to be reckoned with only to the point where my action comports with the ensemble of these possibilities, and no further. The moment the possibilities I am considering are not rigorously involved by my action, I ought to disengage myself from them, because no God, no scheme, can adapt the world and its possibilities to my will. When Descartes said, "Conquer yourself rather than the world," he meant essentially the same thing.

The Marxists to whom I have spoken reply, "You can rely on the support of others in your action, which obviously has certain limits because you're not going to live forever. That means: rely on both what others are doing elsewhere to help you, in China, in Russia, and what they will do later on, after your death, to carry on the action and lead it to its fulfillment, which will be the revolution. You even *have* to rely upon that, otherwise you're immoral." I reply at once that I will always rely on fellow fighters insofar as these comrades are involved with me in a common struggle, in the unity of a party or a group in which I can more or less make my weight felt; that is, one whose ranks I am in as a fighter and whose movements I am aware of at every moment. In such a situation, relying on the unity and will of the party is exactly like counting on the fact that the train will arrive on time or that the car won't jump the track. But, given that man is free and that there is no human nature for me to depend on, I cannot count on men whom I do not know by relying on human goodness or man's concern for the good of society. I don't know what will become of the Russian revolution; I may make an example of it to the extent that at the present time it is apparent that the proletariat plays a part in Russia that it plays in no other nation. But I can't swear that this will inevitably lead to a triumph of the proletariat. I've got to limit myself to what I see.

Given that men are free, and that tomorrow they will freely decide what man will be, I cannot be sure that, after my death, fellow fighters will carry on my work to bring it to its maximum perfection. Tomorrow, after my death, some men may decide to set up Fascism, and the others may be cowardly and muddled enough to let them do it. Fascism will then be the human reality, so much the worse for us.

Actually, things will be as man will have decided they are to be. Does that mean that I should abandon myself to quietism? No. First, I should involve myself; then, act on the old saw, "Nothing ventured, nothing gained." Nor does it mean that I shouldn't belong to a party, but rather that I shall have no illusions and shall do what I can. For example, suppose I ask myself, "Will socialization, as such, ever come about?" I know nothing about it. All I know is that I'm going to do everything in my power to bring it about. Beyond that, I can't count on anything. Quietism is the attitude of people who say, "Let others do what I can't do." The doctrine I am presenting is the very opposite of quietism, since it declares, "There is no reality except in action." Moreover, it goes further, since it adds, "Man is nothing else than his plan; he exists only to the extent that he fulfills himself; he is, therefore, nothing else than the ensemble of his acts, nothing else than his life."

STUDY QUESTIONS

1. What does Sartre mean by saying that human beings are "condemned to be free"?
2. According to Sartre, we never decide solely on the basis of someone else's advice since we ourselves choose to seek that advice from that advisor. Do you think he is right?
3. Sartre says, in effect, "I am responsible for myself and for everyone else. I am creating a certain image of man of my own choosing. In choosing myself, I choose man." What do these assertions mean and how does Sartre argue for them?

Absurd Self-Fulfillment

An Essay on the Perversity of the Gods

Joel Feinberg

Joel Feinberg (1926–2004) was a professor of philosophy at the University of Arizona. Among his numerous books are *Social Philosophy* (1973) and *Harm to Others* (1987). He also coauthored *Doing Philosophy: A Guide to the Writing of Philosophy Papers* (1996).

ABSURD SELF-FULFILLMENT: AN ESSAY ON THE PERVERSITY OF THE GODS By Joel Feinberg from *Time and Cause* © 1980, edited by Peter Inwagen. Dordrecth, Holland: D. Reidel Co. 1980. Reprinted by permission of the author.

Joel Feinberg recommends cultivating a strong sense of irony as a way of coping with "the thought that there should be a kind of joke at the heart of human existence."

Consider a human life that is near-totally fulfilled, yet from a quite accessible imaginary vantage point is apparently absurd. Insofar as the person in question is fulfilled, he ought to "feel good" about his life, and rejoice that he has achieved his good. Suppose that he realizes then how futile it all was, "coming to nothing in the end." What would be the appropriate attitude in that event to hold toward his life? Unchanged pride and satisfaction? Bitterness and despair? Haughty existential scorn? We can call such responsive attitudes taken toward one's whole life and by implication toward the whole human condition, "cosmic attitudes." One of the traditional tasks of philosophy (and what "philosophy" is entirely about in the minds of innocent persons unacquainted with the academic discipline of that name) is to perform a kind of literary criticism of cosmic attitudes. It used to be the custom for philosophers not only to describe the universe in its more general aspects but to recommend cosmic attitudes toward the world as so described.

I welcome the suggestion of Thomas Nagel that the appropriate responsive attitude toward human lives that are both absurd and fulfilled is *irony*, and I shall conclude by elaborating that suggestion somewhat beyond the bare recommendation that Nagel offers.

None of the familiar senses of irony in language or in objective occurrences seem to make any sense out of the advice that we respond to absurdity with irony. What Nagel had in mind clearly was another sense in which irony is a kind of outlook on events, namely, "an attitude of detached awareness of incongruity"[1] This is a state of mind halfway between seriousness and playfulness. It may even seem to the person involved that he is both very serious and playful at the same time. The tension between these opposed elements pulling in their opposite ways creates at least temporarily a kind of mental equilibrium not unlike that of the boy in Lincoln's story who was "too [big to cry and far too badly hurt to laugh]," except that the boy squirms with discomfort whereas irony is on balance an *appreciative* attitude.[2] One appreciates the perceived incongruity much as one does in humor, where the sudden unexpected perception of incongruity produces laughter. Here the appreciation is more deliberate and intellectual. The situation is too unpleasant in some way—sad, threatening, disappointing—to permit the relaxed playfulness of spirit prerequisite to the comic response. There *is* a kind of bittersweet pleasure in

---

[1] *Webster's New Collegiate Dictionary* (1976), based on *Webster's Third New International Dictionary of the English Language*. Of the five English dictionaries I consulted, only this newest one contained any definition of irony as an attitude. Is that because this sense is relatively new or because dictionary-makers have heretofore overlooked it?

[2] "The President takes the result of the New York election [a defeat for his party] philosophically, and will doubtless profit by the lesson. When Colonel Forney inquired of him how he felt about New York, he replied: 'Somewhat like the boy in Kentucky who stubbed his toe while running to see his sweetheart. The boy said he was too big to cry, and far too badly hurt to laugh'" *(Frank Leslie's Illustrated Weekly,* November 22, 1862).

it, but not the pleasure of amusement. The situation is surely not seen as funny, though perhaps it would be if only one could achieve a still more detached outlook on it. One contemplates a situation with irony when one looks the facts in the eye and responds in an appreciative way to their incongruous aspects as such. Irony is quite different from despair-cum-tears, scornful defiance-cum-anger, and amusement-cum-laughter. It is pleasant enough to be expressed characteristically in a smile, but a somewhat tired smile, with a touch both of gentleness and mischievousness in it, as befitting the expression of a tempered pleasure.

In one of the most moving scenes of the twenty-seven–part BBC documentary film on the First World War, a group of British reinforcements is shown marching toward the front. We know that they are cannon fodder marching to their own slaughter, and they know it too. They are foot-sore and bone-weary, and splattered with mud, and a steady rain is falling. The song they sing as they march is not a rousing anthem like *La Marseillaise* or *Rule, Britannia*, not a cocky fight song like *Over There*, not a jolly drinking song like *Waltzing Matilda*, not a sentimental ballad, hymn of lamentation, or a mournful dirge. Instead they sing to the stirring tune of *Auld Lang Syne* the famous nonsense verse they created for the occasion:

> We're here because we're here
> Because we're here because we're here;
> We're here because we're here
> Because we're here because we're here...

The observer of the film feels a sudden pang and finds himself near tears, but quickly he perceives the absurdity in the lyrics and responds appreciatively to it, just as the troops, by selecting those words, are responding to the perceived absurdity in their situation. The sensitive observer sees how fitting the ironic response of the soldiers is (and how dreadfully false any of its standard alternatives would have been) and himself takes a quiet sad pleasure in it. The soldiers were in an inescapably absurd predicament, without hope, and only by their unflinching acceptance of the absurdity of their situation are they saved from absurdity themselves. For us, the unseen audience, there is an inspiration in their example that makes the scene noble.

I do not mean to suggest for a moment that the march of the doomed soldiers is an apt metaphor for the whole of human life. The soldiers' brief lives were tragically wasted. If they had been specially-bred military animals they might have found both a personal and biological fulfillment in their peculiar demises, but they were ordinary humans whose bizarre and untimely deaths climaxed their undeveloped and unfinished lives. In contrast, many individuals do achieve fulfillment in long, active, creative lives. These lives are more than just "worthwhile"; they represent to those who lead them the achievement of the only condition that can plausibly be deemed "their good." So philosophical "Pessimism," the view of Schopenhauer and others that *no* life can *possibly* be worth living given the absurdity of the human condition, must be rejected. Its logical contrary, that cosmic Optimism that holds that all human lives necessarily are, or always can be, good and worth while, must also be rejected, in favor of the common-sense view that fulfillment requires luck, and luck is not always good in a world that contains violent passions, accidents, disease, and war.

...Imagine a person who both through his own virtues and good luck has led a maximally fulfilling life into his final declining years. He has realized his highest

individual potential in a career that perfectly fit his inherited temperamental pro-
clivities. His talents and virtues have unfolded steadily in a life that gave them lim-
itless opportunity for exercise, and he has similarly perfected his generic human
powers of discrimination, sympathy, and judgment in a life full of intermeshing
purposes and goals. All of this is a source of rich satisfaction to him, until in the
philosophical autumn of his days, he chances upon the legend of Sisyphus, the com-
mentary of Camus, and the essays of Taylor and Nagel. In a flash he sees the vanity
of all his pursuits, the total permeability of his achievements by time; the lack of
any long-term rationale for his purposes, in a word the absurdity of his (otherwise
good) life. At first he will feel a keen twinge. But unless he be misled by the sophis-
tries of the philosophical Pessimists who confuse the empty ideal of long-term
coherence with the Good for Man, he will soon recover. And then will come a
dawning bittersweet appreciation of the cosmic incongruities first called to his
attention by the philosophers. The thought that there should be a kind of joke at
the heart of human existence begins to please (if not quite tickle) him. Now he can
die not with a whine or a snarl, but with an ironic smile.

STUDY QUESTIONS

1. Present and justify your own conception of a fulfilled life.
2. Feinberg counsels humility as a way of coping with the human predicament. Camus
   counsels defiance. Discuss and adjudicate.
3. Nagel and Camus describe the human predicament rather differently. In your view,
   whose description is more accurate? Why?
4. Do you agree with Feinberg and Nagel that a sense of irony will mitigate the sense of
   absurdity? Explain.

The Human Search for Meaning

Victor Frankl

> Viktor Frankl (1905–1997) was a professor of psychiatry and neurology at
> the University of Vienna Medical School. He founded a school of psychol-
> ogy called *logotherapy* that treats patients by helping them find meaning
> and purpose in their lives. Frankl spent three years in concentration camps
> during World War II, where his entire family was exterminated by the
> Nazis. He is the author of several books including the classic *Man's
> Search for Meaning* (1959).

During his confinement in the Nazi concentration camps, Frankl's captors were intent on degrading him and his fellow prisoners. The goal was to make the life of the inmates into a meaningless, humiliating torment. But Frankl discovered that even in such conditions, human beings possess an "inner freedom" that allows them to preserve their dignity and to raise themselves above their fate.

In death camps, one cannot find meaning in pleasure, beauty, or creativity. But, says Frankl, there is still the possibility of high moral behavior. There were, for example, inmates who, despite all the terror and deprivation, shared their food and never stopped trying to comfort others. Human beings do not have to be mere playthings of fate. They can choose dignity and responsibility.

Frankl does not believe life has one meaning—different existences bring different challenges and pose different questions. Few will face the challenge of a Nazi death camp, but there will be other challenges. "Life ultimately means taking the responsibility to find the right answer to its problem and to fulfill the tasks which it constantly sets for each individual."

What did the prisoner dream about most frequently? Of bread, cake, cigarettes, and nice warm baths. The lack of having these simple desires satisfied led him to seek wish-fulfillment in dreams. Whether these dreams did any good is another matter; the dreamer had to wake from them to the reality of camp life, and to the terrible contrast between that and his dream illusions.

I shall never forget how I was roused one night by the groans of a fellow prisoner, who threw himself about in his sleep, obviously having a horrible nightmare. Since I had always been especially sorry for people who suffered from fearful dreams or deliria, I wanted to wake the poor man. Suddenly I drew back the hand which was ready to shake him, frightened at the thing I was about to do. At that moment I became intensely conscious of the fact that no dream, no matter how horrible, could be as bad as the reality of the camp which surrounded us, and to which I was about to recall him....

When the last layers of subcutaneous fat had vanished, and we looked like skeletons disguised with skin and rags, we could watch our bodies beginning to devour themselves. The organism digested its own protein, and the muscles disappeared. Then the body had no powers of resistance left. One after another the members of the little community in our hut died....

In attempting this psychological presentation and a psychopathological explanation of the typical characteristics of a concentration camp inmate, I may give the impression that the human being is completely and unavoidably influenced by his surroundings. (In this case the surroundings being the unique structure of camp life, which forced the prisoner to conform his conduct to a certain set pattern.) But what about human liberty? Is there no spiritual freedom in regard to behavior and reaction to any given surroundings? Is that theory true which would have us believe that man is no more than a product of many conditional and environmental factors—be they of a biological, psychological or sociological nature? Is man but an accidental product of these? Most important, do the prisoners' reactions to the singular world of the concentration camp prove that man cannot escape the influences of his surroundings? Does man have no choice of action in the face of such circumstances?

We can answer these questions from experience as well as on principle. The experiences of camp life show that man does have a choice of action. There were enough examples, often of a heroic nature, which proved that apathy could be overcome, irritability suppressed. Man *can* preserve a vestige of spiritual freedom, of independence of mind, even in such terrible conditions of psychic and physical stress.

We who lived in concentration camps can remember the men who walked through the huts comforting others, giving away their last piece of bread. They may have been few in number, but they offer sufficient proof that everything can be taken from a man but one thing: the last of the human freedoms—to choose one's attitude in any given set of circumstances, to choose one's own way.

And there were always choices to make. Every day, every hour, offered the opportunity to make a decision, a decision which determined whether you would or would not submit to those powers which threatened to rob you of your very self, your inner freedom; which determined whether or not you would become the plaything of circumstance, renouncing freedom and dignity to become molded into the form of the typical inmate.

Seen from this point of view, the mental reactions of the inmates of a concentration camp must seem more to us than the mere expression of certain physical and sociological conditions. Even though conditions such as lack of sleep, insufficient food and various mental stresses may suggest that the inmates were bound to react in certain ways, in the final analysis it becomes clear that the sort of person the prisoner became was the result of an inner decision, and not the result of camp influences alone. Fundamentally, therefore, any man can, even under such circumstances, decide what shall become of him—mentally and spiritually. He may retain his human dignity even in a concentration camp. Dostoevski said once, "There is only one thing that I dread: not to be worthy of my sufferings." These words frequently came to my mind after I became acquainted with those martyrs whose behavior in camp, whose suffering and death, bore witness to the fact that the last inner freedom cannot be lost. It can be said that they were worthy of their sufferings; the way they bore their suffering was a genuine inner achievement. It is this spiritual freedom—which cannot be taken away—that makes life meaningful and purposeful.

An active life serves the purpose of giving man the opportunity to realize values in creative work, while a passive life of enjoyment affords him the opportunity to obtain fulfillment in experiencing beauty, art, or nature. But there is also purpose in that life which is almost barren of both creation and enjoyment and which admits of but one possibility of high moral behavior: namely, in man's attitude to his existence, an existence restricted by external forces. A creative life and a life of enjoyment are banned to him. But not only creativeness and enjoyment are meaningful. If there is a meaning in life at all, then there must be a meaning in suffering. Suffering is an ineradicable part of life, even as fate and death. Without suffering and death human life cannot be complete.

The way in which a man accepts his fate and all the suffering it entails, the way in which he takes up his cross, gives him ample opportunity—even under the most difficult circumstances—to add a deeper meaning to his life. It may remain brave, dignified and unselfish. Or in the bitter fight for self-preservation he may forget his human dignity and become no more than an animal. Here lies the chance for a man either to make use of or to forego the opportunities of attaining the moral values that a difficult situation may afford him. And this decides whether he is worthy of his sufferings or not.

Do not think that these considerations are unworldly and too far removed from real life. It is true that only a few people are capable of reaching such high moral standards. Of the prisoners only a few kept their full inner liberty and obtained those values which their suffering afforded, but even one such example is sufficient proof that man's inner strength may raise him above his outward fate. Such men are not only in concentration camps. Everywhere man is confronted with fate, with the chance of achieving something through his own suffering....

A man who let himself decline because he could not see any future goal found himself occupied with retrospective thoughts. In a different connection, we have already spoken of the tendency there was to look into the past, to help make the present, with all its horrors, less real. But in robbing the present of its reality there lay a certain danger. It became easy to overlook the opportunities to make something positive of camp life, opportunities which really did exist. Regarding our "provisional existence" as unreal was in itself an important factor in causing the prisoners to lose their hold on life; everything in a way became pointless. Such people forgot that often it is just such an exceptionally difficult external situation which gives man the opportunity to grow spiritually beyond himself. Instead of taking the camp's difficulties as a test of their inner strength, they did not take their life seriously and despised it as something of no consequence. They preferred to close their eyes and to live in the past. Life for such people became meaningless.

Naturally only a few people were capable of reaching great spiritual heights. But a few were given the chance to attain human greatness even through their apparent worldly failure and death, an accomplishment which in ordinary circumstances they would never have achieved. To the others of us, the mediocre and the half-hearted, the words of Bismarck could be applied: "Life is like being at the dentist. You always think that the worst is still to come, and yet it is over already." Varying this, we could say that most men in a concentration camp believed that the real opportunities of life had passed. Yet, in reality, there was an opportunity and a challenge. One could make a victory of those experiences, turning life into an inner triumph, or one could ignore the challenge and simply vegetate, as did a majority of the prisoners.

Any attempt at fighting the camp's psychopathological influence on the prisoner by psychotherapeutic or psychohygienic methods had to aim at giving him inner strength by pointing out to him a future goal to which he could look forward. Instinctively some of the prisoners attempted to find one on their own. It is a peculiarity of man that he can only live by looking to the future—*sub specie aeternitatis*. And this is his salvation in the most difficult moments of his existence, although he sometimes has to force his mind to the task....

The prisoner who had lost faith in the future—his future—was doomed. With his loss of belief in the future, he also lost his spiritual hold; he let himself decline and became subject to mental and physical decay. Usually this happened quite suddenly, in the form of a crisis, the symptoms of which were familiar to the experienced camp inmate. We all feared this moment—not for ourselves, which would have been pointless, but for our friends. Usually it began with the prisoner refusing one morning to get dressed and wash or to go out on the parade grounds. No entreaties, no blows, no threats had any effect. He just lay there, hardly moving. If this crisis was brought about by an illness, he refused to be taken to the sick-bay or to do anything to help himself. He simply gave up. There he remained, lying in his own excreta, and nothing bothered him any more.

I once had a dramatic demonstration of the close link between the loss of faith in the future and this dangerous giving up. F——, my senior block warden, a fairly well-known composer and librettist, confided in me one day: "I would like to tell you something, Doctor. I have had a strange dream. A voice told me that I could wish for something, that I should only say what I wanted to know, and all my questions would be answered. What do you think I asked? That I would like to know when the war would be over for me. You know what I mean, Doctor—for me! I wanted to know when we, when our camp, would be liberated and our sufferings come to an end."

"And when did you have this dream?" I asked.

"In February, 1945," he answered. It was then the beginning of March.

"What did your dream voice answer?"

Furtively he whispered to me, "March thirtieth."

When F—— told me about his dream, he was still full of hope and convinced that the voice of his dream would be right. But as the promised day drew nearer, the war news which reached our camp made it appear very unlikely that we would be free on the promised date. On March twenty-ninth, F—— suddenly became ill and ran a high temperature. On March thirtieth, the day his prophecy had told him that the war and suffering would be over for him, he became delirious and lost consciousness. On March thirty-first, he was dead. To all outward appearances, he had died of typhus.

Those who know how close the connection is between the state of mind of a man—his courage and hope, or lack of them—and the state of immunity of his body will understand that the sudden loss of hope and courage can have a deadly effect. The ultimate cause of my friend's death was that the expected liberation did not come and he was severely disappointed. This suddenly lowered his body's resistance against the latent typhus infection. His faith in the future and his will to live had become paralyzed and his body fell victim to illness—and thus the voice of his dream was right after all.

The observations of this one case and the conclusion drawn from them are in accordance with something that was drawn to my attention by the chief doctor of our concentration camp. The death rate in the week between Christmas, 1944, and New Year's, 1945, increased in camp beyond all previous experience. In his opinion, the explanation for this increase did not lie in the harder working conditions or the deterioration of our food supplies or a change of weather or new epidemics. It was simply that the majority of the prisoners had lived in the naïve hope that they would be home again by Christmas. As the time drew near and there was no encouraging news, the prisoners lost courage and disappointment overcame them. This had a dangerous influence on their powers of resistance and a great number of them died.

As we said before, any attempt to restore a man's inner strength in the camp had first to succeed in showing him some future goal. Nietzsche's words, "He who has a *why* to live for can bear with almost any *how*" could be the guiding motto for all psychotherapeutic and psychohygienic efforts regarding prisoners. Whenever there was an opportunity for it, one had to give them a *why*—an aim—for their lives, in order to strengthen them to bear the terrible *how* of their existence. Woe to him who saw no more sense in his life, no aim, no purpose, and therefore no point in carrying on. He was soon lost. The typical reply with which such a man rejected all encouraging arguments was, "I have nothing to expect from life any more." What sort of answer can one give to that?

What was really needed was a fundamental change in our attitude toward life. We had to learn ourselves and, furthermore, we had to teach the despairing men, that it did not really matter what we expected from life, but rather what life expected from us. We needed to stop asking about the meaning of life, and instead to think of ourselves as those who were being questioned by life—daily and hourly. Our answer must consist, not in talk and meditation, but in right action and in right conduct. Life ultimately means taking the responsibility to find the right answer to its problems and to fulfill the tasks which it constantly sets for each individual.

These tasks, and therefore the meaning of life, differ from man to man, and from moment to moment. Thus it is impossible to define the meaning of life in a general way. Questions about the meaning of life can never be answered by sweeping statements. "Life" does not mean something vague, but something very real and concrete, just as life's tasks are also very real and concrete. They form man's destiny, which is different and unique for each individual. No man and no destiny can be compared with any other man or any other destiny. No situation repeats itself, and each situation calls for a different response. Sometimes the situation in which a man finds himself may require him to shape his own fate by action. At other times it is more advantageous for him to make use of an opportunity for contemplation and to realize assets in this way. Sometimes man may be required simply to accept fate, to bear his cross. Every situation is distinguished by its uniqueness, and there is always only one right answer to the problem posed by the situation at hand.

When a man finds that it is his destiny to suffer, he will have to accept his suffering as his task; his single and unique task. He will have to acknowledge the fact that even in suffering he is unique and alone in the universe. No one can relieve him of his suffering or suffer in his place. His unique opportunity lies in the way in which he bears his burden.

For us, as prisoners, these thoughts were not speculations far removed from reality. They were the only thoughts that could be of help to us. They kept us from despair, even when there seemed to be no chance of coming out of it alive. Long ago we had passed the stage of asking what was the meaning of life, a naïve query which understands life as the attaining of some aim through the active creation of something of value. For us, the meaning of life embraced the wider cycles of life and death, of suffering and of dying.

Once the meaning of suffering had been revealed to us, we refused to minimize or alleviate the camp's tortures by ignoring them or harboring false illusions and entertaining artificial optimism. Suffering had become a task on which we did not want to turn our backs. We had realized its hidden opportunities for achievement, the opportunities which caused the poet Rilke to write, *"Wie viel ist aufzuleiden!"* (How much suffering there is to get through!) Rilke spoke of "getting through suffering" as others would talk of "getting through work." There was plenty of suffering for us to get through. Therefore, it was necessary to face up to the full amount of suffering, trying to keep moments of weakness and furtive tears to a minimum. But there was no need to be ashamed of tears, for tears bore witness that a man had the greatest of courage, the courage to suffer. Only very few realized that. Shamefacedly some confessed occasionally that they had wept, like the comrade who answered my question of how he had gotten over his edema, by confessing, "I have wept it out of my system."...

Freedom ... is not the last word. Freedom is only part of the story and half of the truth. Freedom is but the negative aspect of the whole phenomenon whose positive aspect is responsibility. In fact, freedom is in danger of degenerating into mere arbitrariness unless it is lived in terms of responsibility. That is why *I recommend that the Statue of Liberty on the East Coast be supplemented by a Statue of Responsibility on the West Coast.*

STUDY QUESTIONS

1. Do Frankl's insights relate to everyday life or only to the extreme circumstances he confronted? Explain.
2. How is it possible for a person to remain "brave, dignified and unselfish even under the most difficult circumstances?" Compare Frankl's experiences as a prisoner with those of James Stockdale (Chapter Five). What similarities and differences do you find when you compare Frankl's philosophy with that of the ancient Stoics?
3. Explain Frankl's remark that "freedom is but the negative aspect of the whole phenomenon whose positive aspect is responsibility."

The Book of Job

The author of the Book of Job is unknown. It is thought to have been written sometime between the seventh and fifth centuries B.C. Job, whose afflictions cause him to curse the day he was born, is engaged in a debate on the mysterious ways of God. The book's arguments and its style make it one of the masterpieces of religious literature.

This selection is from the later chapters of the Book of Job. Job, who is a God-fearing man, is being tested by God. He had been at home in the world, blessed, prosperous, and respected but now he has lost his family, his health, and all of his possessions. He bitterly protests his fate, arguing that he does not deserve so much suffering. Many mock him. He is vulnerable to all malice and evil. But what were his crimes? "Oh … that my accuser would write out his indictment!"

Job's story illustrates the truism that life is sometimes terribly unfair. Good people suffer, while the wicked often live very well. Job's plight and plaint are universal. He begs God for some explanation, some justification.

The Lord addressed Job out of the "whirlwind," neither explaining nor justifying, but pointing out that Job, a finite being, is in no position to understand the workings of the world. It is not fitting for Job to demand an explanation that he could not possibly fathom. Thus, despite all appearances to the contrary, Job must have faith in the ultimate justice of his fate. For he has neither the power to change that fate nor the wisdom to comprehend its meaning in the larger scheme of things. Finally, Job sees that his insistence on moral justification is presumptuous, and he accepts God's will. God then relents. The book ends with Job restored to prosperity and a new family.

29

Job took up his theme anew and said:

Oh, that I were as in the months past!
   as in the days when God watched over me,
While he kept his lamp shining above my head,
   and by his light I walked through darkness;
As I was in my flourishing days,
   when God sheltered my tent;
When the Almighty was yet with me,
   and my children were round about me;
When my footsteps were bathed in milk,
   and the rock flowed with streams of oil;
When I went forth to the gate of the city
   and set up my seat in the square—....

Whoever heard of me blessed me;
   those who saw me commended me.

For I rescued the poor who cried out for help,
   the orphans, and the unassisted;
The blessing of those in extremity came upon me,
   and the heart of the widow I made joyful.
I wore my honesty like a garment;
   justice was my robe and my turban.

I was eyes to the blind,
 and feet to the lame was I;
I was a father to the needy;
 the rights of the stranger I studied,
And I broke the jaws of the wicked man;
 from his teeth I forced the prey.

Then I said: "In my own nest I shall grow old;
 I shall multiply years like the phoenix.
My root is spread out to the waters;
 the dew rests by night on my branches.
My glory is fresh within me,
 and my bow is renewed in my hand!"

30

But now they hold me in derision
 who are younger in years than I;
Whose fathers I should have disdained
 to rank with the dogs of my flock.
Such strength as they had, to me meant nought;
 they were utterly destitute.

  ....

The Lord's Speech

38

Then the LORD addressed Job out of
 the·storm and said:

Who is this that obscures divine plans
 with words of ignorance?
Gird your loins now, like a man;
 I will question you, and you will tell me the answers!
Where were you when I founded the earth?
 Tell me, if you have understanding.
Who determined its size; do you know?
 Who stretched out the measuring line for it?
Into what were its pedestals sunk,
 and who laid the cornerstone,
While the morning stars sang in chorus
 and all the sons of God shouted for joy?

And who shut within doors the sea,
 when it burst forth from the womb;
When I made the clouds its garment
 and thick darkness its swaddling bands?
When I set limits for it
 and fastened the bar of its door,
And said: Thus far shall you come but no farther,
 and here shall your proud waves be stilled!

Have you ever in your lifetime commanded the morning
    and shown the dawn its place
For taking hold of the ends of the earth,
    till the wicked are shaken from its surface?
The earth is changed as is clay by the seal,
    and dyed as though it were a garment;
But from the wicked the light is withheld,
    and the arm of pride is shattered.

Have you entered into the sources of the sea,
    or walked about in the depths of the abyss?
Have the gates of death been shown to you,
    or have you seen the gates of darkness?
Have you comprehended the breadth of the earth?
    Tell me, if you know all:
Which is the way to the dwelling place of light,
    and where is the abode of darkness,
That you may take them to their boundaries
    and set them on their homeward paths?
You know, because you were born before them,
    and the number of your years is great!
Have you entered the storehouse of the snow,
    and seen the treasury of the hail
Which I have reserved for times of stress,
    for the days of war and of battle?
Which way to the parting of the winds,
    whence the east wind spreads over the earth?
Who has laid out a channel for the downpour
    and for the thunderstorm a path
To bring rain to no man's land,
    the unpeopled wilderness;
To enrich the waste and desolate ground
    till the desert blooms with verdure?
Has the rain a father;
    or who has begotten the drops of dew?
Out of whose womb comes the ice,
    and who gives the hoarfrost its birth in the skies,
When the waters lie covered as though with stone
    that holds captive the surface of the deep?

Have you fitted a curb to the Pleiades,
    or loosened the bonds of Orion?
Can you bring forth the Mazzaroth in their season
    or guide the Bear with its train?
Do you know the ordinances of the heavens;
    can you put into effect their plan on the earth?

Can you raise your voice among the clouds,
    or veil yourself in the waters of the storm?
Can you send forth the lightnings on their way,
    or will they say to you, "Here we are"?

Who counts the clouds in his wisdom?
    Or who tilts the water jars of heaven
So that the dust of earth is fused into a mass
    and its clods made solid?
Do you hunt the prey for the lioness
    or appease the hunger of her cubs,
While they crouch in their dens,
    or lie in wait in the thicket?
Who puts wisdom in the heart,
    and gives the cock its understanding?
Who provides nourishment for the ravens
    when their young ones cry out to God,
    and they rove abroad without food?

39

Do you know about the birth of the mountain goats,
    watch for the birth pangs of the hinds,
Number the months that they must fulfill,
    and fix the time of their bringing forth?
They crouch down and bear their young;
    they deliver their progeny in the desert.

.....

Is it by your discernment that the hawk soars,
    that he spreads his wings toward the south?
Does the eagle fly up at your command
    to build his nest aloft?
On the cliff he dwells and spends the night,
    on a spur of the cliff or the fortress.
From thence he watches for his prey;
    his eyes behold it afar off.
His young ones greedily drink blood;
    where the slain are, there is he.

40

The LORD then said to Job:

Will we have arguing with the Almighty by the critic?
    Let him who would correct God give answer!

Then Job answered the LORD and said:

Behold, I am of little account; what can I answer you?
    I put my hand over my mouth.
Though I have spoken once, I will not do so again;
    though twice, I will do so no more.

Then the LORD addressed Job out of the storm and said:

Gird up your loins now, like a man.
    I will question you, and you tell me the answers!

Would you refuse to acknowledge my right?
    Would you condemn me that you may be justified?

Have you an arm like that of God,
    or can you thunder with a voice like his?
Adorn yourself with grandeur and majesty,
    and array yourself with glory and splendor.
Let loose the fury of your wrath;
    tear down the wicked and shatter them.
Bring down the haughty with a glance;
    bury them in the dust together;
    in the hidden world imprison them.
Then will I too acknowledge
    that your own right hand can save you.

See, besides you I made Behemoth,
    that feeds on grass like an ox.
Behold the strength in his loins,
    and his vigor in the sinews of his belly.
He carries his tail like a cedar;
    the sinews of his thighs are like cables.

        ....

41

Rows of scales are on his back,
    tightly sealed together;
They are fitted each so close to the next
    that no space intervenes;
So joined one to another
    that they hold fast and cannot be parted.

When he sneezes, light flashes forth;
    his eyes are like those of the dawn.
Out of his mouth go forth firebrands,
    sparks of fire leap forth.
From his nostrils issues steam,
    as from a seething pot or bowl.
His breath sets coals afire;
    a flame pours from his mouth.
Strength abides in his neck,
    and terror leaps before him.

His heart is hard as stone;
    his flesh, as the lower millstone.
When he rises up, the mighty are afraid;
    the waves of the sea fall back.
Should the sword reach him, it will not avail;
    nor will the spear, nor the dart, nor the javelin.
He regards iron as straw,
    and bronze as rotten wood.
The arrow will not put him to flight;
    slingstones used against him are but straws.

Clubs he esteems as splinters;
    he laughs at the crash of the spear.

His belly is sharp as pottery fragments;
    he spreads like a threshing sledge upon the mire.
He makes the depths boil like a pot;
    the sea he churns like perfume in a kettle.
Behind him he leaves a shining path;
    you would think the deep had the hoary head of age.
Upon the earth there is not his like,
    intrepid he was made.
All, however lofty, fear him;
    he is king over all proud beasts.

42

Then Job answered the LORD and said:

I know that you can do all things,
    and that no purpose of yours can be hindered.
I have dealt with great things that I do not understand;
    things too wonderful for me, which I cannot know.
I had heard of you by word of mouth,
    but now my eye has seen you.
Therefore I disown what I have said,
    and repent in dust and ashes.

STUDY QUESTIONS

1. Job's story illustrates that life is unfair. Does this cast doubts on the foundations of morality? Discuss.
2. Throughout his sufferings Job never doubts God's existence. But many say that the suffering of innocents cannot be squared with the proposition that a benevolent God has created the world. Job himself has no solution to the problem of justifying evil in a world created by God. Why do you think Job's faith in God's existence never wavers?
3. Though Job has no answer to why God permits the suffering of innocents, the Book of Job does have a response to those who raise the question. What is that response? How do you react to it?
4. Job's complaint is that life is unfair; Camus' complaint is that life is absurd. Why did they react so differently to life? Present and justify your own perspective.
5. There's a story that Bertrand Russell went to heaven and met God, who said to him, "You see, Russell, you were wrong to deny that I exist!" To which Russell replied, "Not at all; you should have given us more evidence."

    Now imagine Russell meeting Job. Their conversation is longer and more heated (but they part friends). What is it like?